TO THE STUDENT: Two helpful supplemental study aids for this textbook are available:

☐ *Student Guide* by Dudley W. Curry contains, for each chapter in this textbook, a detailed review of key ideas plus practice questions and problems with solutions.

☐ Applications for Management Accounting Using the TWIN™/ Lotus® 1-2-3® by Ali A. Peyvandi and Wayne D. Robertson is designed to accompany the Seventh Edition of INTRODUCTION TO MANAGEMENT ACCOUNTING by Horngren and Sundem and allows you to solve management accounting problems using spread sheets. This supplement includes partially solved problems, model-building problems, a list of spread sheet commands, and a tutorial. No computer experience is needed to use this supplement.

☐ The TWIN™ (educational version), a work-alike spreadsheet software program that is incredibly similar to Lotus® 1-2-3® at a fraction of the cost.

Introduction to
MANAGEMENT
ACCOUNTING

PRENTICE-HALL SERIES IN ACCOUNTING

Charles T. Horngren, Editor

7th Edition

Introduction to
MANAGEMENT
ACCOUNTING

Charles T. Horngren

Stanford University

Gary L. Sundem

University of Washington–Seattle

Prentice-Hall, Inc., Englewood Cliffs, New Jersey 07632

Library of Congress Cataloging-in-Publication Data

Horngren, Charles T., (date)
  Introduction to management accounting.

  (Prentice-Hall series in accounting)
  Bibliography: p.
    Includes index.
  1. Managerial accounting. I. Sundem, Gary L.
II. Title. III. Series.
HF5635.H814 1987   658.1′511   86–25138
ISBN 0-13-487885-X

Editorial/production supervision: Nancy G. Follender
Interior and cover design: Jayne Conte
Cover photo: John Scowlin/FPG
Manufacturing buyer: Raymond Keating

Printed in the United States of America

10 9 8 7 6 5 4 3 2 1

ISBN 0-13-487885-X   01

Prentice-Hall International (UK) Limited, *London*

Prentice-Hall of Australia Pty. Limited, *Sydney*

Prentice-Hall Canada Inc., *Toronto*

Prentice-Hall Hispanoamericana, S.A., *Mexico*

Prentice-Hall of India Private Limited, *New Delhi*

Prentice-Hall of Japan, Inc., *Tokyo*

Prentice-Hall of Southeast Asia Pte. Ltd., *Singapore*

Editora Prentice-Hall do Brasil, Ltda., *Rio de Janeiro*

To Joan, Scott, Mary, Susie, Cathy
Jenny, Garth, Jens

Charles T. Horngren is the Edmund W. Littlefield Professor of Accounting at Stanford University. A graduate of Marquette University, he received his MBA from Harvard University and his Ph.D. from the University of Chicago. He is also the recipient of honorary doctorates from Marquette University and De Paul University.

A Certified Public Accountant, Horngren served on the Accounting Principles Board for six years, the Financial Accounting Standards Board Advisory Council for five years, and the Council of the American Institute of Certified Public Accountants for three years. He is currently serving as a trustee of the Financial Accounting Foundation.

A member of the American Accounting Association, Horngren has been its President and its Director of Research. He received the Outstanding Accounting Educator Award in 1973, when the association initiated an annual series of such awards.

The California Certified Public Accountants Foundation gave Horngren its Faculty Excellence Award in 1975 and its Distinguished Professor Award in 1983. He is the first person to have received both awards.

In 1985 the American Institute of Certified Public Accountants presented its first Outstanding Educator Award to Horngren.

Professor Horngren is also a member of the National Association of Accountants, where he was on its research planning committee for three years. He was a member of the Board of Regents, Institute of Certified Management Accountants, which administers the Certified Management Accounting examinations.

Horngren is the co-author of two other books published by Prentice-Hall: *Cost Accounting: A Managerial Emphasis*, *Sixth Edition*, 1987 (with George Foster); and *Introduction to Financial Accounting*, *Third Edition*, 1987 (with Gary L. Sundem).

Charles T. Horngren is the Consulting Editor for the Prentice-Hall Series in Accounting.

Gary L. Sundem is Professor of Accounting at the University of Washington, Seattle. He received his B.A. degree from Carleton College and MBA and Ph.D. degrees from Stanford University.

Professor Sundem served as Editor of *The Accounting Review*, 1982–86. His other American Accounting Association positions have included membership on the Executive Committee, Chair of the Planning Committee for the Association's 1981 annual meeting, and Director of the AAA Doctoral Consortium.

A member of the National Association of Accountants, Sundem is past-president of the Seattle chapter. He has served on NAA's Committee on Academic Relations and is currently on the national Board of Directors.

Professor Sundem has numerous publications in accounting and finance journals, including *The Accounting Review*, *Journal of Accounting Research*, and *The Journal of Finance*. He received an award for the most notable contribution to accounting literature in 1978. He has made presentations at over 50 universities in the U.S. and abroad.

Sundem was chairman of the University of Washington's department of accounting in 1978–82. He has been a consultant to industry and government.

CONTENTS

3 INTRODUCTION TO MANUFACTURING COSTS 61

4 RELEVANT COSTS AND SPECIAL DECISIONS— PART ONE 86

5 RELEVANT COSTS AND SPECIAL DECISIONS— PART TWO 121

☐ PART TWO: Accounting for Planning and Control

6 THE MASTER BUDGET: THE OVERALL PLAN 153

7 FLEXIBLE BUDGETS AND STANDARDS FOR CONTROL 186

14 PROCESS-COSTING SYSTEMS 443

15 OVERHEAD APPLICATION: DIRECT AND ABSORPTION COSTING 475

19 UNDERSTANDING CORPORATE ANNUAL REPORTS—PART TWO 638

20 DIFFICULTIES IN MEASURING NET INCOME 678

☐ PART SEVEN: Appendices

PREFACE

Introduction to Management Accounting is the second member of a matched pair of books that provides full coverage of the essentials of financial and managerial accounting. The first book is *Introduction to Financial Accounting*. In combination, the pair can be used throughout two semesters or three quarters of introductory accounting.

This book is an introduction to internal accounting—most often called *management accounting*. It deals with important topics that all students of management and business should study. The book is written primarily for students who have had one or two terms of basic accounting.

It is also appropriate for continuing educational programs of varying lengths in which the students have had no formal training in accounting. Our twin goals have been to choose relevant subject matter and to present it clearly.

The major change in this edition is summarized in one word: *clarity*. Chapter by chapter, the authors have made painstaking revisions that ease understanding and sharpen thought. More than ever, this is a basic book aimed at a reader who has a minimal background in accounting, if any.

This book attempts a balanced, flexible approach. For example, it deals as much with nonprofit, retail, wholesale, selling, and administrative situations as it does with manufacturing. The fundamental accounting concepts and techniques for planning and control are applicable to all types and functions of organizations, not just to manufacturing. This more general approach makes it easier for the student to relate the book's examples and problems to his or her particular interests. Moreover, many valuable concepts (for example, master budgets) are more easily grasped if they are not complicated by intricate manufacturing situations.

Stress is on planning and control, not on product costing for purposes of inventory valuation and income determination. This approach, which excludes the troublesome but unimportant complications introduced by changes in inventory levels, simplifies the presentation of planning and control techniques in the classroom. Instead of the simultaneous discussion of costs for control and for product costing found in most texts, this text concentrates on planning and control without dwelling on product costing at all until Chapter 13. At that point, job costing, process costing, and the implications of overhead application for product costing may be considered in perspective and in relation to management policy decisions regarding the "best" inventory valuation method.

A chapter-by-chapter description of the new features and changes in this edition is given in the front section of the solutions manual. Significant changes include the following:

1. As mentioned earlier, clarity has been the watchword of this revision. For a few examples, consider the explanations in Chapter 2 of cost-volume-profit analysis and also the effects of sales mix; in Chapter 3 of the basic vocabulary of manufacturing costs; in Chapter 4 of the role of costs in pricing; in Chapter 5 of the explanation of opportunity costs; in Chapter 7 of the relationship between a flexible budget and the master (static) budget.

2. Chapters 13 and 14 have been switched in sequence so that job costing precedes process costing. These chapters have been heavily rewritten. They provide a solid grounding in how costs are accumulated and applied to products and services.

3. An international flavor has been added. Suppliers and customers, no matter what their size or country, are increasingly affected by dealings with and within other nations. Each chapter has at least one homework problem that has a setting outside the United States. For example, consider Problems 4–29, 6–24, 9–27, 12–34, 15–36, and 19–32.

4. Improved clarity extends to cross-referencing for the learning of accounting terms. Page numbers are included for each key term in the Accounting Vocabulary section at the end of each chapter and in the glossary. Therefore, readers can easily find the page where the accounting term was initially introduced.

5. The effects of the Internal Revenue Code of 1986 have been included.

6. The student guide (by Dudley W. Curry), a supplement that parallels the textbook chapters, contains numerous changes and additions in the review of key ideas and in the practice test questions and problems, which include many multiple-choice items in quantitative form ("mini problems").

7. The chapter-by-chapter test bank (by Duane Milano), available free to adopters, has been revised and considerably expanded, both in the softcover version and in the computerized option that facilitates the construction of the tailor-made exams in volume.

☐ Alternative Ways of Using This Book

In our opinion, the first nine chapters provide the foundation of the field of management accounting. These nine chapters may be amplified by assigning the subsequent chapters in the given order, or by inserting them after the earlier chapters as desired. Such insertion may be achieved without disrupting the readers' flow of thought. The most obvious candidates for insertion are indicated below:

Chapters	1	2	3	4	5	6	7	8	9 → 10–20
		↑		↑		↑	↑		
		17				11	15		
		18				12			
		19	13						
		20	14						

If some of the basics of financial accounting are to be included in a course in management accounting, any or all of the financial accounting chapters (17–20) may be undertaken anytime. (For example, to provide a change of pace, such chapters have even been used in the midst of a course.)

Instructors tend to disagree markedly about the sequence of topics in a course in management accounting. Criticisms of *any* sequence in a textbook are inevitable. Consequently, this book tries to provide a modular approach that permits hopping and skipping back and forth with minimal inconvenience. In a nutshell, our rationale is to provide a loosely constrained sequence to ease diverse approaches to teaching. Content is of primary importance; sequence is secondary.

Teaching is highly personal and is heavily influenced by the backgrounds and interests of assorted students in miscellaneous settings. To satisfy this audience, a book must be a pliable tool, not a straitjacket.

As the authors, we prefer to assign the chapters in the sequence provided in the book. But we are not enslaved by the sequence. Through the years, we have assigned an assortment of sequences, depending on the readers' backgrounds.

Part One, "Focus on Decision Making," provides a bedrock introduction, so we assign it in its entirety. Sometimes we assign Chapter 17 immediately after Chapter 1, particularly if the readers have little or no background in financial accounting. Moreover, if there is time in the course for students to become more familiar with product costing, we frequently assign Chapter 13 immediately after Chapter 3. Furthermore, there is much logical appeal to studying the chapters on capital budgeting (Chapters 11 and 12) immediately after the chapters on relevant costs (Chapters 4 and 5). However, tradition has prevented our placing such chapters there, plus the fact that capital budgeting is often amply covered in other courses. In addition, the master budget is often covered in finance courses, so Chapter 6 is frequently skipped in courses in accounting.

Part Two, "Accounting for Planning and Control," emphasizes the attention-directing functions of accounting. We often assign Chapter 15 immediately after Chapter 7 because it stresses the product-costing aspects of standard costs, whereas Chapter 7 focuses on the control aspects.

Parts Three, Four, and Five cover capital budgeting, product costing, and quantitative methods, respectively. In particular, the coverage of product costing has been expanded, especially the fundamentals of process and job costing. All of these topics are important. However, the decision to study them will depend on the teacher's preferences, the other courses in the curriculum, and the students' previous course.

Part Six introduces, interprets, and appraises basic financial accounting. These chapters form a unified package that covers all elementary financial accounting in capsule form with heavy stress on interpretation and uses and, except in Chapter 17, with little attention given to the accumulation of the information. In our view, a major objective of basic financial accounting should be to equip the student with enough fundamental concepts and terminology so that he or she can reasonably comprehend any industrial corporate annual report.

Chapters 17–20 may be skipped entirely or may be used in a variety of ways:

1. In courses or executive programs where the students have *no* accounting background but where the main emphasis is on management rather than financial accounting
2. In courses where the chapters may be used as a quick review by students who have had some financial accounting previously
3. In courses where one or two of Chapters 17–20 may be chosen to remedy weaknesses or gaps in the background of the students

Chapters 17–20 need not be used in total, page by page or topic by topic. Teachers are free to pick and choose those topics (particularly in Chapters 19 and 20) that seem most suitable for their students.

On the other hand, some teachers may want to use these chapters to teach the fundamentals of financial accounting to students with no prior background in accounting. Classroom testing has shown that such teaching can be done successfully, provided that the homework material is chosen carefully.

The front of the solutions manual contains several alternate detailed assignment schedules and ample additional recommendations to teachers regarding how best to use this book.

ACKNOWLEDGMENTS

We have received ideas, assistance, miscellaneous critiques, and assorted assignment material in conversations and by mail from many students and professors. Each has our gratitude, but the list is too long to enumerate here.

Professor Dudley W. Curry (Southern Methodist University) has our special thanks for offering many helpful suggestions and for preparing the student guide that is available as supplementary material.

Duane Milano (East Texas State University) has our appreciation for preparing the test bank material.

We are also especially grateful to Jonathan Schiff for his preparation of Instructor Resource Outlines, available to adopters upon request.

The following professors supplied helpful comments and reviews of the previous edition or drafts of this edition: James T. Bristol, William L. Call, Wayne R. Chapin, Biagio G. Coppolella, Paul A. Dierks, Edwin A. Doty, William P. Enderlein, Peter A. Firmin, Lyle E. Jacobsen, John N. McKenna, Elliott Mittler, and David W. Phipps.

Appreciation also goes to The Institute of Certified Management Accountants for their generous permission to use or adapt problems (designated as CMA) from their publications.

Elsie Young has our special appreciation for her cheerful and skillful typing and related help. Valerie Amphlett and Ali Salama have our gratitude for ably performing assorted editorial chores. Barbara Pearson deserves special recognition for her flawless typing of the solutions manual.

And, finally, our thanks to Julie Warner, Nancy Follender, Jayne Conte, Sally Ann Bailey, Nancy McDermott and Bob McGee at Prentice-Hall.

Comments from users are welcome.

Charles T. Horngren
Gary L. Sundem

Chapter 1

PERSPECTIVE: SCOREKEEPING, ATTENTION DIRECTING, AND PROBLEM SOLVING

LEARNING OBJECTIVES

Learning objectives are at the beginning of each chapter. These objectives specify some of the important knowledge and skills you should have after completing your study of the chapter and your solving of the assignment material.

1. List the three major means and ends of the accounting system.
2. Name the basic functions of a management planning and control system and identify the main accounting activities that relate to these functions.
3. Identify the three main characteristics of service organizations that distinguish them from manufacturing organizations.
4. Distinguish between the line and staff roles in an organization.
5. Contrast the functions of controllers and treasurers.
6. Describe the two major themes of this book: cost-benefit and behavioral implications.
7. Identify the major distinctions between management accounting and financial accounting.

This chapter presents an overall view of the accountant's role in an organization. We shall see that the accountant has three main functions: scorekeeping, attention directing, and problem solving.

WHY STUDY ACCOUNTING?

Accounting is a very important subject. This opinion is widely shared, as shown by 1,100 responses to a questionnaire sent to academicians and managers by the American Assembly of Collegiate Schools of Business. Here are the top three courses ranked in terms of how much time and effort should be spent by students on each one of them:

	RANKED BY MANAGERS	RANKED BY PROFESSORS
Accounting	1	2
Finance	2	3
Economics	3	1

Because accounting is so pervasive, an understanding of its usefulness—and its limitations—is desirable for all managers in all types of organizations. Company presidents, production managers, public accountants, hospital administrators, controllers, school administrators, sales managers, and politicians are better equipped to perform their duties when they have a reasonable grasp of accounting data.

The study of management accounting can be especially fruitful because it helps us see through the eyes of those who are subject to accounting measures of performance and who often depend heavily on accounting data for guidance in decision making. There is no escaping the linkage of accounting and management, so the study of management accounting will help you whether you become a manager or an accountant, or whether you will work in retailing, manufacturing, health care, public administration or other activity.

Many production, marketing, and government executives are stronger managers when they have a solid understanding of accounting. Moreover, their performance and their rewards are often determined by how accounting measurements are made, so they have a natural self-interest in gaining knowledge about accounting.

The more that managers know about accounting, the better able they are to plan and control the operations of their organization and its subunits.

Managers will be handicapped in dealing with both inside and outside parties if their comprehension of accounting is sketchy or confused. Therefore the learning of accounting is almost always a wise investment.

APPLICABILITY TO NONPROFIT ORGANIZATIONS

This book is aimed at a variety of readers, including students who aspire to become either managers or professional accountants. The major focus will be on profit-seeking organizations. However, the fundamental ideas also apply to nonprofit organizations. In addition, managers of the latter typically have personal investments in profit-seeking organizations or must interact with businesses in some way.

Managers and accountants in various settings such as hospitals, universities, and government agencies have much in common with their counterparts in profit-seeking organizations. There is money to be raised and spent. There are budgets to be prepared and control systems to be designed and implemented. There is an obligation to use resources wisely. If used intelligently, accounting contributes to efficient operations. The strengthening of the accounting system was a mandatory condition imposed by the federal government in saving New York City from bankruptcy.

The overlap of government and business is everywhere. Government administrators and politicians are much better equipped to deal with problems inside and outside their organizations if they understand accounting. For example, a knowledge of accounting is crucial for decisions regarding research contracts, defense contracts, and loan guarantees. Keep in mind that decisions about loan guarantees have been made with respect to tiny businesses (for instance, through the Small Business Administration) as well as large corporations such as Lockheed and Chrysler.

MEANS AND ENDS OF AN ACCOUNTING SYSTEM

An *accounting system* is a formal means of gathering and communicating data to *aid* and *coordinate* collective decisions in light of the overall goals or objectives of an organization. The accounting system is the major quantitative information system in almost every organization. An effective accounting system provides information for three broad purposes or ends: (1) internal reporting to managers, for use in planning and controlling routine operations; (2) internal reporting to managers, for use in the making of special decisions and the formulating of overall policies and long-range plans; and (3) external reporting to stockholders, government, and other outside parties.

Both management (internal parties) and external parties share an interest in all three important purposes, but the emphases of financial accounting and of management (internal) accounting differ. **Financial accounting** has mainly been concerned with the third purpose and has traditionally been oriented toward the historical, stewardship aspects of external reporting.[1] The distinguishing feature of management accounting is its emphasis on the planning and control purposes. **Management accounting** is the process of identification, measurement, accumulation, analysis, preparation, interpretation, and communication of information that assists executives in fulfilling organizational objectives.

What means do accounting systems use to fulfill the ends? Accounting data can be classified and reclassified in countless ways. A helpful overall classification was proposed in a research study of seven large companies with geographically dispersed operations:

☐ By observation of the actual decision-making process, specific types of data needs were identified at particular organizational levels—the vice-presidential level, the level of the factory manager, and the level of the factory head [foreman], for example—each involving quite distinct problems of communication for the accounting department.[2]

The research team found that three types of information, each serving as different means, often at various management levels, raise and help to answer three basic questions:

1. *Scorecard questions*: Am I doing well or badly?
2. *Attention-directing questions*: Which problems should I look into?
3. *Problem-solving questions*: Of the several ways of doing the job, which is the best?

The scorecard and attention-directing uses of data are closely related. The same data may serve a scorecard function for a manager and an attention-directing function for the manager's superior. For example, many accounting systems provide performance reports in which actual results are compared with previously determined budgets or standards. Such a performance report often helps to answer scorecard questions and attention-directing questions simultaneously. Furthermore, the actual results collected serve not only control purposes but also the traditional needs of financial accounting, which is chiefly concerned with the answering of scorecard questions. This collection, classification, and reporting of data is the task that dominates day-to-day accounting.

Problem-solving data may be used in long-range planning and in making special, nonrecurring decisions, such as whether to make or buy parts, replace an X-ray machine, or add or drop a product. These decisions often require expert advice from specialists such as industrial engineers, budgetary accountants, and statisticians.

---

[1] For a book-length presentation of the subject, see Charles T. Horngren and Gary L. Sundem, *Introduction to Financial Accounting* (Englewood Cliffs, N.J.: Prentice-Hall), the companion to this textbook. For an expanded definition of management accounting, see *Management Accounting*, April 1983, p. 65.

[2] H. A. Simon, *Administrative Behavior*, 2nd ed. (New York: Macmillan), p. 20.

EXHIBIT 1–1

Means and Ends of an Accounting System

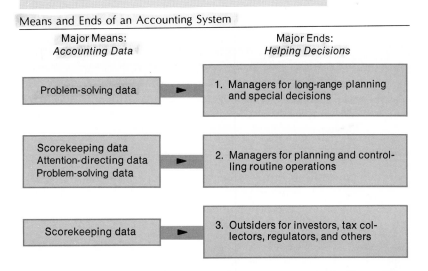

| Major Means:
Accounting Data | Major Ends:
Helping Decisions |

In sum, the accountant's task of supplying information has three facets:

1. **Scorekeeping**. The accumulation of data. This aspect of accounting enables both internal and external parties to evaluate organizational performance and position.
2. **Attention directing**. The reporting and interpreting of information that helps managers to focus on operating problems, imperfections, inefficiencies, and opportunities. This aspect of accounting helps managers to concentrate on important aspects of operations promptly enough for effective action. Attention directing is commonly associated with current planning and control and with the analysis and investigation of recurring routine internal accounting reports.
3. **Problem solving**. This aspect of accounting involves the concise quantification of the relative merits of possible courses of action, often with recommendations as to the best procedure. Problem solving is commonly associated with nonrecurring decisions, situations that require special accounting analyses or reports.

These distinctions sometimes overlap or merge. Consequently, it is often difficult to pinpoint a particular accounting task as being scorekeeping, attention directing, or problem solving. Nevertheless, attempts to make these distinctions provide insight into the objectives and tasks of both accountants and managers. Exhibit 1–1 recapitulates the relationships just described. Above all, accounting systems are the *means*, and better decisions are the *ends*.

THE MANAGEMENT PROCESS AND ACCOUNTING

☐ Nature of Planning and Controlling

The management *process* is a series of activities leading to a definite end. Its nucleus is decision making, the purposeful choosing among a set of alternative courses of action in light of some objective. These decisions range from the routine (making daily production schedules) to the nonroutine (launching a new product line).

Decision making underlies the commonly encountered twofold division of the management process into (1) planning and (2) control. The left side of Exhibit 1–2 clearly demonstrates the planning and control cycle of current operations. **Planning** (the top-box) means deciding on objectives and the means for their attainment. It provides the answers to two questions: What is desired? and When and how is it to be accomplished? **Controlling** (the two boxes labeled "Action" and "Evaluation" immediately below) means implementation of plans and the use of feedback so that objectives are attained. The feedback loop is the central facet of any concept of control, and timely, systematic measurement is the chief means of providing useful feedback. Planning and controlling are so intertwined that it seems artificial to draw rigid lines of separation between them; yet at times we will find it useful to concentrate on one or the other phase of the planning-control cycle.

☐ Management by Exception

The right side of Exhibit 1–2 shows that accounting formalizes plans by expressing them in the language of figures as **budgets**. Accounting formalizes

EXHIBIT 1–2

Accounting Framework for Planning and Control

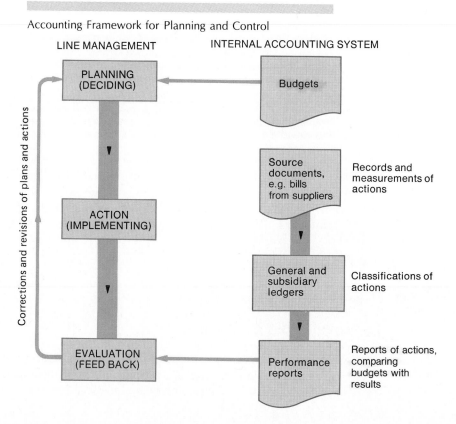

control as **performance reports** (the last box), which provide feedback by comparing results with plans and by highlighting **variances** (i.e., deviations from plans).

Exhibit 1–3 shows the form of a simple performance report for a law firm. Such reports spur investigation of exceptions. Operations are then brought into conformity with the plans, or the plans are revised. This is an example of management by exception.

EXHIBIT 1–3

Performance Report

	BUDGETED AMOUNTS	ACTUAL AMOUNTS	DEVIATIONS OR VARIANCES	EXPLANATION
Revenue from fees	xxx	xxx	xx	—
Various expenses	xxx	xxx	xx	—
Net income	xxx	xxx	xx	—

Management by exception means that the executive's attention and effort are concentrated on the significant deviations from expected results and that the information system highlights the areas most in need of investigation. Management should not ordinarily be concerned with results that conform closely to plans. However, well-conceived plans should incorporate enough discretion or flexibility so that the manager may feel free to pursue any unforeseen opportunities. In other words, the definition of control does not mean that managers should blindly cling to a preexisting plan when unfolding events indicate the desirability of actions that were not authorized specifically in the original plan.

☐ Illustration of the Budget and the Performance Report

An assembly department constructs electric fans. The assembly of the parts and the installation of the electric motor are basically hand operations. Each fan is inspected before being transferred to the painting department. In light of the present sales forecast, a production schedule of 4,000 window fans and 6,000 table fans is planned for the coming month. Cost classifications are shown in Exhibit 1–4, the Assembly Department Budget.

The operating plan, which is crystallized in the form of a department budget for the coming month, is prepared in conferences attended by the department manager, the manager's supervisor, and an accountant. Each of the costs subject to the manager's control is scrutinized. Its average amount for the past few months is often used as a guide, especially if past performance has been reasonably efficient. However, the budget is a *forecast* of costs. Each cost is projected in light of trends, price changes, alterations in product mix, specifications, labor methods, and changes in production volume from month

EXHIBIT 1–4

Assembly Department Budget
For the Month Ended March 31, 19X1

Material (detailed by type: metal stampings, motors, etc.)	$ 68,000
Assembly labor (detailed by job classification, number of workers, etc.)	43,000
Other labor (managers, inspectors)	12,000
Utilities, maintenance, etc.	7,500
Supplies (small tools, lubricants, etc.)	2,500
Total	$133,000

to month. The budget is then formulated, and it becomes the manager's target for the month.

As actual factory costs are incurred during the month, the accounting system collects them and classifies them by departments. At the end of the month (or perhaps weekly, or even daily, for such key items as materials or assembly labor), the accounting department prepares an Assembly Department Performance Report (Exhibit 1–5). In practice, this report may be very detailed and contain explanations of variances from the budget.

Department heads and their superiors use this report to help appraise performance. The spotlight is cast on the variances—the deviations from the budget. It is through management's investigation of these variances that better ways of doing things are discovered. The budget is the tool that aids planning; the performance report is the tool that aids controlling. The accounting system thus helps to direct managerial attention to the exceptions. Exhibit 1–2 shows that accounting does *not* do the controlling. Controlling consists of actions performed by the managers and their subordinates and of the evaluation

EXHIBIT 1–5

Assembly Department Performance Report
For the Month Ended March 31, 19X1

	BUDGET	ACTUAL	VARIANCE
Material (detailed by type: metal stampings, motors, etc.)	$ 68,000	$ 69,000	$1,000 U
Assembly labor (detailed by job classification, number of workers, etc.)	43,000	44,300	1,300 U
Other labor (managers, inspectors)	12,000	11,200	800 F
Utilities, maintenance, etc.	7,500	7,400	100 F
Supplies (small tools, lubricants, etc.)	2,500	2,600	100 U
Total	$133,000	$134,500	$1,500 U

U = Unfavorable.
F = Favorable.

that follows actions. Accounting assists the managerial control function by providing prompt measurements of actions and by systematically pinpointing trouble spots. This management-by-exception approach frees managers from needless concern with those phases of operations that are adhering to plans.

MANAGEMENT ACCOUNTING AND SERVICE ORGANIZATIONS

The basic ideas of management accounting were developed in manufacturing organizations. However, they have evolved so that they are applicable to all types of organizations, including service organizations. Service organizations or industries are defined in various ways. For our purposes, they are all organizations other than manufacturers, wholesalers, and retailers. That is, they are organizations that do not make or sell tangible goods. Examples are public accounting firms, law firms, management consultants, real estate firms, transportation companies, banks, insurance companies, and hotels. Almost all nonprofit organizations are service industries. Examples are hospitals, schools, libraries, museums, and a department of forestry.

The characteristics of service organizations include the following:

1. *Labor is intensive*. For example, the highest proportion of expenses in schools and law firms are wages, salaries, and payroll-related costs, not the costs relating to the use of machinery, equipment, and extensive physical facilities.
2. *Output is usually difficult to define*. For example, the output of a university might be defined as the number of degrees granted, but many critics would maintain that the real output is "what is contained in the students' brains." In such a manner the output of schools and hospitals is often idealized; attempts to measure output are often considered impossible.
3. *Major inputs and outputs cannot be stored*. For example, although raw materials and retail merchandise may be stored, a hotel's available labor force and rooms are either used or unused as each day occurs.

Many activities of nonprofit organizations differ little from those of business organizations. Sales promotion efforts are important. For example, the president of the University of San Francisco launched a "high-powered $100,000 ad campaign" on the grounds that "Universities simply must be more aggressive in their marketing." There was a four-week media blitz in 17 newspapers and 1 magazine, and on 5 radio stations.[3] For other examples, consider the campaigns by The United Way and the money-raising auctions by community television stations.

In this book, references are made to service industry applications as the various management accounting techniques are discussed. A major generalization is worth mentioning at the outset. Simplicity is the watchword for installation of systems in service industries and nonprofit organizations, especially in the health industry, where highly paid professionals such as physicians barely bother with a written medical record, much less a time card. In fact, simplicity is a fine watchword for the design of any accounting system.

---

[3] *San Francisco Chronicle*, March 26, 1985.

Complexity tends to generate costs of gathering and interpreting data that often exceed prospective benefits. Simplicity is sometimes referred to as KISS (which means "keep it simple, stupid").

ROLE OF THE ACCOUNTANT IN THE ORGANIZATION

☐ Line and Staff Authority

The organization chart in Exhibit 1–6 portrays how many manufacturing companies are divided into subunits. In particular, consider the distinction between **line** and **staff authority**. Most organizations specify certain activities as their basic mission, such as the production and sale of goods or services. All subunits of the organization that are *directly* responsible for conducting these basic activities are called *line* departments. The others are called *staff* departments because their principal task is to support or service the line departments. Thus staff activities are *indirectly* related to the basic activities of the organization. For instance, Exhibit 1–6 shows a series of factory-service departments that perform the staff functions of supporting the line functions carried on by the production departments.

The controller fills a staff role, in contrast to the line roles of sales and production executives. The accounting department has responsibility for providing other managers with specialized service, including advice and help in budgeting, analyzing variances, pricing, and the making of special decisions. The accounting department does not exercise direct authority over line departments: its authority to prescribe uniform accounting and reporting methods is delegated to the controller by top-line management. The uniform accounting procedure is authorized by the company president and is installed for her by the controller. When the controller prescribes the line department's role in supplying accounting information, he is not speaking as the controller, a staff person; he is speaking for top-line management.

Theoretically, the controller's decisions regarding the best accounting procedures to be followed by line people are transmitted to the president. In turn, the president communicates these procedures through a manual of instructions, which comes down through the line chain of command to all people affected by the procedures. In practice, however, the daily work of the controller, and his face-to-face relationships with the production manager, may require him to direct how production records should be kept or how time records should be completed. The controller usually holds delegated authority from top-line management over such matters.

Exhibit 1–7 shows how a controller's department may be organized. In particular, note the distinctions among the scorekeeping, attention-directing, and problem-solving roles. Unless some internal accountants are given the last two roles as their primary responsibilities, the scorekeeping tasks tend to be too dominating and the system less responsive to helping management's decision making.

EXHIBIT 1-6

Partial Organization Chart of a Manufacturing Company

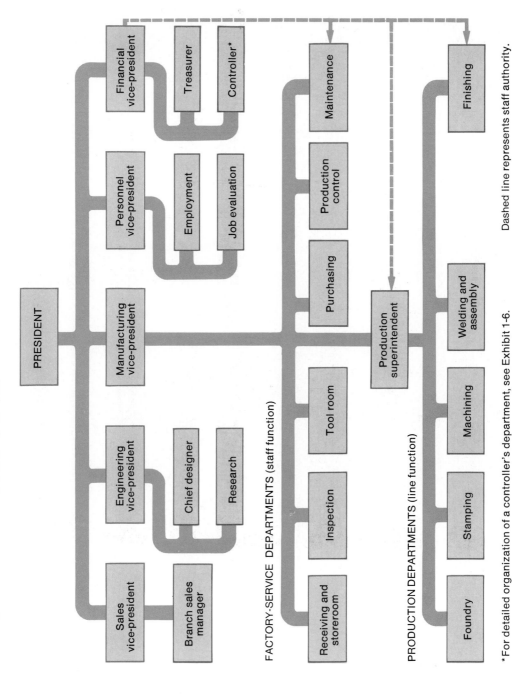

PRESIDENT

Sales vice-president — Branch sales manager

Engineering vice-president — Chief designer, Research

Manufacturing vice-president

Personnel vice-president — Employment, Job evaluation

Financial vice-president — Treasurer, Controller*

FACTORY-SERVICE DEPARTMENTS (staff function)

Receiving and storeroom, Inspection, Tool room, Purchasing, Production control, Maintenance

PRODUCTION DEPARTMENTS (line function)

Production superintendent

Foundry, Stamping, Machining, Welding and assembly, Finishing

Dashed line represents staff authority.

*For detailed organization of a controller's department, see Exhibit 1-6.

11

EXHIBIT 1–7

Organization Chart of a Controller's Department

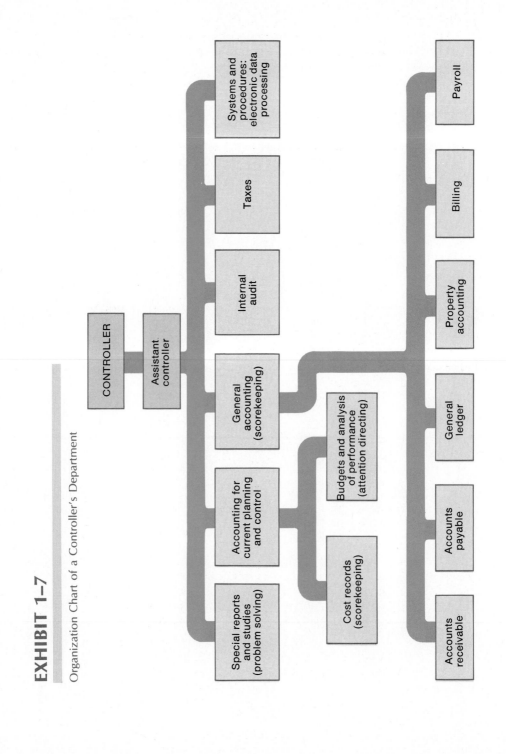

□ The Controller

The controller position varies in stature and duties from company to company. In some firms the controller is little more than a glorified bookkeeper who compiles data, primarily for external reporting purposes. In General Electric the controller is a key executive who aids managerial planning and control in over 160 company subdivisions. In most firms controllers have a status somewhere between these two extremes. For example, their opinions on the tax implications of certain management decisions may be carefully weighed, yet their opinions on other aspects of these decisions may not be sought. In this book, **controller** (sometimes called **comptroller**, derived from the French *compte*, for "account") means the chief management accounting executive. We have already seen that the modern controller does not do any controlling in terms of line authority except over his own department. Yet the modern concept of controllership maintains that, in a special sense, the controller *does* control: by reporting and interpreting relevant data, the controller exerts a force or influence or projects an attitude that impels management toward logical decisions that are consistent with objectives.

□ Distinctions Between Controller and Treasurer

Many people confuse the offices of controller and treasurer. The Financial Executives Institute, an association of corporate treasurers and controllers, distinguishes their functions as follows:

CONTROLLERSHIP	TREASURERSHIP
1. Planning for control	1. Provision of capital
2. Reporting and interpreting	2. Investor relations
3. Evaluating and consulting	3. Short-term financing
4. Tax administration	4. Banking and custody
5. Government reporting	5. Credits and collections
6. Protection of assets	6. Investments
7. Economic appraisal	7. Insurance

Note how management accounting is the controller's primary *means* of implementing the first three functions of controllership.

We shall not dwell at length on the treasurer's functions. As the seven points indicate, the treasurer is concerned mainly with financial, as distinguished from operating, problems. The exact division of various accounting and financial duties obviously varies from company to company.

The controller has been compared to the ship's navigator. The navigator, with the help of his specialized training, assists the captain. Without the navigator, the ship may flounder on reefs or miss its destination entirely, but the captain exerts his right to command. The navigator guides and informs the captain as to how well the ship is being steered. This navigator role is especially evident in points 1 through 3 of the seven functions.

TWO MAJOR THEMES

We have already seen that management accounting is concerned with how accounting systems help collective decisions. This book emphasizes two major themes or philosophies or problems regarding the design of these systems: (1) cost-benefit and (2) behavioral implications. Both will briefly be described now, and because of their importance, both will also be mentioned often in succeeding chapters.

☐ Cost-Benefit Theme

The **cost-benefit theme** (or call it a philosophy or state of mind if you prefer) is our fundamental approach to choosing among accounting systems and accounting methods. It will dominate this book. Systems and methods are economic goods that are available at various costs. Which system does a manager want to buy? A simple file drawer for amassing receipts and canceled checks? An elaborate budgeting system based on computerized descriptive models of the organization and its subunits? Or something in between?

Of course, the answer depends on the buyer's perceptions of the expected incremental (additional) benefits in relation to the incremental costs. For example, a hospital administrator may contemplate the installation of a TECHNICON computerized system for controlling hospital operations. Such a system uses a single document of original entry for automatic accumulation of data for financial records, medical records, costs by departments, nurse staffing requirements, drug administration, billings for patients, revenue generated by physicians, and so forth. This system will lead to more efficiency, less waste, and fewer errors. But the system costs $14 million. Thus the system is not good or bad by itself. It must meet the tests of the economics of information—its value must exceed its cost.

Steak and butter may be "good buys" for many people at 50¢ per pound, but they may become "bad buys" at $5 per pound. Similarly, a particular accounting system may be a wise investment in the eyes of the buyer if it will generate a sufficiently better collective set of decisions to justify its added cost. However, an existing accounting system is only *one* source of information for decision making. In many organizations it may be more economical to gather data by one-shot special efforts than by having a ponderous system that repetitively gathers data that are rarely used.

The cost-benefit theme provides innate appeal to both the hard-headed manager and the theoretician. Managers have been employing the cost-benefit test for years, even though they may not have expressed it as such. Instead, they may have referred to the theme as "having to be practical" despite what theory may say. But the cost-benefit theme has an exceedingly rich underlying theory of information economics. It is good theory that can supply the missing rationale for many management practices.

□ Behavioral Theme

Financial accounting is often looked upon as being a cold, objective discipline. But management accounting is not; it is wrapped up in behavioral ramifications. The buyer of an accounting system should be concerned with how it will affect the decisions (behavior) of the affected managers. Earlier we saw how budgets and performance reports may play a key role in helping management. Emphasis on the future is a major feature of management accounting, whereas it is not as prominent in financial accounting. Budgets are the chief devices for compelling and disciplining management planning. Without budgets, planning may not get the front-and-center focus that it usually deserves.

The performance reports that are so widely used to judge decisions, subunits, and managers have enormous influence on the behavior of the affected individuals. Performance reports not only provide feedback to improve future economic decisions but may also provide desirable or undesirable motivation. The choices of the content, format, timing, and distribution of performance reports are heavily influenced by their probable impact on motivation.

In a nutshell, management accounting can best be understood by using a cost-benefit theme coupled with an awareness of the importance of behavioral effects. Even more than financial accounting, management accounting spills over into related disciplines, such as economics, the decision sciences, and the behavioral sciences.

MANAGEMENT ACCOUNTING AND FINANCIAL ACCOUNTING

□ Freedom of Choice

Financial accounting and management accounting would be better labeled as external accounting and internal accounting, respectively. "Financial accounting" emphasizes the preparation of reports of an organization for external users such as banks and the investing public. "Management accounting" emphasizes the preparation of reports of an organization for its internal users such as company presidents, college deans, and head physicians.

The same basic accounting system compiles the fundamental data for both financial accounting and management accounting. Furthermore, external forces (for example, income tax authorities and regulatory bodies, such as the U.S. Securities and Exchange Commission and the California Health Facility Commission) often limit management's choices of accounting methods. Organizations frequently limp along with a system that has been developed in response to the legal requirements imposed by external parties. In short, many existing systems are externally oriented and neglect the needs of internal users.

Consider our cost-benefit theme that accounting systems are commodities like steak or butter. As just noted, generally accepted accounting standards or principles affect both internal and external accounting. However, change in internal accounting is not inhibited by generally accepted financial accounting standards. The managers who buy an internal accounting system can have anything their hearts desire—as long as they are willing to pay the price. For instance, for its own management purpose, a hospital, a manufacturer, or a university can account for its assets on the basis of *current values*, as measured by estimates of replacement costs. No outside agency can prohibit such accounting.

There are no "generally accepted management accounting principles" that forbid particular measurements. Indeed, the cost-benefit theme refrains from stating that any given accounting is bad or good. Instead, the theme says that any accounting system or method (no matter how crazy it appears at first glance) is desirable as long as it brings incremental benefits in excess of its incremental costs.

Of course, satisfying internal demands for data (as well as external demands) means that organizations may have to keep more than one set of records. At least in the United States, there is nothing immoral or unethical about having many simultaneous sets of books—but they are expensive. The cost-benefit test says that their perceived increases in benefits must exceed their perceived increases in costs. Ultimately, benefits are measured by whether better collective decisions are forthcoming in the form of increased net cost savings or profit (or, in the case of many nonprofit institutions, in the form of increased quality or quantity of service rendered for each dollar spent).

The major distinctions between management accounting and financial accounting are briefly enumerated in Exhibit 1–8. These points will be amplified in succeeding chapters.

☐ Effects of Regulation

The accounting reports to government agencies such as the Internal Revenue Service and the Securities and Exchange Commission are reports to outside parties. Hence such reports have usually been classified as subparts of financial accounting. Nevertheless, the proliferation of government regulation has definitely affected the design of internal accounting systems. Governmental agencies have broad powers, with the force of law, to subpoena any internal document deemed necessary.

An illustration of the effects of government regulation is the requirement that universities and defense contractors allocate costs to government contracts in specified ways or risk failure to get reimbursed.

The most noteworthy illustration is probably the **Foreign Corrupt Practices Act**, which was passed by the U.S. Congress in 1977. The title is misleading because the act's provisions pertain to the internal control systems of *all* publicly held companies, *even if they conduct no business outside the United States*. The act contains not only specific prohibitions against bribery and other corrupt practices but also requirements (1) for maintaining accounting records in reasonable detail and accuracy and (2) for maintaining an appropriate system of internal accounting controls.

The largest impact of the act has been the mandatory documentation of internal control by *management* rather than only by *outside auditors*. To

EXHIBIT 1–8

Distinctions Between Management Accounting and Financial Accounting

	MANAGEMENT ACCOUNTING	FINANCIAL ACCOUNTING
1. Primary users	Organization managers at various levels.	Outside parties such as investors and government agencies but also organization managers.
2. Freedom of choice	No constraints other than costs in relation to benefits of improved management decisions.	Constrained by generally accepted accounting principles (GAAP).
3. Behavioral implications	Concern about how measurements and reports will influence managers' daily behavior.	Concern about how to measure and communicate economic phenomena. Behavioral impact is secondary.
4. Time focus	Future orientation: formal use of budgets as well as historical records. Example: 19X3 **budget** versus 19X3 **actual** performance.	Past orientation: historical evaluation. Example: 19X3 **actual** versus 19X2 **actual** performance.
5. Time span	Flexible, varying from hourly to 10 or 15 years.	Less flexible. Usually one year or one quarter.
6. Reports	Detailed reports: concern about details of parts of the entity, products, departments, territories, etc.	Summary reports: concern primarily with entity as a whole.
7. Delineation of activities	Field is less sharply defined. Heavier use of economics, decision sciences, and behavioral sciences.	Field is more sharply defined. Lighter use of related disciplines.

help management, internal auditing staffs have been markedly increased. Internal auditors help review and evaluate systems with regard to minimizing errors, fraud, and waste. More important, many internal auditing staffs have a primary responsibility for conducting **management audits**, which concentrate on reviewing and evaluating managers' actions to see whether top management's operating policies are being implemented. Incidentally, management audits are not confined to profit-seeking organizations. The General Accounting Office (GAO) of the U.S. government conducts these audits on a massive scale.

The overall impact of government regulation is very controversial. Many managers insist that the extra costs of compliance far exceed any possible benefits. One benefit is that operating managers, now more than ever, must become more intimately familiar with their accounting systems. The resulting changes in the systems sometimes provide stronger controls and more informative reports. In short, outside forces may have more influence on management accounting than appears at first glance. More than ever, managers and accountants are obligated to provide accurate, reliable accounting information to higher-level managers and to outsiders.

Career Opportunities

Accounting deals with all facets of a complex organization. It provides an excellent opportunity for gaining broad knowledge. Senior accountants or controllers in a corporation are sometimes picked as production or marketing executives. Why? Because they may have impressed other executives as having acquired general management skills. Accounting must embrace all management functions, including purchasing, manufacturing, wholesaling, retailing, and a variety of marketing and transportation activities. A number of recent surveys have indicated that more chief executive officers began their careers in an accounting position than in any other area such as marketing, production, or engineering.

Korn/Ferry International, an executive recruiting firm, conducted a survey of 3,600 senior-level executives (excluding presidents) working in several hundred of the largest companies in the United States. The composite executive began in accounting or finance and still believes that to be the "fast track" to the top. In particular, there has been a dominance of accountants near the peak of the corporate pyramid.

Former controllers have risen to the top of such mammoth companies as General Motors, FMC, Fruehauf, and Pfizer. *Business Week* (August 15, 1982, p. 84) pointed out that controllers

are now getting involved with the operating side of the company, where they give advice and influence production, marketing, and investment decisions as well as corporate planning. Moreover, many controllers who have not made it to the top have won ready access to top management. . . . Probably the main reason the controller is getting the ear of top management these days is that he or she is virtually the only person familiar with all the working parts of the company.

Certified Management Accountant

A prominent feature of the field of financial accounting is the use of outside auditors to give assurance about the reliability of the financial information being supplied by managers. These external auditors are called **certified public accountants** in the United States and chartered accountants in many other English-speaking nations. The major U.S. professional association in the private sector that regulates the quality of outside auditors is the American Institute of Certified Public Accountants (AICPA).

The largest association of management accountants in the United States is the **National Association of Accountants** (NAA). The rise of the field of management accounting led the NAA in 1972 to establish the Institute for Certified Management Accountants. The institute administers a program leading to the Certificate in Management Accounting (CMA).[4] The objectives of the program are threefold:

1. To establish management accounting as a recognized profession by identifying the role of the management accountant and the underlying body of knowledge and by outlining a course of study by which such knowledge can be acquired.
2. To foster higher educational standards in the field of management accounting.
3. To establish an objective measure of an individual's knowledge and competence in the field of management accounting.

The highlight of the program is a qualifying examination covering five parts: (1) economics and business finance, (2) organization and behavior, (3) public reporting, (4) periodic reporting for internal and external purposes, and (5) decision analysis, including modeling and information systems. The CMA designation is gaining increased stature in the management community as a credential parallel to the CPA.

SUMMARY

If you understand the overall purposes of the accounting system, you get perspective for the study of the usefulness of accounting to management. The accounting system of the future is likely to be a multiple-purpose system with a highly selective reporting scheme. It will be highly integrated and will serve three main purposes: (1) routine reporting to management, primarily for planning and controlling current operations (scorekeeping and attention directing); (2) special reporting to management, primarily for long-range planning and nonrecurring decisions (problem solving); and (3) routine reporting on financial results, oriented primarily for external parties (scorekeeping). The first two purposes are the distinguishing characteristics of management accounting, which would be better called internal accounting.

Internal accounting is interwoven with management itself. Accounting is a service function. Internal accounting is not management as ordinarily conceived, but it helps management do a better job.

SUMMARY PROBLEMS FOR YOUR REVIEW

Try to solve these problems before examining the solutions that follow.

☐ Problem One

The scorekeeping, attention-directing, and problem-solving duties of the accountant have been described in this chapter. The accountant's usefulness to management is said to be directly influenced by how good an attention director and problem solver he or she is.

Evaluate this contention by specifically relating the accountant's duties to the duties of operating management.

---

[4] Information can be obtained from the Institute, 10 Paragon Drive, Montvale, N.J. 07645–0405.

☐ Problem Two

Using the organization charts in this chapter (Exhibits 1–6 and 1–7), answer the following questions.

1. Do the following have line or staff authority over the machining manager: maintenance manager, manufacturing vice-president, production superintendent, purchasing agent, storekeeper, personnel vice-president, president, chief budgetary accountant, chief internal auditor?
2. What is the general role of service departments in an organization? How are they distinguished from operating or production departments?
3. Does the controller have line or staff authority over the cost accountants? The accounts receivable clerks?
4. What is probably the *major duty* (scorekeeping, attention directing, or problem solving) of the following:

Payroll clerk	Cost analyst
Accounts receivable clerk	Head of special reports and studies
Cost record clerk	Head of internal auditing
Head of general accounting	Head of accounting for planning
Head of taxes	and control
Budgetary accountant	Controller

☐ Solution to Problem One

Operating managers may have to be good scorekeepers, but their major duties are to concentrate on the day-to-day problems that most need attention, to make longer-range plans, and to arrive at special decisions. Accordingly, because managers are concerned mainly with attention directing and problem solving, they will obtain the most benefit from the alert internal accountant who is a useful attention director and problem solver.

☐ Solution to Problem Two

1. The only executives having line authority over the machining manager are the president, the manufacturing vice-president, and the production superintendent.
2. A typical company's major purpose is to produce and sell goods or services. Unless a department is directly concerned with producing or selling, it is called a service or staff department. Service departments exist only to help the production and sales departments with their major tasks: the efficient production and sale of goods or services.
3. The controller has line authority over all members of his own department, all those shown in the controller's organization chart (Exhibit 1–7, p. 12).
4. The major duty of the first five—through the head of taxes—is typically scorekeeping. Attention directing is probably the major duty of the next three. Problem solving is probably the primary duty of the head of special reports and studies. The head of accounting for planning and control and the controller should be concerned with all three duties: scorekeeping, attention directing, and problem solving. However, there is a perpetual danger that day-to-day pressures will emphasize scorekeeping. Therefore accountants and managers should constantly see that attention directing and problem solving are also stressed. Otherwise the major management benefits of an accounting system may be lost.

HIGHLIGHTS TO REMEMBER

This section appears at the end of each chapter. It briefly recapitulates some key ideas, suggestions, comments, or terms that might otherwise be overlooked or misunderstood.

1. This book stresses two major themes: cost-benefit and behavioral implications. The choice of a system or method should be based on weighing the value of the system against its cost. This weighing entails making predictions of how individuals will collectively behave under one system versus another. Therefore the behavioral impact of alternatives is given ample attention throughout this book.

2. Nearly all managers are stronger managers when they attain an understanding of management accounting. Furthermore, their performance and their rewards are often heavily affected by how accounting measurements are made. Consequently, regardless of the size or goals of their organization, managers have a natural self-interest in learning about accounting.

ACCOUNTING VOCABULARY

This section usually immediately precedes the "assignment material" for each chapter. Vocabulary is an essential and often troublesome phase of the learning process. A fuzzy understanding of terms hampers the learning of concepts and the ability to solve accounting problems.

Before proceeding to the assignment material or to the next chapter, be sure you understand the following words or terms. Their meaning is explained in the chapter and also in the Glossary at the end of this book.

Attention Directing *p. 5*   Budget *6*   Certified Management Accountant *18*
Certified Public Accountant *18*   Comptroller *13*   Controller *13*   Controlling *6*
Cost-Benefit Theme *19*   Financial Accounting *3*   Foreign Corrupt Practices
Act *16*   Line Authority *10*   Management Accounting *4*   Management Audit *17*
Management by Exception *7*   National Association of Accountants *18*
Performance Report *7*   Planning *6*   Problem Solving *5*   Scorekeeping *5*   Staff
Authority *10*   Variance *7*

ASSIGNMENT MATERIAL

The assignment material for each chapter is divided into two groups: *fundamental* and *additional*. The first group consists of carefully designed, relatively straightforward material aimed at conveying the essential concepts and techniques of the particular chapter. These assignments provide a solid introduction to the major concepts of accounting for management control.

The second group of assignment material in each chapter should not be regarded as being inferior to the fundamental group. Many of these problems can be substituted for ones in the fundamental group.

FUNDAMENTAL ASSIGNMENT MATERIAL

1-1. **ROLE OF THE ACCOUNTANT IN THE ORGANIZATION: LINE AND STAFF FUNCTIONS.**

   a. Of the following, who have line authority over an assembler: stamping manager, assembly manager, production superintendent, production control chief, storekeeper, manufacturing vice-president, engineering vice-president, president, controller, budgetary accountant, cost record clerk?

   b. Of the following, who have line authority over a cost record clerk: budgetary accountant, head of accounting for current planning and control, head of general accounting, controller, storekeeper, production superintendent, manufacturing vice-president, president, production control chief?

1-2. **SCOREKEEPING, ATTENTION DIRECTING, AND PROBLEM SOLVING.** For each of the following, identify the function the accountant is performing—that is, scorekeeping, attention directing, or problem solving. Also state whether the departments mentioned here are production or service departments. If a department is neither of these, name the particular department and indicate whether it is a staff or a line type.

   (1) Recording overtime hours of the product finishing department.
   (2) Compiling data for a report showing the ratio of advertising expenses to sales for each branch store.
   (3) Investigating reasons for increased returns and allowances for drugs purchased by a hospital.
   (4) Computing and recording end-of-year adjustments for expired fire insurance on the factory warehouse for materials.
   (5) Preparing a schedule of fuel costs by months and government departments.
   (6) Estimating the operating costs and outputs that could be expected for each of two large metal-stamping machines offered for sale by different manufacturers. Only one of these machines is to be acquired by your company.
   (7) Preparing a report of overtime labor costs by production departments.
   (8) Posting daily cash collections to customers' accounts.
   (9) Estimating the costs of moving corporate headquarters to another city.
   (10) Daily recording of material purchase vouchers.
   (11) Analyzing the costs of acquiring and using each of two alternate types of welding equipment.
   (12) Interpreting increases in nursing costs per patient-day.
   (13) Analyzing deviations from the budget of the factory maintenance department.
   (14) Assisting in a study by the manufacturing vice-president to determine whether to buy certain parts needed in large quantities for manufacturing our products or to acquire facilities for manufacturing these parts.
   (15) Allocating factory service department costs to production departments.

ADDITIONAL ASSIGNMENT MATERIAL

1-3. What are the three broad purposes of an accounting system?

1-4. "The emphases of financial accounting and management accounting differ." Explain.

1-5. Distinguish among scorekeeping, attention directing, and problem solving.

1-6. Give examples of special nonrecurring decisions and of long-range planning.

1-7. Briefly describe the probable business information system of the future.

1-8. "Planning is much more vital than control." Do you agree? Explain.

1-9. Distinguish among a source document, a subsidiary ledger, and a general ledger.

1-10. Distinguish among a budget, a performance report, and a variance.

1–11. "Management by exception means abdicating management responsibility for planning and control." Do you agree? Explain.

1–12. "Good accounting provides automatic control of operations." Do you agree? Explain.

1–13. Distinguish between line and staff authority.

1–14. "The controller does control in a special sense." Explain.

1–15. "The importance of accurate source documents cannot be overemphasized." Explain.

1–16. Give three examples of service organizations.

1–17. "Additional government regulation assists the development of management accounting systems." Do you agree? Explain.

1–18. Distinguish between the American Institute of CPAs and the National Association of Accountants.

1–19. What two major themes will be emphasized in succeeding chapters?

1–20. "The Foreign Corrupt Practices Act applies to bribes paid outside the United States." Do you agree? Explain.

1–21. "The accounting system is intertwined with operating management. Business operations would be a hopeless tangle without the paper work that is so often regarded with disdain." Do you agree? Explain, giving examples.

1–22. **ORGANIZATION CHART.** Draw an organization chart for a single-factory company with the following personnel. Which represent factory service departments? Production departments?

Punch press manager   Personnel vice-president
Vice-president and controller   Maintenance manager
Storekeeper   Sales vice-president
Drill press manager   Production control chief
Production superintendent   Production planning chief
Chairman of the board   Assembly manager
Engineering vice-president   Purchasing agent
Manufacturing vice-president   Secretary and treasurer
President

1–23. **OBJECTIVES OF MANAGEMENT ACCOUNTING.** The National Association of Accountants (NAA) is composed of about 100,000 members interested in management accounting. The NAA published "Objectives of Management Accounting" (*Management Accounting*, November 1982). Page 57 states: "The management accountant participates, as part of management, in assuring that the organization operates as a unified whole in its long-run, intermediate, and short-run best interests."

Required: Based on your reading in this chapter, prepare a 100-word description of the principal ways that accountants participate in managing an entity.

1–24. **MANAGEMENT ACCOUNTING AND FINANCIAL ACCOUNTING.** Consider the following short descriptions. Indicate whether each description more closely relates to a major feature of financial accounting (use FA) or management accounting (use MA).

(1) Is constrained by generally accepted accounting principles.
(2) Has a future orientation.
(3) Is characterized by detailed reports.
(4) Field is more sharply defined.
(5) Has less flexibility.
(6) Behavioral impact is secondary.

1-25. **Costs and Benefits.** Marks & Spencer, a huge retailer in the United Kingdom, was troubled by its paper bureaucracy. Looked at in isolation, each form seemed reasonable, but overall a researcher reported that there was substantial effort in each department to verify the information. Basically, the effort seemed out of proportion to any value received, and, eventually, many of the documents were simplified or eliminated.

Describe the rationale that should govern systems design.

1-26. **Focus on Financial Data.** A news story reported:

☐ Rockwell's Anderson, a veteran of the company's automotive operations, recalls that when he sat in on meetings at Rockwell's North American Aircraft Operations in the late 1960s, "there'd be 60 or 70 guys talking technical problems, with never a word on profits." Such inattention to financial management helped Rockwell lose the F-15 fighter to McDonnell Douglas, Pentagon sources say. Anderson brought in profit-oriented executives, and he has now transformed North American's staff meetings to the point that "you seldom hear talk of technical problems any more," he says. "It's all financial."

What is your reaction to Anderson's comments? Are his comments related to management accounting?

1-27. **Nonprofit Systems.** The following comments were made by a certified public accountant who has had extensive experience in consulting in service industries and nonprofit organizations: "Useful accounting is so basic that, once accepted, it seems incredible that there was ever any question. Accounting doesn't advance on theory, only when somebody's money is at stake."

Required:

During the 1980s hospitals hired consultants in droves to install cost-accounting systems. Why hadn't hospitals used much cost accounting before?

INTRODUCTION TO
COST-VOLUME RELATIONSHIPS

LEARNING OBJECTIVES

When you have finished studying this chapter, you should be able to:

1. Define variable costs and fixed costs and compute the effects of changes in volume on each of these costs.
2. Construct a cost-volume-profit graph from appropriate data.
3. From given data, calculate activity volume in both total dollars and total units to (a) break even and (b) achieve a specified target profit.
4. Specify the limiting assumptions that underlie cost-volume analysis.
5. Distinguish between contribution margin and gross margin.
6. Construct and interpret a P/V chart.
7. Explain the effects of sales mix on profits (Appendix 2A).
8. Compute cost-volume-profit relationships on an after-tax basis (Appendix 2B).

IMPORTANCE OF COST-VOLUME-PROFIT ANALYSIS

How do the costs and revenues of a hospital change as one more patient is admitted for a four-day stay? How are the costs and revenue of an airline affected when one more passenger is boarded at the last moment, or when one more flight is added to the schedule? How should the budget request by the California Department of Motor Vehicles be affected by the predicted increase in the state's population? These questions have a common theme: What will happen to financial results if a specified level of activity or volume fluctuates? Their answers are not easy to obtain, and managers usually resort to some simplifying assumptions, especially concerning cost behavior (that is, how total costs are affected as volume changes). Nevertheless, directly or indirectly, managers must frequently answer these questions to reach intelligent decisions.

The managers of profit-seeking organizations usually study the relationships of revenue (sales), expenses (costs), and net income (net profit). This study is commonly called cost-volume-profit analysis. The managers of nonprofit organizations also will benefit from the study of cost-volume-profit relationships. Why? Primarily because knowledge of how costs fluctuate as volume changes is valuable regardless of whether profit is an objective. After all, no organization has unlimited resources. For example, an article on a survey of cost accounting for hospitals (*Journal of Accountancy*, May 1985) said that "variable and fixed cost elements were selected by the majority of respondents as required information for key operating decisions."

The subject matter of this chapter is straightforward. No knowledge of the accountant's assumptions underlying financial reporting is required. After all, in its most fundamental sense, an income statement is merely a presentation of the financial results from matching sales and related costs.

Cost-volume relationships are important to both management and outsiders. For example, the U.S. Securities and Exchange Commission requires the management of all publicly held companies to include a "management's discussion and analysis of the results of operations" in corporate quarterly and annual reports. Some of these analyses are quite detailed, and all focus on the effects of changes in prices and physical quantities sold.

VARIABLE COSTS AND FIXED COSTS

Variable costs and **fixed costs** are usually defined in terms of how a total cost changes in relation to fluctuations in the quantity of some selected activity. Activity bases are diverse: they may be the number of orders processed, the number of lines billed in a billing department, the number of adi a theater, the number of pounds handled in a warehouse, the hou worked in an assembly department, the number of rides in an ai park, the seat-miles on an airline, the dollar sales in a grocery store other index of volume.

If Watkins Products pays its door-to-door sales personnel a 40% commission, then the total cost of sales commissions should be 40% or the total sales dollars. If a sports shop buys bags of fish bait at $2 each, then the total cost of fish bait should be $2 times the total number of bags. These are variable costs. They are uniform *per unit*, but their *total* fluctuates in direct proportion to the total of the related activity or volume. These relationships are depicted graphically in Exhibit 2–1. Examples of variable costs include the costs of most merchandise, materials, parts, supplies, commissions, and many types of labor.

If a manufacturer of picture tubes for color television rents a factory for $100,000 per year, then the unit cost of rent applicable to each tube will depend on the total number of tubes produced. If 100,000 tubes are produced, the unit cost will be $1; if 50,000 tubes are produced, $2. This is an example of a fixed cost, a cost that does not change in *total* but becomes progressively smaller on a *per-unit* basis as volume increases. Examples of fixed costs include real estate taxes, real estate insurance, many executive salaries, and space rentals.

EXHIBIT 2–1

Variable-Cost Behavior

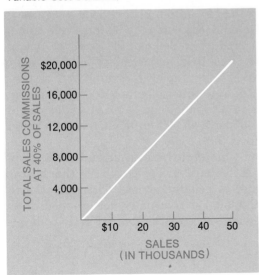

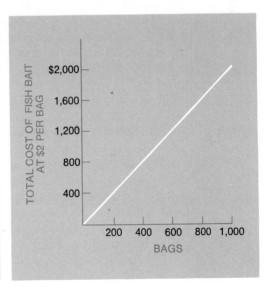

Note carefully from the foregoing examples that the "variable" or "fixed" characteristic of a cost relates to its *total dollar amount* and not to its per-unit amount. A variable cost (the 40% sales commission) is constant per unit, and its *total* dollar amount *changes* proportionally with changes in activity or volume. A fixed cost (the factory rent) varies inversely with activity or volume changes on a per-unit basis but is *constant* in *total* dollar amount. The following table summarizes these relationships:

TYPE OF COST	IF ACTIVITY VOLUME INCREASES (OR DECREASES):	
	Total Cost	Cost Per Unit*
Fixed costs	No change†	Decrease (or increase)
Variable costs	Increase (or decrease)	No change†

* Per unit of activity volume, for example, product units, passenger-miles, sales dollars.

† When using data for making predictions, think of fixed costs as a *total* and variable costs as an amount *per unit* of activity.

☐ Relevant Range

A **relevant range** is the expected band of activity volume for the planning period. For example, the weekly volume of automobiles produced by an assembly plant for a forthcoming year might fluctuate between 10,000 and 20,000 units. A fixed cost is fixed only in relationship to a given time—the budget period—and a given relevant range.

Fixed costs may change from budget year to budget year solely because of changes in insurance and property tax rates, executive salary levels, or rent levels. But these items are highly unlikely to change within a given year. In addition, the total budgeted fixed costs may be for a relevant range of, say, 40,000 to 85,000 units of production per month. However, operations on either side of the range would result in major salary adjustments or in the layoff or hiring of personnel. For example, in Exhibit 2–2 assume the total monthly fixed cost within the relevant range is $100,000. If operations fall below 40,000 units, changes in personnel and salaries would slash fixed costs to $60,000. If operations rise above 85,000 units, increases in personnel and salaries would boost fixed costs to $115,000.

These assumptions—a given time period and a given activity range—are shown graphically at the top of Exhibit 2–2. The possibility that operations will be outside the relevant range is usually remote. Therefore the three-level refinement at the top of Exhibit 2–2 is usually not graphed. A single horizontal line is typically extended through the plotted activity levels, as at the bottom of the exhibit.

EXHIBIT 2–2

Fixed Costs and the Relevant Range

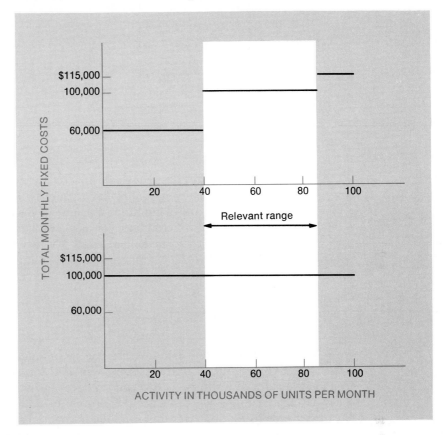

Of course, the basic idea of a relevant range also applies to variable costs. That is, outside a relevant range, some variable costs, such as fuel consumed, may behave differently per unit of activity volume. For example, the efficiency of motors is affected if they are used too much or too little.

☐ Some Simplifying Assumptions

Nearly every organization has some variable costs and some fixed costs. As you may suspect, it is often difficult to classify a cost as exactly variable or exactly fixed. Many complications arise, including the possibility of costs behaving in some nonlinear way (not behaving as a straight line). For example, as workers learn to process incoming tax forms, productivity rises. This means that total costs may actually behave like this:

but not like this:

Moreover, costs may simultaneously be affected by more than one activity base. For example, the costs of shipping labor may be affected by *both* the weight and the number of units handled. We shall investigate various facets of this problem in succeeding chapters; for now, we shall assume that any cost may be classified as either variable or fixed. We assume also that a given variable cost is associated with *only one* measure of volume, and that relationship is *linear*.

ILLUSTRATION OF COST-VOLUME-PROFIT ANALYSIS

The following situation will demonstrate the techniques and the analytical power of cost-volume-profit analysis. Amy Winston, the manager of food services for the state of California, is trying to decide whether to rent a line of food vending machines for the state's Sacramento buildings. Although the unit prices and acquisition costs differ among individual snack items, Winston feels that an average unit selling price of 50¢ and an average unit acquisition cost of 40¢ will suffice for purposes of this analysis. The following revenue and expense relationships are predicted:

	PER UNIT	PERCENT OF SALES
Selling price	$.50	100%
Cost of each item	.40	80
Contribution margin	$.10	20%
Monthly fixed expenses:		
Rent	$1,000	
Wages for replenishing and servicing	4,500	
Other fixed expenses	500	
Total fixed expenses per month	$6,000	

The following six sections will explore various aspects of the foregoing data. A new question or requirement will be stated at the start of each section.

☐ 1. Break-even Point—Two Analytical Techniques

Express the monthly break-even point in number of units and in dollar sales.

The study of cost-volume-profit relationships is often called *break-even analysis*. The latter is a misnomer because the break-even point—the point of zero net income—is often only incidental to the planning decision at hand. Still, knowledge of the break-even point provides insights into the possible riskiness of actions.

The condensed income statement at the break-even point could be presented as follows:

		PER UNIT	PERCENT
Units	60,000		
Sales	$30,000	$.50	100%
Variable expenses	24,000	.40	80
Contribution margin	$ 6,000	$.10	20%
Fixed expenses	6,000		
Net income	$ 0		

The terms *net income* and *net profit* are used interchangeably. Similarly, *expenses* and *costs* are used interchangeably. In this context, costs refer to the costs (whether variable or fixed) expiring during the period in question.

Consider two basic techniques for computing a break-even point: contribution margin and equation.

a. CONTRIBUTION-MARGIN TECHNIQUE. Consider the following commonsense arithmetic approach. Every unit sold generates a **contribution margin** or **marginal income,** which is the excess of the sales price over the variable expenses pertaining to the units in question:

Unit sales price	$.50
Unit variable expenses	.40
Unit contribution margin to fixed expenses and net income	$.10

When is the break-even point reached? When enough units have been sold to generate a total contribution margin equal to the fixed costs. The total fixed expenses are divided by the $.10 unit contribution margin to obtain the number of *units* that must be sold to break even: $6,000 ÷ $.10 = 60,000 units.

The computation in terms of *dollar* sales is 60,000 units × $.50 unit selling price, or $30,000. An alternate computation is

Sales price	100%
Variable expenses as a percentage of dollar sales	80
Contribution-margin percentage	20%

Therefore 20% of each sales dollar is the amount available for the recovery of fixed expenses and the making of net income: $6,000 ÷ .20 = $30,000 sales needed to break even. The contribution-margin percentage is based on dollar sales. This percentage is often expressed as a ratio (for example, 20% expressed as .20).

b. EQUATION TECHNIQUE. This is the most general form of analysis, the one that may be adapted to any conceivable cost-volume-profit situation. You are familiar with a typical income statement. Any income statement can be expressed in equation form, as follows:

$$\text{sales} - \text{variable expenses} - \text{fixed expenses} = \text{net income} \qquad (1)$$

At the break-even point net income is zero:

$$\text{sales} - \text{variable expenses} - \text{fixed expenses} = 0$$

Let

$$X = \text{number of units to be sold to break even. Then}$$

$$\$.50X - \$.40X - \$6,000 = 0$$

$$\$.10X = \$6,000$$

$$X = \frac{\$6,000}{\$.10}$$

$$X = 60,000 \text{ units}$$

Total sales in the equation is a price-times-quantity relationship. In the preceding equation, this was expressed as $\$.50X$. Of course, the *dollar* sales answer in this case could now be obtained by multiplying 60,000 *units* by 50¢, which would yield the break-even dollar sales of $30,000. Another approach is to solve the equation method for total sales *dollars* directly. This method becomes important in those situations where *unit* price and *unit* variable costs are not given. Rather, you must work with variable cost as a *percentage* of each sales *dollar*. Moreover, most companies sell more than one product, and the overall break-even point is often expressed in sales dollars because of the variety of product lines. For example, although radios and television sets cannot be meaningfully added, their sales prices provide an automatic common denominator.

The same equation, this time using the relationship of variable costs and profits as a *percentage* of sales, may be used to obtain the sales in dollars:

$$\text{variable-cost ratio or percentage} = \frac{\text{variable cost per unit}}{\text{sales price per unit}}$$

$$= \frac{\$.40}{\$.50}$$

$$= .80 \text{ or } 80\%$$

Let $\qquad$ X = sales in dollars needed to break even. Then

$$X - .80X - \$6,000 = 0$$

$$.20X = \$6,000$$

$$X = \frac{\$6,000}{.20}$$

$$X = \$30,000$$

c. **RELATIONSHIP OF THE TWO TECHNIQUES.** Reflect on the relationship between the two techniques. The contribution-margin technique is merely a shortcut version of the equation technique. Look at the last three lines in the two solutions given for Equation 1. They read

BREAK-EVEN VOLUME	
In Units	In Dollars
$\$.10X = \$6,000$	$.20X = \$6,000$
$X = \dfrac{\$6,000}{\$.10}$	$X = \dfrac{\$6,000}{.20}$
$X = 60,000 \text{ units}$	$X = \$30,000$

This gives us the shortcut general formulas:

$$\frac{\text{Break-even volume}}{\text{in units}} = \frac{\text{fixed expenses}}{\text{contribution margin per unit}} \qquad (2)$$

$$\frac{\text{Break-even volume}}{\text{in dollars}} = \frac{\text{fixed expenses}}{\text{contribution-margin ratio}} \qquad (3)$$

Which should you use, the equation or the contribution-margin technique?

Use either; the choice is a matter of personal preference or convenience within a particular case.

☐ **2. Graphical Technique**

Graph the cost-volume-profit relationships in Requirement 1.

The break-even point is represented by the intersection of the sales line and the total expenses line in Exhibit 2–3. Exhibit 2–3 was constructed by using a sales line and a total expenses line that combined variable and fixed expenses. The procedure (see Exhibit 2–3) is as follows:

Step 1. Select a convenient sales volume, say, 100,000 units, and plot point A for total sales dollars at that volume: $100,000 \times 50¢ = \$50,000$. Draw the revenue (i.e., sales) line from point A to the origin, point O.

Step 2. Draw the line showing the $6,000 fixed portion of expenses. It should be a horizontal line intersecting the vertical axis at $6,000, point B.

Step 3. Determine the variable portion of expenses at a convenient level of activity: $100,000 \text{ units} \times \$.40 = \$40,000$. Add this to the fixed expenses:

EXHIBIT 2–3

Cost-Volume-Profit Graph

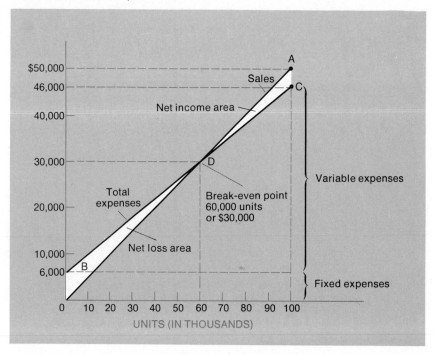

$40,000 + $6,000 = $46,000. Plot point C for 100,000 units and $46,000. Then draw a line between this point and point B. This is the total expenses line. The break-even point is where this line crosses the sales line, 60,000 units or $30,000, namely, where total sales revenues exactly equal total costs, point D.

Exhibit 2–3 is the completed break-even graph. The break-even point is only one facet of this cost-volume-profit graph. More generally, the graph shows the profit or loss at *any* rate of activity. Namely, at any given volume, the vertical distance between the sales line and the total expenses line measures the net income or net loss.

The graph portrays only one of a number of methods for picturing cost-volume-profit relationships. The graph often has educational advantages because it shows potential profits over a wide range of volume more easily than numerical exhibits. Whether graphs or other types of exhibits are used depends largely on management's preference.

The business press frequently refers to break-even points. For example, a news story stated that "the Big Three auto makers have slashed their sales break-even point in North America from 12.2 million cars and trucks to only 9.1 million this year." Another news story described the efforts of International Harvester Company [Navistar] to "lower the sales break-even point 18%."

□ 3. Changes in Fixed Expenses

If the $1,000 monthly rent of the vending machines were doubled, find the monthly break-even point (a) in number of units and (b) in dollar sales.
The fixed expenses would increase from $6,000 to $7,000. Then:

$$\frac{\text{break-even volume}}{\text{in units}} = \frac{\text{fixed expenses}}{\text{contribution margin per unit}} = \frac{\$7,000}{\$.10} = 70,000 \text{ units} \qquad (2)$$

$$\frac{\text{break-even volume}}{\text{in dollars}} = \frac{\text{fixed expenses}}{\text{contribution-margin ratio}} = \frac{\$7,000}{.20} = \$35,000 \qquad (3)$$

Note that a one-sixth increase in fixed expenses altered the break-even point by one-sixth: from 60,000 to 70,000 units and from $30,000 to $35,000. This type of relationship always exists, everything else held constant.

□ 4. Changes in Contribution Margin per Unit

Assume that the fixed rent is unchanged. (a) If the owner is paid 1¢ rental per unit in addition to the fixed rent, find the monthly break-even point in number of units; in dollar sales. (b) If the selling price falls from 50¢ to 45¢ per unit, and the original variable expenses per unit are unchanged, find the monthly break-even point, in number of units; in dollar sales.

a. The variable expenses would be increased from 40¢ to 41¢, the unit contribution margin would be reduced from 10¢ to 9¢, and the contribution-margin ratio would become .18 (9¢ ÷ 50¢).

The original fixed expenses of $6,000 would be unaffected, but the denominators are changed as compared with the denominators used in the solutions to Requirements 1 and 3. Thus,

$$\text{break-even point in units} = \frac{\$6,000}{\$.09} = 66,667 \text{ units} \qquad (2)$$

$$\text{break-even point in dollars} = \frac{\$6,000}{.18} = \$33,333 \qquad (3)$$

b. A change in unit contribution margin can also be caused by a change in selling price. If the selling price fell from 50¢ to 45¢, and the original variable expenses were unchanged, the unit contribution would be reduced from 10¢ to 5¢ (i.e., 45¢ − 40¢) and the break-even point would soar to 120,000 units (6,000 ÷ 5¢). The break-even point in dollars would also change because the selling price and contribution-margin ratio change: the contribution-margin ratio would be .1111 (5¢ ÷ 45¢). The break-even point, in dollars, would be $54,000 (120,000 units × 45¢), or, using the formula:

$$\text{break-even point in dollars} = \frac{\$6,000}{.1111} = \$54,000 \qquad (3)$$

□ 5. Target Net Profit and an Incremental Approach

Refer to the original data on page 30. If Winston considers $480 per month the minimum acceptable net income, how many units will have to be sold to justify the adoption of the vending machine plan? Convert your answer into dollar sales.

INTRODUCTION TO COST-VOLUME RELATIONSHIPS

The method for computing desired or target sales volume in units and the desired or target net income is the same as was used in our earlier break-even computations. However, now the targets are expressed in the equations:

$$\text{target sales} - \text{variable expenses} - \text{fixed expenses} = \text{target net income} \qquad (1)$$

or

$$\text{target sales volume in units} = \frac{\text{fixed expenses} + \text{target net income}}{\text{contribution margin per unit}} \qquad (2)$$

$$= \frac{\$6,000 + \$480}{\$.10} = 64,800 \text{ units}$$

Another way of getting the same answer is to use your knowledge of the break-even point and adopt an incremental approach. The term **incremental** is widely used in accounting. It refers to the *change* in total results (such as revenue, expenses, or income) under a new condition in comparison with some given or known condition.

In this instance, the given condition is assumed to be the 60,000-unit break-even point. All expenses would be recovered at that volume. Therefore the *change* or *increment* in net income for every unit *beyond* 60,000 would be equal to the contribution margin of $.50 − $.40 = $.10. If $480 were the target net profit, $480 ÷ $.10 would show that the target volume must exceed the break-even volume by 4,800 units; it would therefore be 60,000 + 4,800 = 64,800 units.

The answer, in terms of *dollar* sales, can then be computed by multiplying 64,800 units by $.50 or by using the formula:

$$\text{target sales volume in dollars} = \frac{\text{fixed expenses} + \text{target net income}}{\text{contribution-margin ratio}} \qquad (3)$$

$$= \frac{\$6,000 + \$480}{.20} = \$32,400$$

To solve directly for sales dollars with the alternative incremental approach, the break-even point, in dollar sales of $30,000, becomes the frame of reference. Every sales dollar beyond that point contributes 20¢ to net profit. Divide $480 by .20. The dollar sales must therefore exceed the break-even volume by $2,400 to produce a net profit of $480; thus the total dollar sales would be $30,000 + $2,400 = $32,400.

These relationships are recapitulated as follows:

	BREAK-EVEN POINT	INCREMENT	NEW CONDITION
Volume in units	60,000	4,800	64,800
Sales	$30,000	$2,400	$32,400
Variable expenses	24,000	1,920	25,920
Contribution margin	6,000	480	6,480
Fixed expenses	6,000	—	6,000
Net income	$ 0	$ 480	$ 480

☐ 6. Multiple Changes in the Key Factors

Suppose that after the vending machines have been in place awhile, Winston is considering locking them from 6:00 P.M. to 6:00 A.M., which she estimates will save $820 in wages monthly. The cutback from 24-hour service would hurt volume substantially because many nighttime employees use the machines. However, employees could find food elsewhere, so not too many complaints are expected.[1] Should the machines remain available 24 hours per day? Assume that monthly sales would decline by 10,000 units from current sales of (a) 62,000 units and (b) 90,000 units.

First, whether 62,000 or 90,000 units are being sold is irrelevant to the decision at hand. The analysis of this situation consists of constructing and solving equations for conditions that prevail under either alternative and selecting the volume level that yields the highest net profit. However, the incremental approach is much quicker. What is the essence of this decision? We are asking whether the prospective savings in cost exceed the prospective loss in *total* contribution margin in dollars:

Lost total contribution margin, 10,000 units @ $.10	$1,000
Savings in fixed expenses	820
Prospective decline in net income	$ 180

Regardless of the current volume level, be it 62,000 or 90,000 units, if we accept the prediction that sales will decline by 10,000 units as accurate, the closing from 6:00 P.M. to 6:00 A.M. will decrease the income by $180:

	DECLINE FROM 62,000 TO 52,000 UNITS		DECLINE FROM 90,000 TO 80,000 UNITS	
Units	62,000	52,000	90,000	80,000
Sales	$31,000	$26,000	$45,000	$40,000
Variable expenses	24,800	20,800	36,000	32,000
Contribution margin	$ 6,200	$ 5,200	$ 9,000	$ 8,000
Fixed expenses	6,000	5,180	6,000	5,180
Net income	$ 200	$ 20	$ 3,000	$ 2,820
Change in net income	($180)		($180)	

---

[1] The quality of overall working conditions might affect these decisions, even though such factors are difficult to quantify. In particular, if costs or profits do not differ much between alternatives, the nonquantifiable, subjective aspects may be the deciding factors.

USES AND LIMITATIONS OF COST-VOLUME ANALYSIS

☐ **Best Combination of Factors**

The analysis of cost-volume-profit relationships is an important management responsibility. The knowledge of patterns of cost behavior offers insights valuable in planning and controlling short- and long-run operations. This is a major lesson that we will emphasize in this book, so we should regard the current material as introductory. Our purpose in this chapter is to provide perspective rather than to impart an intimate knowledge of the niceties of cost behavior.

The example of the vending machines demonstrated some helpful applications of cost-volume-profit analysis. Managers should try to obtain the most profitable combination of the variable- and fixed-cost factors. For example, automated machinery may be purchased, causing more fixed costs but reducing labor cost per unit. On the other hand, it may be wise to reduce fixed costs to obtain a more favorable combination. Thus, direct selling by a salaried sales force may be supplanted by the use of manufacturer's agents who are compensated via sales commissions (variable costs).

Generally, companies that spend heavily for advertising are willing to do so because they have high contribution-margin percentages (airlines, cigarette, and cosmetic companies). Conversely, companies with low contribution-margin percentages usually spend less for advertising and promotion (manufacturers of industrial equipment). Obviously, two companies with the same unit sales volumes at the same unit prices will have different attitudes toward risking an advertising outlay. Assume:

	PERFUME COMPANY	JANITORIAL SERVICE COMPANY
Unit sales volume	100,000 bottles	100,000 square feet
Dollar sales at $20 per unit	$2,000,000	$2,000,000
Variable costs	200,000	1,700,000
Contribution margin	$1,800,000	$ 300,000
Contribution-margin percentage	90%	15%

Suppose that each company wants to increase sales volume by 10%:

	PERFUME COMPANY	JANITORIAL SERVICE COMPANY
Increase in sales volume, 10,000 × $20	$200,000	$200,000
Increase in contribution margin, 90%, 15%	180,000	30,000

The perfume company would be inclined to increase advertising considerably to boost contribution margin by $180,000. In contrast, the janitorial service company would be foolhardy to spend large amounts to increase contribution margin by $30,000.

Therefore, when the contribution margin is low, great increases in volume are necessary before significant increases in net profits can occur. As sales exceed the break-even point, a high contribution-margin percentage increases profits faster than does a small contribution-margin percentage.

☐ **Limiting Assumptions**

The notion of relevant range, which was introduced when fixed expenses were discussed, is applicable to the entire break-even graph. Almost all break-even graphs show revenue and cost lines extending back to the vertical axis. This is misleading because the relationships depicted in such graphs are valid only within the relevant range that underlies the construction of the graph. Exhibit 2–4 (B), a modification of the conventional break-even graph, partially demonstrates the multitude of assumptions that must be made in constructing the typical break-even graph. Some of these assumptions follow.

1. The behavior of revenues and expenses is accurately portrayed and is linear over the relevant range. The principal differences between the accountant's break-even chart and the economist's are that (a) the accountant's sales line is drawn on the assumption that selling prices do not change with production or

EXHIBIT 2–4

Conventional and Modified Break-even Graphs

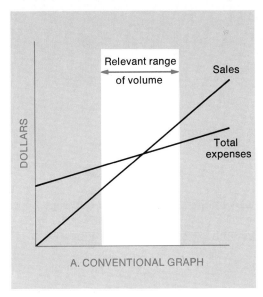

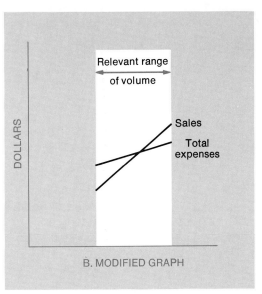

sales, and the economist assumes that reduced selling prices are normally associated with increased sales volume; (b) the accountant usually assumes a constant variable expense per unit, and the economist assumes that variable expense per unit does change with production. Within the relevant range, the accountant's and the economist's sales and expense lines are usually close to one another, although the lines may diverge greatly outside the range.

2. Expenses may be classified into variable and fixed categories. Total variable expenses vary directly with volume. Total fixed expenses do not change with volume.

3. Efficiency and productivity will be unchanged.

4. Sales mix will be constant. The **sales mix** is the relative combination of quantities of a variety of company products that comprise total sales.

5. The difference in inventory level at the beginning and at the end of a period is insignificant. (The impact of inventory changes on cost-volume-profit analysis is discussed in Chapter 15.)

☐ **Contribution Margin and Gross Margin**

Recall that *contribution margin* was defined as the excess of sales over *all* variable expenses. It may be expressed as a *total* absolute amount, a *unit* absolute amount, a *ratio*, and a *percentage*. Sometimes a **variable-expense ratio** or **variable-cost ratio** or **variable-cost percentage** may be encountered; it is defined as the variable expenses divided by sales. Thus a contribution-margin ratio of 20% means that the variable-cost ratio is 80%.

The most confusion about terms seems to be the mix-up between *contribution margin* and **gross margin** (which is also called **gross profit**). *Gross margin* is a widely used concept, particularly in the retailing industry. It is defined as the excess of sales over the **cost of goods sold** (that is, the cost of the merchandise that is acquired and resold). The following comparisons from our chapter illustration show the similarities and differences between the contribution margin and the gross margin in a retail store:

Sales	$.50
Variable costs: acquisition cost of unit sold	.40
Contribution margin and gross margin are equal	$.10

Thus the basic data for Requirement 1 resulted in no difference between the measure of contribution margin and gross margin. However, recall that Requirement 4a introduced a variable portion of rent. There would now be a difference:

	4a	1
Sales		$.50	$.50
Acquisition cost		
of unit sold	$.40		.40
Variable rent	.01		
Total variable expense		.41	
Contribution margin		$.09	
Gross margin			$.10

As the preceding tabulation indicates, and as the next chapter will explain more fully, contribution margin and gross margin are not the same concepts. Contribution margin focuses on sales in relation to *all* variable cost behavior, whereas gross margin focuses on sales in relation to a lone item, the acquisition cost of the *merchandise* that has been sold.

☐ Nonprofit Application

Consider how cost-volume-profit relationships apply to nonprofit organizations. Suppose a city has a $100,000 lump-sum budget appropriation for a government agency to conduct a counseling program for drug addicts. Suppose the variable costs for drug prescriptions are $400 per patient per year. Fixed costs are $60,000. If all of the budget appropriation is spent, how many patients could be served in a year?

Let X = number of patients

$$\text{revenue} - \text{variable expenses} - \text{fixed expenses} = 0$$
$$\$100{,}000 - \$400X - \$60{,}000 = 0$$
$$\$400X = \$100{,}000 - \$60{,}000$$
$$X = \$40{,}000 \div 400$$
$$X = 100$$

Suppose the total budget for the following year is cut 10%. Fixed costs will be unaffected, but service will decline:

$$\text{revenue} - \text{variable expenses} - \text{fixed expenses} = 0$$
$$\$90{,}000 - \$400X - \$60{,}000 = 0$$
$$\$400X = \$90{,}000 - \$60{,}000$$
$$X = \$30{,}000 \div \$400$$
$$X = 75$$

The reduction in service is more than the 10% reduction in the budget. Without restructuring operations, the service volume must be reduced 25%

(from 100 to 75 patients) to stay within budget. Note that revenue is a horizontal line on the graph:

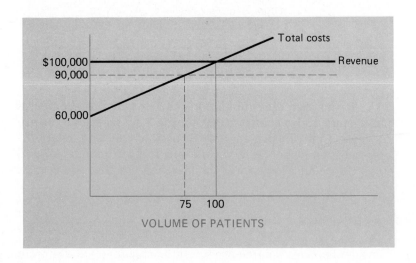

☐ Models and Personal Computers

Cost-volume-profit analysis is based on a mathematical model, the equation

sales — variable expenses — fixed expenses = net income

Consequently, the C-V-P model is widely used as a so-called planning model. Moreover, the increasing use of personal computers has led to expanded applications of C-V-P models in a great variety of organizations and situations. C-V-P analysis is a common management use of personal computers. Various combinations of changes in selling prices, unit variable costs, fixed costs, and desired profits may be studied. Computers readily display such changes, both numerically and graphically.

Computerized C-V-P planning models are used by many nonprofit organizations. For example, some private universities have models that help measure the potential impact on financial results from such decisions as raising tuition, adding programs, and closing dormitories during winter holidays. The reliability of these models depends on the accuracy of their underlying assumptions regarding how revenues and costs will actually be affected.

Throughout this chapter, C-V-P models have been studied as though costs are neatly and readily classified into variable and fixed categories. In the real world, these classifications are highly dependent on the decision situation. For example, the additional cost to an airline of transporting one more passenger on an airplane already at the departure gate is relatively small. Perhaps the costs would go up by only a meal in some instances. In contrast, the costs of adding a new route or a new airplane would be far different.

SUMMARY

An understanding of cost behavior patterns and cost-volume-profit relationships can help guide a manager's decisions.

Variable costs (and expenses) and fixed costs (and expenses) have contrasting behavior patterns. Their relationship to sales, volume, and net profit is probably best seen on a cost-volume-profit graph. However, the graph should be used with great care. The portrayal of all profit-influencing factors on such a graph entails many assumptions that may hold over only the relevant range of activity volume. As a tool, the graph may be compared to a meat-ax rather than to a surgeon's scalpel. Cost-volume-profit analysis, as depicted on a graph, is a framework for analysis, a vehicle for appraising overall performance, and a planning device.

SUMMARY PROBLEM FOR YOUR REVIEW

☐ Problem

The income statement of Wiley Company is summarized as follows:

Net revenue	$800,000
Less: Expenses, including $400,000 of fixed expenses	880,000
Net loss	$ (80,000)

The manager believes that an increase of $200,000 in advertising outlays will increase sales substantially. Her plan was approved by the chairman of the board.

Required:
1. At what sales volume will the company break even?
2. What sales volume will result in a net profit of $40,000?

☐ Solution

1. Note that all data are expressed in dollars. No unit data are given. Most companies have many products, so the overall break-even analysis deals with dollar sales, not units. The variable expenses are $880,000 − $400,000, or $480,000. The variable-expense ratio is $480,000 ÷ $800,000, or .60. Therefore the contribution-margin ratio is .40.

Let $\quad$ S = break-even sales, in dollars

Then

$$S - \text{variable expenses} - \text{fixed expenses} = \text{net profit} \qquad (1)$$

$$S - .60S - (\$400,000 + \$200,000) = 0$$

$$.40S = \$600,000$$

$$S = \frac{\$600,000}{.40} = \frac{\text{fixed expenses}}{\text{contribution-margin ratio}} \qquad (3)$$

$$S = \$1,500,000$$

2.

$$\text{required sales} = \frac{\text{fixed expenses} + \text{target net profit}}{\text{contribution-margin ratio}} \qquad (3)$$

$$\text{required sales} = \frac{\$600,000 + \$40,000}{.40} = \frac{\$640,000}{.40}$$

$$\text{required sales} = \$1,600,000$$

Alternatively, we can use an incremental approach and reason that all dollar sales beyond the $1.5 million break-even point will result in a 40% contribution to net profit. Divide $40,000 by .40. Sales must therefore be $100,000 beyond the $1.5 million break-even point in order to produce a net profit of $40,000.

HIGHLIGHTS TO REMEMBER

1. Check your understanding of basic terms. As a section (p. 40) in the chapter emphasized, gross margin and contribution margin have different meanings.
2. Contribution margin may be expressed as a total amount, as an amount per unit, as a ratio, or as a percentage.
3. The assumptions that underlie typical cost-volume-profit analysis are static. A change in one assumption (e.g., total fixed cost or the unit price of merchandise) will affect all the cost-volume-profit relationships on a given graph. The static nature of these assumptions should always be remembered by the managers who use this valuable analytical technique.

ACCOUNTING VOCABULARY

Contribution Margin *p. 31*   Cost of Goods Sold *40*   Fixed Cost *26*   Gross Margin *40*   Gross Profit *40*   Incremental *36*   Marginal Income *31*   Relevant Range *28*   Sales Mix *40*   Variable Cost *26*   Variable-Cost Percentage *40* Variable-Cost Ratio *40*   Variable-Expense Ratio *40*.

APPENDIX 2A: THE P/V CHART AND SALES-MIX ANALYSIS

THE P/V CHART

Exhibit 2–3 can be recast in another form as a so-called P/V chart (a profit-volume graph). This form is preferred by many managers who are interested mainly in the impact of changes in volume on net income. The first graph in Exhibit 2–5 illustrates the chart, using the data in our example. The chart is constructed as follows:

1. The vertical axis is net income in dollars. The horizontal axis is volume in units (or in sales dollars, in many cases).
2. At zero volume, the net loss would be approximated by the total fixed costs: $6,000 in this example.
3. A net income line will slope upward from the −$6,000 intercept at the rate of the unit contribution margin of 10¢. This line will intersect the volume axis at

EXHIBIT 2–5

P/V Chart

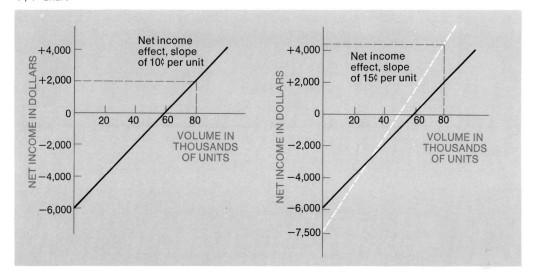

the break-even point of 60,000 units. Each unit sold beyond the break-even point will add 10 cents to net income. For example, at a volume of 80,000 units, the net income would be $(80,000 - 60,000) \times \$.10 = \$2,000$.

The P/V chart provides a quick, condensed comparison of how alternatives on pricing, variable costs, or fixed costs may affect net income as volume changes. For example, the second graph in Exhibit 2–5 shows how net income and the break-even point would be affected by an increase in selling price from 50¢ to 55¢ and a $1,500 increase in rent. The unit contribution would become 15¢, and the break-even point would fall from 60,000 to 50,000 units:

$$\text{new break-even point} = \$7,500 \div \$.15$$
$$= 50,000 \text{ units}$$

Note also that the net income will increase at a much faster rate as volume increases. At a volume of 80,000 units, the net income would be $(80,000 - 50,000) \times \$.15 = \$4,500$.

SALES-MIX ANALYSIS

To emphasize fundamental ideas, the cost-volume-profit analysis in this chapter has focused on a single product. But nearly all companies sell more than one product. **Sales mix** is defined as the relative combination of quantities of products that compose total sales. If the proportions of the mix change, the cost-volume-profit relationships also change.

Suppose that Ramos Company has two products, H and J. H is a wallet subject to heavy competition. J is a key case subject to less competition. The income budget follows:

	H	J	TOTAL
Sales in units	300,000	75,000	375,000
Sales @ $8 and $5	$2,400,000	$375,000	$2,775,000
Variable expenses @ $7 and $3	2,100,000	225,000	2,325,000
Contribution margins @ $1 and $2	$ 300,000	$150,000	$ 450,000
Fixed expenses			180,000
Net income			$ 270,000

For simplicity, ignore income taxes. What would be the break-even point? The typical answer assumes a constant mix of 4 units of H for every unit of J.

Let J = number of units of product J to break even

$4J$ = number of units of product H to break even

sales − variable expenses − fixed expenses = zero net income

$$\$8(4J) + \$5(J) - \$7(4J) - \$3(J) - \$180,000 = 0$$

$$\$32J + \$5J - \$28J - \$3J - \$180,000 = 0$$

$$\$37J - \$31J = \$180,000$$

$$\$6J = \$180,000$$

$$J = 30,000$$

$$4J = 120,000 = H$$

The break-even point is 30,000J + 120,000H = 150,000 units.

This is the only break-even point for a sales mix of 4 units of H for every unit of J. However, clearly, there are other break-even points for other sales mixes. For instance, suppose only J were sold, fixed expenses being unchanged:

$$\text{break-even point} = \frac{\text{fixed expenses}}{\text{contribution margin per unit}}$$

$$= \frac{\$180,000}{\$2}$$

$$= 90,000 \text{ units of J}$$

If only H were sold,

$$\text{break-even point} = \frac{\$180,000}{\$1}$$

$$= 180,000 \text{ units of H}$$

Managers are not primarily interested in the break-even point for its own sake. Instead, they want to know how changes in a planned sales mix will affect net income. When the sales mix changes the break-even point and the expected net income at various sales levels are altered. For example, suppose that overall actual total sales were equal to the budget of 375,000 units. However, only 50,000 units of J were sold:

	H	J	TOTAL
Sales in units	325,000	50,000	375,000
Sales @ $8 and $5	$2,600,000	$250,000	$2,850,000
Variables expenses @ $7 and $3	2,275,000	150,000	$2,425,000
Contribution margins @ $1 and $2	$ 325,000	$100,000	$ 425,000
Fixed expenses			180,000
Net income			$ 245,000

The change in sales mix has resulted in a $245,000 actual net income rather than the $270,000 budgeted net income, an unfavorable difference of $25,000. The total budgeted and actual total sales in number of units were identical, but the proportion of the product bearing the higher unit contribution margin declined.

Managers usually want to maximize the sales of all their products. However, faced with limited resources and time, executives prefer to generate the most profitable sales mix achievable. Different advertising strategies may also affect the sales mix. Clearly, if a sales budget is not actually attained, the budgeted net income will be affected by the individual sales volumes of each product. The fewer the units sold, the less profit, and vice versa. All other things being equal, the higher the proportion of the more profitable products, the higher the profit. For example, Reynolds Industries sells highly profitable cigarettes (such as the Winston brand) and less profitable canned goods (such as the Del Monte brand). For any given level of total sales, the greater the proportion of the cigarettes, the greater the total profit.

Management's discussion and analysis of income statements often refers to the effects of changes in sales mix. For example, consider a recent annual report of Deere & Co., a manufacturer of farm equipment: "The increase in the ratio of cost of goods sold to net sales resulted from higher production costs, a less favorable mix of products sold, and sales incentive programs."

Executives often must decide to emphasize or deemphasize particular products. For example, given limited production facilities or limited time of sales personnel, should we emphasize brand A or brand B fertilizer? These decisions may be affected by other factors beyond the contribution margin per unit of product. Chapters 4 and 16 explore some of these factors, including the importance of the amount of profit per *unit of time* rather than per *unit of product*.

APPENDIX 2B: IMPACT OF INCOME TAXES

Private enterprises are subject to income taxes. Reconsider Requirement 5 of the basic illustration in the chapter, page 35, where the target income before income taxes was $480. If an income tax were levied at 40%, relationships would be:

Income before income tax	$480	100%
Income tax	192	40
Net income	$288	60%

Note that

net income = income before income taxes − .40 (income before income taxes)

net income = .60 (income before income taxes)

$$\text{income before income taxes} = \frac{\text{net income}}{.60}$$

or

$$\text{income before income taxes} = \frac{\text{target after-tax net income}}{1 - \text{tax rate}}$$

$$\text{income before income taxes} = \frac{\$288}{1 - .40} = \frac{\$288}{.60} = \$480$$

Suppose the target net income after taxes were $288. The only change in the general equation approach would be:

$$\text{target sales} - \text{variable expenses} - \text{fixed expenes} = \frac{\text{target after-tax net income}}{1 - \text{tax rate}}$$

Thus, letting X be the number of units to be sold at 50¢ each with a variable cost of 40¢ each and total fixed costs of $6,000:

$$\$.50X - \$.40X - \$6,000 = \frac{\$288}{1 - .4}$$

$$\$.10X = \$6,000 + \frac{\$288}{.6}$$

$$\$.06X = \$3,600 + \$288 = \$3,888$$

$$X = \$3,888 \div \$.06 = 64,800 \text{ units}$$

Sales of 64,800 units produce an *after-tax* profit of $288 as shown here and a *before-tax* profit of $480 as shown in Requirement 5, page 35.

Suppose that the target net income after taxes were $480. The needed volume would rise to 68,000 units, as follows:

$$\$.50X - \$.40X - \$6,000 = \frac{\$480}{1 - .4}$$

$$\$.10X = \$6,000 + \frac{\$480}{.6}$$

$$\$.06X = \$3,600 + \$480 = \$4,080$$

$$X = \$4,080 \div \$.06 = 68,000 \text{ units}$$

Note that after-tax net income rises from $288 to $480, an increase of $192. A shortcut computation of the effects of volume on after-tax income can use the formula:

$$\begin{array}{c}\text{Change} \\ \text{in net} \\ \text{income}\end{array} = \left(\begin{array}{c}\text{Change in volume} \\ \text{in units}\end{array}\right) \times \left(\begin{array}{c}\text{Contribution margin} \\ \text{per unit}\end{array}\right) \times (1 - \text{tax rate})$$

In our example, suppose operations were at a level of 64,800 units and $288 after-tax net income. The manager is wondering how much after-tax net income would increase if sales become 68,000 units:

$$\text{Change in net income} = (68,000 - 64,800) \times \$.10 \times (1 - .4)$$

$$= 3,200 \times \$.10 \times .60 = 3,200 \times \$.06$$

$$= \$192$$

In brief, each unit beyond the break-even point adds to after-tax net profit at the unit contribution margin multiplied by (1 − income tax rate).

Throughout our illustration, the break-even point itself does not change. Why? Because there is no income tax at a level of zero profits.

FUNDAMENTAL ASSIGNMENT MATERIAL

2–1. **PHOTOCOPYING MACHINES.** The Martinez Company operates and services photo-copying machines located in college dormitories, libraries, hotels, and various public places. The machines are rented from the manufacturer. In addition, Martinez must rent the space occupied by the machines. Martinez has an opportunity to place some machines in ten branch libraries of a large city. The following expense and revenue relationships pertain to a contemplated expansion program of ten machines, which are rented by Martinez from a manufacturer at a flat rate per month plus 1 cent per copy:

Fixed monthly expenses:

Machine rental: 10 machines	$1,200
Space rental: 10 locations	400
Wages, including fringe costs, to service the additional 10 machines	700
Other fixed costs	100
Total	$2,400

Other data:

	PER COPY	PER $100 OF SALES
Selling price	$.10	100%
Cost of paper, toner, repair parts, and rental charge per copy	.06	60
Contribution margin	$.04	40%

Required

These questions relate to the above data unless otherwise noted. Ignore income taxes. *Consider each question independently.*

1. Compute the monthly break-even point in number of copies; in dollar sales.
2. Compute the company's monthly net income if 70,000 copies were sold.
3. Suppose the space rental were doubled. Compute the monthly break-even point in number of copies; in dollar sales.
4. Refer to the original data. Suppose the manufacturer increased the rent from 1¢ to 2¢ per copy. Compute the monthly break-even point in number of copies.
5. Refer to the original data. Suppose the libraries were paid 1¢ per copy for each unit sold in excess of the break-even point. Compute the company's net income if 70,000 copies were sold.

2–2. **EXERCISES IN COST-VOLUME-PROFIT RELATIONSHIPS.** (Alternate is 2–13.) The Miller Transportation Company specializes in hauling heavy goods over long distances. Miller's revenue depends on both weights and mileage. Summarized budget data for next year are based on total intercity vehicle revenue-miles of 800,000:

	PER MILE
Average selling price (revenue)	$1.20
Average variable expenses	1.00
Fixed expenses, $120,000	

1. Compute the budgeted net income. Ignore income taxes.

2. Management is trying to decide how various possible conditions or decisions might affect net income. Compute the new net income for each of the following changes. Consider each case independently, referring to the original data.

  a. A 10% increase in revenue-miles.

  b. A 10% increase in sales price.

  c. A 10% increase in variable expenses.

  d. A 10% increase in fixed expenses.

  e. A 10% increase in fixed expenses in the form of more advertising and a 5% increase in revenue-miles.

  f. An average decrease in selling price of 3¢ per mile and a 5% increase in revenue-miles.

  g. An average increase in selling price of 5% and a 10% decrease in revenue-miles.

ADDITIONAL ASSIGNMENT MATERIAL

2–3. "Fixed costs decline as volume increases." Do you agree? Explain.

2–4. "Classification of costs into variable and fixed categories depends on the decision situation." Explain.

2–5. Why is "break-even analysis" a misnomer?

2–6. Distinguish between the equation technique and the unit contribution technique.

2–7. What are the principal differences between the accountant's and the economist's break-even graphs?

2–8. What is the sales mix?

2–9. Explain the *incremental approach* as used in cost-volume-profit analysis.

2–10. NATURE OF VARIABLE AND FIXED COSTS. "As I understand it, costs such as the salary of the vice-president of transportation operations are variable because the more traffic you handle, the less your unit cost. In contrast, costs such as fuel are fixed because each ton-mile should entail consumption of the same amount of fuel and hence bear the same unit cost." Do you agree? Explain.

2–11. BASIC REVIEW EXERCISES. Fill in the blanks for each of the following independent cases (ignore income taxes):

	SALES	VARIABLE EXPENSES	CONTRIBUTION MARGIN	FIXED EXPENSES	NET INCOME
1.	$950,000	$500,000	$ —	$400,000	$ —
2.	800,000	—	360,000	—	80,000
3.	—	550,000	340,000	310,000	—

2–12. BASIC REVIEW EXERCISES. Fill in the blanks for each of the following independent cases:

	(a) SELLING PRICE PER UNIT	(b) VARIABLE COST PER UNIT	(c) TOTAL UNITS SOLD	(d) TOTAL CONTRIBUTION MARGIN	(e) TOTAL FIXED COSTS	(f) NET INCOME
1.	$10	$ 7	100,000	$ —	$300,000	$ —
2.	20	16	—	100,000	—	10,000
3.	30	21	70,000	—	—	10,000
4.	—	8	80,000	160,000	100,000	—
5.	25	—	100,000	500,000	550,000	—

2–13. **BASIC REVIEW EXERCISES.** (Alternate is 2–2.) Each problem is unrelated to the others.

1. Given: Selling price per unit, $20; total fixed expenses, $8,000; variable expenses per unit, $16. Find break-even sales in units.
2. Given: Sales, $40,000; variable expenses, $30,000; fixed expenses, $9,000; net income, $1,000. Find break-even sales.
3. Given: Selling price per unit, $30; total fixed expenses, $32,000; variable expenses per unit, $14. Find total sales in units to achieve a profit of $16,000, assuming no change in selling price.
4. Given: Sales, $50,000; variable expenses, $20,000; fixed expenses, $30,000; net income, zero. Assume no change in selling price; find net income if activity volume increases 10%.
5. Given: Selling price per unit, $40; total fixed expenses, $80,000; variable expenses per unit, $30. Assume that if variable expenses are reduced by 20% per unit, the total fixed expenses will be increased by 10%. Find the sales in units to achieve a profit of $8,000, assuming no change in selling price.

2–14. **EXTENSIONS OF CHAPTER ILLUSTRATION.** Refer to the basic facts in the chapter illustration. Suppose the selling price was changed to 60¢ in response to a rise in unit variable cost from 40¢ to 45¢. The original data are on page 30.

Required:

1. Compute the monthly break-even point in number of units and in dollar sales.
2. Refer to the original data. If the rent were halved, what would be the monthly break-even point in number of units and in dollar sales?

2–15. **FIXED COSTS AND RELEVANT RANGE.** Horizon Computer Consultants has a substantial year-to-year fluctuation in billings to clients. Top management has the following policy regarding the employment of key professional personnel:

IF GROSS ANNUAL BILLINGS ARE	NUMBER OF PERSONS TO BE EMPLOYED	KEY PROFESSIONAL ANNUAL SALARIES AND RELATED EXPENSES
$2,000,000 or less	8	$ 800,000
$2,000,001–2,400,000	9	900,000
$2,400,001–2,800,000	10	1,000,000

Top management believes that a minimum of eight individuals should be retained for a year or more even if billings drop drastically below $2 million.

For the past five years, gross annual billings have fluctuated between $2,020,000 and $2,380,000. Expectations for next year are that gross billings will be between $2,100,000 and $2,300,000. What amount should be budgeted for key professional personnel? Graph the relationships on an annual basis, using the two approaches illustrated in Exhibit 2–2. Indicate the relevant range on each graph. You need not use graph paper; simply approximate the graphical relationships.

2–16. **ESTIMATING COST BEHAVIOR PATTERNS.** The Mideastern Railroad showed the following results (in millions of dollars):

	19X3	19X2
Operating revenues	$218	$196
Operating expenses		
Transportation	$ 87	$ 84
Maintenance of way and structures	34	32
Maintenance of equipment	37	34
Traffic	7	6
General	12	11
Payroll taxes	9	9
Property taxes	7	7
Equipment and other rentals	13	12
Total operating expenses	$206	$195
Net railway operating income	$ 12	$ 1

Required: Examine the figures in their entirety, not item by item. How do total expenses change in relation to total revenues? That is, if total revenues increase by $1,000, by how much will total expenses increase? What is the apparent contribution-margin percentage? Explain any assumptions that underlie your answer.

2-17. HOSPITAL COSTS AND PRICING. A hospital has overall variable costs of 30% of total revenue and fixed costs of $35 million per year.

Required:
1. Compute the break-even point expressed in total revenue.
2. A patient-day is often used to measure the volume of a hospital. Suppose there are going to be 50,000 patient-days next year. Compute the average daily revenue per patient necessary to break even.

2-18. MOTEL RENTALS. The Moraine Motel has annual fixed costs applicable to its rooms of $3 million for its 400-room motel, average daily room rents of $50, and average variable costs of $10 for each room rented. It operates 365 days per year.

Required:
1. How much net income on rooms will be generated (a) if the motel is completely full throughout the entire year? and (b) if the motel is half-full?
2. Compute the break-even point in number of rooms rented. What percentage occupancy for the year is needed to break even?

2-19. BASIC RELATIONSHIPS, HOTEL. (W. Crum, adapted.) Palm Oasis Hotel has 400 rooms, with a fixed cost of $400,000 per month during the busy season. Room rates average $60 per day with variable costs of $12 per rented room per day. Assume a 30-day month.

Required:
1. How many rooms must be occupied per day to break even?
2. How many rooms must be occupied per month to make a profit of $100,000?
3. Assume that Palm Oasis Hotel had these average contribution margins per month from use of space in its hotel:

Leased shops in hotel	$60,000
Meals served, conventions	30,000
Dining room and coffee shop	30,000
Bar and cocktail lounge	20,000

Fixed costs for the total hotel are $400,000 per month. Variable costs are $12 per day per rented room. The hotel has 400 rooms and average 80% occupancy per day. What average rate per day must the hotel charge to make a profit of $100,000 per month?

2–20. **MOVIE MANAGER.** Joan Hartung is the manager of Stanford's traditional Sunday Flicks. Each Sunday a film has two showings. The admission price is deliberately set at a very low $2. A maximum of 500 tickets are sold for each showing. The rental of the auditorium is $100 and labor is $280, including $50 for Hartung. Hartung must pay the film distributor a guarantee, ranging from $200 to $600 or 50% of gross admission receipts, whichever is higher.

Before and during the show, refreshments are sold; these sales average 12% of gross admission receipts and yield a contribution margin of 40%.

1. On June 3, Hartung played *The Graduate*. The film grossed $1,400. The guarantee to the distributor was $500, or 50% of gross admission receipts, whichever is higher. What operating income was produced for the Students Association, which sponsors the showings?
2. Recompute the results if the film grossed $900.
3. The "four-wall" concept is increasingly being adopted by movie producers. This means that the producer pays a fixed rental for the theater for, say, a week's showing of a movie. As a theater owner, how would you evaluate a "four-wall" offer?

2–21. **PROMOTION OF CHAMPIONSHIP FIGHT.** Newspaper accounts of a Joe Frazier–Muhammad Ali boxing match stated that each fighter would receive a flat fee of $2.5 million in cash. The fight would be shown on closed-circuit television. The central promotor would collect 100% of the receipts and would return 30% to the individual local promoters. He expected to sell 1.1 million seats at a net average price of $10 each. He also was to receive $250,000 from Madison Square Garden (which had sold out its 19,500 seats, ranging from $150 for ringside down to $20, for a gross revenue of $1.25 million); he would not share the $250,000 with the local promoters.

Required:
1. The central promoter is trying to decide what amount to spend for advertising. What is the most he could spend and still break even on his overall operations, assuming that he would sell 1.1 million tickets?
2. If the central promoter desired an operating income of $500,000, how many seats would have to be sold? Assume that the average price was $10 and the total fixed costs were $8 million.

2–22. **BASIC RELATIONSHIPS, RESTAURANT.** (W. Crum, adapted.) Juan Castillo owns and operates La Cantina Restaurant. His fixed costs are $10,500 per month. Luncheons and dinners are served. The average total bill (excluding tax and tip) is $7 per customer. Juan's present variable costs average $2.80 per meal.

Required:
1. How many meals must be served to attain a profit before taxes of $4,200 per month?
2. What is Juan's break-even point in number of meals served per month?
3. Juan's rent and his other fixed costs rise to a total of $14,700 per month. Assume that variable costs also rise to $3.75 per meal. If Juan increases his average price to $9, how many meals must he now serve to make $4,200 profit per month?
4. Juan's accountant tells him he may lose 10% of his customers if he increases his prices. If this should happen, what would be Juan's profit per month? Assume that Juan had been serving 3,500 customers per month.
5. Refer to the data in Requirement 4. To help offset the anticipated 10% loss of customers, Juan hires a guitarist to perform for 4 hours each night for $800 per month. Assume that this would increase the total monthly meals to 3,450. Would Juan's total profit change? By how much?

2–23. CHURCH ENTERPRISE. A California law permits a game of chance called BINGO when it is offered by specified nonprofit institutions, including churches. Reverend John O'Toole, the pastor of a new parish in suburban Los Angeles, is investigating the desirability of conducting weekly BINGO nights. The parish has no hall, but a local hotel would be willing to commit its hall for a lump-sum rental of $300 per night. The rent would include cleaning, setting up and taking down the tables and chairs, and so on.

Required:

1. BINGO cards would be provided by a local printer in return for free advertising thereon. Door prizes would be donated by local merchants. The services of clerks, callers, security force, and others would be donated by volunteers. Admission would be $2.50 per person, entitling the player to one card; extra cards would be $1.50 each. Father O'Toole also learns that many persons buy extra cards, so there would be an average of four cards played per person. What is the maximum in total cash prizes that the church may award and still break even if 100 persons attend each weekly session?
2. Suppose the total cash prizes are $400. What will be the church's operating income if 50 persons attend? If 100 persons attend? If 150 persons attend? Briefly explain effects of the cost behavior on income.
3. After operating for ten months, Father O'Toole is thinking of negotiating a different rental arrangement but keeping the prize money unchanged. Suppose the rent is $200 weekly plus $1 per person. Compute the operating income for attendance of 50, 100, and 150 persons, respectively. Explain why the results differ from those in Requirement 2.

2–24. HOSPITAL COST-VOLUME-PROFIT RELATIONSHIPS. Dr. Chan and Dr. Ng, the two radiologists of the Hong Kong Hospital, have submitted the following costs for operating the Department of Radiology:

Radiologists' salaries	30% of gross receipts
Technicians' and clerical salaries	$70,000
Supplies (fixed)	80,000
Depreciation	60,000

This year the department processed 65,000 films with three 200-milliampere X-ray machines. (Their original cost was $200,000 each; their original life expectancy, ten years.) For these processed films the average charge was $6. The 65,000 films represent maximum volume possible with the present equipment.

The physicians have submitted a request for two new 300-milliampere X-ray machines. (Their cost will be $250,000 each; their life expectancy, ten years.) They will increase the capacity of the department by 35,000 films per year. Because of their special attachments (e.g., fluoroscopes), it will be possible to take more intricate films, for which a higher charge will be made. The average charge to the patient for each of these additional 35,000 films is estimated at $10. To operate the new machines, one highly trained technician must be hired at an annual salary of $15,000. The added capacity will increase the cost of supplies by $20,000.

Required:

1. (a) Determine the break-even point in films for the three 200-milliampere X-ray machines. (b) How much do they contribute to the hospital's overall profits?
2. (a) Determine the break-even point if the two new 300-milliampere X-ray machines are added to the department, assuming a sales mix based on maximum capacity. (b) How much will be contributed to the hospital's overall profit, assuming they are operated at maximum volume?

2–25. COST-VOLUME-PROFIT ANALYSIS AND BARBERING. Harry's Barber Shop in Singapore has five barbers. (Harry is not one of them.) Each barber is paid $6 per hour and works a 40-hour week and a 50-week year. Rent and other fixed expenses are $1,000 per month. Assume that the only service performed is the giving of haircuts, the unit price of which is $9.

Required:

1. Find the contribution margin per haircut. Assume that the barbers' compensation is a fixed cost.
2. Determine the annual break-even point, in number of haircuts.
3. What will be operating income if 20,000 haircuts are sold?
4. Suppose Harry revises the compensation method. The barbers will receive $4 per hour plus a 33⅓% commission for each haircut. What is the new contribution margin per haircut? What is the annual break-even point (in number of haircuts)?
5. Ignore Requirements 3 and 4, and assume that the barbers cease to be paid by the hour but receive a 50% commission for each haircut. What is the new contribution margin per haircut? The annual break-even point (in number of haircuts)?
6. Refer to Requirement 5. What would be the operating income if 20,000 haircuts are sold? Compare your answer with the answer in Requirement 3.
7. Refer to Requirement 5. If 20,000 haircuts are sold, at what rate of commission would Harry earn the same operating income as he earned in Requirement 3?

2–26. COST-VOLUME-PROFIT RELATIONSHIPS AND A DOG TRACK. The Multnomah Kennel Club is a dog-racing track. Its revenue is derived mainly from attendance and a fixed percentage of the parimutuel betting. Its expenses for a 90-day season are:

Wages of cashiers and ticket takers	$150,000
Commissioner's salary	20,000
Maintenance (repairs, etc.)	20,000
Utilities	30,000
Other expenses (depreciation, insurance, advertising, etc.)	100,000
Purses: Total prizes paid to winning racers	810,000

The track made a contract with the Auto Parking Association to park the cars. Auto Parking charged the track $1.80 per car. A survey revealed that on the average three persons arrived in each car and that there were no other means of transportation except by private automobiles.

The track's sources of revenue are:

Rights for concession and vending	$50,000
Admission charge (deliberately low)	$.80 per person
Percentage of bets placed	10%

Required:

1. Assuming that each person bets $25 a night,
   a. How many persons have to be admitted for the track to break even for the season?
   b. What is the total contribution margin at the break-even point?

c. If the desired profit for the year is $540,000, how many people would have to attend?

2. If a policy of free admission brought a 10% increase in attendance, what would be the new level of profit? Assume that the previous level of attendance was 600,000 people.

3. If the purses were doubled in an attempt to attract better dogs and thus increase attendance, what would be the new break-even point? Refer to the original data and assume that each person bets $25 a night.

2–27. **GOVERNMENTAL ORGANIZATION.** A social welfare agency has a government budget appropriation for 19X1 of $900,000. The agency's major mission is to help handicapped persons who are unable to hold jobs. On the average, the agency supplements each person's other income by $5,000 annually. The agency's fixed costs are $270,000. There are no other costs.

Required:

1. How many handicapped persons are helped during 19X1?

2. For 19X2, the agency's budget appropriation has been reduced by 15%. If the agency continues the same level of monetary support per person, how many handicapped persons will be helped in 19X2? Compute the percentage decline in the number of persons helped.

3. Assume a budget reduction of 15%, as in Requirement 2. The manager of the agency has discretion as to how much to supplement each handicapped person's income. She does not want to reduce the number of persons served. On the average, what is the amount of the supplement that can be given to each person? Compute the percentage decline in the annual supplement.

2–28. **TRAVELING EXPENSES.** (A. Roberts.) Harold Nuget is a traveling inspector for the Environmental Protection Agency. He uses his own car and the agency reimburses him at 18¢ per mile. Harold claims he needs 21¢ per mile just to break even.

George Barr, the district manager, decides to look into the matter. He is able to compile the following information about Harold's expenses:

Oil change every 3,000 miles	$ 12
Maintenance (other than oil) every 6,000 miles	180
Yearly insurance	400
Auto cost $10,800 with an average cash trade-in value of $6,000; has a useful life of three years.	
Gasoline is approximately $2 per gallon and Harold averages 20 miles per gallon.	

When Harold is on the road, he averages 120 miles a day. The manager knows that Harold does not work Saturdays or Sundays, has 10 working days vacation and 6 holidays, and spends approximately 15 working days in the office.

Required:

1. How many miles per year would the inspector have to travel to break even at the current rate of reimbursement?

2. What would be an equitable mileage rate?

2–29. **ANALYSIS OF AIRLINE RESULTS.** Texas Air Corporation owns Texas International Airlines and Continental Airlines. Its actual operating statistics for the three months ended June 30 in a recent quarterly report follow:

	CURRENT YEAR	PRECEDING YEAR
Revenue passengers carried	946,603	1,044,697
Revenue-passenger-miles (000s)*	549,179	577,071
Scheduled aircraft miles flown	9,472,766	8,595,308
Available seat-miles (000s)	971,028	839,720
Passenger load factor	56.6%	?
Yield per revenue-passenger-mile†	$?	$ .0884

* A revenue-passenger-mile is 1 passenger carried 1 mile. For example, 2 passengers carried 800 miles would be 1,600 revenue-passenger-miles.

† Total revenue divided by revenue-passenger-miles.

The president of Texas Air commented:

☐ In the second quarter, airline revenues were nearly $64 million, a 25.6% increase compared to the preceding year. Revenue-passenger-miles, however, declined 5%, the first quarterly decline since 1976, primarily as a result of weakened economic conditions. Meanwhile, the yield per passenger-mile increased 32% as a result of several fare increases made to counter spiralling costs.

Required:

1. (a) Compute the total passenger revenue in the second quarter of the preceding year. (b) Also compute the passenger load factor.
2. Compute the yield per passenger-mile in the current year.
3. Assume that variable costs during the current quarter were 5¢ per available seat-mile. Also assume that the yield per revenue-passenger-mile was unaffected by the increase in the load factor. Suppose the passenger load factor had increased from 56.6% to 57.6%; compute the increase in operating income that would have been attained.

2–30. **HOSPITAL COSTS.** The Mount Sinai Hospital is unionized. In 19X1 nurses received an average annual salary of $37,000. The hospital administrator is considering how the contract with nurses should be changed for 19X2. In turn, the charging of nursing costs to each department also might be changed.

Each department is accountable for its financial performance. Revenues and expenses are allocated to departments. Consider the expenses of the obstetrics department in 19X1:

Variable expenses (based on patient-days) are:

Meals	$ 320,000
Laundry	160,000
Laboratory	700,000
Pharmacy	400,000
Maintenance	50,000
Other	130,000
Total	$1,760,000

Fixed expenses (based on number of beds) are:

Rent	$2,000,000
General administrative services	1,500,000
Janitorial	100,000
Maintenance	100,000
Other	200,000
Total	$3,900,000

Nurses are assigned to departments on the basis of annual patient-days, as follows:

VOLUME LEVEL IN PATIENT-DAYS	NUMBER OF NURSES
10,000–12,500	30
Over 12,500	35

Total patient-days are the number of patients multiplied by the number of days they are hospitalized.

During 19X1 the obstetrics department had a capacity of 60 beds, billed each patient an average of $500 per day, and had revenues of $8,000,000.

Required:

1. Compute the 19X1 volume of activity in patient-days.
2. Compute the 19X1 patient-days that would have been necessary for the obstetrics department to recoup all fixed expenses except nursing expenses.
3. Compute the 19X1 patient-days that would have been necessary for the obstetrics department to break even.
4. The head of the obstetrics department is considering offering the nursing center a nursing rate of $120 per patient-day. This plan would replace the two-level system employed in 19X1. Compute what the break-even point in patient-days would have been in 19X1 under this plan.

2–31. **CHOOSING EQUIPMENT FOR DIFFERENT VOLUMES.** (CMA, adapted.)

William Company owns and operates a nationwide chain of movie theaters. The 500 properties in the William chain vary from low-volume, small-town, single-screen theaters to high-volume, big-city, multiscreen theaters.

The management is considering installing machines that will make popcorn on the premises. These machines would allow the theaters to sell popcorn that would be freshly popped daily rather than the prepopped corn that is currently purchased in large bags. This proposed feature would be properly advertised and is intended to increase patronage at the company's theaters.

The machines can be purchased in several different sizes. The annual rental costs and the operating costs vary with the size of the machines. The machine capacities and costs are:

	POPPER MODEL		
	Economy	Regular	Super
Annual capacity	50,000 boxes	120,000 boxes	300,000 boxes
Costs:			
Annual machine rental	$8,000	$11,000	$20,000
Popcorn cost per box	.13	.13	.13
Other costs per box	.22	.14	.05
Cost of each box	.08	.08	.08

1. Calculate the volume level in boxes at which the Economy Popper and Regular Popper would earn the same operating profit (loss).
2. The management can estimate the number of boxes to be sold at each of its theaters. Present a decision rule that would enable William's management to select the most profitable machine without having to make a separate cost calculation for each theater. That is, at what anticipated range of unit sales should the Economy model be used? the Regular model? the Super model?
3. Could the management use the average number of boxes sold per seat for the entire chain and the capacity of each theater to develop this decision rule? Explain your answer.

ASSIGNMENT MATERIALS FOR APPENDIXES

2–32. **INCOME TAXES.** Review the illustration in Appendix 2B. Suppose that the income tax rate were 30% instead of 40%.

Required:

How many units would have to be sold to achieve a target net income of (1) $288 and (2) $480? Show your computations.

2–33. **INCOME TAXES AND COST-VOLUME-PROFIT ANALYSIS.** Suppose the Lopez Moving Company has a 40% income tax rate, a contribution-margin ratio of 30%, and fixed costs of $400,000. How much sales are necessary to achieve an after-tax income of $66,000?

2–34. **INCOME TAXES ON HOTELS.** The Grove Hotel is in downtown Chicago. It has annual fixed costs applicable to rooms of $10 million for its 600-room hotel, average daily room rates of $90, and average variable costs of $10 for each room rented. It operates 365 days per year. The hotel is subject to an income tax rate of 30%.

Required:

1. How many rooms must the hotel rent to earn a net income after taxes of $1,400,000? of $420,000?
2. Compute the break-even point in number of rooms rented. What percentage occupancy for the year is needed to break even?
3. Assume that the volume level of rooms sold is 150,000. The manager is wondering how much income could be generated by adding sales of 20,000 rooms. Compute the additional net income after taxes.

2–35. **TAX EFFECTS, MULTIPLE CHOICE.** (CMA.)

DisKing Company is a retailer for video disks. The projected after-tax net income for the current year is $120,000 based on a sales volume of 200,000 video disks. DisKing has been selling the disks at $16 each. The variable costs consist of the $10 unit purchase price of the disks and a handling cost of $2 per disk. DisKing's annual fixed costs are $600,000, and DisKing is subject to a 40% income tax rate.

Management is planning for the coming year when it expects that the unit purchase price of the video disks will increase 30%.

1. DisKing Company's break-even point for the current year in number of video disks is (a) 100,000 units (b) 150,000 units (c) 50,000 units (d) 60,000 units (e) some amount other than those given.
2. An increase of 10% in projected unit sales volume for the current year would result in an increased after-tax income for the current year of (a) $80,000 (b) $32,000 (c) $48,000 (d) $12,000 (e) some amount other than those given.
3. The volume of sales in dollars that DisKing Company must achieve in the coming year to maintain the same after-tax net income as projected for the current year if unit selling price remains at $16 is (a) $12,800,000 (b) $14,-400,000 (c) $11,520,000 (d) $32,000,000 (e) some amount other than those given.

4. To cover a 30% increase in the disk's purchase price for the coming year and still maintain the current contribution-margin ratio, DisKing Company must establish a selling price per disk for the coming year of (a) $19.60 (b) $19.00 (c) $20.80 (d) $20.00 (e) some amount other than those given.

2–36. **P/V Chart.** Consider the example on page 45. Suppose the rent were cut from $1,000 to $504, the cost per item raised from 40¢ to 47¢, and the selling price raised to 55¢.

Required:
1. Compute the new break-even point in units.
2. Draw a new P/V chart similar to the second one in Exhibit 2–5.
3. Compute and plot the new net income at a volume of 80,000 units.

2–37. **Sales-Mix Analysis.** The Frozen Delicacies Company specializes in preparing tasty main courses that are frozen and shipped to the finer restaurants in the Los Angeles area. When a diner orders the item, the restaurant heats and serves it. The budget data for 19X2 are:

| | PRODUCT | |
	Chicken Cordon Bleu	Veal Marsala
Selling price to restaurants	$5	$8
Variable expenses	3	5
Contribution margin	$2	$3
Number of units	250,000	125,000

The items are prepared in the same kitchens, delivered in the same trucks, and so forth. Therefore, the fixed costs of $840,000 are unaffected by the specific products.

Required:
1. Compute the planned net income for 19X2.
2. Compute the break-even point in units, assuming that the planned sales mix is maintained.
3. Compute the break-even point in units if only veal were sold and if only chicken were sold.
4. Suppose 90,000 units of veal and 270,000 units of chicken were sold. Compute the net income. Compute the new break-even point if these relationships persisted in 19X2. What is the major lesson of this problem?

2–38. **Hospital Patient Mix.** Hospitals measure their volume in terms of patient-days, which are defined as the number of patients multiplied by the number of days that the patients are hospitalized. Suppose a large hospital has fixed costs of $15,000,000 per year and variable costs of $300 per patient-day. Daily revenues vary among classes of patients. For simplicity, assume that there are two classes: (1) self-pay patients (S) who pay an average of $500 per day and (2) nonself-pay patients (G) who are the responsibility of insurance companies and government agencies and who pay an average of $400 per day. Twenty percent of the patients are self-pay.

Required:
1. Compute the break-even point in patient-days, assuming that the planned mix of patients is maintained.
2. Suppose that 125,000 patient-days were achieved but that 25% of the patient-days were self-pay (instead of 20%). Compute the net income. Compute the break-even point.

Chapter 3

INTRODUCTION TO

MANUFACTURING COSTS

LEARNING OBJECTIVES

When you have finished studying this chapter, you should be able to:

1. Define the following terms and concepts and explain how they are related: **cost, cost objective, cost accumulation, and cost allocation.**

2. Define and identify examples of each of the three major elements in the cost of a manufactured product.

3. Differentiate between product costs and period costs, identifying examples of each.

4. Explain how the financial statements of merchandisers and manufacturers differ because of the types of goods they sell.

5. Show the effects that the basic transactions of a manufacturing company can have on the balance sheet equation.

6. Construct model income statements of a manufacturing company in both the absorption form and the contribution form.

Some form of cost accounting is applicable to manufacturing companies, retail stores, insurance companies, medical centers, and nearly all organizations. Throughout this book we shall consider both nonmanufacturing and manufacturing organizations, but we shall start with the manufacturing company because it is the most general case—embracing production, marketing, and general administration functions. You can then apply this overall framework to any organization.

CLASSIFICATIONS OF COSTS

☐ Cost Accumulation and Cost Objectives

A **cost** may be defined as a sacrifice or giving up of resources for a particular purpose. Costs are frequently measured by the monetary units (for example, dollars or francs) that must be paid for goods and services. Costs are initially recorded in elementary form (for example, repairs or advertising). Then these costs are grouped in different ways to help managers make decisions, such as evaluating subordinates and subunits of the organization, expanding or deleting products or territories, and replacing equipment.

To aid decisions, managers want the *cost of something*. This something is called a **cost objective**, which may be defined as *any activity for which a separate measurement of costs is desired*. Examples of cost objectives include departments, products, territories, miles driven, bricks laid, patients seen, tax bills sent, checks processed, student hours taught, and library books shelved.

The cost-accounting system typically (1) accumulates costs by some "natural" classification such as materials or labor and (2) then allocates (traces) these costs to cost objectives. **Cost accumulation** is the gathering of costs in some organized way via an accounting system. **Cost allocation** is the assignment or reassignment of a cost or group of costs to one or more cost objectives. Exhibit 3–1 illustrates how a company might use materials in two main departments for manufacturing several different products. The cost of, say, the metal used may be accumulated initially by keeping a tabulation of the amounts withdrawn from the raw-material storage center by each department. In turn, the cost of metal used by each department is allocated to the products worked on in that department.

Cost-accounting systems vary in complexity. They tend to become more detailed as management seeks more accurate data for decision making. Consider this news story about Mark Controls Company, a manufacturer in the valve industry: "The key to Mark's success so far has been tough financial controls and methodical emphasis on profit margins." The company had previ-

ously relied on broad averages. The story continued: "The company set u̲
a computerized costing system that calculated the precise cost and profit margin for each of the 15,000 products the company sold. Since then, about 15%
of those products have been dropped from the company's line because they
were insufficiently profitable."

How "precise" can cost allocations be? Probably never as precise as might
be desired. Nevertheless, managers have increasingly discovered that reliance
on broad averages is not enough in today's competitive world.

This chapter concentrates on the big picture of how manufacturing costs
are accumulated and classified. A variety of cost-accounting systems allocate
these costs to the products worked on. These systems are described in some
detail in three separate chapters (13, 14, and 15) in this book. However, such
detail may be studied at almost any stage of an introductory course.

☐ Elements of Manufacturing Costs

Manufacturing is the transformation of materials into other goods through
the use of labor and factory facilities. Exhibit 3–1 shows a general approach
to accumulating and allocating costs for raw materials. The same approach
pertains to other manufacturing costs: as products are manufactured, costs
are accumulated and allocated to departments and to the physical units produced.

EXHIBIT 3–1

Cost Accumulation and Allocation

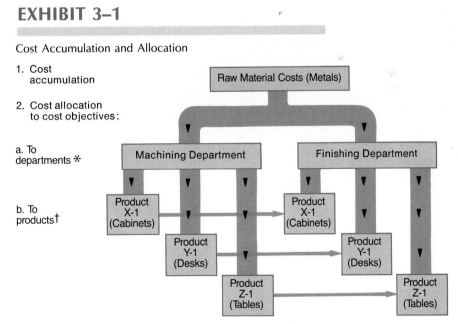

1. Cost
   accumulation

2. Cost allocation
   to cost objectives:

a. To
departments *

b. To
products†

* Purpose: to evaluate performance of manufacturing departments.

† Purpose: to obtain costs of various products for valuing inventory, determining income, and
judging product profitability.

There are three major elements of manufacturing costs: (1) **direct materials**, (2) **direct labor**, and (3) **factory overhead**.

1. **Direct materials.** The acquisition cost of all materials that are physically identified as a part of the finished goods and that may be traced to the finished goods in an economically feasible way. Examples are iron castings, lumber, aluminum sheets, and subassemblies. Direct materials often do not include minor items such as tacks or glue. Why? Because the costs of tracing insignificant items do not seem worth the possible benefits of having more precise product costs. Such items are usually called *supplies* or *indirect materials* and are classified as a part of the factory overhead described in this list.

2. **Direct labor.** The wages of all labor that is physically traceable to the finished goods in an economically feasible way. Examples are the wages of machine operators and of assemblers. Much labor, such as that of janitors, forklift truck operators, plant guards, and storeroom clerks, is considered to be indirect labor because of the impossibility or economic infeasibility of tracing such activity to specific products via physical observation. Indirect labor is classified as a part of factory overhead.

3. **Factory overhead.** All costs other than direct material or direct labor that are associated with the manufacturing process. Other terms used to describe this category are **factory burden**, **manufacturing overhead**, **manufacturing expenses**, and **indirect manufacturing costs**. The last term is a clearer descriptor than factory overhead, but factory overhead will be used most frequently in this book because it is briefer. Two major subclassifications of factory overhead are

   a. **Variable factory overhead.** Examples are power, supplies, and some indirect labor. Whether the cost of a specific category of indirect labor is variable or fixed depends on its behavior in a given company. In this book, unless we specify otherwise, indirect labor will be considered a variable rather than a fixed cost.

   b. **Fixed factory overhead.** Examples are supervisory salaries, property taxes, rent, insurance, and depreciation.

As Exhibit 3–2 shows, two of the three major elements are sometimes combined in cost terminology as follows. **Prime cost** consists of (1) + (2), direct materials plus direct labor. **Conversion cost** consists of (2) + (3), direct labor plus factory overhead.

Manufacturing companies also incur selling and administrative costs. These are accumulated by departments such as advertising and sales departments. However, as the next section explains, the typical accounting system does not allocate these costs to the physical units produced. In short, these costs do not become a part of the inventory cost of the manufactured products.

RELATIONSHIPS OF INCOME STATEMENTS AND BALANCE SHEETS

This section assumes a basic familiarity with income statements and balance sheets, as covered by any beginning course in financial accounting or by Chapter 17. However, the reader can easily understand most of the terms explained here without having such familiarity.

EXHIBIT 3–2

Relationships of Key Elements of Manufacturing Costs

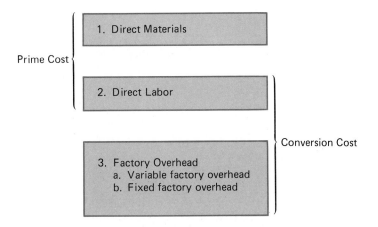

☐ Product Costs and Period Costs

Accountants frequently refer to *product costs* and *period costs*. **Product costs** generally are identified with goods produced or purchased for resale. Product costs are initially identified as part of the inventory on hand; in turn, these product costs (inventoriable costs) become expenses (in the form of *cost of goods sold*) only when the inventory is sold. In contrast, **period costs** are costs that are deducted as expenses during the current period without going through an inventory stage.

The distinctions between product costs and period costs are best understood by example. Examine the top half of Exhibit 3–3. A merchandising company (retailer or wholesaler) acquires goods for resale without changing their basic form. The *only* product cost is the purchase cost of the merchandise. Unsold goods are held as merchandise inventory cost and are shown as an asset on a balance sheet. As the goods are sold, their costs become expense in the form of "cost of goods sold."

A merchandising company also has a variety of selling and administrative expenses, which are the major examples of period costs (noninventoriable costs). They are referred to as period costs because they are deducted from revenue as expenses without ever having been regarded as a part of inventory.

In manufacturing accounting, as the bottom half of Exhibit 3–3 illustrates, direct materials are transformed into salable form with the help of direct labor and factory overhead. All these costs are product costs because

EXHIBIT 3–3

Relationships of Product Costs and Period Costs

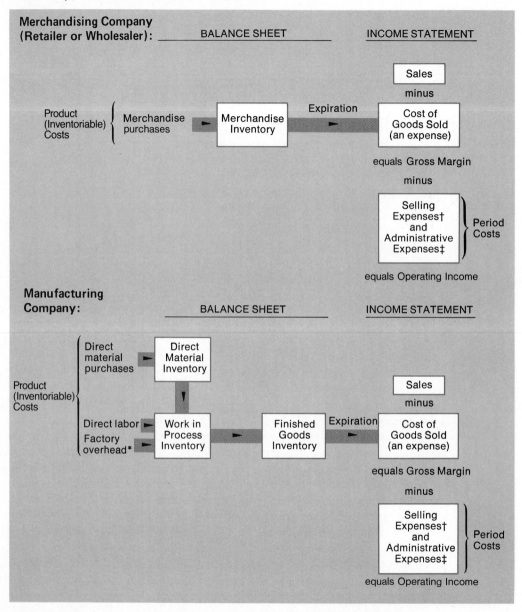

‡ Examples: insurance on corporate headquarters building, depreciation on office equipment, clerical salaries.

* Examples: indirect labor, factory supplies, insurance, and depreciation on plant.

† Examples: insurance on salespersons' cars, depreciation on salespersons' cars, salespersons' salaries.

   Note particularly that where insurance and depreciation relate to the manufacturing function, they are inventoriable, but where they relate to selling and administration, they are not inventoriable.

they are allocated to inventory until the goods are sold. As in merchandising accounting, the selling and administrative expenses are not regarded as product costs but are treated as period costs.

□ Balance Sheet Presentation

As Exhibit 3–3 shows, balance sheets of manufacturers and merchandisers differ with respect to inventories. The merchandise inventory account is supplanted in a manufacturing concern by three inventory classes. The purpose of these various classifications is to trace all product costs through the production process to the time of sale. The classes are:

Direct-material inventory: materials on hand but not yet issued to the production line

Work-in-process inventory: cost of uncompleted goods still on the production line containing appropriate amounts of the three major manufacturing costs (direct material, direct labor, and factory overhead)

Finished-goods inventory: fully completed goods not yet sold

The only essential difference between the structure of the balance sheet of a manufacturer and that of the balance sheet of a retailer or wholesaler would appear in their respective current asset sections (numbers are assumed):

Current Asset Sections of Balance Sheets

MANUFACTURER			RETAILER OR WHOLESALER	
Cash		$ 4,000	Cash	$ 4,000
Receivables		25,000	Receivables	25,000
Finished goods	$32,000			
Work in process	22,000			
Direct material	23,000		Merchandise	
Total inventories		77,000	inventories	77,000
Other current assets		1,000	Other current assets	1,000
Total current assets		$107,000	Total current assets	$107,000

□ Unit Costs for Product Costing

Most often, product costing is accomplished by heavy use of unit costs. Assume the following:

Total cost of goods manufactured	$40,000,000
Total units manufactured	10,000,000
Unit cost of product for inventory purposes ($40,000,000 ÷ 10,000,000)	$4

The unit cost eases the accounting for inventory valuation and income measurement. If some of the 10 million units manufactured are still unsold at the end of the period, a part of the $40 million cost of goods manufactured will be "held back" as a cost of the ending inventory of finished goods (and shown as an asset on a balance sheet). The remainder becomes "cost of goods sold" for the current period (that is, shown as an expense on the income statement).

☐ Costs and Income Statements

In the income statements, the detailed reporting of selling and administrative expenses is typically the same for manufacturing and merchandising organizations, but the cost of goods sold is different:

MANUFACTURER	RETAILER OR WHOLESALER
Manufacturing cost of goods produced and then sold, usually composed of the three major elements of cost: direct materials, direct labor, and factory overhead	Merchandise cost of goods sold, usually composed of the purchase cost of items, including freight in, that are acquired and then resold

Consider the *additional assumed* details as they are presented in the model income statement of Exhibit 3–4. The $40 million cost of goods manufactured is subdivided into the major components of direct materials, direct labor, and factory overhead.

EXHIBIT 3–4

Model Income Statement, Manufacturing Company

Sales (8,000,000 units @ $10)			$80,000,000
Cost of goods manufactured and sold:			
Beginning finished-goods inventory		$ –0–	
Cost of goods manufactured:			
Direct materials used	$20,000,000		
Direct labor	12,000,000		
Factory overhead:			
Variable factory overhead	2,000,000		
Fixed factory overhead	6,000,000	40,000,000	
Cost of goods available for sale		$40,000,000	
Ending finished-goods inventory			
2,000,000 units @ $4		8,000,000	
Cost of goods sold (an expense)			32,000,000
Gross margin or gross profit			$48,000,000
Less: Other expenses			
Selling costs (an expense)		$30,000,000	
General and administrative costs			
(an expense)		8,000,000	38,000,000
Operating income*			$10,000,000

Also net income in this example because other expenses such as interest and income taxes are ignored here for simplicity.

The terms "costs" and "expenses" are often used loosely by accountants and managers. "Expenses" denote all costs deducted from (matched against) revenue in a given period. On the other hand, "costs" is a much broader term; for example, "cost" is used to describe an asset (the cost of inventory) and an expense (the cost of goods sold). Thus manufacturing costs are funneled into an income statement as an expense (in the form of cost of goods sold) via the multistep inventory procedure, as indicated earlier in Exhibit 3–3. In contrast, selling and general administrative costs are commonly deemed expenses immediately as they are incurred.

☐ Common Mistakes

Before proceeding, take a moment to review some key distinctions made in Exhibits 3–3 and 3–4. Otherwise, these new terms and classifications become blurred.

Distinguish sharply between the merchandising accounting and the manufacturing accounting for such costs as insurance, depreciation, and wages. In merchandising accounting, all such items are period costs (expenses of the current period). In manufacturing accounting, many of these items are related to production activities and thus, as factory overhead, are product costs (become expenses as the inventory is sold).

In both merchandising and manufacturing accounting, selling and general administrative costs are period costs. Thus the inventory cost of a manufactured product *excludes* sales salaries, sales commissions, advertising, legal, public relations, and the president's salary. *Manufacturing* overhead is traditionally regarded as a part of finished-goods inventory cost, whereas *selling* expenses and *general administrative* expenses are not.

☐ Relation to Balance Sheet Equation

Exhibit 3–5 relates the theory of product costing to the analysis of the balance sheet equation. For simplicity, all acquisitions and dispositions of resources are assumed to be for cash. The same dollar amounts are used in Exhibits 3–4 and 3–5 except that Exhibit 3–5 introduces the idea of an inventory of materials. That is, $30 million of direct materials were acquired, $20 million were used, and $10 million were left in inventory at the end of the period.

Trace the effects of each summary transaction, step by step, in Exhibit 3–5. As the bottom of Exhibit 3–5 indicates, the ending balance sheet accounts would be:

Cash	$ 92,000,000	Paid-in capital	$100,000,000
Direct-materials inventory	10,000,000	Retained income	10,000,000*
Work-in-process inventory	—		
Finished-goods inventory	8,000,000		
Total assets	$110,000,000	Total equities	$110,000,000

* Retained income arose because of profitable operations, which produced income of $10 million. For the detailed income statement, see Exhibit 3–4.

EXHIBIT 3–5

Analysis of Balance Sheet Equation for Manufacturing Costs (in millions of dollars)

		ASSETS				LIABILITIES & STOCKHOLDERS' EQUITY	
						Stockholders' equity	
		Direct-Materials	Work-in-Process	Finished-Goods		Paid-in	Retained
Transactions	Cash +	Inventory +	Inventory +	Inventory =	Liabilities +	Capital +	Income
Beginning balances	100				=	100	
1. Purchase of direct materials	−30	+30			=		
2. Direct materials used		−20	+20		=		
3. Acquire direct labor	−12		+12		=		
4. Acquire factory overhead	−8		+8		=		
5. Complete the goods			−40	+40	=		
6a. Revenue	+80				=		+80 (Revenue)
6b. Cost of goods sold				−32	=		−32 (Expense)
7. Selling costs	−30				=		−30 (Expense)
8. General and administrative costs	−8				=		−8 (Expense)
Ending balances	92 +	10 +	0 +	8	=	100 +	10

□ Direct and Indirect Costs

Admittedly, the area of manufacturing costs contains a thicket of new terms. One of your main tasks in studying this chapter is to understand these terms. For example, a distinction was made between costs that are "direct" and "indirect" with respect to a *particular* cost objective—the manufactured product. In other settings, the direct-indirect distinction may pertain to a different cost objective, for example, a department. Thus the wages of a janitor who works solely in the assembly department may be regarded as a direct cost of the department but as an indirect cost of the products worked on within that department. However, unless otherwise stated, throughout this book the direct-indirect distinction will pertain only to the *product* as the cost objective.

TWO TYPES OF INCOME STATEMENTS

□ Detailed Costs of a Manufacturing Company

A fresh example may clarify many of the cost terms and distinctions explored thus far. Assume that the Samson Company for 19X2 has direct-material costs of $7 million and direct-labor costs of $4 million. Assume also that the company incurred the indirect manufacturing costs (factory overhead) illustrated in Exhibit 3–6 and the selling and administrative expenses illustrated in Exhibit 3–7. Total sales were $20 million.

Finally, assume that the units produced are equal to the units sold. That is, there is no change in inventory levels. In this way, we avoid some complications that are unnecessary and unimportant at this stage.[1]

---

[1] These complexities are discussed in Chapters 13, 14, and 15. (If preferred, Chapter 13 may be studied immediately after Chapter 3 without loss of continuity.)

EXHIBIT 3–6

SAMSON COMPANY
Schedules of Indirect Manufacturing Costs
(which are product costs)
For the Year Ended December 31, 19X2
(in thousands of dollars)

Schedule 1: Variable Costs

Supplies (lubricants, expendable tools, coolants, sandpaper)	$ 150	
Material-handling labor (forklift operators)	700	
Repairs	100	
Power	50	$1,000

Schedule 2: Fixed Costs

Managers' salaries	$ 200	
Employee training	90	
Factory picnic and holiday party	10	
Supervisory salaries, except foremen's salaries	700	
Depreciation, plant and equipment	1,800	
Property taxes	150	
Insurance	50	3,000
Total indirect manufacturing costs		$4,000

EXHIBIT 3–7

SAMSON COMPANY
Schedules of Selling and Administrative
Expenses (which are period costs)
For the Year Ended December 31, 19X2
(in thousands of dollars)

Schedule 3: Selling Expenses

Variable:		
Sales commissions	$ 700	
Shipping expenses for products sold	300	$1,000
Fixed:		
Advertising	$ 700	
Sales salaries	1,000	
Other	300	2,000
Total selling expenses		$3,000

Schedule 4: Administrative Expenses

Variable:		
Some clerical wages	$ 80	
Computer time rented	20	$ 100
Fixed:		
Office salaries	$ 100	
Other salaries	200	
Depreciation on office facilities	100	
Public-accounting fees	40	
Legal fees	100	
Other	360	900
Total administrative expenses		$1,000

Note that Exhibits 3–6 and 3–7 contain subdivisions of costs between variable and fixed classifications. Many companies do not make such subdivisions. Furthermore, when such subdivisions are made, sometimes arbitrary decisions are necessary as to whether a given cost is variable or fixed, or partially variable and partially fixed (for example, repairs). Nevertheless, to aid decision making, an increasing number of companies are attempting to report the extent to which their costs are approximately variable or fixed.

☐ Absorption Approach

Exhibit 3–8 presents the income statement in the form used by most companies. The theory followed is called the **absorption approach** or **absorption costing** or **traditional costing** or **full costing** or **functional costing**. It is the theory also illustrated in Exhibit 3–4, page 68, whereby all indirect manufacturing costs (both variable plus fixed factory overhead) are considered as inventoriable or product costs that become an expense in the form of manufacturing cost of goods sold only as sales occur.

Take a moment to compare Exhibits 3–4 and 3–8. Note that gross profit or gross margin is the difference between sales and the *manufacturing* cost of goods sold. Note too that the *primary classifications* of costs on the income

EXHIBIT 3–8

SAMSON COMPANY
Absorption Income Statement
For the Year Ended
December 31, 19X2
(in thousands of dollars)

Sales		$20,000
Less: **Manufacturing** costs of goods sold:		
Direct material	$7,000	
Direct labor	4,000	
Indirect **manufacturing costs** (Schedules 1 plus 2)	4,000	15,000
Gross margin or gross profit		$ 5,000
Selling expenses (Schedule 3)	$3,000	
Administrative expenses (Schedule 4)	1,000	
Total **selling** and **administrative** expenses		4,000
Operating income		$ 1,000

Note: Schedules 1 and 2 are in Exhibit 3–6. Schedules 3 and 4 are in Exhibit 3–7.

statement are by three major management *functions*: manufacturing, sel
and administrative.

☐ Contribution Approach

Exhibit 3–9 presents the income statement in the "contribution" form used
by an increasing number of companies for internal (management accounting)
purposes. Even though a standard format is used for external purposes, a
company can and often does adopt a different format for internal purposes
if the expected benefits of making decisions exceed the extra costs of using
different reporting systems simultaneously.

The theory followed by Exhibit 3–9 has been called the **contribution
approach**, **variable costing**, **direct costing**, or **marginal costing**. For decision purposes, the most important difference between the contribution approach and the absorption approach is the emphasis of the former on the
distinction between variable and fixed costs. The *primary classifications* of
costs are by variable and fixed *cost behavior patterns*, not by *business functions*.

The contribution income statement provides a contribution margin,
which is computed after deducting *all* variable costs, *including* variable selling

EXHIBIT 3–9

SAMSON COMPANY
Contribution Income Statement
For the Year Ended
December 31, 19X2
(in thousands of dollars)

Sales		$20,000
Less: **Variable** expenses:		
Direct material	$ 7,000	
Direct labor	4,000	
Variable indirect manufacturing (Schedule 1)	1,000	
Total **variable** manufacturing cost of goods sold	$12,000	
Variable selling expenses (Schedule 3)	1,000	
Variable administrative expenses (Schedule 4)	100	
Total **variable** expenses		13,100
Contribution margin		$ 6,900
Less: **Fixed** expenses:		
Manufacturing (Schedule 2)	$ 3,000	
Selling (Schedule 3)	2,000	
Administrative (Schedule 4)	900	5,900
Operating income		$ 1,000

Note: Schedules 1 and 2 are in Exhibit 3–6. Schedules 3 and 4
are in Exhibit 3–7.

and administrative costs. This approach facilitates the computation of the impact on operating income of changes in sales, and it dovetails neatly with the cost-volume-profit analysis illustrated in the preceding chapter.

The contribution approach stresses the lump-sum amount of fixed costs to be recouped before net income emerges. This highlighting of total fixed costs helps to attract management attention to fixed-cost behavior and control when both short-run and long-run plans are being made. Keep in mind that advocates of this contribution approach do not maintain that fixed costs are unimportant or irrelevant, but they do stress that the distinctions between behaviors of variable and fixed costs are crucial for certain decisions.

The implications of the *absorption approach* and the *contribution approach* for decision making are discussed in the next chapter, using Exhibits 3–8 and 3–9.

SUMMARY

Costs of manufacturing are typically accumulated and then allocated to departments and to products. The three major elements in the inventory costs of a manufactured product are direct materials, direct labor, and factory overhead.

Students of elementary accounting are accustomed to thinking that such costs as utilities, wages, and depreciation are expenses (period costs) and unconnected with inventories. If these costs are related to the manufacturing process, however, they are inventoriable (product costs).

The most important aspect of intelligent cost planning and control is an understanding of cost behavior patterns and influences. The most basic behavior pattern of costs may be described as either variable or fixed. The contribution approach to preparing an income statement emphasizes this distinction and is a natural extension of the cost-volume-profit analysis used in decisions. In contrast, the absorption approach emphasizes the distinction between manufacturing costs and selling and administrative costs.

READERS WHO NOW DESIRE A MORE DETAILED TREATMENT OF PRODUCT COSTING MAY JUMP TO THE STUDY OF CHAPTER 13 WITHOUT LOSING CONTINUITY. IN TURN, CHAPTER 15 MAY BE STUDIED IMMEDIATELY AFTER CHAPTER 7 IF DESIRED. INSTRUCTORS DIFFER REGARDING THE APPROPRIATE SEQUENCE OF CHAPTERS AND TOPICS. MANY INSTRUCTORS PREFER TO ASSIGN CHAPTER 13 NEXT.

SUMMARY PROBLEM FOR YOUR REVIEW

☐ **Problem**

1. Review the illustrations in Exhibits 3–6 through 3–9. Suppose that all variable costs fluctuate in direct proportion to units produced and sold and that all fixed costs are unaffected over a wide range of production and sales. What would operating income have been if sales (at normal selling prices) had been $20.9 million instead of $20.0 million? Which statement, the absorption income statement or the contribution income statement, did you use as a framework for your answer? Why?

2. Suppose that employee training (Exhibit 3–6) was regarded as a variable rather than a fixed cost at a rate of $90,000 ÷ 1,000,000 units, or 9¢ per unit. How would your answer in part 1 change?

1. Operating income would increase from $1,000,000 to $1,310,500, computed as follows:

Increase in revenue	$ 900,000
Increase in total contribution margin:	
Contribution-margin ratio in contribution income	
statement (Exhibit 3–9) is $6,900,000 ÷ $20,000,000 = .345	
Ratio times revenue increase is .345 × $900,000	$ 310,500
Increase in fixed expenses	–0–
Operating income before increase	1,000,000
New operating income	$1,310,500

Computations are easily made by using data from the contribution income statement. In contrast, the traditional absorption costing income statement must be analyzed and divided into variable and fixed categories before the effect on operating income can be estimated.

2. The contribution-margin ratio would be lower because the variable costs would be higher by 9¢ per unit: ($6,900,000 − $90,000) ÷ $20,000,000 = .3405.

	Given Level	Higher Level	Difference
Revenue	$20,000,000	$20,900,000	$900,000
Variable expenses ($13,100,000 + $90,000)	13,190,000	13,783,550	593,550
Contribution margin at .3405	$ 6,810,000	$ 7,116,450	$306,450
Fixed expenses ($5,900,000 − $90,000)	5,810,000	5,810,000	—
Operating income	$ 1,000,000	$ 1,306,450	$306,450

HIGHLIGHTS TO REMEMBER

1. Many new terms were introduced in this chapter. Review those in bold print to make sure you know their exact meaning.
2. Manufacturing costs (direct material, direct labor, and factory overhead) are traditionally regarded as product costs (inventoriable costs).
3. In contrast, selling and administrative costs are accounted for as period costs; hence they are typically deducted from revenue as expenses in the period incurred.

ACCOUNTING VOCABULARY

Absorption Approach, *p.* 72   Absorption Costing 72   Contribution Approach 73
Conversion Cost *64*   Cost *62*   Cost Accumulation *62*   Cost Allocation *62*   Cost
Objective *62*   Direct Costing *73*   Direct Labor *64*   Direct Material *64*   Factory
Burden *64*   Factory Overhead *64*   Full Costing *72*   Functional Costing *72*   Idle
Time *77*   Indirect Labor *76*   Indirect Manufacturing Costs *64*   Manufacturing

APPENDIX 3: CLASSIFICATION OF LABOR COSTS

The terms for labor costs are usually the most confusing. Each organization seems to develop its own interpretation of various labor-cost classifications. We begin by considering some commonly encountered labor-cost terms:

> Direct labor (already defined)
> Factory overhead (examples of prominent labor components of these indirect
>   manufacturing costs follow):
>   Indirect labor (wages):
>   Forklift truck operators (internal handling of materials)
>   Janitors
>   Plant guards
>   Rework labor (time spent by direct laborers redoing defective work)
>   Overtime premium paid to *all* factory workers
>   Idle time
>   Managers' salaries
>   Payroll fringe costs (for example, health care premiums, pension costs)

All factory labor wages, other than those for direct labor and manager salaries, are usually classified as **indirect labor** costs, a major component of indirect manufacturing costs. The term *indirect labor* is usually divided into many subsidiary classifications. The wages of forklift truck operators are generally not commingled with janitors' salaries, for example, although both are regarded as indirect labor.

Costs are classified in a detailed fashion primarily to associate a specific cost with its specific cause, or reason for incurrence. Two classes of indirect labor need special mention: overtime premium and idle time.

Overtime premium paid to all factory workers is usually considered a part of overhead. If a lathe operator earns $8 per hour for straight time and time and one-half for overtime, the premium is $4 per overtime hour. If the operator works 44 hours, including 4 overtime hours, in one week, the gross earnings are classified as follows:

Direct labor: 44 hours × $8	$352
Overtime premium (factory overhead): 4 hours × $4	16
Total earnings for 44 hours	$368

Why is overtime premium considered an indirect cost rather than direct? After all, it can usually be traced to specific batches of work. It is usually not considered a direct charge because the scheduling of production jobs is generally random. For example, assume that jobs 1 through 5 are scheduled for a specific workday of ten hours, including two overtime hours. Each job requires two hours. Should the job scheduled during hours 9 and 10 be assigned the overtime premium? Suppose that you brought your automobile to a shop for repair by 8:00 A.M. Through random scheduling, your auto was repaired during hours 9 and 10 as job 5. When you came to get your car, you learned that all the overtime premium had been added to your bill. You probably would not be overjoyed.

Thus, in most companies, the overtime premium is not allocated to any specific job. Instead, the overtime premium is considered to be attributable to the heavy overall volume of work, and its cost is thus regarded as indirect manufacturing costs (factory overhead). The latter approach does not penalize a particular batch of work solely because it happened to be worked on during the overtime hours.

Another subsidiary classification of indirect-labor costs is **idle time**. This cost typically represents wages paid for unproductive time caused by machine breakdowns, material shortages, sloppy production scheduling, and the like. For example, if the same lathe operator's machine broke down for 3 hours during the week, the operator's earnings would be classified as follows:

Direct labor: 41 hours × $8	$328
Overtime premium (factory overhead): 4 hours × $4	16
Idle time (factory overhead): 3 hours × $8	24
Total earnings for 44 hours	$368

Manager salaries usually are not classified as a part of indirect labor. Instead, the compensation of supervisors, department heads, and all others who are regarded as part of manufacturing management are placed in a separate classification of factory overhead. The classification of factory **payroll fringe costs** (e.g., employer contributions to employee benefits such as social security, life insurance, health insurance, and pensions) differs from company to company. In most companies these are classified as indirect manufacturing costs. In some companies, however, the fringe benefits related to direct labor are charged as an additional direct-labor cost. For instance, a direct laborer, such as a lathe operator whose gross wages are computed on the basis of $8 an hour, may enjoy fringe benefits totaling, say, $1 per hour. Most companies tend to classify the $8 as direct-labor cost and the $1 as factory overhead. Other companies classify the entire $9 as direct-labor cost. The latter approach is conceptually preferable, because most of these costs are a fundamental part of acquiring labor services.

Chapter 13, which may be studied now if desired, describes how the accounting system allocates factory overhead to products. An averaging technique assures that all products bear their share of factory overhead, including the components just described.

FUNDAMENTAL ASSIGNMENT MATERIAL

3–1. **STRAIGHTFORWARD INCOME STATEMENTS.** (Alternate is **3–34**.) The Gardena Company had the following manufacturing data for the year 19X1 (in thousands of dollars):

Beginning inventories	None	Indirect labor, variable portion	$50
Direct material used	$180	Indirect labor, fixed portion	20
Direct labor	200	Depreciation	60
Supplies	10	Property taxes	12
Utilities, variable portion	20	Supervisory salaries	50
Utilities, fixed portion	6		

Selling expenses were $172,000 (including $40,000 that were variable), and general administrative expenses were $100,000 (including $20,000 that were variable). Sales were $1 million.

Supplies are regarded as variable costs.

1. Prepare two income statements, one using the contribution approach and one the absorption approach.
2. Suppose that all variable costs fluctuate directly in proportion to sales and that fixed costs are unaffected over a very wide range of sales. Compute the operating income if sales had been $1,150,000 instead of $1,000,000. Which income statement did you use to help obtain your answer? Why?

3–2. **MEANING OF TYPICAL LANGUAGE.** Refer to the absorption income statement of your solution to the preceding problem. Give the amounts of the following: (1) factory burden, (2) conversion costs, (3) manufacturing expenses, and (4) prime costs.

ADDITIONAL ASSIGNMENT MATERIAL

3–3. Distinguish between "costs" and "expenses."

3–4. "Departments are not cost objects or objects of costing." Do you agree? Explain.

3–5. "Manufacturing cost of goods sold is a special category of expense." Do you agree? Explain.

3–6. "Unexpired costs are always inventory costs." Do you agree? Explain.

3–7. "Advertising is noninventoriable." Explain.

3–8. "Miscellaneous supplies are always indirect costs." Do you agree? Explain.

3–9. Distinguish between the two prime costs.

3–10. "Glue or tacks become an integral part of the finished product, so they would be direct material." Do you agree? Explain.

3–11. What is the advantage of the contribution approach as compared with the absorption approach?

3–12. Distinguish between manufacturing and merchandising.

3–13. "The primary classifications of costs are by variable- and fixed-cost behavior patterns, not by business functions." Name three commonly used terms that describe this type of income statement.

3–14. **COST ACCUMULATION AND ALLOCATION.** The Rohr Company incurred raw-material costs of $500,000. The machining department used $400,000, and the finishing department, $100,000. Product M flowed through both departments, incurring 10% of the machining department's raw-material costs and 5% of the finishing department's raw-material costs. What was the raw-material cost of product M?

3–15. **MEANING OF TECHNICAL TERMS.** Refer to Exhibit 3–4, page 68. Give the amounts of the following with respect to the cost of goods available for sale: (1) prime costs, (2) conversion costs, (3) factory burden, and (4) manufacturing expenses.

3–16. **PRODUCT AND PERIOD COSTS.** Refer to Exhibit 3–4, page 68. Suppose that $30 million of direct material had been purchased.

Using Exhibit 3–3 as a guide, sketch how the costs in Exhibit 3–4 are related to balance sheets and income statements. In other words, prepare an exhibit like 3–3, inserting the numbers from Exhibit 3–4 to the extent you can.

3–17. **PRESENCE OF ENDING WORK IN PROCESS.** Refer to Exhibits 3–4 and 3–5. Suppose that manufacturing costs were the same, but there was an ending work-in-process inventory of $5 million. The cost of the completed goods would therefore be $35 million instead of $40 million. Suppose also that sales and the cost of goods sold are unchanged.

1. Recast the income statement of Exhibit 3–4, page 68.
2. What lines and ending balances would change in Exhibit 3–5 and by how much?

3–18. **BALANCE SHEET EQUATION.** Review Exhibit 3–5, page 70. Assume that the G Company had a beginning balance of $800,000 cash and paid-in capital. The following transactions occurred in 19X2 (in thousands):

1. Purchase of direct materials for cash	$350
2. Direct materials used	300
3. Acquire direct labor for cash	160
4. Acquire factory overhead for cash	200
5. Complete all goods that were started	?
6a. Revenue (all sales are for cash)	600
6b. Cost of goods sold (half of the goods completed were sold)	?
7. Selling costs for cash	100
8. General and administrative costs for cash	40

Required: Prepare an analysis similar to Exhibit 3–5. What are the ending balances of cash, direct materials, finished goods, paid-in capital, and retained income?

3–19. **BALANCE SHEET EQUATION.** Refer to the preceding problem. Suppose that some goods were still in process that cost $100,000. Half the goods completed were sold. However, the same revenue was generated even though fewer goods were sold. What are the balances of all the accounts in the ending balance sheet?

3–20. **STRAIGHTFORWARD ABSORPTION STATEMENT.** Consider the following data (in thousands) for a given period:

Sales	$900
Direct materials	300
Direct labor	150
Indirect manufacturing costs	170
Selling and administrative expenses	160

Required: There were no beginning or ending inventories. Compute the (1) manufacturing cost of goods sold, (2) gross profit, (3) operating income, (4) conversion cost, and (5) prime cost. Assume an absorption approach.

3–21. **STRAIGHTFORWARD CONTRIBUTION INCOME STATEMENT.** Consider the following data (in thousands) for a given period:

Sales	$970
Direct materials	400
Direct labor	140
Variable factory overhead	60
Variable selling and administrative expenses	100
Fixed factory overhead	110
Fixed selling and administrative expenses	60

Required: There were no beginning or ending inventories. Compute the (1) variable manufacturing cost of goods sold, (2) contribution margin, and (3) operating income.

3–22. **STRAIGHTFORWARD ABSORPTION AND CONTRIBUTION STATEMENT.** Consider the following data (in millions) and fill in the blanks. There were no beginning or ending inventories.

a. Sales	$990
b. Direct materials used	300
c. Direct labor	200
Factory overhead:	
d. Variable	100
e. Fixed	50
f. Variable manufacturing cost of goods sold	_____
g. Manufacturing cost of goods sold	_____
Selling and administrative expenses:	
h. Variable	90
i. Fixed	80
j. Gross profit	_____
k. Contribution margin	_____
l. Prime costs	_____
m. Conversion costs	_____
n. Operating income	_____

3–23. **ABSORPTION STATEMENT.** Consider the following data (in thousands) for a given period. Assume there are no inventories. Assume an absorption approach. Fill in the blanks.

Gross margin	$200
Selling and administrative expenses	_____
Operating income	110
Conversion cost	_____
Prime cost	600
Sales	_____
Direct materials	370
Direct labor	_____
Factory overhead	_____
Manufacturing cost of goods sold	780

3–24. **CONTRIBUTION INCOME STATEMENT.** Consider the following data (in thousands) for a given period. Assume there are no inventories.

Contribution margin	$200
Fixed selling and administrative expenses	100
Operating income	15
Sales	995
Direct labor	200
Direct materials	210
Variable factory overhead	80

Required: Compute the (1) variable manufacturing cost of goods sold, (2) variable selling and administrative expenses, and (3) fixed factory overhead.

3–25. **COST ACCUMULATION AND ALLOCATION.** A company has two departments, machining and finishing. For a given period, suppose that the following costs were incurred by the company as a whole: direct material, $180,000; direct labor, $60,000; and manufacturing overhead, $78,000. The grand total costs were $318,000.

The machining department incurred 80% of the direct-material costs, but only 30% of the direct-labor costs. As is commonplace, manufacturing overhead incurred by each department was allocated to products in proportion to the direct-labor costs of products within the departments.

Three products were produced:

PRODUCT	DIRECT MATERIAL	DIRECT LABOR
H–1	50%	$33\frac{1}{3}$%
J–1	25	$33\frac{1}{3}$
K–1	25	$33\frac{1}{3}$
Total, machining department	100%	100%
H–1	$33\frac{1}{3}$%	40%
J–1	$33\frac{1}{3}$	40
K–1	$33\frac{1}{3}$	20
Total, finishing department	100%	100%

The manufacturing overhead incurred by departments amounted to machining, $36,000; finishing, $42,000.

Required:

1. Compute the total costs incurred by the machining department and added by the finishing department.
2. Compute the total costs of each product that would be shown as finished-goods inventory if all the products were transferred to finished stock upon completion and held there at the end of the period.

3–26. **RELATING COSTS TO COST OBJECTIVES.** A company uses an absorption cost system. Prepare headings for two columns: (1) assembly department costs and (2) products assembled. Fill in the two columns for each of the costs below. If a specific cost is direct to the department but indirect to the product, place a *D* in column 1 and an *I* in column 2. The costs are: materials used, supplies used, assembly labor, material-handling labor (transporting materials between and within departments), depreciation—building, assembly supervisor's salary, and the building and grounds supervisor's salary.

3–27. **CLASSIFICATION OF MANUFACTURING COSTS.** Classify each of the following as direct or indirect (*D* or *I*) with respect to product and as variable or fixed (*V* or *F*) with respect to whether the cost fluctuates in total as activity or volume changes over wide ranges of activity. You will have two answers, *D* or *I* and *V* or *F*, for *each* of the ten items:

(1) Salary of a factory storeroom clerk
(2) Workers' compensation insurance in a factory
(3) Cement for a roadbuilder
(4) Steel scrap for a blast furnace
(5) Paper towels for a factory washroom
(6) Supervisor training program
(7) Abrasives (sandpaper, etc.)
(8) Cutting bits in a machinery department
(9) Food for a factory cafeteria
(10) Factory rent

3–28. **VARIABLE COSTS AND FIXED COSTS; MANUFACTURING AND OTHER COSTS.** For each of the numbered items, choose the appropriate classifications for a job-order manufacturing company (e.g., custom furniture, job printing). If in doubt about whether the cost behavior is basically variable or fixed, decide on the basis of whether the total cost will fluctuate substantially over a wide range of volume. Most items have two answers among the following possibilities with respect to the cost of a particular job:

a. Variable cost
b. Fixed cost
c. General and administrative cost
d. Selling cost
e. Manufacturing costs, direct
f. Manufacturing costs, indirect
g. Other (specify)

Sample answers:

Direct material	a, e
President's salary	b, c
Bond interest expense	b, g (financial expense)

Items for your consideration:

(1) Factory power for machines
(2) Salespersons' commissions
(3) Salespersons' salaries
(4) Welding supplies
(5) Fire loss
(6) Sandpaper
(7) Supervisory salaries, production control
(8) Supervisory salaries, assembly department
(9) Supervisory salaries, factory storeroom
(10) Company picnic costs
(11) Overtime premium, punch press
(12) Idle time, assembly
(13) Freight out
(14) Property taxes
(15) Paint for finished products
(16) Heat and air-conditioning, factory
(17) Material-handling labor, punch press
(18) Straight-line depreciation, salespersons' automobiles

3–29. **OVERTIME PREMIUM.** Study the chapter appendix. An automobile dealer has a service department. You have brought your car for repair at 8:00 A.M. When you come to get your car after 6:00 P.M., you notice that your bill contains a charge under "labor" for "overtime premium." When you inquire about the reason for the charge, you are told, "We worked on your car from 5:00 P.M. to 6:00 P.M. Our union contract calls for wages to be paid at time-and-a-half after eight hours. Therefore our ordinary labor charge of $40 per hour was billed to you at $60."

Required:

1. Should the overtime premium be allocated only to cars worked on during overtime hours? Explain.
2. Would your preceding answer differ if the dealer arranged to service your car at 8:00 P.M. as a special convenience to you? Explain.

3–30. **PAYROLL FRINGE COSTS.** Study the chapter appendix. Direct labor is often accounted for at the gross wage rate, and the related "fringe costs" such as employer payroll taxes and employer contributions to health care plans are accounted for as part of overhead. Therefore the $9 gross pay per hour being paid to Mary Locke, a direct laborer, might cause related fringe costs of $3 per hour.

Required:

1. Suppose Locke works 40 hours during a particular week as an auditor for a public accounting firm, 30 hours for Client A and 10 for Client B. What would be the cost of direct labor? Of general overhead?
2. The firm allocates costs to each client. What would be the cost of "direct labor" on the Client A job? The Client B job?
3. How would you allocate general overhead to the Client A job? The Client B job?
4. Suppose Locke works a total of 50 hours (30 for A and 20 for B), 10 of which are paid on the basis of time-and-one-half. What would be the cost of direct labor? Of general overhead?
5. Given the facts in Requirement 4, what would be the cost of "direct labor" on the Client A job? The Client B job?

3–31. **REVIEW OF CHAPTERS 2 AND 3.** Consider the following miscellaneous data regarding operations in 19X3 of the Gombiner Manufacturing Company (in millions):

Gross profit	$ 25	Net loss	$12
Fixed selling and		Fixed manufacturing	
administrative expenses	21	overhead	30
Direct material used	60	Direct labor	25
Sales	150		

There were no beginning or ending inventories.

Required:

Compute the following (listed in no particular sequence):

1. Contribution margin in dollars.
2. Break-even point in sales dollars.
3. Manufacturing cost of goods sold.
4. Variable selling and administrative expenses.
5. Variable manufacturing overhead.
    Hint: Prepare an income statement. Fill in the known items; then solve for the unknowns.

3–32. **REVIEW OF CHAPTERS 2 AND 3.** Consider the following data of the Belmont Corporation regarding operations for 19X4:

Variable manufacturing overhead	$ 50,000
Direct labor	140,000
Break-even point (in sales dollars)	600,000
Gross profit	240,000
Direct material used	200,000
Sales	800,000
Contribution margin	360,000

There were no beginning or ending inventories. Ignore income taxes.

INTRODUCTION TO MANUFACTURING COSTS

Required: Compute (1) variable selling and administrative expenses, (2) fixed manufacturing overhead, and (3) fixed selling and administrative expenses. Computations need not be made in any specific order. Probably the easiest way to obtain the answers is to prepare an income statement, filling in the known items, and then solving for the unknowns.

3–33. **REVIEW OF CHAPTERS 2 AND 3.** (D. Kleespie.) A. Lee Company manufactured and sold 1,000 "Sams" during November. Selected data for this month follow:

Sales	$110,000
Direct materials used	21,000
Direct labor	16,000
Variable manufacturing overhead	13,000
Fixed manufacturing overhead	14,000
Variable selling and administrative expenses	?
Fixed selling and administrative expenses	?
Contribution margin	40,000
Operating income	22,000

There were no beginning or ending inventories.

Required:
1. What were the variable selling and administrative expenses for November?
2. What were the fixed selling and administrative expenses for November?
3. What was the cost of goods sold during November?
4. Without prejudice to your earlier answers, assume that the fixed selling and administrative expenses for November amounted to $14,000.
   a. What was the break-even point in units for November?
   b. How many units must be sold to earn a target operating income of $12,000?
   c. What would the selling price per unit have to be if the company wanted to earn an operating income of $17,000 on the sale of 900 units?

3–34. **CONTRIBUTION AND ABSORPTION INCOME STATEMENTS.** (Alternate is 3–1.) The records of the Atlanta Company for the year ended December 31, 19X2, revealed the following:

Long-term rent, factory	$ 200,000	Inventories	None
Factory super-intendent's salary	90,000	Indirect labor (variable)	$1,400,000
Direct labor	4,000,000	Fire insurance on factory equipment	10,000
Sales	26,000,000	Abrasives for matching	200,000
Supervisors' salaries	200,000	Factory methods studies, fixed	90,000
Advertising	5,690,000		
Cutting bits used	110,000	Property taxes on factory equipment	20,000
Administrative expenses (variable)	400,000	Administrative executive salaries	300,000
Direct material used	7,000,000		
Shipping expenses	590,000	Sales commissions	1,900,000
Depreciation on equipment, fixed	800,000		

Required:
1. Prepare a contribution income statement and an absorption income statement. If you are in doubt about any cost behavior pattern, decide on the basis of whether the total cost in question will fluctuate substantially over a wide range of volume. Prepare a separate supporting schedule of indirect manufacturing costs subdi-

vided between variable and fixed costs. Prepare your statements in thousands of dollars.

2. Suppose that all variable costs fluctuate directly in proportion to sales, and that fixed costs are unaffected over a very wide range of sales. What would operating income have been if production and sales had been $27 million instead of $26 million? Which income statement did you use to help get your answer? Why?

3–35. **FREQUENTLY ENCOUNTERED TERMS.** Refer to the absorption income statement of your solution to the preceding problem. Give the amounts of the following: (1) manufacturing expenses, (2) factory burden, (3) prime costs, and (4) conversion costs.

3–36. **ANALYSIS WITH CONTRIBUTION INCOME STATEMENT.** The following data have been condensed from Rhone Corporation's report of 19X3 operations [in millions of French francs (FF)]:

	VARIABLE	FIXED	TOTAL
Manufacturing cost of goods sold	FF400	FF180	FF580
Selling and administrative expenses	140	60	200
Sales			900

Required:

1. Prepare the 19X3 income statement in contribution form, ignoring income taxes.
2. Rhone operations have been fairly stable from year to year. In planning for the future, top management is considering several options for changing the annual pattern of operations. You are asked to perform an analysis of their estimated effects. Use your contribution income statement as a framework to compute the estimated operating income (in millions) under each of the following separate and unrelated assumptions:
   a. Assume that a 10% reduction in selling prices would cause a 30% increase in the physical volume of goods manufactured and sold.
   b. Assume that an annual expenditure of FF30 million for a special sales promotion campaign would enable the company to increase its physical volume by 10% with no change in selling prices.
   c. Assume that a basic redesign of manufacturing operations would increase annual fixed manufacturing costs by FF80 million and decrease variable manufacturing costs by 15% *per product unit*, but with no effect on physical volume or selling prices.
   d. Assume that a basic redesign of selling and administrative operations would double the annual fixed expenses for selling and administration and increase the variable expenses for selling and administration by 25% *per product unit*, but would also increase physical volume by 20%. Selling prices would be increased by 5%.

Chapter 4

RELEVANT COSTS AND SPECIAL

DECISIONS—PART ONE

Learning Objectives

When you have finished studying this chapter, you should be able to:

1. Diagram the relationships among the main elements of the decision process: information, predictions, decisions, implementation, and feedback.

2. Discriminate between relevant and irrelevant information for making decisions.

3. Analyze data by the contribution approach to support a decision for accepting or rejecting a special sales order.

4. Compute a target sales price by various approaches and identify their advantages and disadvantages in determining sales prices.

5. Analyze data by the relevant-cost approach to support a decision for adding or deleting a product line.

6. Analyze data to determine how to maximize profits within the limits of a given productive capacity.

Managers' special decisions pervade a variety of areas and time spans. By definition, special decisions occur with less regularity than do the typical daily or weekly operating decisions of a hotel, hospital, or manufacturer. The pricing of an unusual sales order is an example of a special decision. Other examples are adding new programs, services, or products; replacing old equipment; selling products at a particular stage of manufacturing or processing them further; and repairing municipal automobiles internally or buying the repair service from outside suppliers.

Unique factors bear on all these special decisions. However, there is a general approach that will help executives make wise decisions in *any* problem-solving situation. The term "relevant" has been overworked in recent years; nevertheless the general approach herein will be labeled as the *relevant-cost approach*. Coupled with the contribution approach, the ability to distinguish relevant from irrelevant items is the key to making special decisions.

Throughout this and the next chapter, to concentrate on the fundamental ideas, we shall ignore the time value of money (discussed in Chapter 11) and income taxes (discussed in Chapter 12).

THE ACCOUNTANT'S ROLE IN SPECIAL DECISIONS

☐ Accuracy and Relevance

Accountants have an important role in the problem-solving process, not as the decision makers but as collectors and reporters of **relevant information**, data pertinent to the decision at hand. Many managers want the accountant to recommend the proper decision, even though the final choice always rests with the operating executive.

The distinction between precision and relevance should be kept in mind. Ideally, the data should be *precise* (accurate) and *relevant* (pertinent). However, as we shall see, figures can be precise but irrelevant, or imprecise but relevant. For example, the university president's salary may be $140,000 per year, to the penny, but may have no bearing on the question of whether to buy or rent data processing equipment. As has often been said, it is better to be roughly right than precisely wrong.

☐ Qualitative and Quantitative Factors

The aspects bearing on each alternative may be divided into two broad categories, *qualitative* and *quantitative*. Qualitative factors are those for which measurement in dollars and cents is difficult and imprecise; yet a qualitative factor may easily be given more weight than a measurable saving in cost. For example, the opposition of a militant union to new labor-saving machinery may cause an executive to defer or even reject completely the contemplated installation. Or the chance to manufacture a component oneself for less than the supplier's selling price may be rejected because acceptance might lead to the company's long-run dependency on the supplier for other subassemblies. Quantitative factors are those that may more easily be expressed in dollars and cents—for example, projected costs of alternative materials, of direct labor, and of overhead. The accountant, statistician, and mathematician try to express as many decision factors as feasible in quantitative terms. This approach reduces the number of qualitative factors to be judged.

MEANING OF RELEVANCE: THE MAJOR CONCEPTUAL LESSON

Decision making is essentially choosing among several courses of action. The available actions are the result of an often time-consuming formal or informal search and screening process, perhaps carried on by a company team that includes engineers, accountants, and operating executives.

The accountant's role in problem solving is primarily that of a technical expert on cost analysis. The accountant's responsibility is to help the manager focus on relevant data, information that will lead the manager to the best decision.

☐ Definition of Relevance

Consider the final stages of the decision-making process. Two (or more) courses of action are aligned, and a comparison is made. The decision is based on the difference in the effect of the two on future performance. The key question is, What difference does it make? The **relevant information** is the *expected future data* that will *differ* among alternatives.

The ideas in the preceding paragraph deserve elaboration because they have such wide application. Historical, or past, data have no *direct* bearing on the decision. Historical data may help in formulating *predictions*. But past figures, in themselves, are irrelevant to the decision itself. Why? Because the decision will not affect them. Past data simply are not the expected future data that managers must use in intelligent decision making. Decisions affect the future. Nothing can alter what has already happened; all past costs are down the drain as far as current or future decisions are concerned.

Of the expected future data, only those that will differ among alternatives are relevant to the decision. Any item is irrelevant if it will remain the same regardless of the alternative selected. For instance, if the department manager's salary will be the same regardless of the products stocked, his or her salary is irrelevant to the selection of products.

The following examples will help us to summarize the sharp disti[n] needed for proper cost analysis for special decisions.

You habitually buy gasoline from either of two nearby gasoline stati[on]. Yesterday you noticed that one station is selling gasoline at $2.00 per gall[on] the other, at $1.90. Your automobile needs gasoline, and, in making yo[ur] choice of stations, you *assume* that these prices are unchanged. The relevan[t] costs are $2.00 and $1.90, the expected future costs that will differ between the alternatives. You use your past experience (i.e., what you observed yesterday) for predicting today's price. Note that the relevant cost is not what you paid in the past, or what you observed yesterday, but what you *expect to pay* when you drive in to get gasoline. This cost meets our two criteria: (1) it is the expected future cost, and (2) it differs between the alternatives.

You may also plan to have your car lubricated. The recent price at each station was $8.50, and this is what you anticipate paying. This expected future cost is irrelevant because it will be the same under either alternative. It does not meet our second criterion.

Exhibit 4–1 sketches the decision process and uses the following decision as an illustration. A manufacturer is thinking of using aluminum instead of copper in a line of ash trays. The cost of direct material will decrease from 30¢ to 20¢. The elaborate mechanism in Exhibit 4–1 seems unnecessary for this decision. After all, the analysis in a nutshell is:

	ALUMINUM	COPPER	DIFFERENCE
Direct material	$.20	$.30	$.10

The cost of copper used for this comparison undoubtedly came from historical-cost records, but note that the relevant costs in the foregoing analysis are both expected future costs.

The direct-labor cost will continue to be 70¢ per unit regardless of the material used. It is irrelevant because our second criterion—an element of difference between the alternatives—is not met:

	ALUMINUM	COPPER	DIFFERENCE
Direct material	$.20	$.30	$.10
Direct labor	.70	.70	—

Therefore, we can safely exclude direct labor. There is no harm in including irrelevant items in a formal analysis, provided that they are included properly. However, clarity is usually enhanced by confining the reports to the relevant items only.

Busy managers often make decisions on the basis of informal analysis,

Process and Role of Information

...n is whether to use aluminum instead of copper.
...tive is to minimize costs.

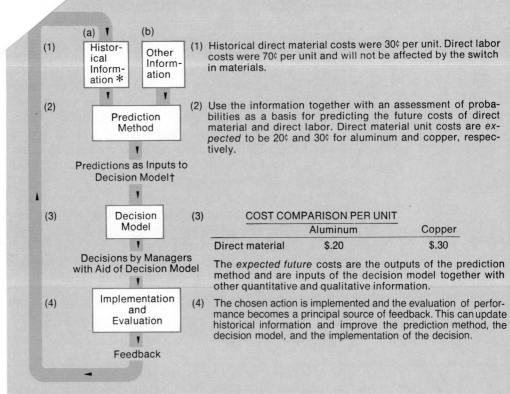

(a)   (b)

(1)   Histor-   Other   (1) Historical direct material costs were 30¢ per unit. Direct labor
      ical   Inform-   costs were 70¢ per unit and will not be affected by the switch
      Inform-   ation   in materials.
      ation *

(2)   Prediction   (2) Use the information together with an assessment of proba-
      Method   bilities as a basis for predicting the future costs of direct
                                 material and direct labor. Direct material unit costs are *ex-
Predictions as Inputs to   pected* to be 20¢ and 30¢ for aluminum and copper, respec-
Decision Model†   tively.

(3)   Decision   (3)   COST COMPARISON PER UNIT
      Model
                                            Aluminum   Copper
Decisions by Managers   Direct material $.20 $.30
with Aid of Decision Model
                              The *expected future* costs are the outputs of the prediction
                              method and are inputs of the decision model together with
                              other quantitative and qualitative information.

(4)   Implementation   (4) The chosen action is implemented and the evaluation of perfor-
      and   mance becomes a principal source of feedback. This can update
      Evaluation   historical information and improve the prediction method, the
                                decision model, and the implementation of the decision.

Feedback

* Note that historical data may be relevant for prediction methods.

† Historical data are never relevant per se for decision models. Only those expected future data
that differ between alternatives are really relevant. For instance, in this example, direct material
makes a difference and direct labor does not. Therefore, *under our definition here*, direct labor
is irrelevant.

intuition, and limited information. These managers should not clutter their thinking with irrelevant data such as the direct labor in this example.

Role of Predictions

Study Exhibit 4–1. It provides a helpful overview. Box 1(a) represents historical data from the accounting system. Box 1(b) represents other data, such as price indices or industry statistics, gathered from outside the accounting system. Regardless of their source, the historical data in step 2 help the formulation of *predictions*. Although historical data are often used as a guide to predicting, they are irrelevant per se to the decision itself.

In step 3 these predictions become inputs to the **decision model**. A decision model is defined as *any* method for making a choice. These models are often assumed to require elaborate quantitative procedures, such as a petroleum refinery's mathematical method for choosing what products to manufacture for any given day or week. But a decision model may be confined to a simple comparison of costs for choosing between two materials. In this instance our decision model has a simple form: compare the predicted unit costs and select the alternative with the lesser cost.

Exhibit 4–1 will be referred to frequently. It displays the major conceptual lesson in this chapter. This and the next chapter will show how the notion of relevant costs combined with the contribution approach applies to various particular decisions. The analytical approach is consistent, regardless of the particular decision encountered. The contribution approach to cost analysis, which was introduced in Chapter 3, assists analysis for a variety of decisions. In this chapter we shall examine the following decisions: (1) special sales orders, (2) pricing policies, (3) deleting or adding product lines or departments, and (4) using available capacity.

THE SPECIAL SALES ORDER

Illustrative Example

Consider the special sales order decision by selecting data from Exhibits 3–8 and 3–9, page 72. We are deliberately returning to these exhibits to underscore their general importance. The main data are summarized again in Exhibit 4–2.

The differences in the emphasis and format of the two income statements in Exhibit 4–2 may be unimportant as long as the accompanying cost analysis leads to the same set of decisions. But these two approaches sometimes lead to different unit costs that must be interpreted warily.

In our illustration, suppose that 1 million units of product, such as some automobile replacement part, were made and sold. Under the absorption costing approach, the unit manufacturing cost of the product would be $15,000,000 ÷ 1,000,000, or $15 per unit. Suppose a mail-order house near year end offered Samson $13 per unit for a 100,000-unit special order that (1) would not affect

EXHIBIT 4–2

Absorption and Contribution Forms of the Income Statement

SAMSON COMPANY
Income Statement
For the Year Ended December 31, 19X2
(in thousands of dollars)

ABSORPTION FORM		CONTRIBUTION FORM		
Sales	$20,000	Sales		$20,000
Less: Manufacturing cost of goods sold	15,000	Less: Variable expenses:		
Gross margin or gross profit	$ 5,000	Manufacturing	$12,000	
Less: Selling and administrative expenses	4,000	Selling and administrative	1,100	13,100
Operating income	$ 1,000	Contribution margin		$ 6,900
		Less: Fixed expenses:		
		Manufacturing	$ 3,000	
		Selling and administrative	2,900	5,900
		Operating income		$ 1,000

Samson's regular business in any way, (2) would not raise any antitrust issues concerning price discrimination, (3) would not affect total fixed costs, (4) would not require any additional variable selling and administrative expenses, and (5) would use some otherwise idle manufacturing capacity. Should Samson accept the order? Perhaps the question should be stated more sharply: What is the difference in the short-run financial results between not accepting and accepting? Again, the key question is, What difference does it make?

☐ Correct Analysis

The correct analysis employs the contribution approach and concentrates on the final overall results. As Exhibit 4–3 shows, only the variable manufacturing costs are affected by the particular order, at a rate of $12 per unit. All other variable costs and all fixed costs are unaffected and may therefore be safely ignored in making this special-order decision. Note how the necessary cost analysis is aided by the contribution approach's distinction between variable- and fixed-cost behavior patterns. The total short-run income will increase by $100,000 if the order is accepted—despite the fact that the unit selling price of $13 is less than the absorption manufacturing cost of $15 computed below:

Total manufacturing costs from Exhibit 4–2	$15,000,000
Divided by units produced	1,000,000
Unit manufacturing cost of product	$15

EXHIBIT 4–3

Comparative Predicted Income Statements, Contribution Approach

SAMSON COMPANY
For the Year Ended December 31, 19X2

	WITHOUT SPECIAL ORDER, 1,000,000 UNITS	WITH SPECIAL ORDER, 1,100,000 UNITS	SPECIAL-ORDER DIFFERENCE, 100,000 UNITS Total	Per Unit
Sales	$20,000,000	$21,300,000	$1,300,000	$13
Less: Variable expenses:				
Manufacturing	$12,000,000	$13,200,000	$1,200,000	$12
Selling and administrative	1,100,000	1,100,000	—	—
Total variable expenses	$13,100,000	$14,300,000	$1,200,000	$12
Contribution margin	$ 6,900,000	$ 7,000,000	$ 100,000	$ 1
Less: Fixed expenses:				
Manufacturing	$ 3,000,000	$ 3,000,000	—	—
Selling and administrative	2,900,000	2,900,000	—	—
Total fixed expenses	$ 5,900,000	$ 5,900,000	—	—
Operating income	$ 1,000,000	$ 1,100,000	$ 100,000	$ 1

☐ Incorrect Analysis

Faulty cost analysis sometimes occurs because of misinterpretation of unit fixed costs. Some managers may erroneously use the $15 absorption manufacturing cost per unit to make the following prediction for the year:

	WITHOUT SPECIAL ORDER 1,000,000 Units	WITH SPECIAL ORDER 1,100,000 Units	SPECIAL-ORDER DIFFERENCE 100,000 Units
Sales	$20,000,000	$21,300,000	$1,300,000
Less: Manufacturing cost of goods sold @ $15	15,000,000	16,500,000	1,500,000
Gross margin	5,000,000	4,800,000	(200,000)
Selling and administrative expenses	4,000,000	4,000,000	—
Operating income	$ 1,000,000	$ 800,000	$ (200,000)

The $1.5 million increase in costs is computed by multiplying $15 times 100,000 units. Of course, the fallacy in this approach is the regarding of a fixed cost (fixed manufacturing cost) as though it behaved in a variable manner. Avoid the assumption that unit costs may be used indiscriminately as a basis for predicting how total costs will behave.

To underscore the basic ideas, focus on the relationship between total fixed manufacturing costs and a fixed manufacturing cost per unit of product:

$$\text{fixed cost per unit of product} = \frac{\text{total fixed manufacturing costs}}{\text{some selected volume level used as the denominator}}$$

$$= \frac{\$3,000,000}{1,000,000} = \$3$$

The typical cost-accounting system serves two purposes simultaneously: *planning and control* and *product costing*. The total fixed cost for *budgetary planning and control purposes* can be graphed as a lump sum:

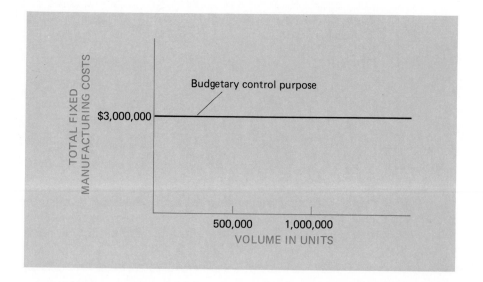

For *product-costing purposes*, however, the absorption costing approach implies that these *fixed* costs have a *variable*-cost behavior pattern:

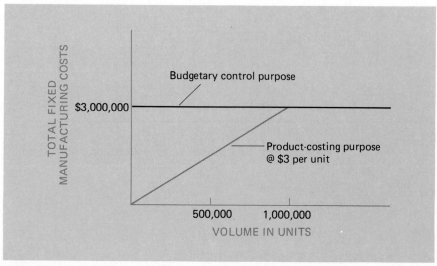

The addition of 100,000 units will *not* add any *total* fixed costs. However, the analytical pitfall is to include 100,000 × $3 = $300,000 in the predictions of increases in total costs.

In short, the increase in manufacturing costs should be computed by multiplying 1,000,000 units by $12, not by $15. The $15 includes a $3 component that will not affect the total manufacturing costs as volume changes.

□ Spreading Fixed Costs

As we just saw, the unit cost–total cost distinction can become particularly troublesome when analyzing fixed-cost behavior. Assume the same facts concerning the special order as before, except that the order was for 250,000 units at a selling price of $11.50. The analytical pitfalls of unit-cost analysis can be avoided by using the contribution approach and concentrating on totals (in thousands of dollars):

	WITHOUT SPECIAL ORDER 1,000,000 Units	WITH SPECIAL ORDER 1,250,000 Units	SPECIAL-ORDER DIFFERENCE 250,000 Units
Sales	20,000	22,875	2,875*
Variable manufacturing costs	12,000	15,000	3,000†
Other variable costs	1,100	1,100	—
Total variable costs	13,000	16,100	3,000
Contribution margin	6,900	6,775	(125)‡

* 250,000 × $11.50 selling price of special order.
† 250,000 × $12.00 variable manufacturing cost per unit of special order.
‡ 250,000 × $.50 negative contribution margin per unit of special order.

Short-run income will fall by $125,000 (that is, 250,000 units × $.50) if the special order is accepted. No matter how the fixed manufacturing costs are "unitized" and "spread" over the units produced, their total of $3 million will be *unchanged* by the special order (in thousands of dollars):

	WITHOUT SPECIAL ORDER 1,000,000 Units	WITH SPECIAL ORDER 1,250,000 Units	SPECIAL-ORDER DIFFERENCE 250,000 Units
Contribution margin (as above)	6,900	6,775	(125)
Total fixed costs:			
At an average rate of $3,000,000 ÷ 1,000,000 = $3.00	3,000	} 3,000	—
At an average rate of $3,000,000 ÷ 1,250,000 = $2.40			—
Contribution to other fixed costs and operating income	3,900	3,775	(125)

No matter how fixed costs are spread for *unit* product-costing purposes, the *total* fixed costs will be unchanged. This is true even though fixed costs *per unit* have fallen from $3.00 to $2.40.

The lesson here is important. Do not be deceived. Follow what was called Robert McNamara's First Law of Analysis when he was U.S. secretary of defense: "Always start by looking at the grand total. Whatever problem you are studying, back off and look at it in the large." In this context, that law means, "Beware of unit costs. When in doubt, convert all unit costs into the total costs under each alternative to get the big picture." In particular, beware of unit costs when analyzing fixed costs. Think in terms of totals instead.

SUMMARY PROBLEMS FOR YOUR REVIEW

☐ Problem One

1. Return to the basic illustration in Exhibit 4–3, page 93. Suppose a special order like that described in conjunction with Exhibit 4–3 had the following terms: selling price would be $13.50 instead of $13.00, but a manufacturer's agent who had obtained the potential order would have to be paid a flat fee of $40,000 if the order were accepted. What would be the new operating income if the order were accepted?

2. Assume the same facts concerning the special order as before, except that the order was for 250,000 units at a selling price of $11.50. Some managers have been known to argue for acceptance of such an order as follows: "Of course, we will lose 50¢ each on the variable manufacturing costs, but we will gain 60¢ per unit by spreading our fixed manufacturing costs over 1.25 million units instead of 1 million units. Consequently, we should take the offer because it represents an advantage of 10¢ per unit."

Old fixed manufacturing cost per unit, $3,000,000 ÷ 1,000,000	$3.00
New fixed manufacturing cost per unit, $3,000,000 ÷ 1,250,000	2.40
"Saving" in fixed manufacturing costs per unit	$ .60
Loss on variable manufacturing costs per unit, $11.50 − $12.00	.50
Net saving per unit in manufacturing costs	$ .10

Explain why this is faulty thinking.

☐ Solution to Problem One

1. The easiest way to solve this part is to work from the $100,000 increase in income already shown in the final column of Exhibit 4–3, page 93:

Operating income based on $13 price	$100,000
Increase in selling price per unit is $13.50 minus $13, or $.50. Increase in revenue, $.50 × 100,000 units	50,000
Increase in fixed expenses, special fee	(40,000)
New operating income	$110,000

2. Regardless of how the fixed manufacturing costs are "unitized" or "spread" over the units produced, their *total* of $3 million will be *unchanged* by the special order. As the tabulation on page 95 indicates, short-run income will fall by 250,000 units × ($12.00 − $11.50) = $125,000 if the special order is accepted.

ROLE OF COSTS IN PRICING

☐ Influencing Prices: Customers and Competitors

Three major factors influence pricing decisions: customers, competitors, and costs. *Customers* have alternative sources of supply, can substitute one material for another, and may make their own part rather than buy it if the vendor's price is too high. *Competitors* will usually react to the price changes of their rivals. Tinkering with prices often is most heavily affected by the price setter's expectations of competitors' reactions and of the overall effects on the total industry demand for the good or service in question. For example, an airline might cut prices even if it expects price cuts from its rivals. A justification for the price cut may be the prediction that total customer demand for the tickets of all airlines will increase sufficiently to offset the reduction in the price per ticket.

☐ Influencing Prices: Cost

Costs influence the deliberate setting of prices in some industries, but not in others. Frequently, the market price is regarded as a given. Examples include the prices of metals and agricultural commodities. Consider gold. A mining company sells at the established market prices. Whether profits or losses are forthcoming depends on how well the company controls its costs and volume.

The influence of costs on the setting of prices is often overstated. Nevertheless, many managers say that their prices are set by cost-plus pricing. For example, consider the construction and automobile industries. Their executives describe the procedure as computing an average unit cost and then adding a "reasonable" markup that will generate a target return on investment. But the key is the "plus" in cost plus. It is rarely an unalterable markup. Its magnitude depends on the behavior of competitors and customers.

Prices are most directly related to costs in industries where revenue is based on cost reimbursement. A prime example is defense contracting. Cost-reimbursement contracts generally specify how costs should be measured and what costs are allowable. For example, only coach-class (not first-class) air travel is reimbursable.

In short, the market sets prices after all. Why? Because the target price as set by a cost-plus formula is inevitably adjusted "in light of market conditions."

The maximum price that may be charged is the one that does not drive the customer away. The minimum price is zero; companies may give out free samples to gain entry into a market. A more practical guide is that, in the short run, the *minimum* price to be quoted, *subject to consideration of long-run effects*, should be the costs that may be avoided by not landing the order—often all variable costs.

☐ Target Pricing

Target prices might be based on a host of different markups based on a host of different definitions of cost. Thus there are many ways to arrive at the *same target price*. They simply reflect different arrangements of the components of the same income statement.

Exhibit 4–4 displays the relationships of costs to target selling prices. The percentages there represent four popular markup formulas for pricing: (1) as a percentage of variable manufacturing costs, (2) as a percentage of total variable costs, (3) as a percentage of all costs, and (4) as a percentage of absorption manufacturing costs. Of course, the percentages differ. For instance, the markup on variable manufacturing costs is 66.67% and on absorption manufacturing costs is 33.33%. Regardless of the formula used, the pricing decision maker will be led toward the *same* target price. For a volume of 1 million units, assume that the target selling price is $20 per unit. If the decision maker is unable to obtain such a price consistently, the company will not achieve its $1 million operating income objective or its desired operating income percentage of sales.

☐ Advantages of Contribution Approach

When it is used intelligently, the contribution approach has some advantages over the absorption costing approach or the all-costs approach. Most often, the last two fail to highlight different cost behavior patterns.

EXHIBIT 4–4

Relationships of Costs to Target Selling Prices

		ALTERNATIVE MARKUP PERCENTAGES TO ACHIEVE TARGET SALES (dollars in thousands)
Target sales	$20,000,000	
Variable costs:		
(1) Manufacturing	$12,000,000*	($20,000 − $12,000) ÷ $12,000 = 66.67%
Selling and administrative	1,100,000	
(2) Total variable costs	$13,100,000	($20,000 − $13,100) ÷ $13,100 = 52.67%
Fixed costs:		
Manufacturing	$ 3,000,000*	
Selling and administrative	2,900,000	
Total fixed costs	$ 5,900,000	
(3) Total of all costs	$19,000,000	($20,000 − $19,000) ÷ $19,000 = 5.26%
Operating income	$ 1,000,000	

* A frequently used formula is based on absorption *manufacturing* costs:
[$20,000 − ($12,000 + $3,000)] ÷ $15,000 = 33.33%.

First, the contribution approach offers more detailed information because variable- and fixed-cost behavior patterns are explicitly delineated. Since the contribution approach is sensitive to cost-volume-profit relationships, it is a helpful basis for developing pricing formulas.

plus better control of activity.

Second, a normal or target-pricing formula can be as easily developed by the contribution approach as by absorption-costing approaches, as was shown in Exhibit 4–4.

Third, the contribution approach offers insight into the short-run versus long-run effects of cutting prices on special orders. For example, assume the same cost behavior patterns as in Exhibit 4–3, page 93. The 100,000-unit order added $100,000 to operating income at a selling price of $13, which was $7 below the target selling price of $20 and $2 below the absorption manufacturing cost of $15. The implication there, given all the stated assumptions, favored accepting the order. No general answer can be given, but the relevant information was more easily generated by the contribution approach. Recall the possible analyses:

	CONTRIBUTION APPROACH	ABSORPTION COSTING APPROACH
Sales, 100,000 units @ $13	$1,300,000	$1,300,000
Variable manufacturing costs @ $12	1,200,000	
Absorption manufacturing costs @ $15		1,500,000
Apparent change in operating income	$ 100,000	$−200,000

Should the offer be accepted? Compare the two approaches. Under the absorption approach, the decision maker has no direct knowledge of cost-volume-profit relationships. The decision maker makes the decision by hunch. On the surface the offer is definitely unattractive because the price of $13 is $2 below absorption manufacturing costs.

Under the contribution approach, the decision maker sees a short-run advantage of $100,000 from accepting the offer. Fixed costs will be unaffected by whatever decision is made and operating income will increase by $100,000. Still, there often are long-run effects to consider. Will acceptance of the offer undermine the long-run price structure? In other words, is the short-run advantage of $100,000 more than offset by high probable long-run financial disadvantages? The decision maker may think so and may reject the offer. But— and this is important—by doing so the decision maker is, in effect, saying that he or she is willing to forgo $100,000 now in order to protect his or her long-run market advantages. Generally, the decision maker can assess problems of this sort by asking whether the probability of long-run benefits is worth an "investment" equal to the forgone contribution margin ($100,000 in this case). Under absorption approaches, the decision maker must ordinarily conduct a special study to find the immediate effects. Under the contribution approach, the manager has a system that will routinely and more surely provide such information.

☐ Advantages of Absorption-Cost or All-Costs Approaches

Our general theme of focusing on relevant costs also extends into the area of pricing. To say that either a contribution approach or an absorption-cost approach or an all-costs approach provides the preferable guide to pricing decisions is a dangerous over-simplification of one of the most perplexing problems in business. Lack of understanding and judgment can lead to unprofitable pricing regardless of the kind of cost data available or cost-accounting system used.

Frequently, managers do not employ a contribution approach because they fear that variable costs will be substituted indiscriminately for all costs and will therefore lead to suicidal price cutting. This should *not* occur if the data are used wisely. However, if the top managers perceive a pronounced danger of underpricing when variable-cost data are revealed, they may justifiably prefer an absorption-costing approach or an all-costs approach for guiding pricing decisions.

Cost-plus pricing based on absorption costs or all costs entails circular reasoning. That is, price, which influences sales volume, is often based upon an average absorption cost per unit, which in turn is partly determined by the underlying volume of sales.

Despite these criticisms, absorption costs or all costs are far more widely used in practice than is the contribution approach. Why? In addition to the reasons already mentioned, the following have been offered:

1. In the long run, all costs must be recovered to stay in business.
2. Computing target prices based on cost-plus may indicate what competitors might charge, especially if they have approximately the same level of efficiency as you and also aim at recovering all costs in the long run.
3. Absorption-cost or all-cost formula pricing meets the cost-benefit test. It is too costly to conduct individual cost-volume tests for the many products (sometimes thousands) that a company offers.
4. There is much uncertainty about the shape of the demand curves and the correct price-output decisions. Absorption-cost pricing copes with this uncertainty by not encouraging managers to take too much marginal business.
5. Absorption-cost or all-cost pricing tends to promote price stability. Managers prefer price stability because it eases their professional lives, primarily because planning is more dependable.
6. Absorption-cost pricing or all-cost pricing provides the most defensible basis for justifying prices to all interested parties, including government antitrust investigators.

In brief, absorption-cost or all-cost pricing provides convenient reference points to simplify hundreds or thousands of pricing decisions. The resulting target prices are at least a first step as a basis for setting prices. A complete discussion of pricing is beyond the scope of this book.[1] However, a contribution

---

[1] For example, many laws prohibit price discrimination—that is, quoting different selling prices for identical goods or services. Obviously there are also many other complications, which are explored in books on economics and marketing.

approach should clarify the major classes of information that bear on the pricing decision.

The history of accounting reveals that most companies' systems have gathered costs via some form of all-cost system. In recent years, when systems are changed, variable costs and fixed costs are identified. But managers have regarded this change as an addition to the existing all-cost system. That is, many managers insist on having information regarding *both* variable costs per unit and the allocated fixed costs per unit before setting selling prices. If the accounting system routinely gathers data regarding both variable and fixed costs, such data can be readily provided. However, most absorption costing systems in practice do not organize their data collection so as to distinguish between variable and fixed costs. As a result, special studies or special guessing must be used to designate costs as variable and fixed.

DELETION OR ADDITION OF PRODUCTS OR DEPARTMENTS

Consider a discount department store that has three major departments: groceries, general merchandise, and drugs. Management is considering dropping groceries, which have consistently shown a net loss. The present annual net income is reported in the following table (in thousands of dollars):

	Total	Groceries	DEPARTMENTS General Merchandise	Drugs
Sales	$1,900	$1,000	$800	$100
Variable cost of goods sold and expenses*	1,420	800	560	60
Contribution margin	$ 480 (25%)	$ 200 (20%)	$240 (30%)	$ 40 (40%)
Fixed expenses (salaries, depreciation, insurance, property taxes, etc.):				
Avoidable	$ 265	$ 150	$100	$ 15
Unavoidable	180	60	100	20
Total fixed expenses	$ 445	$ 210	$200	$ 35
Operating income	$ 35	$ (10)	$ 40	$ 5

* Examples of variable expenses include paper bags and sales commissions.

Sometimes the terms *avoidable* and *unavoidable* costs are used in conjunction with special decision making. **Avoidable costs** are those costs that will not continue if an ongoing operation is changed or deleted; in contrast, **unavoidable costs** are those costs that will continue. Avoidable costs include department salaries and other costs that could be avoided by not operating the specific department. Unavoidable costs include many **common costs**, which are defined as those costs of facilities and services that are shared by user departments. Examples are store depreciation, heating, air conditioning, and general management expenses.

Assume first that the only alternatives to be considered are to drop or continue the grocery department. Assume further that the total assets invested would be unaffected by the decision. The vacated space would be idle, and the unavoidable costs would continue. Which alternative would you recommend? An analysis follows (in thousands of dollars):

| INCOME STATEMENTS | STORE AS A WHOLE | | |
	a Keep Groceries	b Drop Groceries	a − b Difference
Sales	$1,900	$900	$1,000
Variable expenses	1,420	620	800
Contribution margin	$ 480	$280	$ 200
Avoidable fixed expenses	265	115	150
Profit contribution to common space and other unavoidable costs	$ 215	$165	$ 50
Common space and other unavoidable costs	180	180	—
Operating income	$ 35	$ (15)	$ 50

The preceding analysis shows that matters would be worse, rather than better, if groceries were dropped and the vacated facilities left idle. In short, as the income statement shows, groceries bring in a contribution margin of $200,000, which is $50,000 more than the $150,000 fixed expenses that would be saved by closing the grocery department.

Assume now that the space made available by the dropping of groceries would be used by an expanded general merchandise department. The space would be occupied by merchandise that would increase sales by $500,000, generate a 30% contribution-margin percentage, and have avoidable fixed costs of $70,000. The $80,000 increase in operating income of general merchandise more than offsets the $50,000 decline from eliminating groceries, providing an overall increase in operating income of $65,000 − $35,000 = $30,000:

	TOTAL	GENERAL MERCHANDISE (in thousands of dollars)	DRUGS
Sales	$1,400	$800 + $500	$100
Variable expenses	970	560 + 350	60
Contribution margin	$ 430	$240 + $150	$ 40
Avoidable fixed expenses	185	100 + 70	15
Contribution to common space and other unavoidable costs	$ 245	$140 + $ 80	$ 25
Common space and other unavoidable costs*	180		
Operating income	$ 65		

* Includes the $60,000 of former grocery fixed costs, which were allocations of common costs that will continue regardless of how the space is occupied.

As the following summary analysis demonstrates, the objective is to obtain, from a given amount of space or capacity, the maximum contribution to the payment of those costs that remain unaffected by the nature of the product sold (in thousands of dollars):

	PROFIT CONTRIBUTION OF GIVEN SPACE		
	Groceries	Expansion of General Merchandise	Difference
Sales	$1,000	$500	$500 U
Variable expenses	800	350	450 F
Contribution margin	$ 200	$150	$ 50 U
Avoidable fixed expenses	150	70	80 F
Contribution to common space and other unavoidable costs	$ 50	$ 80	$ 30 F

F = Favorable difference resulting from replacing groceries with general merchandise.
U = Unfavorable difference.

In this case, the general merchandise will not achieve the dollar sales volume that groceries will, but the higher markups and the lower wage costs (mostly because of the diminished need for stocking and checkout clerks) will bring more favorable net results.

This illustration contains another lesson. Avoid the idea that relevant-cost analysis merely says, "Consider all variable costs, and ignore all fixed costs." In this case, *some* fixed costs are relevant because they differ under each alternative.

To make intelligent decisions, managers want reliable measurements. An extremely large U.S. grocery chain, A&P, ran into profit difficulties during the 1970s. It began retrenching by closing many stores. Management's lack of adequate information about individual store operations made the closing program a hit-or-miss affair. A news story reported:

☐ Because of the absence of detailed profit-and-loss statements, and a cost-allocation system that did not reflect true costs, A&P's strategists could not be sure whether an individual store was really unprofitable. For example, distribution costs were shared equally among all the stores in a marketing area without regard to such factors as a store's distance from the warehouse. Says one close observer of the company: "When they wanted to close a store, they had to wing it. They could not make rational decisions, because they did not have a fact basis."

CONTRIBUTION TO PROFIT PER UNIT OF LIMITING FACTOR

When a multiple-product plant is being operated at capacity, decisions about which orders to accept must often be made. The contribution approach also applies here, because the product to be emphasized or the order to be accepted is the one that makes the biggest *total* profit contribution per unit of the **limiting factor** or **scarce resource**.

The contribution approach must be used wisely, however. Sometimes a major pitfall is the erroneous tendency to favor those products with the biggest contribution-margin or gross margin per sales dollar.

Assume that a company has two products: a plain portable heater and a fancier heater with many special features. Unit data follow:

	PLAIN HEATER	FANCY HEATER
Selling price	$20	$30
Variable costs	16	21
Contribution margin	$ 4	$ 9
Contribution-margin ratio	20%	30%

Which product is more profitable? The correct answer is "It depends." If sales are restricted by demand for only a limited *number* of heaters, fancy heaters are more profitable. Why? Because sale of a plain heater adds $4 to profit; sale of a fancy heater adds $9. The limiting factor is *units* of sales, so the more profitable product is the one with the higher contribution *per unit*.

But suppose that there is demand for more heaters of both types than the company can produce. Now productive capacity is the limiting factor. If 10,000 hours of capacity are available, and three plain heaters can be produced per hour in contrast to one fancy heater, the plain heater is more profitable. Why? Because it contributes more profit *per hour*.

	PLAIN HEATER	FANCY HEATER
1. Units per hour	3	1
2. Contribution margin per unit	$4	$9
Contribution margin per hour (1) × (2)	$12	$9
Total contribution for 10,000 hours	$120,000	$90,000

The criterion for maximizing profits, for a given capacity, is to obtain the greatest possible contribution to profit for each unit of the limiting or scarce factor.

Many different capacity factors might limit sales. In a manufacturing firm, labor-hours and machine-hours may limit production and hence sales; in department stores, square feet of floor space or cubic meters of display space may limit sales. When there are capacity limitations, the conventional contribution-margin or gross-margin-per-sales-dollar ratios provide an insufficient clue to profitability.

EXHIBIT 4–5

	REGULAR DEPARTMENT STORE	DISCOUNT DEPARTMENT STORE
Retail price	$4.00	$3.50
Cost of merchandise and other variable costs	3.00	3.00
Contribution to profit per unit	$1.00 (25%)	$ .50 (14+%)
Units sold per year	10,000	22,000
Total contribution to profit, assuming the same space allotment in both stores	$10,000	$11,000

Consider an example of two department stores. The conventional gross profit percentage (gross profit ÷ selling price) is an insufficient clue to profitability because profits also depend on the space occupied and the **inventory turnover** (number of times the average inventory is sold per year).

The success of suburban discount department stores illustrates the concept of the contribution to profit per unit of limiting factor. These stores have been satisfied with subnormal markups because they have been able to increase turnover and thus increase the contribution to profit per unit of space. Exhibit 4–5 illustrates the same product, taking up the same amount of space, in each of two stores. The contribution margins per unit and per sales dollar are less in the discount store, but faster turnover makes the same product a more profitable use of space in the discount store.

The illustrations here have focused on one scarce factor rather than on several simultaneously, such as the maximum available machine-hours, labor-hours, and materials. The latter complications are analyzed by using linear programming decision models, as introduced in Chapter 16.

Throughout this discussion, fixed costs have been correctly ignored. They are irrelevant unless their total is affected by the choices.

SUMMARY

The accountant's role in problem solving is primarily that of a technical expert on cost analysis. The accountant's responsibility is to help the manager use **relevant data** as guidance for decisions. Accountants and managers must have a penetrating understanding of relevant costs.

To be relevant to a particular decision, a cost must meet two criteria: (1) it must be an expected *future* cost, and (2) it must be an element of *difference* among the alternatives. All *past* (*historical* or *sunk*) costs are in themselves irrelevant to any *decision* about the future, although they often provide the best available basis for the *prediction* of expected future data.

The combination of the relevant-costing and contribution approaches is a fundamental framework, based on economic analysis, that applies to a vast range of problems.

SUMMARY PROBLEMS FOR YOUR REVIEW

Problem One appears earlier in this chapter.

☐ Problem Two

Consider the following news story:

☐ SALT LAKE CITY (UPI)—Mayor Ted Wilson says Sen. William Proxmire, D-Wis., had better stop taking his daily $12 federally funded showers before he criticizes Salt Lake City's $145,000 wave-making machine.

Wilson awarded Proxmire a "Golden Hypocrisy" award Tuesday in exchange for the "Golden Fleece" award the senator gave the U.S. Interior Department for spending taxpayers' money to make waves in a Salt Lake swimming pool so that desert dwellers could have an aquatic experience known only to coastal swimmers.

Proxmire gives out a Golden Fleece award monthly to people, projects, and organizations he believes are ripping off the taxpayers through wasteful spending.

But Wilson predicted that 180,000 people—the city's entire population—would use the pool annually. He also criticized Proxmire for taking advantage of luxuries provided for senators.

The mayor said it cost taxpayers $12.35 a day for Proxmire to shower in the Senate gymnasium after he jogs to work.

"If he showers every day the Senate is in session, it costs the taxpayer $2,470 a year for a publicly paid shower," said Wilson.

"I am giving him my Golden Hypocrisy Award in recognition of the senator's ability to find fault in others and myopically overlook his own waste."

Wilson, who was a congressional aide before his election as mayor, said he calculated the cost of a Senate shower through his own observations. He said only about 15 of the 100 senators use the gym, which costs about $200,000 a year to operate.

"This means Sen. Proxmire costs the taxpayers $12.35 every time he takes a shower."

Proxmire attacked the wave-making machine as the "biggest, most ridiculous" example of wasteful government spending during November.

He said if the government follows the rationale used to justify the wave-making machine, "hard-pressed taxpayers will next be asked to fund ski slopes in Florida, mountain scenery in Indiana, igloos in Death Valley and tropical rain forests in Wisconsin."

Required:

1. Compute the total cost and the unit cost per swim per year for making waves. Assume that the equivalent of (a) 180,000 and (b) 90,000 swimmers use the pool once during the year. Also assume that the machine will last five years and will have annual fixed operating costs of $11,000 for power and maintenance.
2. Analyze Mayor Wilson's response to Senator Proxmire. Using the mayor's data, compute the number of days the Senate is usually in session per year.
3. Compute the total cost and the unit cost per visit to the gymnasium if (a) 15, (b) 30, and (c) 90 of the senators use the gym and shower each day the Senate is in session.
4. (a) How does your computation of unit cost in Requirement 3a compare with the $12.35 calculated by Wilson? (b) Give a possible explanation for the difference between Wilson's and your computations.

☐ Solution to Problem Two

This problem is worthwhile because (a) it underscores the roles of total costs and unit costs in evaluating frequently encountered discussions and (b) it is amusing.

1. Annual costs in total:

Depreciation, $145,000 ÷ 5	$29,000
Fixed operating costs	11,000
Total	$40,000

    a. Unit costs, $40,000 ÷ 180,000 = $.2222
    b. Unit costs, $40,000 ÷ 90,000 = $.4444

2. Number of days in session = $2,470 ÷ $12.35 = 200. The total cost is probably entirely fixed except for soap, water, towels, and slight fluctuations in energy bills because of variations in hot-water usage. Wilson's analysis seems unjustified. He implies that each visit by Proxmire increases the *total* expenses of operating the gym by $12.35. In fact, each visit has virtually no effect on *total* expenses.

Students should also ponder how Wilson might have accused Proxmire of incurring a higher unit cost per shower if the senator took only 1 or 10 showers per year instead of 200. When a fixed cost is divided by some unit measure of activity, the lower the activity, the higher the unit cost. See the next part for examples.

3. a.

Total operating costs per year	$200,000
Visits per year, 15 senators × 200 days	3,000
Unit cost per visit and shower	$66.67

    b. If 30 senators visit, the unit cost would drop to $200,000 ÷ (30 × 200) = $200,000 ÷ 6,000 = $33.33.
    c. If 90 senators visit, $200,000 ÷ (90 × 200) = $11.11.

4. a. The $66.67 is obviously much higher than the $12.35 quoted by Wilson.
    b. Two possible explanations are:

Wilson erred in his computations. Wilson's criticisms of Proxmire would have been even more dramatic if they had been based on the analysis in 3a.

Another possible explanation is that Wilson conducted a sophisticated analysis and somehow decided that $12.35 represented the true variable portion of the operating costs.

HIGHLIGHTS TO REMEMBER

The following are among the more important generalizations regarding various decisions:

1. Wherever feasible, think in terms of total costs rather than unit costs. Too often, unit costs are regarded as an adequate basis for predicting changes in total costs. This assumption is satisfactory when analyzing variable costs, but it is frequently misleading when analyzing fixed costs.

2. A common error is to regard all unit costs indiscriminately, as if all costs were variable costs. Changes in volume will affect *total* variable costs but not *total* fixed costs. The danger then is to predict total costs assuming that all unit costs are variable. The correct relationships are:

	BEHAVIOR AS VOLUME FLUCTUATES	
	Variable Cost	Fixed Cost
Cost per unit	No change	Change
Total cost	Change	No change

3. The contribution approach to pricing special sales orders offers helpful information because the forgone contribution can be quantified as the investment currently being made to protect long-run benefits.

4. The key to obtaining the maximum profit from a given capacity is to obtain the greatest possible contribution to profit per unit of the limiting or scarce factor.

ACCOUNTING VOCABULARY

All-costs Approach *p. 98*   Avoidable Cost *101*   Common Cost *101*   Decision Model *91*   Inventory Turnover *105*   Limiting Factor *104*   Relevant Information *87*   Scarce Resource *104*   Unavoidable Cost *101*.

FUNDAMENTAL ASSIGNMENT MATERIAL

4–1. **SPECIAL ORDER.**   In late 19X3, General Motors Corporation (GM) offered to buy 200,000 pens on a special order from the Ultra Pen Company. To fill the order, a special clip bearing the GM emblem was to have been added to each ordinary pen regularly manufactured and sold by Ultra. GM planned to use the pens in special promotions in early 19X4.

Ultra's income statement for the year ended December 31, 19X3 (before considering the special order) was:

Sales (2,000,000 pens @ $5)	$10,000,000
Less: Manufacturing cost of goods sold	6,000,000
Gross margin or gross profit	$ 4,000,000
Less: Selling and administrative expenses	3,100,000
Operating income	$ 900,000

Ultra's fixed manufacturing costs were $2.4 million, and its fixed selling and administrative costs were $2.3 million. Sales commissions of 3% of sales are included in selling and administrative expenses.

Even though Ultra had enough idle plant capacity to handle the special order, the president rejected GM's offer of $600,000 for the 200,000 pens. He said:

☐   The GM offer is too low. We'd avoid paying sales commissions, but we'd have to incur an extra cost of 20¢ per clip for the emblem and its assembly with the pens. If Ultra sells below its regular selling prices, it will begin a chain reaction of competitors' price cutting and of customers wanting special deals. I believe in pricing at no lower than 5% above our full costs of $9,100,000 ÷ 2,000,000 units = $4.55 per unit plus the extra 20¢ per clip less the savings in commissions.

Required:

1. Using the contribution approach, prepare an analysis similar to that in Exhibit 4–3. Use four columns without the special order, with the special order, and the special-order difference shown in total and per unit. Exhibit 4–3 is on page 93.
2. By what percentage would operating income increase or decrease if the order had been accepted? Do you agree with the president's decision? Why?

4–2. **CHOOSING PRODUCTS.**   The Rossi Company has two products: A, a plain electric coffee maker, and B, a fancy electric coffee maker. Unit data follow:

Selling price	$30	$40
Variable costs	24	30
Contribution margin	$ 6	$10

Required:

1. Compute the contribution margin ratios for A and B.
2. The demand is for more units than the company can produce. There are only 20,000 machine hours of manufacturing capacity available. Two plain coffee makers can be produced in the same average time (one hour) needed to produce one fancy coffee maker. Compute the total contribution margin for 20,000 hours for A only and for B only.
3. Use two or three sentences to state the major lesson of this problem.

ADDITIONAL ASSIGNMENT MATERIAL

4–3. "The distinction between precision and relevancy should be kept in mind." Explain.

4–4. Distinguish between the quantitative and qualitative aspects of decisions.

4–5. "Any future cost is relevant." Do you agree? Explain.

4–6. Why are historical or past data irrelevant to special decisions?

4–7. Give four examples of limiting or scarce factors.

4–8. "A ratio such as the conventional gross profit percentage is an insufficient clue to profitability." Do you agree? Explain.

4–9. What three major factors influence pricing decisions?

4–10. Why are customers one of the three factors influencing price decisions?

4–11. "Basing pricing on only the variable costs of a job results in suicidal underpricing." Do you agree? Why?

4–12. **REVIEW OF KEY EXHIBIT.**   Exhibit 4–1, page 90, is important because it displays the key steps in management activities and the related role of information. Note how historical information is an input to the prediction method, but historical information is not an input to the decision model. Review the exhibit to be sure you understand these relationships.

4–13. **PINPOINTING RELEVANT COSTS.**   Today you are planning to see a motion picture and you can attend either of two theaters. You have only a small budget for entertainment, so prices are important. You have attended both theaters recently. One charges $5 for admission; the other charges $6. You habitually buy popcorn in the theater—each theater charges $2. The motion pictures now being shown are equally attractive to you, but you are virtually certain that you will never see the picture that you reject today.

Required: | Identify the relevant costs. Explain your answer.

4–14. **INFORMATION AND DECISIONS.** Suppose a company's historical costs for the manufacture of a calculator were as follows: direct materials, $2.20 per unit; direct labor, $3.00 per unit. Management is trying to decide whether to replace some materials with different materials. The replacement should cut material costs by 10% per unit. However, direct-labor time will increase by 5% per unit. Moreover, direct-labor rates will be affected by a recent 10% wage increase.

Prepare an exhibit like Exhibit 4–1, showing where and how the data about direct material and direct labor fit in the decision process.

4–15. **PROFIT PER UNIT OF SPACE.**

a. Several successful chains of discount department stores have merchandising policies that differ considerably from those of the traditional downtown department stores. Name some characteristics of these discount stores that have contributed to their success.

b. Food chains have typically regarded, perhaps, 20% of selling price as an average target gross profit on canned goods and similar grocery items. What are the limitations of such an approach? Be specific.

4–16. **A&P's CLOSING OF STORES.** The text on page 103 refers to the A&P's closing of stores.

a. The company's labor costs as a percentage of sales increased in some markets, such as the Long Island and Pittsburgh divisions, even after allowing for normal increases in wage rates. How could this effect occur?

b. The company manufactured many of its own products. In the mid-1970s the company operated 46 plants. Twenty-one were bakeries. The others manufactured a variety of goods, from frozen potatoes to mouthwash. What impact would the store closings probably have on the manufacturing plants and on the total operating income?

4–17. **UNIT COSTS AND TOTAL COSTS.** You are a college professor who belongs to a faculty club. Annual dues are $120. You use the club solely for lunches, which cost $6 each. You have not used the club much in recent years and are wondering whether to continue your membership.

Required: | 1. You are confronted with a variable cost plus a fixed cost behavior pattern. Plot each on a graph, where the vertical axis is total cost and the horizontal axis is volume in number of lunches. Also plot a third graph that combines the previous two graphs.

2. What is the cost per lunch if you pay for your own lunch once a year? Twelve times a year? Two hundred times a year?

3. Suppose the average price of lunches elsewhere is $8. (a) How many lunches must you have at the faculty club so that the total costs of the lunches would be the same regardless of where you ate for that number of lunches? (b) Suppose you ate 250 lunches a year at the faculty club. How much would you save in relation to the total costs of eating elsewhere?

4–18. **VARIABLE COSTS AND PRICES.** A supplier to an automobile manufacturer has the following conversation with the manufacturer's purchasing manager:

SUPPLIER: You did not predict the heavy demands. To keep up with your unforeseen demands over the coming quarter, we will have to work six days per week instead of five. Therefore, I want a price increase in the amount of the overtime premium that I must pay.

MANUFACTURER: You have already recouped your fixed costs, so you are enjoying a hefty contribution margin on the sixth day. So quit complaining!

Required: Should the supplier get an increase in price? Explain.

4–19. **ACCEPTING A LOW BID.**   The Moravia Company, a maker of a variety of metal and plastic products, is in the midst of a business downturn and is saddled with many idle facilities. The National Hospital Supply Company has approached Moravia to produce 300,000 nonslide serving trays. National will pay $1.20 each.

Moravia predicts that its variable costs will be $1.30 each. However, its fixed costs, which had been averaging $1 per unit on a variety of other products, will now be spread over twice as much volume. The president commented, "Sure we'll lose 10¢ each on the variable costs, but we'll gain 50¢ per unit by spreading our fixed costs. Therefore, we should take the offer, because it represents an advantage of 40¢ per unit."

Required: Do you agree with the president? Why? Suppose the regular business had a current volume of 300,000 units, sales of $600,000, variable costs of $390,000, and fixed costs of $300,000.

4–20. **PRICING BY AUTO DEALERS.**   Many automobile dealers have an operating pattern similar to that of Lance Motors, a dealer in Ohio. Each month, Lance initially aims at a unit volume quota that approximates a break-even point. Until the break-even point is reached, Lance has a policy of relatively lofty pricing, whereby the "minimum deal" must contain a sufficiently high markup to ensure a contribution to profit of no less than $250. After the break-even point is attained, Lance tends to quote lower prices for the remainder of the month.

Required: What is your opinion of this policy? As a prospective customer, how would you react to this policy?

4–21. **TARGET SELLING PRICES.**   Consider the following data from a budgeted income statement (in thousands of dollars):

Target sales	$30,000
Variable costs:	
Manufacturing	15,000
Selling and administrative	5,000
Total variable costs	20,000
Fixed costs:	
Manufacturing	3,000
Selling and administrative	4,000
Total fixed costs	7,000
Total of all costs	27,000
Operating income	$ 3,000

Required: Compute the following markup percentages that would be used for obtaining the same target selling prices as a percentage of (1) total variable costs, (2) all costs, (3) variable manufacturing costs, and (4) absorption manufacturing costs.

4–22. **FORMULAS FOR PRICING.**   Galento Corporation, a building contractor, constructs houses in tracts, often building as many as 20 homes simultaneously.

The president of the corporation, Ms. Galento, has budgeted costs for an expected number of houses in 19X7 as follows:

Direct materials	$2,000,000
Direct labor	1,000,000
Job construction overhead	1,000,000
Cost of jobs	$4,000,000
Selling and administrative costs	1,000,000
Total costs	$5,000,000

The job construction overhead includes approximately $400,000 of fixed costs, such as the salaries of supervisors and depreciation on equipment. The selling and administrative costs include $200,000 of variable costs, such as sales commissions and bonuses that depend fundamentally on overall profitability.

Ms. Galento wants an operating income of $2 million for 19X7.

Required:

Compute the average markup percentage for setting prices as a percentage of:

1. Prime costs (direct materials plus direct labor).
2. The full "cost of jobs."
3. The variable "cost of jobs."
4. The full "cost of jobs" plus selling and administrative costs.
5. The variable "cost of jobs" plus variable selling and administrative costs.

4–23. **PRICING AND CONTRIBUTION APPROACH.** The Trusty Transportation Company has the following operating results to date for 19X3:

Operating revenues	$40,000,000
Operating costs	30,000,000
Operating income	$10,000,000

A large Chicago manufacturer has inquired about whether Trusty would be interested in trucking a large order of its parts to Detroit. Sid Goldfarb, operations manager, investigated the situation and estimated that the "fully distributed" costs of servicing the order would be $30,000. Using his general pricing formula, he quoted a price of $40,000. The manufacturer replied, "We'll give you $28,000, take it or leave it. If you do not want our business, we'll truck it ourselves or go elsewhere."

A cost analyst had recently been conducting studies of how Trusty's operating costs tended to behave. She found that $24 million of the $30 million could be characterized as variable costs. Goldfarb discussed the matter with her and decided that this order would probably generate cost behavior little different from Trusty's general operations.

Required:

1. Using a contribution format, prepare an analysis for Goldfarb.
2. Should Trusty accept the order? Explain.

4–24. **PRICING OF EDUCATION.** You are the director of continuing education programs for a well-known university. Courses for executives are especially popular, and you have developed an extensive menu of one-day and two-day courses that are presented in various locations throughout the nation. The performance of these courses for the current fiscal year, which is almost ended, is:

Tuition revenue	$2,000,000
Costs of courses	800,000
Contribution margin	1,200,000
General administrative expenses	300,000
Operating income	$ 900,000

The costs of the courses include fees for instructors, rentals of classrooms, advertising, and any other items, such as travel, that can be easily and exclusively identified as being caused by a particular course.

The general administrative expenses include your salary, your secretary's compensation, and related expenses, such as a lump-sum payment to the university's central offices as a share of university overhead.

The enrollment for your final course of the year is 40 students, who have paid $150 each. Two days before the course is to begin, a city manager phones your office. "Do you offer discounts to nonprofit institutions?" he asks. "If so, we'll send 10 managers. But our budget will not justify our spending more than $100 per person." The extra cost of including these 10 managers would entail lunches at $10 each and course materials at $20 each.

Required:

1. Prepare a tabulation of the performance for the full year, including the final course. Assume that the costs of the final course for the 40 enrollees' instruction, travel, advertising, rental of hotel classroom, lunches, and course materials would be $2,500. Show a tabulation in four columns: before final course, final course with 40 registrants, effect of 10 more registrants, and grand totals.
2. What major considerations would probably influence the pricing policies for these courses? For setting regular university tuition in private universities?

4–25. **UTILIZATION OF PASSENGER JETS.** In 19X2 Continental Air Lines, Inc., filled 50% of the available seats on its Boeing 727 jet flights, a record about 15% below the national average.

Continental could have eliminated about 4% of its runs and raised its average load considerably. But the improved load factor would have reduced profits. Give reasons for or against this elimination. What factors should influence an airline's scheduling policies?

When you answer this question, suppose that Continental had a basic package of 3,000 flights per month that had an average of 100 seats available per flight. Also suppose that 52% of the seats were filled at an average ticket price of $200 per flight. Variable costs are about 70% of revenue.

Continental also had a marginal package of 120 flights per month that had an average of 100 seats available per flight. Suppose that only 20% of the seats were filled at an average ticket price of $100 per flight. Variable costs are about 50% of this revenue. Prepare a tabulation of the basic package, marginal package, and total package, showing percentage of seats filled, revenue, variable expenses, and contribution margin.

4–26. **PRICING A SPECIAL ORDER.** The Lee Corporation has an annual plant capacity of 2,400 product units. Its predicted operations for the year are:

Manufacturing costs:	
Fixed (total)	$ 30,000
Variable (per unit)	$14
Selling and administrative expenses:	
Fixed (total)	$ 15,000
Variable (per unit)	$4
Production and sales of 2,000 units, total sales	$100,000

Compute the following, ignoring income taxes:

1. If the company accepts a special order for 200 units at a selling price of $19 each, how would the *total* predicted operating income for the year be affected, assuming no effect on regular sales at regular prices?
2. Without decreasing its total operating income, what is the lowest *unit price* for which the Lee Corporation could sell an additional 100 units not subject to any variable selling and administrative expenses, assuming no effect on regular sales at regular prices?
3. In solving Requirement 2, list the numbers given in the problem that are irrelevant.
4. Compute the expected annual operating income (with no special orders) if plant capacity can be doubled by adding additional facilities at a cost of $250,000. Assume that these facilities have an estimated life of five years with no residual scrap value and that the current unit selling price can be maintained for all sales. Total sales are expected to equal the new plant capacity each year. No changes are expected in variable costs per unit or in total fixed costs except for depreciation.

4–27. **PRICING CONFUSION OF VARIABLE AND FIXED COSTS.** A manufacturer had a fixed factory overhead budget for 19X2 of $12 million. The company planned to make and sell 2 million units of the product, a communications device. All variable manufacturing costs per unit were $11. The budgeted income statement contained the following:

Sales	$40,000,000
Manufacturing cost of goods sold	34,000,000
Gross margin	6,000,000
Deduct selling and administrative expenses	5,000,000
Operating income	$ 1,000,000

For simplicity, assume that the actual variable costs per unit and the total fixed costs were exactly as budgeted.

1. Compute the budgeted fixed factory overhead per unit.
2. Near the end of 19X2 a large computer manufacturer offered to buy 100,000 units for $1.2 million on a one-time special order. The president of the manufacturing firm stated: "The offer is a bad deal. It's foolish to sell below full manufacturing costs per unit. I realize that this order will have only a modest effect on selling and administrative costs. They will increase by a $10,000 fee paid to our sales agent."

   Compute the effect on operating income if the offer is accepted.
3. What factors should the president consider before finally deciding whether to accept the offer?
4. Suppose the original budget for fixed manufacturing costs was $12 million, but budgeted units of product were 1 million. How would your answers to Requirements 1 and 2 change? Be specific.

4–28. **DEMAND ANALYSIS.** (SMA, adapted.) The Aurora Manufacturing Limited produces and sells one product. During 19X4 the company manufactured and sold 50,000 units at $25 each. Existing production capacity is 60,000 units per year.

In formulating the 19X5 budget, management is faced with a number of decisions concerning product pricing and output. The following information is available:

(1) A market survey shows that the sales volume is very much dependent on the selling price. For each $1 drop in selling price, sales volume would increase by 10,000 units.

(2) The company's expected cost structure for 19X5 is as follows:
(a) Fixed cost (regardless of production or sales activities), $360,000
(b) Variable costs per unit (including production, selling, and administrative expenses), $16
(3) To increase annual capacity from the present 60,000 to 90,000 units, additional investment for plant, building, equipment, and the like, of $200,000 would be necessary. The estimated average life of the additional investment would be ten years, so the fixed costs would increase by an average of $20,000 per year. (Expansion of less than 30,000 additional units of capacity would cost only slightly less than $200,000.)

Required: Indicate, with reasons, what the level of production and the selling price should be for the coming year. Also indicate whether the company should approve the plant expansion. Show your calculations. Ignore income tax considerations and the time value of money.

4–29 **DROPPING A PRODUCT LINE.** A London Woolworth's store sells many products. It has a restaurant with a counter that extends almost the length of the store. Management is considering dropping the restaurant, which has consistently shown an operating loss. The predicted income statements, in thousands of pounds (£), follow (for ease of analysis, only three product lines are shown):

	TOTAL	GENERAL MERCHANDISE	GARDEN PRODUCTS	RESTAURANT
Sales	£5,000	£4,000	£400	£600
Variable expenses	3,390	2,800	200	390
Contribution margin	£1,610 (32%)	£1,200 (30%)	£200 (50%)	£210 (35%)
Fixed expenses (compensation, depreciation, property taxes, insurance, etc.)	1,110	750	50	(310)
Operating income	£ 500	£ 450	£150	£(100

The £310,000 of fixed expenses include the compensation of restaurant employees of £100,000. These employees will be released if the restaurant is abandoned. All counters and equipment are fully depreciated, so none of the £310,000 pertains to such items. Furthermore, their disposal values will be exactly offset by the costs of removal and remodeling.

If the restaurant is dropped, the manager will use the vacated space for either more general merchandise or more garden products. The expansion of general merchandise would not entail hiring any additional salaried help, but more garden products would require an additional person at an annual cost of £25,000. The manager thinks that sales of general merchandise would increase by £300,000; garden products, by £200,000. The manager's modest predictions are partially based on the fact that she thinks the restaurant has helped lure customers to the store and thus improved overall sales. If the restaurant is closed, that lure would be gone.

Required: Should the restaurant be closed? Explain, showing computations.

4–30. **UNIT COSTS AND CAPACITY.** (CMA.) Moorehead Manufacturing Company produces two products for which the following data have been tabulated. Fixed manufacturing cost is applied to product at a rate of $1.00 per machine-hour.

PER UNIT	XY-7	BD-4
Selling price	$4.00	$3.00
Variable manufacturing cost	2.00	1.50
Fixed manufacturing cost	.75	.20
Variable selling cost	1.00	1.00

The Sales Manager has had a $160,000 increase in her budget allotment for advertising and wants to apply the money on the most profitable product. The products are not substitutes for one another in the eyes of the company's customers.

Required:

Suppose Moorehead has only 100,000 machine-hours that can be made available to produce XY-7 and BD-4. If the potential increase in sales units for either product resulting from advertising is far in excess of these production capabilities, which product should be produced and advertised and what is the estimated increase in contribution margin earned?

4–31. **UNIT COSTS AND CAPACITY.** The Ogura Company manufactures small appliances, such as electric can openers, toasters, food mixers, and irons. The peak season is at hand, and the president is trying to decide whether to produce more of the company's standard line of can openers or its premium line that includes a built-in knife sharpener, a better finish, and a higher-quality motor. The unit data follow:

	PRODUCT	
	Standard	Premium
Selling price	$12	$20
Direct material	$ 2	$ 4
Direct labor	2	1
Variable factory overhead	2	4
Fixed factory overhead	2	4
Total cost of goods sold	$ 8	$13
Gross profit per unit	$ 4	$ 7

The sales outlook is very encouraging. The plant could operate at full capacity by producing either product or both products. Both the standard and the premium products are processed through the same departments. Selling and administrative costs will not be affected by this decision, so they may be ignored.

Many of the parts are produced on automatic machinery. The factory overhead is allocated to products by developing separate rates per machine-hour for variable and fixed overhead. For example, the total fixed overhead is divided by the total machine-hours to get a rate per hour. Thus the amount of overhead allocated to products is dependent on the number of machine-hours allocated to the product. It takes one hour of machine time to produce six units of the standard product.

Direct labor may not be proportionate with overhead because many workers operate two or more machines simultaneously.

Which product should be produced? If more than one should be produced, indicate the proportions of each. Show computations. Explain your answer briefly.

4–32. UTILIZATION OF CAPACITY. (CMA, adapted.) Anchor Company manufactures several different styles of jewelry cases. Management estimates that during the third quarter of 19X6 the company will be operating at 80 percent of normal capacity. Because the company desires a higher utilization of plant capacity, it will consider a special order.

Anchor has received special-order inquiries from two companies. The first is from JCP, Inc., which would like to market a jewelry case similar to one of Anchor's cases. The JCP jewelry case would be marketed under JCP's own label. JCP, Inc., has offered Anchor $5.75 per jewelry case for 20,000 cases to be shipped by October 1, 19X6. The cost data for the Anchor jewelry case, which would be similar to the specifications of the JCP special order, are as follows:

Regular selling price per unit	$9.00
Costs per unit:	
Raw materials	$2.50
Direct labor .5 hr @ $6	3.00
Overhead .25 machine-hr @ $4	1.00
Total costs	$6.50

According to the specifications provided by JCP, Inc., the special-order case requires less expensive raw materials, which will cost only $2.25 per case. Management has estimated that the remaining costs, labor time, and machine time will be the same as those for the Anchor jewelry case.

The second special order was submitted by the Krage Co. for 7,500 jewelry cases at $7.50 per case. These cases would be marketed under the Krage label and would have to be shipped by October 1, 19X6. The Krage jewelry case is different from any jewelry case in the Anchor line; its estimated per-unit costs are as follows:

Raw materials	$3.25
Direct labor .5 hr @ $6	3.00
Overhead .5 machine-hr @ $4	2.00
Total costs	$8.25

In addition, Anchor will incur $1,500 in additional setup costs and will have to purchase a $2,500 special device to manufacture these cases; this device will be discarded once the special order is completed.

The Anchor manufacturing capabilities are limited to the total machine-hours available. The plant capacity under normal operations is 90,000 machine-hours per year, or 7,500 machine-hours per month. The budgeted *fixed* overhead for 19X6 amounts to $216,000. All manufacturing overhead costs are applied to production on the basis of machine-hours at $4 per hour.

Anchor will have the entire third quarter to work on the special orders. Management does not expect any repeat sales to be generated from either special order. Company practice precludes Anchor from subcontracting any portion of an order when special orders are not expected to generate repeat sales.

Required:
Should Anchor Company accept either special order? Justify your answer and show your calculations. *Hint*: Distinguish between variable and fixed overhead.

TERMINOLOGY AND STRAIGHTFORWARD INTERPRETATIONS OF UNIT COSTS.
Following is the income statement of a manufacturer of slacks:

ROSENBERG COMPANY
Income Statement
For the Year Ended December 31, 19X4

	TOTAL	PER UNIT
Sales	$36,000,000	$36
Less: Manufacturing cost of goods sold	20,000,000	20
Gross margin	$16,000,000	$16
Less: Selling and administrative expenses	13,000,000	13
Operating income	$ 3,000,000	$ 3

Rosenberg manufactured 1 million units in 19X4, which had been sold to various clothing wholesalers and department stores. At the start of the year, the president, Sarah Rosenberg, dropped dead of a stroke. Her son, Theodore, became the new president. Ted has worked for 15 years in the marketing phases of the business. He knows very little about accounting and manufacturing, which were his mother's strengths. Ted has several questions for you, including inquiries regarding the pricing of special orders.

Required:

1. To prepare better answers, you decide to recast the income statement in contribution form. Last year variable manufacturing cost was $15 million. Variable selling and administrative expenses, which were mostly sales commissions, shipping expenses, and advertising allowances paid to customers based on units sold, were $9 million.
2. Ted asks, "I can't understand financial statements until I know the meaning of various terms. In scanning my mother's notes, I found the following pertaining to both total and unit costs: *absorption manufacturing cost, absorption cost, variable cost, all cost, full cost, fully allocated cost, fully distributed cost, gross margin, contribution margin.* Using our data for 19X4, please give me a list of these costs, their total amounts, and their per unit amounts."
3. "Near the end of 19X4 I brought in a special order from Macy's for 50,000 slacks at $30 each. I said I'd accept a flat $8,000 sales commission instead of the usual 6% of selling price, but my mother refused the order. She usually upheld a relatively rigid pricing policy, saying that it was bad business to accept orders that did not at least generate full manufacturing cost plus 80% of full manufacturing cost.

   "That policy bothered me. We had idle capacity. The way I figured, our manufacturing costs would go up by 50,000 × $20 = $1,000,000, but our selling and administrative expenses would only go up by $8,000. That would mean additional operating income of 50,000 × ($30 − $20) minus $8,000, or $500,000 minus $8,000, or $492,000. That's too much money to give up just to maintain a general pricing policy. Was my analysis of the impact on operating income correct? If not, please show me the correct additional operating income."
4. After receiving the explanations offered in Requirements 2 and 3, Ted said, "Forget that I had the Macy's order. Suppose I had an even bigger order from J. C. Penney. It was for 250,000 units and would have filled the plant completely. I told my mother I'd settle for no commission. There would have been no selling and administrative costs whatsoever because J. C. Penney would pay for the shipping and would not get any advertising allowances.

   "J. C. Penney offered $14.40 per unit. Our fixed manufacturing costs would have been spread over 1.25 million instead of 1 million units. Wouldn't it have been advantageous to accept the offer? Our old fixed manufacturing costs were $5 per unit. The added volume would reduce that cost more than our loss on our variable costs per unit.

"Am I correct? What would have been the impact on total operating income if we had accepted the order?"

4–34. **USING AVAILABLE CAPACITY.**   The Penske Company manufactures electronic subcomponents that can be sold at the end of Process H or can be processed further in Process J and sold as special parts for a variety of intricate electronic equipment. The entire output of Process H can be sold at a market price of $2.00 per unit. The output of Process J has been generating a sales price of $5.70 for three years, but the price has recently fallen to $5.30 on assorted orders.

Amy Schramka, the vice-president of marketing, has analyzed the markets and the costs. She thinks that the J output should be dropped whenever its price falls below $5.10 per unit. The total available capacity of H and J is interchangeable, so all facilities should currently be devoted to producing J. She has cited the following data:

OUTPUT OF H

Selling price, after deducting relevant selling costs		$2.00
Direct materials	$1.00	
Direct labor	.20	
Manufacturing overhead	.60	
Cost per unit		1.80
Operating profit		$ .20

OUTPUT OF J

Selling price, after deducting relevant selling costs		$5.30
Transferred-in cost from A	$1.80	
Additional direct materials	1.50	
Direct labor	.40	
Manufacturing overhead	1.20*	
Cost per unit		4.90
Operating profit		$ .40

* For additional processing to make J.

Direct-materials and direct-labor costs are variable. The total overhead is fixed; it is allocated to units produced by predicting the total overhead for the coming year and dividing this total by the total hours of capacity available.

The total hours of capacity available are 500,000. It takes our hour to make 60 units of H and two hours of additional processing to make 60 units of J.

Required:

1. If the price of J for the coming year is going to be $5.30, should H be dropped and all facilities devoted to the production of J? Show computations.
2. Prepare a report for the vice-president of marketing to show the lowest possible price for J that would be acceptable.
3. Suppose that 50% of the manufacturing overhead were variable. Repeat Requirements 1 and 2. Do your answers change? If so, how?

4–35. REVIEW OF CHAPTERS 2, 3, 4. The Lorenzo Corporation has the following cost behavior patterns:

Production range in units	0–10,000	10,001–20,000	20,001–30,000	30,001–40,000
Fixed costs	$400,000	$560,000	$670,000	$760,000

Maximum production capacity is 40,000 units per year. Variable costs per unit are $50 at all production levels.

Required:

Each situation described here is to be considered independently.

1. Production and sales are expected to be 21,000 units for the year. The sales price is $80 per unit. How many additional units need to be sold, in an unrelated market, at $70 per unit to show a total overall operating income of $60,000 for the year?
2. The company has orders for 45,000 units at $80. If it desired to make a minimum overall operating income of $500,000 on these 45,000 units, what unit purchase price would it be willing to pay a subcontractor for 5,000 units? Assume that the subcontractor would act as Lorenzo's agent, deliver the units to customers directly, and bear all related costs of manufacture, delivery, and so forth. The customers, however, would pay Lorenzo directly as the goods were delivered.
3. Production is currently expected to be 12,000 units for the year at a selling price of $80. By how much may advertising or special promotion costs be increased to bring production up to 25,000 units and still earn a total operating income of 3% of dollar sales?
4. Operating income is currently $330,000. Fixed costs are $670,000. However, competitive pressures are mounting. A 4% decrease in price will not affect sales volume but will decrease operating income by $90,000. Compute the present volume in units and the selling price per unit (which is *not* $80). Refer to the original data.

Chapter 5

RELEVANT COSTS AND SPECIAL DECISIONS—PART TWO

LEARNING OBJECTIVES

When you have finished studying this chapter, you should be able to:

1. Analyze given data to support a decision to make or buy certain parts or products.
2. Identify the opportunity-cost concept and apply it to an analysis for choosing the best use of available facilities.
3. Identify the uses and limitations of allocating joint costs.
4. Use either a differential analysis or an opportunity-cost analysis to determine whether individual joint products should be processed beyond the split-off point.
5. Distinguish between relevant and irrelevant items in arriving at decisions concerning disposal of obsolete inventory and replacement of equipment.
6. Identify the nature, causes, and remedies of a serious motivational problem that might block a desirable decision to dispose of old equipment and replace it with new equipment.

The key question in relevant-cost analysis was introduced and explained in the preceding chapter: What difference does it make? This chapter extends the application of such analysis. The contribution approach is illustrated for make-or-buy decisions and sell-or-process-further decisions. Particular attention is given to the relationships between past and future data, using the decision to replace equipment as an illustration

MAKE OR BUY

☐ **Make or Buy and Idle Facilities**

Manufacturers often face the question of whether to make or buy a product. For example, should we manufacture our own parts and subassemblies or buy them from vendors? The qualitative factors may be paramount. Sometimes the manufacture of parts requires special know-how, unusually skilled labor, rare materials, and the like. Therefore, some manufacturers often make parts because they desire to control quality. On the other hand, companies want to protect mutually advantageous long-run relationships with their suppliers. These companies may deliberately avoid the practice of making their parts during slack times and buying them only during prosperous times. Otherwise, they may have difficulty in obtaining needed parts during boom times, when there may well be shortages of material and workers but no shortage of sales orders.

What quantitative factors are relevant to the decision of whether to make or buy? The answer, again, depends on the situation. A key factor is whether there are idle facilities. Many companies make parts only when their facilities cannot be used to better advantage.

Assume that the following costs are reported:

GENERAL ELECTRIC COMPANY (GE)
Cost of Making Part No. 900

	TOTAL COST FOR 20,000 UNITS	COST PER UNIT
Direct material	$ 20,000	$ 1
Direct labor	80,000	4
Variable factory overhead	40,000	2
Fixed factory overhead	80,000	4
Total costs	$220,000	$11

Another manufacturer offers to sell GE the same part for $10. Should GE make or buy the part?

Although the $11 unit cost shown seemingly indicates that the company should buy, the answer is rarely obvious. The essential question is the difference in expected future costs as between the alternatives. If the $4 fixed overhead per unit consists of costs that will continue regardless of the decision, the entire $4 becomes irrelevant. Examples of such costs include depreciation, property taxes, insurance, and allocated executive salaries.

Again, are only the variable costs relevant? No. Perhaps $20,000 of the fixed costs will be saved if the parts are bought instead of made. This might be the salary of a supervisor who will be released or transferred to another productive assignment. In other words, fixed costs that may be avoided in the future are relevant.

For the moment, suppose that the capacity now used to make parts will become idle if the parts are purchased. The relevant computations follow:

	PER UNIT		TOTALS	
	Make	Buy	Make	Buy
Direct material	$1		$ 20,000	
Direct labor	4		80,000	
Variable factory overhead	2		40,000	
Fixed factory overhead that can be avoided by not making (supervisor's salary)	1		20,000	
Total relevant costs	$8	$10	$160,000	$200,000
Difference in favor of making		$2		$40,000

☐ Essence of Make or Buy: Utilization of Facilities

The choice in our example is not only whether to make or buy; it is how best to use available facilities. Although the data indicate that making the part is the better choice, the figures are not conclusive—primarily because we have no idea of what can be done with the manufacturing facilities if the component is bought. Only if the released facilities are to remain idle are the figures above valid.

Suppose that the released facilities can be used advantageously in some other manufacturing activity (to produce a contribution to profits of, say, $55,000) or can be rented out (say, for $35,000). These alternatives merit consideration. The two courses of action now become four (figures are in thousands):

	MAKE	BUY AND LEAVE FACILITIES IDLE	BUY AND RENT	BUY AND USE FACILITIES FOR OTHER PRODUCTS
Rent revenue	$ —	$ —	$ 35	$ —
Contribution from other products	—	—	—	55
Obtaining of parts	(160)	(200)	(200)	(200)
Net relevant costs	$(160)	$(200)	$(165)	$(145)

The final column indicates that buying the parts and using the vacated facilities for the production of other products should yield the best results in this case.

In sum, the make-or-buy decision should focus on relevant costs in a particular decision situation. In all cases, companies should relate make-or-buy decisions to the long-run policies for the use of capacity:

☐ One company does subcontract work for *other* manufacturers during periods when sales of its own products do not fully use the plant, but such work could not be carried on regularly without expansion of its plant. The profit margin on subcontracts would not be large enough to cover the additional costs of operating an expanded plant, and hence work is accepted only when other business is lacking. The same company sometimes meets a period of high volume by *purchasing* parts or having them made by subcontractors. While the cost of such parts is usually higher than the cost to make them in the company's own plant, the additional cost is less than it would be if they were made on equipment which could be used only part of the time.[1]

OPPORTUNITY COSTS

Consider a homeowner who has finally made the last payment on the mortgage. While celebrating, the owner says, "It's a wonderful feeling to know that future occupancy is free of any interest cost!" Many owners have the same thoughts. Why? Because no future *outlay costs* for interest are required. An **outlay cost** is defined as a cost that requires a cash disbursement sooner or later.

Accountants and economists maintain that the homeowner will not be living free of interest cost in the mortgage-free home. Why? Because an *opportunity cost* exists. An **opportunity cost** is defined as the *maximum* available contribution to profit forgone by using scarce resources for a particular purpose. It is measured by examining the *best* forsaken alternative; it is not an outlay cost because cash is neither received nor disbursed.

Suppose the owner could sell the home for $150,000, realizing no gain subject to income taxes. Suppose also that the owner considers tax-free munici-

---

[1] *The Analysis of Cost-Profit Relationships,* National Association of Accountants, Research Series No. 17, p. 552.

pal bonds (paying 10% annual interest) as the best alternative investment for the $150,000. An analysis of relevant items follows:

	HOLD THE HOME	SELL AND INVEST IN BONDS
Revenue, .10 × $150,000	$ —	$15,000
Expenses	—	—
Income effects	$ —	$15,000

The owner who continued to live in the home has rejected the next-best alternative, either directly or indirectly. He or she bears an opportunity cost of $15,000. The point here is important: *do not overlook the possible existence of opportunity costs.*

Numerical effects of alternatives may be framed in more than one way. Consider Maria Morales, a certified public accountant employed by a large accounting firm at $50,000 per year. She is yearning to have her own independent practice. She has narrowed her consideration to two alternatives:

	EMPLOYEE	INDEPENDENT PRACTICE
Revenues	$50,000	$200,000
Operating expenses	—	130,000
Income effects	$50,000	$ 70,000

The difference of $20,000 favors Maria's choosing independent practice.

Focus on the meaning of opportunity cost. What is the contribution to profit if the next-best alternative is rejected? Independent practice has an opportunity cost of $50,000, the forgone salary.

These facts may also be presented as follows:

		CHOOSE INDEPENDENT PRACTICE
Revenue		$200,000
Expenses:		
Outlay costs (operating expenses)	$130,000	
Opportunity cost of employee salary	50,000	180,000
Income effects		$ 20,000

Ponder the two preceding tabulations. Each produces the key difference between alternatives, $20,000. The first tabulation does not mention opportunity cost because the economic impacts are individually measured for each of the alternatives (two in this case). Neither alternative has been excluded from consideration. The second tabulation mentions opportunity cost because the $50,000 economic impact of the best excluded alternative is included as a cost of the chosen alternative. The failure to recognize opportunity cost will misstate the difference between alternatives.

Suppose that Morales prefers less risk and chooses to stay as an employee:

		EMPLOYEE
Revenue		$ 50,000
Expenses:		
Outlay costs	$ 0	
Opportunity cost of independent practice	70,000	70,000
Decrease in income		$(20,000)

If the employee alternative is selected, the key difference in favor of independent practice is again $20,000. The opportunity cost is $70,000, the operating income forgone by rejecting the best alternative. Morales is sacrificing $20,000 to avoid the risks of an independent practice. In sum, the measure of the opportunity cost depends on the best alternative that is excluded from consideration.

Note that opportunity costs are seldom incorporated into formal accounting systems, particularly for external reporting. Such costs represent incomes forgone by rejecting alternatives; therefore, opportunity costs do not involve cash receipts or outlays. Accountants usually confine their recording to those events that ultimately involve exchanges of assets. Thus, the historical records are limited to alternatives actually selected rather than those rejected, primarily because of the impracticality or impossibility of accumulating meaningful data on what might have been.

JOINT PRODUCT COSTS AND INCREMENTAL COSTS

☐ Nature of Joint Products

Joint products are two or more manufactured products (1) that have relatively significant sales values and (2) that are not separately identifiable as individual products until their split-off point. The **split-off point** is that juncture of manufacturing where the joint products become individually identifiable. Any costs beyond that stage are called *separable costs* because they are not part of the joint process and can be exclusively identified with individual products. Examples of joint products include chemicals, lumber, flour, and the products of petroleum refining and meat packing. A meat-packing company cannot kill a sirloin steak; it has to slaughter a steer, which supplies various cuts of dressed meat, hides, and trimmings.

Sometimes **common costs** are used as synonyms for **joint costs**. The former were described in Chapter 4 as the cost of facilities and services shared by user departments. However, most accountants (and this book) confine *joint costs* to the narrower meaning of the costs of manufacturing joint products prior to the split-off point.

An illustration should clarify the meaning of these new terms. Suppose Dow Chemical Company produces two chemical products, X and Y, as a result of a particular joint process. The joint processing cost is $100,000. This includes raw-material costs and the cost of processing to the point where X and Y go their separate ways. Both products are sold to the petroleum industry to be used as ingredients of gasoline. The relationships follow:

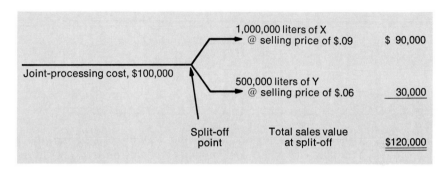

☐ Sell or Process Further

Management frequently faces decisions of whether to sell joint products at split-off or to process some or all products further. Suppose the 500,000 liters of Y can be processed further and sold to the plastics industry as product YA, an ingredient for plastic sheeting, at an additional cost of 8¢ per liter for manufacturing and distribution, a total of $40,000. The net sales price of YA would be 16¢ per liter, a total of $80,000 for 500,000 liters.

Product X will be sold at the split-off point, but management is undecided about Product Y. Should Y be sold or should it be processed into YA? The joint costs must be incurred to reach the split-off point. They do not differ between alternatives and are completely irrelevant to the question of whether The only approach that will yield valid results is to concentrate on the separable costs and revenue *beyond* split-off, as shown in Exhibit 5–1.

EXHIBIT 5–1

	SELL AT SPLIT-OFF AS Y	PROCESS FURTHER AS YA	DIFFERENCE
Revenue	$30,000	$80,000	$50,000
Separable costs beyond split-off @ $.08	—	40,000	40,000
Income effects	$30,000	$40,000	$10,000

This analysis shows that it would be $10,000 more profitable to process Y beyond split-off than to sell Y at split-off. Briefly, it is profitable to extend processing or to incur additional distribution costs on a joint product if the additional revenue exceeds the additional expenses.

For decisions regarding whether to sell or process further, the most straightforward analysis is as shown. Alternatively, an opportunity cost format would be:

		PROCESS FURTHER
Revenue		$80,000
Outlay cost: separable cost beyond		
split-off, @ $.08	$40,000	
Opportunity cost: sales		
value of Y at split-off	30,000	70,000
Income effects		$10,000

This format is merely a different way of recognizing another alternative (sell Y at split-off) when considering the decision to process further. When decision alternatives are properly analyzed, they may be compared either (1) by excluding the idea of opportunity costs altogether, as Exhibit 5–1 shows, or (2) by including opportunity costs, derived from the best excluded alternative, as is shown here. The key difference, $10,000, is generated either way.

☐ Differential Costs and Similar Terms

Exhibit 5–2 illustrates still another way to compare the alternatives of (1) selling Y at the split-off point and (2) processing Y beyond split-off. The title of the last column in Exhibit 5–2 refers to "differential" effects, a term frequently encountered in cost analysis for special decisions. In this situation, the *differential* revenue is $50,000, the **differential cost** is $40,000, and the *differential* income is $10,000. Each is the difference between the corresponding items under the alternatives being considered. In an analysis that showed

EXHIBIT 5–2

Firm as a Whole

	(1) ALTERNATIVE ONE			(2) ALTERNATIVE TWO			(3) DIFFERENTIAL EFFECTS
	X	Y	Total	X	YA	Total	
Revenue	$90,000	$30,000	$120,000	$90,000	$80,000	$170,000	$50,000
Joint costs			$100,000		—	$100,000	—
Separable costs			—		40,000	40,000	40,000
Total costs			$100,000			$140,000	$40,000
Income effects			$ 20,000			$ 30,000	$10,000

only the differences, called a *differential analysis*, only column 3 would be shown. In a *total analysis*, all three sets of columns are shown. The choice of a differential or a total analysis is a matter of individual preference.

Incremental cost is a widely used term. Defined narrowly, incremental cost is the additional cost associated with increases in a given set of costs. For example, the incremental costs of increasing production from 1,000 units to 1,200 units per week would be the additional costs of the extra 200 units. Defined broadly, incremental is a synonym for differential; that is, an increment may be a positive or negative amount. For example, the decline in costs caused by reducing production from 1,200 to 1,000 units per week would be called differential savings by many accountants. Other accountants would refer to the decline as incremental savings.

□ Danger of Allocation

Earlier discussions in this and the preceding chapter have emphasized the desirability of concentrating on totals and of carefully examining unit costs and allocations of fixed costs. For example, the total common costs may be only slightly affected by changes in departments or products. Similarly, the allocation of joint product costs to units of product is fraught with analytical perils.

The allocation of joint costs would not affect the decision, as Exhibit 5–2 demonstrates. The joint costs are not allocated in the exhibit, but no matter how they might be allocated, the total income effects would be unchanged.

Nevertheless, joint product costs are routinely allocated to products for purposes of *inventory valuation* and *income determination*. For example, some of the costs attributable to Product X will ordinarily be allocated to any ending inventory of X. Such allocations are useful for inventory purposes *only*. For decisions of selling a joint product or processing it further, joint cost allocations should be ignored. Not only are they irrelevant, they may be downright misleading.

Two conventional ways of allocating joint costs to products are widely used: *physical units* and *relative sales values*. If physical units were used, the joint costs would be allocated as follows:

	LITERS	WEIGHTING	ALLOCATION OF JOINT COSTS	VALUE AT SPLIT-OFF
X	1,000,000	10/15 × $100,000	$ 66,667	$ 90,000
Y	500,000	5/15 × $100,000	33,333	30,000
	1,500,000		$100,000	$120,000

This approach shows that the $33,333 joint cost of producing Y exceeds its $30,000 value at split-off, seemingly indicating that Y should not be produced. However, such an allocation is not helpful in making production decisions. Neither of the two products could be produced separately.

A decision to produce Y must be a decision to produce X *and* Y. Because total revenue of $120,000 exceeds the total joint cost of $100,000, both will be produced. The allocation was not useful for this decision. Furthermore, as we have already seen, the allocation of joint costs would not be relevant in deciding what to do with each product individually after split-off.

Costing in proportion to *relative sales values* at split-off is another popular way of allocating joint costs:

	RELATIVE SALES VALUE	WEIGHTING	ALLOCATION OF JOINT COSTS
X	$ 90,000	90/120 × $100,000	$ 75,000
Y	30,000	30/120 × $100,000	25,000
	$120,000		$100,000

Now each product would be assigned a joint cost portion that is less than its value at split-off. Note how the allocation of a cost to a particular product such as Y depends not only on the sales value of Y but also on the sales value of X. However, here again the joint cost allocation has no bearing on whether Y should be sold as Y or processed further to become YA.

☐ By-product Costs

The general concepts of relevant costs just presented pertain equally to by-products and joint products. Why? Because, like joint products, **byproducts** are not individually identifiable until manufacturing reaches a split-off point. However, joint products have relatively significant sales values in comparison with the other products emerging at split-off. In contrast, by-products have relatively insignificant sales values in comparison with such other products. Examples of byproducts are glycerine from soap making and mill ends of cloth and carpets.

If an item is accounted for as a by-product, only separable costs are allocated to it. All joint costs are allocated to the main product. Any revenues from by-products, less their separable costs, are deducted from the cost of the main product.

IRRELEVANCE OF PAST COSTS

As defined early in Chapter 4, a relevant cost is (1) an expected future cost (2) that will differ among alternatives. The contribution aspect of relevant-cost analysis has shown that those expected future costs that will not differ are irrelevant to choosing among alternatives. Now we return to the idea that all past costs are also irrelevant to such decisions.

□ Obsolete Inventory

A company has 100 obsolete missile parts that are carried in inventory at a manufacturing cost of $100,000. The parts can be (1) remachined for $30,000 and then sold for $50,000 or (2) scrapped for $5,000. Which should be done?

This is an unfortunate situation; yet the $100,000 past cost is *irrelevant* to the decision to remachine or scrap. The only relevant factors are the expected future revenue and costs:

	REMACHINE	SCRAP	DIFFERENCE
Expected future revenue	$ 50,000	$ 5,000	$45,000
Expected future costs	30,000	—	30,000
Relevant excess of revenue over costs	$ 20,000	$ 5,000	$15,000
Accumulated historical inventory costs*	100,000	100,000	—
Net overall loss on project	$ (80,000)	$ (95,000)	$15,000

* Irrelevant because it is unaffected by the decision.

We could completely ignore the **historical cost** and still arrive at the $15,000 difference, the key figure in the analysis.

□ Book Value of Old Equipment

For now, we shall not consider all aspects of equipment-replacement decisions, but we shall turn to one that is widely misunderstood—the role of the book value of the old equipment. **Book value** is defined here as the original (historical) acquisition cost of a fixed asset less its accumulated depreciation. Book value is often called *net book value*. Consider the following data:

	OLD MACHINE	REPLACEMENT MACHINE
Original cost	$10,000	$8,000
Useful life in years	10	4
Current age in years	6	0
Useful life remaining in years	4	4
Accumulated depreciation	$ 6,000	0
Book value	$ 4,000	Not acquired yet
Disposal value (in cash) now	$ 2,500	Not acquired yet
Disposal value in 4 years	0	0
Annual cash operating costs (maintenance, power, repairs, coolants, etc.)	$ 5,000	$3,000

We have been asked to prepare a comparative analysis of the two alternatives. Before proceeding, consider some important concepts. The most widely misunderstood facet of replacement analysis is the role of the book value of the old equipment in the decision. The book value, in this context, is sometimes called a **sunk cost**, which is really just another term for historical or past cost. All historical costs are always irrelevant to choosing among alternative courses of action. Therefore the book value of the old equipment is always irrelevant to replacement decisions. At one time or another, we all like to think that we can soothe our wounded pride arising from having made a bad purchase decision by using the item instead of replacing it. The fallacy here is in erroneously thinking that a current or future action can influence the long-run impact of a past outlay. All past costs are down the drain. *Nothing* can change what has already happened.

We can apply our definition of decision relevance to four commonly encountered items:

> *Book value of old equipment*. Irrelevant, because it is a past (historical) cost. Therefore depreciation on old equipment is irrelevant.
>
> *Disposal value of old equipment*. Relevant (ordinarily), because it is an expected future inflow that usually differs among alternatives.
>
> *Gain or loss on disposal*. This is the algebraic difference between 1 and 2. It is therefore a meaningless combination of book value, which is always irrelevant, and disposal value, which is usually relevant. The combination form, *loss (or gain) on disposal*, blurs the distinction between the irrelevant book value and the relevant disposal value. Consequently, it is best to think of each separately.
>
> *Cost of new equipment*. Relevant, because it is an expected future outflow that will differ among alternatives. Therefore depreciation on new equipment is relevant.

Exhibit 5–3 should clarify the foregoing assertions. It deserves close study. Book value of old equipment is irrelevant regardless of the decision-making technique used. The "difference" column in Exhibit 5–3 shows that the $4,000 book value of the *old* equipment is not an element of difference between alternatives; it could be completely ignored for decision-making purposes. No matter what the *timing* of the charge against revenue, the amount charged is still $4,000, regardless of any available alternative. In either event, the undepreciated cost will be written off with the same ultimate effect on profit.[2] The $4,000 creeps into the income statement either as a $4,000 offset against the $2,500 proceeds to obtain a $1,500 *loss on disposal* in one year or as $1,000 depreciation in each of four years. But how it appears is irrelevant to the replacement decision. In contrast, the $2,000 annual depreciation on the *new* equipment *is* relevant because the total $8,000 depreciation is a future cost that may be avoided by not replacing.

☐ **Examining Alternatives over the Long Run**

The foregoing is the first example that has looked beyond one year. A useful technique is to view the alternatives over their entire lives and then compute average annual results. In this way, peculiar nonrecurring items (such as

---

[2] For simplicity, we ignore income tax considerations and the effects of the interest value of money in this chapter. But book value is irrelevant even if income taxes are considered, because the relevant item is then the tax cash flow, not the book value. The book value is essential information for predicting the amount and timing of future tax cash flows, but, by itself, the book value is irrelevant. For elaboration, see Chapter 12, page 391.

EXHIBIT 5–3

Cost Comparison—Replacement of Equipment
Including Relevant and Irrelevant Items

	FOUR YEARS TOGETHER		
	Keep	Replace	Difference
Cash operating costs	$20,000	$12,000	$8,000
Old equipment (book value):			
Periodic write-off as depreciation	4,000	—	—
or			
Lump-sum write-off	—	4,000*	—
Disposal value	—	−2,500*	2,500
New machine acquisition cost	—	8,000†	−8,000
Total costs	$24,000	$21,500	$2,500

The advantage of replacement is $2,500 for the four years together.

* In a formal income statement, these two items would be combined as "loss on disposal" of $4,000 − $2,500 = $1,500.
† In a formal income statement, written off as straight-line depreciation of $8,000 ÷ 4 = $2,000 for each of four years.

loss on disposal) will not obstruct the long-run view that must necessarily be taken in almost all special managerial decisions.

Exhibit 5–4 concentrates on relevant items only. Note that the same answer (the $2,500 net difference) will be produced even though the book value is completely omitted from the calculations. The only relevant items are the cash operating costs, the disposal value of the old equipment, and the depreciation on the new equipment. To demonstrate that the amount of the book value will not affect the answer, suppose the book value of the old equipment is $500,000 rather than $4,000. Your final answer will not change. The cumulative advantage of replacement is still $2,500. (If you are in doubt, rework this example, using $500,000 as the book value.)

EXHIBIT 5–4

Cost Comparison—Replacement of Equipment,
Relevant Items Only

	FOUR YEARS TOGETHER		
	Keep	Replace	Difference
Cash operating costs	$20,000	$12,000	$8,000
Disposal value of old machine	—	−2,500	2,500
New machine, acquisition cost	—	8,000	−8,000
Total relevant costs	$20,000	$17,500	$2,500

MOTIVATION AND CONFLICT OF MODELS

☐ Influence of Loss

Reconsider our replacement example in light of the following sequence, which was originally presented in a vertical format in Exhibit 4–1, page 90:

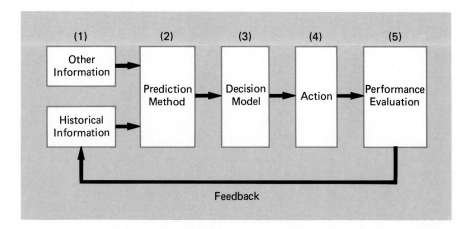

Assume that the decision model (box 3) specifies choose the alternative with the lower cumulative total costs over the four years. The analysis in Exhibit 5–4 indicates replace rather than keep. In the "real world," would the manager replace? The answer frequently depends on whether the manager believes that the decision model is consistent with the performance evaluation model (box 5). Conflict arises when managers are told to use one model for decision making, and their performance is then evaluated via a performance evaluation model that is inconsistent with the decision model. In this instance, if the manager's performance were to be evaluated by the typical accrual accounting model, a loss of $1,500 on the disposal of the old equipment would appear for the first year under the "replace" choice, but not under the "keep" choice:

	KEEP	REPLACE
Cash operating costs	$5,000	$3,000
Depreciation	1,000	2,000
Loss on disposal ($4,000 − $2,500)	—	1,500
Total charges against revenue	$6,000	$6,500

The performance evaluation model for the first year indicates lower charges against revenue of $6,500 − $6,000 = $500. The manager would be inclined to keep.

Note the motivational factors here. Managers may be reluctant to replace simply because the large loss on disposal would severely harm their reported profit performance in the first year. **Many managers and accountants would not replace the old machine because it would recognize the $1,500 "loss on disposal," whereas retention would allow spreading the $4,000 book value over four years in the form of "depreciation expense" (a more appealing term than "loss on disposal").** This demonstrates how overemphasis on short-run income may conflict with the objective of maximizing income over the long run, especially if managers are transferred periodically to different responsibilities.

Reconciling the Models

The conflict between decision models and performance evaluation models is a widespread problem in practice. Unfortunately, there are no easy solutions. In theory, the synchronization of these models seems obvious. Merely design a performance evaluation model that harmonizes exactly with the decision model. In our equipment example, this would mean predicting year-by-year income effects over the planning horizon for four years, noting that the first year would be poor, and following up accordingly.

The trouble is that evaluating performance, decision by decision, is costly. Therefore, aggregate measures are used. For example, an income statement shows the results of many decisions, not just the single decision of buying a machine. Consequently, in many cases like our equipment example, managers may be most heavily influenced by the first-year effects on the income statement. Thus, managers often refrain from taking the longer view that their superiors prefer.

This one-year-at-a-time approach is especially prevalent in many nonprofit organizations where budgets are approved on a year-to-year basis and the use of feedback is not well developed. Occasionally, managers will be tempted to underestimate costs to obtain initial approval. Then the managers come back year after year for supplementary amounts that were not contained in the original budget request. A related situation is the acceptance by many colleges and universities of donations for new facilities such as buildings and research equipment without budgeting sufficiently for lifelong maintenance and repairs. There is a danger that the value of such resources will be exceeded by the costs of operating them.

Distinguishing Between Decisions

Consider the following relationships:

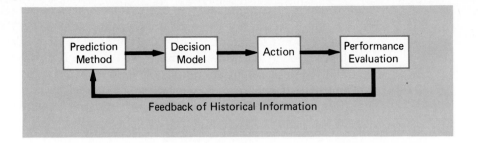

Prediction Method → Decision Model → Action → Performance Evaluation

Feedback of Historical Information

Refer to the data summarized in the table on page 131. The old machine was bought six years ago for $10,000. Its expected useful life was ten years. Call this original purchase Decision A. The feedback from this decision should affect the future decision process. How? By affecting predictions. Now consider Decision B, the replacement of the old machine by a new machine. However, if a better machine is now available, then the useful life of the old machine was really six years instead of ten. Given this feedback, how believable is the new prediction that the new machine will have a four-year useful life? Thus, the evaluation of the performance of Decision A provides vital feedback that should improve Decision B.

Although the feedback regarding the performance of Decision A is helpful, avoid confusing the financial impact of Decision A with the financial impact of Decision B. Above all, Decision B should not be forced to bear any "loss" already suffered by Decision A. In the machine example, thinking of the $1,500 loss on disposal (or the $4,000 book value) as affecting the measurement of Year 1's performance for Decision B (replacing) would be faulty. The relationships should be kept in perspective: the financial consequences of Decision A should be separated from Decision B. Mixing them together may lead to the wrong choice when Decision B is made.

IRRELEVANCE OF FUTURE COSTS THAT WILL NOT DIFFER

The past costs in the preceding two examples were not elements of difference among the alternatives. As noted in these examples, the $100,000 inventory of obsolete parts and the $4,000 book value of old equipment were irrelevant because they were the same for each alternative under consideration.

There are also expected *future* costs that may be irrelevant because they will be the same under all feasible alternatives. These, too, may be safely ignored for a particular decision. The salaries of many members of top management are examples of expected future costs that will be unaffected by the decision at hand.

Other irrelevant future costs include fixed costs that will be unchanged by such considerations as whether Machine X or Machine Y is selected, or whether a special order is accepted. However, it is not merely a case of saying that fixed costs are irrelevant and variable costs are relevant. Variable costs can be irrelevant. For instance, sales commissions might be paid on an order regardless of whether the order was filled from Plant G or Plant H. Variable costs are irrelevant whenever they do not differ among the alternatives at hand. Our preceding example showed that fixed costs (cost of new equipment) can be relevant. Fixed costs are relevant whenever they differ under the alternatives at hand.

BEWARE OF UNIT COSTS

The pricing illustration in the preceding chapter showed that unit costs should be analyzed with care in decision making. There are two major ways to go wrong: (1) the inclusion of irrelevant costs, such as the $3 allocation of unavoidable fixed costs in the make-or-buy example that would result in a unit cost of $11 instead of the relevant unit cost of $8, and (2) comparisons of unit costs not computed on the same volume basis, as the following example demonstrates. Generally, be wary of unit fixed costs. Use total costs rather than unit costs. Then, if desired, the totals may be unitized. Machinery sales personnel, for example, often brag about the low unit costs of using the new machines. Sometimes they neglect to point out that the unit costs are based on outputs far in excess of the volume of activity of their prospective customer.

Assume that a new $100,000 machine with a five-year life can produce 100,000 units a year at a variable cost of $1 per unit, as opposed to a variable cost per unit of $1.50 with an old machine. A sales representative claims that it will reduce cost by $.30 per unit. Is the new machine a worthwhile acquisition?

The new machine is attractive at first glance. If the customer's expected volume is 100,000 units, unit-cost comparisons are valid, provided that new depreciation is also considered. Assume that the disposal value of the old equipment is zero. Because depreciation is an allocation of *historical* cost, the depreciation on the old machine is irrelevant. In contrast, the depreciation on the new machine is relevant because the new machine entails a *future* cost that can be avoided by not acquiring it:

	OLD MACHINE	NEW MACHINE
Units	100,000	100,000
Variable costs	$150,000	$100,000
Straight-line depreciation	—	20,000
Total relevant costs	$150,000	$120,000
Unit relevant costs	$ 1.50	$ 1.20

Apparently, the sales representative is correct. However, if the customer's expected volume is only 30,000 units per year, the unit costs change in favor of the old machine:

	OLD MACHINE	NEW MACHINE
Units	30,000	30,000
Variable costs	$45,000	$30,000
Straight-line depreciation	—	20,000
Total relevant costs	$45,000	$50,000
Unit relevant costs	$ 1.50	$1.6667

DECISION MODELS AND UNCERTAINTY

The decision models illustrated in this and the preceding chapter employed accrual accounting models, whereby the effects on operating income under various alternatives were compared and the alternative with the best income effect was chosen. Other decision models are discussed in later chapters. (For example, Chapters 11 and 12 cover discounted-cash-flow models for equipment-replacement decisions. Many readers may prefer to jump directly to Chapters 11 and 12 immediately after completing their study of this chapter. This can be done without breaking continuity.)

Throughout this and other chapters, dollar amounts of future sales and operating costs are assumed to be known with certainty. This assumption highlights and simplifies various important points. In practice, the forecasting of these key figures is generally the most difficult aspect of decision analysis. For elaboration, see Chapter 16, which explores the implications of uncertainty in decision contexts.

SUMMARY

Relevant-cost analysis, which makes heavy use of the contribution approach, concentrates on expected future data that will differ among alternatives. As Exhibit 4–1 (p. 90) shows, clear distinctions should be made between past data, which may be helpful in formulating predictions, and the predicted data that are the inputs to decision models. Numerous illustrations in Chapters 4 and 5 underscore these fundamental ideas.

SUMMARY PROBLEM FOR YOUR REVIEW

☐ **Problem**

Exhibit 5–5 contains data for the Block Company for the year just ended. The company makes parts used in the final assembly of its finished product.

Required: 1. During the year, a prospective customer in an unrelated market offered $82,000 for 1,000 finished units. The latter would be in addition to the 100,000 units sold. The regular sales commission rate would have been paid. The president rejected the order because "it was below our costs of $97 per unit." What would operating income have been if the order had been accepted?

EXHIBIT 5–5

	A + B COMPANY AS A WHOLE	A FINISHED PRODUCT*	B PARTS
Sales: 100,000 units, @ $100	$10,000,000		
Variable costs:			
Direct material	$ 4,900,000	$4,400,000	$ 500,000
Direct labor	700,000	400,000	300,000
Variable factory overhead	300,000	100,000	200,000
Other variable costs	100,000	100,000	—
Sales commissions, @ 10% of sales	1,000,000	1,000,000	—
Total variable costs	$ 7,000,000	$6,000,000	$1,000,000
Contribution margin	$ 3,000,000		
Separable fixed costs	$ 2,300,000	$1,900,000	$ 400,000
Common fixed costs	400,000	320,000	80,000
Total fixed costs	$ 2,700,000	$2,220,000	$ 480,000
Operating income	$ 300,000		

* Not including the costs of parts (column B).

2. A supplier offered to manufacture the year's supply of 100,000 parts for $13.50 each. What would be the effect on operating income if the Block Company purchased rather than made the parts? Assume that $350,000 of the separable fixed costs assigned to parts would have been avoided if the parts were purchased.
3. The company could have purchased the parts for $13.50 each and used the vacated space for the manufacture of a deluxe version of its major product. Assume that 20,000 deluxe units could have been made (and sold in addition to the 100,000 regular units) at a unit variable cost of $70, exclusive of parts and exclusive of the 10% sales commission. The sales price would have been $110. All the fixed costs pertaining to the parts would have continued, because these costs related primarily to the manufacturing facilities used. What would operating income have been if Block had bought the necessary parts and made and sold the deluxe units?

☐ **Solution**

1. Costs of filling special order:

Direct material	$49,000
Direct labor	7,000
Variable factory overhead	3,000
Other variable costs	1,000
Sales commission @ 10% of $82,000	8,200
Total variable costs	$68,200
Selling price	82,000
Contribution margin	$13,800

Operating income would have been $300,000 + $13,800, or $313,800, if the order had been accepted. In a sense, the decision to reject the offer implies that the Block Company is willing to invest $13,800 in immediate gains forgone (an opportunity cost) in order to preserve the long-run selling-price structure.

2. Assuming that $350,000 of the fixed costs could have been avoided by not making the parts and that the other fixed costs would have been continued, the alternatives can be summarized as follows:

	MAKE	BUY
Purchase cost		$1,350,000
Variable costs	$1,000,000	
Avoidable fixed costs	350,000	
Total relevant costs	$1,350,000	$1,350,000

If the facilities used for parts became idle, the Block Company would be indifferent as to whether to make or buy. Operating income would be unaffected.

3.

Sales would increase by 20,000 units, @ $110		$2,200,000
Variable costs exclusive of parts would increase by 20,000 units, @ $70	$1,400,000	
Plus: Sales commission, 10% of $2,200,000	220,000	1,620,000
Contribution margin on 20,000 units		$ 580,000
Parts: 120,000 rather than 100,000 would be needed		
Buy 120,000 @ $13.50	$1,620,000	
Make 100,000 @ $10 (only the variable costs are relevant)	1,000,000	
Excess cost of outside purchase		620,000
Fixed costs, unchanged		—
Disadvantage of making deluxe units		$ (40,000)

Operating income would decline to $260,000 ($300,000 − $40,000, the disadvantage of selling the deluxe units). The deluxe units bring in a contribution margin of $580,000, but the additional costs of buying rather than making parts is $620,000, leading to a net disadvantage of $40,000.

HIGHLIGHTS TO REMEMBER

The following are among the more important generalizations regarding various decisions:

1. Make-or-buy decisions are, fundamentally, examples of obtaining the most profitable utilization of given facilities.
2. Sometimes the notion of an opportunity cost is helpful in cost analysis. An opportunity cost is the maximum sacrifice in rejecting an alternative; it is the maximum earning that might have been obtained if the productive good, service, or capacity had been applied

to some alternative use. The opportunity-cost approach does not affect the important final differences between the courses of action, but the format of the analysis differs.

3. Joint product costs are irrelevant in decisions about whether to sell at split-off or process further.

4. Differential costs are the differences in the total costs under each alternative.

5. The book value of old equipment is always irrelevant in replacement decisions. This cost is often called a *sunk cost.* Disposal value, however, is generally relevant.

6. Generally, use total costs, rather than unit costs, in cost analysis.

7. Managers are often motivated to reject desirable economic decisions because of a conflict between the measures used in the decision model and the performance evaluation model.

ACCOUNTING VOCABULARY

Book Value *p. 131*   Byproducts *130*   Differential Cost *128*   Historical Cost *131* Incremental Cost *129*   Joint Costs *126*   Joint Products *126*   Joint Product Costs *126*   Opportunity Cost *124*   Outlay Cost *124*   Split-off Point *126*   Sunk Cost *132*

FUNDAMENTAL ASSIGNMENT MATERIAL

5–1. **REPLACING OLD EQUIPMENT.** (Alternates are **5–30** and **5–31.**) Consider these data regarding a hospital's photocopying requirements:

	OLD EQUIPMENT	PROPOSED REPLACEMENT EQUIPMENT
Useful life, in years	5	2
Current age, in years	3	0
Useful life remaining, in years	2	2
Original cost	$25,000	$9,000
Accumulated depreciation	15,000	0
Book value	10,000	Not acquired yet
Disposal value (in cash) now	2,000	Not acquired yet
Disposal value in 2 years	0	0
Annual cash operating costs for power, maintenance, toner, and supplies	12,500	7,500

The hospital administrator is trying to decide whether to replace the old equipment. Because of rapid changes in technology, she expects the replacement equipment to have only a two-year useful life.

Required:

1. Tabulate a cost comparison that includes both relevant and irrelevant items for the next two years together. *Hint*: See Exhibit 5–3, page 133.

2. Tabulate a cost comparison of all relevant items for the next two years together. Which tabulation is clearer, this one or the one in Requirement 1? *Hint*: See Exhibit 5–4, page 133.

3. Prepare a simple "shortcut" or direct analysis to support your choice of alternatives.

5–2. DECISION AND PERFORMANCE MODELS. (Alternate is 5–32.) Refer to the preceding problem.

1. Suppose that the "decision model" favored by top management consisted of a comparison of a two-year accumulation of cash under each alternative. As the manager of office operations, which alternative would you choose? Why?

2. Suppose that the "performance evaluation model" emphasized the minimization of overall costs of photocopying operations for the first year. Which alternative would you choose?

ADDITIONAL ASSIGNMENT MATERIAL

5–3. "Choices are often mislabeled as *make or buy*." Do you agree? Explain.

5–4. "Joint products and byproducts are essentially the same types of products." Do you agree? Explain.

5–5. "Evaluating performance, decision by decision, is costly. Aggregate measures, like the income statement, are frequently used." How might the wide use of income statements affect managers' decisions about buying equipment?

5–6. "Past costs are indeed relevant in most instances because they provide the point of departure for the entire decision process." Do you agree? Why?

5–7. Which of the following items are relevant to replacement decisions? Explain.
(1) Book value of old equipment.
(2) Disposal value of old equipment.
(3) Cost of new equipment.

5–8. "No technique applicable to the problem of joint product costing should be used for management decisions regarding whether a product should be sold at the split-off point or processed further." Do you agree? Explain.

5–9. "Incremental cost is the addition to costs from the manufacture of one unit." Do you agree? Explain.

5–10. "I had a chance to rent my summer home for two weeks for $800. But I chose to have it idle. I didn't want strangers living in my summer house." What term in this chapter describes the $800? Why?

5–11. There are two major reasons why unit costs should be analyzed with care in decision making. What are they?

5–12. "Accountants do not ordinarily record opportunity costs in the formal accounting records." Why?

5–13. Distinguish between an opportunity cost and an outlay cost.

5–14. Distinguish between an incremental cost and a differential cost.

5–15. RELEVANT INVESTMENT. Mike Lacey had obtained a new truck with a list price, including options, of $14,000. The dealer had given him a "generous trade-in allowance" of $4,000 on his old truck that had a wholesale price of $3,000. Sales tax was $780.

The annual cash operating costs of the old truck were $3,000. The new truck was expected to reduce these costs by one-third.

Required: | Compute the original investment in the new truck. Explain your reasoning.

5–16. WEAK DIVISION. (S. Goodman.) The Goodman Company paid $5 million in cash four years ago to acquire a company manufacturing magnetic tape drives. This company has been operated as a division of Goodman and has lost $500,000 each year since its acquisition.

The minimum desired return for this division is that, when a new product is fully developed, it should return a net profit of $500,000 per year for the foreseeable future.

Recently the IBM Corporation offered to purchase the division from Goodman for $3 million. The president of Goodman commented, "I've got an investment of $7 million to recoup ($5 million plus losses of $500,000 for each of four years). I have finally got this situation turned around, so I oppose selling the division now."

Prepare a response to the president's remarks. Indicate how to make this decision. Be as specific as possible.

5–17. OPPORTUNITY COSTS. Sheila Epstein is a certified public accountant employed by a large accounting firm at $70,000 per year. She is considering whether to become a sole practitioner, which would probably generate annually $400,000 in operating revenues and $300,000 in operating expenses.

Required:

1. Present two tabulations of the income effects of these alternatives. The second tabulation should include the opportunity cost of Epstein's compensation as an employee.
2. Suppose Epstein prefers less risk and chooses to stay as an employee. Show a tabulation of the income effects of rejecting the opportunity of independent practice.

5–18. HOSPITAL OPPORTUNITY COST. A hospital administrator is considering how to use some space vacated by the children's clinic. She has narrowed her choices as follows:

a. Use the space to expand laboratory testing. Expected future annual revenue would be $200,000; future costs, $160,000.
b. Use the space to expand the eye clinic. Expected future annual revenue would be $500,000; future costs, $490,000.
c. The gift shop is rented by an independent retailer who wants to expand into the vacated space. The retailer has offered a $9,000 yearly rental for the space. All operating expenses will be borne by the retailer.

The administrator's planning horizon is unsettled. However, she has decided that the yearly data given will suffice for guiding her decision.

Required:

Tabulate the total relevant data regarding the decision alternatives. Omit the concept of opportunity cost in one tabulation, but use the concept in a second tabulation. As the administrator, which tabulation would you prefer to get if you could receive only one?

5–19. OPPORTUNITY COST. Francine Abrams, M.D., is a psychiatrist who is in heavy demand. Even though she has raised her fees considerably during the past five years, Dr. Abrams still cannot accommodate all the patients who wish to see her.

Abrams has conducted 6 hours of appointments a day, 6 days a week, for 48 weeks a year. Her fee averages $130 per hour.

Her variable costs are negligible and may be ignored for decision purposes. Ignore income taxes.

Required:

1. Abrams is weary of working a 6-day week. She is considering taking every other Saturday off. What would be her annual income (a) if she worked every Saturday and (b) if she worked every other Saturday?
2. What would be her opportunity cost for the year of not working every other Saturday?
3. Assume that Dr. Abrams has definitely decided to take every other Saturday off. She loves to repair her sports car by doing the work herself. If she works on her car during half a Saturday when she otherwise would not see patients, what is her opportunity cost?

5–20. HOTEL ROOMS AND OPPORTUNITY COSTS. The Sheraton Corporation operates many hotels throughout the world. One of its Dallas hotels is facing difficult times because of the opening of several new competing hotels.

To accommodate its flight personnel, American Airlines has offered Sheraton a contract for the coming year that provides a rate of $50 per night per room for a minimum of 50 rooms for 365 nights. This contract would assure Sheraton of selling 50 rooms of space nightly, even if some of the rooms are vacant on some nights.

The Sheraton manager has mixed feelings about the contract. On several peak nights during the year, the hotel could sell the same space for $95 per room.

Required:
1. Suppose that the contract is signed. What is the opportunity cost of the 50 rooms on October 20, the night of a big convention of retailers when every midtown hotel room is occupied? What is the opportunity cost on December 28, when only 10 of these rooms would be expected to be rented at an average rate of $75?
2. If the year-round rate per room averaged $90, what percentage of occupancy of the 50 rooms in question would have to be rented to make Sheraton indifferent about accepting the offer?

5–21. **EXTENSION OF PRECEDING PROBLEM.** (A. Wheelock.) Assume the same facts as in the preceding problem. However, also assume that the variable costs per room per day are $10.

Required:
1. Suppose that the best estimate is a 54% general occupancy rate at an average $90 room rate for the next year. Should Sheraton accept the contract?
2. What percentage of occupancy of the 50 rooms in question would have to make Sheraton indifferent about accepting the offer?

5–22. **HOTEL PRICING AND DISCOUNTS.** (A. Wheelock.) A growing corporation in a large city has offered a 200-room Holiday Inn a one-year contract to rent 40 rooms at reduced rates of $45 per room instead of the regular rate of $80 per room. The corporation will sign the contract for 365-day occupancy because its visiting manufacturing and marketing personnel are virtually certain to use all the space each night.

Each room occupied has a variable cost of $5 per night (for cleaning, laundry, lost linens, and extra electricity).

The hotel manager expects an 85% occupancy rate for the year, so she is reluctant to sign the contract.

Required:
1. Compute the total contribution margin for the year with and without the contract.
2. Compute the lowest room rate that the hotel should accept on the contract so that the total contribution margin would be the same with or without the contract.

5–23. **SPECIAL AIR FARES.** The manager of operations of United Airlines is trying to decide whether to adopt a new discount fare. Focus on one 134-seat 727-200 airplane now operating at a 55.2% load factor. That is, on the average the airplane has .552 × 134 = 74 passengers. The regular fares produce an average revenue of 12¢ per passenger-mile.

Suppose that an average 40% fare discount (which is subject to restrictions regarding time of departure and length of stay) will produce three new additional passengers. Also suppose that three of the previously committed passengers accept the restrictions and switch to the discount fare from the regular fare.

Required:
1. Compute the total revenue per airplane mile with and without the discount fares.
2. Suppose the maximum allowed allocation to new discount fares is 50 seats. These will be filled. As before, some previously committed passengers will accept the restrictions and switch to the discount fare from the regular fare. How many will have to switch so that the total revenue per mile will be the same either with or without the discount plan?

5–24. MEANING OF ALLOCATION OF JOINT COSTS.

1. Examine the illustration on joint costs that appears on pages 127–130. Suppose that the joint costs were allocated on the basis of liters. Prepare an income statement by product line on the assumption that product Y was (a) sold at split-off or (b) processed further.
2. Repeat Requirement 1, assuming that the joint costs were allocated on the basis of net realizable values (relative sales values) at split-off.
3. Which set of income statements is more meaningful, those in Requirement 1 or in 2? Why?

5–25. JOINT COSTS.
Two products, A and B, had been allocated $30,000 of joint costs each, using the net-realizable-value method. Net realizable value is the ultimate selling price less separable costs of completion and marketing. The products' ultimate sales values were $70,000 and $90,000, respectively. The separable costs for A were $20,000. What were the separable costs for B?

5–26. SELL OR PROCESS JOINT PRODUCTS.
The Raymond Company manufactured three joint products at a joint cost of $600,000. These products were processed further and sold as follows:

PRODUCT	SALES	ADDITIONAL PROCESSING COSTS
X	$ 400,000	$100,000
Y	700,000	320,000
Z	300,000	130,000
	$1,400,000	$550,000

If the company had pursued its opportunities to sell at split-off directly to other processors, sales would have been X, $250,000; Y, $400,000; and Z, $100,000.

The company expects to operate at the same level of production and sales in the forthcoming year.

Required:

Consider all the available information, and assume that all costs incurred after split-off are variable.

1. Could the company increase operating income by altering its processing decisions? If so, what would be the expected overall operating income?
2. Which products would be processed further and which should be sold at split-off?

5–27. JOINT COSTS AND DECISIONS.
The Coast Chemical Company has a batch process whereby 1,400 gallons of raw material are transformed into 200 pounds of X-1 and 600 pounds of X-2. Although the joint costs of their production are $1,200, both products are worthless at their split-off point. Additional separable costs of $350 are necessary to give X-1 a sales value of $1,000 as product A. Similarly, additional separable costs of $150 are necessary to give X-2 a sales value of $1,000 as product B.

Required:

You are in charge of the batch process and the marketing of both products. (Show your computations for each answer.)

1. a. Assuming that you believe in assigning joint costs on a physical basis, allocate the operating profit of $300 per batch to products A and B.
   b. Would you stop processing one of the products? Why?

2. a. Assuming that you believe in assigning joint costs on a net-realizable-value (relative-sales-value) basis, allocate the operating profit of $300 per batch to products A and B. If there is no market for X-1 and X-2 at their split-off point, a net realizable value is usually imputed by taking the ultimate sales values at the point of sale and working backward to obtain approximated "synthetic" relative sales values at the split-off point. These synthetic values are then used as weights for allocating the joint costs to the products.

b. You have internal product-profitability reports in which joint costs are assigned on a net-realizable-value basis. Your chief engineer says that, after seeing these reports, he has developed a method of obtaining more of product B and correspondingly less of product A from each batch, without changing the per-pound cost factors. Would you approve of this new method? Why? What would the overall operating profit be if 100 more pounds of B were produced and 100 less pounds of A?

5–28. **NEW MACHINE.** A new $360,000 machine is expected to have a four-year life and a terminal value of zero. It can produce 90,000 units a year at a variable cost of $2 per unit. The variable cost is $3 per unit with an old machine, which has a book value of $180,000. It is being depreciated on a straight-line basis at $45,000 per year. It too is expected to have a terminal value of zero. Its current disposal value is also zero because it is highly specialized equipment.

The salesman of the new machine prepared the following comparison:

	NEW MACHINE	OLD MACHINE
Units	90,000	90,000
Variable costs	$180,000	$270,000
Straight-line depreciation	90,000	45,000
Total cost	$270,000	$315,000
Unit cost	$ 3.00	$ 3.50

He said, "The new machine is obviously a worthwhile acquisition. You will save 50¢ for every unit you produce."

Required:

Do you agree with the salesman's analysis? If not, how would you change it? Be specific.

Prepare an analysis of total and unit costs if the annual volume is 60,000 units. At what annual volume would both the old and new machines have the same total relevant costs?

5–29. **CONCEPTUAL APPROACH.** A large automobile-parts plant was constructed four years ago in an Ohio city served by two railroads. The PC Railroad purchased 40 specialized 60-foot freight cars as a direct result of the additional traffic generated by the new plant. The investment was based on an estimated useful life of 20 years.

Now the competing railroad has offered to service the plant with new 86-foot freight cars, which would enable more efficient shipping operations at the plant. The automobile company has threatened to switch carriers unless PC Railroad buys 10 new 86-foot freight cars.

The PC marketing management wants to buy the new cars, but PC operating management says, "The new investment is undesirable. It really consists of the new outlay plus the loss on the old freight cars. The old cars must be written down to a low salvage value if they cannot be used as originally intended."

Evaluate the comments. What is the correct conceptual approach to the quantitative analysis in this decision?

5–30. BOOK VALUE OF OLD EQUIPMENT. (Alternates are 5–1 and 5–31.) Consider the following data:

	OLD EQUIPMENT	PROPOSED NEW EQUIPMENT
Original cost	$32,000	$27,000
Useful life in years	8	3
Current age in years	5	0
Useful life remaining in years	3	3
Accumulated depreciation	$20,000	0
Book value	12,000	*
Disposal value (in cash) now	3,000	*
Disposal value in 3 years	0	0
Annual cash operating costs (maintenance, power, repairs, lubricants, etc.)	$30,000	$20,000

* Not acquired yet.

Required:

1. Prepare a cost comparison of all relevant items for the next three years together.
2. Prepare a cost comparison that includes both relevant and irrelevant items.
3. Prepare a comparative statement of the total charges against revenue for the first year. Would the manager be inclined to buy the new equipment? Explain.

5–31. ROLE OF OLD EQUIPMENT IN REPLACEMENT. (Alternates are 5–1 and 5–30.) On January 2, 19X1, the Buxton Company installed a brand-new $81,000 special molding machine for producing a new product. The product and the machine have an expected life of three years. The machine's expected disposal value at the end of three years is zero.

On January 3, 19X1, Jim Swain, a star salesman for a machine tool manufacturer, tells Mr. Buxton: "I wish I had known earlier of your purchase plans. I can supply you with a technically superior machine for $100,000. The old machine can be sold for $16,000. I guarantee that our machine will save $35,000 per year in cash operating costs, although it too will have no disposal value at the end of three years."

Mr. Buxton examines some technical data. Although he had confidence in Swain's claims, Buxton contends: "I'm locked in now. My alternatives are clear: (a) disposal will result in a loss, (b) keeping and using the 'old' equipment avoids such a loss. I have brains enough to avoid a loss when my other alternative is recognizing a loss. We've got to use that equipment till we get our money out of it."

The annual operating costs of the old machine are expected to be $60,000, exclusive of depreciation. Sales, all in cash, will be $900,000 per year. Other annual cash expenses will be $800,000 regardless of this decision. Assume that the equipment in question is the company's only fixed asset. Note that the facts in this problem are probed more deeply in Problems 11–34 and 12–35.

Required:

Ignore income taxes and the time value of money.

1. Prepare statements of cash receipts and disbursements as they would appear in each of the next three years under both alternatives. What is the total cumulative increase or decrease in cash for the three years?

2. Prepare income statements as they would appear in each of the next three years under both alternatives. Assume straight-line depreciation. What is the cumulative increase or decrease in net income for the three years?

3. Assume that the cost of the "old" equipment was $1 million rather than $81,000. Would the net difference computed in Requirements 1 and 2 change? Explain.

4. As Jim Swain, reply to Buxton's contentions.

5. What are the irrelevant items in each of your presentations for Requirements 1 and 2? Why are they irrelevant?

5–32. **DECISION AND PERFORMANCE MODELS.** (Alternate is 5–2.) Refer to the preceding problem.

1. Suppose the "decision model" favored by top management consisted of a comparison of a three-year accumulation of wealth under each alternative. Which alternative would you choose? Why? (Accumulation of wealth means cumulative increase in cash.)

2. Suppose the "performance evaluation model" emphasized the net income of a subunit (such as a division) each year rather than considering each project, one by one. Which alternative would you choose? Why?

3. Suppose the same quantitative data existed, but the "enterprise" was a city-owned waste disposal area open to the public for an entrance fee per visit. Would your answers to the first two parts change? Why?

5–33. **MAKE OR BUY.** A Ford Motor Company executive in Germany is trying to decide whether Ford should continue to manufacture an engine component or purchase it from Dresden Corporation for 20 Deutschemarks (DM) each. Demand for the coming year is expected to be the same as for the current year, 200,000 units. Data for the current year follow:

Direct material	DM2,000,000
Direct labor	800,000
Factory overhead, variable	400,000
Factory overhead, fixed	1,000,000
Total costs	DM4,200,000

If Ford makes the components, the unit costs of direct material will increase 10%.

If Ford buys the components, 40% of the fixed costs will be avoided. The other 60% will continue regardless of whether the components are manufactured or purchased.

Required:

1. Tabulate a comparison of the make-and-buy alternatives. Show totals and amounts per unit. Compute the numerical difference between making and buying. Assume that the capacity now used to make the components will become idle if the components are purchased.

2. Assume also that the Ford capacity in question can be rented to a local electronics firm for DM500,000 for the coming year. Tabulate a comparison of the net relevant costs of the three alternatives: make, buy and leave capacity idle, buy and rent. Which is the most favorable alternative? By how much in total?

5–34 **MAKE OR BUY.** Dana Corporation manufactures automobile parts. It frequently subcontracts work to other manufacturers, depending on whether Dana's facilities are fully occupied. Dana is about to make some final decisions regarding the use of its manufacturing facilities for the coming year.

The following are the costs of making part M431, a key component of an emission control system:

	TOTAL COST FOR 60,000 UNITS	COST PER UNIT
Direct material	$ 300,000	$ 5
Direct labor	480,000	8
Variable factory overhead	180,000	3
Fixed factory overhead	300,000	5
Total manufacturing costs	$1,260,000	$21

Another manufacturer has offered to sell the same part to Dana for $21 each. The fixed overhead consists of depreciation, property taxes, insurance, and supervisory salaries. All the fixed overhead would continue if Dana bought the component except that the costs of $120,000 pertaining to some supervisory and custodial personnel could be avoided.

Required:
1. Assume that the capacity now used to make parts will become idle if the parts are purchased. Should the parts be made or bought? Show computations.
2. Assume that the capacity now used to make parts will either (a) be rented to a nearby manufacturer for $60,000 for the year or (b) be used to make oil filters that will yield a profit contribution of $250,000. Should part M431 be made or bought? Show computations.

5–35. **MAKE OR BUY.** The Rohr Company's old equipment for making subassemblies is worn out. The company is considering two courses of action: (a) completely replacing the old equipment with new equipment or (b) buying subassemblies from a reliable outside supplier, who has quoted a unit price of $1 on a seven-year contract for a minimum of 50,000 units per year.

Production was 60,000 units in each of the past two years. Future needs for the next seven years are not expected to fluctuate beyond 50,000 to 70,000 units per year. Cost records for the past two years reveal the following unit costs of manufacturing the subassembly:

Direct material	$ .25
Direct labor	.40
Variable overhead	.10
Fixed overhead (including $.10 depreciation and $.10 for direct departmental fixed overhead)	.25
	$1.00

The new equipment will cost $188,000 cash, will last seven years, and will have a disposal value of $20,000. The current disposal value of the old equipment is $10,000.

The salesman for the new equipment has summarized his position as follows: The increase in machine speeds will reduce direct labor and variable overhead by 35¢ per unit. Consider last year's experience of one of your major competitors with identical equipment. They produced 100,000 units under operating conditions very comparable to yours and showed the following unit costs:

Direct material	$.25
Direct labor	.10
Variable overhead	.05
Fixed overhead, including depreciation of $.24	.40
	$.80

For purposes of this case, assume that any idle facilities cannot be put to alternative use. Also assume that 5¢ of the old Rohr unit cost is allocated fixed overhead that will be unaffected by the decision.

1. The president asks you to compare the alternatives on a total-annual-cost basis and on a per-unit basis for annual needs of 60,000 units. Which alternative seems more attractive?
2. Would your answer to Requirement 1 change if the needs were 50,000 units? 70,000 units? At what volume level would Rohr be indifferent between make and buy? Show your computations.
3. What factors, other than the above, should the accountant bring to the attention of management to assist them in making their decision? Include the considerations that might be applied to the outside supplier.
For additional analysis, see Problem 11–47.

5–36. **RELEVANT-COST ANALYSIS.** Following are the unit costs of making and selling a single product at a normal level of 5,000 units per month and a current unit selling price of $75:

Manufacturing costs:	
Direct material	$20
Direct labor	12
Variable overhead	8
Fixed overhead	
(total for the year, $300,000)	5
Selling and administrative expenses:	
Variable	15
Fixed (total for the year, $540,000)	9

Consider each requirement separately. Label all computations, and present your solutions in a form that will be comprehensible to the company president.

1. This product is usually sold at a rate of 60,000 units per year. It is predicted that a rise in price to $85 will decrease volume by 10%. How much may advertising be increased under this plan without having annual operating income fall below the current level?
2. The company has received a proposal from an outside supplier to make and ship this item directly to the company's customers as sales orders are forwarded. Variable selling and administrative costs would fall 40%. If the supplier's proposal is accepted, the company will use its own plant to produce a new product. The new product would be sold through manufacturer's agents at a 10% commission based on a selling price of $20 each. The cost characteristics of this product, based on predicted yearly normal volume, are as follows:

	PER UNIT
Direct material	$ 3
Direct labor	6
Variable overhead	4
Fixed overhead	3
Manufacturing costs	$16
Selling and administrative expenses:	
Variable	10% of selling price
Fixed	$ 1

What is the maximum price per unit that the company can afford to pay to the supplier for subcontracting the entire old product? This is not easy. Assume the following:

(1) Total fixed factory overhead and total fixed selling expenses will not change if the new product line is added.

(2) The supplier's proposal will not be considered unless the present annual net income can be maintained.

(3) Selling price of the old product will remain unchanged.

5–37. **RELEVANT COSTS OF AUTO OWNERSHIP.** Joan Krantz, a dairy inspector for the state of Wisconsin, used her private automobile for work purposes and was reimbursed by the state at a rate of 22¢ per mile. Krantz was unhappy about the rate, so she was particularly interested in a publication of the Federal Highway Administration, "The Cost of Owning and Operating an Automobile."

The publication contained a "worksheet for first-year auto costs":

1. Amount paid for your car	$ . . . . . .
2. First-year mileage	. . . . . .
3. First-year depreciation	$ . . . . . .
4. Insurance	$ . . . . . .
5. License, other fees or taxes	$ . . . . . .
6. Interest on auto loan	$ . . . . . .
7. Maintenance, repairs, tires	$ . . . . . .
8. Fuel and oil	$ . . . . . .
9. Parking, garaging, tolls	$ . . . . . .
10. Total of Lines 3 through 9	$ . . . . . .
11. Line 10 divided by Line 2	$ . . . . . .
Line 11 is your first-year per-mile cost.	

Krantz paid $9,000 for her new small car. She expected to drive it 20,000 miles per year. The highway administration worksheet calls for depreciation at 33% of original cost for the first year, 25% the second year, and 20% the third year.

Insurance is $400. License and other fees amount to $200. Interest on her $6,000 auto loan is $720 for the first year, $480 for the second year, and $240 for the third year. The highway booklet said that the following charges might be expected for maintenance for every 10,000 miles: $120 for the first year, $240 for the second year, and $480 for the third year. Parking and tolls would cost an average of 1¢ per mile and fuel and oil 6¢ per mile.

1. Compute the total first-year cost of automobile ownership. Compute the cost per mile if the following miles were driven: 10,000, 20,000, and 30,000.
2. Is the reimbursement rate of 22¢ a "fair" rate?
3. Krantz and a friend use her car for a 400-mile journey. They agree in advance "to split the costs of using the car, fifty-fifty." How much should Joan's friend pay?
4. What if Krantz had paid cash for her car rather than borrowed $6,000? Would the costs change? By how much? Explain.
5. Suppose Krantz was thinking of buying a second car exactly like the first and on the same financial terms, but she would confine the second car to personal use of 5,000 miles per year. The total mileage of the two cars taken together would still be 20,000 miles. What would be the first-year cost of operating a second car? The average unit cost? What costs are relevant? Why?
6. Krantz has owned the car one year. She has switched to a local job that does not require a car. What costs are relevant to the question of selling the car and using other means of transportation?

Chapter 6

THE MASTER BUDGET:
THE OVERALL PLAN

LEARNING OBJECTIVES

When you have finished studying this chapter, you should be able to:

1. Define budget and identify its major advantages to an organization.
2. Distinguish between master budgets and long-range plans.
3. Distinguish between operating budgets and financial budgets.
4. List the principal steps in preparing a master budget.
5. Construct the supporting schedules and main statements for a master budget.
6. Identify the uses of a financial-planning model.

Managers—and many investors and bank loan officers—have become increasingly aware of the merits of formal business plans. This chapter provides a condensed view of the overall business plan for the forthcoming year (or less)—the master budget. The major technical work of the budgetary accountant involves expected future data rather than historical data. There is also a major philosophical difference: the advocates of budgeting maintain that the process of preparing the budget forces executives to become better administrators. Budgeting puts planning where it belongs—in the forefront of the manager's mind.

In some organizations, especially governmental agencies, a budget primarily sets limits on various expenditures. But the budget in an effectively managed entity must be much more than a spending authorization. We will see that a budget helps managers to make better planning and control decisions. Budgeting is primarily attention directing because it helps managers to focus on operating or financial problems early enough for effective planning or action.

This book stresses how accounting helps the *operating* performance of management (how effectively assets are acquired and used). But the *financing* function (how funds for investment in assets are obtained) is also important. That is why this chapter examines cash budgets as well as operating budgets. Business failures are frequently traceable to management's shirking of the financial aspects of its responsibilities.

CHARACTERISTICS OF BUDGETS

☐ Definition of Budget

A **budget** is a formal quantitative expression of management plans. The **master budget** summarizes the goals of all subunits of an organization—sales, production, distribution, and finance. It quantifies targets for sales, production, net income, and cash position, and for any other objective that management specifies. The master budget is a coordinated set of detailed financial schedules and statements. It includes forecasts of sales and expenses, cash receipts and disbursements, balance sheets, and a statement of changes in financial position.

Of course, individuals also use budgets. For instance, a student may budget food expenses for the coming week or month, hours of study before examinations, and so forth.

☐ Advantages of Budgets

All managers do some kind of planning. Often the plans are vague and are never written down. This might work in a small organization. But as an organization grows, informal seat-of-the-pants planning is not enough. A more formal budgetary system becomes an attractive alternative.

Skeptical managers have claimed, "I face too many uncertainties and complications to make budgeting worthwhile for me." Be wary of such claims. Planning and budgeting are especially important in uncertain environments. A budget allows systematic rather than chaotic reaction to change. For example, the Natural Resources Group of W. R. Grace & Co. greatly reduced capital expenditures in reaction to an oversupply of oil and gas in 1983. A top executive, quoted in the company's annual report, stated that "management used the business planning process to adjust to changes in operating conditions."

Three major benefits of budget programs are:

1. Budgeting, by formalizing the managers' responsibilities for planning, compels them to think ahead.
2. Budgeting provides definite expectations that are the best framework for judging subsequent performance.
3. Budgeting aids managers in coordinating their efforts, so that the objectives of the organization as a whole harmonize with the objectives of its parts.

☐ Formalization of Planning

Budgeting forces managers to think ahead—to anticipate and prepare for changing conditions. The budgeting process makes planning an explicit management responsibility. Too often, managers operate from day to day, extinguishing one business brush fire after another. They simply have no time for any tough-minded thinking beyond the next day's problems. Planning takes a back seat or is actually obliterated by workaday pressures.

The trouble with the day-to-day approach to managing an organization is that objectives are never crystallized. Without goals, company operations lack direction, problems are not foreseen, and results are hard to interpret.

In a recent interview, Carl E. Reichardt, chief executive officer of Wells Fargo, commented:

☐ I say our budget is the most important thing we do. I like to have all the debates over with when it is adopted. I'm not too sympathetic about hearing a lot of excuses after the fact. If budget planning is done well, there is no room for infighting and personality conflicts.

☐ Expectations as a Framework for Judging Performance

As a basis for judging actual results, budgeted goals and performance are generally regarded as being more appropriate than past performance. The news that a company had sales of $10 million this year, as compared with

$8 million the previous year, may or may not indicate that the company has been effective and has achieved maximum success. Perhaps sales should have been $11 million this year. The major drawback of using historical data for judging performance is that inefficiencies may be concealed in the past performance. Moreover, the usefulness of comparisons with the past is also limited by intervening changes in economic conditions, technology, competitive maneuvers, personnel, and so forth.

Another benefit of budgeting is that key personnel are informed of what is expected of them. Nobody likes to drift along, not knowing what his or her boss expects or hopes to achieve.

☐ Coordination and Communication

Coordination is the meshing and balancing of an organization's resources so that its overall objectives are attained—so that the goals of the individual manager harmonize with goals of the organization as a whole. The budget is the means for communicating overall objectives and for blending the objectives of all departments.

Coordination requires, for example, that purchasing officers integrate their plans with production requirements, and that production officers use the sales budget to help them anticipate and plan for the employees and plant facilities they will require. The budgetary process obliges executives to visualize the relationship of their department to other departments, and to the company as a whole.

A good budget process communicates both from the top down and from the bottom up. Top management makes clear the goals and objectives of the organization in its budgetary directives to middle- and lower-level managers. Conversely, managers inform top executives how they plan to achieve the objectives.

HUMAN RELATIONS

Middle management's attitude toward budgets will be heavily influenced by the attitude of top management. Top-level executives must offer whole-hearted support if a budgetary program is to achieve maximum benefits.

Managers often compare actual results to the budget in evaluating subordinates. Few individuals are immediately ecstatic about techniques used by the boss to check their performance. Middle managers sometimes regard budgets as embodiments of nickle-nursing, restrictive, negative top management attitudes. Accountants reinforce this view if they use a budget only to point out managers' failings.

To avoid negative attitudes toward budgets, accountants and top management must stress that budgets can *help each manager* achieve better results. Only then will the budget become a positive aid in setting standards of performance, in motivating toward goals, in metering results, and in directing attention to the areas that need investigation.

The supreme importance of the human relations aspects of budgeting cannot be overemphasized. Too often, top management and its accountants are overly concerned with the mechanics of budgets, whereas the effectiveness of any budgeting system depends directly on whether the managers it affects understand it and accept it. Budgets formulated with the active participation of managers are more effective than budgets imposed on subordinates.

TYPES OF BUDGETS

☐ Time Span

The planning horizon for budgeting may vary from one day to many years, depending on the budget objectives and the uncertainties involved. The most forward-looking budget is the strategic plan. **Strategic planning** sets the goals and objectives of the organization. Some would not call a strategic plan a budget because it covers no specific time period and it does not produce forecasted financial statements.

Long-range planning produces forecasted financial statements for five- or ten-year periods. Long-range plans are coordinated with *capital budgets* to assure that the facilities needed are acquired in time. Decisions made during long-range planning include addition of product lines, design and location of new plants, acquisitions of buildings and equipment, and other long-term commitments.

This chapter covers primarily *master budgets*, which consolidate an organization's overall plans for short periods of time, usually one year. The master budget is essentially a more extensive analysis of the first year of the long-range plan. Management might prepare monthly budgets for the year or perhaps monthly budgets for only the first quarter and quarterly budgets for the three remaining quarters. The master budget is the most detailed budget that is coordinated across the whole organization, but individual managers also prepare daily or weekly *task-oriented budgets* to help them carry out their particular functions.

Continuous budgets are increasingly being used. These are master budgets that add a month in the future as the month just ended is dropped. Continuous budgets compel managers to think specifically about the forthcoming 12 months and thus maintain a stable planning horizon. As you add a new twelfth month to a continuous budget, you might update the other 11 months as well. In such cases actual monthly results can be compared to *both* the original plan and the most recently revised plan.

☐ Components of the Master Budget

The terms used to describe assorted budget schedules vary from company to company. Sometimes budgets are called **pro forma statements.** They are *forecasted* financial statements, in contrast to statements of actual results.

The master budget, accompanied by subsidiary schedules, can be classified as follows:

A. Operating budget
   1. Sales budget
   2. Production budget (for manufacturing companies)
      a. Materials used and material purchases
      b. Direct labor
      c. Indirect manufacturing costs (factory overhead)
      d. Changes in inventory levels
   3. Cost of goods sold budget (for merchandising and manufacturing companies)
   4. Selling expense budget
   5. Administrative expense budget
   6. Budgeted income statement
B. Financial budget
   1. Capital budgets (long-range expectations for specific projects)
   2. Cash budget (cash receipts and disbursements)
   3. Budgeted balance sheet
   4. Budgeted statement of changes in financial position.

EXHIBIT 6–1

Master Budget for Nonmanufacturing Company

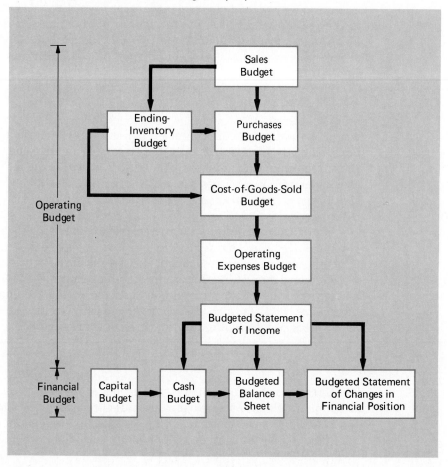

Exhibit 6–1 presents a condensed diagram of the various parts of the master budget for a nonmanufacturing company. The two major parts of the master budget are the operating budget and the financial budget. The **operating budget** focuses on the income statement and its supporting schedules. Some call the operating budget the **profit plan.** Despite the name, the plan might show a budgeted *loss*, or even be used to budget expenses in an organization or agency with no revenues.

The **financial budget** focuses on the effect that the operating budget and other plans (such as capital expenditures and repayments of debt) will have on cash.

In addition to the master budget there are countless forms of special budgets and related reports. For example, a report might be prepared containing various cost-volume-profit forecasts that might be encountered under different management decisions and economic conditions.

ILLUSTRATION OF PREPARATION OF A MASTER BUDGET

☐ Description of Problem

Try to prepare the master budget schedules required for the solution of this illustrative problem. Use the basic steps described after the problem. Do not rush. This comprehensive illustration will require some step-by-step thinking and some reflection before a full understanding can be achieved. Although the illustration may seem largely mechanical, remember that the master-budgeting process generates key decisions regarding pricing, product lines, capital expenditures, research and development, personnel assignments, and so forth. Therefore, the first draft of a budget leads to decisions that prompt subsequent drafts before a final budget is chosen. Suppose that R Company is a retailer of a wide variety of household items. The company rents a number of retail stores and also has a local door-to-door sales force.

The R Company's newly hired accountant has persuaded management to prepare a budget to aid financial and operating decisions. Because this is the company's first attempt at formal budgeting, the planning horizon is only four months, April through July. In the past, sales have increased during the spring season. Collections lag behind and cash is needed for purchases, wages, and other operating outlays. In the past, the company has met this cash squeeze with the help of short-term loans from banks.

Exhibit 6–2 is the closing balance sheet for the fiscal year just ended. Sales in March were $40,000. Monthly sales are forecasted as follows:

April	$50,000	July	$50,000
May	$80,000	August	$40,000
June	$60,000		

Sales consist of 60% cash and 40% credit. All credit accounts are collected in the month following the sales. The $16,000 of accounts receivable on March 31 represents credit sales made in March (40% of $40,000). Uncollectible accounts are negligible and are to be ignored.

EXHIBIT 6–2

R COMPANY
Balance Sheet
March 31, 19X1

ASSETS

Current assets:		
Cash	$10,000	
Accounts receivable, net (.4 × March sales of $40,000)	16,000	
Merchandise inventory, $20,000 + .8 (.7 × April sales of $50,000)	48,000	
Unexpired insurance	1,800	$ 75,800
Plant assets:		
Equipment, fixtures, and other	$37,000	
Accumulated depreciation	12,800	24,200
Total assets		$100,000

LIABILITIES AND OWNERS' EQUITY

Current liabilities:		
Accounts payable (.5 × March purchases of $33,600)	$16,800	
Accrued wages and commissions payable ($1,250 + $3,000)	4,250	$ 21,050
Owners' equity		78,950
Total liabilities and owners' equity		$100,000

At the end of any month, the R Company wants a basic inventory of $20,000 plus 80% of the cost of goods to be sold in the following month. The cost of merchandise sold averages 70% of sales. Therefore the inventory on March 31 is $20,000 + .8 (.7 × April sales of $50,000) = $20,000 + $28,000 = $48,000. The purchase terms available to the R Company are net, 30 days. Each month's purchases are paid as follows: 50% during that month and 50% during the next month.

Wages and commissions are paid semimonthly, half a month after they are earned. They are divided into two portions: monthly fixed wages of $2,500 and commissions, equal to 15% of sales, which are uniform throughout each month. Therefore the March 31 balance of Accrued Wages and Commissions Payable consists of (.5 × $2,500) + .5 (.15 × $40,000) = $1,250 + $3,000 = $4,250. This $4,250 will be paid on April 15.

A used delivery truck will be purchased for $3,000 cash in April. Other monthly expenses are:

Miscellaneous expenses	5% of sales, paid as incurred
Rent	$2,000, paid as incurred
Insurance	$200 expiration per month
Depreciation, including truck	$500

The company wants a minimum cash balance of $10,000 at the end of each month. Money can be borrowed or repaid in multiples of $1,000. Management plans to borrow no more cash than necessary and to repay as promptly as possible. Assume that borrowing takes place at the beginning, and repayment at the end, of the months in question. Interest is paid when the related loan is repaid. The interest rate is 18% per annum.

[*Special note*: By now it may be obvious that a basic knowledge of financial accounting (see Chapter 17) is necessary to cope with this illustration problem.]

1. Using the data given, prepare the following detailed schedules:
   a. Sales budget
   b. Cash collections from customers
   c. Purchases budget
   d. Disbursements for purchases
   e. Operating expense budget
   f. Disbursements for operating expenses
2. Using the data given and the schedules you have compiled, prepare the following major statements:
   a. Budgeted income statement for the four months ending July 31, 19X1
   b. Budgeted statement of cash receipts and disbursements by months, including details of borrowings, repayments, and interest
   c. Budgeted balance sheet as of July 31, 19X1

For consistency with the numbering scheme used in this book, label your responses to Requirement 2 as Exhibits 6–3, 6–4, and 6–5, respectively. Note that Schedules *a*, *c*, and *e* will be needed to prepare Exhibit 6–3 and Schedules *b*, *d*, and *f* will be needed to prepare Exhibit 6–4.

□ Basic Steps in Preparing Operating Budget

Organizations with effective budget systems have a budget manual with specific guidelines for the steps and timing of budget preparation. Although the details differ, the manuals invariably include the following steps. Use the steps to prepare your own schedules. Then examine the schedules in the solution.

Step 1. The sales budget (Schedule *a* on the next page) is the starting point for budgeting, because inventory levels, purchases, and operating expenses are generally geared to the rate of sales activity. Trace the final column in Schedule *a* to Exhibit 6–3, page 164. In nonprofit organizations, forecasts of revenue or some level of services are also the focal point for budgeting. Examples are patient revenues expected by hospitals and donations to be received by churches. If no revenues are generated, as in the case of municipal fire protection, a desired level of service is predetermined.

	MARCH	APRIL	MAY	JUNE	JULY	APRIL–JULY TOTAL
Schedule a: Sales Budget						
Credit sales, 40%	$16,000	$20,000	$32,000	$24,000	$20,000	
Cash sales, 60%	24,000	30,000	48,000	36,000	30,000	
Total sales, 100%	$40,000	$50,000	$80,000	$60,000	$50,000	$240,000
Schedule b: Cash Collections						
Cash sales this month		$30,000	$48,000	$36,000	$30,000	
100% of last month's credit sales		16,000	20,000	32,000	24,000	
Total collections		$46,000	$68,000	$68,000	$54,000	

Step 2. After sales are budgeted, the purchases budget (Schedule *c*) can be prepared. The total merchandise needed will be the sum of the desired ending inventory plus the amount needed to fulfill budgeted sales demand. The total need will be partially met by the beginning inventory; the remainder must come from planned purchases. Therefore these purchases are computed as follows: Purchases = Desired ending inventory + Cost of goods sold − Beginning inventory. Trace the final column of Schedule *c* to Exhibit 6–3, page 164.

	MARCH	APRIL	MAY	JUNE	JULY	APRIL–JULY TOTAL
Schedule c: Purchases Budget						
Ending inventory	$48,000	$64,800	$ 53,600	$48,000	$42,400	
Cost of goods sold	28,000*	35,000	56,000	42,000	35,000	$168,000
Total needed	$76,000	$99,800	$109,600	$90,000	$77,400	
Beginning inventory	42,400†	48,000	64,800	53,600	48,000	
Purchases	$33,600	$51,800	$ 44,800	$36,400	$29,400	
Schedule d: Disbursements for Purchases						
50% of last month's purchases		$16,800	$ 25,900	$22,400	$18,200	
50% of this month's purchases		25,900	22,400	18,200	14,700	
Disbursements for merchandise		$42,700	$ 48,300	$40,600	$32,900	

* .7 × March sales of $40,000 = $28,000.

† $20,000 + .8(.7 × March sales of $40,000) = $20,000 + $22,400 = $42,400.

Step 3. The budgeting of operating expenses depends on various factors. Month-to-month fluctuations in sales volume directly influence many operating expenses. Examples are sales commissions and delivery expenses. Other expenses are not directly influenced (e.g., rent, insurance, depreciation, certain types of payroll). In this solution, Schedule *e* summarizes these expenses. Trace the final column of Schedule *e* to Exhibit 6–3, the budgeted income statement.

	MARCH	APRIL	MAY	JUNE	JULY	APRIL–JULY TOTAL
Schedule e: Operating Expense Budget						
Wages, all fixed*	$ 2,500	$ 2,500	$ 2,500	$ 2,500	$ 2,500	
Commission (15% of current month's sales)	6,000	7,500	12,000	9,000	7,500	
Total wages and commissions	$ 8,500	$10,000	$14,500	$11,500	$10,000	$46,000
Miscellaneous expenses (5% of current month's sales)		2,500	4,000	3,000	2,500	12,000
Rent*		2,000	2,000	2,000	2,000	8,000
Insurance*		200	200	200	200	800
Depreciation*		500	500	500	500	2,000
Subtotal		$ 5,200	$ 6,700	$ 5,700	$ 5,200	$22,800
Total operating expenses		$15,200	$21,200	$17,200	$15,200	$68,800

* Monthly amounts are given in the statement of the problem.

	APRIL	MAY	JUNE	JULY
Schedule f: Disbursements for Operating Expenses				
Wages and commissions:				
50% of last month's expenses	$ 4,250	$ 5,000	$ 7,250	$ 5,750
50% of this month's expenses	5,000	7,250	5,750	5,000
Total wages and commissions	$ 9,250	$12,250	$13,000	$10,750
Miscellaneous expenses	2,500	4,000	3,000	2,500
Rent	2,000	2,000	2,000	2,000
Total disbursements	$13,750	$18,250	$18,000	$15,250

Step 4. Steps 1 through 3 provide enough information for a budgeted statement of income from operations (Exhibit 6–3). The income statement is complete except for interest expense, which cannot be computed until the cash budget is prepared.

The Financial Budget

The second major part of the master budget is the financial budget, which consists of the capital budget, cash budget, ending balance sheet, and statement of changes in financial position. This chapter focuses on the cash budget and the ending balance sheet. Chapters 11 and 12 discuss the capital budget. In our illustration, the $3,000 purchase of the used truck would be included in the capital budget. The statement of changes in financial position (Chapter 18) is beyond the scope of this illustration.

Basic Steps in Preparing Cash Budget

The **cash budget** is a statement of planned cash receipts and disbursements. It is heavily affected by the level of operations summarized in the budgeted income statement.

EXHIBIT 6–3

R COMPANY
Budgeted Income Statement
For the Four Months Ended July 31, 19X1

	DATA		SOURCE OF DATA
Sales		$240,000	Schedule **a**
Cost of goods sold		168,000	Schedule **c**
Gross margin		$ 72,000	
Operating expenses:			
Wages and commissions	$46,000		Schedule **e**
Rent	8,000		Schedule **e**
Miscellaneous expenses	12,000		Schedule **e**
Insurance	800		Schedule **e**
Depreciation	2,000	68,800	Schedule **e**
Income from operations		$ 3,200	
Interest expense		675	Exhibit 6–4*
Net income		$ 2,525	

* For May, June, and July: $30 + $405 + $240 = $675.

The cash budget has the following major sections:

w. The beginning cash balance plus cash receipts yield the total cash available for needs, before financing. Cash receipts depend on collections from customers' accounts receivable and cash sales (Schedule b) and on other operating sources such as miscellaneous rental income. Trace Schedule b to Exhibit 6–4. Studies of the collectibility of accounts receivable are a prerequisite to accurate forecasting. Key factors include collection experience and average time lag between sales and collections.

x. Cash disbursements:
  (1) Purchases depend on the credit terms extended by suppliers and the bill-paying habits of the buyer (Schedule d, which should be traced to Exhibit 6–4).
  (2) Payroll depends on wage, salary, or commission terms and on payroll dates (Schedule f, which should be traced to Exhibit 6–4).
  (3) Other costs and expenses (Schedule f) depend on timing and credit terms. Note that depreciation and the expiration of insurance do not entail a cash outlay.
  (4) Other disbursements include outlays for fixed assets, long-term investments, installment payments on purchases, cash dividends, and the like. In this problem, the only "other disbursement" is $3,000 for the truck.

y. Financing requirements depend on how the total cash available w (in Exhibit 6–4) compares with the total cash needed. Needs include the disbursements x plus the desired ending cash balance z. If total cash available is less than the cash needed, borrowing is necessary; $14,000 is borrowed in April (see Exhibit 6–4). If there is an excess, loans may be repaid; $1,000, $9,000, and $4,000 are repaid in May, June, and July, respectively. The pertinent outlays for interest expenses are usually contained in this section of the cash budget. Trace the calculated interest expense to Exhibit 6–3, which will then be complete (ignoring income taxes).

z. The ending cash balance is $w + y - x$. Financing y may have a positive (borrowing) or a negative (repayment) effect on the cash balance. The illustrative cash

EXHIBIT 6–4

R COMPANY
Budgeted Statement of Cash Receipts and Disbursements
For the Four Months Ended July 31, 19X1

	APRIL	MAY	JUNE	JULY
Cash balance, beginning	$10,000	$10,550	$10,970	$10,965
Cash receipts:				
Collections from customers (Schedule **b**)	46,000	68,000	68,000	54,000
w.* Total cash available for needs, before financing	56,000	78,550	78,970	64,965
Cash disbursements:				
Merchandise (Schedule **d**)	42,700	48,300	40,600	32,900
Operating expenses (Schedule **f**)	13,750	18,250	18,000	15,250
Truck purchase (given)	3,000	—	—	—
x. Total disbursements	59,450	66,550	58,600	48,150
Minimum cash balance desired	10,000	10,000	10,000	10,000
Total cash needed	69,450	76,550	68,600	58,150
Excess (deficiency) of total cash available over total cash needed before current financing	(13,450)	2,000	10,370	6,815
Financing:				
Borrowings (at beginning)	14,000†			
Repayments (at end)	—	(1,000)	(9,000)	(4,000)
Interest (at 18% per annum)‡	—	(30)	(405)	(240)
y. Total cash increase (decrease) from financing	14,000	(1,030)	(9,405)	(4,240)
z. Cash balance, ending (w + y − x)	$10,550	$10,970	$10,965	$12,575

Note: Expired insurance and depreciation do not entail cash outlays.

* Letters are keyed to the explanation in the text.

† Borrowings and repayments of principal are made in multiples of $1,000, at an interest rate of 18% per annum.

‡ Interest computations: .18 × $1,000 × 2/12 = $30; .18 × $9,000 × 3/12 = $405; .18 × $4,000 × 4/12 = $240

budget shows the pattern of short-term, self-liquidating financing. Seasonal peaks often result in heavy drains on cash, for merchandise purchases and operating expenses, before the sales are made and cash is collected from customers. The resulting loan is self-liquidating—that is, the borrowed money is used to acquire merchandise for sale, and the proceeds from the sale are used to repay the loan. This "working capital cycle" moves from cash to inventory to receivables and back to cash.

Cash budgets help management to avoid having unnecessary idle cash, on the one hand, and unnecessary nerve-racking cash deficiencies, on the other. An astutely mapped financing program keeps cash balances from becoming too large or too small.

☐ Budgeted Balance Sheet

The final step is the preparation of the budgeted balance sheet (Exhibit 6–5). Each item is projected in accordance with the business plan as expressed in the previous schedules. Specifically, the beginning balances at March 31

EXHIBIT 6–5

R COMPANY
Budgeted Balance Sheet
July 31, 19X1

ASSETS

Current assets:		
Cash (Exhibit 6-4)	$12,575	
Accounts receivable (.40 × July sales of $50,000)		
(Schedule **a**)	20,000	
Merchandise inventory (Schedule **c**)	42,400	
Unexpired insurance ($1,800 old balance − $800 expired)	1,000	$ 75,975
Plant:		
Equipment, fixtures, and other ($37,000 + truck, $3,000)	$40,000	
Accumulated depreciation ($12,800 + $2,000 depreciation)	14,800	25,200
Total assets		$101,175

LIABILITIES AND OWNERS' EQUITY

Current liabilities:		
Accounts payable (.5 × July purchases of $29,400)		
(Schedule **d**)	$14,700	
Accrued wages and commissions payable (.5 × $10,000)		
(Schedule **e**)	5,000	$ 19,700
Owners' equity ($78,950 + $2,525 net income)		81,475
Total liabilities and owners' equity		$101,175

Note: Beginning balances were used as a start for the computations of unexpired insurance, plant, and owners' equity.

would be increased or decreased in light of the expected cash receipts and disbursements in Exhibit 6–4 and in light of the effects of noncash items appearing on the income statement in Exhibit 6–3. For example, unexpired insurance would decrease from its balance of $1,800 on March 31 to $1,000 on July 31, even though it is a noncash item.

When the complete master budget is formulated, management can consider all the major financial statements as a basis for changing the course of events. For example, the initial formulation may prompt management to try new sales strategies to generate more demand. Or management may explore the effects of various ways of adjusting the timing of receipts and disbursements. The large cash requirement in April may lead to an emphasis on cash sales or an attempt to speed up collection of accounts receivable. In any event, the first draft of the master budget is rarely the final draft. In this way, the budgeting process becomes an integral part of the management process itself in the sense that *planning* and *budgeting* are indistinguishable.

THE DIFFICULTIES OF SALES FORECASTING

As you have seen in the foregoing illustration, the sales budget is the foundation of the entire master budget. The accuracy of estimated production schedules and costs depends on the detail and accuracy, in dollars and in units, of the budgeted sales.

Sales forecasting is a key to preparing the sales budget, but a forecast and a budget are not necessarily identical. A **sales forecast** is a *prediction* of sales under a given set of conditions. A **sales budget** is the result of *decisions* to create conditions that will generate a *desired* level of sales. For example, you may have forecasts of sales at various levels of advertising; the forecast for the one level you decide to implement becomes the budget.

Sales forecasts are usually prepared under the direction of the top sales executive. All the following factors are important: (1) past patterns of sales, (2) the estimates made by the sales force, (3) general economic and competitive conditions, (4) specific relationships of sales with economic indicators such as gross national product or industrial production indexes, (5) changes in prices, (6) market research studies, and (7) advertising and sales promotion plans.

Sales forecasting usually combines various techniques. Opinions of the sales staff are sought. Statistical methods are often used. Correlations between sales and economic indicators help to make sales forecasts more reliable. In most cases, the quantitative analysis provided by economists and members of the market research staff provide valuable help but not outright answers. The opinions of line management heavily influence the final sales forecasts. No matter how many technical experts are used in forecasting, the *sales budget* is the responsibility of line management.

Pricing policies can have pronounced effects on sales. Management's assessment of price elasticities (the effect of price changes on the physical volume sold) will influence the sales forecast. A company may not offer the same unit price to all customers (because of differences in costs of serving different markets). In such cases, a detailed analysis of both units to be sold as well as dollar sales is needed for each price category before a final sales forecast can be aggregated.

Sales forecasting is still somewhat mystical, but its procedures are becoming more formal and are being reviewed more seriously because of the intensity of competitive pressures. Although this book does not include a detailed discussion of the preparation of the sales budget, the importance of an accurate sales forecast cannot be overstressed.

In recent years, the formal use of statistical probabilities has been applied to the problem of sales forecasting. (See Chapter 16 for an elaboration.) Moreover, managers have used financial-planning models and simulation methods to get a quantitative grasp on the ramifications of various sales strategies.

Governments and other nonprofit organizations also face a problem similar to sales forecasting. For example, the budget for city revenues may depend on a variety of items such as predicted property taxes, traffic fines, parking fees, and city income taxes. In turn, property taxes depend on the extent of new construction and general increases in real estate values. Thus the budget is based on a variety of assumptions and past results.

FINANCIAL-PLANNING MODELS

In most cases, the master budget is the best practical approximation to a formal model of the total organization: its objectives, its inputs, and its outputs. If the master budget serves as a "total decision model" for top management, then decisions about strategies for the forthcoming period may be formulated and altered during the budgetary process. Traditionally, this has been a step-by-step process whereby tentative plans are gradually revised as executives exchange views on various aspects of expected activities.

In the future, much of the interaction and interdependence of the decisions will probably be formalized in mathematical simulation models—sometimes called **financial-planning models**. These models are mathematical statements of the relationships in the organization among all the operating and financial activities, and of other major internal and external factors that may affect decisions.

Many organizations have developed computer-based financial-planning models. These models contain mathematical expressions of the interaction and interdependence among various internal and external factors that affect the results of decisions. Financial-planning models allow managers to assess the predicted impacts of various alternatives before a final decision is selected.

For example, a manager might want to predict the consequences of adding a new product line. A financial-planning model provides budgeted financial statements for several years into the future under any set of assumptions and predictions the manager desires. Most important, managers can get answers to "what if" questions: *What if* sales are 10% below projections? *What if* inflation is 8% rather than 4%, as predicted? *What if* the new union contract grants a 6% raise? a 4% raise?

Use of financial-planning models expanded greatly during the 1980s. The use of spreadsheets on personal computers has made it possible for even small firms to construct such models. Village Shoe Store, a local retailer, has a simple model to show the effects of various marketing strategies. On the other hand, *Business Week* described a Dow Chemical model that uses 140 separate, constantly-revised cost inputs.

The computer has enabled managers to shorten their reaction times. A revised plan that took accountants days to prepare by hand can be prepared in minutes by a computer. Companies such as Public Service Electric & Gas, a New Jersey utility, run their total corporate plan as often as once a day. The executive vice-president of Public Service said that within 24 hours of an announcement of an oil embargo, PSE & G would know the major impact of it and could begin reacting.

Financial-planning models are a great aid to managers. But heed one warning: GIGO—garbage-in, garbage-out! The predicted results from a model are only as good as the model itself and the predictions fed into it. A 1985 article in *CFO*, a magazine for chief financial officers, pointed out several actual cases of terrible decisions resulting from reliance on inaccurate financial-planning models.

SUMMARY

The master budget expresses management's overall operating and financing plan. It outlines company objectives and steps for achieving them. The budgetary process compels managers to think ahead and to prepare for changing conditions. Budgets are aids in setting standards of performance, motivating personnel toward goals, measuring results, and directing attention to the areas that most need investigation.

SUMMARY PROBLEM FOR YOUR REVIEW

☐ Problem

Before attempting to solve the homework problems, review the R Company illustration in this chapter.

HIGHLIGHTS TO REMEMBER

1. Budgets deserve more respect than they often receive. Some companies use different words to emphasize the positive nature of budgeting. They will refer to *profit planning* or *targeting* instead of plain old *budgeting*. Nevertheless, the nature of the process is the same regardless of the label.
2. For most organizations, budgets meet the cost-benefit test. That is, they are installed voluntarily because top management believes they can help managers throughout the organization.
3. The cornerstone of the master budget is the sales budget. All current operating and financial planning is generally tied to the expected volume of sales.
4. The human factors in budgeting are more important than the mechanics. Top management must support a budgetary program wholeheartedly. The job of educating personnel and selling them on the budget is everlasting, but essential, if those who are affected by the budget are to understand it and accept it. The master budget should be a powerful aid to the most crucial decisions of top management. Often it falls far short of that role because its potential is misunderstood. Instead of being regarded as a management tool, in many cases the budget is unfortunately looked upon as a necessary evil.

ACCOUNTING VOCABULARY

Budget *p. 154*   Cash Budget *163*   Continuous Budget *157*   Financial Budget *159*   Financial Planning Models *168*   Long-range Planning *157*   Master Budget *154*   Operating Budget *159*   Pro forma Statements *157*   Sales Budget *167*   Sales Forecast *167*   Strategic Planning *157*

FUNDAMENTAL ASSIGNMENT MATERIAL

Special note: Problem 6–1 provides a single-problem review of most of the chapter topics. Those readers who prefer to concentrate on the fundamentals in smaller chunks should consider Problems 6–16, 6–17, and 6–20 or 6–23.

6–1. **MASTER BUDGET.** (Alternates are 6–31 and 6–34.) A subsidiary of a major retailing company has a strong belief in using highly decentralized management. You are the new manager of one of its small "Arrow" stores in Spokane, Washington. You know much about how to buy, how to display, how to sell, and how to reduce shoplifting. However, you know little about accounting and finance.

Top management believes that store managers should participate in the budgeting process. You have been asked to prepare a complete master budget for your store for April, May, and June. All accounting is done centrally, so you have no expert help on the premises. In addition, tomorrow the branch manager and the assistant controller will be here to examine your work; at that time they will assist you in formulating the final budget document. The idea is to have you prepare the budget a few times so that you gain more confidence about accounting matters. You want to make a favorable impression on your superiors, so you gather the following data as of March 31, 19X7:

		RECENT AND PROJECTED SALES	
Cash	$ 11,000		
Inventory	300,000		
Accounts receivable	261,000	February	$200,000
Net furniture and fixtures	150,000	March	250,000
Total assets	$722,000	April	500,000
		May	300,000
Accounts payable	$340,000	June	300,000
Owners' equity	382,000	July	200,000
Total equities	$722,000		

Credit sales are 90% of total sales. Credit accounts are collected 80% in the month following the sale and 20% in the next following month. Assume that bad debts are negligible and can be ignored. The accounts receivable on March 31 are the result of the credit sales for February and March: (.20 × .90 × $200,000 = $36,000) + (1.00 × .90 × $250,000 = $225,000) = $261,000. The average gross profit on sales is 40%.

The policy is to acquire enough inventory each month to equal the following month's projected sales. All purchases are paid for in the month following purchase.

Salaries, wages, and commissions average 20% of sales; all other variable expenses total 4% of sales; and fixed expenses for rent, property taxes, and miscellaneous payroll and other items are $40,000 monthly. Assume that these expenses require cash disbursements each month. Depreciation is $2,000 monthly.

In April, $40,000 is going to be disbursed for fixtures acquired in March. The March 31 balance of accounts payable includes this amount.

Assume that a minimum cash balance of $10,000 is to be maintained. Also assume that all borrowings are effective at the beginning of the month and that all repayments are made at the end of the month of repayment. Interest is paid only at the time of repaying principal. Interest rate is 8% per annum; round out interest computations to the nearest $10.00. All loans and repayments of principal must be made in multiples of a thousand dollars.

1. Prepare a budgeted income statement for the coming quarter, a budgeted statement of monthly cash receipts and disbursements (for the next three months), and a budgeted balance sheet for June 30, 19X7. All operations are evaluated on a before-income-tax basis. Also, because income taxes are disbursed from corporate headquarters, they may be ignored here.
2. Explain why there is a need for a bank loan and what operating sources supply cash for repaying the bank loan.

ADDITIONAL ASSIGNMENT MATERIAL

6–2. What factors influence the sales forecast?

6–3. What is the major technical difference between historical and budgeted financial statements?

6–4. What are the major benefits of budgeting?

6–5. Why is budgeted performance better than past performance, as a basis for judging actual results?

6–6. "Budgets are primarily a tool used to limit expenditures." Do you agree? Explain.

6–7. "Education and salesmanship are key features of budgeting." Explain.

6–8. "Capital budgets are plans for managing long-term debt and common stock." Do you agree? Explain.

6–9. "Pro forma statements are those statements prepared in conjunction with continuous budgets." Do you agree? Explain.

6–10. What is the difference between an operating budget and a financial budget?

6–11. Why is the sales forecast the starting point for budgeting?

6–12. "Budgets are okay in relatively certain environments. But everything changes so quickly in the electronics industry that budgeting is a waste of time." Comment on this statement.

6–13. What is the principal objective of a cash budget?

6–14. How do strategic planning, long-range planning, and budgeting differ?

6–15. What is the difference between a sales forecast and a sales budget?

6–16. **SALES BUDGET.** A retail store has the following data:

(1) Accounts receivable, May 31, are .6 × May sales of $300,000 = $180,000.
(2) Monthly forecasted sales are: June, $200,000; July, $220,000; August, $280,000; September, $310,000.
(3) Sales consist of 40% cash and 60% credit. All credit accounts are collected in the month following the sales. Uncollectible accounts are negligible and may be ignored.

Required:

Prepare a sales budget schedule and a cash collections budget schedule for June, July, and August.

6–17. **PURCHASE BUDGET.** In 19X7 Goldilocks Toy Store plans the following:

(1) Inventory levels are (at cost) at the end of June, $150,000; July, $190,000; August, $160,000; September, $200,000.
(2) Sales are expected to be: July, $250,000; August, $330,000; September, $300,000.
(3) Cost of goods sold is 60% of sales.
(4) Purchases in May had been $160,000; in June, $190,000. A given month's purchases are paid as follows: 10% during that month; 80% the next month; and the final 10% the next month.

Required:

Prepare budget schedules for July, August, and September for purchases and for disbursements for purchases.

6–18. PURCHASE BUDGET. The inventory of a retail clothing store was $160,000 on May 31. The manager was upset because the inventory was too high. She has adopted the following policies regarding merchandise purchases and inventory. At the end of any month, the inventory should be $10,000 plus 90% of the cost of goods to be sold during the following month. The cost of merchandise sold averages 60% of sales. Purchase terms are generally net, 30 days. A given month's purchases are paid as follows: 20% during that month and 80% during the following month.

Purchases in May had been $150,000. Sales are expected to be: June, $250,000; July, $220,000; August, $280,000; and September, $310,000.

Required:
1. Compute the amount by which the inventory on May 31 exceeded the manager's policies.
2. Prepare budget schedules for June, July, and August for purchases and for disbursements for purchases.

6–19. INVENTORY PLANNING. Ramirez Company manufactures many furniture items, including four-legged tables for playing games. Each table is assembled from one square top, four legs, and eight supporting crosspieces (two between each pair of legs). The following data pertain to the budgeted production of tables for the fourth quarter of a given year. The budgeted sales are 18,000 tables.

	ITEM TO BE PRODUCED	
	Tables	Legs
Budgeted inventory, September 30	2,400	4,000
Budgeted inventory, December 31	2,800	3,500

Required: Prepare a schedule of budgeted production of tables and legs.

6–20. CASH BUDGET. Consider the following:

EAGLETON COMPANY
Budgeted Income Statement
For the Month Ended June 30, 19X9
(in thousands)

Sales		$240
Inventory, May 31	$ 40	
Purchases	160	
Available for sale	$200	
Inventory, June 30	30	
Cost of goods sold		170
Gross margin		$ 70
Operating expenses:		
Wages	$ 30	
Utilities	2	
Advertising	9	
Depreciation	1	
Office expenses	3	
Insurance and property taxes	2	47
Operating income		$ 23

(1) The cash balance, May 31, 19X9, is $68,000. Sales proceeds are collected as follows: 25% month of sale, 50% second month, 25% third month.

(2) Accounts receivable are $120,000 on May 31, 19X9, consisting of $30,000 from April sales and $90,000 from May sales.

(3) Accounts payable on May 31, 19X9, are $120,000.

Eagleton Company pays 25% of purchases during the month of purchase and the remainder during the following month. All operating expenses requiring cash are paid during the month of recognition. However, insurance and property taxes are paid annually in December.

Required: | Prepare a cash budget for June. Confine your analysis to the given data. Ignore income taxes and other possible items that might affect cash.

6–21. CASH COLLECTION BUDGET. Volyum Company's experience indicates that cash collections from customers tend to occur in the following pattern:

Collected within cash discount period in month of sale	50%
Collected within cash discount period in first month after month of sale	10
Collected after cash discount period in first month after month of sale	25
Collected after cash discount period in second month after month of sale	13
Never collected	2
Total sales in any month (before cash discounts)	100%
Cash discount allowable as a percentage of invoice price	1%

Compute the total cash budgeted to be collected in March if sales are predicted as $200,000 for January, $300,000 for February, and $350,000 for March.

6–22. BUDGET COMPUTATIONS FOR PURCHASES AND BORROWING. Nuts & Bolts, Inc., needs your help in computing two of the estimates for its budget for a certain period.

a. The company plans to produce during the period 15,000 units of Product X and 20,000 units of Product Y. It uses 5 units of material K for each X and 3 units of K for each Y. The beginning inventory of K is 12,000 units, and the desired ending inventory is 18,000 units. How many K units must your company purchase during the period?

b. The company forecasts cash receipts of $330,000 and cash disbursements of $365,000. If the beginning cash balance is $26,000 and the desired ending cash balance is $20,000, how much cash must be borrowed during the period?

6–23. CASH BUDGET. Consider the following cash budget (in dollars). Compute amounts for the lettered spaces.

	MAY	JUNE
Cash balance, beginning	20,000	E
Cash receipts from customers	A	140,000
Total cash available before financing	100,000	F
Cash disbursements:		
Merchandise	70,000	60,000
Operating expenses	20,000	25,000
Acquisition of equipment	30,000	—
Total disbursements	120,000	85,000
Minimum cash balance desired	B	B
Total cash needed	130,000	G
Excess (deficiency) of total cash available over total cash needed before current financing	C	H
Financing:		
Borrowings (at beginning)*	D	—
Repayments (at end)	—	I
Interest (at 12% per annum)	—	J
Total cash increase (decrease) from financing	D	K
Cash balance, ending	E	L

* Borrowings and repayments of principal are made in multiples of $1,000. Interest is to be paid when loans are paid.

6–24. **MULTIPLE CHOICE.** (CPA.) The Zel Co., a small wholesaler in Mexico City, budgeted the following sales for the indicated months (in pesos):

	JUNE 19X1	JULY 19X1	AUGUST 19X1
Sales on account	1,500,000	1,600,000	1,700,000
Cash sales	200,000	210,000	220,000
Total sales	1,700,000	1,810,000	1,920,000

All merchandise is marked up to sell at its invoice cost plus 25%. Merchandise inventories at the beginning of each month are at 30% of that month's projected cost of goods sold.

Select the best answer for each of the following items:

a. The cost of goods sold for the month of June 19X1 is anticipated to be (i) 1,530,000 pesos, (ii) 1,402,500 pesos, (iii) 1,275,000 pesos, (iv) 1,190,000 pesos, (v) none of these.

b. Merchandise purchases for July 19X1 are anticipated to be (i) 1,605,500 pesos, (ii) 1,474,400 pesos, (iii) 1,448,000 pesos, (iv) 1,382,250 pesos, (v) none of these.

6–25. **CASH BUDGET.** Barbara Lucas and Olga Washington are partners in Balloon Bouquets, a firm that sells and delivers balloons. Although business has been booming, they are concerned about their ability to meet certain payment deadlines in February 19X8. An $8,000 bank loan plus $960 of interest is due on February 28. They have asked you to prepare a cash budget for February. You have been able to gather the following information:

(1) A large inventory of balloons was purchased in January in anticipation of Valentine's Day. Of the $25,000 of purchases, only $6,000 was paid for in January; the remainder is due in February. The $12,000 of purchases in

February will be primarily in the first half of the month, so 60% will be paid in February.

(2) February is their busiest month; sales of $48,000 are expected. However, most sales are made over the phone, and it is usually a week or two before a bill is sent and then another two weeks until a cash collection is received. Only 20% of February's sales will be collected by the end of the month.

(3) Accounts receivable on sales before February are $9,000. Two-thirds of this is likely to be collected in February. Most of the remainder will never be collected.

(4) Normal salaries and wages are $4,500 per month. Payment is twice monthly, on the fifth and twentieth. An additional person will work 40 hours in the week of Valentine's Day at $6 an hour; he will be paid immediately upon completion of his work.

(5) The regular $400 monthly payment on a compressor purchased last year is due on February 22.

(6) Accrued payroll taxes and other expenses of January to be paid in February are $800.

(7) Expected cash balance on February 1 is $1,500.

(8) Utilities and other expenses to be paid in February are $2,100.

(9) Depreciation on the building and equipment for February is $450.

Required:

1. Prepare a cash budget showing the expected cash receipts and disbursements for February and the cash balance at the end of the month.
2. Compute the percentage of February sales that must be collected by the end of the month to maintain an ending cash balance of $1,000.

6–26. **CASH COLLECTIONS AND DISBURSEMENTS.** The following information was available from Mathis Corporation's books:

19X2	PURCHASES	SALES
June	$42,000	$72,000
July	48,000	66,000
August	36,000	60,000
September	50,000	70,000

Collections from customers are normally 70% in the month of sale, 20% in the month following the sale, and 9% in the second month following the sale. The balance is expected to be uncollectible. Mathis takes full advantage of the 2% discount allowed on purchases paid for by the tenth of the following month. Purchases for October are budgeted at $60,000 (before the cash discount), while sales for October are forecasted at $66,000. Cash disbursements for expenses are expected to be $14,400 for the month of October. Mathis's cash balance at October 1 was $22,000.

Required:

Prepare the following schedules:

1. Expected cash collections during October.
2. Expected cash disbursements during October.
3. Expected cash balance at October 31.

6–27. **PURCHASES AND SALES BUDGETS.** (CMA, adapted.) The Russon Corporation is a retailer whose sales are all made on credit. Sales are billed twice monthly, on the tenth of the month for the last half of the prior month's sales and on the twentieth of the month for the first half of the current month's sales. The terms of all sales are 2/10, net 30. Based on past experience, the collection experience of accounts receivable is as follows:

Within the discount period	80%
On the 30th day	18%
Uncollectible	2%

The sales value of shipments for May 19X0 and the forecast for the next four months are:

May (actual)	$500,000
June	600,000
July	700,000
August	700,000
September	400,000

Russon's average markup on its products is 20% of the sales price.

Russon purchases merchandise for resale to meet the current month's sales demand and to maintain a desired monthly ending inventory of 25% of the next month's sales. All purchases are on credit with terms of net 30. Russon pays for one-half of a month's purchases in the month of purchase and the other half in the month following the purchase.

All sales and purchases occur uniformly throughout the month.

Required:

1. How much cash can Russon Corporation plan to collect from accounts receivable collections during July 19X0?
   a. $574,000
   b. $662,600
   c. $619,000
   d. $608,600
   e. None of these
2. How much cash can Russon plan to collect in September from sales made in August 19X0?
   a. $337,400
   b. $343,000
   c. $400,400
   d. $280,000
   e. None of these
3. The budgeted dollar value of Russon's inventory on August 31, 19X0 will be
   a. $110,000
   b. $80,000
   c. $112,000
   d. $100,000
   e. Some amount other than those given
4. How much merchandise should Russon plan to purchase during June 19X0?
   a. $520,000
   b. $460,000
   c. $500,000
   d. $580,000
   e. None of these
5. The amount Russon should budget in August 19X0 for the payment of merchandise is
   a. $560,000
   b. $500,000
   c. $667,000
   d. $600,000
   e. None of these

6–28. **IMPORTANCE OF SALES FORECAST.** Yokahama Florists specializes in bonsai plants. Its most popular variety, Ginkgo biloba, is sold in both a plain pot and in a decorative oriental planter. Yokahama purchases the plants in bulk and replants them into pots or planters. Bonsai plants are especially popular as Christmas gifts. Purchasing and selling prices have been stable, and no price changes are anticipated.

Wholesale nurseries require a two-month lead time to assure delivery, and shipping time for the decorative planters is eight weeks. Plain pots can be obtained in a couple of hours, if needed, so a minimal inventory is maintained.

Yokahama wants enough bonsai plants and planters for the entire Christmas season to be in stock by November 15, so it is making plans in early September.

The September issue of the local Chamber of Commerce publication shows retail plant and flower sales up 3% over last year, for the period January 1 to August 31. Industry specialists predict Christmas sales of common plants to be 2% above last year's level and those of specialty plants to be up 7%. Interest in bonsai plants seems to be especially strong. The proprietor of Yokahama, Mr. Harui, thinks bonsai sales will increase by three percentage points more than plants in general. That would mean sales 5% above last year for those in pots and 10% for those in decorative planters. The selling price per plant is $20 in plain pots and $30 in planters. The wholesale cost of the plants is $8.00. Pots cost $2.00 each, and decorative planters are $7.00.

Other data are:

	SALES LAST YEAR	
	Nov. 15–30	Dec. 1–31
Plants sold		
In regular pots	200	300
In decorative planters	300	450

	PROJECTED INVENTORY LEVELS	
	Expected November 15	Target December 31
Inventory levels		
Bonsai plants	40	20
Decorative planters	30	10

Required:

Prepare the following:

1. Budgeted sales of plants in regular pots, in number of plants and in total dollars, for November 15 through December 31.
2. Budgeted sales of plants in decorative planters, in number of plants and in total dollars, for November 15 through December 31.
3. Number and total cost of plants to be purchased.
4. Number and total cost of needed plain pots.
5. Number and total cost of needed decorative planters.

6–29. **SALES FORECASTING.** In each of the accompanying diagrams A through E (page 178), the dollar value of a sales order is contrasted with the quantity of product or service sold. Assume a single product in each case.

Required:

1. What pricing policy is reflected by each of these order patterns (assuming that all customers are rational)?
2. Why are these patterns relevant to a sales forecast?

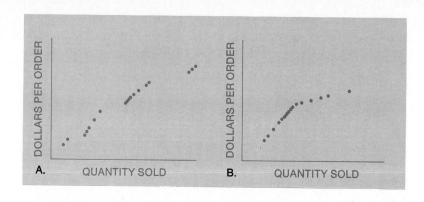

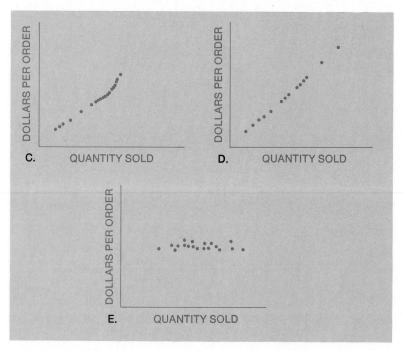

6–30. CASH BUDGET. Prepare a statement of estimated cash receipts and disbursements for October 19X2 for the Wilcox Company, which sells one product. On October 1, 19X2, certain balances were:

Cash	$ 9,000	
Accounts receivable	19,500	
Allowance for bad debts		$2,400
Merchandise inventory	12,000	
Accounts payable, merchandise		9,000

The company's purchases are payable within ten days. Assume that one-third of the purchases of any month are due and paid for in the following month.

The unit invoice cost of the merchandise purchased is $10. At the end of each month it is desired to have an inventory equal in units to 50% of the following month's sales in units.

Sales terms include a 1% discount if payment is made by the end of the calendar month. Past experience indicates that 60% of the billings will be collected during the month of the sale, 30% in the following calendar month, 6% in the next following calendar month. Four percent will be uncollectible. The company's fiscal year begins August 1.

Unit selling price	$ 15
August actual sales	20,000
September actual sales	45,000
October estimated sales	36,000
November estimated sales	27,000
Total sales expected in the fiscal year	450,000

Exclusive of bad debts, total budgeted selling and general administrative expenses for the fiscal year are estimated at $80,500, of which $33,000 is fixed expense (inclusive of a $9,000 annual depreciation charge). These fixed expenses are incurred uniformly throughout the year. The balance of the selling and general administrative expenses vary with sales. Expenses are paid as incurred.

6–31. **PREPARE MASTER BUDGET.** (Alternates are 6–1 and 6–34.) The Techno/Electra Company wants a master budget for the next three months, beginning January 1, 19X2. It desires an ending minimum cash balance of $4,000 each month. Sales are forecasted at an average selling price of $4 per unit. Inventories are supposed to equal 120% of the next month's sales in units except for the end of March. The March 31 inventory in units should be 75% of the next month's sales. Merchandise costs are $2 per unit. Purchases during any given month are paid in full during the following month. All sales are on credit, payable within 30 days, but experience has shown that 40% of current sales is collected in the current month, 40% in the next month, and 20% in the month thereafter. Bad debts are negligible.

Monthly operating expenses are as follows:

Wages and salaries	$11,000
Insurance expired	100
Depreciation	500
Miscellaneous	2,000
Rent	200 + 12% of sales

Cash dividends of $1,000 are to be declared and paid quarterly, beginning January 15. All operating expenses are paid as incurred, except insurance, depreciation, and rent. Rent of $200 is paid at the beginning of each month, and the additional 12% of sales is paid quarterly on the tenth of the month following the quarter. The next settlement is due January 10.

The company plans to buy some new fixtures, for $2,000 cash, in March.

Money can be borrowed and repaid in multiples of $500, at an interest rate of 15% per annum. Management wants to minimize borrowing and repay rapidly. Interest is computed and paid when the principal is repaid. Assume that borrowing takes place at the beginning, and repayments at the end, of the months in question. Compute interest to the nearest dollar.

ASSETS AS OF DECEMBER 31		LIABILITIES AS OF DECEMBER 31	
Cash	$ 4,000	Accounts payable	
Accounts receivable	16,000	(merchandise)	$28,000
Inventory	30,000	Rent payable	8,400
Unexpired insurance	1,200		$36,400
Fixed assets, net	10,000		
	$61,200		

Recent and budgeted sales are:

October	$30,000	December	$20,000	February	$60,000	April	$36,000
November	20,000	January	50,000	March	40,000		

Required: 1. Prepare a master budget, including a budgeted income statement, balance sheet, statement of cash receipts and disbursements, and supporting schedules.
2. Explain why there is a need for a bank loan and what operating sources provide the cash for the repayment of the bank loan.

6–32. **BUDGETING, PRICING, AND SERVICE INDUSTRIES.** Most law firms have two broad ranks of attorneys: associates, who work for salaries, and partners, who share any income generated before taxes. You are an experienced associate of Juanita Ortez and Company, a small but prestigious law firm. Ortez, the senior partner, has asked you to analyze the following budget data with the aim of setting a fee structure for 19X4:

	DEPARTMENT		
	Probate	Tax	TOTAL
Number of partners	2	3	5
Budgeted partner-hours billable to clients	3,200	4,500	7,700
Number of associates	2	6	8
Budgeted associate-hours billable to clients	3,000	8,400	11,400
Total hours	6,200	12,900	19,100
Budgeted expenses for the firm:			
Secretarial staff and receptionist			$141,400
Library services			40,000
Rent			52,000
Janitorial services			14,000
Supplies and photocopying			36,000
Telephone			11,000
General expenses			20,000
			$314,400

Associates receive salaries and benefits of $48,000 per person per year.

Ortez kept abreast of the general pricing practices of other law firms. The billing rate for associates was $45 per hour, and she said it would be unthinkable for her firm to do otherwise. However, because of the general high quality of the work performed by her firm, the senior partner was confident that a partner could be billed out at $85 to $135 per hour. Ortez also told you that, on an average, the partners expected an income after all expenses, but before income taxes, of $120,000 each.

Required:
1. Compute the average billing rate per partner-hour for 19X4.
2. All expenses for 19X4 were exactly the same as budgeted. You have been asked to repeat for 19X5 what you did in Requirement 1. All expenses are expected to be the same as the actual expenses for 19X4. However, because of their superior work in 19X4, the associates will be provided greater responsibility and greater breadth of experience. What that entailed, you learned, was that the associates will work more hours and the partners will work fewer. The budgeted billable hours for 19X5 were:

| | DEPARTMENT | | |
	Probate	Tax	TOTAL
Partners	2,400	3,300	5,700
Associates	3,800	9,600	13,400
Total hours	6,200	12,900	19,100

You also learned that the partners still expected to receive $120,000 each on the average. The market remained such that an associate could still only be billed out at $45 per hour.

6–33. **CASH BUDGETING FOR A HOSPITAL.** (CMA, adapted). Voorhees Hospital provides a wide range of health services in its community. Voorhees's board of directors has authorized the following capital expenditures:

Interaortic balloon pump	$1,100,000
CT scanner	700,000
X-ray equipment	600,000
Laboratory equipment	1,400,000
	$3,800,000

The expenditures are planned for October 1, 19X7, and the board wishes to know the amount of borrowing, if any, necessary on that date. Marc Kelly, hospital controller, has gathered the following information to be used in preparing an analysis of future cash flows.
(1) Billings, made in the month of service, for the first six months of 19X7 are:

MONTH	ACTUAL AMOUNT
January	$4,400,000
February	4,400,000
March	4,500,000
April	4,500,000
May	5,000,000
June	5,000,000

Ninety percent of Voorhees' billings are made to third parties such as Blue Cross, federal or state governments, and private insurance companies. The remaining 10% of the billings are made directly to patients. Historical patterns of billing collections are:

	THIRD-PARTY BILLINGS	DIRECT PATIENT BILLINGS
Month of service	20%	10%
Month following service	50	40
Second month following service	20	40
Uncollectible	10	10

Estimated billings for the last six months of 19X7 are listed next. The same billing and collection patterns that have been experienced during the first six months of 19X7 are expected to continue during the last six months of the year.

MONTH	ESTIMATED AMOUNT
July	$4,500,000
August	5,000,000
September	5,500,000
October	5,700,000
November	5,800,000
December	5,500,000

(2) The purchases that have been made during the past three months and the planned purchases for the last six months of 19X7 are presented in the following schedule.

MONTH	AMOUNT
April	$1,100,000
May	1,200,000
June	1,200,000
July	1,250,000
August	1,500,000
September	1,850,000
October	1,950,000
November	2,250,000
December	1,750,000

All purchases are made on account, and accounts payable are remitted in the month following the purchase.

(3) Salaries for each month during the remainder of 19X7 are expected to be $1,500,000 per month plus 20% of that month's billings. Salaries are paid in the month of service.

(4) Voorhees' monthly depreciation charges are $125,000.

(5) Voorhees incurs interest expense of $150,000 per month and makes interest payments of $450,000 on the last day of each calendar quarter.
(6) Endowment fund income is expected to continue to total $175,000 per month.
(7) Voorhees has a cash balance of $300,000 on July 1, 19X7 and has a policy of maintaining a minimum end-of-month cash balance of 10% of the current month's purchases.
(8) Voorhees Hospital employs a calendar year reporting period.

Required:

1. Prepare a schedule of budgeted cash receipts by month for the third quarter of 19X7.
2. Prepare a schedule of budgeted cash disbursements by month for the third quarter of 19X7.
3. Determine the amount of borrowing, if any, necessary on October 1, 19X7, to acquire the capital items totaling $3,800,000.

6–34. **DEVIATIONS FROM MASTER BUDGET.** (Alternates are 6–1 and 6–31.) Review the major illustration in the chapter. It is the end of July. Operations have been exactly in accordance with the budget except that July sales were $40,000 instead of $50,000. Purchases for July were not affected by the drop in sales, but commissions, cash, accounts receivable, and notes payable were among the accounts affected.

Prepare a summary analysis of the effects. That is, how would Schedules *a*, *b*, *e*, and *f* be affected, as well as Exhibits 6–3, 6–4, and 6–5? Include a list of all new balances in Exhibit 6–5.

6–35. **COMPREHENSIVE BUDGETING FOR A UNIVERSITY.** (CPA, adapted). Suppose that you are the controller of Northern Alaska University. The university president, George Kanglilyok, is preparing for his annual fund-raising campaign for 19X8–X9. To set an appropriate target, he has asked you to prepare a budget for the academic year. You have collected the following data for the current year (19X7–X8):
(1)

	UNDERGRADUATE DIVISION	GRADUATE DIVISION
Average salary of faculty member	$40,000	$40,000
Average faculty teaching load in semester credit hours per year (eight undergraduate or six graduate courses)	24	18
Average number of students per class	30	20
Total enrollment (full-time and part-time students)	3,000	1,200
Average number of semester credit hours carried each year per student	25	20
Full-time load, semester hours per year	30	24

For 19X8–X9, all faculty and staff will receive a 5% salary increase. Undergraduate enrollment is expected to increase by 10%, but no change in graduate enrollment is expected.
(2) The 19X7–X8 budget for operation and maintenance of facilities is $450,000, which includes $220,000 for salaries and wages. Experience so far this year indicates that the budget is accurate. Salaries and wages will increase by 5% and other operating costs by $10,000 in 19X8–X9.
(3) The 19X7–X8 and 19X8–X9 budgets for the remaining expenditures are

	19X7–X8	19X8–X9
General administrative	$455,000	$475,000
Library:		
Acquisitions	136,000	140,000
Operations	172,000	180,000
Health services	43,000	45,000
Intramural athletics	51,000	55,000
Intercollegiate athletics	218,000	220,000
Insurance and retirement	475,000	510,000
Interest	70,000	70,000

(4) Tuition is $60 per credit hour. In addition, the state legislature provides $700 per full-time-equivalent student. (A full-time equivalent is 30 undergraduate hours or 24 graduate hours.) Tuition scholarships are given to 30 *full-time* undergraduates and 50 *full-time* graduate students.

(5) Revenues other than tuition and the legislative apportionment are

	19X7–X8	19X8–X9
Endowment income	$180,000	$190,000
Net income from		
auxiliary services	295,000	305,000
Intercollegiate athletic		
receipts	260,000	270,000

(6) The chemistry/physics classroom building needs remodeling during the 19X8–X9 period. Projected cost is $500,000.

Required:

1. Prepare a schedule for 19X8–X9 giving by division (a) expected enrollment, (b) total credit hours, (c) full-time-equivalent enrollment, and (d) number of faculty members needed. Assume that part-time faculty can be hired at the same salary per credit hour as full-time faculty.
2. Calculate the budget for faculty salaries for 19X8–X9 by division.
3. Calculate the budget for tuition revenue and legislative apportionment for 19X8–X9 by division.
4. Prepare a schedule for President Kanglilyok showing the amount that must be raised by the annual fund-raising campaign.

6–36. **PRODUCTION AND LABOR BUDGETS.** Sherman Drill Company makes and sells a special electric drill developed by Adele Sherman. Josh Berg, controller, is responsible for preparing Sherman's master budget and has accumulated the following information for 19X5.

	MARCH	APRIL	MAY	JUNE	JULY
Estimated unit					
sales	10,000	12,000	9,000	11,000	10,000
Sales price per					
unit	$50.00	$47.50	$47.50	$47.50	$47.50
Direct labor-hours					
per unit	2.0	2.0	1.5	1.5	1.5
Wage per direct					
labor-hour	$8.50	$9.00	$9.00	$9.00	$9.00

Sherman has a labor contract that calls for a wage increase to $9.00 per hour on April 1, 19X5. New labor-saving machinery is being installed and will be fully operational by May 1, 19X5.

Sherman expects to have 16,000 drills on hand at February 28, 19X5, and has a policy of carrying an end-of-month inventory of 100% of the following month's sales plus 50% of the second following month's sales.

Required: Prepare a schedule showing the units to be produced, direct-labor-hours required, and direct-labor cost for March, April, and May.

Chapter 7

FLEXIBLE BUDGETS
AND STANDARDS FOR CONTROL

LEARNING OBJECTIVES

When you have finished studying this chapter, you should be able to:

1. Distinguish between static budgets and flexible budgets.
2. Compute and use a budget formula in the construction of a flexible budget.
3. Use the flexible-budget approach to compute (a) sales volume variances and (b) flexible budget variances.
4. Distinguish between budget amounts and standard amounts.
5. Distinguish between perfection standards and currently attainable standards.
6. Compute the price and efficiency variances for direct material and direct labor.
7. Identify the typical responsibilities for controlling variances in material and labor costs.

The essence of control is feedback—the comparison of actual performance with planned performance. Flexible budgets and standard costs are major attention-directing techniques for planning and for providing feedback regarding individual costs. Throughout this chapter, to stress some basic ideas, we shall continue to assume that each cost is either variable or fixed; in the next chapter we shall consider various cost behavior patterns in more detail.

This chapter has two major sections. Part One provides a general overview of flexible budgets without getting into details of the analysis of variances. Part Two introduces price and efficiency variances.

☐ PART ONE: Flexible Budgets

STATIC-BUDGET COMPARISONS

As Chapter 6 shows, budgets may be developed on a companywide basis to cover all activities, from sales to direct material usage to sweeping compound usage, and from spending on a new plant to expected drains on petty cash. A budget may be expressed on an accrual basis or on a cash-flow basis; it may be highly condensed or exceedingly detailed. All the budgets discussed in Chapter 6 are *static* (inflexible). A **static budget** is defined as a budget prepared for only one level of activity (e.g., volume of sales). To illustrate, a typical master-planning budget is a plan tailored to a single target volume level of, say, 100,000 units. All results would be compared with the original plan, regardless of changes in ensuing conditions—even though, for example, volume turned out to be only 90,000 units instead of the original 100,000. Therefore, the terms *static budget* and *master budget* will be regarded as synonyms in this book.

Consider a simplified illustration. Suppose the Dominion Company, a one-department firm in Singapore, manufactured and sold a special kind of carry-on flight luggage that required several hand operations. The product had some variations, but it was viewed essentially as a single product bearing one selling price.

The master budget for June 19X1 included the condensed income statement shown in Exhibit 7–1, column 2. The actual results are in column 1. The master budget called for the production and sales of 9,000 units, but only 7,000 units were actually produced and sold. There were no beginning or ending inventories.

The master budget was based on detailed expectations for the month, including a careful forecast of sales. The performance report in Exhibit 7–1

EXHIBIT 7-1

DOMINION COMPANY
Performance Report Using Static Budget
For the Month Ended June 30, 19X1

	ACTUAL	MASTER (STATIC) BUDGET	MASTER (STATIC) BUDGET VARIANCE
Units	7,000	9,000	2,000
Sales	$168,000	$216,000	$48,000 U
Variable costs:			
Direct material	$ 21,350	$ 27,000	$ 5,650 F
Direct labor	61,500	72,000	10,500 F
Labor to transport materials internally and provide general support	11,100	14,400	3,300 F
Idle time	3,550	3,600	50 F
Cleanup time	2,500	2,700	200 F
Other indirect labor	800	900	100 F
Miscellaneous supplies	4,700	5,400	700 F
Variable manufacturing costs	$105,500	$126,000	$20,500 F
Shipping expenses (selling)	5,000	5,400	400 F
Duplication, telephone, etc. (administrative)	2,000	1,800	200 U
Total variable costs	$112,500	$133,200	$20,700 F
Contribution margin	$ 55,500	$ 82,800	$27,300 U
Fixed costs:			
Factory supervision	$ 14,700	$14,400	$ 300 U
Rent of factory	5,000	5,000	—
Depreciation of factory equipment	15,000	15,000	—
Other fixed factory costs	2,600	2,600	—
Fixed manufacturing costs	$ 37,300	$ 37,000	$ 300 U
Fixed selling and administrative costs	33,000	33,000	—
Total fixed costs	$ 70,300	$ 70,000	$ 300 U
Operating income (loss)	$ (14,800)	$ 12,800	$27,600 U

F = **Favorable cost variances** occur when actual costs are less than budgeted costs.

U = **Unfavorable cost variances** occur when actual costs are greater than budgeted costs.

compares the actual results with the master budget. *Performance report* is a general term that usually means a comparison of actual results with some budget. Recall that Chapter 1 (page 7) defined *variance* (or **budget variance**) as a deviation of an actual result from the expected or budgeted amount. Exhibit 7-1 shows variances from a static budget.

Suppose the president of Dominion Company asks you to explain *why* there was an operating loss of $14,800 when a profit of $12,800 was budgeted. Clearly, sales are below expectations, but the favorable variances regarding the variable costs are deceptive. Considering the lower-than-projected level of activity, was cost control really satisfactory? The comparison of actual results with a static budget does not give much help in answering that question.

FLEXIBLE-BUDGET COMPARISONS

How would you answer the Dominion Company president? You need to prepare a performance report that gives better information than a simple listing of variances between the master budget and the actual results. A helpful framework for analysis can be provided by a flexible budget. A **flexible budget** (also called **variable budget**) is based on knowledge of cost behavior patterns. It is prepared for a range, rather than a single level, of activity; it is essentially a budget formula that shows the revenue and costs expected at *any* level of activity in the relevant range. It recognizes that revenue and variable costs differ for various activity levels whereas fixed costs do not. In contrast, the *master budget* is static. It lists revenues and costs at only the *planned* activity level.

Ideally, the flexible budget is compiled after obtaining a detailed analysis of how each cost is affected by changes in activity. Exhibit 7–2 shows a sample flexible budget.

The costs in Exhibit 7–2 can be graphed as in Exhibit 7–3. As these exhibits show, a mathematical function or formula can summarize the cost behavior as $70,000 per month plus $14.80 per unit. We have assumed that the graph is valid for the relevant range of 7,000 to 9,000 units. Costs are unlikely to behave in accordance with such a simple formula beyond either side of this range. Inasmuch as the actual activity level was 7,000 units, the pertinent flexible budget is in the 7,000-unit column of Exhibit 7–2.

Flexible budgets have the following distinguishing features: (a) they are prepared for a range of activity instead of a single level; (b) they supply a dynamic basis for comparison because they are automatically geared to changes in volume.

The flexible-budget approach says, "Give me any activity level you choose, and I'll provide a budget tailored to that particular volume." Flexible budgets may be useful both before and after the period in question. They may help managers to choose from among various ranges of activity for planning purposes. The may also help managers to analyze actual results at the end of the period. The cost-volume-profit relationships you used in Chapter 2 were essentially flexible budgets.

ISOLATING THE VARIANCES

Pause a moment to reflect on your report to the Dominion Company president. How can you provide a more penetrating analysis of the master (static) budget variances in Exhibit 7–1? You can use a flexible budget to subdivide each

EXHIBIT 7–2 *(Place a clip on this page for easy reference.)*

DOMINION COMPANY
Flexible Budget
For the Month Ended June 30, 19X1

	BUDGET FORMULA PER UNIT	FLEXIBLE BUDGET FOR VARIOUS LEVELS OF ACTIVITY		
Units	—	7,000	8,000	9,000
Sales	$24.00	$168,000	$192,000	$216,000
Variable costs:				
Direct material	$ 3.00	$ 21,000	$ 24,000	$ 27,000
Direct labor	8.00	56,000	64,000	72,000
Labor to transport materials internally and provide general support	1.60	11,200	12,800	14,400
Idle time	.40	2,800	3,200	3,600
Cleanup time	.30	2,100	2,400	2,700
Other indirect labor	.10	700	800	900
Miscellaneous supplies	.60	4,200	4,800	5,400
Variable manufacturing costs	$14.00	$ 98,000	$112,000	$126,000
Shipping expenses (selling)	.60	4,200	4,800	5,400
Duplication, telephone, etc.	.20	1,400	1,600	1,800
Total variable costs	$14.80	$103,600	$118,400	$133,200
Contribution margin	$ 9.20	$ 64,400	$ 73,600	$ 82,800
Fixed costs:				
Factory supervision		$ 14,400	$ 14,400	$ 14,400
Rent of factory		5,000	5,000	5,000
Depreciation of factory equipment		15,000	15,000	15,000
Other fixed factory costs		2,600	2,600	2,600
Fixed manufacturing costs		$ 37,000	$ 37,000	$ 37,000
Fixed selling and administrative costs		33,000	33,000	33,000
Total fixed costs*		$ 70,000	$ 70,000	$ 70,000
Operating income (loss)		$ (5,600)	$ 3,600	$ 12,800

* Note that the budget formula for fixed costs is $70,000 per month. Therefore the budget formula for total costs is $14.80 per unit plus $70,000 per month. The graph in Exhibit 7–3 portrays these relationships.

variance into two components, the flexible-budget variance and the sales volume variance:

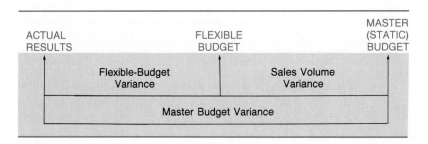

EXHIBIT 7–3

Dominion Company Graph of Flexible Budget of Costs

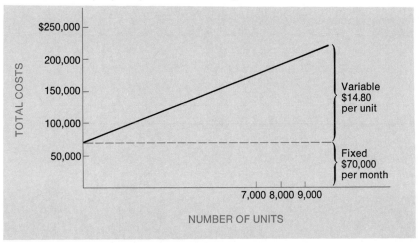

The flexible budget in this diagram includes the revenues and costs expected for the *actual* sales volume over the period. The difference between the master budget and the flexible budget is caused solely by a difference between the actual sales volume and the target volume in the master budget. We will call this variance a **sales volume variance**, although its label will vary from company to company. It measures how effective managers have been in meeting the predetermined sales objective. Marketing managers usually have the primary responsibility for reaching the sales level called for in the master budget. The sales volume variance provides information about their performance.

Differences between the actual results and the flexible budget arise for two reasons: (1) actual unit prices or costs differ from those budgeted, and (2) the amount of inputs used for the actual volume of output differs from the flexible budget. The first are *price variances*, the second, *efficiency variances*. Together they comprise the *flexible-budget variance*.

To summarize, the sales volume variance measures *effectiveness*—how well the sales objectives were met. The flexible-budget variance reflects both price changes and *efficiency*. To assess effectiveness, compare accomplishments to goals. To assess efficiency, compare inputs to outputs. The less input used to produce a given output, the more efficient the operation.

Performance may be both effective and efficient, but either condition can occur without the other. For example, suppose a company's sales target is 100,000 units. Subsequently, only 75,000 are sold, but producing them required exactly the inputs specified in the flexible budget. Performance is ineffective but efficient. In contrast, 100,000 units may be sold, but production of them might have wasted materials and labor—performance would be effective but inefficient.

The master budget variances in Exhibit 7–1 fail to separate sales volume effects from efficiency and price effects. However, Exhibit 7–4 gives a condensed

EXHIBIT 7–4 *(Place a clip on this page for easy reference.)*

DOMINION COMPANY
Summary of Performance
For the Month Ended June 30, 19X1

	(1) ACTUAL RESULTS AT ACTUAL PRICES*	(2) (1) − (3) FLEXIBLE- BUDGET VARIANCES†	(3) FLEXIBLE BUDGET FOR ACTUAL OUTPUT ACHIEVED‡	(4) (3) − (5) SALES VOLUME VARIANCES	(5) MASTER (STATIC) BUDGET*	(6) (1) − (5) or (2) + (4) MASTER (STATIC) BUDGET VARIANCE
Physical units	7,000	—	7,000	2,000 U	9,000	2,000 U
Sales	$168,000	$ —	$168,000	$48,000 U	$216,000	$48,000 U
Variable costs	112,500	8,900 U	103,600	29,600 F	133,200	20,700 F
Contribution margin	$ 55,500	$8,900 U	$ 64,400	$18,400 U	$ 82,800	$27,300 U
Fixed costs	70,300	300 U	70,000	—	70,000	300 U
Operating income	$ (14,800)	$9,200 U	$ (5,600)	$18,400 U	$ 12,800	$27,600 U

U = Unfavorable. F = Favorable.
* Figures are from Exhibit 7–1.
† Figures are shown in more detail in Exhibit 7–5.
‡ Figures are from the 7,000-unit column in Exhibit 7–2.

view of how these variances can be subdivided. The flexible budget is an explanatory bridge between the master (static) budget and the actual results. The unfavorable master (static) budget variance of $27,600 is divided into an unfavorable sales volume variance of $18,400 and an unfavorable flexible-budget variance of $9,200. We discuss the division of the flexible-budget variance into price and efficiency components in Part Two of this chapter.

Column 4 in Exhibit 7–4 focuses on the sales volume variance. It shows that the underachievement of sales by 2,000 units and $48,000 resulted in an $18,400 decrease in attained contribution margin and hence an $18,400 decrease in operating income. Note that unit prices are held constant in this part of the analysis—that is, the sales volume variance is computed by using the budgeted contribution margin per unit:

$$\text{sales volume variance} = \text{budgeted unit contribution margin} \times$$
$$\text{difference between the master budgeted}$$
$$\text{sales in units and the actual sales in units}$$
$$= \$9.20 \times (9,000 - 7,000)$$
$$= \$18,400, \text{ unfavorable}$$

Without the flexible budget in column 3, this sales volume variance cannot be isolated.

Column 2 presents the **flexible-budget variances**, which are the differences between actual amounts and the flexible-budget amounts for the actual output achieved. These variances arise from *price* changes and *inefficient* uses of inputs. The focus is on the difference between actual costs and flexible budgeted costs when *both* are at the 7,000-unit level of activity. Again, without the flexible budget in column 3, these variances cannot be separated from the effects of changes in sales volume.

The variances for operating income can be summarized as follows:

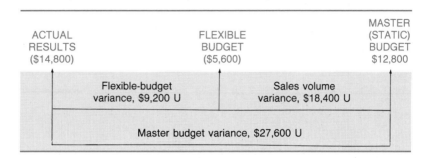

ACTUAL RESULTS ($14,800)	FLEXIBLE BUDGET ($5,600)	MASTER (STATIC) BUDGET $12,800
Flexible-budget variance, $9,200 U	Sales volume variance, $18,400 U	
Master budget variance, $27,600 U		

If the president wants to pursue this analysis of cost control beyond the summary in Exhibit 7–4, the cost performance report in Exhibit 7–5 may be of help. Even if the president were not interested in probing further, some lower-level managers might be so inclined. Exhibit 7–5 gives a line-by-line sizeup, showing how most of the costs that had seemingly favorable variances when a static budget was used as a basis for comparison have, in reality, unfavorable variances. These flexible-budget variances may be analyzed in even more depth by being subdivided further, at least for the more important material and labor costs, as shown later in the section "Standards for Material and Labor."

DEVELOPMENT OF CONTROL SYSTEMS

In most organizations, systems for accumulating and analyzing data evolve gradually. For example, when small businesses are founded, planning and control decisions are based at first almost wholly on the manager's *personal observations* of operations. It does not take long for the manager to realize that keeping some *historical records* would be a net benefit. That is, the additional bookkeeping costs are clearly outweighed by the greater likelihood of a series of better decisions regarding extensions of trade credit to customers, negotiating with suppliers and bankers, and so on. Furthermore, comparing the current period's sales, costs, or income with the preceding period's helps in the evaluation of performance and the preparation of new plans.

Personal observation and historical records, however, are often not enough. Managers desire to reduce emergency decision making by planning more carefully, and the *master (static) budget* helps this process. Furthermore, the master budget provides a better benchmark for evaluating performance. That is, managers want to know more than how they have done currently in relation to last period's performance; they also want to know how they have done *currently* in relation to their *current targeted* performance.

EXHIBIT 7–5

DOMINION COMPANY
Cost Control Performance Report
For the Month Ended June 30, 19X1

	ACTUAL COSTS INCURRED	FLEXIBLE BUDGET*	FLEXIBLE- BUDGET VARIANCES†	EXPLANATION
Units	7,000	7,000	—	
Variable costs:				
Direct material	$ 21,350	$ 21,000	$ 350 U	Lower prices, but higher usage
Direct labor	61,500	56,000	5,500 U	Higher wage rates and higher usage
Labor to transport materials internally and provide general support	11,100	11,200	100 F	
Idle time	3,550	2,800	750 U	Excessive machine breakdowns
Cleanup time	2,500	2,100	400 U	Needs more investigation
Other indirect labor	800	700	100 U	
Miscellaneous supplies	4,700	4,200	500 U	Higher prices and higher usage
Variable manufacturing costs	$105,500	$ 98,000	$7,500 U	
Shipping expenses (selling)	5,000	4,200	800 U	Use of air freight
Duplication, telephone, etc.	2,000	1,400	600 U	Needs more investigation
Total variable costs	$112,500	$103,600	$8,900 U	
Fixed costs:				
Factory supervision	$ 14,700	$ 14,400	$ 300 U	Unanticipated salary increase
Rent of factory	5,000	5,000	—	
Depreciation of factory equipment	15,000	15,000	—	
Other fixed factory costs	2,600	2,600	—	
Fixed manufacturing costs	$ 37,300	$ 37,000	$ 300 U	
Fixed selling and administrative costs	33,000	33,000	—	
Total fixed costs	$ 70,300	$ 70,000	$ 300 U	
Total variable and fixed costs	$182,800	$173,600	$9,200 U	

F = Favorable. U = Unfavorable.

* From 7,000-unit column in Exhibit 7–2, page 190.

† This represents a line-by-line breakdown of the variances in column 2 of Exhibit 7–4.

This chapter has shown that some managers are willing to pay for more help in the form of *flexible budgets*, which are key aids in mapping an explanatory trail from the master budget to the actual results.

Thus the evolution of control systems is often from personal observation, to historical records, to master (static) budgets, to flexible budgets (and standard costs, which are described in the next section). Note that one control tool does not *replace* another; instead, each control tool is *added* to the others. The systems become more costly, but they provide the managers who buy them with net benefits in the form of a better set of collective operating decisions.

This concludes the presentation of an overall view of flexible budgets. Subsequent sections probe the subject more deeply.

SUMMARY PROBLEM FOR YOUR REVIEW

☐ Problem One

Refer to the data contained in Exhibits 7–1 and 7–2. Suppose actual production and sales were 8,500 units instead of 7,000 units, actual variable costs were $129,300, and actual fixed costs were $71,200. (a) Compute the master (static) budget variance. What does this tell you about the efficiency of operations? (b) Compute the sales volume variance. Is the performance of the marketing function the sole explanation for this variance? Why? (c) Using a flexible budget, compute the budgeted contribution margin, budgeted operating income, budgeted direct material, budgeted direct labor, and the flexible-budget variance. What do you learn from this variance?

☐ Solution to Problem One

(a)   actual operating income = (8,500 × $24) − $129,300 − $71,200 = $3,500

master budget operating income = $12,800 (from Exhibit 7–1)

master budget variance = $12,800 − $3,500 = $9,300 U

The master budget variance alone does not provide information about the effects of three key factors on operations: sales volume, efficiency, and price changes.

(b)   sales volume variance = budgeted unit contribution margin × difference between the master-budgeted sales in units and the actual sales in units
= $9.20 × (9,000 − 8,500) = $4,600 U

This variance is labeled as a sales volume variance because it quantifies the impact on operating income of the deviation from an original sales target, while holding price and efficiency factors constant. Of course, the failure to reach target sales may be traceable to a number of causes beyond the control of the marketing force, including strikes, material shortages, and storms.

(c) The budget formulas in Exhibit 7–2 are the basis for the following answers:

budgeted contribution margin	= $9.20 × 8,500 = $78,200
flexible budget operating income	= $78,200 − $70,000 fixed costs = $8,200
budgeted direct material	= $3.00 × 8,500 = $25,500
budgeted direct labor	= $8.00 × 8,500 = $68,000
actual operating income (requirement a)	= $3,500
flexible budget variance	= $8,200 − $3,500 = $4,700 U

The flexible budget variance shows that Dominion Company spent $4,700 more to produce and sell the 8,500 units than it should have if operations had been efficient and unit prices had not changed. Note that this variance plus the $4,600 U sales volume variance total to the $9,300 U master budget variance.

PART TWO: Flexible-Budget Variances in Detail

This part of the chapter shows how to subdivide flexible-budget variances into price and efficiency components.

STANDARDS FOR MATERIAL AND LABOR

Standard costs are the building blocks of a budgeting and feedback system. A **standard cost** is a carefully predetermined cost that should be attained, usually expressed per unit.

☐ Difference Between Standards and Budgets

How does a standard amount differ from a budget amount? If standards are currently attainable, as they are assumed to be in this book, there is no conceptual difference. However, the term *standard cost* usually refers to a *single* unit. In contrast, *budgeted cost* refers to a *total*. For example, the standard cost of direct material in Exhibit 7–2 shows:

	BUDGET FORMULA PER UNIT	FLEXIBLE BUDGET FOR VARIOUS LEVELS OF ACTIVITY		
Units	1	7,000	8,000	9,000
Direct material	$3.00	$21,000	$24,000	$27,000

The standard cost is $3 per unit. The budgeted cost is $21,000 if 7,000 units are to be produced. It may help to think of a standard as a budget for the production of a single unit. In many companies, the terms *budgeted performance* and *standard performance* are used interchangeably.

In practice, direct material and direct labor are often said to be controlled with the help of *standard costs*, whereas all other costs are usually said to be controlled with the help of *departmental overhead budgets*. This distinction probably arose because of different timing and control techniques for various costs. Direct material and direct labor generally are easily identifiable for control purposes. Therefore, techniques for planning and controlling these costs are relatively refined. Overhead costs are combinations of many individual items, none of which by itself justifies an elaborate control system. In consequence, use of direct material may be closely watched on an hourly basis; direct labor, on a daily basis; and factory overhead, on a weekly or monthly basis.

All this leads to the following straightforward approach that we will pursue throughout the remainder of this book. The *standard* is a *unit* idea; the *budget* is a *total* idea. Using the data in Exhibit 7–2, page 190:

| | STANDARDS | | |
	(1) Standard Inputs Allowed for Each Unit of Output Achieved	(2) Standard Price per Unit of Input	BUDGET FOR 7,000 UNITS OF OUTPUT*
Direct material	5 pounds	$ .60	$21,000
Direct labor	2 hours	4.00	56,000
Other costs (detailed)	Various	Various	96,600

* Col. (1) × (2) × 7,000.

☐ Role of Past Experience

The study of past cost behavior patterns is typically a fundamental step in formulating a standard or a budgeted cost. Although the study of past cost behavior is a useful starting point, a budgeted cost should not be merely an extension of past experience. Inefficiencies may be reflected in prior costs. Changes in technology, equipment, and methods also limit the usefulness of comparisons with the past. Performance should be judged in relation to some currently attainable goal, one that may be reached by skilled, diligent, superior effort. Concern with the past is justified only insofar as it helps prediction. Management wishes to plan what costs *should be*, not what costs *have been*.

☐ Current Attainability: The Most Widely Used Standard

What standard of expected performance should be used? Should it be so severe that it is rarely, if ever, attained? Should it be attainable 50% of the time? 80%? 20%? Individuals who have worked a lifetime in setting standards for performance disagree, so there are no universal answers to these questions.

Two types of standards deserve mention here, perfection standards and currently attainable standards. *Perfection standards* (often also called *ideal standards*) are expressions of the absolute minimum costs possible under the best conceivable conditions, using existing specifications and equipment. No provision is made for waste, spoilage, machine breakdowns, and the like. Those who favor this approach maintain that the resulting unfavorable variances will constantly remind managers of the perpetual need for improvement in all phases of operations. These standards are not widely used, however, because they have an adverse effect on employee motivation. Employees tend to ignore unreasonable goals.

Currently attainable standards are those that can be achieved by *very efficient* operations. Expectations are set high enough so that employees regard their fulfillment as possible, though perhaps not probable. Allowances are made for normal spoilage, waste, and machine breakdowns. Variances tend to be unfavorable, but managers accept the standards as being reasonable but tough goals.

The major reasons for using currently attainable standards are:

1. The resulting standard costs serve multiple purposes. For example, the same cost may be used for cash budgeting, inventory valuation, and budgeting departmental performance. In contrast, perfection standards cannot be used per se for cash budgeting because financial planning will be inaccurate.[1]
2. They have a desirable motivational impact on employees. The standard represents reasonable future performance, not fanciful ideal goals or antiquated goals geared to past performance.

☐ Focus on Both Inputs and Outputs

To see how the analysis of variances can be pursued more fully, reconsider the direct material and direct labor in Exhibit 7–5 (p. 194). We continue our illustration and assume that the following actually occurred:

Direct material: 36,810 pounds of inputs were purchased and used at an actual unit price of 58¢ for a total actual cost of $21,350.

Direct labor: 15,000 hours of inputs were used at an actual hourly price (rate) of $4.10, for a total actual cost of $61,500.

These additional data enable us to subdivide the flexible-budget variances into separate price and efficiency variances:

	ACTUAL COSTS INCURRED	FLEXIBLE BUDGET	FLEXIBLE-BUDGET VARIANCE	PRICE VARIANCE*	EFFICIENCY VARIANCE*
Direct material	$21,350	$21,000	$ 350 U	$ 736 F	$1,086 U
Direct labor	61,500	56,000	5,500 U	1,500 U	4,000 U

* Computations to be explained shortly.

The flexible-budget totals for direct material and direct labor are the amounts that would have been spent with normal efficiency. They are sometimes expressed as total *standard costs allowed*, computed as follows:

$$\text{units of good output} \times \text{input allowed per unit of output} \times \text{standard unit price of input} = \text{total standard cost allowed}$$

Direct material: 7,000 units × 5 pounds × $.60 per pound = $21,000
Direct labor: 7,000 units × 2 hours × $4.00 per hour = $56,000

Before reading on, note particularly that the flexible budget amounts (that is, the standard costs allowed) are tied to an initial question, What

---

[1] If you use perfection standards rather than currently attainable standards, the amount budgeted for financial (cash) planning purposes must differ from the standard. Otherwise, projected income and cash disbursements will be forecasted incorrectly. In such cases, perfection standards may be used for compiling performance reports, but "expected variances" are stipulated in the master budget for financial planning. For example, if unusually strict labor standards are used, the standard cost per finished unit may be $8 despite the fact that top management anticipates an unfavorable performance variance of $.40 per unit. In the master budget, the total labor costs would be $8.40 per unit: $8 plus an expected variance of $.40.

was the *output* achieved? Always first ask yourself, What was the good output? Then proceed with your computations of the total standard cost allowed for the good output achieved.

☐ Price and Efficiency Variances

Two commonly encountered variances are:

Price variance—the difference between actual unit prices and budgeted unit prices multiplied by the actual quantity of goods or services purchased. It is often called a **rate variance** when referring to labor.

Efficiency variance—the difference between the quantity of actual inputs (such as pounds of materials or number of direct-labor-hours) and the quantity of inputs that *should have been used* for the actual output achieved (such as finished goods) multiplied by the budgeted unit price. It is also called a **quantity variance** or **usage variance**.

Where feasible, you should separate the items that are subject to the manager's direct influence from those that are not. This aids performance assessment. **The general approach is to separate** *price* **factors from** *efficiency* **factors. Price factors are less subject to immediate control than are efficiency factors, principally because of external forces, such as general economic conditions and unforeseeable price changes.** Even when price factors are regarded as being outside of company control, isolating them helps to focus on the efficient usage of the goods or services in question.

☐ Price and Efficiency Variance Computations

Consider the detailed computations of price and efficiency variances. The objective of these variance calculations is to hold either price or efficiency constant so that the effect of the other can be isolated. **When calculating the price variance, you hold efficiency constant at the** *actual level of efficiency*; **when calculating the efficiency variance, you hold price constant at the** *standard price*.

Price variance: The difference between actual and standard unit prices of inputs *multiplied by the actual quantity of inputs*:

$$\text{price variance} = \begin{array}{c} \text{difference in} \\ \text{unit price} \\ \text{of inputs} \end{array} \times \begin{array}{c} \text{actual} \\ \text{inputs} \\ \text{purchased} \end{array}$$

For direct material:

$$= (\$.58 - \$.60) \times 36{,}810 \text{ pounds}$$
$$= \$736 \text{ F}$$

For direct labor:

$$= (\$4.10 - \$4.00) \times 15{,}000 \text{ hours}$$
$$= \$1{,}500 \text{ U}$$

Efficiency variance: For any given level of output (e.g., units produced), the efficiency variance is the difference between the inputs that should have been used and the inputs that were actually used—holding unit input prices constant at the standard unit price:[2]

$$\text{efficiency variance} = \begin{pmatrix} \text{inputs} \\ \text{actually} \\ \text{used} \end{pmatrix} - \begin{pmatrix} \text{inputs that} \\ \text{should have} \\ \text{been used} \end{pmatrix} \times \begin{pmatrix} \text{standard} \\ \text{unit price} \\ \text{of inputs} \end{pmatrix}$$

$$= \begin{pmatrix} \text{actual} \\ \text{pounds or} \\ \text{hours used} \end{pmatrix} - \begin{pmatrix} \text{standard} \\ \text{allowed pounds} \\ \text{or hours for} \\ \text{good output} \end{pmatrix} \times \begin{pmatrix} \text{standard} \\ \text{unit price} \\ \text{of inputs} \end{pmatrix}$$

For direct materials:

$$= [36{,}810 - (7{,}000 \text{ units} \times 5 \text{ pounds})] \times \$.60$$
$$= (36{,}810 - 35{,}000) \times \$.60$$
$$= 1{,}810 \times \$.60$$
$$= \$1{,}086 \text{ U}$$

For direct labor:

$$= [15{,}000 - (7{,}000 \text{ units} \times 2 \text{ hours})] \times \$4.00$$
$$= (15{,}000 - 14{,}000) \times \$4.00$$
$$= 1{,}000 \times \$4.00$$
$$= \$4{,}000 \text{ U}$$

☐ Meaning of the Variances

To determine whether a variance is favorable or unfavorable, use logic rather than memorizing a formula. A price variance is *favorable* if the actual price is less than the standard; an efficiency variance is favorable if the actual quantity used is less than the standard amount allowed. The opposite relationships imply *unfavorable* variances.

Variances do not, by themselves, show why the budgeted operating income was not achieved. But they raise questions, provide clues, and direct attention. For instance, one possible explanation, among many, for this set of variances is that a manager might have made a trade-off and lost—that is, the manager might have purchased, at a favorable price, some materials that were slightly substandard, saving $736. Excessive waste may have offset this savings, as indicated by the $1,086 U material efficiency variance. The waste also may have caused at least part of the excess use of labor. Evidently, the direct-labor efficiency variance warrants further investigation because it is easily the largest variance of all.

☐ Effects of Inventories

Analysis of the Dominion Company was simplified by two main factors: (1) there were no finished-goods inventories—any units produced were sold in

---

[2] Expressed algebraically, these variances are $V_p = (AP - SP) \times AQ$ and $V_e = (AQ - SQ) \times SP$, where V_p = price variance, V_e = efficiency variance, AP = actual unit price of inputs, SP = standard unit price of inputs, AQ = actual quantity of inputs, and SQ = standard quantity of inputs allowed for good output.

the same period—and (2) there was no raw-material inventory—the materials were purchased and used in the same period.

What if production does not equal sales? The sales volume variance then is the difference between the master budget and the flexible budget *for the number of units sold*. In contrast, the flexible-budget variances compare actual costs to the flexible budget for the *number of units produced*. Chapter 15 provides details about the effects of inventories in a standard cost system.

What if the quantity of raw materials purchased differs from the quantity used? Generally, managers want quick feedback. They want variances to be pinpointed as early as practical. In the case of direct material prices, that point is when the materials are purchased rather than when they are used, often much later. Therefore, the material price variance is usually based on the quantity purchased and the material efficiency variance on the quantity used. For instance, if the purchasing manager for Dominion Company had bought 40,000 pounds at $.58 per pound in June, the material price variance would be (actual price − standard price) × pounds *purchased* = ($.58 − $.60) × 40,000 = $800 F. The material efficiency variance would remain at $1,086 U because it is based on the pounds used.

A General Approach

Exhibit 7–6 presents the foregoing analysis in a format that deserves close study. The general approach is at the top of the exhibit; the specific applications then follow. Even though the exhibit may seem unnecessarily complex at first, its repeated use will solidify your understanding of variance analysis. Of course, the other budget variances in Exhibit 7–5 could be further analyzed in the same manner in which direct material and direct labor are analyzed in Exhibit 7–6. The pursuit of such a detailed investigation depends on the manager's perception as to whether the extra benefits will exceed the extra cost of such detective work.

Graphical Approach

A graphical approach sometimes clarifies the relationships. For example, the direct-labor analysis in the middle of Exhibit 7–6 is also portrayed in Exhibit 7–7. The cost function is linear, sloping upward at a standard rate (price) of $4 per hour.

Note that volume is expressed in hours instead of in physical units of product. This is a common practice. Most departments have a variety of products; when the variety of units is added together, the result is frequently a nonsensical sum. Therefore, all units of output are expressed in terms of the standard inputs of hours allowed for their production. Hours thus become the common denominator for measuring total volume. Production, instead of being expressed as, say, 12,000 chairs and 3,000 tables, is frequently expressed as 14,000 *standard hours allowed* (or *standard hours worked,* or *standard hours earned,* or most accurately as *standard hours of input allowed for outputs achieved*). Remember that standard hours *allowed* is a measure of *actual output* achieved.

EXHIBIT 7–6   *(Place a clip on this page for easy reference.)*

General Approach to Analysis of Direct-material and Direct-labor Variances

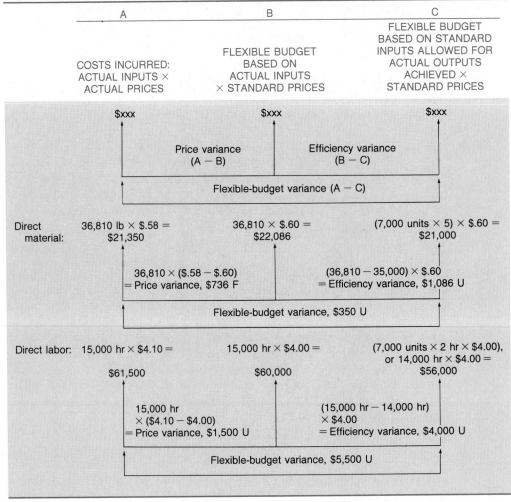

A	B	C
		FLEXIBLE BUDGET BASED ON STANDARD INPUTS ALLOWED FOR ACTUAL OUTPUTS ACHIEVED × STANDARD PRICES
COSTS INCURRED: ACTUAL INPUTS × ACTUAL PRICES	FLEXIBLE BUDGET BASED ON ACTUAL INPUTS × STANDARD PRICES	

$xxx $xxx $xxx

Price variance
(A − B)

Efficiency variance
(B − C)

Flexible-budget variance (A − C)

Direct material:

36,810 lb × $.58 =
$21,350

36,810 × $.60 =
$22,086

(7,000 units × 5) × $.60 =
$21,000

36,810 × ($.58 − $.60)
= Price variance, $736 F

(36,810 − 35,000) × $.60
= Efficiency variance, $1,086 U

Flexible-budget variance, $350 U

Direct labor:

15,000 hr × $4.10 =

$61,500

15,000 hr × $4.00 =

$60,000

(7,000 units × 2 hr × $4.00),
or 14,000 hr × $4.00 =
$56,000

15,000 hr
× ($4.10 − $4.00)
= Price variance, $1,500 U

(15,000 hr − 14,000 hr)
× $4.00
= Efficiency variance, $4,000 U

Flexible-budget variance, $5,500 U

U = Unfavorable.
F = Favorable.

Another key idea illustrated in Exhibits 7–6 and 7–7 is the versatility of the flexible budget. A flexible budget is geared to volume, and Exhibit 7–7 shows that volume can be measured in terms of either *actual inputs* or *actual outputs achieved*. Both measures are shown on the *x* axis of the graph; they are necessary to obtain separate identification of price and efficiency variances.

When used in this book, unless stated otherwise, the term *flexible-budget variance* will mean the difference between columns A and C in Exhibit 7–6, the difference between actual costs and the flexible budget based on the standard inputs allowed for actual outputs achieved.

EXHIBIT 7–7

Graphical Analysis of Direct Labor

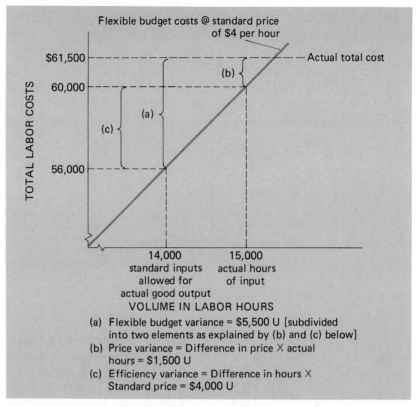

Flexible budget costs @ standard price of $4 per hour

Actual total cost

TOTAL LABOR COSTS

$61,500

60,000

(b)

(a)

(c)

56,000

14,000
standard inputs
allowed for
actual good output

15,000
actual hours
of input

VOLUME IN LABOR HOURS

(a) Flexible budget variance = $5,500 U [subdivided into two elements as explained by (b) and (c) below]
(b) Price variance = Difference in price × actual hours = $1,500 U
(c) Efficiency variance = Difference in hours × Standard price = $4,000 U

Please reread the preceding four paragraphs before going on. They contain key ideas and terms that warrant scrutiny.

☐ Overhead Variances

Direct-material and direct-labor variances are typically subdivided into price and efficiency components. In contrast, most organizations believe that it is too costly to monitor individual overhead items to the same extent. Therefore, overhead variances often are not subdivided beyond the flexible budget variances.[3]

In some cases it is worthwhile to subdivide the flexible budget variance for variable overhead. Suppose that variable overhead costs fluctuate in direct proportion to direct-labor hours. When actual direct-labor hours differ from the standard hours allowed for the output achieved, a related **variable overhead efficiency variance** will occur. Consider the miscellaneous supplies in Exhibit 7–5. The $.60 per unit cost is equivalent to $.30 per direct-labor

---

[3] Fixed overhead has some peculiarities that generate an additional variance in absorption costing systems. This matter is discussed in detail in Chapter 15, pages 481–489.

hour. Of the $500 U variance, $300 U is due to using 15,000 direct-labor-hours when only 14,000 were allowed:

$$
\begin{aligned}
\text{variable-overhead efficiency variance} = {} & \text{standard variable overhead rate per hour} \times \\
& \text{(actual direct-labor hours of inputs} \\
& - \text{standard direct-labor hours allowed)} \\
= {} & \$.30 \times (15{,}000 - 14{,}000) \\
= {} & \$300 \text{ unfavorable}
\end{aligned}
$$

This $300 excess use of supplies is attributable entirely to labor inefficiency. The other $200 is called a **variable overhead spending variance**. It measures control over both efficiency and price of the variable overhead items themselves:

Actual costs		$4,700
Efficiency variance: The amount that would be expected to be incurred *because of the inefficient use of direct labor*, 1,000 hr × $.30 =	$300	
Spending variance: The amount unexplained by the efficiency variance. It could arise from unit price changes for various supplies, but it could also arise simply from the general waste and sloppy use of these supplies, that is, inadequate control of the overhead itself, as distinguished from control of the related direct labor.	200	
Flexible budget variance		500
Budgeted amount in flexible budget		$4,200

The flexible-budget variances for fixed overhead items are not subdivided here. Fixed overhead variances are discussed in more detail in Chapter 15. Note that the sales volume variance for fixed overhead is zero. Why? Because the fixed overhead budget is the same at both planned and actual levels of activity.

Exhibit 7–8 summarizes overhead variances. Like other variances, the overhead variances by themselves cannot identify causes for results that differ from the budget. The *only* way to discover why overhead performance did not agree with the budget is to investigate possible causes, line item by line item. However, the distinction between spending and efficiency provides a springboard for a more rigorous analysis.

CONTROLLABILITY AND VARIANCES

☐ **Responsibility for Material Variances**

In most companies, the *acquisition* of materials or merchandise entails different control decisions than their *use*. The purchasing executive of a manufacturing company worries about getting raw materials at favorable prices, whereas the production executive concentrates on using them efficiently. The merchandise manager of a large grocery company will be responsible for skillful buying of foodstuffs, but the store manager will be responsible for their sale and for minimizing losses from spoilage, shoplifting, and the like. Thus the responsibility for price variances usually rests with the purchasing officer, and the

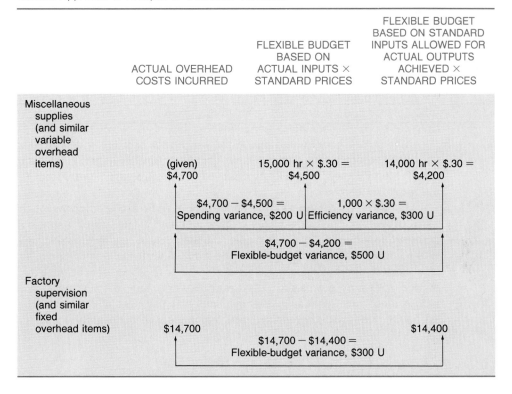

	ACTUAL OVERHEAD COSTS INCURRED	FLEXIBLE BUDGET BASED ON ACTUAL INPUTS × STANDARD PRICES	FLEXIBLE BUDGET BASED ON STANDARD INPUTS ALLOWED FOR ACTUAL OUTPUTS ACHIEVED × STANDARD PRICES
Miscellaneous supplies (and similar variable overhead items)	(given) $4,700	15,000 hr × $.30 = $4,500	14,000 hr × $.30 = $4,200

$4,700 − $4,500 = Spending variance, $200 U | 1,000 × $.30 = Efficiency variance, $300 U

$4,700 − $4,200 = Flexible-budget variance, $500 U

| Factory supervision (and similar fixed overhead items) | $14,700 | | $14,400 |

$14,700 − $14,400 = Flexible-budget variance, $300 U

responsibility for efficiency variances usually rests with the production manager or sales manager.

Price variances are often regarded as measures of forecasting ability rather than of failure to buy at specified prices. Some control over the price variance is obtainable by getting many quotations, buying in economical lots, taking advantage of cash discounts, and selecting the most economical means of delivery. Price variances may lead to decisions to change suppliers or freight carriers.

However, failure to meet price standards may result from a sudden rush of sales orders or from unanticipated changes in production schedules, which in turn may require the purchasing officer to buy at uneconomical prices or to request delivery by air freight. In such cases, the responsibility may rest with the sales manager or the head of production scheduling rather than with the purchasing officer.

The general approach to analyzing efficiency variances is probably best exemplified by the control of direct materials in standard cost systems. The budget of the production department manager is usually based on a *standard formula* or a Standard Bill of Materials. This specifies the physical quantities allowed for producing a given number of acceptable finished units. These quantities are then compared with the quantities actually used.

What does the manager do with the variances? The manager seeks explanations for their existence. Common causes of efficiency variances include improper handling, inferior quality of material, poor workmanship, changes in methods, new workers, slow machines, broken cutting tools, and faulty blueprints.

☐ Responsibility for Labor Variances

In most companies, because of union contracts or other predictable factors, labor prices can be foreseen with much greater accuracy than can prices of materials. Therefore, labor price variances tend to be relatively insignificant.

Labor, unlike material and supplies, cannot ordinarily be stored for later use. The acquisition and use of labor occur simultaneously. For these reasons, labor rate variances are usually charged to the same manager who is responsible for labor usage.

Labor price variances may be traceable to faulty predictions of the labor rates. However, the more likely causes include (1) the use of a single average standard labor price for a given operation that is, in fact, performed by individuals earning slightly different rates because of seniority and (2) the assignment of a worker earning, perhaps, $9 per hour to a given operation that should be performed by a less-skilled worker earning, say, $7 per hour. If labor is paid a piece rate, that is, a specified amount per unit of output, rather than an hourly rate, no labor price (rate) variance will ordinarily occur.

☐ Trade-offs Among Variances

Variance analysis can be useful for focusing on how various aspects of operations are meeting expectations. However, a standard cost system should not be a straitjacket that prevents the manager from aiming at the overall organization objectives. Too often, each unfavorable variance is regarded as, ipso facto, bad, and each favorable variance is regarded as, ipso facto, good.

Managers sometimes deliberately acquire off-standard material at unusually low prices. They predict that the favorable price variances will exceed any resulting unfavorable efficiency variances caused by heavy spoilage or unusual labor-hours. Thus, if the manager guesses correctly, the decision was favorable despite the unfavorable label pinned on the efficiency variances. Because there are so many interdependencies among activities, an "unfavorable" or a "favorable" label should not lead the manager to jump to conclusions. By themselves, such labels merely raise questions and provide clues. They are attention directors, not answer givers.

☐ When to Investigate Variances

When should variances be investigated? Frequently the answer is based on subjective judgments, hunches, guesses, and rules of thumb. The most troublesome aspect of feedback is in deciding when a variance is significant enough to warrant management's attention. For some items, a small deviation may prompt follow-up. For other items, a minimum dollar amount or 5%, 10%, or 25% deviations from budget may be necessary before investigations commence. Of course, a 4% variance in a $1 million material cost may deserve more attention than a 20% variance in a $10,000 repair cost. Therefore, rules such as "Investigate all variances exceeding $5,000 or 25% of standard cost, whichever is lower," are common.

Variance analysis is subject to the same cost-benefit test as other phases of an information system. The trouble with the foregoing rules of thumb is that they are too frequently based on subjective assessments, guesses, or hunches. The field of statistics offers tools to help reduce these subjective features. These tools help answer the cost-benefit question, and they help to separate variances caused by random events from variances that are controllable. A manager investigates only those situations for which the expected cost savings from correcting a process is greater than the cost of investigating.

Accounting systems have traditionally implied that a standard is a single acceptable measure. Practically, the accountant (and everybody else) realizes that the standard is a band or range of possible acceptable outcomes. Consequently, the accountant expects variances to fluctuate randomly within some normal limits. A random variance, by definition, calls for no corrective action to an existing process. In short, random variances are attributable to chance rather than to management's implementation decisions. The more a cost randomly fluctuates, the larger the variance required to make investigation worthwhile.

SUMMARY

Management is best aided by carefully prepared standards and budgets representing what should be accomplished. These standards should be based on material specifications and on work measurement rather than on past performance, because the latter too often conceals past inefficiencies.

Currently attainable standards are the most widely used because they usually have the most desirable motivational impact and because they may be used for a variety of accounting purposes, including financial planning, as well as for monitoring department performance.

When standards are currently attainable, there is no logical difference between standards and budgets. A standard is a unit concept, whereas a budget is a total concept. In a sense, the standard is the budget for one unit.

Flexible budgets are geared to changing levels of activity rather than to a single static level. They may be tailored to a particular level of sales or production volume—before or after the fact. They tell how much cost should be or should have been incurred for any level of output, which is usually expressed either in product units of output or in standard direct-labor-hours allowed for that output.

The evaluation of performance is aided by feedback that compares actual results with budgeted expectations, as summarized in Exhibit 7–4. The flexible-budget idea helps managers to get an explanation of why the master budget was not achieved. Variances are often divided into sales volume and flexible-budget variances. Direct-material and direct-labor variances can be further subdivided into price and efficiency variances and variable overhead into spending and efficiency variances.

Chapter 15, which may be studied now if desired, probes the analysis of variances in more depth, particularly with respect to fixed overhead and inventories.

SUMMARY PROBLEM FOR YOUR REVIEW

(Problem One appeared earlier in this chapter.)

☐ Problem Two

The following questions are based on the data contained in the illustration used in the chapter, page 198:

1. Suppose the following were the actual results for the production of 8,500 units:
   (a) Direct material: 46,000 pounds of inputs were purchased and used at an actual unit price of 55¢, for a total actual cost of $25,300.
   (b) Direct labor: 16,500 hours of inputs were used at an actual hourly price (rate) of $4.20, for a total actual cost of $69,300.
   Compute the flexible-budget variance and the price and efficiency variances for direct material and direct labor. Present your answers in the form shown in Exhibit 7–6, page 202.
2. Suppose the company is organized so that the purchasing manager bears the primary responsibility for the acquisition prices of materials, and the production manager bears the primary responsibility for efficient use of materials but no responsibility for unit prices. Assume the same facts as in Requirement 1 except that the purchasing manager acquired 60,000 pounds of materials. This means that there is an ending inventory of 14,000 pounds. Would your variance analysis of materials in Requirement 1 change? Why? Show computations to support your answer.

☐ Solution to Problem Two

1. The variances are:

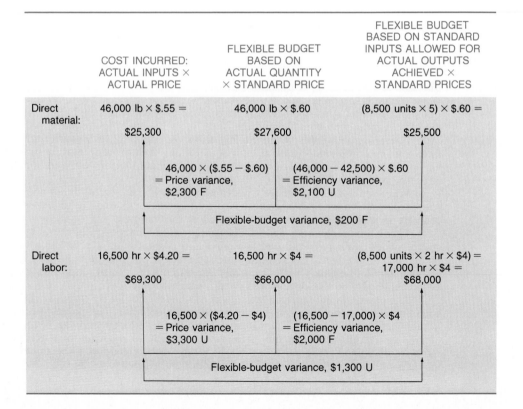

2. Price variances for materials are isolated at the most logical control point—time of purchase rather than time of use. In turn, the production or operating departments that later use the materials are always charged at some predetermined so-called budget or standard unit price, never at actual unit prices. Under this procedure the price-variance analysis would be conducted in the purchasing department and the efficiency-variance analysis in the production department. This represents a slight modification of the approach in Requirement 1 as follows:

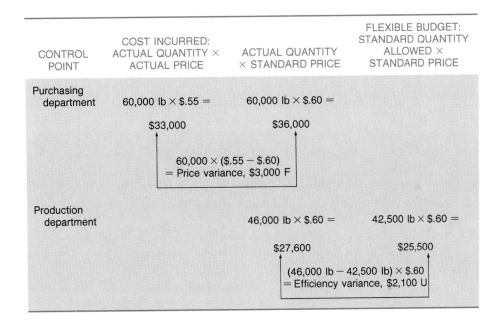

CONTROL POINT	COST INCURRED: ACTUAL QUANTITY × ACTUAL PRICE	ACTUAL QUANTITY × STANDARD PRICE	FLEXIBLE BUDGET: STANDARD QUANTITY ALLOWED × STANDARD PRICE
Purchasing department	60,000 lb × $.55 = $33,000	60,000 lb × $.60 = $36,000	
	60,000 × ($.55 − $.60) = Price variance, $3,000 F		
Production department		46,000 lb × $.60 = $27,600	42,500 lb × $.60 = $25,500
		(46,000 lb − 42,500 lb) × $.60 = Efficiency variance, $2,100 U	

Note that the efficiency variance is the same in Requirements 1 and 2. However, the flexible-budget variance would not now be the algebraic sum of the price and efficiency variances because here the price variance is computed by using the actual quantity *purchased* instead of the actual quantity *used*.

HIGHLIGHTS TO REMEMBER

1. There is a similarity in approach to the control of direct material and direct labor. The price variance is the difference in price multiplied by actual quantity. The efficiency variance is the difference in quantity multiplied by standard price.

2. The master budget variances can be subdivided as follows:

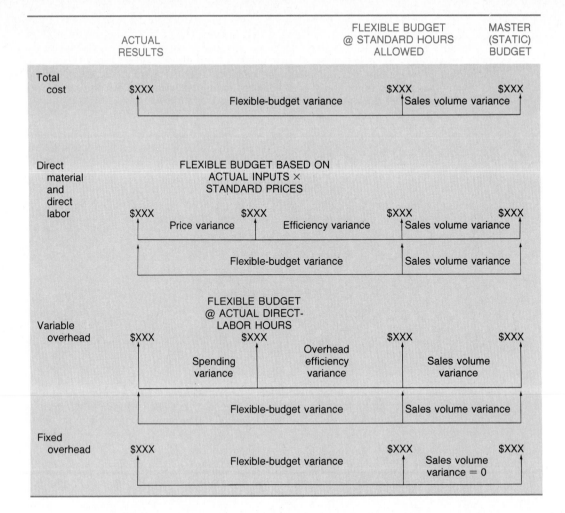

3. Price variances for materials are usually based on the quantity of materials *purchased* rather than on the quantity used as inputs to production.

4. Price variances help managers to gauge the impact of price fluctuations on actual results. Moreover, price variances permit the exclusion of price effects from all *other* variances.

5. The first question to ask in solving standard-cost problems is, "What was the good output achieved?" The second question often asked is, "What were the standard direct-labor-hours allowed for the good output achieved?"

ACCOUNTING VOCABULARY

Budget Variance *p. 188*   Currently Attainable Standards *197*   Efficiency Variance *199*   Favorable Cost Variance *188*   Flexible Budget *189*   Flexible-budget Variances *192*   Price Variance *199*   Quantity Variance *199*   Rate Variance *199*   Sales Volume Variance *191*   Standard Cost *196*   Static Budget *187*   Unfavorable Cost Variance *188*   Usage Variance *199*   Variable Budget *189*   Variable Overhead Efficiency Variance *203*   Variable Overhead Spending Variance *204*.

APPENDIX 7: MUTUAL PRICE AND EFFICIENCY EFFECTS

The usual breakdown of variances into price and efficiency is not theoretically perfect because there may be a small mutual price-usage effect. A production manager and a purchasing agent might argue over the following situation. The standard direct material to produce 1,000 good finished units is 1,000 pounds @ $1. The performance report shows the use of 1,150 pounds @ $1.20 to produce 1,000 good finished units.

The ordinary analysis of variances would appear as follows:

Actual quantity × Actual price, or 1,150 × $1.20 =		$1,380
Price variance = Difference in price ×		
Actual pounds = ($1.20 − $1) × 1,150 =	$230 U	
Efficiency variance = Difference in quantity ×		
Standard price = (1,150 − 1,000) × $1 =	150 U	
Total variance explained		380 U
Standard quantity of inputs allowed for units		
produced × Standard price = 1,000 × $1 =		$1,000

The small area in the upper right-hand corner of the graphic analysis (Exhibit 7–9)

EXHIBIT 7–9

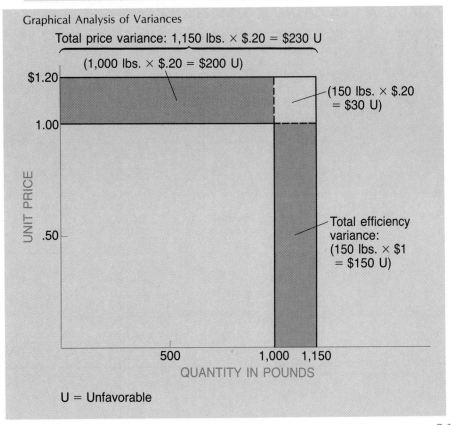

Graphical Analysis of Variances

Total price variance: 1,150 lbs. × $.20 = $230 U

(1,000 lbs. × $.20 = $200 U)

(150 lbs. × $.20 = $30 U)

Total efficiency variance: (150 lbs. × $1 = $150 U)

UNIT PRICE

QUANTITY IN POUNDS

U = Unfavorable

211

is the area of possible controversy. The purchasing officer might readily accept responsibility for the price variance on the 1,000 pounds in the standard allowance but might also claim that the extra $30 buried in the $230 total variance is more properly attributable to the production manager. After all, if the production manager had produced in accordance with the standard, the extra 150 pounds would not have been needed. But this distinction is not often made, simply because it usually involves a small sum. However, we should be aware that the conventional variance analysis arbitrarily assigns the joint price-efficiency variance ($30 in this case) as a part of an overall price variance.

In practice, the efficiency variance is considered more important than the price variance because the manager can exert more direct influence over the efficiency variance. Consequently, the performance report on efficiency should minimize the possibility of the production manager's criticisms of any accounting or measurement methods. The joint price-efficiency variance is less likely to cause arguments if it is assigned to the total price variance than if it is buried in the efficiency variance.

ASSIGNMENT MATERIAL

Special note: Problem 7–1 covers topics in Part One of the chapter; 7–2 covers Part Two. Similarly, Problems 7–20 through 7–30 relate to Part One; 7–31 through 7–46 relate to Part Two. Problem 7–48 is a review and is accompanied by answers. Problem 7–44 covers most of the major points in the chapter.

FUNDAMENTAL ASSIGNMENT MATERIAL

7–1. **FLEXIBLE AND STATIC BUDGETS.** (Alternates are 7–25, 7–26, and 7–27.) The early and middle 1980s were difficult for Redwood Timber Company. Demand for lumber varied widely year to year and even month to month. The company had traditionally used a quarterly master budget based on detailed analyses of the market and expected costs. Managers compared actual quarterly results to the budget. For example, the condensed performance report for the Timberlands Division for a recent quarter was:

	BUDGET	ACTUAL	VARIANCE
Net revenue	$9,000,000	$7,500,000	$1,500,000 U
Variable costs:			
Salaries and wages	$4,140,000	$3,740,000	$ 400,000 F
Transportation	900,000	790,000	110,000 F
Repairs and maintenance	720,000	670,000	50,000 F
Supplies and miscellaneous	1,080,000	1,050,000	30,000 F
Total variable costs	$6,840,000	$6,250,000	$ 590,000 F
Fixed costs:			
Depreciation	$1,200,000	$1,200,000	$ 0
Supervisory salaries	400,000	380,000	20,000 F
Administrative support	200,000	210,000	10,000 U
Other fixed costs	50,000	50,000	0
Total fixed costs	$1,850,000	$1,840,000	$ 10,000 F
Total costs	$8,690,000	$8,090,000	$ 600,000 F
Operating income (loss)	$ 310,000	$ (590,000)	$ 900,000 U

U = Unfavorable.
F = Favorable.

The executives were concerned about their budget system. Control of costs was critical, and they did not think the variances produced by their system gave much information about cost control.

The Timberlands Division manager explained that his profit was $900,000 below budget, but if it were not for his cost control, profits would have been $600,000 more below budget. His superior, the vice-president of operations, was skeptical. She remarked, "I know it is important to compare our actual results to the budget. And I see your $600,000 favorable variance on costs. But I understand our operations well enough to know that you did not save $600,000 through superior cost control."

Required:
1. Prepare a columnar flexible budget for the Timberlands Division at revenue levels of $8,000,000, $9,000,000, and $10,000,000. Use the format of the last three columns of Exhibit 7–2, page 190. Assume that the prices and mix of products sold are equal to the budgeted prices and mix.
2. Express the flexible budget in formula form.
3. Prepare a condensed table showing the master (static) budget variance, the sales volume variance, and the flexible budget variance. Use the format of Exhibit 7–4, page 192.

7–2. **DIRECT-MATERIAL AND DIRECT-LABOR VARIANCES.** The Suquamish Company manufactures glassware that is hand-shaped and hand-painted. The following standards were developed for a luxury line of vases:

	STANDARD INPUTS ALLOWED FOR EACH UNIT OF OUTPUT ACHIEVED	STANDARD PRICE PER UNIT OF INPUT
Direct materials	.75 lb	$ 4.00 per lb
Direct labor	.5 hr	20.00 per hr

During April, 20,000 vases were scheduled for production. However, 22,000 were actually produced.

Direct materials used amounted to 17,800 pounds at a unit price of $3.50 per pound. Direct labor actually was paid $21.00 per hour, and 11,900 hours were used.

Required:
1. Compute the standard cost per vase for direct materials and direct labor.
2. Compute the price variances and efficiency variances for direct materials and direct labor.
3. Based on these sketchy data, what clues for investigation are provided by the variances?

ADDITIONAL ASSIGNMENT MATERIAL

7–3. "The flex in the flexible budget relates solely to variable costs." Do you agree? Explain.

7–4. "We want a flexible budget because costs are hard to predict. We need the flexibility to change budgeted costs as input prices change." Does a flexible budget serve this purpose? Explain.

7–5. Why are standard hours superior to actual hours as an index of activity?

7–6. "A standard is a band or range of acceptable outcomes." Criticize.

7–7. "Direct material and direct labor may be included in a flexible budget." Do you agree? Explain.

7–8. Why should a budgeted cost not be merely an extension of past experience?

7-9. Distinguish between perfection and currently attainable standards.

7-10. What is the difference between a standard amount and a budget amount?

7-11. "Price variances should be computed even if prices are regarded as being outside of company control." Do you agree? Explain.

7-12. "Failure to meet price standards is the responsibility of the purchasing officer." Do you agree? Explain.

7-13. Why do labor price variances tend to be insignificant?

7-14. What are the key questions in the analysis and follow-up of variances?

7-15. What are some common causes of efficiency variances?

7-16. Why is the joint price-efficiency variance buried in the price variance rather than in the efficiency variance?

7-17. Why do the techniques for controlling overhead differ from those for controlling direct material and direct labor?

7-18. How does the variable-overhead spending variance differ from the direct-labor price variance?

7-19. What are expected variances?

7-20. NATIONAL PARK SERVICE. The National Park Service prepared the following budget for one of its national parks for 19X4:

Revenue from fees	$4,000,000
Variable costs (miscellaneous)	400,000
Contribution margin	$3,600,000
Fixed costs (miscellaneous)	3,600,000
Operating income	$ 0

The fees were based on an average of 50,000 vehicle-admission days (vehicles multiplied by number of days in parks) per week for the 20-week season, multiplied by average entry and other fees of $4 per vehicle-admission day.

The season was booming for the first four weeks. However, there was a wave of thievery and violence during the fifth week. Grizzly bears killed four campers during the sixth week and two during the seventh week. As a result, the number of visitors to the park dropped sharply during the remainder of the season.

Total revenue fell by $1 million. Moreover, extra rangers and police had to be hired at a cost of $200,000. The latter was regarded as a fixed cost.

Required:

Prepare a columnar summary of performance, showing the original (master) budget, sales volume variances, flexible budget, flexible-budget variances, actual results, and master budget variances.

7-21. FLEXIBLE BUDGET. Sukova Toy Company made 75,000 stuffed animals in 19X7. The total manufacturing costs of $170,000 included $50,000 of fixed costs. Assume that no price changes will occur in the following year and that no changes in production methods are applicable. Compute the budgeted cost for producing 80,000 stuffed animals in 19X8.

7-22. BASIC FLEXIBLE BUDGET. The superintendent of police of the city of Santa Clara is attempting to predict the costs of operating a fleet of police cars. Among the items of concern are fuel, 15¢ per mile, and depreciation per car per year, $4,000.

Required:

The manager is preparing a flexible budget for the coming year. Prepare the flexible-budget amounts for fuel and depreciation for ten cars at a level of 30,000, 40,000, and 50,000 miles.

7–23. FLEXIBLE BUDGET. Consider the following data for a given month:

	BUDGET FORMULA PER UNIT	VARIOUS LEVELS OF VOLUME		
Units	—	4,000	5,000	6,000
Sales	?	$?	$?	$120,000
Variable costs:				
Direct material	?	48,000	?	?
Fuel	?	?	5,000	?
Fixed costs:				
Depreciation		?	12,000	?
Executive salaries		?	?	50,000

Required:
1. Fill in the unknowns.
2. Draw a freehand graph of the flexible budget for the cost items shown here.

7–24. BASIC FLEXIBLE BUDGET. The president of Cabrillo Fabricating was delighted at the results for April. The cost of direct materials was only $55,000 compared to $60,000 in the master budget. All direct materials purchased in April were used that same month. Direct labor was only $23,500, whereas $25,000 was budgeted.

Cabrillo had just started a policy that paid managers a bonus of 10% of any cost savings in their departments. Before the president authorized a check for $650 (that is, 10% of the total favorable variance of $6,500), he asked the controller to verify the savings.

Required:
Prepare a report to the president indicating whether the performance justifies the bonus. Output in April was 8,500 pounds. Budgeted direct-material and direct-labor costs per pound of output were $6.00 and $2.50, respectively.

7–25. SUMMARY PERFORMANCE REPORT. (Alternates are 7–1, 7–26, and 7–27.) Consider the following data for Mohawk Escrow Company:

(1) Master budget data: sales, 2,000 clients at $30 each; variable costs, $20 per client; fixed costs, $15,000.
(2) Actual results at actual prices: sales, 2,400 clients at $31 per client; variable costs, $52,500; fixed costs, $15,500.

Required:
1. Prepare a summary performance report similar to Exhibit 7–4, page 192.
2. Fill in the blanks:

Master budget operating income		$ —
Variances:		
Sales volume variances	$ —	
Flexible-budget variances	—	—
Actual operating income		$ —

7–26. SUMMARY EXPLANATION. (Alternates are 7–1, 7–25, and 7–27.) Consider the following data. Except for physical units, all quantities are in dollars:

	ACTUAL RESULTS AT ACTUAL PRICES	FLEXIBLE-BUDGET VARIANCES	FLEXIBLE BUDGET	SALES VOLUME VARIANCES	MASTER (STATIC) BUDGET	MASTER (STATIC) BUDGET VARIANCES
Physical units	100,000	—	?	?	90,000	?
Sales	?	?	?	?	900,000	108,000 F
Variable costs	620,000	?	600,000	?	?	?
Contribution margin	?	?	?	?	?	?
Fixed costs	?	?	?	?	260,000	10,000 U
Operating income	?	?	?	?	?	?

Required:

1. Fill in the unknowns.
2. Give a brief summary explanation of why the original target operating income was not attained.

7–27. **EXPLANATION OF VARIANCE IN INCOME.** (Alternates are 7–1, 7–25, and 7–26.) Everyday Legal Services (ELS) was founded by John Jefferson after the legal profession removed its ban on advertising. The firm seeks to provide brief legal consultation on a variety of topics at a reasonable price. Offices are now open in 21 major cities. The staff is a mix of attorneys and para-professionals. The average client requires one-half hour of time and is billed $50 for the service. Attorneys are paid a percentage of the revenue generated, whereas para-professionals are on a straight salary. Standard contribution margins averaged 40% of billed sales.

The ELS master budget for 19X8 had predicted volume of 600,000 clients, but only 500,000 were served. Fixed costs were $6 million, which exceeded the budget by $800,000, primarily because of an extra advertising campaign. There were no variances from the average selling prices, but attorneys handled a higher percentage of clients than planned, causing a flexible-budget variance for variable costs of $750,000 unfavorable.

John Jefferson was disappointed when he learned that operating income for 19X8 was less than half of the $6.8 million budgeted. He said, "I knew that profit would be lower than expected. After all, I authorized the extra advertising. I also realize that volume is down a little. But why is operating income *so much* below budget?"

Required:

1. Explain why the budgeted operating income was not attained. Use a presentation similar to Exhibit 7–4, page 192. Enough data have been given to permit you to construct the complete exhibit by filling in the known items and then computing the unknown.
2. Complete your explanation by summarizing what happened, using no more than three sentences.

7–28. **SUMMARY OF RAILROAD PERFORMANCE.** Consider the following performance of a division of the Amtrack railroad system during 19X4 (in thousands of dollars):

	ACTUAL RESULTS AT ACTUAL PRICES	MASTER BUDGET	VARIANCE
Revenue	?	150,000	?
Variable expenses	100,000	97,500*	2,500 U
Contribution margin	?	52,500	?
Fixed expenses	38,500	37,500	1,000 U
Operating income	?	15,000	?

* Includes diesel fuel of $45,000.

The master budget had been based on budgeted revenue per passenger-mile of 10¢. A passenger-mile is one paying passenger traveling 1 mile. An average rate decrease of 8% had helped generate an increase in volume. Actual passenger-miles were 10% in excess of the master budget for the year.

The price per gallon of diesel fuel fell below the price used to formulate the master budget. The average price decline for the year was 10%.

Required:

1. As an explanation for the president, prepare a summary performance report that is similar to Exhibit 7–4, page 192.
2. Assume that the use of fuel was at the same level of efficiency as predicted in the master budget. What portion of the flexible-budget variance for variable expenses is attributable to diesel fuel expenses? Explain.

7–29. **FLEXIBLE AND STATIC BUDGETS.** The Alpha sorority recently held a dinner dance. The original (static) budget and actual results were as follows:

	BUDGET	ACTUAL	VARIANCE
Attendees	100	126	
Revenue	$3,500	$4,340	$840 F
Chicken dinners @ $15.51	1,551	1,970	419 U
Beverages:			
Wine, $2 per person	200	368	168 U
Cocktails, $6 per person	600	507	93 F
Tax and service charge @ 24%	192	210	18 U
Club rental, $150 plus 7.9% tax	162	162	0
Music, 4 hours @ $250 per hour	1,000	1,250	250 U
Profit (loss)	$ (205)	$ (127)	$ 78 F

Required:

1. Subdivide each variance into a sales volume variance portion and a flexible-budget variance portion. Use the format of Exhibit 7–4, page 192.
2. Provide possible explanations for the variances.

7–30. **UNIVERSITY FLEXIBLE BUDGETING.** (CMA, adapted.) The University of Boyne offers an extensive continuing education program in many cities throughout the state. For the convenience of its faculty and administrative staff and also to save costs, the university operates a motor pool. The motor pool operated with 20 vehicles until February of this year, when an additional automobile was acquired. The motor pool furnishes gasoline, oil, and other supplies for the cars and hires one mechanic who does routine maintenance and minor repairs. Major repairs are done at a nearby commercial garage. A supervisor manages the operations.

Each year the supervisor prepares an operating budget, informing university management of the funds needed to operate the pool. Depreciation on the automobiles is recorded in the budget in order to determine the costs per mile.

The schedule below presents the annual budget approved by the university. The actual costs for March are compared with one-twelfth of the annual budget.

UNIVERSITY MOTOR POOL
Budget Report
For March 19X6

	ANNUAL BUDGET	ONE-MONTH BUDGET	MARCH ACTUAL	OVER (UNDER)
Gasoline	$ 72,000	$ 6,000	$ 9,100	$3,100
Oil, minor repairs, parts,				
and supplies	3,600	300	380	80
Outside repairs	2,700	225	50	(175)
Insurance	6,000	500	525	25
Salaries and benefits	30,000	2,500	2,500	—
Depreciation	26,400	2,200	2,310	110
	$140,700	$11,725	$14,865	$3,140
Total miles	600,000	50,000	63,000	
Cost per mile	$ .2345	$ .2345	$ .2360	
Number of automobiles	20	20	21	

The annual budget was based on the following assumptions:
a. 20 automobiles in the pool
b. 30,000 miles per year per automobile
c. 15 miles per gallon per automobile
d. $1.80 per gallon of gas
e. $.006 per mile for oil, minor repairs, parts, and supplies
f. $135 per automobile in outside repairs
   The supervisor is unhappy with the monthly report comparing budget and actual costs for March; he claims it presents his performance unfairly. His previous employer used flexible budgeting to compare actual costs with budgeted amounts.

Required:
1. Employing flexible-budgeting techniques, prepare a report that shows budgeted amounts, actual costs, and monthly variances for March.
2. Explain briefly the basis of your budget figure for outside repairs.

7–31. MATERIAL AND LABOR VARIANCES. Consider the following data:

	DIRECT MATERIAL	DIRECT LABOR
Costs incurred: actual inputs × actual		
prices incurred	$100,000	$70,000
Actual inputs × standard prices	112,000	72,000
Standard inputs allowed for actual		
outputs achieved × standard prices	115,000	61,000

Required:
Compute the price, efficiency, and flexible-budget variances for direct material and direct labor. Use U or F to indicate whether the variances are unfavorable or favorable.

7–32. MATERIAL AND LABOR VARIANCES. Consider the following data:

	DIRECT MATERIAL	DIRECT LABOR
Actual price per unit of input (pounds and hours)	$14	$ 9
Standard price per unit of input	$12	$10
Standard inputs allowed per unit of output	5	2
Actual units of input	48,000	23,000
Actual units of output (product)	10,000	10,000

1. Compute the price, efficiency, and flexible-budget variances for direct material and direct labor. Use U or F to indicate whether the variances are unfavorable or favorable.
2. Prepare a plausible explanation for the performance.

7–33. **EFFICIENCY VARIANCES.** Assume that 10,000 units of a particular item were produced. Suppose the standard direct-material allowance is 3 pounds per unit, at a cost per pound of $3. Actually, 31,000 pounds of materials (input) were used to produce the 10,000 units (output).

Similarly, assume that it is supposed to take four direct-labor-hours to produce one unit and that the standard hourly labor cost is $8. But 41,000 hours (input) were used to produce the 10,000 units in this Hong Kong factory.

Compute the efficiency variances for direct material and direct labor.

7–34. **STRAIGHTFORWARD VARIANCE ANALYSIS.** The Ramirez Company uses a standard cost system. The month's data regarding its single product follow:

(1) Material purchased and used, 6,700 pounds.
(2) Direct-labor costs incurred, 9,000 hours, $34,200.
(3) Variable overhead costs incurred, $9,500.
(4) Finished units produced, 2,000.
(5) Actual material cost, $.95 per pound.
(6) Variable overhead rate, $.90 per hour.
(7) Standard direct-labor cost, $4 per hour.
(8) Standard material cost, $1 per pound.
(9) Standard pounds of material in a finished unit, 3.
(10) Standard direct-labor hours per finished unit, 5.

Prepare schedules of all variances, using the format of Exhibit 7–6, page 202.

7–35. **STANDARD MATERIAL ALLOWANCES.** (CMA.) Danson Company is a chemical manufacturer that supplies industrial users. The company plans to introduce a new chemical solution and needs to develop a standard product cost for this new solution.

The new chemical solution is made by combining a chemical compound (nyclyn) and a solution (salex), boiling the mixture, adding a second compound (protet), and bottling the resulting solution in 10-liter containers. The initial mix, which is 10 liters in volume, consists of 12 kilograms of nyclyn and 9.6 liters of salex. A 20% reduction in volume occurs during the boiling process. The solution is then cooled slightly before 5 kilograms of protet are added; the addition of protet does not affect the total liquid volume.

The purchase prices of the raw materials used in the manufacture of this new chemical solution are as follows:

Nyclyn	$1.30 per kilogram
Salex	1.80 per liter
Protet	2.40 per kilogram

Determine the standard quantity for each of the raw materials needed to produce a 10-liter container of Danson Company's new chemical solution and the standard materials cost of a 10-liter container of the new product.

7–36. **DIRECT-MATERIAL VARIANCES.** The Gamma Company uses a special fabric in the production of jackets. During August Gamma purchased 9,000 square yards of the fabric @ $7.40 per yard and used 7,500 square yards in the production of 3,600 jackets. The standard allows 2 yards @ $7.50 per yard for each jacket.

Calculate the material price variance and the material efficiency variance.

7–37. SIMILARITY OF DIRECT-LABOR AND VARIABLE-OVERHEAD VARIANCES. The Y. K. Li Company has had great difficulty controlling costs in Singapore during the past three years. Last month a standard cost and flexible-budget system was installed. A condensation of results for a department follows:

	EXPECTED BEHAVIOR PER STANDARD DIRECT-LABOR-HOUR	FLEXIBLE BUDGET VARIANCE
Lubricants	$. 30	$200 F
Other supplies	.20	150 U
Rework	.40	300 U
Other indirect labor	.50	300 U
Total variable overhead	$1.40	$550 U

F = Favorable.
U = Unfavorable

The department had initially planned to manufacture 6,000 units in 4,000 standard direct-labor-hours allowed. However, material shortage and a heat wave resulted in the production of 5,400 units in 3,800 actual direct-labor-hours. The standard wage rate is $3.50 per hour, which was 20¢ higher than the actual average hourly rate.

Required:
1. Prepare a detailed performance report with two major sections: direct labor and variable overhead.
2. Prepare a summary analysis of price and efficiency variances for direct labor and spending and efficiency variances for variable overhead, using the format of Exhibit 7–6, page 202.
3. Explain the similarities and differences between the direct-labor and variable-overhead variances. What are some of the likely causes of the overhead variances?

7–38. GRAPHICAL ANALYSIS OF DIRECT LABOR. An air-conditioning service company uses "mechanics" to rebuild and maintain equipment. It has developed flexible budgets and standards for much of its work. The partially completed graph at the top of page 221 displays a recent month's performance of direct labor regarding the jobs subject to these standards.

The standard inputs allowed for the actual output achieved were 70,000 hours. The mechanics have a strong union. They earn $30 per hour. Apprentices earn less, and they do some of the same work as the mechanics; thus the average standard price per hour is $25. Because a higher than usual proportion of apprentices worked last month, the actual amounts paid were $23 per hour for a total of 80,000 hours of input, or $1,840,000.

Required:
1. Compute the price and efficiency variances for direct labor.
2. Complete and fully label the graph. Enter and identify the flexible-budget variance, the price variance, and the efficiency variance.

7–39. VARIANCE ANALYSIS. The Zurich Company uses standard costs and a flexible budget. The purchasing agent is responsible for material price variances, and the production manager is responsible for all other variances. Operating data for the past week are summarized as follows:

GRAPH FOR PROBLEM 7–38

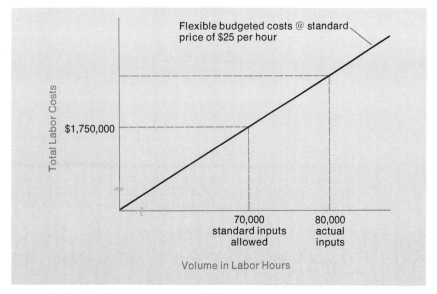

Flexible budgeted costs @ standard price of $25 per hour

Total Labor Costs

$1,750,000

70,000
standard inputs
allowed

80,000
actual
inputs

Volume in Labor Hours

(1) Finished units produced: 5,000.
(2) Direct material: Purchases, 10,000 pounds @ 15 Swiss francs (SF) per pound; standard price is 16 SF per pound. Used, 5,400 pounds. Standard allowed per unit produced, 1 pound.
(3) Direct labor: Actual costs, 8,000 hours @ 30.5 SF, or 244,000 SF. Standard allowed per good unit produced, 1½ hours. Standard price per direct-labor-hour, 30 SF.
(4) Variable manufacturing overhead: Actual costs, 88,000 SF. Budget formula is 10 SF per standard direct-labor-hour.

Required:
1. **a.** Material purchase-price variance.
   b. Material efficiency variance.
   c. Direct-labor price variance.
   d. Direct-labor efficiency variance.
   e. Variable manufacturing-overhead spending variance.
   f. Variable manufacturing-overhead efficiency variance.
   Hint: For a format, see Requirement 2 of the solution to the second Summary Problem for Your Review, page 209.

2. **a.** What is the budget allowance for direct labor?
   b. Would it be any different if production were 6,000 good units?

7–40. **Multiple Choice.**   (CPA.)

(1) Information on Westcott Company's direct-labor costs is as follows:

Standard direct-labor rate	$3.75
Actual direct-labor rate	$3.50
Standard direct-labor-hours	10,000
Direct-labor usage (efficiency) variance, unfavorable	$4,200

What were the actual hours worked, rounded to the nearest hour? (a) 10,714, (b) 11,120 (c) 11,200, (d) 11,914.
(2) Information on Kennedy Company's direct-material costs is as follows:

Standard unit price	$3.60
Actual quantity purchased	1,600
Standard quantity allowed for actual production	1,450
Materials purchase price variance, favorable	$ 240

What was the actual purchase price per unit, rounded to the nearest penny? (a) $3.06, (b) $3.11, (c) $3.45, (d) $3.75.

7–41. LABOR VARIANCES. The city of Detroit has a sign shop where street signs of all kinds are manufactured and repaired. The manager of the shop uses standards to judge performance. However, because a clerk mistakenly discarded some labor records, the manager has only partial data for October. She knows that the total direct-labor variance was $880, favorable, and that the standard labor price was $6 per hour. Moreover, a recent pay raise produced an unfavorable labor price variance for October of $.20 per hour. The standard hours allowed for the output achieved were 1,800.

Required:

1. Find the actual labor price per hour, actual total labor cost, and actual labor-hours.
2. Determine the price and efficiency variances.

7–42. VARIABLE-OVERHEAD VARIANCES. You have been asked to prepare an analysis of the overhead costs in the billing department of a health clinic for 19X6. As an initial step, you prepare a summary of some events that bear on overhead for the year. The variable-overhead flexible budget variance was $4,000, unfavorable. The standard variable-overhead cost per billing was 5¢. Ten bills per hour is regarded as standard productivity per clerk. The total overhead incurred was $168,500, of which $110,000 was fixed. There were no variances for fixed overhead. A total of 1,090,000 bills were processed in 121,000 hours.

Required:

Find the following:

1. Standard hours allowed for output achieved
2. Variable-overhead efficiency variance
3. Variable-overhead spending variance

7–43. MATERIAL AND LABOR VARIANCES. Consider the following data:

	DIRECT MATERIAL	DIRECT LABOR
a. Actual price per unit of input (pounds and hours)	$ 9	?
b. Standard price per unit of input	$10	$12
c. Standard inputs per unit of output	4	?
d. Actual units of input	?	?
e. Actual units of output (product)	?	?
f. Actual inputs × actual prices	?	?
g. Actual inputs × standard prices	?	$114,000
h. Standard inputs allowed for actual output achieved × standard prices	$200,000	?
i. price variance	$ 23,000 F	?
j. Efficiency variance	?	$ 6,000 F
k. Flexible-budget variance	$ 7,000 U	$ 1,250 F

Required:

1. Solve for the unknowns. (You may be helped by following the format in Exhibit 7–6, page 202.)
2. Prepare a plausible explanation for the performance.

7–44. REVIEW OF MATERIAL AND LABOR VARIANCES. The following questions are based on the data contained in the illustration used in the chapter, page 188:

1. Suppose actual production and sales were 8,000 units instead of 7,000 units.
   (a) Compute the sales volume variance. Is the performance of the marketing function the sole explanation for this variance? Why?
   (b) Using a flexible budget, compute the budgeted contribution margin, the budgeted operating income, budgeted direct material, and budgeted direct labor.
2. Suppose the following were the actual results for the production of 8,000 units:
   (a) Direct material: 42,000 pounds were used at an actual unit price of 57¢, for a total actual cost of $23,940.
   (b) Direct labor: 16,400 hours were used at an actual hourly rate of $4.10, for a total actual cost of $67,240.
   (c) Compute the flexible-budget variance and the price and efficiency variances for direct materials and direct labor. Present your answers in the form shown in Exhibit 7–6, page 202.
3. Suppose the company is organized so that the purchasing manager bears the primary responsibility for the acquisition prices of materials, and the production manager bears the primary responsibility for efficiency but no responsibility for unit prices. Assume the same facts as in Requirement 2, except that the purchasing manager acquired 60,000 pounds of materials. This means that there is an ending inventory of 18,000 pounds. Would your variance analysis of materials in Requirement 2 change? Why? Show computations.

7–45. COMBINED OR JOINT PRICE-QUANTITY VARIANCE AND INCENTIVES. Study the chapter appendix. The Howell Company had an incentive system that rewarded managers each Christmas for cost savings on materials. The manager of purchasing received 10% of any favorable price variance accumulated for the fiscal year ending November 30. Similarly, the production manager received 10% of the favorable efficiency (quantity) variances. In addition, each manager received 10% of the favorable net material variances. Note, however, that all variances were included in the computations—that is, an unfavorable variance in one month would offset a favorable variance in another month.

In the opinion of the company president, this system had worked reasonably well in past years. Of course, because of the sensitivity of the incentive system, the standards were carefully specified and adjusted each quarter. Only minimal inventories were kept at any time. Bonuses had varied from zero to 20% of the managers' base salaries. The purchasing manager's base salary for a recent fiscal year ending November 30 was $24,000; the production manager's was $30,000.

The operating results on material A for a recent month were:

Purchase price variance	$ 72,000 U
Efficiency variance	36,000 U
Net material variance	$108,000 U

Two pounds of material A was the standard quantity allowed for every unit of a particular finished product, a chemical used in petroleum refining. One hundred thousand units of the chemical had been manufactured. The average price actually paid for material A was 30¢ per pound in excess of the standard price.

Required: 1. What number of pounds of material A was purchased?
2. Find the standard price per pound of material A.

3. What is the total standard cost allowed for material components of the finished product?
4. As the purchasing manager, what is your opinion of the bonus system? Would your answer be the same if the actual raw-material price paid had been 70¢ per pound? Explain fully.
5. As the production manager, what is your opinion of the bonus system? Why?
6. Why does part of the bonus depend on the net material variance?
7. Assume that some bonus system tied to variance analysis is maintained. What changes would you recommend?

7–46. **HOSPITAL COSTS AND EXPLANATION OF VARIANCES.** A hospital emergency room uses a flexible budget based on patients seen as a measure of volume. An adequate staff of attending and on-call physicians must be maintained at all times, so physician scheduling is unaffected by volume. However, nurse scheduling varies as volume changes. A standard of .5 nurse-hours per patient visit was set. Average hourly pay for nurses is $12, ranging from $7 to $15 per hour. All materials are considered to be supplies, a part of overhead; there are no direct materials. A statistical study showed that the cost of supplies and other variable overhead is more closely associated with nurse hours than with patient visits. The standard for supplies and other variable overhead is $8 per nursing hour.

The head physician of the emergency room unit, Kathy Walkowski, is responsible for control of costs. During December the emergency room unit treated 3,750 patients. The budget and actual costs were as follows:

	BUDGET	ACTUAL	VARIANCE
Patient visits	3,200	3,750	550
Nursing hours	1,600	1,925	325
Nursing cost	$ 19,200	$ 25,025	$5,825
Supplies and other variable overhead	$ 12,800	$ 15,015	$2,215
Fixed costs	$ 78,000	$ 78,000	0
Total cost	$110,000	$118,040	$8,040

Required:
1. Calculate price and efficiency variances for nursing costs.
2. Calculate spending and efficiency variances for supplies and other variable overhead.
3. Dr. Walkowski has been asked to explain the variances to the Chief of Staff. Provide possible explanations.

7–47. **FLEXIBLE-BUDGET AND SALES-VOLUME VARIANCES.** R. J. Reynolds sold 10,450 million packages of cigarettes in 1982 and recognized revenue of $6,655 million. This yielded an operating income of $1,160 million. Reynolds's market share was 33.6% of the 31,100 million packages of cigarettes sold in 1982. During 1982 it was announced that the excise tax per pack of cigarettes would double from $.08 to $.16 beginning in 1983. Suppose R. J. Reynolds then predicted a 6.0% decline in unit sales volume for 1983, based on a similar predicted decline in overall sales of cigarettes. Assume that variable costs were 70% of total costs in 1982 and prices and costs for 1983 are expected to continue at the same level as in 1982. The excise tax is not included in either revenue or variable costs.

Required:
1. What were R. J. Reynolds's budgeted sales (in packages and dollars), fixed cost, variable cost, and operating income for 1983? Round answers to the nearest million dollars.

2. Now suppose actual sales were 9,400 million packs of cigarettes out of a market of 29,750 million packages in 1983. Revenue was $5,986 million and profit was $1,127 million. Prepare a report giving the master (static) budget variance, the sales-volume variance, and the flexible-budget variance.

7–48. REVIEW PROBLEM ON STANDARDS AND FLEXIBLE BUDGETS; ANSWERS ARE PROVIDED. The Singapore Company makes a variety of leather goods. It uses standard costs and a flexible budget to aid planning and control. Budgeted variable overhead at a 60,000-direct-labor-hour level is $36,000.

During April the company had an unfavorable variable-overhead efficiency variance of $1,200. Material purchases were $322,500. Actual direct-labor costs incurred were $187,600. The direct-labor efficiency variance was $6,000, unfavorable. The actual average wage rate was 20¢ lower than the average standard wage rate.

The company uses a variable-overhead rate of 20% of standard direct-labor *cost* for flexible-budgeting purposes. Actual variable overhead for the month was $41,000.

Required:

Compute the following amounts; then use U or F to indicate whether requested variances are unfavorable or favorable.

1. Standard direct-labor cost per hour.
2. Actual direct-labor-hours worked.
3. Total direct-labor price variance.
4. Total flexible budget for direct-labor costs.
5. Total direct-labor variance.
6. Variable-overhead spending variance in total.

Answers to Problem 7–48.

1. $3. The variable-overhead rate is $.60, obtained by dividing $36,000 by 60,000 hours. Therefore the direct-labor rate must be $.60 ÷ .20 = $3.
2. 67,000 hours. Actual costs, $187,600 ÷ ($3 − $.20) = 67,000 hours.
3. $13,400 F. 67,000 actual hours × $.20 = $13,400.
4. $195,000. Efficiency variance was $6,000, unfavorable. Therefore, excess hours must have been $6,000 ÷ $3 = 2,000. Consequently, standard hours allowed must be 67,000 − 2,000 = 65,000. Flexible budget = 65,000 × $3 = $195,000.
5. $7,400 F. $195,000 − $187,600 = $7,400 F; or $13,400 F − $6,000 U = $7,400 F.
6. $800 U. Flexible budget = 65,000 × $.60 = $39,000. Total variance = $41,000 − $39,000 = $2,000 U. Price variance = $2,000 − $1,200 efficiency variance = $800 U.

Chapter 8

VARIATIONS OF COST BEHAVIOR PATTERNS

LEARNING OBJECTIVES

When you have finished studying this chapter, you should be able to:

1. Distinguish between committed and discretionary fixed costs and between engineered and discretionary variable costs.
2. Use the engineered-cost approach to compute the flexible-budget cost and the budget variance for a given expense.
3. Describe the basic ideas of zero-base budgeting.
4. Identify the two major assumptions on which the determination of cost behavior patterns is usually based.
5. Identify each of the elements in the mathematical formula for a linear cost function.
6. Identify the two principal criteria for accepting and using a particular cost function.
7. Use the high-low method for estimating the fixed and variable elements of a mixed cost.
8. Interpret the results of a least-squares regression analysis, including the coefficient of determination.

When we refer to cost behavior patterns, we generally mean the relationship between costs and various factors that influence costs. Until this chapter, we have considered only one such factor, the volume of activity, and two basic linear cost behavior patterns, fixed and variable. Now we shall examine an additional factor, management discretion over costs, and expand our understanding of how the level of activity affects costs. Then we explore how to determine cost behavior patterns so that useful predictions and evaluations can be made.

MANAGEMENT DISCRETION OVER COSTS

The term "cost" can have many different modifiers to identify more precisely the type of cost. Fixed and variable costs can be further classified as follows:

FIXED COSTS	VARIABLE COSTS
Committed	Engineered
Discretionary	Discretionary

These classifications indicate that management policy, as well as activity level, can influence costs. We shall describe these costs, beginning with committed fixed costs.

☐ Fixed Costs and Capacity

Fixed costs, also called **capacity costs**, measure the cost of providing the capability to operate at a particular volume level for such activities as manufacturing, sales, administration, and research. Organizations incur such costs to provide the capability for sustaining a *planned* volume of activity, but the costs are unaffected by the *actual* activity level achieved.

The size of fixed costs is influenced by long-run marketing conditions, technology, and the methods and strategies of management. Examples of the latter include sales salaries versus sales commissions and one-shift versus two-shift operations. Examples of strategies include having lower variable costs in exchange for higher fixed costs. For instance, automatic equipment may be acquired by banks, post offices, or hospitals to reduce labor costs.

Generally, a heavier proportion of fixed to variable costs lessens management's ability to respond to short-run changes in economic conditions and opportunities. Still, unwillingness to incur fixed costs reveals an aversion to risk that may exclude a company from profitable ventures. For instance, the launching of new products often requires very large fixed costs for research, advertising, equipment, and working capital.

☐ Committed Fixed Costs

For planning and control, fixed costs may be usefully subdivided into committed and discretionary categories. **Committed fixed costs** consist largely of fixed costs arising from the possession of plant, equipment, and a basic organization. Examples are depreciation, property taxes, rent, insurance, and the salaries of key personnel. These costs are affected primarily by long-run sales forecasts that, in turn, indicate the long-run capacity needs.

The behavior of committed fixed costs can best be viewed by assuming a zero volume of activity in an enterprise that fully expects to resume normal activity (for example, during a strike or a shortage of materials that forces a complete shutdown of activity). The committed fixed costs are all those organization and plant costs that continue to be incurred and that cannot be reduced without injuring the organization's ability to meet long-range goals. Committed fixed costs are not only independent of volume changes; they cannot be affected much by month-to-month or even year-to-year management decisions.

In planning, the focus is on the impact of these costs over a number of years. Such planning usually requires tailoring the capacity to future demand for the organization's products in the most economical manner. For example, should the store size be 50,000 square feet, or 80,000, or 100,000? Should the gasoline station have one, or two, or more stalls for servicing automobiles? Such decisions usually involve selecting the point of optimal trade-off between present and future operating costs. That is, constructing excess capacity now may save costs in the long run because construction costs per square foot may be much higher if done piecemeal over the years. On the other hand, if the forecast demand never develops, the organization may have to bear the costs of owning idle facilities.

These decisions regarding capital expenditures are generally shown in the *capital budget* or *capital-spending budget*. As you will recall, the *master budget* is based primarily on the annual sales forecast, the cornerstone of budgeting. Similarly, all capital-spending decisions are ultimately based on long-range sales forecasts. Capital budgeting is discussed in Chapters 11 and 12.

Once buildings are constructed and equipment is installed, little can be done in day-to-day operations to affect the *total level* of committed costs. From a control standpoint, the objective is usually to increase current utilization of facilities because this will ordinarily increase net income.

There is another aspect to the control problem, however. A follow-up, or audit, is needed to find out how well the actual use of capacity compares to the use predicted when the facilities were acquired. Such a comparison helps management to evaluate the wisdom of its past long-range decisions and, in turn, should improve the quality of future decisions.

☐ Discretionary Fixed Costs

Discretionary fixed costs (sometimes called **managed** or **programmed costs**) are fixed costs (1) that arise from periodic (usually yearly) *budget appropriation* decisions that directly reflect top-management policies regarding the desired amounts to be incurred and (2) that do not have a demonstrable optimum relationship between inputs (as measured by the costs) and outputs (as measured by sales, services, or production). Discretionary costs may have no necessary relation to the current volume of activity. Examples vary among organizations and include child day care services, staging an opera, research and development, advertising, sales promotion, charitable donations, management consulting services, and many employee-training programs. Conceivably, such costs could be reduced almost entirely for a given year in dire times, whereas the committed costs could not.

Discretionary fixed costs are decided upon by management at the start of the budget period. Goals are selected, the means for their attainment are chosen, the desired expense to be incurred is specified, and the total amount to be spent is appropriated. For example, a state government may appropriate $5 million for an advertising campaign to encourage tourism. In the give-and-take process of preparing the master budget, the discretionary costs are the most likely to be revised.

Discretionary fixed costs represent an assortment of manufacturing, selling, administrative, and research items. For example, a large portion of discretionary fixed costs may consist of salaries for sales personnel, accountants, clerks, and engineers and often appear in the income statement lumped under the heading "General Selling and Administrative Expense." As in the case of committed costs, the resources acquired should be carefully planned and effectively used if net income is to be maximized. Unlike committed costs, discretionary costs can be influenced more easily from period to period. It is also harder to measure the utilization of resources acquired via discretionary costs, principally because the results of services such as creative personnel, advertising, research, and training programs are much more difficult to identify and quantify than are the results of using plants and equipment to make products.

The behavior of some discretionary fixed costs is easy to describe. Advertising, research, donations, and training programs, for example, are usually formulated with certain objectives in mind. The execution of such projects is measured by comparing total expenditures with the appropriation. Because the tendency is to spend the entire budget appropriation, the resulting dollar variances are generally trivial. But planning is far more important than this kind of day-to-day control. The perfect execution of an advertising program—in the sense that the full amount authorized was spent in specified media at predetermined times—will be fruitless if the advertisements are unimaginative and lifeless and if they reach the wrong audience.

The most noteworthy aspect of discretionary fixed costs is that, unlike most other costs, they are not subject to ordinary input-output analysis. For example, an optimum relationship between inputs and outputs can be specified for direct materials because it takes 3 pounds or 5 liters or 2 square feet to make a finished product. In contrast, we are usually unsure of the "correct" amount of advertising, research, management training, donations, management consulting costs, police protection, and programs for health care, education, or consumer protection.

The prominent Philadelphia retailer, John Wanamaker, supposedly said (quoted in *Wharton Magazine*): "Fifty percent of my advertising budget is wasted. I know that. My problem is I don't know which half is being wasted."

The U.S. Department of Education can quantify the inputs (for example, the amount spent on planning, research, and evaluation and on writing regulations), but the outputs and the relation between inputs and outputs are harder to quantify. Systems can be designed to ensure that the research and the regulations are concerned with the subjects deemed most important by the decision makers, but there is no convincing way of knowing how much is enough in any absolute sense.

☐ Engineered and Discretionary Variable Costs

An **engineered cost** is any cost that has an explicit, specified physical relationship with a selected measure of activity. Most variable costs fit this classification. An "engineered" variable cost exists when an optimal relationship between inputs and outputs has been carefully determined by work-measurement techniques, which are described shortly. For example, an automobile may have exact specifications: one battery, one radiator, two fan belts, and so forth. Direct material and direct labor are prime examples of engineered costs. You can easily measure the *efficiency* of engineered variable costs by looking at the inputs used and the outputs achieved.

Many managers and accountants use "variable cost" and "engineered cost" interchangeably, as if they were synonymous. Usually, this error is harmless. However, although most variable costs are engineered, some fit a discretionary classification. Such costs go up and down with sales (or production) merely because management has predetermined that the organization can afford to spend a certain percentage of the sales dollar for such items as research, donations, and advertising. Such discretionary costs would have a graphical pattern of variability, but not for the same reasons as direct materials or direct labor. An increase in these costs may be due only to management's authorization to spend "because we can afford it" rather than to an engineered cause-and-effect relationship between such costs and sales.

ENGINEERED VERSUS DISCRETIONARY COSTS

☐ Work Measurement for Control

Work measurement is the systematic analysis of a task, its size, the methods used in its performance, and its efficiency. Its objective is to determine the workload in an operation and the number of employees necessary to perform that work efficiently.

The work-measurement approach is based on a fundamental premise: permanent improvement in performance is impossible unless efficiency can be *measured*. To know whether an operation is efficient, we must quantify both inputs and outputs and compare their actual relationship to an optimal one.

□ Origins of Work Measurement

Work-measurement techniques were initially developed for planning and control of manufacturing rather than of nonmanufacturing activities. This occurred because inputs and outputs in the manufacturing areas are easier to identify and measure. The measurement of direct material used and finished units produced is straightforward. It is much more difficult to obtain a measurement for relating the inputs of advertising and sales promotion activities to the outputs of sales or contribution margins.

As the input-output relationships become less defined, management tends to abandon any formal work-measurement techniques and, instead, relies almost wholly on individuals and their supervisors for successful control. Consequently, the role of personal observation is paramount and formal cost control is approached from a discretionary-cost rather than from an engineered-cost (work-measurement) viewpoint, especially in many areas of nonmanufacturing. However, despite the difficulties of implementation, work measurement is getting more attention from nonmanufacturing organizations as they seek to improve their efficiency.

During the 1980s, many financial services organizations, such as banks and insurance companies, turned to work measurement. For example, American Express has conducted extensive work-measurement programs that increased productivity in replacing lost credit cards, issuing new cards, responding to inquiries, and performing other functions. For example, American Express now takes one week instead of four weeks to issue new credit cards.

Work measurement is used in nonprofit organizations as well as in the selling and administrative clerical areas of profit-seeking organizations. In fact, federal government agencies are heavy users of work measurement in such diverse areas as the auditing of income tax returns, the processing of social security checks, and the sorting of mail.

□ Control-Factor Units

The specific techniques used to measure the work include time and motion study, observation of a random sample of the work (work sampling), and the estimation, by a work-measurement analyst and a line supervisor, of the amount of time required for the work (time analysis).

The work accomplished (output) is often expressed in **control-factor units**, which are used in formulating the budget. Possible control-factor units in a payroll department include time cards processed, employee promotion notices handled, employment and termination notices prepared, and routine weekly and monthly reports completed. Each control-factor unit is timed and a level of optimal efficiency established. The estimated workload in each factor is then used to determine the required labor force and budgetary allowance.

Examples of other operations and appropriate control-factor units include:

OPERATION	UNIT OF MEASURE (CONTROL-FACTOR UNIT)
Billing	Lines per hour
Warehouse labor	Pounds or cases handled per day
Packing	Pieces packed per hour
Posting accounts receivable	Postings per hour
Mailing	Pieces mailed per hour
Clearing of checks	Checks processed per hour

Control-factor units aid control. Based on work measurement, standards are set for activities. For example, Pan American World Airways set the following standards:

1. Answering reservations: pick up 85% of all calls within 20 seconds.
2. Checking passengers in: process 85% of the passengers within 5 minutes.
3. Handling baggage: deliver the last bag stowed in the belly of a large airplane within 35 minutes.

Actual work accomplished can be compared to these standards.

☐ **The Engineered-Cost Approach**

There is much disagreement about how clerical costs should be controlled. Advocates of work measurement favor a more rigorous approach, which essentially regards these costs as engineered. In practice, a discretionary-fixed-cost approach is more often found.

Assume that 10 payroll clerks are employed by a government agency and that each clerk's operating efficiency *should be* the processing of the payroll records of 500 employees per month. This might be called the *perfection standard* for the work. In the month of June, the payroll records of 4,700 individuals were processed by these 10 clerks. Each clerk earns $1,800 per month.

The engineered-cost approach to this situation is to base the budget formula on the unit cost of the individual pay record processed: $1,800 ÷ 500 records, or $3.60. Therefore the budget allowance for payroll-clerk labor would be $3.60 × 4,700, or $16,920. Assume that the 10 employees worked throughout the month. The following performance report would be prepared (*U* means unfavorable):

	ACTUAL COST (10 × $1,800)	FLEXIBLE BUDGET: TOTAL STANDARD INPUTS ALLOWED FOR ACTUAL OUTPUT PRODUCED (4,700 × $3.60)	BUDGET VARIANCE
Payroll-clerk labor	$18,000	$16,920	$1,080 U

The engineered-cost approach generates a budget variance that assumes a comparison of actual costs with the perfection standard—the cost that would be incurred if payroll-clerk labor could be turned on and off like a faucet. In this case, the variance of $1,080 informs management that there was over-staffing. The workload capability was 5,000 pay records, not the 4,700 actually processed. The extra cost of $1,080 resulted from operating in a way that does not attain the lowest possible cost. The $1,080 might also be considered as the amount that management is currently investing to provide stability in the work force.

Critics of work measurement often assert that such a formal approach is not worth its cost because strong labor unions and other forces prevent managers from fine-tuning the size of the work force. Defenders of work mea-surement will respond that managers must know the costs of various labor policies. For instance, if the cost of overstaffing becomes exorbitant, the perti-nent provisions in a labor contract may become key bargaining issues when the contract is about to be renewed. In recent years, airlines have provided numerous illustrations of this bargaining.

□ The Discretionary-Fixed-Cost Approach

Work-measurement techniques are not used in the vast majority of organiza-tions. Consequently, they rely on the experience of the department head and his or her superior for judging the size of the work force needed to carry out the department's functions. There is a genuine reluctance to overhire. Why? Because discharging or laying off people when volume slackens is diffi-cult. As a result, temporary peak loads are often met by hiring temporary workers or by having the regular employees work overtime.

In most cases, the relevant range of activity during the budget period can be predicted with assurance, and the work force needed for the marketing and administrative functions can readily be determined. These costs are discre-tionary—that is, their total amount is relatively fixed and unresponsive to short-run variations in volume.

The practical effects of the discretionary-fixed-cost approach are that the budgeted costs and the actual costs tend to be very close, so that resulting budget variances are small. In our example, a performance report would show a zero variance. Why? Because the budget of $18,000 would equal the actual cost incurred. Follow-ups to see that the available resources are being fully and efficiently used are regarded as the managers' responsibility, a duty that can be carried through by face-to-face control and by records of physical quanti-ties (for example, pounds handled per day in a warehouse, pieces mailed per hour in a mailing room) that do not have to be formally integrated into the accounting records in dollar terms.

Hence there is a conflict between common practice and the objective of work measurement, which is to treat most costs as engineered and to there-fore subject them to short-range management control. The moral is that man-agement's attitudes and its planning and controlling decisions often determine whether a cost is discretionary fixed or engineered variable. A change in policy can transform a budgeted fixed cost into a budgeted variable cost, and vice versa.

BUDGETING OF DISCRETIONARY FIXED COSTS

☐ Negotiated Static Budgets

The most popular ways of controlling discretionary fixed costs are personal observation and negotiated static budgets. Salaries are the major component of most budgets for discretionary costs. Because of the difficulties of identifying a convincing relationship between inputs and outputs, most organizations rely heavily on appropriate hiring and supervision to control a department's discretionary costs. That is, personal observation by supervisors is a key to ensuring that human resources are used appropriately.

Managers and their superiors tend to negotiate an appropriate lump sum that forms the static budget for discretionary costs. By definition, the "appropriate" amounts of discretionary costs are difficult to establish. Hence tradition, rules of thumb, industry custom, and formulas often determine the final budget figures. For example, the forthcoming year's research budget might be a lump sum of 2% of last year's sales.

Negotiated static budgets can be subclassified as incremental and zero-base. Each will be discussed in sequence.

☐ Incremental Budgets

Ordinary incremental budgets are by far the most popular. The budget is based on the previous period's budget and actual results. The budget amount is then changed in accordance with expectations for the next period. For example, a budget for a research department might be increased because of increases in salaries or additions of new personnel for a new project, or both.

Priority incremental budgets are similar to ordinary incremental budgets; however, they require managers to specify the activities that would be added or deleted if the budgetary appropriation were increased or decreased by, say, 10%. This procedure is an inexpensive way of forcing managers to indicate some key priorities. Superior managers can then evaluate the stated priorities before approving the final budget.

☐ Zero-Base Budgeting

Zero-base budgeting (ZBB) is an elaborate, time-consuming practice of having managers justify all their activities and costs as if they were being undertaken for the first time. Zero-base budgeting gets at fundamental questions by requiring managers to document the following steps:

1. Determine goals, operations, and costs of all activities under the manager's jurisdiction.
2. Explore alternative means of conducting each activity. (This is a desirable attribute of any budgeting system for discretionary costs.)
3. Evaluate budgetary implications of increasing or decreasing the level of each activity.
4. Establish measures of workload and performance.
5. Rank all activities in order of their importance to the organization.

Zero-base budgeting is successfully used in many nonprofit organizations. Why? Because most costs in many nonprofit organizations are discretionary. Zero-base budgeting forces managers to define the output of various programs of expenditures and relate inputs to the output.

Zero-base budgeting became fashionable after President Jimmy Carter installed the practice for all federal government agencies. Although ZBB yields benefits, it requires much time and effort. It has lost some popularity as a yearly endeavor, but its basic ideas are probably worth applying sequentially through various departments every five years or so. Meanwhile, priority incremental budgeting warrants annual use.

DETERMINING HOW COSTS BEHAVE

☐ **Major Assumptions**

Before costs can be classified and appropriately controlled, managers must be familiar with how the costs in question behave. As we know, costs often do not fit snugly into strictly variable and strictly fixed categories. Instead, there are a variety of **cost behavior patterns**, more technically described as *cost functions*. A **cost function** is a relationship between a cost and one or more variables. The dependent variable is frequently denoted as y (for example, some measure of total cost of repairs), and the independent variable as x (for example, some measure of related activity or volume of inputs or outputs). The problem facing the accountant or manager is frequently called **cost estimation** or **cost approximation**, which is the attempt to specify some underlying relation between x and y over a stipulated *relevant range* of x that may be of interest. That is, given the value of the independent variable x (e.g., total miles driven), what is the value of the dependent variable y (e.g., total repair costs)?

In practice, such cost approximations are typically based on two major simplifying and often heroic assumptions:

1. The cost behavior can be sufficiently explained by only a single independent variable (miles driven) instead of a combination of several independent variables (miles driven, weather, weight carried, model year of the vehicle, and so forth).
2. The cost function is linear over the relevant range.

☐ Focus on Costs and Benefits

As this book has stressed, whether these simplifying assumptions are justified is a cost-benefit question to be answered on a situation-by-situation basis. Managers rely on rough approximations of costs until a finer estimation method promises additional benefits (through better decisions) that exceed the cost of using the method.

Given assumptions of a single independent variable and linearity, each item of cost has some underlying behavior pattern, whose expected value, $E(y)$, has the form

$$E(y) = A + Bx$$

where A and B are parameters representing total fixed cost and variable cost per unit, respectively. (A **parameter** is a constant, such as A, or a coefficient, such as B, in a model or system of equations.)

A and B are generally unknown, and the cost analyst develops approximations to them for each item of cost. We call these approximations a and b, respectively. They are used to calculate predicted or estimated cost, y', for any given level of volume, x:

$$y' = a + bx$$

The predicted cost, y', might differ from the actual cost, y, for three reasons: (1) y is not perfectly determined by its linear relation to x, (2) a and b are only *approximations* of A and B, and (3) random, unpredictable factors affect cost.

☐ Variety of Cost Functions

To illustrate the major types of cost functions, we now examine graphic solutions to the basic cost-approximation formula: $y' = a + bx$.

A *proportionately variable cost* is the classical variable cost that was introduced in Chapter 2. Its total fluctuates in direct proportion to changes in x:

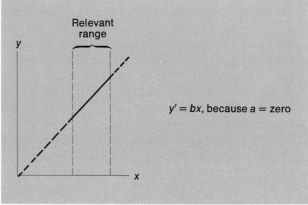

A *fixed cost* does not fluctuate in total as x changes within the relevant range:

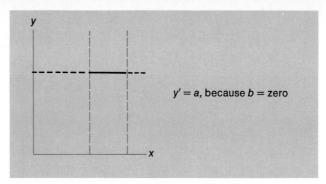

$y' = a$, because b = zero

A **mixed cost** or *semivariable cost* is a combination of variable and fixed elements. That is, its total fluctuates as x changes within the relevant range, but not in direct proportion. Instead, its behavior accords with the basic formula:

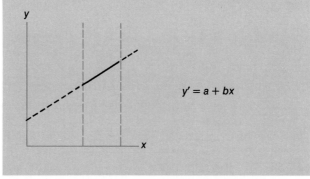

$y' = a + bx$

A *step-function cost* is nonlinear. Costs change abruptly at intervals of activity because the acquisition of resources comes in indivisible chunks:

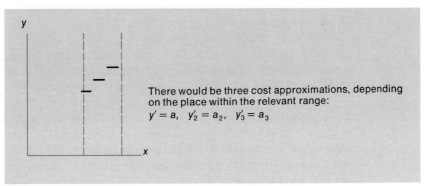

There would be three cost approximations, depending on the place within the relevant range:
$y' = a, \quad y'_2 = a_2, \quad y'_3 = a_3$

☐ Mixed Costs

Exhibit 8–1 gives a closer look at a mixed cost. The fixed portion is usually the result of *providing* the capability to operate at a particular capacity, whereas the variable portion is the result of *using* the available capacity. For example, a copy-making machine often has a fixed monthly rental plus a variable cost based on the copies produced. Other examples include costs of rented trucks, power, telephone, repairs and maintenance, clerks, accountants, and janitors.

EXHIBIT 8–1

Mixed Cost

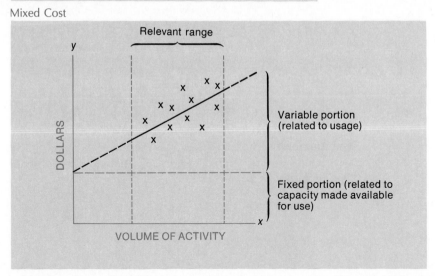

Ideally, there should be no accounts for mixed costs. All such costs should be subdivided into two accounts, one for the variable portion and one for the fixed portion. In practice, these distinctions are rarely made in the recording process because of the difficulty of separating day-to-day costs into variable and fixed components. Costs such as power, indirect labor, repairs, and maintenance are generally accounted for in total. It is typically very difficult to decide, as such costs are incurred, whether a particular invoice or time record represents a variable or fixed item. Moreover, even if it were possible to make such distinctions, the advantages might not be worth the additional clerical effort and costs.

In sum, mixed costs are merely a blend of two unlike cost behavior patterns; they do not entail new conceptual approaches. Anybody who obtains a working knowledge of the planning and controlling of variable and fixed costs, separately, can adapt to a mixed-cost situation when necessary.

In practice, where a report is divided into only two main cost classifications, variable and fixed, mixed costs tend to be included in the variable category even though they may not have purely variable behavior. At first glance, such arbitrary classification may seem undesirable and misleading. However, within a particular organization, the users of the reports usually have an intimate knowledge of the fundamental characteristics of the cost in question. Therefore they can temper their interpretation accordingly.

☐ Budgeting Mixed Costs

How should mixed costs be budgeted? Sometimes it is relatively easy to separate the cost into its fixed and variable elements. For example, the rental for a leased computer or photocopy machine may be subdivided:

| Photocopying costs, variable @ 3¢ per copy | XXXX |
| Photocopying costs, fixed @ $200 per month | XXXX |

Alternatively, a flexible budget may be prepared that contains a single-line item:

| Photocopying costs ($200 per month plus 3¢ per copy) | XXXX | XXXX | XXXX |

Other mixed costs are harder to analyze. For example, how do repairs and maintenance, indirect factory labor, clerical labor, and miscellaneous overhead relate to decisions concerning changes in general volume of work in the form of more sales, more inquiries, more telephone calls, more letters, and so forth? The relationships are often hazy and difficult to pinpoint in any systematic way. Still, decision makers want to know how these costs are affected by volume so that they can weigh their operating alternatives more intelligently.

APPROXIMATING A COST FUNCTION

☐ Criteria for Choosing Functions

To determine a cost function you must approximate the slope coefficient (defined as the amount of increase in y for each unit increase in x) and the constant or intercept (defined as the value of y when x is zero). The cost function is based on some plausible theory that supports the relationship between the dependent variable, y, and the independent variable, x—not on sample observations alone. Many variables tend to move together and are therefore referred to as being highly correlated. But no conclusions about causes and effects are warranted. For instance, studies have shown a high positive correlation between sunspot activity and stock market averages, but no cause-and-effect relationship has been demonstrated.

Two overriding criteria are important in obtaining accurate approximations of cost functions:

1. *Economic plausibility*. The relationship must be credible. Personal observation, when it is possible, probably provides the best evidence of a relationship. The engineered-cost approach described earlier is an example of heavy reliance on observed technical relationships between inputs and outputs.
2. *Goodness of fit*. The relationship must fit past data. A cost analyst compares cost function estimates to actual past data for reassurance that the cost function is plausible. Goodness-of-fit tests, which are briefly described later, may be limited to scatter diagrams or may entail full-fledged formal statistical analyses.

Note especially that these criteria are used *together* in choosing a cost function: each is a check on the other. Knowledge of both cost accounting and operations is helpful in interpreting observed relationships. For example, repairs are often made when output is low because that is when the machines can be taken out of service. If repair costs were recorded as each repair was made, it would appear that repair costs decline as output increases. But you observe this relationship because the timing of the repair is often discretionary—using the true cause-and-effect relationship, repair costs increase as activity increases. Consequently, economic plausibility should dominate the observed relationship; otherwise, the true extent of variability of costs with output will be masked.

As another example, a clerical overhead cost may show a high correlation with the number of records processed and an even higher correlation with the number of factory machine-hours worked. Our knowledge of operations confirms the plausibility of only the first relationship, so it should be used.

☐ Methods of Linear Approximation

There are many methods of approximating cost functions, including (1) *the industrial engineering method*, (2) *account analysis*, (3) *high-low points*, (4) *visual fit*, (5) *simple regression*, and (6) *multiple regression*. These methods are not mutually exclusive; frequently, two or more are used to avoid major blunders. In many organizations, each of these six methods is used in succession over the years as the need for more accuate approximations becomes evident. The first two methods are based only on logical analysis, while the last four involve analysis of past costs.

The *industrial engineering method*, sometimes called the *analytic method*, searches for the most efficient means of obtaining wanted output. It entails a systematic review of materials, supplies, labor, support services, and facilities. Time and motion studies are sometimes used. Any input-output relationship that is observable is an obvious candidate for the engineering method. For example, in the manufacturing of bicycles, one handlebar and two wheels are needed per bicycle. But the engineering method is of little help when relationships between cost (y) and volume (x) cannot be personally observed. Examples are relationships between various overhead costs and output.

In *account analysis*, the analyst proceeds through the detailed ledger accounts, one by one, and classifies each into one of two categories, variable or fixed. In so doing, analysts may use their past experience intuitively and nothing else. More likely, they will also use one of the methods of analyzing past data for each account. An examination of the accounts is a necessary first step for each of the remaining methods. Familiarity with the data avoids the pitfalls that abound in analyzing past costs.

A major disadvantage of the account analysis method is its inherent subjectivity. The *high-low* method is slightly less subjective because at least it employs two actual observations of cost and volume, those representing the highest cost and the lowest cost. It will be illustrated in a subsequent section.

The *visual-fit*, *simple-regression*, and *multiple-regression* methods have a distinct advantage because *all sample points* (not just two) are used in determining the cost function. A visual fit is applied by drawing a straight line through the cost points on a scatter diagram, which consists of a plotting on a graph of individual dots that represent various costs experienced at various activity levels. The line in Exhibit 8–1 could have been fitted visually.

There are no objective tests to ensure that the line fitted visually is the most accurate representation of the underlying data. Consequently, regression analysis is a more systematic approach. **Regression analysis** refers to the measurement of the average amount of change in one variable (e.g., shipping cost) that is associated with unit increases in the amounts of one or more other variables. In addition to providing a cost function, regression analysis supplies statistics that reveal how well that function approximates the past cost and volume relationship. When only two variables are studied (e.g., shipping costs in relation to units shipped), the analysis is called *simple regression*; when more than two variables are studied (e.g., shipping costs in relation to units shipped and to the weight of those units shipped), it is called *multiple regression*.

☐ **Data for Illustration**

The city of Northvale operates several municipal golf courses that require varying maintenance attention, depending on the season of the year. The assistant city manager has begun to collect data on the cost of repairing the various types of power equipment used (for example, golf carts and power lawn mowers). She is concerned because repairs have been billed individually by an outside firm as each piece of equipment fails to perform. She is considering various alternatives, including buying a service contract for a flat fee or creating her own equipment repair department.

To date, she has compiled the following data:

	GROUNDSKEEPER LABOR-HOURS (x)	REPAIR EXPENSE (y)
August	2,200	$2,300
September	2,300	2,500
October	1,900	2,000
November	1,200	1,700
December	1,200	2,000
January	900	1,500
February	1,100	1,600
March	1,100	1,400
April	1,400	1,600

She realizes that many more months of data should be gathered before jumping to conclusions about how costs behave. She also wishes that more detailed classifications were available (for example, by acreage in specific golf courses, by types and age of equipment, and perhaps by number of rounds played at each course). But she has decided to use the foregoing data as a start.

EXHIBIT 8–2

High-Low Method

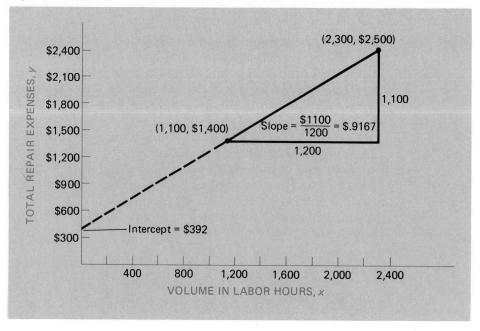

☐ High-Low Method

The high-low method uses only the highest-cost and lowest-cost points. If one of these points is an "outlier" that seems nonrepresentative, the next-highest- or next-lowest-cost point should be used. The line between the two points is extended back to intersect the vertical axis as in Exhibit 8–2. The intercept becomes the "fixed" portion and the slope becomes the "variable" portion of the formula for the mixed cost.

The same results can be achieved via algebra:

	LABOR-HOURS (x)	REPAIR EXPENSES (y)
High	2,300	$2,500
Low	1,100	1,400
Difference	1,200	$1,100

$$\text{variable rate} = \frac{\text{change in costs}}{\text{change in activity}} = \frac{\$2,500 - \$1,400}{2,300 - 1,100} = \frac{\$1,100}{1,200} = \$.9167 \text{ per labor-hour}$$

$$\text{fixed component} = \text{total mixed cost less variable component}$$
$$\text{at } x \text{ (high)} = \$2,500 - \$.9167 \,(2,300)$$
$$= \$2,500 - \$2,108 = \$392$$

or

$$\text{at } x \text{ (low)} = \$1,400 - \$.9167 \,(1,100)$$
$$= \$1,400 - \$1,008 = \$392$$

Therefore,

mixed-cost formula = $392 per month plus $.9167 per labor-hour

The high-low method is statistically inefficient. It uses only 2 of the 9 pairs of data available. Even if 100 data pairs were available, it would use only 2. Because of the danger that the 2 points are not representative of normal situations, the high-low method is not recommended.

☐ **Visual-Fit Method**

The simplest method that uses all data points is the visual-fit method. Exhibit 8–3 is a scatter diagram of the preceding data. The analyst should scrutinize the data to see whether a strong relationship exists between the costs of repair and groundskeeper labor-hours. Also, the analyst uses the scatter diagram as a key to deciding whether the relationship is approximately *linear*—that is, whether a straight line fits reasonably close to all the dots.

The line in Exhibit 8–3 was fit visually, trying to come as close to as many dots as possible. The intercept of $600 and slope of $.825 were read directly from the graph. The visual-fit method is better than the high-low,

EXHIBIT 8–3

Scatter Diagram With Visual Fit

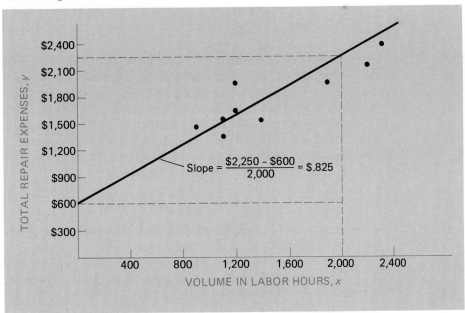

EXHIBIT 8–4

Least-Squares Regression Analysis

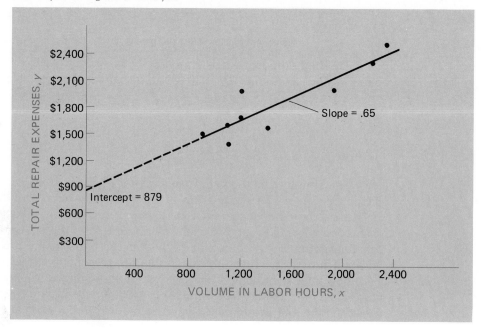

but it suffers from being highly subjective. For example, your visual fit will differ from your neighbor's.

☐ Least-Squares Regression Analysis

You should prepare a scatter diagram and visually fit a line to the data points as a first step in applying least-squares regression analysis. Any data point falling far from the line should be investigated. If it represents abnormal conditions, perhaps a period when there was a strike or a devastating storm, it should be eliminated. In our illustration there are no such "outliers."

Exhibit 8–4 shows the straight line that has been fitted by the *statistical method of least squares*, which is described in more detail in the appendix to this chapter. The formula for the straight line is:

$$y' = a + bx$$
$$y' = \$879 + \$.65x$$

The constant, a, is the fixed cost, and the regression coefficient, b, is the variable cost rate. That is, repair costs over the relevant range of 900 to 2,300 hours have averaged $879 per month plus $.65 per labor-hour.

Three methods that use past costs to determine fixed and variable costs produce three different estimates:

	TOTAL FIXED COST	VARIABLE COST RATE
High-low method	$392	$.92
Visual fit	$600	$.825
Least-squares regression	$879	$.65

The high-low method is unreliable because it uses only two data points. The visual fit method may be appropriate when used by a skilled analyst, but it requires much judgment. **Least-squares regression analysis** is an objective way of using all available data points to determine a cost function. It also provides statistics that show how well the regression line fits the data.

One goodness-of-fit statistic is the **coefficient of determination**, r^2. It reveals the percentage of variation in cost (y) that is explained by changes in volume (x). The appendix shows that $r^2 = .806$ in our illustration. That is, 80.6% of the fluctuation in repair cost is explained by groundskeeper labor-hours. A statistician can use r^2 and other goodness-of-fit statistics to determine how much faith you should put in the fixed and variable cost estimates from a regression analysis.

☐ **Focus on Relevant Range**

The line in Exhibit 8–4 is extended backward from the relevant range to intersect the *y* axis at $879. The extension is deliberately shown as a dashed line to emphasize the focus on the relevant range. The manager is concerned with how costs behave within the relevant range, not with how they behave at zero volume. Therefore the $879 intercept must be kept in perspective. It is often called simply the fixed cost, but it is really a fixed or constant component of the formula that provides the best available linear approximation of how a mixed cost behaves within the relevant range. This analysis does not reveal how costs behave at volumes below or above the relevant range.

SUMMARY

Managers who know cost behavior patterns are better equipped to make intelligent planning and control decisions. The division of costs into engineered, discretionary, and committed categories highlights the major factors that influence cost incurrence. Management policies often determine whether a cost will be planned and controlled as an engineered cost or as a discretionary cost.

Predictions of how costs will behave in response to various actions usually have an important bearing on a wide number of decisions. The cost function used to make these predictions is usually a simplification of underlying relationships. Whether this simplification is justified depends on how sensitive the manager's decisions are to the errors that the simplifications may generate. In some cases, additional accuracy may not make any difference; in other cases, it may be significant. The choice of a cost function is a decision concerning the costs and benefits of information.

SUMMARY PROBLEM FOR YOUR REVIEW

☐ Problem

The Delite Company has its own power plant. All costs related to the production of power have been charged to a single account, Power. We know that the total cost for power was $24,000 in one month and $28,000 in another month. Total machine-hours in those months were 120,000 and 160,000, respectively. Express the cost behavior pattern of the Power account in formula form.

☐ Solution

$$\text{variable rate} = \frac{\text{change in mixed cost}}{\text{change in volume}} = \frac{\$28,000 - \$24,000}{160,000 - 120,000}$$

$$= \frac{\$4,000}{40,000} = \$.10 \text{ per machine-hour}$$

$$\text{fixed component} = \text{total mixed cost less variable component}$$

$$\text{at 160,000-hour level} = \$28,000 - \$.10(160,000) = \$12,000$$

or

$$\text{at 120,000-hour level} = \$24,000 - \$.10(120,000) = \$12,000$$

$$\text{cost formula} = \$12,000 \text{ per month} + \$.10 \text{ per machine-hour}$$

HIGHLIGHTS TO REMEMBER

1. Costs may be divided for planning and control purposes as follows:

TYPE OF COST	MAJOR CONTROL TECHNIQUES	TIME SPAN AND FEEDBACK
Engineered	Flexible budgets and standards	Short
Discretionary	Personal observation and negotiation of static budgets	Longer
Committed	Capital budgeting*	Longest

* Discussed in Chapters 11 and 12.

2. From time to time, you will undoubtedly find that these distinctions among engineered, discretionary, and committed costs are useful. However, these are subjective decisions, so expect some difference of opinion as to whether a given cost is, say, committed or discretionary. For example, the salaries of supervisory or other highly prized personnel who would be kept on the payroll at zero activity levels are often regarded as committed costs, but some organizations may classify them as discretionary costs. Arguments about whether such types of costs should be classified as committed or discretionary are a waste of time—these matters must be settled on a case-by-case basis. In a given organization, quick agreement regarding an appropriate classification is usually achieved.

3. The comparison of engineered cost and discretionary cost approaches illustrates the overall theme of this book regarding control systems. Two alternative systems have been

described, but note that one is not *advocated* here as being superior to the other. Such judgments can safely be made only in the specific circumstances facing a given organization.

4. Although a particular *system* has not been advocated here, a *method for choosing* among the systems is favored. Essentially, it is the cost-benefit method. That is, the manager or systems designer should assess (1) the expected benefits from, say, a proposed clerical work-measurement system in the form of a better collective set of operating behaviors or decisions against (2) the expected costs of a more formal system, including behavioral costs and the costs of educating employees.

ACCOUNTING VOCABULARY

Capacity Cost *p. 227*   Coefficient of Determination *245*   Committed Fixed Costs *228*   Control-factor Unit *231*   Cost Approximation *235*   Cost Behavior Pattern *235*   Cost Estimation *235*   Cost Function *235*   Discretionary Fixed Costs *229*   Engineered Cost *230*   Least-squares Regression Analysis *245* Managed Costs *229*   Mixed Cost *237*   Ordinary Incremental Budget *234* Parameter *236*   Priority Incremental Budget *234*   Programmed Cost *229*   Regression analysis *241*   Step-Function Cost *237*   Work Measurement *230*   Zero-base Budgeting *234*.

APPENDIX 8: METHOD OF LEAST SQUARES

The method of least squares is the most accurate device for formulating the *past behavior* of a mixed cost.

The linear cost function is approximated by using two simultaneous linear equations:

$$\Sigma xy = a\Sigma x + b\Sigma x^2 \tag{1}$$
$$\Sigma y = na + b\Sigma x \tag{2}$$

where a is the fixed component, b is the variable cost rate, x is the activity measure, y is the mixed cost, n is the number of observations, and the Greek letter Σ (sigma) means summation.

For example, assume that nine monthly observations of repair costs are to be used as a basis for developing a budget formula. A scatter diagram indicates a mixed cost behavior in the form $y' = a + bx$. Computation of the budget formula by the method of least squares is shown in Exhibit 8–5. Substitute the values from Exhibit 8–5 into Equations 1 and 2:

$$25{,}940{,}000 = 13{,}300a + 21{,}810{,}000b \qquad (1)$$

$$16{,}600 = \quad 9a + \quad 13{,}300b \qquad (2)$$

Repeat equation 1:

$$25{,}940{,}000 = 13{,}300a + 21{,}810{,}000b$$

Multiply equation 2
by 1,477.7778
(which is $13{,}300 \div 9$):
subtract.

$$\begin{array}{l} 24{,}531{,}111 = 13{,}300a + 19{,}654{,}444b \\ \hline 1{,}408{,}889 = \quad 0 \quad + \ 2{,}155{,}556b \end{array}$$

$$b = \frac{1{,}408{,}889}{2{,}155{,}556} = .6536$$

Substitute $.6536
for b in equation 2:

$$16{,}600 = 9a + 13{,}300(.6536)$$

$$16{,}600 = 9a + 8{,}692.99$$

$$9a = 7{,}907.01$$

$$a = 878.56$$

Therefore the formula for the total repair expenses is $y' = 878.56 + .6536x$, or (rounding) $879 per month plus $.65 per labor-hour.

A scatter diagram and goodness-of-fit statistics should also be prepared to see whether the derived line seems to fit the existing cost data to a satisfactory degree. If not, then factors other than volume or activity have also significantly affected total cost behavior. In such instances, multiple regression techniques may have to be used.

EXHIBIT 8–5

Least-Squares Computation of Budget Formula for Mixed Cost

MONTH	LABOR-HOURS x	TOTAL MIXED COST y	xy	x^2	$(y - y')^2$	$(y - \bar{y})^2$
August	2,200	2,300	5,060,000	4,840,000	272	207,535
September	2,300	2,500	5,750,000	5,290,000	13,962	429,759
October	1,900	2,000	3,800,000	3,610,000	14,496	24,199
November	1,200	1,700	2,040,000	1,440,000	1,378	20,863
December	1,200	2,000	2,400,000	1,440,000	113,650	24,199
January	900	1,500	1,350,000	810,000	1,102	118,639
February	1,100	1,600	1,760,000	1,210,000	6	59,751
March	1,100	1,400	1,540,000	1,210,000	39,014	197,527
April	1,400	1,600	2,240,000	1,960,000	37,481	59,751
	13,300	16,600	25,940,000	21,810,000	221,361	1,142,223

SOURCE: Adapted from "Separating and Using Costs as Fixed and Variable," *N.A.A. Bulletin*, Accounting Practice Report No. 10 (New York, June 1960), p. 13. For a more thorough explanation, see any basic text in statistics or Horngren and Foster, *Cost Accounting*, Chap. 24.

One goodness-of-fit statistic, the coefficient of determination, r^2, shows the percentage of variation in cost that is explained by volume:

$$r^2 = 1 - \frac{\Sigma (y - y')^2}{\Sigma (y - \bar{y})^2}$$

where y is the observed cost, y' is the cost predicted by the regression equation, $\bar{y}$ is the average cost over all observations, and Σ means summation over all observed values of y.

In the illustration, $y' = 878.56 + .6536x$ and $\bar{y} = 1,844.44$. From the last two columns of Exhibit 8.5 we find

$$r^2 = 1 - \frac{221,361}{1,142,223} = .806$$

FUNDAMENTAL ASSIGNMENT MATERIAL

8–1. CLERICAL WORK MEASUREMENT. (Alternate is 8–25.) The underwriting department of Union General Life Insurance Company recently installed a work measurement program. Each underwriter is expected to process 250 applications per month, and he or she earns $2,200 per month. During January six underwriters processed 1,250 applications.

Required:

1. Prepare a performance report that presents actual, budgeted, and budget variance columns for the month. Use (a) a discretionary-cost approach and (b) an engineered-cost approach.
2. Suppose the workers have been reasonably efficient. What do the budget variances in 1(a) and 1(b) tell the manager?
3. Assume that an engineered-cost approach to control is used, even though management has deliberately overstaffed. This means that management must provide for an "expected variance" or "budgeted variance" for cash-planning purposes. For preparing a budgeted statement of cash receipts and disbursements, what amount would be budgeted for payroll-clerk labor?

8–2. TYPES OF COST BEHAVIOR. Identify the following as (a) proportionately variable costs, (b) discretionary fixed costs, (c) committed fixed costs, (d) mixed or semivariable costs, (e) step-function costs, (f) discretionary variable costs, and (g) engineered variable costs.

(1) Compensation of lawyers employed internally for Ford Motor Company.
(2) Total costs of renting trucks by the city of Palo Alto. Charge is a lump sum of $300 per month plus 20¢ per mile.
(3) Advertising allowances granted to wholesalers by Stroh Brewing Company on a per-case basis.
(4) Total repairs and maintenance of a school building.
(5) Sales commissions based on revenue dollars. Payments made to advertising salespersons employed by radio station KCBS, San Francisco.
(6) Advertising costs, a lump sum budgeted and paid by Coca-Cola.
(7) Crew supervisor in a Sears mail-order house. A new supervisor is added for every seven workers employed.
(8) Public relations employee compensation paid by Mobil Oil Company.
(9) Jet fuel costs of United Airlines.
(10) Straight-line depreciation on desks in the office of a certified public accountant.
(11) Rental payment by the Federal Bureau of Investigation on a five-year lease for office space in a private office building.

8-3. Division of Mixed Costs into Variable and Fixed Components. The president of Ramayya Metal Works has asked for information about the cost behavior of overhead costs. Specifically, she wants to know how much overhead cost is fixed and how much is variable. The following data are the only records available:

MONTH	LABOR-HOURS	OVERHEAD COST
May	1,200	$10,000
June	1,500	11,200
July	1,100	9,300
August	900	8,700
September	1,300	10,800

Required:

1. Find total fixed cost and the variable cost per labor-hour by the high-low method.
2. Suppose a least-squares regression analysis gave the following output:

   Regression equation: $y = 4,600 + \$4.50x$
   Coefficient of determination: .95

   What answer would you give the president based on this output?

ADDITIONAL ASSIGNMENT MATERIAL

8-4. Why are committed costs the stickiest of the fixed costs?

8-5. "An unfavorable variance for discretionary costs would measure the failure to spend the entire appropriation." Do you agree? Explain.

8-6. What is the primary determinant of the level of committed costs?

8-7. What is the primary determinant of the level of discretionary costs?

8-8. "Planning is far more important than day-to-day control of discretionary costs." Do you agree? Explain.

8-9. What is *work measurement*?

8-10. Why are fixed costs also called capacity costs?

8-11. How do committed costs differ from discretionary costs?

8-12. How do the methods and philosophies of management affect cost behavior?

8-13. "Variable costs should fluctuate directly in proportion to sales." Do you agree? Explain.

8-14. How does the basic behavior of the cost of raw materials differ from the cost behavior of clerical services?

8-15. "For practical budgeting purposes, costs do not have to be proportionately variable to be regarded as variable." Explain.

8-16. "The objective in controlling step costs is to attain activity at the highest volume for any given step." Explain.

8-17. "Ideally, there should be no accounts for mixed costs." Explain.

8-18. Describe how mixed costs are budgeted.

8-19. Why is least-squares regression analysis usually preferred to the high-low method?

8-20. "You never know how good your fixed and variable cost approximations are if you use account analysis or if you visually fit a line on a scatter diagram. That's why I like least-squares regression analysis." Explain.

8-21. **Attitudes Toward Work Measurement.** At a management conference, a proponent of work measurement stated, "Before you can control, you must measure." Another executive complained, "Why bother to measure when work rules and guaranteed employment provisions in labor union contracts prevent discharging workers, using part-time employment, and using overtime!"

Required: Evaluate these comments. Summarize your personal attitudes toward the use of work measurement.

8–22. GOVERNMENT WORK MEASUREMENT. The auditor general of the state of California conducted a study of the Department of Motor Vehicles. The auditor's report said that the department's work standards, which were set in 1939, allow 10 minutes for typing and processing a driver's license application. But a 1977 study of 40 of its 147 field offices showed that it takes only 6 minutes. The report said, "The continued use of the 10-minute standard results in the overstaffing of 158 positions at an unnecessary annual cost of $1.9 million."

Required: Name four government activities that are likely candidates for using work measurement as a means for control.

8–23. GOVERNMENT WORK MEASUREMENT. The Internal Revenue Service has an auditing system whereby an auditor scrutinizes income tax returns after they have been prescreened with the help of computer tests for normal ranges of deductions claimed by taxpayers. A standard cost of $5 per tax return has been used, based on work-measurement studies that allow 20 minutes per return. Each agent has a workweek of 5 days at 8 hours per day.

The audit supervisor has the following data regarding performance for the most recent 4-week period, when 8,000 returns were processed.

	ACTUAL COSTS	FLEXIBLE BUDGET	VARIANCE
Salaries	$48,000*	?	?

* 20 auditors × $600 salary per week × 4 weeks.

Required:
1. Compute the flexible-budget allowance and the variance.
2. The supervisor believes that audit work should be conducted more productively and that superfluous personnel should be transferred to field audits. If the foregoing data are representative, how many auditors should be transferred?
3. Enumerate some possible reasons for the variance.

8–24. ZERO-BASE BUDGETING. (CMA adapted.) Zero-base budgeting can be applied in governmental, nonprofit, and profit-making organizations. Its proponents believe it represents a significant change in the budgeting process for most types of organizations and that it therefore leads to more effective use of limited resources.

Required:
1. Describe the zero-base budgeting system.
2. Explain how the proponents of zero-base budgeting say it differs from the traditional budgeting process.
3. Identify the advantages and disadvantages of the zero-base budgeting system.

8–25. CLERICAL WORK MEASUREMENT. (Alternate is 8–1.) Bill Cody Western Gear Co. is a mail-order firm. Order-filling labor used to be controlled by careful personal observation, but a year ago a formal system of work measurement was added to aid control.

A management consultant developed work standards that allowed 75 orders per day per clerk. The company employs 20 clerks at a salary of $300 per 5-day week.

To avoid confusion regarding comparisons from month to month, interim

VARIATIONS OF COST BEHAVIOR PATTERNS

performance focuses on reporting periods of 4 weeks each. A recent 4-week period showed that 27,000 orders had been processed by the 20 clerks.

Required:
1. How would a performance report show the budget variance for the four-week period under (a) a discretionary-fixed-cost approach and (b) an engineered-cost approach?
2. What factors might influence management regarding the size of the clerical force for the order-filling operation?
3. Sometimes top management uses one budget for cash-planning purposes and a second budget for cost-control purposes. If an engineered-cost approach is used, the cash-planning budget might include an "expected variance." What would be the "expected" or "budgeted" variance in this case?

8–26. **NONLINEAR BEHAVIOR.** The following graph contains a linear function, which is the linear approximation of the nonlinear "true" cost function also shown.

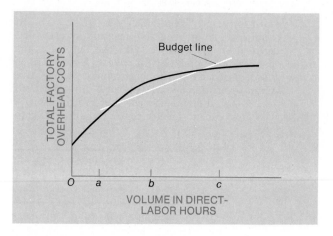

Required:
1. Will the flexible budget be higher or lower than the budgeted "true" costs at volume level a? at b? at c?
2. Would you prefer to use the "true" cost curve for budgeting and for decision purposes? Why?

8–27. **FIXED COSTS AND CAPACITY.** Diego Garcia started Garcia Marine several years ago to make a specialized 21-foot sailboat. These boats have become very popular, and Mr. Garcia sees the opportunity to expand. He could hire additional workers and keep his operation labor intensive. Alternatively, he could invest in machinery to automate many processes, making the operation more capital intensive.

Mr. Garcia predicts sales of 400 boats in 19X9 and each year thereafter if he can produce that many. Annual fixed costs for the current capacity of 200 boats per year are $300,000, and variable costs are $7,500 per boat. At a selling price of $10,000 per boat, Garcia Marine will make $200,000 operating profit on revenue of $2,000,000 and expenses of $1,800,000 in 19X8. To make 400 boats, Mr. Garcia could purchase robot-type machines to automate several processes, increasing annual fixed costs to $2,000,000 and reducing variable costs to $4,000 per boat. Alternatively, he could double current operations, leaving variable costs at $7,500 per boat and increasing fixed costs to only $600,000.

Required:
1. Calculate the predicted operating profit for 19X9 for each alternative under three different predictions of production and sales: 300 boats, 400 boats, and 500 boats.
2. Comment on how Mr. Garcia's confidence in his prediction of annual sales of 400 boats might affect his decision.

8–28. **DIVISION OF MIXED COSTS INTO VARIABLE AND FIXED COMPONENTS.** The president and the controller of the Istanbul Transformer Company have agreed that refinement of the company cost classifications will aid planning and control decisions. They have asked you to approximate the formula for variable- and fixed-cost behavior of repairs and maintenance from the following sparse data. Currency is the Turkish lira (TL).

MONTHLY ACTIVITY IN DIRECT-LABOR HOURS	MONTHLY REPAIR AND MAINTENANCE COSTS INCURRED
300	85,000 TL
500	115,000 TL

8–29. **SEPARATION OF HOSPITAL X-RAY MIXED COSTS INTO VARIABLE AND FIXED COMPONENTS.** A staff meeting has been called at Providence Hospital by the new administrator. She has examined the income statement and is particularly interested in the X-ray department. The chief radiologist, Dr. Martinez, has demanded an increase in prices to cover the increased repair costs because of the opening of an outpatient clinic. He claims that it is costing more per X-ray for this expense.

The administrator has asked you to approximate the fundamental variable- and fixed-cost behavior of repairs and maintenance for the X-ray department and to prepare a graphic report she can present to Dr. Martinez. Data for the relevant range follow:

	X-RAYS PER MONTH	MONTHLY REPAIR AND MAINTENANCE COST INCURRED
Low volume	8,000	$4,400
High volume	12,000	6,400

Required:

Prepare the requested information. Also prepare a freehand graph to show the administrator.

8–30. **NONPROFIT BUDGETING.** Meadow Day School, a private elementary school, is preparing a budgeted income statement for the coming academic year ending August 31, 19X8. Tuition revenues for the past two years ending August 31 were 19X7, $700,000; and 19X6, $750,000. Total expenses in 19X7 were $710,000 and in 19X6 were $730,000. No tuition rate changes occurred in 19X6 or 19X7, nor are any expected to occur in 19X8. Tuition revenue is expected to be $720,000 for the year ending August 31, 19X8. What net income should be budgeted for next year, assuming that the implied cost behavior patterns remain unchanged?

8–31. **COLLEGE INCOME.** Many private universities try to recover about one-third of their total costs from tuition revenue. The remainder is recovered via endowment income and charitable donations. Stanford University is preparing a budgeted income statement for the coming fiscal year, which will end on August 31, 19X6. Tuition revenue for fiscal 19X5 was $54 million; and for 19X4, $48 million. Total expenses for 19X5 were $165.6 million; and for 19X4, $153.6 million. No tuition rate changes occurred in 19X4 or 19X5. If the tuition rate is not changed in 19X6, tuition revenue is expected to be $60 million.

1. What is the implied cost behavior pattern faced by the university? That is, what is the university's fixed- and variable-cost equation in relation to tuition revenue?
2. If historical patterns persist, what total expenses are expected by the university in 19X6?
3. What are the analytical defects in using the volume of tuition revenue as a basis for predicting costs? As financial vice-president of the university, what basis would you prefer?

8–32. **WORK MEASUREMENT IN A HOSPITAL.** The billing procedures in a hospital require ponderous detail. University Hospital introduced a work-measurement program and established a standard rate of four bills per hour. Extensive studies had concluded that the typical bill contains 40 lines. Each billing clerk received an hourly labor rate of $9 and worked 5 days per week, 8 hours per day.

1. The billing supervisor has asked you to prepare a performance report for billing labor for a recent 8-week period when twelve clerks were employed and 13,000 bills were processed. Show the actual cost, flexible budget, and the variance.
2. The hospital administrator has followed the work-measurement application with intense interest. A consultant had suggested that all variances should be expressed in terms of "equivalent persons" in addition to dollar amounts. The administrator has asked you to compute the variance in terms of "equivalent persons."
3. The administrator told the supervisor: "As you know, the trustees, the government agencies, and the patients are really criticizing us for soaring hospitalization costs. This work-measurement system leads me to think we are overstaffed with billing labor. As a start, we ought to reduce the work force by the number of equivalent persons shown by the variance analysis."

The supervisor was upset. She then took a careful random sample of 500 of the bills that were processed. Her count showed a total of 25,000 lines in the sample. As the supervisor, prepare a reply to the administrator.

8–33. **IDENTIFYING COST BEHAVIOR PATTERNS.** Ann Falk, administrator of City Art Museum, attended a seminar on the classification of different kinds of cost behavior. She identified several museum costs and classified them. After her classification, Falk presented you with the following list of costs and asked you to classify their behavior as one of the following: variable, step, mixed, discretionary fixed, or committed fixed:

(1) Straight-line depreciation of display cases.
(2) Costs incurred by Dr. Witherspoon in researching the origins of some Pacific Northwest Coast Indian artifacts.
(3) Costs of services of Museum Financial Consultants, Inc.
(4) Repairs made on furniture.
(5) Salaries for supervisors of volunteer docents (a docent is a teacher or guide, and a supervisor is added for each 25 docents).
(6) Leasing costs of ticket selling equipment ($4,500 a year plus $.05 per ticket).
(7) Training costs of an administrative assistant.
(8) Blue Cross insurance for all full-time employees.

8–34. **VARIOUS COST BEHAVIOR PATTERNS.** In practice, there is often a tendency to simplify approximations of cost behavior patterns, even though the "true" underlying behavior is not simple. Choose from the accompanying graphs A through H the one that matches the numbered items. Indicate by letter which graph best fits each of the situations described.

The vertical axes of the graphs represent total dollars of factory costs incurred, and the horizontal axes represent total production. The graphs may be used more than once.

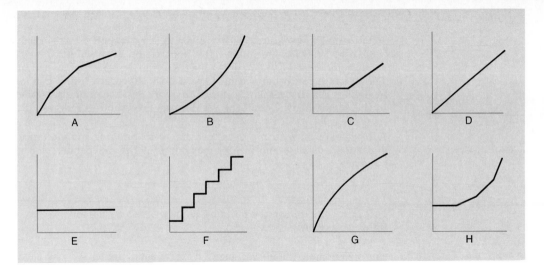

(1) Cost of sheet steel for a manufacturer of refrigerators.
(2) Guaranteed annual wage plan, whereby workers get paid for 40 hours of work per week at zero or low levels of production that require working only a few hours weekly.
(3) Cost of machining labor that tends to decrease per unit as workers gain experience.
(4) Depreciation on a straight-line basis.
(5) Water bill under drought conditions, which entails a flat fee for the first 10,000 gallons and then an increasing unit cost for every additional batch of 10,000 gallons used.
(6) Salaries of assistant supervisors, where one assistant supervisor is added for every ten assembly workers added.
(7) Natural gas bill consisting of a fixed component, plus a constant variable cost per thousand cubic feet after a specified number of cubic feet are used.
(8) Availability of quantity discounts, where the cost per unit falls as each price break is reached.
(9) Price rise of an increasingly scarce raw material as the volume used increases.

8-35. **INTERPRETING A LEAST-SQUARES REGRESSION ANALYSIS.** Elliott Bay Tarp and Tent (EBTT) Company has difficulty controlling its use of supplies. The company has traditionally regarded supplies as a variable cost. But nearly every time volume was above average, EBTT had a favorable supplies variance; when volume was below average, the variance was unfavorable. This suggested to Margarite Brown, the new controller, that part of the supplies cost was probably fixed. EBTT uses square feet of materials as a measure of volume.

    Brown decided to use least-squares regression analysis to explore this issue. She obtained the following regression results with supplies cost as the dependent variable and square feet of materials as the independent variable:

Constant: 1,800
Regression coefficient: .072
Coefficient of determination: .58

Required: Suppose that 100,000 square feet of materials are produced in an average month. What percentage of overhead cost is variable in an average month? What percentage is fixed? Do fluctuations in supplies costs depend on anything other than square feet of materials? What proportion of the fluctuations are *not* associated with square feet of materials?

8–36. ECONOMIC PLAUSIBILITY OF REGRESSION ANALYSIS RESULTS. The head of the Industrial Products Manufacturing Department of the Mottl Co. was concerned about some cost behavior data given to him by the new assistant controller. The assistant controller was hired because of his recent training in mathematical modeling. His first assignment was to apply regression analysis to various costs in the department. One of the results was presented as follows:

☐ A regression on monthly data was run with building maintenance cost as the dependent variable and direct-labor hours as the independent variable. The results are

$$y = \$7,542 - \$.54X; \quad r^2 = .89$$

I suggest that we use the building as intensively as possible to keep the maintenance costs down.

The department head was puzzled. How could increased use cause decreased maintenance costs? His comment to the controller was, "It just doesn't seem logical. But how can we argue with the numbers?"

Required: Explain this counterintuitive result to the department head. What step did the assistant controller omit in applying and interpreting the regression analysis?

8–37. NONLINEAR COSTS AND FLEXIBLE-BUDGET VARIANCES. The U.S. Government Printing Office has used a flexible budget for the overhead of one of its press departments. At a level of 15,000 direct-labor-hours, its total overhead is budgeted at $75,000; at a level of 23,000 hours, at $95,000.

In March, the department took 21,000 hours of input for work that should have taken 19,000 standard allowed hours. Actual overhead costs incurred were $98,000.

Required:
1. Compute the flexible-budget variance for March. Subdivide the variance into a spending variance and an efficiency variance. (See chapter 7, page 204.)
2. Special cost studies were conducted later in the year that developed the following approximation for relating overhead to direct-labor-hours (DL):

$$\text{Total overhead} = \$53,000 + \$1.25\text{DL} + \$100\sqrt{\text{DL}}$$

If this cost function had been used in March as the flexible-budget formula (instead of the linear budget used previously), what would have been the flexible-budget variance for March? the spending variance? the efficiency variance? Round your square roots to the nearest hour.

8–38. NONLINEAR BEHAVIOR AND BANKING. Managers are often troubled by not really knowing how overhead is affected by their operating decisions. As a result, they are uncomfortable when they use the simple "linear approximations" that are commonly encountered. Suppose that a bank is contemplating the introduction of a new "one-price" banking service, whereby a flat monthly fee will provide a combination of "free" checking, safety deposit, and other services.

Suppose the underlying (but unidentified) overhead-cost behavior would be:

VOLUME LEVEL IN NUMBER OF ACCOUNTS	TOTAL OVER-HEAD COSTS PER YEAR
1,000	$34,000
2,000	40,000
3,000	45,000
4,000	49,000
5,000	64,000
6,000	85,000

Required:

1. A committee is trying to predict what costs are relevant. After much heated discussion, predictions were made for two "representative" volumes: 2,000 accounts and 5,000 accounts. A flexible budget was to be constructed based on a "high-low" analysis of these two volumes. Compute the formula for the flexible-budget line.
2. What predictions would be produced by the flexible budget developed in Requirement 1 for each of the tabulated levels of activity? Use a table to compare these predictions with the "true" cost behavior, showing the difference between the "true" and the linear approximation.
3. Plot the two sets of predictions on a graph.
4. Assume that the new service has been introduced. The manager in charge is convinced that a special television campaign can increase volume from the current level of 2,000 accounts to a level of 4,000 accounts. These additional accounts would bring an additional contribution to income of $64,000 before considering the predicted increase in total overhead cost and before considering the cost of $50,000 for the television campaign. If the manager were guided by the linear flexible-budget formula, would she launch the campaign? Show computations. If she did launch the campaign, by how much would income change if 2,000 more accounts were achieved?
5. As an operating manager responsible for budgetary control of overhead, would you regard the linear budget allowances for 4,000 and 6,000 accounts as too tight or too loose? Why?
6. A top executive of the bank commented, "I think we should have a more accurate budgetary system." Do you agree? Explain.

8–39. **TEMPORARY VERSUS PERMANENT HELP.** The Central States Division of Lawrence's Famous Candies, Inc., is responsible for filling all orders in an area comprising 15 midwestern states. The company's product is a high-grade candy that is retailed in many fine stores from coast to coast. The clerical work incidental to filling an order has traditionally been done by a staff of 7 persons who work a 5-day week of 8 hours per day. Their salary and fringe benefits total $1,800 each per month. To uphold quality, the company has a long-standing policy of not using overtime. Assume, for simplicity, that each month consists of exactly 20 working days.

Sheila Matson, the division manager, has noticed that the workers are idle during part of the day during some parts of the year. A strong union prevents the division from sending permanent employees home early in order to reduce their compensation. However, the union will provide temporary help (one-day minimum) for $120 per worker per day. In turn, the workers pay some of their compensation to the union. Matson is considering reducing the permanent staff and hiring temporary help during peak periods.

Matson learned that the New York division routinely hires temporary help for the same duty, but with some loss of efficiency. Temporary help can process only 35 orders per day, whereas permanent help can process 40 orders per day.

The month-to-month sales record, expressed in terms of orders filled, has been as follows for the past five years:

January	4,800	May	4,400	September	4,400
February	4,800	June	4,000	October	4,800
March	4,800	July	4,000	November	5,600
April	5,600	August	4,000	December	5,600

Required:

Should the division manager retain all seven clerks? If not, how many should she retain? Sales fluctuate significantly from month to month, but not from year to year. Any fluctuation within a given month is so minor that it can be absorbed by a slight delay. For computational simplicity, the manager assumes that sales are constant throughout the month.

8-40. **LEAST SQUARES.** Study the chapter appendix. Assume that total operating overhead of a trucking company is a function of the gross ton-miles of work to be performed. The past records show (in thousands):

	DATE			
	10/1	10/2	10/3	10/4
Gross ton-miles	800	1,200	400	1,600
Total operating costs	$350	$350	$150	$550

Required:

1. Draw a scatter diagram.
2. Use simple regression to fit a line to the data. What is the equation of the line? Calculate the coefficient of determination. Plot the line. This example is used only to illustrate the least-squares method. When the number of observations is small, as in this example, additional analysis should be performed to determine whether the results are reliable.

8-41. **LEAST-SQUARES ANALYSIS.** Study the chapter appendix. Suppose a manufacturer is troubled by fluctuations in labor productivity and wants to compute how direct-labor costs are related to the various sizes of batches of output. The workers in question set up their own jobs on complex machinery. The following data show the results of a random sample of ten batches of a given kind:

BATCH SIZE	DIRECT-LABOR COSTS	BATCH SIZE	DIRECT-LABOR COSTS
x	y	x	y
15	$180	25	$300
12	140	22	270
20	230	9	110
17	190	18	240
12	160	30	320

Required:

1. Prepare a scatter diagram.
2. Using least-squares analysis, compute the equation of the line relating labor costs and size of batch.
3. Predict the labor costs for a lot size of 20.
4. Using a high-low method, repeat Requirements 2 and 3. Should the manager use the high-low method or the least-squares method? Explain.

Chapter 9

RESPONSIBILITY ACCOUNTING
AND COST ALLOCATION

LEARNING OBJECTIVES

When you have finished studying this chapter, you should be able to:

1. Define and contrast cost centers, profit centers, and investment centers, and explain how a responsibility accounting structure can promote desirable management behavior.

2. Recognize the major purposes for allocating costs.

3. Prepare a segmented income statement, using the contribution approach to cost allocation.

4. Distinguish between the economic performance of an organization segment and the performance of the segment manager.

5. Use recommended guidelines to allocate the variable and fixed costs of service departments to other organizational segments.

6. Identify the principal approaches to solving the allocation problem for the central costs of an organization.

7. Use the direct and step-down methods to allocate service department costs to user departments.

This chapter is the first of a two-chapter overview of how management accounting systems are designed. It describes some typical approaches and focuses on the factors that influence management's choice of systems. We learn that no single system is inherently superior to another. The "best" system is the one that consistently leads to a collective set of subordinate managers' decisions that are desired by higher-level managers. The relative costs of each system must also be considered.

GENERAL IDEAS OF RESPONSIBILITY ACCOUNTING

☐ **Responsibility Accounting and Motivation**

Executives in well-managed organizations identify each subordinate's responsibilities. A **responsibility center** is defined as a set of activities assigned to a manager or group of managers. A small collection of machines may be a responsibility center for a production supervisor, a full department for the department head, and the entire organization for the president.

A **responsibility accounting system** measures the financial results of responsibility centers. Executives use responsibility accounting information to evaluate managers and thereby motivate them to act in the organization's best interests.

Responsibility accounting emphasizes a major lesson for both managers and accountants—that is, the behavior of managers is often heavily influenced by how their performance is measured. Thus accounting is far from being a sterile, secondary part of a manager's professional life. Instead, the accounting system often plays a key role in motivating managers toward or away from the desires of top management. The motivational impact of the responsibility approach is described in the following:

☐ The sales department requests a rush production. The plant scheduler argues that it will disrupt his production and cost a substantial though not clearly determined amount of money. The answer coming from sales is: "Do you want to take the responsibility of losing the X Company as a customer?" Of course the production scheduler does not want to take such a responsibility, and he gives up, but not before a heavy exchange of arguments and the accumulation of a substantial backlog of ill feeling. Analysis of the payroll in the assembly department, determining the costs involved in getting out rush orders, eliminated the cause for argument. Henceforth, any rush order was accepted with a smile by the production scheduler, who made sure that the extra cost would be duly recorded and charged to the sales department—"no questions asked." As a result, the tension created by rush orders disappeared completely; and, somehow, the number of rush orders requested by the sales department was progressively reduced to an insignificant level.[1]

A news story regarding quality control in the automobile industry also illustrates the motivational impact of responsibility accounting. A former Ford engineer said that he often watched suspect vehicles being manufactured: "Bonuses were figured on how many cars we produced, not how well we made them. When the customer discovered the defect, it was charged to warranties, not to our plant."

COST CENTERS AND PROFIT CENTERS

Responsibility centers take many forms, including

1. **Cost centers**—reporting of costs only.
2. **Profit centers**—reporting of revenues and expenses.
3. **Investment centers**—reporting of revenues, expenses, and related investment.

A **cost center** is the smallest responsibility center for which costs are accumulated. Typically, cost centers are departments, but in some instances a department may contain several cost centers. For example, although an assembly department may be supervised by one manager, it may contain several assembly lines. Sometimes each assembly line is regarded as a separate cost center with its own assistant manager.

Profit center managers are responsible for both revenue and expenses.[2] An **investment center** goes a step farther; its success is measured not only by its income but also by relating that income to its invested capital. In practice, the term *investment center* is not widely used. Instead, *profit center* is used indiscriminately to describe centers that are always assigned responsibility for revenue and expenses but may or may not be assigned responsibility for the related invested capital.

☐ Illustration of Responsibility Accounting

The simplified organization chart in Exhibit 9–1 will be the basis for our illustration of how responsibility accounting is used in the motel industry. The manager at the motel level has freedom to make many operating decisions, including some repairs and building improvements.

Exhibit 9–2 provides an overall view of responsibility reporting. Start

---

[1] Raymond Villers, "Control and Freedom in a Decentralized Company," *Harvard Business Review*, XXXII, No. 2, 95.

[2] A profit center can exist in nonprofit organizations when a responsibility center receives revenue for its services, but it might not be referred to as such. For example, an army motor pool is a profit center if it charges users for its vehicles, as is a university printing department that charges for its services. All profit centers are responsible for both revenues and costs, but they may not be expected to maximize profit.

EXHIBIT 9–1

Siesta Motels, Inc., Simplified Organization Chart

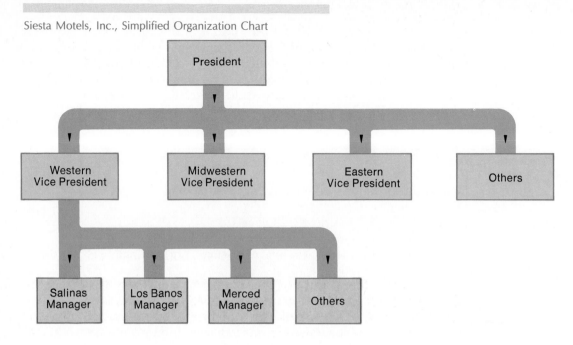

with the lowest level and work toward the top. See how the reports are integrated through three levels of responsibility. All the variances may be subdivided for further analysis, either in these reports or in more detailed reports.

Trace the $38,000 total from the Los Banos manager's report to the Western vice-president's report. The vice-president's report merely summarizes the final results of the motels under his jurisdiction. He may also want copies of the detailed statements for each motel manager reporting to him.

Also trace the $297,000 total from the Western vice-president's report to the president's report. The president's report includes data for her own corporate office plus a summarization of the entire company's operating income performance.

☐ Format of Feedback Reports

Exhibit 9–2 shows only the budgeted amounts and the variances, which are defined as the differences between the budgeted and the actual amounts. This places the focus on the variances and illustrates *management by exception*, which means that the executive's attention is concentrated on the important deviations from budgeted items. In this way, managers do not waste time on those parts of the reports that reflect smoothly running phases of operations.

Of course, this illustration represents only one possible means of presenting a report of performance. Another common reporting method shows actual results in addition to the budget and variances. Moreover, the variances could

EXHIBIT 9–2

SIESTA MOTELS, INC.
Responsibility Accounting at Various Levels
(in thousands of dollars)

| | PRESIDENT'S MONTHLY RESPONSIBILITY REPORT | | | |
| | Budget | | Variance: Favorable (Unfavorable) | |
	This Month	Year to Date	This Month	Year to Date
President's office	$ (90)	$ (300)	$ (9)	$ (30)
Western vice-president	297	850	(8)	50
Midwestern vice-president	400	1,300	20	(100)
Eastern vice-president	350	1,050	46	130
Others	300	1,000	50	100
Operating income	$1,257	$3,900	$99	$150

| | WESTERN VICE-PRESIDENT'S MONTHLY RESPONSIBILITY REPORT | | | |
| | Budget | | Variance: Favorable (Unfavorable) | |
	This Month	Year to Date	This Month	Year to Date
Vice-president's office	$ (20)	$ (40)	$(2)	$ 4
Salinas	29	(20)	(1)	(5)
Los Banos	38	133	3	16
Merced	30	90	2	10
Others	220	687	(10)	25
Operating income	$297	$850	$(8)	$50

| | LOS BANOS MANAGER'S MONTHLY RESPONSIBILITY REPORT | | | |
| | Budget | | Variance: Favorable (Unfavorable) | |
	This Month	Year to Date	This Month	Year to Date
Revenues	$80	$250	$ 5	$15
Housekeeping and supplies	$12	$ 30	$ 1	$ 4
Heat, light, power	3	10	(1)	(2)
Advertising and promotion	2	7	—	(2)
Repairs and maintenance	4	10	(2)	(1)
General	11	30	—	2
Depreciation	10	30	—	—
Total expenses	$42	$117	$(2)	$ 1
Operating income	$38	$133	$ 3	$16

also be expressed in terms of percentages of budgeted amounts. For example, revenue in Los Banos could appear as follows:

	BUDGET		ACTUAL RESULTS		VARIANCE: FAVORABLE (UNFAVORABLE)		VARIANCE: PERCENT OF BUDGETED AMOUNT	
	This Month	Year to Date	This Month	Year to Date	This Month	Year to Date	This Month	Year to Date
Revenue	$80	$250	$85	$265	$5	$15	6.3%	6.0%

The full performance report would contain a similar line-by-line analysis of all items.

Other data are often included in performance evaluation reports. For example, the motel industry characteristically includes the percentage of occupancy of rooms and the average rate per room. Restaurants will show the number of meals served and the average selling price per meal.

The exact format adopted in a particular organization depends heavily on user preferences. For instance, some companies focus on the budgeted income statement for the year. As each month unfolds, the managers receive the original plan *for the year* compared with the revised plan *for the year*. The revised plan provides management with the best available prediction of how the year's results will eventually turn out.

Even though formats and intent of responsibility reports may be geared to satisfy the preferences of the managers in a particular organization, the following fundamentals are typically followed:

1. Keep the terminology, time spans, and various internal reports consistent. In this way, budgeted figures can easily be compared with actual results and with budgets and actual results of previous and future periods.

2. Detailed reports that include total costs, unit costs, and physical amounts of inputs and outputs are useful at lower levels of management. Upper levels of management generally want highly summarized reports. A favorite saying of the chairman of CSX Corporation, a large transportation company, illustrates this: "If you can't put it on one page, it's not worth writing."[3]

☐ **Information Focus**

A responsibility accounting system should inform top management about *what* is happening in each responsibility center and *why* it is happening. Such a system has innate appeal for most top managers because it helps the delegation of decision making. Each middle manager is given responsibility for a group of activities. The responsibility accounting system should report on (1) the financial results of the activities and (2) the manager's influence on those results.

---

[3] *FE: The Magazine for Financial Executives* (June 1985), p. 27.

Often responsibility center managers are in the best position to explain their center's results even if the managers had little influence over them. Consider the responsibility accounting system at Johnson & Johnson. In 1982 seven people died after taking Extra-Strength Tylenol capsules laced with cyanide. Tylenol's market share dropped from 35% to 7%. Management spent $50 million to recall 31 million bottles of Tylenol and increased the advertising budget by $13 million. When additional deaths were linked to Tylenol capsules in 1986, management withdrew all capsules from the market. J & J has 170 operating "companies," each with great autonomy. Certainly the Tylenol managers knew more than top management about the effects in these situations. Although the Tylenol managers may not have been responsible for the disastrous financial results, they were responsible for explaining the results and reacting to the crises. The responsibility accounting system measured both the total financial results of the situations and the effects of management's responses.

The focus of responsibility accounting is information gathering. Top management often uses the information to evaluate and reward managers. But beware of using the total financial results of a responsibility center for such an evaluation. The results are affected by many factors that managers cannot influence. For example, a hurricane or a strike at a key supplier may upset a manager's plans. A well-designed responsibility accounting system separates, as much as possible, the effects of manager's decisions and actions from uncontrollable effects. Managers must explain the uncontrollable events and the actions taken to be prepared for and in response to such events. However, the uncontrollable events themselves should not affect manager's evaluations.

☐ Controllable and Uncontrollable Costs

Responsibility accounting systems often distinguish between controllable and uncontrollable costs. An **uncontrollable cost** is any cost that cannot be affected by a manager of a responsibility center within a given time span. For example, a production supervisor's performance report may be confined to usage of direct material, direct labor, and supplies and exclude depreciation, rent, and property taxes. In a prison, hospital, or hotel, the only costs on a laundry department performance report might be soap and labor; depreciation on the building and equipment would be excluded.

Controllable costs should include all costs that are influenced by a manager's decisions and actions, even if some uncontrollable events can also affect those costs. For example, warehouse managers on the Florida Gulf Coast should be prepared for hurricanes. Although the occurrence of a hurricane is beyond anybody's control, the resulting costs depend on managers' preparation. The distinction between controllable and uncontrollable costs serves an *information* purpose. Costs that are completely uncontrollable tell nothing about a manager's decisions and actions because nothing the manager does will affect the costs. Such costs should be ignored in evaluating the manager. In contrast, controllable costs provide evidence about a manager's performance. Thus, they are helpful in judging the manager.

Managers are expected to take risks even though they may have limited control over many outcomes. Indeed, in some service organizations, the rationale for working in teams is to avoid actions being controllable by a single person. Performance evaluation cannot be confined to factors that a manager can literally "control." A manager is supposed to cope with uncertainty as skillfully as possible. A responsibility accounting system should report on all factors affected by, not necessarily controlled by, a manager.

☐ Who Gets Blamed?

Responsibility accounting, budgets, variances, and the entire library of accounting techniques are basically neutral devices. However, they are frequently misused as negative weapons to place blame or find fault. Viewed positively, they assist managers to improve decisions. Moreover, they aid the delegation of decision making to lower levels, providing the autonomy that is almost always treasured by managers. Used negatively, they pose a threat to managers, and their use will be resisted and undermined.

The "blame-placing" attitude reveals a misunderstanding of the rationale of responsibility accounting, which basically asks, "Which individual in the organization is in the best position to *explain why* a specific outcome occurred? Let's trace costs down to that level so that the feedback coming from the responsibility accounting system is as well informed as feasible."

In many circumstances, the degree of the manager's control or influence over the outcome may be minimal—but responsibility accounting still is appropriate. For example, the price of gold to a jewelry manufacturer may be beyond the influence of anybody within the organization. Still, somebody usually is in the best position to predict the uncontrollable *price* of gold and report on the uncontrollable price changes. Another person is in the best position to explain the *quantity* of gold consumed. The latter individual typically has a budget based on a standard (budgeted) unit price of gold rather than on its actual unit price. In sum, one manager has *the most information* about prices and the other about quantities.

☐ Budgets and Responsibility Accounting

Responsibility accounting systems are usually built around budgets. The budgets help managers to identify the various factors affecting financial results. For example, a flexible budget separates the effects of sales volume from the other elements affecting income. A production manager who is not responsible for volume can be evaluated by comparing actual costs to the flexible budget at the actual volume level.

A budget also helps identify superior managerial actions in a less successful responsibility center. For example, a loss of $15 million in a responsibility center with a budgeted loss of $40 million may show excellent performance by the manager. In contrast, income of $15 million when income of $40 million is budgeted may indicate substandard performance.

In sum, responsibility accounting presses accountability down to the person who has the most information and the greatest potential day-to-day influence over the revenue or cost in question. This person's fundamental reporting responsibility is to explain the outcome regardless of the personal influence over the result. Once the causes of the outcome are known, the manager can be evaluated on the basis of his or her effect on that outcome. That is, the key to responsibility accounting is information gathering, not controllability over outcomes.

COST ALLOCATION IN GENERAL

To be credible, responsibility accounting depends on appropriate cost allocations. The term *cost allocation* is used here as a general label for all tracing of various costs to cost objectives such as departments or products. Like air and water, problems of cost allocation are everywhere. University presidents, city managers, hospital administrators, and corporate executives inevitably face these difficult problems. This section describes some general approaches to the solutions, but there are no easy answers.

☐ Cost Allocation as a Term

As Chapter 3 pointed out, cost allocation is fundamentally a problem of linking (1) some cost or groups of costs with (2) one or more cost objectives (examples are products, departments, and divisions). Ideally, cost allocation should assign each cost to the cost objective that *caused* it. In short, cost allocation tries to identify (1) with (2) via some function representing causation.

The linking of (1) with (2) is accomplished by a **cost-allocation base**. Such a base is the common denominator used to trace the cost or costs in question to the cost objectives. For example, the total direct-labor cost and many indirect costs are frequently expressed as costs *per hour*. Direct-labor hours are an illustration of a cost-allocation base.

Major costs, such as newsprint for a newspaper and direct professional labor for a law firm, may be allocated to departments, jobs, and projects on an item-by-item basis, using obvious cost-allocation bases such as tonnage consumed or direct-labor-hours used. Other costs, taken one at a time, are not important enough to justify being allocated individually. These costs are *pooled* and then allocated together A **cost pool** is a group of individual costs that is allocated to *cost objectives* using a single cost-allocation base. For example, building rent, utilities cost, and janitorial services may be in the same cost pool because all are allocated on the basis of square footage of space occupied. Or a university could pool all the operating costs of its registrar's office and allocate them to its colleges on the basis of the number of students in each college.

The use of terms in this area is not consistent, so be sure to pinpoint the meaning of terms in specific situations. You may encounter terms such as *allocate*, *reallocate*, *trace*, *assign*, *distribute*, *redistribute*, *load*, *burden*, *apportion*, and *reapportion* being used interchangeably to describe the same cost-accounting practice. The terms *apply* or *absorb* tend to have the narrower meaning of costs traced to *products* rather than to *departments*.

There are three basic types of cost allocations:

1. *Allocation of costs to the appropriate responsibility center*. Direct costs are physically traced to the center, but costs used jointly by more than one center are allocated using a cost-allocation base. Examples are allocating rent to departments based on floor space occupied, depreciation on jointly used machinery based on machine-hours, and general administrative expense based on total direct cost.

2. *Reallocation of costs from one responsibility center to another*. When one center provides products or services to another center, the costs are reallocated. Some centers, called **service departments**, exist only to support other departments, and their costs are totally reallocated. Examples are personnel departments, laundry departments in hospitals, and legal departments in industrial firms.

3. *Allocation of the costs of a responsibility center to products or services*. The pediatrics department of a medical clinic allocates its costs to patient visits, the assembly department of a manufacturing firm to units assembled, and the tax department of a CPA firm to clients served. The costs allocated to products or services will include those allocated to the responsibility center in (1) and (2).

☐ Four Purposes of Allocation

What logic should be used for allocating costs? This question bothers many internal users and suppliers of services in all organizations, including nonprofit organizations. The answer depends on the principal purpose or purposes of the cost allocation.

Costs are allocated for four major purposes:

1. *To predict the economic effects of planning and control decisions*. Managers within a responsibility center should be aware of all the consequences of their decisions, even consequences outside of their center. Examples are the addition of a new course in a university that causes additional work in the registrar's office, the addition of a new flight or an additional passenger on an airline that requires reservation and booking services, and the addition of a new specialty in a medical clinic that produces more work for the medical records department.

2. *To obtain desired motivation*. Cost allocations are sometimes made to promote goal coordination and managerial effort. Top management may allocate a cost to influence management behavior. Consequently, in some organizations there is no cost allocation for legal or internal auditing services or internal management consulting services because top management wants to encourage their use. In other organizations there is a cost allocation for such items to spur managers to take an interest in a particular activity or to compare the costs and benefits of the use of specified services.

3. *To compute income and asset valuations*. Costs are allocated to products and projects to measure their inventory costs and their profit contributions. These allocations may primarily serve financial accounting purposes, but the resulting costs are often used by managers in planning and in performance evaluation.

4. *To obtain a mutually agreeable price*. Sometimes prices are based directly on costs. The best examples are in regulated industries and in government contracts based on a negotiated price that provides for costs plus some profit margin. These contracts are used when ordinary market prices do not seem applicable. In these instances, cost allocations become substitutes for the usual working of

the marketplace. That is, cost allocations are a way of using a "cost-accounting pricing system" as a substitute for the "free-market pricing system."

Ideally, all four purposes would be served simultaneously by a single cost allocation. But thousands of managers and accountants will testify that for most costs the ideal is rarely achieved. Instead, cost allocations are often a major source of discontent and confusion to the affected parties. Allocating fixed costs usually causes the greatest problems. When all four purposes are unattainable simultaneously, the manager and the accountant should start attacking a cost-allocation problem by trying to identify which of the purposes should dominate in the particular situation at hand.

Too often purposes three and four dominate by default because they are externally imposed. When allocated costs are used in decision making and performance evaluation, managers should consider adjusting the allocations used to satisfy purposes three and four. Often the added benefit of using separate allocations for internal and external purposes is much greater than the cost.

THE CONTRIBUTION APPROACH TO ALLOCATION

Many organizations combine the contribution approach and responsibility accounting; they report by cost behavior pattern as well as by degrees of controllability. To do so, they must contend with problems of cost allocation. Consider an illustration of a retail grocery company. It might have the basic organizational design shown in Exhibit 9–3.

Exhibit 9–4 displays the contribution approach to reporting and cost allocation. Study this important exhibit carefully. It provides perspective on how a reporting system can be designed to stress cost behavior patterns, controllability, manager performance, and responsibility center performance simultaneously.

☐ Contribution Margin

As demonstrated in previous chapters, the contribution margin, which is revenues minus all variable expenses (line (a) in Exhibit 9–4), is especially helpful for predicting the impact on income of short-run changes in volume. Incidentally, in this case, if management prefers, a gross margin or gross profit (revenue minus the cost of the merchandise sold) could be inserted just after cost of merchandise sold. This is a good example of how gross margin and contribution margin differ. The principal example of variable operating expenses is the wages and payroll-related costs for most store personnel.

Any expected changes in income may be quickly calculated by multiplying increases in dollar sales by the contribution-margin ratio. The contribution-margin ratio for meats in Branch B is 20%. Thus a $1,000 increase in sales of meats should produce a $200 increase in income (.20 × $1,000 = $200). (This assumes, of course, no changes in selling prices, operating conditions, or mix of sales between stores 1 and 2.)

EXHIBIT 9–3

Organization Chart of a Retail Grocery Company

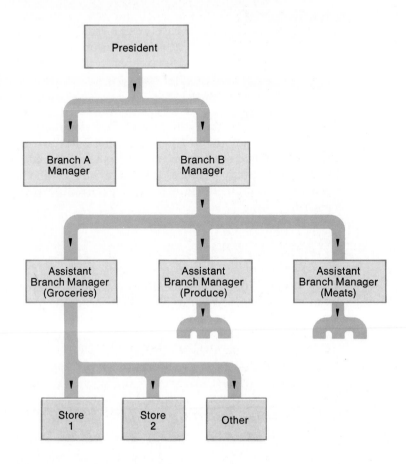

☐ Segment and Manager Performance

A **segment** (or *subunit*) is defined as any part of an organization or line of activity for which separate determination of revenue or costs is obtained. When they analyze performance, many proponents of responsibility accounting distinguish sharply between the *segment* (department, division, store, motel) as an economic investment and the *manager* as a professional decision maker. Managers frequently have little influence over many factors that affect economic performance. For instance, the manager of a motel may be relatively helpless if an energy crisis reduces automobile traffic or if unseasonable weather ruins the ski season.

Similarly, the manager of a retail store may have influence over some local advertising but not other advertising, some fixed salaries but not other salaries, and so forth. Moreover, the meat manager at both the branch and store levels for the retail grocery company may have zero influence over store

EXHIBIT 9-4

The Contribution Approach:
Model Income Statement, by Segments*
(in thousands of dollars)

	RETAIL FOOD COMPANY AS A WHOLE	COMPANY BREAKDOWN INTO TWO DIVISIONS		POSSIBLE BREAKDOWN OF BRANCH B ONLY				POSSIBLE BREAKDOWN OF BRANCH B, MEATS ONLY		
		Branch A	Branch B	Not Allocated†	Groceries	Produce	Meats	Not Allocated†	Store 1	Store 2
Net sales	$4,000	$1,500	$2,500	—	$1,300	$300	$900	—	$600	$300
Variable costs:										
Cost of merchandise sold	$3,000	$1,100	$1,900	—	$1,000	$230	$670	—	$450	$220
Variable operating expenses	260	100	160	—	100	10	50	—	35	15
Total variable costs	$3,260	$1,200	$2,060	—	$1,100	$240	$720	—	$485	$235
(a) Contribution margin	$ 740	$ 300	$ 440	—	$ 200	$ 60	$180	—	$115	$ 65
Less: Fixed costs controllable by segment managers‡	260	100	160	$ 20	40	10	90	$ 30	35	25
(b) Contribution controllable by segment managers	$ 480	$ 200	$ 280	$(20)	$ 160	$ 50	$ 90	$(30)	$ 80	$ 40
Less: Fixed costs controllable by others§	200	90	110	20	40	10	40	10	22	8
(c) Contribution by segments	$ 280	$ 110	$ 170	$(40)	$ 120	$ 40	$ 50	$(40)	$ 58	$ 32
Less: Unallocated costs‖	100									
(d) Income before income taxes	$ 180									

* Three different types of segments are illustrated here: branches, product lines, and stores. As you read across, note that the focus becomes narrower: from branch A and B, to branch B only, to meats in branch B only.

† Only those costs clearly identifiable to a product line should be allocated.

‡ Examples are certain advertising, sales promotion, salespersons' salaries, management consulting, training and supervision costs.

§ Examples are depreciation, property taxes, insurance, and perhaps the segment manager's salary.

‖ These costs are not clearly or practically allocable to any segment except by some highly questionable allocation base.

depreciation and the president's salary. When a performance report fails to distinguish controllable from uncontrollable costs, it is especially important not to use the report alone to judge the manager.

☐ Contribution Controllable by Segment Managers

Exhibit 9–4 distinguishes between the segment contribution (item (c)) and the contribution that is controllable by segment managers (item (b)). Managers are asked to explain the total segment contribution, but are held responsible only for the controllable contribution.

Note that fixed costs controllable by the segment manager are deducted from the contribution margin to obtain the contribution controllable by segment managers. These are usually discretionary fixed costs. Examples of these discretionary costs are some local advertising but not all advertising and some fixed salaries but not the manager's own salary.

In many organizations, managers have some latitude to trade off some variable costs for fixed costs. To save variable material and labor costs, managers might make heavier outlays for machinery, labor-saving devices, quality control inspectors, maintenance, management consulting fees, employee training programs, and so on. Moreover, decisions on advertising, research, and sales promotion have effects on sales volumes and hence on contribution margins. That is why the contribution margin alone is not a satisfactory measure of manager performance. However, the controllable contribution attempts to capture the results of these trade-offs.

The distinctions in Exhibit 9–4 among which items belong in what cost classification are inevitably not clear-cut. For example, determining controllability is always a problem when service department costs are allocated to other departments. Should the store manager bear a part of the branch headquarters costs? If so, how much and on what basis? How much, if any, store depreciation or lease rentals should be deducted in computing the controllable contribution? There are no easy answers to these questions. They are worked out in various ways from organization to organization. Again, for management control purposes there are no constraints of external accounting principles on designing acceptable management accounting systems. The answers depend fundamentally on what reporting system will bring the most net benefits in terms of motivation and collective decisions.

Consider the fixed costs controllable by segment managers (deducted between items (a) and (b) in Exhibit 9–4). The "not allocated" columns show amounts of $20,000 and $30,000, respectively. This approach recognizes that perphaps some clusters of costs should not be allocated below specified levels in the organization's hierarchy. Of the $160,000 fixed cost that is controllable by the manager of Branch B, $140,000 is also controllable by subordinates (grocery, produce, and meats managers), but $20,000 is not. The latter could be the secretarial salaries of the Branch B general manager. Similarly, the $30,000 in that same line may include costs of general meat advertisements that may not be allocated to individual stores.

☐ Contribution by Segments

The contribution by segments, line (c) in Exhibit 9–4, is an attempt to approximate the economic *performance of the segment*, as distinguished from the *performance of its manager*. The "fixed costs controllable by others" typically include committed costs (such as depreciation and property taxes) and discretionary costs (such as the segment manager's salary). These costs are examples of items that are minimally influenced by the segment manager within a reporting period of a year or less.

Exhibit 9–4 shows "unallocated costs" immediately before line (d). They might include central corporate costs such as the costs of the president's office and many costs of the legal and accounting activities. When a persuasive "cause-and-effect" or "benefits-received" justification for allocating such costs cannot be found, many organizations favor not allocating them to segments.

The contribution approach highlights the relative objectivity of various measures of performance evaluation. The contribution margin tends to be the most objective. As you read downward, the allocations become more difficult, and the resulting measures of contributions or income become more subject to dispute. In contrast, the traditional approach to income statements rarely hesitates to use full-cost allocations. Therefore, it tends to offer less sharp distinctions between variable and fixed costs and between controllable and uncontrollable costs.

HOW TO ALLOCATE FOR PLANNING AND CONTROL

☐ General Guides

What causes costs? Organizations incur costs to support the operations of their segments and the production of goods and services. Essentially, costs are *caused* by the very same activities that are usually chosen as cost objectives. Examples are products produced, patients seen, personnel records processed, and legal advice given. The *effects* of these activities are various costs. Therefore the manager and the accountant should search for some cost-allocation base that establishes a convincing relationship between the cause and the effect and that permits reliable predictions of how costs will be affected by decisions regarding the activities.

This important principle will be illustrated by considering allocation of service department costs. The preferred guides for allocating service department costs are:

1. Use responsibility accounting and flexible budgets for each service (staff) department, just as they are used for each production or operating (line) department. The performance of a service department is evaluated by comparing actual costs to a flexible budget, independent of how the costs are later allocated. From the flexible budget, variable-cost pools and fixed-cost pools can be identified for use in allocation.

2. Allocate variable- and fixed-cost pools separately. This is sometimes called the dual method of allocation. Note that one service department (such as a computer department) can contain a variable-cost pool and a fixed-cost pool. That is, costs may be pooled within and among departments if desired.
3. Establish part or all of the details regarding cost allocation in advance of rendering the service rather than after the fact.

☐ Using the Guides

To illustrate these guides, consider a simplified example of a computer department of a university that serves two major users, the School of Earth Sciences and the School of Engineering. The computer mainframe was acquired on a five-year lease that is not cancelable unless prohibitive cost penalties are paid.

How should costs be allocated to the user departments? Suppose there are two major purposes for the allocation: (1) predicting economic effects of the use of the computer and (2) motivating toward optimal usage. Apply the guides enumerated earlier:

1. Analyze the costs of the computer department in detail. Suppose the flexible-budget formula for the forthcoming fiscal year is $100,000 monthly fixed costs plus $200 variable cost per hour of computer time used.
2. *Allocate separately* the variable-cost pool and the fixed-cost pool.
3. *Establish in advance* the details regarding the cost allocation.

Guides (2) and (3) will be considered together in the following sections on variable-cost pools and fixed-cost pools.

☐ Variable-Cost Pool

Ideally, the variable-cost pool should be allocated as follows:

$$\text{budgeted unit rate} \times \text{actual quantities of service units used}$$

The cause-and-effect relationship is clear: the heavier the usage, the higher the total costs. In this example, the rate used would be the budgeted rate of $200 per hour.

The use of *budgeted* cost rates rather than *actual* cost rates for allocating variable costs of service departments protects the using departments from intervening price fluctuations and also often protects them from inefficiencies. An organization that allocates *actual* total service department cost holds user department managers responsible for costs beyond their control and provides less incentive for service departments to be efficient. Both effects are undesirable.

The best procedure for allocating variable-cost pools is to predict the complete cost of routine services in advance. For example, the cost of a specific repair job would be predetermined based on budgeted cost rates multiplied by the budgeted or standard hours of input allowed for accomplishing the repairs. User department managers sometimes complain more vigorously about uncertainty over allocations and the poor management of a service department than about the choice of a cost-allocation base (such as direct-labor dollars or number of employees). Such complaints are less likely if the service department managers have budget responsibility and the user departments are protected from short-run price fluctuations and inefficiencies.

□ Fixed-Cost Pool

Ideally, the fixed-cost pool should be allocated as follows:

budgeted fraction of capacity available for use × total budgeted fixed costs

Before exploring the implications of this approach, consider our example. Suppose the deans had originally predicted the following long-run average monthly usage: earth sciences, 210 hours, and engineering, 490 hours, a total of 700 hours. The fixed-cost pool would be allocated as follows:

	EARTH SCIENCES	ENGINEERING
Fixed costs per month:		
210/700, or 30% of $100,000	$30,000	
490/700, or 70% of $100,000		$70,000

This predetermined lump-sum approach is based on the long-run capacity *available* to the user, regardless of actual usage from month to month. The reasoning is that the level of fixed costs is affected by long-range planning regarding the overall level of service and the *relative expected* usage, not by *short-run* fluctuations in service levels and relative *actual* usage.

A major strength of the use of capacity *available* rather than capacity *used* for allocating *budgeted* fixed costs is that short-run allocations to user departments are not affected by the *actual* usage of *other* user departments. Such a budgeted lump-sum approach is more likely to have the desired motivational effects with respect to the ordering of services in both the short run and the long run.

□ Fixed Pool and Actual Usage

In practice, fixed-cost pools often are inappropriately allocated on the basis of capacity used, not capacity available. Suppose the computer department allocated the total actual costs after the fact. At the end of the month, total *actual* costs would be allocated in proportion to the *actual* hours used by the consuming departments. Compare the costs borne by the two schools when Earth Sciences uses 200 hours and Engineering 400 hours:

Total costs incurred, $100,000 + 600($200) = $220,000	
Earth Sciences: 200/600 × $220,000 =	$ 73,333
Engineering: 400/600 × $220,000 =	146,667
Total cost allocated	$220,000

What happens if Earth Sciences uses only 100 hours during the following month while Engineering still uses 400 hours?

Total costs incurred, $100,000 + 500($200) = $200,000	
Earth Sciences: 100/500 × $200,000	$ 40,000
Engineering: 400/500 × $200,000 =	160,000
Total cost allocated	$200,000

Engineering has done nothing differently, but it must bear higher costs of $13,333, an increase of 9%. Its short-run costs depend on what *other* consumers have used, not solely on its own actions. This phenomenon is caused by a faulty allocation method for the *fixed* portion of total costs, a method whereby the allocations are highly sensitive to fluctuations in the actual volumes used by the various consuming departments. This weakness is avoided by the dual approach that provides for a predetermined lump-sum allocation of fixed costs.

To consider further the use of *budgeted* rates for allocating *variable* costs, return to our data for 600 hours of use. Suppose inefficiencies in the computer department caused the variable costs to be $140,000 instead of the 600 hours × $200, or $120,000 budgeted. A common weakness of cost allocation is to allocate the costs of inefficiencies to the consumer departments. To remedy this weakness, a good cost-allocation scheme would allocate only the $120,000 to the consuming departments and would let the $20,000 remain as an unallocated unfavorable budget variance of the computer department. This is responsibility accounting in action, and it reduces the resentment of user managers. The allocation of costs of inefficiency seems unjustified because the "consuming departments" have to bear another department's cost of waste.

Most consumers prefer to know the total price in advance. They become nervous when an automobile mechanic or a contractor undertakes a job without specifying prices. As a minimum, they like to know the hourly rates that they must bear. Therefore, predetermined unit prices (at least) should be used. Where feasible, predetermined total prices should be used for various kinds of work based on flexible budgets and standards.

To illustrate, when we have our automobiles repaired, we are routinely given firm total prices for various types of services. Furthermore, these prices are not affected by the volume of work handled on a particular day. Imagine your feelings if you came to an automobile service department to get your car and were told, "Our daily fixed overhead is $1,000. Yours was the only car in our shop today, so we are charging you the full $1,000. If we had processed 100 cars today, your charge would have been only $10."

☐ Troubles with Using Lump Sums

If fixed costs are allocated on the basis of long-range plans, there is a natural tendency on the part of consumers to underestimate their planned usage and thus obtain a smaller fraction of the cost allocation. Top management can counteract these tendencies by monitoring predictions and by following up and using feedback to keep future predictions more honest.

In some organizations there are even definite rewards in the form of salary increases for managers who are skillful as accurate predictors. Moreover, some cost-allocation methods provide for penalties for underpredictions. For example, if a manager predicts usage of 210 hours and then demands 300 hours, either he doesn't get the hours or he pays a dear price for every hour beyond 210.

☐ Allocating Central Costs

Many central costs, such as the president's salary and related expenses, public relations, legal, income tax planning, companywide advertising, and basic research, are difficult to allocate on the basis of cause and effect. Therefore many companies do not allocate them at all. Other companies use allocation bases such as the revenue of each division, the cost of goods sold of each division, the total assets of each division, or the total costs of each division (before allocation of the central costs).

The desperate search for such allocation bases is a manifestation of a widespread, deep-seated belief that all costs must somehow be fully allocated to the revenue-producing (operating) parts of the organization. The flimsy assumptions that might underlie such allocations are widely recognized, but most managers accept them as a fact of a manager's life—as long as all managers seem to be treated alike and thus "fairly."

The use of the foregoing bases might provide a *rough* indication of cause-and-effect relationships. Basically, however, they represent a "soak-the-rich" or "ability-to-bear" philosophy of cost allocation. For example, the costs of companywide advertising, such as the goodwill sponsorship of a program on a noncommercial television station, might be allocated to all products and divisions on the basis of the dollar sales in each. But such costs precede sales. They are discretionary costs as determined by management policies, not by sales results.

☐ Choices of Allocation Bases

An attractive allocation base for central services is usage, either actual or estimated. Many organizations, however, regard such measurements as infeasible. For example, 60% of the companies in a large survey use sales revenue as an allocation base.

Not all central services are allocated in the same manner. The costs of such services as public relations, top corporate management overhead, real estate department, and corporate-planning department are the least likely to be allocated on the basis of usage; the most likely are data processing, advertising, and operations research.

Companies that allocate central costs by usage tend to generate less resentment. Consider the experience of J. C. Penney Co. (*Business Week*, April 12, 1982, p. 107):

□	The controller's office wanted subsidiaries such as Thrift Drug Co. and the insurance operations to base their share of corporate personnel, legal, and auditing costs on their revenues. The subsidiaries contended that they maintained their own personnel and legal departments, and should be assessed far less.

. . . The subcommittee addressed the issue by asking the corporate departments to approximate the time and costs involved in servicing the subsidiaries. The final allocation plan, based on these studies, cost the divisions less than they were initially assessed but more than they had wanted to pay. Nonetheless, the plan was implemented easily.

□ Using Budgeted Allocation Bases

Again, if the costs of central services are to be allocated, the use of *budgeted* sales or some other *budgeted* allocation base is preferred to the use of *actual* sales. At least this method means that the short-run costs of a given consuming department will not be affected by the fortunes of other consuming departments.

For example, suppose central advertising were allocated on the basis of potential sales in two territories:

| | TERRITORIES | | | |
	A	B	TOTAL	PERCENT
Budgeted sales	$500	$500	$1,000	100%
Central advertising allocated	$ 50	$ 50	$ 100	10%

Consider the possible differences in allocations when actual sales become known:

| | TERRITORIES | |
	A	B
Actual sales	$300	$600
Central advertising:		
1. Allocated on basis of budgeted sales	$ 50	$ 50
or		
2. Allocated on basis of actual sales	$ 33	$ 67

Compare allocation 1 with 2. Allocation 1 is preferable. It indicates a low ratio of sales to advertising in territory A. It directs attention to where it is deserved. In contrast, allocation 2 soaks territory B with more advertising cost because of the *achieved* results and relieves territory A because it had lesser success. This is another example of the analytical confusion that can arise when cost allocations to one consuming department depend on the activity of other consuming departments.

THE PRODUCT-COSTING PURPOSE

☐ Relating Costs to Outputs

Until this point, we have concentrated on cost allocation to divisions, departments, and similar segments of an entity. Cost allocation is often carried one step farther—to the outputs of these departments, however defined. Examples are *products* such as automobiles, furniture, and newspapers. Other examples are personal *services* such as hospitalization and education.

Costs are allocated to products for inventory valuation purposes and for decision purposes such as pricing, adding products, and promoting products. Cost allocation is also performed for cost-reimbursement purposes. For example, many defense contractors are reimbursed for the "costs" of producing products for the government.

The general approach to allocating costs to final products or services is:

1. Prepare budgets for all departments, including (a) the *operating (line)* or *production* or *revenue-producing* departments that work directly on the final product or service and (b) the *service (staff* or *support)* departments that help the operating departments.
2. Choose the most logical cost-allocation bases that seem economically feasible. Usually no more than two allocation bases are used for a given service department, one for its variable-cost pool and one for its fixed-cost pool. Often all the costs of a service department are allocated using only one base.
3. Allocate the costs of the service departments to the operating departments. The operating departments have now been allocated all the costs: their direct department costs and the service department costs.
4. Allocate (apply) the total costs accumulated in item 3 to the products or services that are the outputs of the operating departments.

☐ Allocation of Service Department Costs

The foregoing steps can be illustrated in a hospital setting. The output of a hospital is not as easy to define as the output of a factory. The objective is the improved health of patients, but that is hard to quantify. Consequently, the output of revenue-producing departments might be the following:

DEPARTMENT	MEASURES OF OUTPUT*
Radiology	X-ray films processed
Laboratory	Tests administered
Daily patient services†	Patient-days of care (that is, the number of patients multiplied by the number of days of each patient's stay)

* These become the product cost objectives, the various revenue-producing activities of a hospital.

† There would be many of these departments, such as obstetrics, pediatrics, and orthopedics. Moreover, there may be both in-patient and out-patient care.

As you undoubtedly suspect, the allocation of hospital costs to cost objectives is marked by trade-offs between costs and the possible benefits to be derived from more elaborate cost allocations. During the 1970s, hospitals found it worthwhile to develop elaborate cost-allocation methods. Why? Because the government and insurance companies paid for services based on the hospital's costs. The cost-allocation directly affected a hospital's revenue.

During the 1980s, government agencies began paying hospitals fixed fees for many medical services. Yet, more than ever before, hospitals are continuing to invest in better methods of allocating costs. Why? Because hospital managers want to know the cost of various services to help decide which to emphasize or deemphasize. For example, a major health maintenance organization in Portland, Oregon, recently decided to select a single local hospital to provide open heart surgery services to its members. Each hospital submitted a bid, indicating what it would charge for such a procedure. Knowing the cost of open heart surgery was crucial to submitting a competitive bid that was also financially attractive to the hospital.

☐ **Applying the Steps**

To keep the data manageable, suppose there are only three service departments in addition to the revenue-producing departments just mentioned: Administrative and Fiscal Services, Plant Operations and Maintenance, and Laundry.

1. *Prepare departmental budgets*. All six departments would prepare responsibility-center budgets for operating their own areas as efficiently and effectively as possible. These budgets would be confined to their "direct departmental costs" that are the primary responsibility of the particular department manager. Examples of such costs are salaries and supplies.
2. *Choose allocation bases*. Common allocation bases for various hospital service departments are shown in Exhibit 9–5. Exhibit 9–6 shows the allocation bases and relationships of our sample hospital.

EXHIBIT 9–5

Hospital Cost-allocation Bases*

Purchasing—Costs of supplies used by each center; "other" direct expenses.
Nursing service, administrative office—Hours of nursing service supervised; estimated supervision time.
Pharmacy—Amount of requisitions priced at retail; number of requisitions; special studies.
Medical records—Estimated time spent on records; number of patient-days; number of admissions.
Admitting—Number of admissions.
Plant operations and maintenance—Square feet of area occupied; work orders.
Laundry and linens—Pounds of soiled laundry processed; pounds weighted by degree of care (nurses' uniforms would be double- or triple-weighted to allow for starching or pressing).
Administrative and Fiscal Services—Accumulated costs in each department before these costs are allocated; number of personnel. This is a general cost center that should be subdivided into several cost centers and be allocated on different bases.

* For a thorough discussion, see *Cost Finding and Rate Setting for Hospitals* (Chicago: American Hospital Association).

EXHIBIT 9–6

Cost-Allocation Bases by Department

| | SERVICE DEPARTMENTS | | | REVENUE DEPARTMENTS | | |
	Adminis- trative and Fiscal Services	Plant Operations and Maintenance	Laundry	Radiology	Laboratory	Daily Patient Services
Direct departmental costs	$ —	$800,000	$200,000	$1,000,000	$400,000	$1,600,000
Square feet occupied	—	—	5,000	12,000	3,000	80,000
Pounds	—	—	—	80,000	20,000	300,000

3. *Allocate service department costs.* There are two popular ways to allocate:

Method 1, **Direct Method**. As the name implies, this method ignores other service departments when any given service department's costs are allocated to the revenue-producing (operating) departments. For example, as Exhibit 9–7 shows, the service rendered by Plant Operations and Maintenance to Laundry is not considered. The direct method is popular. Its outstanding virtue is simplicity.

Method 2, **Step-down Method**. Hospitals are increasingly being required to use this method, which has been used by many manufacturing companies for years. As Exhibit 9–7 shows, the step-down method recognizes that service departments support the activities in other service departments as well as in revenue-producing departments. A sequence of allocations is chosen, usually by starting with the service department that renders the greatest service (as measured by costs) to the greatest number of other service departments. The last service department in the sequence is the one that renders the least service to the least number of other service departments. Once a department's costs are allocated to other departments, no subsequent service department costs are allocated back to it.

Administrative and Fiscal Services will be allocated on the basis of the relative costs of other departments and will be allocated first. Because a department's own costs are not allocated to itself, its costs are not included in the allocation base.

Plant Operations and Maintenance will be allocated second on the basis of square feet occupied, and none will be allocated to itself or back to Administrative and Fiscal Services. Therefore no square footage is presented for these two departments in Exhibit 9–6.

Laundry will be allocated third; none will be allocated back to the first two departments, *even though the first two departments may have used laundry services*.

Sometimes special studies of relative usage of services are made to establish what percentage should go to various consuming departments. For example, the hospital administrator's salary might be allocated separately in proportion to the average time she spends on each department. This allocation might be unchanged for a year or two. Similarly, laundry might be weighed periodically on a sampling basis and the results used as a predetermined means of allocation for a year regardless of interim usage.

EXHIBIT 9–7

Allocation of Service Department Costs: Two Methods

	ADMINISTRATIVE AND FISCAL SERVICES	PLANT OPERATIONS AND MAINTENANCE	LAUNDRY	RADIOLOGY	LABORATORY	DAILY PATIENT SERVICES
Allocation base—from Exhibit 9-6	Accumulated costs	Sq. footage	Pounds			
Method One, Direct Method						
Direct departmental costs before allocation	$1,000,000	$ 800,000	$200,000	$1,000,000	$400,000	$1,600,000
Administrative and fiscal services	(1,000,000)	—	—	333,333*	133,333	533,334
Plant operations and maintenance		(800,000)	—	101,052†	25,263	673,685
Laundry			(200,000)	40,000‡	10,000	150,000
Total costs after allocation				$1,474,385	$568,596	$2,957,019
Product output in films, tests, and patient-days, respectively				60,000	50,000	30,000
Cost per unit of output				$24.573	$11.372	$98.567
Method Two, Step-Down Method						
Direct departmental costs before allocation	$1,000,000	$ 800,000	$200,000	$1,000,000	$400,000	$1,600,000
Administrative and fiscal services	(1,000,000)	200,000§	50,000	250,000	100,000	400,000
Plant operations and maintenance		(1,000,000)	50,000¶	120,000	30,000	800,000
Laundry			(300,000)	60,000#	15,000	225,000
Total costs after allocation				$1,430,000	$545,000	$3,025,000
Product output in films, tests, and patient-days, respectively				60,000	50,000	30,000
Cost per unit of output				$23.833	$10.900	$100.833

Notes: The cost-allocation bases are from Exhibit 9-6.

* $1,000,000 ÷ ($1,000,000 + $400,000 + $1,600,000) = 33⅓%; 33⅓% × $1,000,000 = $333,333; etc.

† $800,000 ÷ (12,000 + 3,000 + 80,000) = $8.4210526; $8.4210526 × 12,000 sq. ft. = $101,052; etc.

‡ $200,000 ÷ (80,000 + 20,000 + 300,000) = $.50; $.50 × 80,000 = $40,000; etc.

§ $1,000,000 ÷ ($800,000 + $200,000 + $1,000,000 + $400,000 + $1,600,000) = 25%; 25% × $800,000 = $200,000; etc.

¶ $1,000,000 ÷ (5,000 + 12,000 + 3,000 + 80,000) = $10.00; $10.00 × 5,000 sq. ft. = $50,000; etc.

\# $300,000 ÷ (80,000 + 20,000 + 300,000) = $.75; $.75 × 80,000 = $60,000; etc.

4. *Allocate (apply) the total costs to products*. The final step is sometimes called **cost application**, whereby total departmental costs are applied to the revenue-producing products. Our illustation in Exhibit 9–7 is a hospital, but the same fundamental approach is used for manufactured products, for research projects in universities, and for client cases in social welfare departments.

Compare Methods One and Two in Exhibit 9–7. In many instances, the final product costs may not differ enough to warrant investing in a cost-allocation method that is any fancier than the direct method.[4] But sometimes even small differences may be significant to a government agency or anybody paying for a large volume of services based on costs. For example, in Exhibit 9–7 the "cost" of an "average" laboratory test is either $11.37 or $10.90. This may be significant for the fiscal committee of the hospital's board of trustees, who must decide on hospital prices. Thus cost allocation often is a technique that helps answer the vital question, "Who should pay for what, and how much?"

SUMMARY

Responsibility accounting assigns particular revenues and costs to the individual in the organization who has the greatest potential day-to-day influence over them.

Costs are allocated for four major purposes: (1) Prediction of economic effects of decisions, (2) motivation, (3) income and asset measurement, and (4) pricing.

The contribution approach to the income statement and to the problems of cost allocation is accounting's most effective method of helping management to evaluate performance and make decisions. Allocations are made with thoughtful regard for the purpose of the information being compiled. Various subdivisions of net income are drawn for different purposes. The contribution approach distinguishes sharply between various degrees of objectivity in cost allocations.

Where feasible, fixed costs of service departments should be reallocated by using predetermined monthly lump sums for providing a basic capacity to serve. Variable costs should be reallocated by using a predetermined standard unit rate for the services actually used.

SUMMARY PROBLEM FOR YOUR REVIEW

☐ **Problem**

Review the section "How to Allocate for Planning and Control," pages 273–278, especially the example of the use of the computer by the university. Recall that the flexible-budget formula was $100,000 monthly plus $200 per hour of computer time used. Based on long-run predicted usage, the fixed costs were allocated on a lump-sum basis, 30% to earth sciences and 70% to engineering.

1. Show the total allocation if earth sciences used 210 hours and engineering used 420 hours in a given month. Assume that the actual costs coincided exactly with the flexible-budgeted amount.

2. Assume the same facts as in Requirement 1 except that the fixed costs were allocated on the basis of actual hours of usage. Show the total allocation of

---

[4] The most defensible theoretical accuracy is generated by the *reciprocal method*, which is rarely used in practice because of its complexity. Simultaneous equations and linear algebra are used to solve for the impact of mutually interacting services, such as between Administrative and Fiscal Services and Plant Operations and Maintenance.

costs to each school. As the dean of Earth Sciences, would you prefer this method or the method in requirement 1? Explain.

□ Solution

1.

	EARTH SCIENCES	ENGINEERING
Fixed costs per month:		
210/700, or 30% of $100,000	$30,000	
490/700, or 70% of $100,000		$70,000
Variable costs @ $200 per hour:		
210 hours	42,000	
420 hours		84,000
Total costs	$72,000	$154,000

2.

	EARTH SCIENCES	ENGINEERING
Fixed costs per month:		
210/630 × $100,000	$33,333	
420/630 × $100,000		$ 66,667
Variable costs, as before	42,000	84,000
Total costs	$75,333	$150,667

The dean of Earth Sciences would probably be unhappy. His school has operated exactly in accordance with the long-range plan. Nevertheless, Earth Sciences is bearing an extra $3,333 of fixed costs because of what *another* consumer is using. He would prefer the method in requirement 1 because it insulates Earth Sciences from short-run fluctuations in costs caused by the actions of other users.

HIGHLIGHTS TO REMEMBER

1. Cost, profit, and investment centers are responsibility centers where managers control cost, cost and revenues, and cost, revenues, and investment, respectively.
2. The aim of responsibility accounting is *not* to place blame. Instead, it is to evaluate performance and provide feedback so that future operations can be improved. The central question is, Who has the most information? not who bears the blame?
3. Ideally, cost-allocation bases should measure a cause-effect relationship between costs and cost objectives.
4. Costs to be allocated are assigned to cost pools, preferably keeping variable costs and fixed costs in separate pools.
5. The selection of a cost-allocation method should be influenced by how the results of the alternative allocation methods affect decisions. Full-cost allocations are wide-spread, apparently because accountants and managers feel that these methods generally induce better decisions than partial-cost allocations.

ACCOUNTING VOCABULARY

Cost-Allocation Base, *p. 267*   Cost Application *283*   Cost Centers *261*   Cost Pool *267*   Direct Method *281*   Investment Centers *261*   Profit Centers *261* Responsibility Accounting System *260*   Responsibility Center *260*   Segment *271* Service Department *268*   Step-Down Method *281*   Uncontrollable Cost *265*.

ASSIGNMENT MATERIAL

☐ Fundamental Assignment Material

9–1. **RESPONSIBILITY OF PURCHASING DEPARTMENT.**   (Alternate is 9–19). Hazleton Electronics Company, a privately held enterprise, has a subcontract from a large computer company on the West Coast. Although Hazleton was low bidder, the computer company was reluctant to award the business to Hazleton, a newcomer to this kind of activity. Consequently, Hazleton assured the company of its financial strength by submitting its audited financial statements. Moreover, Hazleton agreed to a penalty clause of $4,000 per day to be paid by Hazleton for each day of late delivery for whatever cause.

Amy Chang is the Hazleton manager responsible for acquiring materials and parts in time to meet production schedules. She placed an order with a Hazleton supplier for a critical manufactured component. The supplier, which had a reliable record for meeting schedules, gave Chang an acceptable delivery date. Chang checked up several times and was assured that the component would arrive at Hazleton on schedule.

On the date specified by the supplier for shipment to Hazleton, Chang was informed that the component had been damaged during final inspection. It was delivered ten days late. Chang had allowed four extra days for possible delays, but Hazleton was six days late in delivering to the computer company. Hence a penalty of $24,000 was paid.

Required: | What department should bear the penalty? Why?

9–2. **ALLOCATING AUTOMOBILE COSTS.**   (Alternates are 9–26 and 9–28.) The motor pool of a major city provides automobiles for the use of various city departments. Currently, the motor pool has 50 autos. A recent study showed that it costs $3,600 of annual fixed cost per automobile plus $.10 per mile variable cost to own, operate, and maintain autos such as those provided by the motor pool.

Each month, the costs of the motor pool are allocated to the user departments on the basis of miles driven. On average, each auto is driven 24,000 miles annually, although wide month-to-month variations occur. In April 19X7, the 50 autos were driven a total of 50,000 miles. The motor pool's total costs for April were $21,500.

The chief planner for the city always seemed concerned about her auto costs. She was especially upset in April when she was charged $6,450 for the 15,000 miles driven in the department's five autos. This is the normal monthly mileage in the department. Her memo to the head of the motor pool stated, "I can certainly get autos at less than the $.43 per mile you charged in April." The response was, "I am under instructions to allocate the motor pool costs to the user departments. Your department was responsible for 30% of the April usage (15,000 miles ÷ 50,000 miles), so I allocated 30% of the motor pool's April costs to you (.30 × $21,500). That just seems fair."

1. Calculate the city's average annual cost per mile for owning, maintaining, and operating an auto.
2. Explain why the allocated cost in April ($.43 per mile) exceeds the average in Requirement 1.
3. Describe any undesirable behavioral effects of the cost allocation method used.
4. How would you improve the cost allocation method?

9–3. **ALLOCATING CENTRAL COSTS.** The Midwest Baking Company allocates all central corporate overhead costs to its divisions. Some costs, such as specified internal auditing and legal costs, are identified on the basis of time spent. However, other costs are harder to allocate, so the revenue achieved by each division is used as an allocation base. Examples of such costs are executive salaries, travel, secretarial, utilities, rent, depreciation, donations, corporate planning, and general marketing costs.

Allocations on the basis of revenue for 19X7 were (in millions):

DIVISION	REVENUE	ALLOCATED COSTS
Breads	$200	$20
Pastries	100	10
Health Foods	50	5
Total	$350	$35

In 19X8, revenue from breads remained unchanged. However, revenue from health foods soared to $90 million. The latter are troublesome to forecast because this market is so influenced by fads. Midwest had expected a sharp rise in pastry revenue, but severe competitive conditions resulted in a decline to $60 million. The total cost allocated on the basis of revenue was again $35 million, despite rises in other costs. The president was pleased that central costs did not rise for the year.

1. Compute the allocations of costs to each division for 19X8.
2. How would each division manager probably feel about the cost allocation in 19X8 as compared with 19X7? What are the weaknesses of using revenue as a basis for cost allocation?
3. Suppose the budgeted revenues for 19X8 were $200, $100, and $70 million for breads, pastries, and health foods, respectively, and the budgeted revenues were used as a cost-allocation base. Compute the allocations of costs to each division for 19X8. Do you prefer this method to the one used in Requirement 1? Why?
4. Many accountants and managers oppose allocating any central costs. Why?

☐ **Additional Assignment Material**

9–4. "Variable costs are controllable and fixed costs are uncontrollable." Do you agree? Explain.
9–5. "Managers may trade off variable costs for fixed costs." Give three examples.
9–6. Name two major factors that influence controllability.
9–7. "The contribution margin is the best measure of short-run performance." Do you agree? Why?
9–8. What is the most controversial aspect of the contribution approach to cost allocation?
9–9. What is *dual allocation*?
9–10. "A commonly misused basis for allocation is dollar sales." Explain.
9–11. Give three guides for the allocation of service department costs.
9–12. How should national advertising costs be allocated to territories?

9-13. Give five terms that are sometimes used as substitutes for the term *allocate*.

9-14. "Managers of profit centers should be held responsible for the center's entire profit. They are responsible for profit even if they cannot control all factors affecting it." Discuss.

9-15. How does the term *cost application* differ from *cost allocation*?

9-16. Give four examples of segments.

9-17. "Always try to distinguish between the performance of a segment and its manager." Why?

9-18. **HOSPITAL DEPRECIATION ALLOCATION.** Many hospital accounting systems are designed so that depreciation on buildings and fixed equipment is collected in a separate cost pool and then allocated to departments, usually on the basis of square feet of space occupied. In contrast, depreciation of major movable equipment is allocated directly to the departments that use such equipment.

Is square feet a logical allocation base? Explain.

9-19. **RESPONSIBILITY ACCOUNTING.** (Alternate is 9-1.) The Lucchini Company makes modular furniture. It has three departments: Material Receiving and Preparation, Wood Shop, and Finishing. Standards are set for each department. Variances are measured and are reported to both departmental managers and top management. Everyone recognizes that the variances play an important part in performance evaluation.

John Sandberg was recently appointed manager of the Finishing Department. After just two months on the job, John approached the executive vice-president of Lucchini with a complaint. Already his department had received two unfavorable variance reports. John maintained that both cases were a result of sloppy work in the other departments. The first resulted from substandard materials. Because of blemishes in the wood, an extra coat of paint was needed on a whole batch of units. The second occurred because a nail-set machine in the wood shop had malfunctioned, making extra deep holes. The finishing process required two passes to fill such deep holes.

Required:
1. Is John Sandberg's complaint valid? Explain the reason(s) for your answer.
2. What would you recommend that Lucchini Company do to solve the problem with John Sandberg and his complaint?

9-20. **MUNICIPAL RESPONSIBILITY ACCOUNTING.** In 1975 New York City barely avoided bankruptcy. By 1985 it had one of the most sophisticated budgeting and reporting systems of any municipality, and its budgetary problems had nearly disappeared. The Integrated Financial Management System (IFMS) "clearly identifies managers in line agencies, and correlates allocations and expenditures with organizational structure. . . . In addition, managers have more time to take corrective measures when variances between budgeted and actual expenditures start to develop." (*FE—The Magazine for Financial Executives*, August 1985, p. 26.)

Discuss how a responsibility accounting system like IFMS can help manage a municipality such as New York City.

9-21. **RESPONSIBILITY FOR A STABLE EMPLOYMENT POLICY.** The Fast-Weld Metal Fabricating Company has been manufacturing machine tools for a number of years and has an industrywide reputation for doing high-quality work. The company has been faced with irregularity of output over the years. It has been company policy to lay off welders as soon as there was insufficient work to keep them busy and to rehire them when demand warranted. The company, however, now has poor labor relations and finds it very difficult to hire good welders because of its layoff policy. Consequently, the quality of the work has continually been declining.

The plant manager has proposed that the welders, who earn $8 per hour, be retained during slow periods to do menial plant maintenance work that is normally performed by workers earning $5.85 per hour in the plant maintenance department.

You, as controller, must decide the most appropriate accounting procedure to handle the wages of the welders doing plant maintenance work. What department or departments should be charged with this work, and at what rate? Discuss the implications of your plan.

9–22. **COST OF PASSENGER TRAFFIC.** Southern Pacific Railroad (SP) has a commuter operation that services passengers along a route between San Jose and San Francisco. Problems of cost allocation were highlighted in a news story about SP's application to the Public Utilities Commission (PUC) for a rate increase. The PUC staff claimed that the "avoidable annual cost" of running the operation was $700,000, in contrast to SP officials' claim of a loss of $9 million. PUC's estimate was based on what SP would be able to save if it shut down the commuter operation.

The SP loss estimate was based on a "full-allocation-of-costs" method, which allocates a share of common maintenance and overhead costs to the passenger service.

If the PUC accepted its own estimate, a 25% fare increase would have been justified, whereas SP sought a 96% fare increase.

The PUC stressed that commuter costs represent less than 1% of the system-wide costs of SP and that 57% of the commuter costs are derived from some type of allocation method—sharing the costs of other operations.

SP's representative stated that "avoidable cost" is not an appropriate way to allocate costs for calculating rates. He said that "it is not fair to include just so-called above-the-rail costs" because there are other real costs associated with commuter service. Examples are maintaining smoother connections and making more frequent track inspections.

Required:

1. As Public Utilities commissioner, what approach toward cost allocation would you favor for making decisions regarding fares? Explain.
2. How would fluctuations in freight traffic affect commuter costs under the SP method?

9–23. **RESPONSIBILITY ACCOUNTING, PROFIT CENTERS, AND THE CONTRIBUTION APPROACH.** Consider the 19X6 income statement for Broadway Auto:

BROADWAY AUTO

Income Statement

For the Year Ended December 31, 19X6

(in thousands of dollars)

Revenues:		
Sales of vehicles	$2,000	
Parts and service	500	
Total revenues		$2,500
Cost of sales:		
Cost of vehicles sold	$1,600	
Parts and service materials	150	
Parts and service labor	200	
Total cost of sales		1,950
Gross margin		$ 550
Other operating expenses:		
Sales commissions	$ 60	
Sales salaries	70	
Advertising	80	
Parts and service overhead	50	
General dealership overhead	100	
Total other operating expenses		360
Operating income		190

The president of Broadway Auto has long regarded the markup on material and labor for the parts and service activity as the amount that is supposed to cover all parts and service overhead plus all general overhead of the dealership. In other words, the parts and service department is viewed as a cost-recovery operation, and the sales of vehicles as the income-producing activity.

Required:

1. Prepare a departmentalized operating statement that harmonizes with the views of the president.
2. Prepare an alternative operating statement that would reflect a different view of the dealership operations. Assume that $10,000 and $50,000 of the $100,000 general dealership overhead can be allocated with confidence to the parts and service department and to sales of vehicles, respectively. The remaining $40,000 cannot be allocated except in some highly arbitrary manner.
3. Comment on the relative merits of Requirements 1 and 2.

9–24. **DIVISIONAL CONTRIBUTION, PERFORMANCE, AND SEGMENT MARGINS.** Alfredo Ortez has just purchased a struggling regional airline, Bloomington Air. He hopes to achieve profitability by applying techniques he recently learned in an executive MBA program. He is especially excited about applying some new "contribution" approaches to cost allocations that emphasize cost behavior patterns and so-called *contribution margins*, *contributions controllable by segment managers*, and *contributions by segments*. Pertinent data for the year ended December 31, 19X6, follow.

Total revenue was $100 million, of which $60 million was freight traffic and $40 million was passenger traffic. Fifty percent of the latter was generated by Division 1; 40% by Division 2; and 10% by Division 3.

Total variable costs were $56 million, of which $18 million pertained to freight traffic. Of the $38 million allocable to passenger traffic, $18.4 million, $13.7 million, and $5.9 million could be allocated to Divisions 1, 2, and 3, respectively.

Total separable discretionary fixed costs were $10 million, of which $7.5 million applied to freight traffic. Of the remainder, $500,000 could not be allocated to specific divisions, although it was clearly traceable to passenger traffic in general. Divisions 1, 2, and 3 should be allocated $1,500,000, $350,000, and $150,000, respectively.

Total separable committed costs, which were not regarded as being controllable by segment managers, were $33 million, of which 80% was allocable to freight traffic. Of the 20% traceable to passenger traffic, Divisions 1, 2, and 3 should be allocated $3.6 million, $840,000, and $360,000, respectively; the balance was unallocable to a specific division.

The common fixed costs not clearly allocable to any part of the company amounted to $2 million.

Required:

1. The president asks you to prepare statements, dividing the data for the company as a whole between the freight and passenger traffic and then subdividing the passenger traffic into three divisions.
2. Some competing airlines actively promote discount passenger service on night-time freight flights. Currently Bloomington Air's freight flights have empty passenger compartments. What costs are relevant for making decisions to offer such passenger service? Some other airlines facing the same general cost picture, refuse to offer such discount fares. Why?
3. For purposes of this analysis, even though the numbers may be unrealistic, suppose that Division 2's figures represented a specific flight instead of a division. Suppose further that Bloomington Air is considering dropping the flight. What would be the effect on overall company net income for 19X7, assuming that the figures are accurate and that 19X7 operations are in all other respects a duplication of 19X6 operations?

9–25. **INCENTIVES IN THE SOVIET UNION.** Officials in the Soviet Union had been rewarding managers for exceeding a five-year-plan target for production quantities. But a problem arose because managers naturally tended to predict low volumes so that the targets would be set low. This hindered planning; good information about production possibilities was lacking.

The Soviets then devised a new performance evaluation measure. Suppose F is the forecast of production, A is actual production, and X, Y, and Z are positive constants set by top officials, with $X < Y < Z$.

$$\text{performance} = \begin{cases} (Y \times F) + X \times (A - F) & \text{if } F \leq A \\ (Y \times F) - Z \times (F - A) & \text{if } F > A \end{cases}$$

This performance measure was designed to motivate both high production and accurate forecasts.

Consider the Siberian Automotive Factory. During 1987 the factory manager, Katrina Rubinov, had to predict the number of automobiles that could be produced during the next year. She was confident that at least 800,000 autos could be produced in 1988, and most likely they could produce 900,000 autos. With good luck, they might even produce 1,000,000. Government officials told her that the new performance evaluation measure would be used, and that $X = .50$, $Y = .80$, and $Z = 1.00$ for 1988 and 1989.

Required:

1. Suppose Katrina predicted production of 900,000 autos and 900,000 were produced. Calculate the performance measure.
2. Suppose again that 900,000 autos were produced. Calculate the performance measure if Katrina had been conservative and predicted only 800,000 autos. Also calculate the performance measure if she had predicted 1,000,000 autos.
3. Now suppose it is November 1988 and it is clear that the 900,000 target cannot be achieved. Does the performance measure motivate continued efforts to increase production? Suppose it is clear that the 900,000 target will be met easily. Will the system motivate continued effort to increase production?

9–26. ALLOCATION OF COSTS. (Alternates are 9–2 and 9–28.) Southeast Electric Company allocates corporate overhead to residential and commercial departments based on kilowatt hours. A flexible budget is used. The budgeted cost behavior pattern for corporate overhead is $500,000 monthly plus $.80 per 1,000 kilowatt hours. The actual monthly costs of corporate overhead are allocated on the basis of actual kilowatt hours.

Required:

1. Southeast produced 400 million kilowatt hours in April, half for the commercial department and half for residential. The actual corporate overhead costs were exactly equal to those predicted by the flexible budget. Compute the costs that would be allocated to each department.
2. Suppose the commercial department's customers were plagued by strikes, so that commercial sales were much lower than originally anticipated, only 100 million kilowatt hours. The residential department sold 200 million kilowatt hours. The actual corporate overhead costs were exactly the same as the flexible budget for this lower level of activity. Compute the costs that would be allocated to commercial and residential departments.
3. Refer to the facts in Requirement 1. Various inefficiencies caused the corporate overhead to be $900,000. Compute the costs to be allocated to residential and commercial departments. Are the allocations justified? If not, what improvements do you suggest?
4. Refer to the facts of Requirement 2. Assume that assorted investment outlays for equipment and space in the corporate staff departments were made to provide a basic maximum capacity to serve the commercial department at a level of 390 million kilowatt hours and the residential department at a level of 210 million kilowatt hours. Suppose fixed costs are allocated on the basis of this capacity to serve. Variable costs are allocated by using a predetermined standard rate per 1,000 kilowatt hours. Compute the costs to be allocated to each department. What are the advantages of this method over other methods?

9–27. HOSPITAL COST ALLOCATION. The laboratory of Copenhagen City Hospital has developed the following relative value weightings based on the amount of time necessary to complete specific types of tests:

	WEIGHTING	NUMBER OF TESTS PERFORMED
Sugar, quantitative	1.0	1,375
Bleeding time	0.8	2.340
White cell count	0.6	4,675
Chlorides	1.9	584
Sedimentation rate	0.5	3,280
Tissues, surgical, frozen section	10.0	603

For example, a white cell count takes $.6 \div 1.9 = .316$ times as long as a chlorides test. The total costs of these tests were 1,334,880 Dkr. (Dkr stands for Danish kroner.) You are to allocate the costs to the tests as a basis for reimbursements from health care agencies. Compute the cost rate per individual test.

9–28. HOSPITAL EQUIPMENT. (Alternates are 9–2 and 9–26.) Many states have a hospital commission that must approve the acquisition of specified medical equipment before the hospitals in the state can qualify for cost-based reimbursement related to that equipment. That is, hospitals cannot bill government agencies for the later use of the equipment unless the commission originally authorized the acquisition.

Two hospitals in one such state proposed the acquisition and sharing of some expensive X-ray equipment to be used for unusual cases. The depreciation and related fixed costs of operating the equipment were predicted at $10,000 per month. The variable costs were predicted at $20 per patient procedure.

The commission asked each hospital to predict its usage of the equipment over its expected useful life of five years. Hospital A predicted an average usage of 60 X-rays per month; B, of 40 X-rays. The commission regarded this information as critical to the size and degree of sophistication that would be justified. That is, if the number of X-rays exceeded a certain quantity per month, a different configuration of space, equipment, and personnel would be acquired that would mean higher fixed costs per month.

Required:

1. Suppose fixed costs are allocated on the basis of the hospitals' predicted average use per month. Variable costs are allocated on the basis of $20 per X-ray, the budgeted variable-cost rate for the current fiscal year. In October, A had 40 X-rays and B had 40 X-rays. Compute the total costs allocated to A and to B.
2. Suppose the manager of the equipment had various operating inefficiencies so that the total October costs were $12,400. Would you change your answers in Requirement 1? Why?
3. A traditional method of cost allocation does not use the method in Requirement 1. Instead, an allocation rate depends on the actual costs and actual volume encountered. The actual costs are totaled for the month and divided by the actual number of X-rays during the month. Suppose the actual costs agreed exactly with the flexible budget for a total of 80 actual X-rays. Compute the total costs allocated to A and to B. Compare the results with those in Requirement 1. What is the major weakness in this traditional method? What are some of its possible behavioral effects?
4. Describe any undesirable behavioral effects of the method described in Requirement 1. How would you counteract any tendencies toward deliberate false predictions of long-run usage?

9–29. **ALLOCATION OF DATA PROCESSING COSTS.** (CMA, adapted.) The Independent Underwriters Insurance Co. (IUI) established a Systems Department two years ago to implement and operate its own data processing systems. IUI believed that its own system would be more cost effective than the service bureau it had been using.

IUI's three departments—Claims, Records, and Finance—have different requirements with respect to hardware and other capacity related resources and operating resources. The system was designed to recognize these differing needs. In addition, the system was designed to meet IUI's long-term capacity needs. The excess capacity designed into the system would be sold to outside users until needed by IUI. The estimated resource requirements used to design and implement the system are shown in the following schedule.

	HARDWARE AND OTHER CAPACITY RELATED RESOURCES	OPERATING RESOURCES
Records	30%	60%
Claims	50	20
Finance	15	15
Expansion (outside use)	5	5
Total	100%	100%

IUI currently sells the equivalent of its expansion capacity to a few outside clients.

At the time the system became operational, management decided to redistribute total expenses of the Systems Department to the user departments based upon actual computer time used. The actual costs for the first quarter of the current fiscal year were distributed to the user departments as follows:

DEPARTMENT	PERCENTAGE UTILIZATION	AMOUNT
Records	60%	$330,000
Claims	20	110,000
Finance	15	82,500
Outside	5	27,500
Total	100%	$550,000

The three user departments have complained about the cost distribution method since the Systems Department was established. The Records Department's monthly costs have been as much as three times the costs experienced with the service bureau. The Finance Department is concerned about the costs distributed to the outside user category because these allocated costs form the basis for the fees billed to the outside clients.

James Dale, IUI's controller, decided to review the cost-allocation method. The additional information he gathered for his review is reported in Tables 1, 2, and 3.

TABLE 1

Systems Department Costs and Activity Levels

| | ANNUAL BUDGET | | FIRST QUARTER | | | |
| | | | BUDGET | | ACTUAL | |
	Hours	Dollars	Hours	Dollars	Hours	Dollars
Hardware and other capacity related costs	—	$ 600,000	—	$150,000	—	$155,000
Software development	18,750	562,500	4,725	141,750	4,250	130,000
Operations:						
Computer related	3,750	750,000	945	189,000	920	187,000
Input/output related	30,000	300,000	7,560	75,600	7,900	78,000
		$2,212,500		$556,350		$550,000

TABLE 2

Historical Usage

| | Hardware and Other Capacity Needs | SOFTWARE DEVELOPMENT | | OPERATIONS | | | |
| | | | | COMPUTER | | INPUT/OUTPUT | |
		Range	Average	Range	Average	Range	Average
Records	30%	0–30%	12%	55–65%	60%	10–30%	20%
Claims	50	15–60	35	10–25	20	60–80	70
Finance	15	25–75	45	10–25	15	3–10	6
Outside	5	0–25	8	3–8	5	3–10	4
	100%		100%		100%		100%

TABLE 3
Usage of Systems Department's Services
First Quarter (in hours)

	Software Development	OPERATIONS Computer Related	Input/ Output
Records	425	552	1,580
Claims	1,700	184	5,530
Finance	1,700	138	395
Outside	425	46	395
Total	4,250	920	7,900

Dale has concluded that the method of cost allocation should be changed. He believes that the hardware and capacity related costs should be allocated to the user departments in proportion to the planned, long-term needs. Any difference between actual and budgeted hardware costs would not be allocated to the departments but remain with the Systems Department.

The costs for software development and operations would be charged to the user departments based on actual hours used. A predetermined hourly rate based on the annual budget data would be used. The hourly rates that would be used for the current fiscal year are as follows:

FUNCTION	HOURLY RATE
Software development	$ 30
Operations:	
Computer related	$200
Input/output related	$ 10

Dale plans to use first quarter activity and cost data to illustrate his recommendations. The recommendations will be presented to the Systems Department and the user departments for their comments and reactions. He then expects to present his recommendations to management for approval.

Required:

1. Calculate the amount of data processing costs that would be included in the Claims Department's first quarter *budget* according to the method James Dale has recommended.
2. Prepare a schedule to show how the actual first quarter costs of the Systems Department would be charged to the users if James Dale's recommended method were adopted.
3. Explain whether James Dale's recommended system for charging costs to the user departments will:
   a. Improve cost control in the Systems Department.
   b. Improve planning and cost control in the user departments.

9–30. **DIRECT AND STEP-DOWN ALLOCATIONS METHODS.** The James Company has two production departments—molding and finishing—and two service departments—building services (rent, heat, light, etc.) and personnel. You have been asked to allocate the service department costs to the production departments and calculate a cost per direct labor dollar (after allocation) in each production department. Use the following data:

| | SERVICE DEPARTMENTS | | PRODUCTION DEPARTMENTS | | |
	Building Services	Personnel	Molding	Finishing	Total
Direct department costs	$241,000	$24,000	$100,000	$171,000	$536,000
Square feet	—	7,500	14,500	3,000	25,000
Direct labor-hours	—	—	22,500	32,500	55,000
Number of employees	—	30	80	320	430

Building services are allocated on the basis of square footage occupied and personnel costs on the basis of number of employees.

Required:

1. Use the direct method to compute the total cost of the molding and finishing departments. The total cost includes costs initially assigned to each department plus those allocated from the service departments. Calculate the cost per direct labor-hour in each producing department.
2. Repeat Requirement 1 using the step-down method.
3. Compare the results in Requirements 1 and 2. Which method of allocation do you prefer? Why?

9–31. **DIRECT AND STEP-DOWN METHODS OF ALLOCATION.** The X Company has prepared departmental overhead budgets for normal activity levels before reapportionments, as follows:

Building and grounds	$ 10,000
Personnel	1,000
General factory administration*	26,090
Cafeteria operating loss	1,640
Storeroom	2,670
Machining	34,700
Assembly	48,900
	$125,000

* To be reapportioned before cafeteria.

Management has decided that the most sensible product costs are achieved by using departmental overhead rates. These rates are developed after appropriate service department costs are reapportioned to production departments.

Bases for reapportionment are to be selected from the following data:

DEPARTMENT	DIRECT-LABOR HOURS	NUMBER OF EMPLOYEES	SQUARE FEET OF FLOOR SPACE OCCUPIED	TOTAL LABOR-HOURS	NUMBER OF REQUISITIONS
Building and grounds	—	—	—	—	
Personnel*		—	2,000	—	
General factory administration		35	7,000	—	
Cafeteria operating loss		10	4,000	1,000	
Storeroom		5	7,000	1,000	
Machining	5,000	50	30,000	8,000	2,000
Assembly	15,000	100	50,000	17,000	1,000
	20,000	200	100,000	27,000	3,000

* Basis used is number of employees.

Required:

1. Allocate service department costs by the step-down method. Develop overhead rates per direct labor-hour for machining and assembly.
2. Same as in Requirement 1, using the direct method.
3. What would be the blanket plantwide factory-overhead application rate, assuming that direct labor-hours are used as a cost-allocation base?
4. Using the following information about two jobs, prepare three different total overhead costs for each job, using rates developed in Requirements 1, 2, and 3.

	DIRECT LABOR-HOURS	
	Machining	Assembly
Job 88	18	2
Job 89	3	17

9–32. **REVIEW OF CHAPTERS 1–9.** (H. Schaefer.) As you are about to depart on a business trip, your accountant hands you the following information about your Singapore division:

a. Master budget for the fiscal year just ended on October 31, 19X1:

Sales	$700,000
Manufacturing cost of goods sold	560,000
Manufacturing margin	$140,000
Selling and administrative expenses	90,000
Operating income	$ 50,000

b. Budgeted sales and production mix:

Product A   40,000 units
Product B   60,000 units

c. Standard variable manufacturing cost per unit:

Product A
Direct material	10 pieces	@ $0.25	$2.50
Direct labor	1 hour	@ $3.00	3.00
Variable overhead	1 hour	@ $2.00	2.00
			$7.50

Product B
Direct material	5 pounds	@ $0.10	$0.50
Direct labor	.3 hours	@ $2.50	0.75
Variable overhead	.3 hours	@ $2.50	0.75
			$2.00

d. All budgeted selling and administrative expenses are common, fixed expenses; 60% are discretionary expenses.

e. Actual income statement for the fiscal year ended October 31, 19X1:

Sales	$700,000
Manufacturing cost of goods sold	571,400
Manufacturing margin	$128,600
Selling and administrative expenses	87,000
Operating income	$ 41,600

f. Actual sales and production mix:

Product A	42,000 units
Product B	56,000 units

g. Budgeted and actual sales prices:

Product A	$10
Product B	5

h. Schedule of the actual *variable* manufacturing cost of goods sold by product; actual quantities in parentheses:

Product A:	Material	$106,800	(427,200 pieces)
	Labor	123,900	(42,000 hours)
	Overhead	86,100	(42,000 hours)
Product B:	Material	33,600	(280,000 pounds)
	Labor	42,500	(17,000 hours)
	Overhead	42,500	(17,000 hours)
		$435,400	

i. Products A and B are manufactured in separate facilities. Of the *budgeted* fixed manufacturing cost, $120,000 is separable as follows: $40,000 to product A and $80,000 to product B. Ten percent of these separate costs is discretionary. All other budgeted fixed manufacturing expenses, separable and common, are committed.

The purpose of your business trip is a board of directors meeting. During the meeting it is quite likely that some of the information from your accountant will be discussed. In anticipation you set out to prepare answers to possible questions. (There are no beginning or ending inventories.)

Required:

1. Determine the firm's *budgeted* break-even point, overall contribution-margin ratio, and contribution margins per unit by product.
2. Considering products A and B as *segments* of the firm, find the *budgeted* "contribution by segments" for each.
3. It is decided to allocate the *budgeted* selling and administrative expenses to the segments (in Requirement 2) as follows: committed costs on the basis of budgeted unit sales mix and discretionary costs on the basis of actual unit sales mix. What are the final expense allocations? Briefly appraise the allocation method.
4. How would you respond to a proposal to base commissions to salespersons on the sales (revenue) value of orders received? Assume all salespersons have the opportunity to sell both products.
5. Determine the firm's *actual* "contribution margin" and "contribution controllable by segment managers" for the fiscal year ended October 31, 19X1. Assume *no* variances in committed fixed costs.
6. Determine the "sales volume variance" for each product for the fiscal year ended October 31, 19X1.
7. Determine and identify all variances in *variable* manufacturing costs by product for the fiscal year ended October 31, 19X1.

Chapter 10

PROFIT CENTERS
AND TRANSFER PRICING

LEARNING OBJECTIVES

When you have finished studying this chapter, you should be able to:

1. Describe the role of management accounting systems in relation to top management goals and subgoals and in relation to organization structure.
2. Explain the implications of goal congruence and managerial effort in the design of systems.
3. Define decentralization and identify its expected benefits and costs.
4. Distinguish between profit centers and decentralization.
5. Define transfer prices and identify their purpose.
6. Identify the relative advantages and disadvantages of basing transfer prices on total costs, variable costs, and market prices.
7. Compute ROI and residual income and contrast them as criteria for judging the performance of organization segments.
8. Identify the relative advantages and disadvantages of using various bases for measuring the invested capital used by organization segments.

This chapter continues the overview of management control systems that was introduced in the preceding chapter. Special attention is given to judging one system versus another and to using (1) transfer prices and (2) rate of return on investment (usually called ROI) in measuring performance.

JUDGING A MANAGEMENT CONTROL SYSTEM

How should managers and accountants judge a management control system? Too often, judgments focus on technical details of data processing or external financial reporting, emphasizing compliance with legal requirements or detection of fraud. However, a broader focus is preferable. Systems exist primarily to improve the collective decisions within an organization.

☐ Top Management Goals and Subgoals

The starting point for judging a system is the specification of top management's goals. Some managements will set a single goal, such as the maximization of profit over the long run. Such a lofty overall goal is too vague for most subordinates. Consequently, most organizations specify multiple goals and accompany them with some form of measurement for evaluating performance. Some organizations use the term *goals* to mean long-term, unmeasurable aims and the term *objectives* to mean short-term, measurable targets that lead toward fulfilling the goals. This book makes no such distinction.

Top management's subgoals are frequently called by other names, such as *key-result areas*, *critical success factors*, *key variables*, or *critical variables*. Some critics maintain that they should not be called goals at all; instead they should be labeled as key *means* of obtaining a single, dominant overall goal such as long-run profitability.

To illustrate the use of multiple goals, consider the General Electric Company, which has stated that organizational performance will be measured in the following eight areas:

1. Profitability
2. Market position
3. Productivity
4. Product leadership
5. Personnel development
6. Employee attitudes
7. Public responsibility
8. Balance between short-range and long-range goals.

Note that the first goal, profitability, usually is measured in terms of a single year's results. The thrust of the other goals is to offset the inclination of managers to maximize short-run profits to the detriment of long-run profits.

Overemphasis on any single goal, be it short-run profits or some other goal, seldom promotes long-run profitability. Some critics insist that many U.S. companies stress short-run profits too much. They point to successful Japanese companies as examples of long-run–oriented firms. The generalization that *all* U.S. firms are short-run oriented is certainly not true. But examples of a short-run focus abound. Consider a news story about Campbell Soup Company: "Management was resorting increasingly to short-term methods to improve the bottom line. In weak quarterly periods, the advertising budget was pared—sometimes eliminated. Marketing employees recall that expensive new products were often discouraged."

Another example of short-run emphasis comes from the Soviet Union:

Example The Moscow Cable Company decided to reduce copper wastage and actually slashed it by 60% in a given year. The value of the scrap recovered was only $40,000 instead of the $100,000 originally budgeted. However, when top management in the central government perceived this to be an undesirable shortfall of value, the plant was fined $45,000 for not meeting its scrap budget.

As the Moscow Cable example illustrates, the design of a system includes choosing accounting reports that evaluate performance and affect rewards or penalties. Managers often face trade-off decisions. That is, which goals should be emphasized or deemphasized? For example, one way to increase market share, at least in the short run, is to cut selling prices. In turn, however, profitability may be hurt. These trade-offs, this juggling of goals, are major keys to the successes or failures of the managers and the segments they oversee.

☐ **Working Within Constraints**

Management control *systems* should be distinguished from *goals* and from **organization structures**. The latter are defined here as the way top management has arranged the lines of responsibility within an entity. For example, one company may be organized primarily by *functions*, such as manufacturing and sales; another company by *divisions* bearing profit responsibility, such as the eastern and western divisions; and other companies by some hybrid arrangement.

Occasionally the systems designer may be in a position to persuade top management that goals or organization structures deserve revamping before the system is redesigned. But most of the time, changes in control systems are piecemeal improvements rather than grandiose replacements. Thus, typically the designer must work within the constraints of given goals and organization structures.

To recapitulate, the judge or designer of systems should ordinarily consider the following:

1. Top-management goals
2. Subgoals or key-result areas
3. Trade-offs among the goals in items 1 and 2
4. Organization structure
5. Systems design in light of the foregoing

An illustration may clarify these distinctions. Suppose top managers specify their goal: earnings for the coming year should be $50 million. They may use the accounting system to communicate and enforce this goal. Near the end of the year, if the earnings prospects are gloomy, top managers may exert immense pressure to reach the budgeted target. To reach the earnings goal, subordinates may be inclined to reduce current expenses by postponing outlays for maintenance, sales promotion, or research, even though such decisions could cripple future earning power.

We may deplore these decisions, but our criticism should be aimed at top management's choice of goals rather than at the system. Given the goal, the accounting system performed admirably. It provided the earnings information desired by top management. The system should be judged in light of the goals, whatever they may be. In this example, the top management goal was actually achieved; the trouble was that the goal may not have been appropriate.

Similarly, top management may be heavily committed to a favored organization structure, such as a university's heavy or light use of formal departments organized by subject area (for example, a department of marketing, a department of statistics). Most often, the design of the system must be made within the given structure.

☐ Internal Control

One of the few external constraints on management control systems was imposed by the Foreign Corrupt Practices Act, passed in 1977. Despite its title, it requires *all* publicly held U.S. companies to maintain accurate and detailed accounting records and a documented system of *internal control*. An **internal control system** consists of methods and procedures that are concerned with the authorization of transactions, safeguarding of assets, and accuracy of the financial records. Both managers and accountants are responsible for developing and evaluating internal control systems.

The three goals of an internal control system are:

1. To prevent errors and irregularities by a system of authorization for transactions, accurate recording of transactions, and safeguarding of assets.
2. To detect errors and irregularities by reconciling accounting records with independently kept records and physical counts and reviewing accounts for possible write-downs of values.

3. To promote operating efficiency by examining policies and procedures for possible improvements.

An internal control system is part of the management control system. That is, a management control system encompasses administrative controls (such as budgets for planning and controlling operations) and accounting controls (such as the common internal control procedure of separating the duties of the person who counts cash from the duties of the person who has access to the accounts receivable records). Top management has the ultimate responsibility for both administrative and accounting controls.

☐ Cost, Congruence, Managerial Effort

The final selection of a management accounting system should be affected by three major criteria: cost-benefit, goal congruence, and managerial effort.

1. The primary criterion in judging System A versus System B is *cost-benefit*. The choice of a system should be governed by weighing the collective costs and benefits, given the circumstances of the specific organization. The benefits are often difficult to measure. The overall cost-benefit theme basically says that all systems are imperfect and that System A is superior to System B if A is likely to generate a more desirable set of collective operating decisions after due consideration is given to the costs of A and B.

2. Two additional criteria help make the primary criterion more concrete: congruence and effort. **Goal congruence** exists when individuals and groups aim at the goals desired by top management. Goal congruence is achieved as managers, when working in their own perceived best interests, make decisions that harmonize with the overall objectives of top management. The challenge is to specify segment goals (or behaviors) that induce (or at least do not discourage) decisions that would achieve top management goals.

3. **Managerial effort** is defined here as exertion toward a goal. Effort is not confined to its common meaning of a worker producing faster; it includes all conscientious actions (such as watching or thinking) that result in more efficiency and effectiveness. Managerial effort is a matter of degree; it is maximized when individuals and groups *strive* (run rather than walk) toward their goals. Goal congruence can exist with little accompanying effort, and vice versa. For example, students can enroll for a university course because their goal is to learn about, say, managing a government agency. The dean of the school, the professors, and the students may share the same goal. But goal congruence is not enough. Educators also introduce incentives in the form of a grading system to spur student effort.

Grading is a formal tool of *performance evaluation*, as are accounting performance reports in various organizations. Performance evaluation is a widely used means of improving congruence and effort because most individuals tend to perform better when they expect such feedback.

During the course some students may be irresistibly tempted to skip class sessions and play tennis instead. This would be an example of having plenty of effort aimed at a different and less important goal. Similarly, managers may eagerly pursue sales in the aggregate without paying sufficient attention to the specified and most important goal of profits, which may be affected differently by different products.

☐ Behavioral Focus

Motivation has been defined as aiming for some *selected goal* (goal congruence) together with the *resulting drive* (managerial effort) that influences action toward that goal. The systems designer's problems of congruence and effort may be wrapped together as subparts of the problem of motivation.

Obtaining goal congruence and effort is essentially a behavioral problem. The incessant focus is on the motivational impact of a particular accounting system or method versus another system or method. It may seem strange to judge accounting systems in terms of their behavioral effects, but the accountant's task is more complex, more ill-structured, and more affected by the human aspects than many people believe at first glance. A simple awareness of the importance of goal congruence and the effort impacts of systems is at least a first step toward getting a perspective on the design of accounting systems and the selection of accounting techniques.

EVOLUTION OF ACCOUNTING TECHNIQUES

Reconsider the ideas introduced in Chapter 7 in the section on page 193, "Development of Control Systems." As organizations grow, managers cope with their responsibilities by delegating their decision-making powers to subordinates and by coordinating activities through informal and formal control systems, most notably the accounting system. The initial stages of organizations are usually marked by heavy reliance on personal observation and light reliance on formal accounting techniques. But the founders soon learn that accounting techniques can improve decisions. The evolution occurs as follows:

1. *Personal observation*. Managers rely on their eyes and ears to obtain their objectives.
2. *Historical records*. Managers quickly find that records help operations. Moreover, assorted records must be kept to satisfy legal requirements such as income tax laws. The cost-benefit tests of system design are easily met; without such records, the manager faces lawsuits, fines, or worse.
3. *Static budgets*. Managers find that historical records are often insufficient because they do not draw attention to the right questions. For example, a manager may be depressed if she discovers that her hospital's actual revenue in 19X1 was only $50 million instead of the $55 million of the previous year. But she may be even more depressed if the budgeted 19X1 revenue was $62 million. The key question, then, is not, "How did we do in comparison with last year?" but "How did we do in comparison with our targets for the current year?"
4. *Flexible budgets and standards*. Many organizations introduce these techniques to obtain a sharper focus on explaining the separate impact on operations of price, efficiency, and volume factors.
5. *Profit centers*. Organizations use these devices to evaluate the performance of segments that are assigned responsibility for revenue as well as costs and to provide better motivation.

Reflect on this evolution. Steps 3 through 5 are usually taken voluntarily rather than being imposed by outside forces. Thus the cost-benefit tests induce managers to invest in more sophisticated accounting systems as their organizations become harder to control. Furthermore, new features are *additions* to the old features instead of *replacements* for them. Above all, remember that personal observation is fundamental to management control.

The conceptual overview here is that systems are typically changed on an incremental basis when top management predicts that the benefits from better collective decisions (improved goal congruence and managerial effort) will exceed the additional costs.

DECENTRALIZATION

☐ Costs and Benefits

Decentralization is the delegation of the freedom to make decisions. The lower in the organization that this freedom exists, the greater the decentralization. Decentralization is a matter of degree along a continuum:

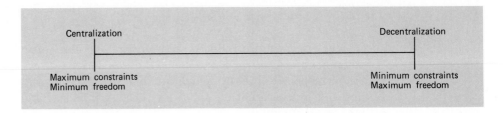

The benefits of decentralization include the following: (1) the lower-level managers have the best information concerning local conditions and therefore are able to make better decisions than their superiors; (2) managers acquire the ability to make decisions and other management skills that assist their movement upward in the organization; and (3) managers enjoy higher status from being independent and thus are better motivated.

The costs of decentralization include the following: (1) managers may make dysfunctional decisions by (a) focusing on and acting to improve their own subunit's[1] performance at the expense of the organization or (b) not being aware of relevant facts from other subunits; (2) managers tend to duplicate services that might be less expensive when centralized (accounting, advertising, and personnel are examples); and (3) costs of accumulating and processing information frequently rise. The last is exemplified by responsibility accounting reports that represent a necessary counterbalance to the extension of freedom to make decisions. It is also exemplified by the time that subunit managers often spend with one another in negotiating prices for goods or services that are transferred internally.

---

[1] We will use subunit as a synonym for segment, a part of an organization for which revenues or costs are identified.

Decentralization is more popular in profit-seeking organizations (where outputs and inputs can be measured) than in nonprofit organizations. Managers can be given freedom when their results are measurable so that they can be held accountable for them. Poor decisions in a profit-seeking firm become apparent from the inadequate profit generated. Most nonprofit organizations lack such a reliable performance indicator, so granting managerial freedom is more risky.

☐ Middle Ground

Philosophies of decentralization differ considerably. Cost-benefit considerations usually require that some management decisions be highly decentralized and others centralized. To illustrate, much of the controller's problem-solving and attention-directing functions may be found at the lower levels, whereas income tax planning and mass scorekeeping such as payroll may be highly centralized.

Decentralization is most successful when an organization's segments are relatively independent of one another—that is, the decisions of one manager will not affect the fortunes of another manager. If segments do much internal buying or selling, much buying from the same outside suppliers, or much selling to the same outside markets, they are candidates for heavier centralization.

An earlier part of this chapter stressed cost-benefit tests, goal congruence, and managerial effort as three major criteria that must be considered when designing a control system. A fourth criterion, *segment autonomy*, must be added if management has decided in favor of heavy decentralization. **Segment autonomy** is defined here as the possession of decision-making power by managers of segments of an organization. The control system should be designed to respect segment autonomy to the extent specified by top management. In other words, when top managers openly commit themselves to heavy decentralization, they should rarely interfere in decisions by segment managers.

☐ Profit Centers and Decentralization

Do not confuse *profit centers* (accountability for revenue and expenses) with *decentralization* (freedom to make decisions). They are entirely separate concepts, although profit centers clearly are accounting devices that aid decentralization. However, one can exist without the other. Some profit center managers possess vast freedom to make decisions concerning labor contracts, supplier choices, equipment purchases, personnel decisions, and so on. In contrast, other profit center managers may need top management approval for almost all the decisions just mentioned. Indeed, some cost centers may be more heavily decentralized than profit centers if the cost center managers have more freedom to make decisions.

The literature contains many criticisms of profit centers on the grounds that managers are given profit responsibility without commensurate authority. Therefore, the criticism continues, the profit center is "artificial" because the manager is not free to make a sufficient number of the decisions that affect profit.

Such criticisms confuse profit centers and decentralization. The fundamental question in deciding between using a cost center or a profit center for a given subunit is not whether heavy decentralization exists. Instead, the fundamental question is, "Will a profit center better solve the problems of goal congruence and management effort than a cost center? In other words, do I predict that a profit center will induce the managers to make a better collective set of decisions from the viewpoint of the organization as a whole?"

All control systems are imperfect. Judgments about their merits should concentrate on which alternative system will bring the actions top management seeks. For example, a plant may seem to be a "natural" cost center because the plant manager has no influence over decisions concerning the marketing of its products. Still, some companies evaluate a plant manager by the plant's profitability. Why? Because such a broader evaluation base will affect the plant manager's behavior. How? Instead of being concerned solely with running an efficient cost center, the plant manager now "naturally" considers quality control more carefully and reacts to customers' special requests more sympathetically. The profit center obtained the desired plant-manager behavior that the cost center failed to achieve.

From the viewpoint of top management, plant managers often have more influence on sales than is apparent at first glance. This is an example of how systems may evolve from cost centers to profit centers and an example of the first-line importance of predicting behavioral effects when an accounting control system is designed.

TRANSFER PRICING

☐ Nature of Transfer Pricing

Transfer prices are the amounts charged by one segment of an organization for a product or service that it supplies to another segment of the same organization. Most often, the term is associated with materials, parts, or finished goods. The transfer price is revenue to the segment producing the product or service, and it is a cost to the acquiring department.

In a most fundamental sense, cost allocation and transfer pricing are synonyms. In practice, however, the term *transfer price* is confined to exchanges of products or services between the profit centers of an organization. An example of a cost-allocation problem is how to charge a state government's personnel department costs to the various state agencies. An example of a transfer pricing problem is how to charge the marketing segments of Hewlett-Packard for the products supplied by the manufacturing segments.

Why do transfer-pricing systems exist? The principal reason is to communicate data that will lead to goal-congruent decisions. For example, transfer prices should guide managers to make the best possible decisions regarding whether to buy or sell products and services inside or outside the total organization. Another important reason is to evaluate segment performance to motivate both the selling manager and the buying manager toward goal-congruent decisions. These are easy aims to describe, but they are difficult aims to achieve.

Organizations solve their problems by using market prices for some transfers, cost-based prices for other transfers, and negotiated prices for others. Therefore, do not expect to obtain a lone, universally applicable answer in the area of transfer pricing. It is a subject of continuous concern to top management. Whenever there is a lull in a conversation with a manager, try asking, "Do you have any transfer-pricing problems?" The response is usually, "Let me tell you about the peculiar transfer-pricing difficulties in my organization." A manager in a large wood products firm called transfer pricing his firm's most troublesome management control issue.

☐ Transfer at Cost

When the "transfer price" is some version of cost, such transfer pricing is nearly identical to the "cost allocation" of interdepartmental services that was discussed in Chapter 9, pages 279–283. Therefore, you can study the options and pitfalls of cost-based transfer prices by substituting "transfer pricing at cost" for "cost allocation" as you review those pages.

As an example of a pitfall, transferring at *actual* cost is generally not recommended because actual cost cannot be known in advance and thus fails to provide the buying segment with a reliable basis for planning. More important, it fails to provide the supplying division with the incentive to control its costs. Inefficiencies are merely passed along to the buying division. Thus the general recommendation of using budgeted or standard costs instead of actual costs applies to all forms of cost allocation, whether the allocation is called transfer pricing, cost reallocation, or some other name.

☐ Market Price

When an organization has profit centers, market price should be the prime candidate for setting transfer prices. In this way, the buyers and sellers systematically keep abreast of their internal and external opportunities, and problems of congruence, effort, and autonomy are minimized.

Frequently, internal transfers are made at "market-price-minus." That is, the supplier division may avoid some shipping or marketing costs by transferring goods to another division instead of marketing them to outside customers. These savings are often deducted when the transfer price is agreed upon.

Sometimes market prices do not exist, are inapplicable, or are impossible to determine. For example, no intermediate markets may exist for specialized parts, or markets may be too thin or scattered to permit the determination of a credible price. In these instances, versions of "cost-plus-a-profit" are often used in an attempt to provide a "fair" or "equitable" substitute for regular market prices.

☐ Variable Cost

Market prices have innate appeal in a profit-center context, but they are not cure-all answers to transfer-pricing problems. To illustrate, consider the analysis in Exhibit 10–1. Division A produces a part that may be sold either to outside customers or to Division B, which incorporates the part into a finished product that is then sold to outside customers. The selling prices and variable costs per unit are shown in the exhibit. In this example the variable costs are the only costs affected by producing the additional units for transfer to division B. Whether the part should be manufactured by Division A and transferred to Division B depends on the existence of idle capacity in Division A (insufficient demand from outside customers).

As Exhibit 10–1 shows, if there were *no idle capacity* in Division A, the optimum action would be for A to sell outside at $19, because Division B would incur $8 of variable costs but add only $2 to the selling price of the product ($21 − $19). Using market price would provide the correct motivation for such a decision because, if the part were transferred, Division B's cost would rise to $19 + $8 = $27, which would be $6 higher than B's prospective revenue of $21 per unit. So B would choose not to buy from A at the $19 market price.

What if Division A has idle capacity? The optimum action would be to produce the part and transfer it to Division B. If there were no production and transfer, Division B and the company as a whole would forgo a total contribution of $30,000. In this situation, variable cost would be the better basis for transfer pricing and would lead to the optimum decision for the firm as a whole. To be more precise, the transfer price should be all additional costs that will be incurred by the production of the units to be transferred. For example, if a lump-sum setup cost is required to produce the 10,000 units, it should be added to the variable cost in calculating the appropriate transfer price. In the example there is no such cost.

EXHIBIT 10–1

Analysis of Market Prices

DIVISION A		DIVISION B			
Market price of finished part to outsiders	$19	Sales price of finished product			$21
Variable costs per unit	10	Variable costs:			
Contribution margin	$ 9	Division A		$10	
Total contribution for 10,000 units	$90,000	Division B:			
		Processing	$5		
		Selling	3	8	18
		Contribution margin			$ 3
		Total contribution for 10,000 units			$30,000

Both market-price and variable-cost rules for transfer prices can lead to dysfunctional behavior. **Dysfunctional behavior** is defined as actions taken in conflict with top management goals.

Reconsider the situation depicted in Exhibit 10–1. Suppose that transfers are made at *market price* and that Division A has *idle capacity*. If you were the Division B manager, would you pay $19 to A for the product? No—each unit transferred would decrease B's profit by $6:

	DIVISION B WITHOUT TRANSFER	DIVISION B WITH TRANSFER
Revenue	$x	$x + 21
Cost	y	y + 27*
Operating income	$z	$z − 6

* $19 transfer price + $5 processing + $3 selling.

Does top management want Division B to buy the part from A? Yes—each unit transferred would increase the firm's profit by $3:

	FIRM AS A WHOLE WITHOUT TRANSFER	FIRM AS A WHOLE WITH TRANSFER
Revenue	$a	$a + 21
Cost	b	b + 18*
Operating income	$c	$c + 3

* $10 additional cost in A + $5 processing + $3 selling.

This example illustrates how dysfunctional behavior could occur—the Division B manager makes a decision that is best for his division but hurts the firm as a whole. If A were allowed to offer the part to B at a transfer price below market price, the managers of A and B could agree to a price between $10 and $13 that would increase the profit of both divisions and the total firm's profit as well.

A conflict between divisional goals and top management goals can arise under a *variable-cost transfer-pricing method* as well. Suppose that Division A has *no idle capacity*, Division B can sell the finished product for $29, and all other facts are as given in Exhibit 10–1. Would you, as the Division A manager, produce and transfer the part to B for the variable cost of $10? No—if you transfer the part, you sacrifice the opportunity to sell it:

	DIVISION A WITHOUT TRANSFER	DIVISION A WITH TRANSFER
Revenue	$r	$r − 19 + 10*
Cost	s	s
Operating income	$t	$t − 9

* Eliminate market revenue of $19 and get transfer price of $10.

But what does top management prefer? The part should be transferred; this would increase profit by $2:

	FIRM AS A WHOLE WITHOUT TRANSFER	FIRM AS A WHOLE WITH TRANSFER
Revenue	$a	$a + 29 − 19*
Cost	b	b + 8†
Operating income	$c	$c + 2

* B sells the finished part for $29 instead of A selling it for $19.
† $5 processing + $3 selling.

Thus, dysfunctional behavior could be motivated by a variable-cost transfer-pricing method if the producing segment has no idle capacity.

To summarize, when Division A has idle capacity, variable-cost transfers provide goal congruence, and market price transfers create dysfunctional behavior. When Division A has no idle capacity, market price transfers promote goal congruence, and variable-cost transfers lead to dysfunctional behavior. No single transfer-pricing method creates goal congruence in all types of situations. However, a good rule of thumb to *minimize* dysfunctional decisions is usually the following: use market prices whenever they exist.

A dysfunctional behavior is sometimes overcome by having top management impose a "fair" transfer price and insist that a transfer be made. But the managers of segments within an organization that has an announced policy of decentralization often regard such orders as undermining their autonomy. So the imposition of a price may satisfy the congruence and managerial effort criteria but not satisfy the autonomy criterion. Transfer pricing thus becomes a delicate balancing act in systems design.

The general difficulties are exemplified by the following about Gulf Oil:

☐ Segments tried to make their results look good at each other's expense. One widespread result: Inflated transfer payments among the Gulf segments as each one vied to boost its own bottom line. A top manager, quoted in *Business Week*, commented, "Gulf doesn't ring the cash register until we've made an outside sale."

☐ **Use of Incentives**

What should top management of a decentralized organization do if it sees dysfunctional decisions being made at the segment level? As usual, the answer is "It depends." If top management steps in and forces transfers, it undermines autonomy. This may have to be done occasionally, but if top management imposes its will too often, the organization is in substance being recentralized. Of course, if the decision were indeed not to give autonomy, the organization could be redesigned by combining the two segments.

Top managers who are proponents of decentralization will be more reluctant to impose their desires. Instead, they will make sure that both A and B managers understand all the facts and then allow the division managers to negotiate a transfer price. Well-trained and informed segment managers, who understand opportunity costs and fixed and variable costs, will often make better decisions than will top managers. The Division A manager knows best the various uses of its capacity, and the Division B manager knows best what profit can be made on the parts to be transferred.

Keep in mind that a decentralized setup is usually initiated primarily because top managers think that the segment managers have more information at the local level that permits these subordinates to make better collective decisions about all sorts of options. Therefore, second-guessing the local managers really means that the top manager is saying, "I know more than you do about the condition of the local markets." Even when top managers suspect that a dysfunctional decision might be made, they may swallow hard and accept the segment manager's judgment.

Conflicts between segment actions and top-management goals are inevitable in a decentralized organization. Some top managers deal with this by asking segment managers to be good company citizens, to sacrifice results for the good of the organization. They may enhance this request by basing performance evaluation and rewards on companywide as well as segment results. But such a policy is seldom as effective as well-designed formal incentives tied to a specific manager's performance. As a result, some companies would try various incentives in reaction to our illustration in Exhibit 10–1. For example, the contribution to the company as a whole, $30,000 in the idle capacity case, could be split between A and B, perhaps equally, perhaps in proportion to the variable costs of each, or perhaps via negotiation.[2]

☐ Motivation, Performance, Reward

Exhibit 10–2 shows the criteria and choices faced by top management when designing a management control system. Using the criterion of cost-benefit and the motivational criteria of congruence and effort, top management chooses responsibility centers (e.g., cost center versus profit center), performance measures, and rewards. The term *incentives* was used in the preceding paragraph. As used in this context, **incentives** are defined as those informal and formal performance measures and rewards that enhance goal congruence and managerial effort. For example, how the $30,000 contribution in Exhibit

---

[2] Other examples include using the dual allocation described in the preceding chapter—that is, transfer at standard variable cost. In addition, a predetermined lump-sum charge is made for fixed costs, based on a long-run commitment of the buyer to support the supplier. In this way the buyer's month-to-month decisions are not influenced by the supplier's fixed costs.

EXHIBIT 10–2

Criteria and Choices

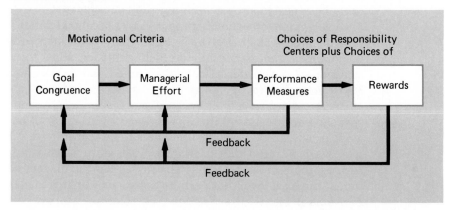

10–1 is split between A and B affects the measures of their performance. In turn, the performance measures may affect the managers' rewards.

Numerous performance measurement choices have been described in this book. Examples include whether to use tight or loose standards, whether to measure divisional performance by contribution margins or operating incomes, and whether to allocate central corporate costs to divisions.

Research about rewards has generated a basic principle that is simple and important: individuals are motivated to perform in a way that leads to rewards. Managers tend to focus their efforts in areas where performance is measured and where their performance affects rewards. Rewards are both monetary and nonmonetary. Examples include pay raises, bonuses, promotion, praise, self-satisfaction, elaborate offices, and private dining rooms.

Research also shows that the more objective the measures of performance, the more likely the manager will provide effort. That is why accounting measures are important. They provide relatively objective evaluations of performance. Moreover, if individuals believe that their behavior fails to affect their measure of performance, they will not see the connection between performance and rewards.

The choice of rewards clearly belongs with an overall system of management control. However, the design of a reward system is mainly the concern of top managers, who frequently get advice from many sources besides accountants.

☐ Agency Theory, Performance, Rewards, and Risk

Linking rewards to performance is desirable. But often a manager's performance cannot be measured directly. For example, responsibility center results may be measured easily, but a manager's effect on those results (that is, managerial performance) may not. Ideally, rewards should be based on managerial performance, but in practice the rewards usually depend on the financial results in the manager's responsibility center. Managerial performance and responsibility center results are certainly related, but factors beyond a manager's control also affect results. The greater the influence of noncontrollable factors on responsibility center results, the more problems there are in using the results to represent a manager's performance.

Economists describe the choices of performance measures and rewards as **agency theory**. For top management to hire a manager, both need to agree to an employment contract that includes specification of a performance measure and how it will affect rewards.[3] For example, a manager might receive a bonus of 15% of her salary if her responsibility center achieves its budgeted profit. According to agency theory, employment contracts will trade off three factors:

1. *Incentive*. The more a manager's reward depends on a performance measure, the more incentive there is to improve that measure. Top management should define the performance measure to promote *goal congruence* and base enough reward on it to achieve *managerial effort*.
2. *Risk*. The greater the influence of uncontrollable factors on a manager's reward, the more risk the manager bears. People generally avoid risk, so managers must be paid more if they are expected to bear more risk. Creating incentive by linking rewards to responsibility center results has the undesirable effect of imposing risk on managers.
3. *Cost of measuring performance*. The incentive versus risk trade-off is not necessary if a manager's performance is perfectly measured. Why? Because rewarding a manager based on performance creates no risk if only controllable factors affect the performance measure. But directly measuring a manager's performance is usually expensive and sometimes infeasible. Responsibility center results are more readily available. The cost-benefit criterion usually indicates that perfect measurement of a manager's performance is not worth its cost.

Consider a concert manager hired by a group of investors to promote and administer an outdoor rock performance. If the investors cannot directly measure the manager's effort and judgment, they would probably pay a bonus that depended on the economic success of the concert. The bonus would motivate the manager to put his effort toward generating a profit. On the other hand, it creates risk. Factors such as bad weather also could affect the concert's economic success. The manager might do an outstanding job and still not receive a bonus. Suppose the investors offer a contract with part guaranteed pay and part bonus. A larger bonus portion compared to the guaranteed portion creates more incentive, but it also means a larger expected total payment to compensate the manager for the added risk.

☐ **The Need for Many Transfer Prices**

Previous sections have pointed out that there is seldom a single transfer price that will ensure the desired decisions. The "correct" transfer price depends on the economic and legal circumstances and the decision at hand. We may

---

[3] Often performance measures and rewards are implicit. For example, promotion is a reward, but usually the requirements for promotion are not explicit.

want one transfer price for congruence and a second to spur managerial effort. Furthermore, the optimal price for either may differ from that employed for tax reporting or for other external needs.

Income taxes, property taxes, and tariffs often influence the setting of transfer prices so that the firm as a whole will benefit, even though the performance of a segment may suffer. To minimize tariffs and domestic income taxes, a company may want to set an unusually low selling price for a domestic division that ships goods to foreign subsidiaries in countries where the prevailing tax rates are lower. To maximize tax deductions for percentage depletion allowances, which are based on revenue, a petroleum company may want to transfer crude oil to other segments at as high a price as legally possible.

Transfer pricing is also influenced in some situations by state fair-trade laws and national antitrust acts. Because of the differences in national tax structures around the world or because of the differences in the incomes of various divisions and subsidiaries, the firm may wish to shift profits and "dump" goods, if legally possible. These considerations are additional illustrations of the limits of decentralization where heavy interdependencies exist and of why the same company may use different transfer prices for different purposes.

SUMMARY PROBLEM FOR YOUR REVIEW

☐ **Problem One**

Examine Exhibit 10–1, page 308. In addition to the data there, suppose Division A has fixed manufacturing costs of $400,000 and expected annual production of 100,000 units. The "fully allocated cost" per unit was computed as follows:

Variable costs per unit	$10
Fixed costs, $400,000 ÷ 100,000 units	4
Fully allocated cost per unit	$14

Required: Assume that Division A has idle capacity. Division B is considering whether to buy 10,000 units to be processed further and sold for $21. The additional costs shown in Exhibit 10–1 for Division B would prevail. If transfers were based on fully allocated cost, would the B manager buy? Why? Would the company as a whole benefit if the B manager decided to buy? Why?

☐ **Solution to Problem One**

B would not buy. Fully allocated costing may occasionally lead to dysfunctional decisions. The resulting transfer price of $14 would make the acquisition of parts unattractive to B:

Division B:		
Sales price of final product		$ 21
Deduct costs:		
Transfer price per unit paid to A (fully allocated cost)	$14	
Additional costs (from Exhibit 10–1):		
Processing	$5	
Selling	3	8
Total costs to B		22
Contribution to profit of B		$–1
Contribution to company as a whole (from Exhibit 10–1)		$ 3

As Exhibit 10–1 shows, the company as a whole would benefit by $30,000 (10,000 units × $3) if the units were transferred.

The major lesson here is that, when idle capacity exists in the supplier division, transfer prices based on fully allocated costs may induce the wrong decisions. Working in his own best interests, the B manager has no incentive to buy from A.

MEASURES OF PROFITABILITY

☐ Return on Investment

A favorite objective of top management is to maximize profitability. The trouble is that profitability does not mean the same thing to all people. Is it net income? Income before taxes? Net income percentage based on revenue? Is it an absolute amount? A percentage?

Too often, managers stress net income or income percentages without tying the measure into the investment associated with the generating of the income. A better test of profitability is the rate of **return on investment (ROI)**, defined as a measure of income or profit divided by the investment required to help obtain the income or profit. That is, given the same risks, for any given amount of resources required, the investor wants the maximum income. To say that Project A has an income of $200,000 and Project B has an income of $150,000 is an insufficient statement about profitability. The required investment in A may be $500,000, and the required investment in B may be only $150,000. Based on rate of return, all other things being equal, A's return is much less than B's.

The ROI measure is a useful common denominator. It can be compared with rates inside and outside the organization and with opportunities in other projects and industries. It is affected by two major ingredients:

$$\text{rate of return on invested capital} = \frac{\text{income}}{\text{invested capital}}$$
$$= \frac{\text{income}}{\text{revenue}} \times \frac{\text{revenue}}{\text{invested capital}}$$
$$= \text{income percentage of revenue} \times \text{capital turnover}$$

The terms of this equation are deliberately vague at this point because various versions of income, revenue, and invested capital are possible. Ponder the components of the equation. The rate of return is the result of the combination of two items, **income percentage of revenue** and **capital turnover**. An improvement in either without changing the other will improve the rate of return on invested capital.

Consider an example of these relationships:

	RATE OF RETURN ON INVESTED CAPITAL		$\dfrac{\text{INCOME}}{\text{REVENUE}}$	$\times$	$\dfrac{\text{REVENUE}}{\text{INVESTED CAPITAL}}$
Present outlook	20%	=	$\dfrac{16}{100}$	$\times$	$\dfrac{100}{80}$
Alternatives:					
1. Increase income percentage by reducing expenses	25%	=	$\dfrac{20}{100}$	$\times$	$\dfrac{100}{80}$
2. Increase turnover by decreasing investment in inventories	25%	=	$\dfrac{16}{100}$	$\times$	$\dfrac{100}{64}$

Alternative 1 is a popular way to improve performance. An alert management tries to decrease expenses without reducing sales in proportion or to boost sales without increasing related expenses in proportion. Alternative 2 is less obvious, but it may be a quicker way to improve performance. Increasing the turnover of invested capital means generating higher revenue for each dollar invested in such assets as cash, receivables, inventories, or equipment. There is an optimal level of investment in these assets. Having too much is wasteful, but having too little may hurt credit standing and the ability to compete for sales.

☐ ROI or Residual Income?

Most managers agree that measuring return in relation to investment provides the ultimate test of profitability. ROI is one such comparison. However, some companies favor emphasizing an *absolute amount* of income rather than a *percentage rate* of return. They use **residual income**, defined as net income less imputed interest. For example, suppose that divisional net income was $900,000, the average invested capital in the division for the year was $10 million, and the corporate headquarters assesses an "imputed" interest charge of 8%:

	FIGURES ASSUMED
Divisional net income after taxes	$900,000
Minus imputed interest on average invested capital (.08 × $10,000,000)	800,000
Equals residual income	$100,000

The word "imputed" means that the charge is made regardless of whether the corporation as a whole has actually incurred an interest cost in the ordinary sense of a cash disbursement. The rate represents the minimum acceptable rate for investments in that division, called the *cost of capital*. Modern finance theory has shown that the cost of capital depends on the risk of the investment. If divisions have different levels of risk, they should have different imputed interest rates.

Why do some companies prefer residual income to ROI? The ROI approach shows:

Divisional net income after taxes	$ 900,000
Average invested capital	$10,000,000
Return on investment	9%

Residual income is favored for reasons of goal congruence and managerial effort. Under ROI, the basic message is, "Go forth and maximize your rate of return, a percentage." Thus, if performance is measured by ROI, managers of highly profitable divisions may be reluctant to invest in projects at, say, 15% if their division is currently earning, say, 20%, because their average ROI would be reduced.

However, from the viewpoint of the company as a whole, top management may want this division manager to accept projects that earn 15%. If performance is measured by residual income, managers would be inclined to invest in any project earning more than the imputed interest rate. Regardless of the current profitability level of the division, residual income would be increased by such an investment. Goal congruence and managerial effort would thus be accomplished by using residual income with an 8% imputed interest rate. The basic message is, "Go forth and maximize residual income, an absolute amount."

DEFINITIONS OF INVESTED CAPITAL AND INCOME

☐ **Many Investment Bases**

To apply either ROI or residual income, a manager must measure invested capital. Consider the following balance sheet classifications:

Current assets	$ 400,000	Current liabilities	$ 200,000
Property, plant, and		Long-term liabilities	400,000
equipment	800,000		
Construction in progress	100,000	Stockholders' equity	700,000
Total assets	$1,300,000	Total liab. and stk. eq.	$1,300,000

Possible definitions of invested capital include:

1. *Total assets*. All assets are included, $1,300,000.
2. *Total assets employed*. All assets except agreed-upon exclusions of vacant land or construction in progress, $1,300,000 − $100,000 = $1,200,000.
3. *Total assets less current liabilities*. All assets except that portion supplied by short-term creditors, $1,300,000 −$200,000 = $1,100,000. This is sometimes expressed as *long-term invested capital*; note that it can also be computed by adding the long-term liabilities and the stockholders' equity, $400,000 + $700,000 = $1,100,000.
4. *Stockholders' equity*. Focuses on the investment of the owners of the business, $700,000.

All the above are computed as averages for the period under review. These averages may be based on simply the beginning and ending balances or on more complicated averages that weigh changes in investments through the months.

For measuring the performance of division managers, any of the three asset bases is recommended rather than stockholders' equity. If the division manager's mission is to use *all* assets as best he or she can without regard to their financing, then base 1 is best. If top management directs the manager to carry extra assets that are not currently productive, then base 2 is best. If the manager has direct control over obtaining short-term credit and bank loans, then base 3 is best. A key behavioral factor in choosing an investment base is that managers will focus attention on reducing those assets and increasing those liabilities that are included in the base. In practice, most companies using ROI or residual income include all assets in invested capital, and about half deduct some portion of current liabilities.

A few companies allocate long-term debt to their divisions and thus have an approximation of the stockholders' equity in each division. However, this practice has doubtful merit. Division managers typically have little responsibility for the long-term *financial* management of their divisions, as distinguished from *operating* management. You might compare how the investment base of a division manager of Company A could differ radically from the investment base of a comparable division manager of Company B if A bore heavy long-term debt and B were debt-free.

☐ Allocation to Divisions

Various definitions of income for the segments of an organization were discussed in Chapter 9, page 270, so they will not be repeated here. Just as cost allocations affect income, asset allocations affect the invested capital of particular divisions. The aim is to allocate in a manner that will be goal congruent, will spur managerial effort, and will recognize segment autonomy insofar as possible. Incidentally, as long as the managers feel that they are being treated uniformly, they tend to be more tolerant of the imperfections of the allocation.

A frequent criterion for asset allocation is avoidability. That is, the amount allocable to any given segment for the purpose of evaluating the division's performance is the amount that the corporation as a whole could avoid by not having that segment. Commonly used bases for allocation, when assets are not directly identifiable with a specific division, include:

ASSET CLASS	POSSIBLE ALLOCATION BASE
Corporate cash	Budgeted cash needs, as discussed shortly
Receivables	Sales weighted by payment terms
Inventories	Budgeted sales or usage
Plant and equipment	Usage of services in terms of long-run fore-casts of demand or area occupied

The allocation of central corporate assets often parallels the allocation of central corporate costs. Where the allocation of an asset would indeed be arbitrary, many managers feel that it is better not to allocate.

Should cash be included in a division's investment if the balances are strictly controlled by corporate headquarters? Arguments can be made for both sides, but the manager is usually regarded as being responsible for the volume of business generated by the division. In turn, this volume is likely to have a direct effect on the overall cash needs of the corporation.

A popular allocation base for cash is sales dollars. However, the allocation of cash on the basis of sales dollars seldom gets at the economic rationale of cash holdings. As Chapter 6 explains, cash needs are influenced by a host of factors, including payment terms of customers and creditors.

Central control of cash is usually undertaken to reduce the holdings from what would be used if each division had a separate account. Fluctuations in cash needs of each division will be somewhat offsetting, and backup borrow-ing power is increased. For example, Division A might have a cash deficiency of $1 million in February, but Division B might have an offsetting cash excess of $1 million. Taken together for the year, Divisions A, B, C, D, and E might require a combined investment in cash of, say, $16 million if each were inde-pendent entities, but only $8 million if cash were controlled centrally. Hence, if Division C would ordinarily require a $4 million investment in cash as a separate entity, it would be allocated an investment of only $2 million as a subunit of a company where cash was controlled centrally.

MEASUREMENT ALTERNATIVES

☐ Valuation of Assets

There is a widespread tendency to have one asset measure serve many masters. Should the assets contained in the investment base be valued at net book value (original cost less accumulated depreciation), some version of current value, or some other way? Practice is overwhelmingly in favor of using net book value. In 1978 Reece and Cool reported the following in the *Harvard Business Review*:

	NUMBER	PERCENTAGE
Gross book value	63	14%
Net book value	389	85
Replacement cost	10	2
Other	2	0
No answer	8	2
Total	472*	103%

* Number of responding companies was 459. Includes multiple responses. Note that only 2% used replacement cost, a remarkably low percentage in light of the inflation of the 1970s.

Historical cost has been widely criticized for many years as providing a faulty basis for decision making and performance evaluation. As Chapters 4 and 5 point out, historical costs are irrelevant per se for making economic decisions. Despite these criticisms, and despite the increasing external requirements for using current values such as replacement costs for asset valuation, managers have been slow to depart from historical cost.

Why is historical cost so widely used? Some critics would say that sheer ignorance is the explanation. But a more persuasive answer comes from cost-benefit analysis. Accounting systems are costly. Historical records must be kept for many legal purposes; therefore they are already in place. No additional money must be spent to obtain an evaluation of performance based on the historical-cost system. Furthermore, many managements believe that such a system provides the desired goal congruence and managerial effort. That is, a more sophisticated system will not radically improve collective operating decisions.

Historical costs may even improve some decisions because they are more objective. Moreover, managers will be better able to predict the historical-cost effects of their decisions, so their decisions may be more influenced by the control system. Further, the uncertainty involved with current-cost measures may impose undesirable risks on the managers. In short, the historical-cost system may be superior for the *routine* evaluation of performance. In nonroutine instances, such as replacing equipment or deleting a product line, managers will conduct special studies to gather any current valuations that seem relevant.

Sooner or later the required disclosures of "current costs" in American external reporting will probably also cause their wider use internally.[4] Such current-value information must be gathered in a routine manner by many large companies to satisfy external requirements. When current values are already available, the incremental costs (including the high cost of educating personnel) of using such values for internal performance measurement purposes are much less imposing than when current values must be installed from scratch.

---

[4] See Chapter 20 for a discussion of the use of current values and general price-level indexes as a basis of asset valuation and income measurement for external reporting.

Budgets and Inflation

Surveys and interviews have shown time and again that managers do not believe that the routine collection of current-value data will significantly affect collective decisions. Why? Because managers are already predicting the effects of inflation when they prepare their budgets.

Put another way, most well-managed organizations do not use a historical-cost system by itself. The alternatives available to managers are not:

| Historical-
Cost
System | versus | Current-
Value
System |

More accurately stated, the alternatives are:

| Historical Cost:
Budget versus Actual | versus | Current Value:
Budget versus Actual |

A budget system, whether based on historical cost or current value, causes managers to worry about inflation. Most managers seem to prefer to concentrate on improving their existing historical-cost budget system.

Plant and Equipment: Gross or Net?

Net book value is the carrying amount of an asset, net of any related accounts (such as *accumulated depreciation*). **Gross book value** is the carrying amount of an asset before deducting any related amounts. Most companies use net book value in calculating their investment base. However, according to a recent survey, 14% use gross book value. The proponents of gross book value maintain that it facilitates comparisons between years and between plants or divisions.

Consider an example of a $600,000 piece of equipment with a three-year life and no residual value:

| | OPERATING
INCOME
BEFORE | | OPERATING | AVERAGE INVESTMENT | | | |
YEAR	DEPRECIATION	DEPRECIATION	INCOME	Net Book Value	Rate of Return	Gross Book Value	Rate of Return
1	$260,000	$200,000	$60,000	$500,000	12%	$600,000	10%
2	260,000	200,000	60,000	300,000	20%	600,000	10%
3	260,000	200,000	60,000	100,000	60%	600,000	10%

The rate of return on net book value goes up as the equipment ages; note that it could increase even if operating income gradually declined through the years. In contrast, the rate of return on gross book value is unchanged if operating income does not change; moreover, the rate would decrease if operating income gradually declined through the years.

The advocates of using net book value maintain:

1. It is less confusing because it is consistent with the assets shown on the conventional balance sheet and with the net income computations.
2. The major criticism of net book value is not peculiar to its use for ROI purposes. It is really a criticism of using historical cost as a basis for evaluation.

The effect on motivation should be considered when choosing between net and gross book value. Managers evaluated using gross book value will tend to replace assets sooner than those in firms using net book value. Consider a four-year-old machine with an original cost of $1,000 and net book value of $200. It can be replaced by a new machine for $1,500. The choice of net or gross book value does not affect net income, but the investment base increases from $200 to $1,500 in a net book value firm, but only from $1,000 to $1,500 in a gross-book-value firm. To motivate managers to use state-of-the-art production technology, gross asset value is preferred. Net asset value promotes a more conservative approach to asset replacement.

DISTINCTION BETWEEN MANAGERS AND INVESTMENTS

☐ Focus on Controllability

As Chapter 9 explained (see Exhibit 9–4, p. 270), a distinction should be made between the performance of the division manager and the performance of the division as an investment by the corporation. Managers should be evaluated on the basis of their controllable performance (in many cases some controllable contribution in relation to controllable investment). However, decisions such as increasing or decreasing investment in a division are based on the economic viability of the *division*, not the performance of its *managers*.

This distinction helps to clarify some vexing difficulties. For example, top management may want to use an investment base to gauge the economic performance of a retail store, but the *manager* may best be judged by focusing on income and forgetting about any investment allocations. If investment is assigned to the manager, the aim should be to assign controllable investment only. Controllability depends on what *decisions* managers can make regarding the size of the investment base. In a highly decentralized company, for instance, the manager can influence the size of all his or her assets and can exercise judgment regarding the appropriate amount of short-term credit and perhaps some long-term credit.

☐ Management by Objectives

Management by objectives (MBO) describes the joint formulation by a manager and his or her superior of a set of goals and of plans for achieving the goals for a forthcoming period. For our purposes here, the terms *goals* and *objectives* are synonyms. The plans often take the form of a responsibility accounting budget (together with supplementary goals such as levels of management training and safety that may not be incorporated into the accounting budget). The manager's performance is then evaluated in relation to these agreed-upon budgeted objectives.

Regardless of whether it is so labeled, a management-by-objectives approach lessens the complaints about lack of controllability because of its stress on *budgeted results*. That is, a budget is negotiated between a particular manager and his or her superior for a *particular* time period and a *particular* set of expected outside and inside influences. In this way, a manager may more readily accept an assignment to a less successful subunit. This is preferable to a system that emphasizes absolute profitability for its own sake. Unless focus is placed on currently attainable results, able managers will be reluctant to accept responsibility for subunits that are in economic trouble.

Thus, skillful budgeting and intelligent performance evaluation will go a long way toward overcoming the common lament: "I'm being held responsible for items beyond my control."

☐ **Tailoring Budgets for Managers**

Many of the troublesome motivational effects of performance evaluation systems can be minimized by the astute use of budgets. The desirability of tailoring a budget to particular managers cannot be overemphasized. For example, either an ROI or a residual income system can promote goal congruence and managerial effort if top management gets everybody to focus on what is currently attainable in the forthcoming budget period. Typically, divisional managers do not have complete freedom to make major investment decisions without checking with senior management.

In sum, our cost-benefit approach provides no universal answers with respect to such controversial issues as historical values versus current values or return on investment versus residual income. Instead, using a cost-benefit test, each organization must judge for itself whether an alternative control system or accounting technique will improve collective decision making. The latter is the primary criterion.

Too often, the literature engages in pro-and-con discussions about which alternative is more perfect or truer than another in some logical sense. The cost-benefit approach is not concerned with "truth" or "perfection" by itself. Instead, it asks, "Do you think your perceived 'truer' or 'more logical' system is worth its added cost? Or will our existing imperfect system provide about the same set of decisions if it is skillfully administered?"

ALTERNATIVES OF TIMING

Accounting textbooks, including this one, do not discuss at length the problem of timing. However, timing is an important factor to consider when an information system is designed. For instance, the costs of gathering and processing information and the need for frequent feedback for controlling current operations may lead to using historical-cost measures rather than replacement costs. The need for replacement costs, realizable values, and economic values tends to be less frequent, so the systems are not designed for providing such information routinely. The essence of the matter is that management seems unwilling to pay for more elegant information because its extra costs exceed its prospective benefits.

Another aspect of timing underscores why management accounting systems are seldom static. A system that works well in 1987 may not suffice in 1990. Why? Because top management's desires and the attitudes of various managers may change. For example, top management may not allocate the costs of the internal auditing department in 1987 in order to encourage all managers to use auditing services. In 1990 top management may begin allocating auditing services in order to discourage use.

CONTROL SYSTEMS IN NONPROFIT ORGANIZATIONS

Most nonprofit organizations have more difficulty in identifying objectives or goals than do profit-seeking organizations. There is no profit, no "bottom line" that so often serves as a powerful incentive in private industry. Furthermore, monetary incentives are generally less effective in nonprofit organizations. For example, many managers seek positions in nonprofit organizations primarily for nonmonetary rewards.

Control systems in nonprofit organizations will never be as highly developed as in profit-seeking organizations for several reasons, including:

1. Organizational goals or objectives are less clear. Moreover, they are often multiple, requiring trade-offs.
2. Professionals (for example, teachers, attorneys, physicians, scientists, economists) tend to dominate nonprofit organizations. They are usually less receptive to the installation or improvement of formal control systems.
3. Measurements are more difficult:
   a. There is no profit measure.
   b. There are heavy amounts of discretionary fixed costs.
   c. The relationships of inputs to outputs are hard to specify and measure. Attempts to relate inputs to outputs via work measurement are often resisted.

Additional difficulties arise because of the lesser role of the marketplace, the greater role of politics, and the vague sense of responsibility because "ownership" of nonprofit organizations is often ill-defined.

Budgeting was originally developed in the public sector as a way of providing fiscal accountability. However, the management uses of budgets have been unimpressive. Because most nonprofit organizations are centralized, the budget process should be an important means of communicating expectations to middle- and lower-level managers. However, too often, the budget is regarded as a means of obtaining money, not as a means of planning and control. Thus the process of budgeting in the public sector is often a matter of playing bargaining games with higher authorities to get the largest possible authorization of discretionary fixed costs.

SUMMARY

The starting point for judging a management accounting or management control system is the specification of top-management goals and subgoals. Systems typically are designed within the constraints of a given set of goals and a given organization structure. The final selection of a system depends on criteria of cost-benefit, goal congruence, and managerial effort. Above all, top management should predict which alternative system is more likely to produce the best collective set of operating decisions in light of the costs of the systems.

As organizations grow, decentralization of some management functions becomes desirable. Decentralization immediately raises problems of obtaining decisions that are coordinated with the objectives of the organization as a whole. Ideally, planning and control systems should provide information that (a) aims managers toward decisions that are goal congruent, (b) provides feedback (evaluation of performance) that improves managerial effort, and (c) preserves subunit autonomy. Note that the common thread of these problems is motivation.

Transfer-pricing systems are often used as a means of communicating information among subunits and of measuring their performance. Problems of transfer pricing and cost allocations are similar. Proper choices vary from situation to situation.

Choices of performance measures (such as return on investment and residual income) and rewards (such as bonuses and increases in salaries) can heavily affect goal congruence and managerial effort. To affect managerial behavior, strong links must exist between effort, performance, and rewards.

SUMMARY PROBLEM FOR YOUR REVIEW

Problem One appeared earlier in this chapter.

☐ Problem Two

A division has assets of $200,000 and operating income of $60,000.
1. What is the division's ROI?
2. If interest is imputed at 14%, what is the residual income?
3. What effects on management behavior can be expected if ROI is used to gauge performance?
4. What effects on management behavior can be expected if residual income is used to gauge performance?

☐ Solution to Problem Two

1. $60,000 \div $200,000 = 30\%$.
2. $60,000 - .14($200,000) = $60,000 - $28,000 = $32,000$.
3. If ROI is used, the manager is prone to reject projects that do not earn an ROI of at least 30%. From the viewpoint of the organization as a whole, this may be undesirable because its best investment opportunities may lie in that division at a rate of, say, 22%. If a division is enjoying a high ROI, it is less likely to expand if it is judged via ROI than if it is judged via residual income.
4. If residual income is used, the manager is inclined to accept all projects whose expected ROI exceeds the minimum desired rate. The manager's division is more likely to expand because his or her goal is to maximize a dollar amount rather than a rate.

HIGHLIGHTS TO REMEMBER

1. Choices must usually be made between two or more imperfect systems. Incremental rather than radical improvements are typically achieved. That is, there is no immaculate substitution whereby a perfect System A replaces an imperfect System B.

2. When arguments arise regarding whether current values should be a routine part of performance measurement, the role of budgets should not be overlooked. Budgets deserve more respect because they do induce managers to consider the effects of future price changes.

3. Profit centers are usually associated with heavily decentralized organizations, whereas cost centers are usually associated with heavily centralized organizations. However, profit centers and decentralization are separate ideas; one can exist without the other.

4. Although this point was not mentioned in the chapter, any control system requires enthusiastic support from senior management if it is to be taken seriously by subordinates. Indeed, top-management support is so important that it deserves nearly as much prominence as goal congruence as a major criterion in designing systems.

ACCOUNTING VOCABULARY

Agency Theory *p. 313*   Capital Turnover *316*   Decentralization *304*   Dysfunctional Behavior *309*   Goal Congruence *302*   Gross Book Value *321*   Incentive *311*   Income Percentage of Revenue *316*   Internal Control System *301*   Management by Objectives (MBO) *322*   Managerial Effort *302*   Net Book Value *321*   Organization Structure *300*   Residual Income *316*   Return on Investment (ROI) *315*   Segment Autonomy *305*   Transfer Price *306*.

FUNDAMENTAL ASSIGNMENT MATERIAL

10–1. **RATE OF RETURN AND TRANSFER PRICING.** The Athletic Footware Division of Exotic Shoe Company prepared the following budget data:

Average available assets:	
Receivables	$100,000
Inventories	200,000
Plant and equipment, net	300,000
Total	$600,000
Fixed overhead	$200,000
Variable costs	$10 per pair
Desired rate of return on average available assets	25%
Selling price	$45 per pair

Required:

1. **a.** How many pairs of shoes must be sold to obtain the desired rate of return on average available assets?
   b. What would be the expected capital turnover?
   c. What would be the operating income percentage on dollar sales?

2. **a.** What rate of return will be earned on available assets if sales volume is 12,000 pairs of shoes?

   b. If sales volume is 8,000 pairs?

3. Assume that 3,000 pairs of shoes are to be sold to another division of the same company and that only 7,000 pairs of shoes can be sold to outside customers. The other division manager has balked at a tentative selling price of $40. She has offered $22.50, claiming that she can manufacture the shoes herself for that price. The manager of the selling division has examined his own data. He has decided that he could eliminate $40,000 of inventories, $60,000 of plant and equipment, and $20,000 of fixed overhead if he did *not* sell to the other division and sold only 7,000 pairs of shoes to outside customers. Should he sell for $22.50? Show computations to support your answer.

10–2. **TRANSFER-PRICING DISPUTE.** A computer equipment manufacturer, Eptek Corporation, is heavily decentralized. Each division head has full authority on all decisions regarding sales to internal or external customers. The Printer Division has always acquired a certain equipment component from the Parts Manufacturing Division. However, when informed that Parts was increasing its unit price from $18 to $20, the Printer Division management decided to purchase the component from outside suppliers at a price of $19.

 The Parts Manufacturing Division has recently acquired some specialized equipment that was used primarily to make this component. The manager cited the resulting high depreciation charges as the justification for the price boost. He asked the president of the company to instruct the Printer Division to buy from Parts at the $20 price. He supplied the following:

Printer's annual purchases of component	100,000 units
Part's variable costs per unit	$17
Part's fixed costs per unit	$ 3

Required:

1. Suppose that there are no alternative uses of the Parts facilities. Will the company as a whole benefit if the Printer Division buys from the outside suppliers for $19 per unit? Show computations to support your answer.
2. Suppose that internal facilities of Parts would not otherwise be idle. The equipment and other facilities would be assigned to other production operations that would otherwise require an additional annual outlay of $29,000. Should the Printer Division purchase from outsiders at $19 per unit?
3. Suppose that there are no alternative uses for Parts' internal facilities and that the selling price of outsiders drops to $16. Should the Printer Division purchase from outsiders?
4. As the president, how would you respond to the request of the manager of the Parts Division? Would your response differ, depending on the specific situations described in Requirements 1 through 3? Why?

☐ **Additional Assignment Material**

10–3. "There are corporate objectives other than profit." Name four.

10–4. "As a company grows, it is necessary to use accounting measures instead of personal observation to achieve management control." Do you agree? Why?

10–5. What is the most important criterion in judging the effectiveness of a measure of performance?

10–6. "The essence of decentralization is the use of profit centers." Do you agree? Explain.

10–7. Why are cost-based transfer prices in common use?

10–8. Why are transfer-pricing systems needed?

10–9. Give three examples of how managers may improve short-run performance to the detriment of long-run results.

10–10. Why are interest expense and income taxes ordinarily excluded in computing incomes that are related to asset bases?

10–11. What is the major benefit of the ROI technique for measuring performance?

10–12. "We budget different rates of return for different divisions in the short run. But in the long run our desired rate of return for all divisions is the same." Do you agree with this policy? Why?

10–13. "Managers who use a historical-cost accounting system look backward, at what something cost yesterday, instead of forward to what it will cost tomorrow." Do you agree? Why?

10–14. The head of the public library in a major city said, "Budgeting is a necessary evil for us. We would rather spend the time providing help to library users, but we have to prepare a budget to get city funding." Discuss this statement.

10–15. **SIMPLE CALCULATIONS.** You are given the following data:

Sales	$150,000
Invested capital	30,000
Net income	3,000

Required:
1. Turnover of capital.
2. Return on investment.
3. Net income as a percentage of sales.

10–16. **SIMPLE CALCULATIONS.** Fill in the blanks:

	DIVISION		
	A	B	C
Income percentage of revenue	___%	2%	6%
Capital turnover	2	10	
Rate of return on invested capital	16%	___	24%

10–17. **SIMPLE CALCULATIONS.** Consider the following data:

	DIVISION		
	X	Y	Z
Invested capital	$ 300,000	$200,000	$ 250,000
Revenue	1,200,000	600,000	2,500,000
Income	36,000	36,000	25,000

Required:
1. For each division, compute the income percentage of revenue, the capital turnover, and the rate of return on invested capital.
2. Which division is the best performer? Explain.
3. Suppose each division is assessed an imputed interest rate of 12% on invested capital. Compute the residual income for each divison.

10–18. **SIMPLE CALCULATIONS.** Consider the following data:

	DIVISION		
	L	M	N
Invested capital	$1,000,000	$ _____	$1,500,000
Income	$ _____	$ 360,000	$ 150,000
Revenue	$5,000,000	$6,000,000	$ _____
Income percentage of revenue	3%	_____ %	_____ %
Capital turnover	_____	_____	2
Rate of return on invested capital	_____ %	12%	_____ %

Required:

1. Prepare a similar tabular presentation, filling in all blanks.
2. Which division is the best performer? Explain.
3. Suppose each division is assessed an imputed interest rate of 8% on invested capital. Compute the residual income for each division.

10–19. **MARGINS AND TURNOVER.** Return on investment is often expressed as the product of two components—capital turnover and margin on sales. You are considering investing in one of three companies, all in the same industry, and are given the following information:

	COMPANY		
	I	II	III
Sales	$5,000,000	$ 2,500,000	$50,000,000
Income	250,000	250,000	250,000
Capital	2,000,000	20,000,000	20,000,000

Required:

1. Why would you desire the breakdown of return on investment into margin on sales and turnover on capital?
2. Compute the margin on sales, turnover on capital, and return on investment for the three companies, and comment on the relative performance of the companies as thoroughly as the data permit.

10–20. **COMPARISON OF ASSET AND EQUITY BASES.** Company A has assets of $1 million and long-term, 9% debt of $600,000. Company B has assets of $1 million and no long-term debt. The annual operating income (before interest) of both companies is $150,000.

Required:

1. Compute the rate of return on
   a. Assets available.
   b. Stockholders' equity.

2. Evaluate the relative merits of each base for appraising operating management.

10–21. **FINDING UNKNOWNS.** Consider the following data:

		DIVISION	
	J	K	L
Income	$210,000	$ _____	$ _____
Revenue	$ _____	$ _____	$ _____
Invested capital	$ _____	$5,000,000	$21,000,000
Income percentage of revenue	10%	5%	_____ %
Capital turnover	3	_____	2
Rate of return on invested capital	_____ %	20%	12%
Imputed interest rate on invested capital	25%	15%	_____ %
Residual income	$ _____	$ _____	$ 420,000

Required: 1. Prepare a similar tabular presentation, filling in all blanks.
2. Which division is the best performer? Explain.

10–22. **ROI OR RESIDUAL INCOME.** J. Peter & Co. is a large integrated conglomerate with shipping, metals, and mining operations throughout the world. The general manager of the ferrous metals division has been directed to submit his proposed capital budget for 19X1 for inclusion in the companywide budget.

The division manager has for consideration the following projects, all of which require an outlay of capital. All projects have equal risk.

PROJECT	INVESTMENT REQUIRED	RETURN
1	$6,000,000	$1,380,000
2	4,800,000	1,632,000
3	1,750,000	245,000
4	1,200,000	216,000
5	800,000	96,000
6	350,000	98,000

The division manager must decide which of the projects to take. The company has a cost of capital of 15%. An amount of $15 million is available to the division for investment purposes.

Required: 1. What will be the total investment, total return, return on capital invested, and residual income of the rational division manager if
   a. The company has a rule that all projects promising at least 20% or more should be taken.
   b. The division manager is evaluated on his ability to maximize his return on capital invested (assume that this is a new division with no invested capital).
   c. The division manager is expected to maximize residual income as computed by using the 15% cost of capital.

2. Which of the three approaches will induce the most effective investment policy for the company as a whole?

10–23. **EVALUATING DIVISIONAL PERFORMANCE.** As the chief executive officer of J. L. Fernandez Company, you examined the following measures of the performance of three divisions (in thousands of dollars):

DIVISION	NET ASSETS BASED ON Historical Cost	NET ASSETS BASED ON Replacement Cost	OPERATING INCOME BASED ON* Historical Cost	OPERATING INCOME BASED ON* Replacement Cost
Northeast	$15,000	$15,000	$2,600	$2,600
Midwest	30,000	37,500	4,500	4,100
Southwest	20,000	32,000	3,200	2,600

* The differences in operating income between historical and replacement cost are attributable to the differences in depreciation expenses.

Required:

1. Calculate for each division the rate of return on net assets and the residual income based on historical cost and on replacement cost. For purposes of calculating residual income, use 10% as the minimum desired rate of return.
2. Rank the performance of each division under each of the four different measures computed in Requirement 1.
3. What do these measures indicate about the performance of the divisions? Of the division managers? Which measure do you prefer? Why?

10–24. **USING GROSS OR NET BOOK VALUE OF FIXED ASSETS.** Lou LaBossiere was recently promoted and placed in charge of a new product. In his new position he will be evaluated on income from the product in relation to the fixed assets used in production. He expects to acquire one $100,000 machine at the beginning of each year for seven years. Each machine has a useful life of four years and no residual value. The business volume will be increasing for the first three years, stable in years 4–7, and declining in years 8, 9, and 10 as the product reaches the end of its life cycle.

Straight-line depreciation is $25,000 per year on each machine. All sales and expenses (except depreciation) are on a cash basis. Headquarters provides cash needed for investment, and cash generated is remitted to headquarters. The production from each machine is expected to generate $35,000 of cash (sales less cash expenses) each year. Therefore, net income per machine should be $35,000 − $25,000 = $10,000.

Lou prepared the following analysis:

YEAR	NO. OF MACHINES	BOOK VALUE, BEGINNING	ANNUAL DEPRECIATION	BOOK VALUE, ENDING	AVERAGE BOOK VALUE	NET INCOME
1	1	$100,000	$ 25,000	$ 75,000	$ 87,500	$10,000
2	2	175,000	50,000	125,000	150,000	20,000
3	3	225,000	75,000	150,000	187,500	30,000
4	4	250,000	100,000	150,000	200,000	40,000
5	4	250,000	100,000	150,000	200,000	40,000
6	4	250,000	100,000	150,000	200,000	40,000
7	4	250,000	100,000	150,000	200,000	40,000
8	3	150,000	75,000	75,000	112,500	30,000
9	2	75,000	50,000	25,000	50,000	20,000
10	1	25,000	25,000	0	12,500	10,000

The company measures the asset value used in managerial evaluations as the average net book value (i.e., original cost less accumulated depreciation) for the year. LaBossiere has heard that other companies use gross book value (i.e., original cost) for this purpose. He wonders what difference this measurement might make.

1. Prepare a tabulation of the product's annual rates of return based on:
   a. Gross book value of assets.
   b. Net book value of assets.
2. For each of the four years of an individual machine's useful life, show the annual rate of return based on:
   a. Gross book value of assets.
   b. Net book value of assets.
3. Evaluate the relative merits of gross assets and net book value of assets as investment bases.

10–25. MANAGEMENT BY OBJECTIVES. (CMA, adapted.) Eric McDonald is the chief executive officer of Farmers' Insurance Company. McDonald has a financial management background and is known throughout the organization as a "no-nonsense" executive. When McDonald became chief executive officer, he emphasized cost reduction and savings and introduced a comprehensive cost control and budget system. The company goals and budget plans were established by McDonald and given to his subordinates for implementation. Some of the company's key executives were dismissed or demoted for failing to meet projected budget plans. Under the leadership of McDonald, Farmers' Insurance has once again become financially stable and profitable after several years of poor performance.

Recently McDonald has become concerned with the human side of the organization and has become interested in the management technique referred to as "management by objectives" (MBO). If there are enough positive benefits of MBO, he plans to implement the system throughout the company. However, he realizes that he does not fully understand MBO because he does not understand how it differs from the current system of establishing firm objectives and budget plans.

1. Briefly explain what "management by objectives" entails and identify its advantages and disadvantages.
2. Does McDonald's management style incorporate the human value premises and goals of MBO? Explain your answer.

10–26. MANAGEMENT CONTROL SYSTEMS AND INNOVATION. The president of a fast-growing high-tech firm remarked, "Developing budgets and comparing performance to the budgets may be fine for some firms. But we want to encourage innovations and entrepreneurship. Budgets go with bureaucracy, not innovation." Do you agree? How can a management control system encourage innovation and entrepreneurship?

10–27. MULTIPLE GOALS AND PROFITABILITY. The following are multiple goals of the General Electric Company:

Profitability   Employee attitudes
Market position   Public responsibility
Productivity   Balance between short-range and long-
Product leadership   range goals
Personnel development

General Electric is a huge, highly decentralized corporation with sales of about $28 billion and assets of $26 billion in 1985. It had approximately 170 responsibility centers called "departments," but that is a deceiving term. In most other companies, these departments would be called divisions. For example, some GE departments have sales of over $500 million.

Each department manager's performance is evaluated annually in relation to the specified multiple goals. A special measurements group was set up in 1952 to devise ways of quantifying accomplishments in each of the areas. In this way, the evaluation of performance would become more objective as the various measures were developed and improved.

1. How would you measure performance in each of these areas? Be specific.
2. Can the other goals be encompassed as ingredients of a formal measure of profitability? In other words, can profitability per se be defined to include the other goals?

10–28. SALESCLERK'S COMPENSATION PLAN. You are manager of the clothing department of a major retail store. Sales are subject to month-to-month variations, depending on the individual salesclerk's efforts. A new salary-plus-bonus plan has been in effect for four months, and you are reviewing a sales performance report. The plan provides for a base salary of $400 per month, a $500 bonus each month if the monthly sales quota is met, and an additional commission of 5% of all sales over the monthly quota. The quota is set approximately 3% above the previous month's sales to motivate clerks toward increasing sales.

		SALESCLERK A	SALESCLERK B	SALESCLERK C
January	Quota	$30,000	$10,000	$50,000
	Actual	10,000	10,000	60,000
February	Quota	$10,300	$10,300	$61,800
	Actual	20,000	10,300	20,000
March	Quota	$20,600	$10,600	$20,600
	Actual	35,000	5,000	60,000
April	Quota	$36,050	$ 5,150	$61,800
	Actual	10,000	5,200	27,000

1. Compute the compensation for each salesclerk for each month.
2. Evaluate the compensation plan. Be specific. What changes would you recommend?

10–29. INTERNAL CONTROL. The Matsuhita Company keeps careful control over its inventory. An important factor in its internal control is *separation of duties*. The purchasing personnel are not authorized to sign for the receipt of physical inventories, and those in charge of inventory records do not perform the regular count of the physical inventory.

Briefly describe an irregularity that would probably be discovered or prevented by each of the two separations of duties described.

10–30. PROFIT CENTERS AND TRANSFER PRICING IN AN AUTOMOBILE DEALERSHIP. A large automobile dealership is installing a responsibility accounting system and three profit centers: parts and service; new vehicles; and used vehicles. Each department manager has been told to run his shop as if he were in business for himself. However, there are interdepartmental dealings. For example:

a. The parts and service department prepares new cars for final delivery and repairs used cars prior to resale.

b. The used-car department's major source of inventory has been cars traded in as part payment for new cars.

   The owner of the dealership has asked you to draft a company policy statement on transfer pricing, together with specific rules to be applied to the examples cited. He has told you that clarity is of paramount importance because your statement will be relied upon for settling transfer-pricing disputes.

10–31. ROLE OF ECONOMIC VALUE AND REPLACEMENT VALUE. (This problem requires understanding of the concept of present values.) "To me, economic value is the only justifiable basis for measuring plant assets for purposes of evaluating performance. By economic value, I mean the present value of expected future services. Still, we do not even do this upon acquisition of new assets—that is, we may compute a positive net present value, using discounted cash flow; but we record the asset at no more than its cost. In this way, the excess present value is not shown in the initial balance sheet. Moreover, the use of replacement costs in subsequent years is also unlikely to result in showing economic values; the replacement cost will probably be less than the economic value at any given instant of an asset's life.

"Market values are totally unappealing to me because they represent a second-best alternative value—that is, they ordinarily represent the maximum amount obtainable from an alternative that has been rejected. Obviously, if the market value exceeds the economic value of the assets in use, they should be sold. However, in most instances, the opposite is true; market values of individual assets are far below their economic value in use.

"The obtaining and recording of total present values of individual assets based on discounted-cash-flow techniques is an infeasible alternative. I, therefore, conclude that replacement cost (less accumulated depreciation) of similar assets producing similar services is the best practical approximation of the economic value of the assets in use. Of course, it is more appropriate for the evaluation of the division's performance than the division manager's performance."

Required: Critically evaluate these comments. Please do not wander; concentrate on the issues described by the quotation.

10–32. **VARIABLE COST AS A TRANSFER PRICE.** A product's variable cost is $4 and its market value is $5 at a transfer point from Division S to Division P. Division P's variable cost of processing the product further is $3.25, and the selling price of the final product is $7.75. Transfer prices are set at variable cost.

Required:
1. Prepare a tabulation of the contribution margin per unit for Division P performance and overall performance under the two alternatives of (a) processing further and (b) selling to outsiders at the transfer point.
2. As Division P manager, which alternative would you choose? Explain.

10–33. **TRANSFER PRICING.** Refer to Problem 10–2, Requirement 1 only. Suppose that the Parts Manufacturing Division could modify the component at an additional variable cost of $1.00 per unit and sell the 100,000 units to other customers for $20.50. Then would the entire company benefit if P purchased the 100,000 components from outsiders at $19 per unit?

10–34. **TRANSFER PRICING.** The Kenosha Division of Elk Farm Equipment Company is the sole supplier of radiators to the Tractor Division. The Kenosha Division charges $100 per unit, the current market price for large wholesale lots. The Kenosha Division also sells to outside retail outlets, but at $125 per unit. Normally, outside sales amount to 25% of a total sales volume of 100,000 radiators per year. Typical combined annual data for the division follow:

Sales	$10,625,000
Variable costs, @ $80 per radiator	$ 8,000,000
Fixed costs	1,000,000
Total costs	$ 9,000,000
Gross margin	$ 1,625,000

The Sure Life Radiator Company, an entirely separate entity, has offered the Tractor Division comparable radiators at a firm price of $90 per unit. The Kenosha Division claims that it can't possibly match this price because it could not earn any margin at $90.

Required: 1. Assume you are the manager of the Tractor Division. Comment on the Kenosha Division's claim. Assume that normal outside volume cannot be increased.
2. The Kenosha Division feels that it can increase outside sales by 75,000 radiators per year by increasing fixed costs by $1 million and variable costs by $10 per unit while reducing the selling price to $120. Assume that maximum capacity remains at 100,000 radiators per year. Should the division reject intracompany business and concentrate on outside sales?

10–35. TRANSFER PRICING. International Food Company (IFC) makes a variety of food products. In addition, it owns a chain of Crab Pot restaurants. The manager of each restaurant is told to act as if he or she owned the restaurant and is judged on his profit performance.

Various divisions of IFC supply much of the food to Crab Pot restaurants. One such item is the sirloin steak that is part of the restaurants' "Crab 'n Slab" specialty. It is produced by the Omaha Packing Division. Omaha currently supplies 2 million pounds annually at $3.00 per pound to the 13 Crab Pot restaurants. The meat costs Omaha $1.40 a pound, and it is put through a process to make it especially compatible with the crab. This process is not useful for any other meat that the Omaha Packing Division sells. The process has a variable cost of $.20 a pound and a fixed cost of $1 million.

The manager of the New York City Crab Pot restaurant, Luci Magellan, has found a supplier who promises to provide a sirloin steak that is just as compatible with crab for $2.40 a pound. Her restaurant uses 400,000 pounds of the steak per year. She has sent a memo to you, controller of IFC, requesting permission to buy from the outside supplier. You determine that Omaha's fixed costs can be decreased by $100,000 if this 20% reduction in volume takes place.

The Omaha Packing Division manager is balking at selling to New York at $2.40 a pound. He says that such a sale would make his profit $240,000 below budget ($.60 lost revenue per pound × 400,000 pounds).

Required: What is the appropriate transfer price?

10–36. TRANSFER-PRICING CONCESSION. (CMA, adapted.) The Ajax Division of Gunnco Corporation, operating at capacity, has been asked by the Defco Division of Gunnco to supply it with Electrical Fitting No. 521. Ajax sells this part to its regular customers for $7.50 each. Defco, which is operating at 50% capacity, is willing to pay $5 each for the fitting. Defco will put the fitting into a brake unit that it is manufacturing on essentially a cost-plus basis for a commercial airplane manufacturer.

Ajax has a variable cost of producing fitting No. 521 of $4.25. The cost of the brake unit as being built by Defco is as follows:

Purchased parts from outside vendors	$22.50
Ajax fitting No. 521	5.00
Other variable costs	14.00
Fixed overhead and administration	8.00
	$49.50

Defco believes the price concession is necessary to get the job.

The company uses return on investment and dollar profits in the measurement of division and division-manager performance.

Required: 1. Consider that you are the division controller of Ajax. Would you recommend that Ajax supply fitting No. 521 to Defco? Why or why not? (Ignore any income tax issues.)

2. Would it be to the short-run economic advantage of the Gunnco Corporation for the Ajax Division to supply the Defco Division with fitting No. 521 at $5 each? (Ignore any income tax issues.) Explain your answer.

3. Discuss the organizational and manager-behavior difficulties, if any, inherent in this situation. As the Gunnco controller, what would you advise the Gunnco Corporation president to do in this situation?

10–37. REVIEW OF MAJOR POINTS IN CHAPTER. (D. Kleespie.) The Tomãs Company uses the decentralized form of organizational structure and considers each of its divisions as an investment center. Division L is currently selling 10,000 air filters annually, although it has sufficient productive capacity to produce 14,000 units per year. Variable manufacturing costs amount to $20 per unit, while the total fixed costs amount to $80,000. These 10,000 air filters are sold to outside customers at $40 per unit.

Division M, also a part of the Tomãs Company, has indicated that it would like to buy 1,000 air filters from Division L, but at a price of $39 per unit. This is the price Division M is currently paying an outside supplier.

Required:

1. Compute the effect on the operating income of the company as a whole if Division M purchases the 1,000 air filters from Division L.
2. What is the minimum price that Division L should be willing to accept for these 1,000 air filters?
3. What is the maximum price that Division M should be willing to pay for these 1,000 air filters?
4. Suppose instead that Division L is currently producing and selling 14,000 air filters annually to outside customers. What is the effect on the overall Tomãs Company operating income if Division L is required by top management to sell 1,000 air filters to Division M at (a) $20 per unit and (b) $39 per unit?
5. For this question only, assume that Division L is currently earning an annual operating income of $33,000, and the division's average invested capital is $300,000. The division manager has an opportunity to invest in a proposal that will require an additional investment of $20,000 and will increase annual operating income by $2,000. (a) Should the division manager accept this proposal if the Tomãs Company uses ROI in evaluating the performance of its divisional managers? (b) If the company uses residual income? (Assume an "imputed interest" charge of 8%.)

10–38. TRANSFER-PRICING PRINCIPLES. A consulting firm, INO, is decentralized with 25 offices around the country. The headquarters is based in Orange County, California. Another operating division is located in Los Angeles, 50 miles away. A subsidiary printing operation, We Print, is located in the headquarters building. Top management has indicated the desirability of the Los Angeles office's using We Print for printing reports. All charges are eventually billed to the client, but INO was concerned about keeping such charges competitive.

We Print charges Los Angeles the following:

Photographing page for offset printing (a setup cost)	$.30
Printing cost per page	.015

At this rate, We Print sales have a 60% contribution margin to fixed overhead.

Outside bids for 50 copies of a 135-page report needed immediately have been:

EZ Print	$145.00
Quick Service	128.25
Fast Print	132.00

These three printers are located within a five-mile radius of INO Los Angeles and can have the reports ready in two days. A messenger would have to be sent to drop off the original and pick up the copies. The messenger usually goes to headquarters, but in the past, special trips have been required to deliver the original or pick up the copies. It takes three to four days to get the copies from We Print (because of the extra scheduling difficulties in delivery and pickup).

Quality control at We Print is poor. Reports received in the past have had wrinkled pages and have occasionally been miscollated or had pages deleted. (In one circumstance an intracompany memorandum indicating INO's economic straits was inserted in a report. Fortunately, the Los Angeles office detected the error before the report was distributed to the clients.) The degree of quality control in the three outside print shops is unknown.

(Although the differences in costs may seem immaterial in this case, regard the numbers as significant for purposes of focusing on the key issues.)

Required:
1. If you were the decision maker at INO Los Angeles, to which print shop would you give the business? Is this an optimal economic decision from the entire corporation's point of view?
2. What would be the ideal transfer price in this case, if based only on economic considerations?
3. Time is an important factor in maintaining the goodwill of the client. There is potential return business from this client. Given this perspective, what might be the optimal decision for the company?
4. Comment on the wisdom of top management in indicating that We Print should be used.

10–39. **AGENCY THEORY.** The Mobutu Company plans to hire a manager for its division in Kenya. The president and vice-president/personnel of Mobutu Company are trying to decide on an appropriate incentive employment contract. The manager will operate far from the London corporate headquarters, so evaluation by personal observation will be limited. The president insists that a large incentive to produce profits is necessary; he favors a salary of £10,000 and a bonus of 10% of the profits above £100,000. If operations proceed as expected, profits will be £400,000, and the manager will receive £40,000. But both profits and compensation might be more or less than planned.

The vice-president/personnel responds that £40,000 is more than most of Mobutu's division managers make. She is sure that a competent manager can be hired for a guaranteed salary of £30,000. "Why pay £40,000 when we can probably hire the same person for £30,000?" she argued.

Required:
1. What factors would affect Mobutu Company's choice of employment contract? Include a discussion of the pros and cons of each proposed contract.
2. Why is the expected compensation more with the bonus plan than with the straight salary?

10–40. **PROFIT CENTERS AND CENTRAL SERVICES.** Easthall Company, a manufacturer of a variety of small appliances, has an Engineering Consulting Department (ECD). The department's major task has been to help the production departments improve their operating methods and processes.

For several years the consulting services have been charged to the production departments based on a signed agreement between the managers involved. The agreement specifies the scope of the project, the predicted savings, and the number of consulting hours required. The charge to the production departments is based on the costs to the Engineering Department of the services rendered. For example, senior engineer hours cost more per hour than junior engineer hours. An overhead cost is included. The agreement is really a "fixed-price" contract. That is, the production manager knows his total cost of the project in advance. A recent survey revealed that production managers have a high level of confidence in the engineers.

The ECD department manager oversees the work of about 40 engineers and 10 draftsmen. She reports to the engineering manager, who reports to the vice-president of manufacturing. The ECD manager has the freedom to increase or decrease the number of engineers under her supervision. The ECD manager's performance is based on many factors, including the annual incremental savings to the company in excess of the costs of operating the ECD department.

The production departments are profit centers. Their goods are transferred to subsequent departments, such as a sales department or sales division, at prices that approximate market prices for similar products.

Top management is seriously considering a "no-charge" plan. That is, engineering services would be rendered to the production departments at absolutely no cost. Proponents of the new plan maintain that it would motivate the production managers to take keener advantage of engineering talent. In all other respects, the new system would be unchanged from the present system.

Required:
1. Compare the present and proposed plans. What are their strong and weak points? In particular, will the ECD manager tend to hire the "optimal" amount of engineering talent?
2. Which plan do you favor? Why?

Chapter 11

CAPITAL BUDGETING:

AN INTRODUCTION

LEARNING OBJECTIVES

When you have finished studying this chapter, you should be able to:

1. Compute a project's net present value (NPV).
2. Compute a project's internal rate of return (IRR).
3. Identify the assumptions of the two discounted-cash-flow models: NPV and IRR.
4. Apply the decision rules for the DCF models.
5. Use sensitivity analysis in evaluating projects.
6. Use the differential approach in determining the NPV difference between two projects.
7. Use the payback model and the accounting rate-of-return model and compare them with the DCF models.
8. Identify the methods for reconciling the conflict between using a DCF model for making a decision and the accrual accounting model for evaluating the related performance.

Should we replace the equipment? Should we add this product to our line? Managers must make these and similar decisions having significant financial effects beyond the current year; they are called **capital-budgeting** decisions. Capital-budgeting decisions are faced by managers in all types of organizations, including religious, medical, and governmental subunits.

Capital budgeting has three phases: (1) identification of potential investments, (2) selection of the investments to undertake (including the gathering of data to aid the decision), and (3) post-audit (or follow-up or monitoring) of investments. Accountants usually are not involved in the first phase, but they play important roles in phases 2 and 3.

Managers use many different capital-budgeting models in the *selection* of investments. Each model summarizes facts and forecasts about an investment in a way that provides information for a decision maker. Accountants contribute to this choice process in their problem-solving role. In this chapter we compare the uses and limitations of various capital-budgeting models, with particular attention to relevant-cost analysis. Accountants' score-keeping is important to the *post-audit* of investments; later in the chapter we will briefly discuss how accountants help to monitor investments.

FOCUS ON PROGRAMS OR PROJECTS

The planning and controlling of operations typically have a *time-period* focus. For example, the chief administrator of a university will be concerned with all activities for a given academic year. But the administrator will also be concerned with longer-range matters that tend to have an individual *program* or *project* focus. Examples are new programs in educational administration or health care education, joint law-management programs, new athletic facilities, new trucks, or new parking lots. In fact, many organizations may be perceived as a collection of individual investments.

This chapter concentrates on the planning and controlling of those programs or projects that affect more than one year's financial results. Such decisions require investments of resources that are often called *capital outlays*. Hence the term *capital budgeting* has arisen to describe the long-term planning for making and financing such outlays.

Capital-budgeting problems affect almost all organizations. Some examples are:

1. Northwest Hospital decides whether to purchase new X-ray equipment.
2. The partners of Stone, Goldberg, and Gomez (a law firm) decide whether to buy a word processor and what type to buy.

3. General Foods, Inc., decides whether to introduce a proposed new instant dessert into its product line.

All these decisions involve *risk*. An investment commitment is made immediately, but future predicted returns are uncertain. Because many factors affecting future returns are unknowable, well-managed organizations try to gather and quantify as many knowable or predictable factors as possible before making a decision. Capital-budgeting models facilitate this process.

Most large organizations use more than one capital-budgeting model. Why? Because each model summarizes information in a different way and reveals various useful perspectives on investments. There are three general types of capital-budgeting models:

1. Discounted-cash-flow (DCF) models, conceptually the most attractive models, are used by over 85% of the large industrial firms in the United States and are the best measures of financial effects of an investment.
2. Payback models indicate how fast an initial investment is likely to be recovered, thus providing a rough measure of riskiness, especially in decisions involving areas of rapid technological change.
3. Accounting rate-of-return models are based on the accrual accounting model, and they show the effect of an investment on an organization's financial statements.

DISCOUNTED-CASH-FLOW MODEL

☐ Major Aspects of DCF

The old adage that a bird in the hand is worth two in the bush is applicable to the management of money. A dollar in the hand today is worth more than a dollar to be received (or spent) five years from today, because the use of money has a cost (interest), just as the use of a building or an automobile may have a cost (rent). Because the discounted-cash-flow model explicitly and systematically weighs the time value of money, it is the best method to use for long-range decisions.

Another major aspect of DCF is its focus on *cash* inflows and outflows rather than on *net income* as computed in the accrual accounting sense. As we shall see, students without a strong accounting background have an advantage here. They do not have to unlearn the accrual concepts of accounting, which accounting students often incorrectly try to inject into discounted-cash-flow analysis.

There are two main variations of DCF: (a) net present value (NPV) and (b) internal rate of return (IRR). Both variations are based on the theory of compound interest. A brief summary of the tables and formulas used is included in Appendix B, pages 723–730. Before reading on, be sure you understand Appendix B.

Example   The following example will be used to illustrate the concepts. A buildings and grounds manager of a campus of the University of California is contemplating the purchase of some lawn maintenance equipment that will increase efficiency and produce cash operating savings of $2,000 per year. The useful life of the equipment is four years, after which it will have a net disposal value of zero. Assume that the equipment will cost $6,075 now and that the minimum desired rate of return is 10% per year.

Required:
1. Compute the project's net present value.
2. Compute the expected internal rate of return on the project.

☐ Net Present Value (NPV)

One type of discounted-cash-flow approach is the **net-present-value (NPV) method**. A manager determines some minimum desired rate of return. The minimum rate is often called the **required rate**, **hurdle rate**, **cutoff rate**, **discount rate**, **target rate**, or **cost of capital**. All expected future cash flows are discounted to the present, using this minimum desired rate. If the result is zero or positive, the project is desirable, and if negative it is undesirable. When choosing among several investments, the one with the largest net present value is most desirable.

The NPV method is applied in three steps. Consider Requirement 1 of our example and examine approach 1 in Exhibit 11–1:

1. Prepare a diagram of relevant expected cash inflows and outflows, including the outflow at time zero, the date of acquisition. The right-hand side of Exhibit 11–1 shows how these cash flows are sketched. Outflows are in parentheses. Although a sketch is not essential, it clarifies thought.
2. Find the present value of each expected cash inflow or outflow. Examine Table 1 on page 728. Find the discount factor from the correct row and column of Table 1. Multiply each expected cash inflow or outflow by the appropriate discount factor.
3. Sum the individual present values. If the total is zero or positive, the project should be accepted; if negative, it should be rejected.

Exhibit 11–1 shows a positive net present value of $265, so the investment is desirable. The value today (that is, at time zero) of the four $2,000 cash inflows is $6,340. The manager can obtain these cash inflows for only $6,075. Thus, a favorable difference can be achieved at time zero: $6,340 − $6,075 = $265.

The higher the minimum desired rate of return, the lower the present value of each future cash inflow and thus the lower the net present value of the project. At a rate of 16%, the net present value would be −$479 (i.e., $2,000 × 2.7982 = $5,596, which is $479 less than the required investment of $6,075). (Present-value factor, 2.7982, is taken from Table 2, page 729.) When the desired rate of return is 16%, rather than 10%, the project is undesirable at a price of $6,075.

EXHIBIT 11-1

Net-Present-Value Technique

Original investment, $6,075. Useful life, 4 years. Annual cash inflow from operations, $2,000. Minimum desired rate of return, 10%. Cash outflows are in parentheses; cash inflows are not. Total present values are rounded to the nearest dollar.

	PRESENT VALUE OF $1, DISCOUNTED AT 10%	TOTAL PRESENT VALUE	SKETCH OF CASH FLOWS AT END OF YEAR				
			0	1	2	3	4

APPROACH 1: DISCOUNTING EACH YEAR'S CASH INFLOW SEPARATELY*

Cash flows:							
Annual savings	.9091	$ 1,818		$2,000			
	.8264	1,653			$2,000		
	.7513	1,503				$2,000	
	.6830	1,366					$2,000
Present value of future inflows		$ 6,340					
Initial outlay	1.0000	(6,075)	$(6,075)				
Net present value		$ 265					

APPROACH 2: USING ANNUITY TABLE†

Annual savings	3.1699	$ 6,340		$2,000	$2,000	$2,000	$2,000
Initial outlay	1.0000	(6,075)	$(6,075)				
Net present value		$ 265					

* Present values from Table 1, Appendix B, at the end of this book. (You may wish to put a paper clip on page 728.)
† Present values of annuity from Table 2, page 729. (Incidentally, hand-held programmed calculators may give slightly different answers than tables due to rounding differences.)

☐ Choosing the Correct Table

Compare Approach 2 with Approach 1 in Exhibit 11–1. The basic steps are the same for both approaches. The only difference is that Approach 2 uses Table 2, page 729, instead of Table 1. Table 2 is a shortcut to reduce hand calculations.

Table 2 is an annuity table. That is, it provides discount factors for computing the present value of a *series* of *equal* cash flows at equal intervals. Table 2 is merely a summation of the pertinent present-value factors of Table 1:[1]

$$.9091 + .8264 + .7513 + .6830 = 3.1698$$

In this example, Table 2 accomplishes in one computation what Table 1 accomplishes in four multiplications and one summation.

Beware of using the wrong table. Table 1 should be used for discounting individual amounts, Table 2 for a *series* of equal amounts. Of course, Table 1 is the fundamental table. If shortcuts are not desired, Table 1 can be used for all present-value calculations.

☐ Internal Rate of Return (IRR)

Now consider Requirement 2. The **internal rate of return (IRR)** has been defined as the discount rate that makes the net present value of a project equal to zero, as Exhibit 11–2 shows. Expressed another way, the internal rate of return can be defined as the discount rate that makes the present value of a project's expected cash inflows equal to the present value of the expected cash outflows, including the investment in the project.

Exhibit 11–2 shows why 12% is the IRR in our example. The 12% rate produces an NPV of zero. There are three steps:

1. Prepare a diagram of the expected cash inflows and outflows exactly as you did in calculating the NPV (see Exhibit 11–1).
2. Find an interest rate that equates the present value of the cash inflows to the present value of the cash outflows. If one outflow is followed by a series of equal inflows, use the following equation:

$$\text{initial investment} = \text{annual cash inflow} \times \text{annuity PV factor (F)}$$

$$\$6,075 = \$2,000 \times F$$

$$F = \frac{\$6,075}{\$2,000} = 3.0375$$

Scan the row in Table 2 (p. 729) that represents the relevant life of the project, row 4 in our example. Select the column with an entry closest to the annuity PV factor that was calculated. The factor closest to 3.0375 is 3.0373 in the 12% column. Because these factors are extremely close, the IRR is 12%.

---

[1] Rounding error causes a .0001 difference between the Table 2 factor and the summation of Table 1 factors.

EXHIBIT 11–2

Two Proofs of Internal Rate of Return

Original investment, $6,075. Useful life, 4 years. Annual cash inflow from operations, $2,000. Internal rate of return (selected by trial-and-error methods), 12%. Total present values are rounded to the nearest dollar.

	PRESENT VALUE OF $1, DISCOUNTED AT 12%	TOTAL PRESENT VALUE
APPROACH 1: DISCOUNTING EACH YEAR'S CASH INFLOW SEPARATELY*		
Cash flows:		
Annual savings	.8929	$ 1,786
	.7972	1,594
	.7118	1,424
	.6355	1,271
Present value of future inflows		$ 6,075
Initial outlay	1.0000	(6,075)
Net present value (the zero difference proves that the rate of return is 12%)		$ 0
APPROACH 2: USING ANNUITY TABLE‡		
Annual savings	3.0373	$ 6,075
Initial outlay	1.0000	(6,075)
Net present value		$ 0

SKETCH OF CASH FLOWS AT END OF YEAR

```
          0       1       2       3       4
                $2,000
                        $2,000
                                $2,000
                                        $2,000
        $(6,075)


        $(6,075)——————$2,000  $2,000  $2,000  $2,000
```

* Present values from Table 1, Appendix B, page 728.

‡ Present values of annuity from Table 2, Appendix B, page 729.

345

3. Compare the IRR to the minimum desired rate of return. If the IRR is equal to or greater than the minimum desired rate, the project should be accepted; otherwise, it should be rejected.

☐ Interpolation and Trial and Error

Suppose that the expected cash inflow in step 1 were $1,800 instead of $2,000. The equation in step 2 produces

$$\$6,075 = \$1,800 \times F$$

$$F = \frac{\$6,075}{\$1,800} = 3.3750$$

On the period 4 line of Table 2, the column closest to 3.3750 is 7%. This may be close enough for most purposes. To obtain a more accurate rate, interpolation is needed:

	PRESENT-VALUE FACTORS	
7%	3.3872	3.3872
True rate		3.3750
8%	3.3121	
Difference	.0751	.0122

$$\text{true rate} = 7\% + \frac{.0122}{.0751}(1\%) = 7.16\%$$

These hand computations become more complex when the cash inflows and outflows are not uniform. Then trial-and-error methods are needed. See the appendix to this chapter for examples. Of course, in practice, canned computer programs are commonly available for such computations, and spreadsheets on personal computers can greatly simplify trial-and-error procedures.

☐ Meaning of Internal Rate

Exhibit 11–2 shows that $6,075 is the present value, at a rate of return of 12%, of a four-year stream of inflows of $2,000 in cash. Twelve percent is the rate that equates the amount invested ($6,075) with the present value of the cash inflows ($2,000 per year for four years). In other words, if money were borrowed at an effective interest rate of 12%, as Exhibit 11–3 shows, the cash inflow produced by the project would exactly repay the hypothetical loan plus the interest over the four years. If the cost of borrowing is less than 12%, the organization will have cash left over after repaying the hypothetical loan and interest.

Exhibit 11–3 highlights how the internal rate of return is computed on the basis of the investment tied up in the project from period to period

EXHIBIT 11–3

Rationale Underlying Internal Rate-of-Return Model
(*Same data as in Exhibit 11–2*)

Original investment, $6,075. Useful life, 4 years. Annual cash savings from operations, $2,000. Internal rate of return, 12%. Amounts are rounded to the nearest dollar.

YEAR	(1) UNRECOVERED INVESTMENT AT BEGINNING OF YEAR	(2) ANNUAL CASH SAVINGS	(3) INTEREST AT 12% PER YEAR (1) × 12%	(4) AMOUNT OF INVESTMENT RECOVERED AT END OF YEAR (2) − (3)	(5) UNRECOVERED INVESTMENT AT END OF YEAR (1) − (4)
1	$6,075	$2,000	$729	$1,271	$4,804
2	4,804	2,000	576	1,424	3,380
3	3,380	2,000	406	1,594	1,786
4	1,786	2,000	214	1,786	0

Assumptions: Unrecovered investment at beginning of each year earns interest for whole year. Annual cash inflows are received at the end of each year. For simplicity in the use of tables, all operating cash inflows are assumed to take place at the end of the years in question. This is unrealistic because such cash flows ordinarily occur uniformly throughout the given year, rather than in lump sums at the end of the year. Compound interest tables especially tailored for these more stringest conditions are available, but we shall not consider them here.

instead of solely the initial investment. The internal rate is 12% of the capital invested during each year. The $2,000 inflow is composed of two parts, as analyzed in columns 3 and 4. Consider Year 1. Column 3 shows the interest on the $6,075 invested capital as .12 × $6,075 = $729. Column 4 shows that $2,000 − $729 = $1,271, the amount of investment recovered at the end of the year. By the end of Year 4, the series of four cash inflows exactly recovers the initial investment plus annual interest at a rate of 12% on the as yet unrecovered capital.

Exhibit 11–3 can be interpreted from either the borrower's or the lender's vantage point. Suppose the university borrowed $6,075 from a bank at an interest rate of 12% per annum, invested in the project, and repaid the loan with the $2,000 saved each year. Each $2,000 payment would represent interest of 12% plus a reduction of the loan balance. At a rate of 12%, the borrower would end up with an accumulated wealth of zero. Obviously, if the borrower could borrow at 12%, and the project could generate cash at more than the 12% rate (that is, in excess of $2,000 annually), the borrower would be able to keep some cash—and the internal rate of return, *by definition*, would exceed 12%. Again the internal rate of return is the discount rate that would provide a net present value of zero (no more, no less).

☐ Assumptions of the DCF Model

Two major assumptions underlie the DCF model. First, we have a world of certainty. That is, we are absolutely sure that the predicted cash inflows and outflows will occur at the times specified. Second, we have perfect capital markets. That is, if we have extra cash or need cash at any time, we can borrow or lend money at the same interest rate. This rate is our minimum desired rate of return. If these assumptions are met, no model could possibly be better than a DCF model.

Unfortunately, our world has neither certainty nor perfect capital markets. Nevertheless, the DCF model is usually preferred to other models. The assumptions of most other models are even more unrealistic. The DCF model is not perfect, but it generally meets our cost-benefit criterion. The payoff from better decisions is greater than the cost of applying the DCF model. More sophisticated models do not generally improve decisions enough to be worth their cost.

To apply the DCF model, we use *expected* cash inflows and outflows. Further, the minimum desired rate of return is adjusted according to the risk of a proposed project—the higher the risk, the higher the minimum desired rate of return.

□ Depreciation and Discounted Cash Flow

Accounting students are sometimes mystified by the apparent exclusion of depreciation from discounted-cash-flow computations. A common homework error is to deduct depreciation from cash inflows. This is a misunderstanding of one of the basic ideas involved in the concept of the discounting. Because the discounted-cash-flow approach is fundamentally based on inflows and outflows of *cash* and not on the *accrual* concepts of revenues and expenses, no adjustments should be made to the cash flows for the periodic allocation of cost called depreciation expense (which is not a cash flow). In the discounted-cash-flow approach, the initial cost of an asset is usually regarded as a *lump-sum* outflow of cash at time zero. Therefore it is wrong to deduct depreciation from operating cash inflows before consulting present-value tables. To deduct periodic depreciation would be a double-counting of a cost that has already been considered as a lump-sum outflow.

□ Review of Decision Rules

Review the basic ideas of discounted cash flow. The decision maker cannot readily compare an outflow of $6,075 with a series of future inflows of $2,000 each because the outflows and inflows do not occur simultaneously. The net-present-value model expresses all amounts in equivalent terms (in today's dollars at time zero). An interest rate is used to measure the decision maker's time preference for money. At a rate of 12%, the comparison would be:

Outflow in today's dollars	$(6,075)
Inflow equivalent in today's dollars @ 12%	6,075
Net present value	$ 0

Therefore, at a time preference for money of 12%, the decison maker is indifferent between having $6,075 now or having a stream of four annual inflows of $2,000 each. If the interest rate were 16%, the decision maker would find the project unattractive because the net present value would be negative:

Outflow	$(6,075)
Inflow equivalent in today's dollars @ 16% = $2,000 × 2.7982 (from Table 2) =	5,596
Net present value	$ (479)

At 10%, the NPV is positive, and the project is desirable:

Outflow	$(6,075)
Inflow equivalent in today's dollars @ 10% = $2,000 × 3.1699 from Table 2 =	$ 6,340
Net present value	$ 265

We can summarize the decision rules offered by these two models as follows:

NET-PRESENT-VALUE MODEL

1. Calculate the net present value, using the minimum desired rate of return as the discount rate.
2. If the net present value is zero or positive, accept the project; if negative, reject the project.

INTERNAL RATE-OF-RETURN MODEL

1. Using present-value tables, compute the internal rate of return by trial and error.
2. If this rate equals or exceeds the minimum desired rate of return, accept the project; if not, reject the project.

A report in *Business Week* provided an example of using a net-present-value model:

☐ Like many of the amounts being paid in big acquisitions of the last year, the $350 million that Eaton Corp. will have paid this January to acquire Cutler-Hammer, Inc., appears to be a stiff price. . . . Eaton is justifying the price in large part by using an old but increasingly popular financial tool: discounted cash flow analysis (DCF). To set the price, Eaton projected the future cash flows it expects from Cutler over the next 5 to 10 years and then discounted them, using a rate that reflects the risks involved in the investment and the time value of the money used. Eaton figures that, based on DCF, Cutler will return at least 12% on its $350 million outlay.

There are two key aspects of capital budgeting: investment decisions and financing decisions. *Investment decisions* focus on whether to acquire an asset, a project, a company, a product line, and so on. *Financing decisions* focus on whether to raise the required funds via some form of debt or equity or both. This textbook concentrates on the investment decision. Finance textbooks provide ample discussions of financing decisions.

Depending on a project's risk (that is, the probability that the expected cash inflows will not be achieved) and what alternative investments are available, investors usually have some notion of a minimum rate of return that would make various projects desirable investments. The problem of choosing this required rate of return is complex and is really more a problem of finance than of accounting. In general, the higher the risk, the higher the required rate of return. In this book we shall assume that the minimum acceptable rate of return is the opportunity-cost rate. It is given to the accountant by management. It represents the rate that can be earned by the best alternative investments of similar risk.

Note too that the minimum desired rate is not affected by whether the *specific project* is financed by all debt, all ownership capital, or some of both. Thus the cost of capital is not "interest expense" on borrowed money as the accountant ordinarily conceives it. For example, a mortgage-free home still has a cost of capital—the maximum amount that could be earned with the proceeds if the home were sold.[2]

CAPITAL BUDGETING AND NONPROFIT ORGANIZATIONS

Religious, educational, health care, governmental, and other nonprofit organizations face a variety of capital-budgeting decisions. Examples include investments in buildings, equipment, national defense systems, and research programs. Thus, even when no revenue is involved, organizations try to choose projects with the least cost for any given set of objectives.

The unsettled question of the appropriate discount rate plagues all types of organizations, profit-seeking and nonprofit. One thing is certain: as all cash-strapped organizations soon discover, capital is not cost-free. A discussion of the appropriate hurdle rate is beyond the scope of this book. Often departments of the federal government use 10%. It represents a crude approximation of the opportunity cost to the economy of having investments made by public agencies instead of by private organizations.

---

[2] Avoid a piecemeal approach. It is near-sighted to think that the appropriate hurdle rate is the interest expense on any financing associated with a specific project. Under this faulty approach, a project will be accepted as long as its expected internal rate of return exceeds the interest rate on funds that might be borrowed to finance the project. Thus a project would be desirable if it has an expected internal rate of 11% and a borrowing rate of 9%. The trouble here is that a series of such decisions will lead to a staggering debt that will cause the borrowing rate to skyrocket or will result in an inability to borrow at all. Conceivably, during the next year, some other project might have an expected internal rate of 16% and will have to be rejected, even though it is the most profitable in the series, because the heavy debt permits no further borrowing.

Progress in management practices and in the use of sophisticated techniques has generally tended to be faster in profit-seeking organizations. Although DCF is used by federal departments, it is less frequently used at state and local levels of government. Thus there are many opportunities to introduce improved analytical techniques. In general, managers have more opportunities in nonprofit than in profit-seeking organizations to contribute to improved decision making by introducing newer management decision models such as DCF.[3]

UNCERTAINTY AND SENSITIVITY ANALYSIS

☐ Uncertainty

Capital investments entail risk. Why? Because the actual cash inflows may differ from what was expected or predicted. When considering a capital-budgeting project, a manager should first determine the riskiness of the investment. Then the inputs to the capital-budgeting model should be adjusted to reflect the risk.

There are three ways to recognize risk. They can be used singly or in combination:

1. Increase the minimum desired rate of return for riskier projects.
2. Reduce individual expected cash inflows or increase expected cash outflows by an amount that depends on their riskiness.
3. Change the expected life of the project.

In the examples in this book we assume that an appropriate risk adjustment is included in the minimum desired rate of return.

One method of determining the riskiness of a project is sensitivity analysis, a "what-if" technique that measures how decisions would be affected by changes in the data. Another approach is to compare the results of different capital-budgeting models. A manager can compare the NPV and IRR results to those of simpler measures such as the payback period and accounting rate-of-return (discussed later in this chapter).

☐ Sensitivity Analysis

Sensitivity analysis shows the financial consequences that occur if actual cash inflows and outflows differ from those expected. It can be usefully applied whenever a decision requires predictions. It answers the question: "How will my net present value or internal rate of return be changed if my predictions of useful life or cash flows are inaccurate?"

---

[3] An extensive study by the General Accounting Office cited the U.S. Post Office as being the best of the federal agencies regarding capital budgeting. The Post Office uses discounted cash flow, sensitivity analysis, and postaudits. See *Federal Capital Budgeting: A Collection of Haphazard Practices* (GAO, P.O. Box 6015, Gaithersburg, Md., PAO-81-19, February 26, 1981), p. 6.

We examine two types of sensitivity analysis: (1) comparing the optimistic, pessimistic, and most likely predictions and (2) determining the amount of deviation from expected values before a decision is changed.

(1) Suppose that the forecasts of annual cash inflows in Exhibit 11–1 could range from a low of $1,700 to a high of $2,300. To calculate a pessimistic prediction of NPV, you use the low cash inflow prediction, $1,700. The present value of cash inflows @ 10% is $1,700 × 3.1699 = $5,389, and the NPV is $5,389 − $6,075 = −$686. The optimistic prediction of NPV is ($2,300 × 3.1699) − $6,075 = $1,216. Recall that the expected NPV is $265. Although the expected NPV is positive, it is possible for the actual NPV to be as low as −$686 or as high as $1,216.

(2) A manager would reject a project if its NPV were negative. How far below $2,000 must the cash inflow drop before the NPV becomes negative? The cash inflow at the point where NPV = 0 is the "break-even" cash flow:

$$NPV = 0$$
$$(3.1699 \times \text{cash flow}) - \$6,075 = 0$$
$$\text{cash flow} = \$6,075 \div 3.1699$$
$$= \$1,916$$

If the annual cash inflow is less than $1,916, the project should be rejected. Therefore, cash inflows can drop only $2,000 − $1,916, or $84, annually before the manager would change the decision. He or she must decide whether this margin of error is acceptable or whether undertaking the project represents too great a risk.

Sensitivity analysis can also be performed on the useful life prediction. Suppose three years is a pessimistic prediction and five years is optimistic. Using present value factors from the third, fourth, and fifth rows of the 10% column of Table 2, page 729, the NPV's are:

Pessimistic:	(2.4869 × $2,000) − $6,075 =	−$1,101
Expected:	(3.1699 × $2,000) − $6,075 =	$ 265
Optimistic:	(3.7908 × $2,000) − $6,075 =	$1,507

If the useful life is even one year less than predicted, the investment will be undesirable.

Sensitivity analysis provides an immediate financial measure of the consequences of possible errors in forecasting. Why is this useful? It helps to identify decisions that may be affected by prediction errors. These are the decisions for which it may be most worthwhile to gather additional information about cash flows or useful life.

THE NET-PRESENT-VALUE COMPARISON OF TWO PROJECTS

☐ **Differential versus Total Project Approach**

The mechanics of compound interest may appear formidable to those readers who are encountering them for the first time. However, a little practice with the interest tables should easily clarify the mechanical aspect. We now combine some relevant-cost analysis with the discounted-cash-flow approach. Consider an example.

A company owns a packaging machine, which was purchased three years ago for $56,000. It has a remaining useful life of five years but will require a major overhaul at the end of two more years at a cost of $10,000. Its disposal value now is $20,000; in five years its disposal value is expected to be $8,000, assuming that the $10,000 major overhaul will be done on schedule. The cash operating costs of this machine are expected to be $40,000 annually.

A sales representative has offered a substitute machine for $51,000, or for $31,000 plus the old machine. The new machine will reduce annual cash operating costs by $10,000, will not require any overhauls, will have a useful life of five years, and will have a disposal value of $3,000.

Required: Assume that the minimum desired rate of return is 14%. Using the net-present-value technique, show whether the new machine should be purchased, using (1) a **total project approach**, (2) a **differential approach.** Try to solve before examining the solution.

The total project approach compares two or more alternatives by computing the *total* impact on cash flows of *each* alternative and then converting these total cash flows to their present values.

The differential approach compares two alternatives by computing the *differences* in cash flows between alternatives and then converting these differences in cash flows to their present values.

A difficult part of long-range decision making is the structuring of the data. We want to see the effects of each alternative on future cash inflows and outflows. The following steps apply to either the total project or the differential approach:

Step 1. Arrange the relevant cash flows by project, so that a sharp distinction is made between total project flows and differential flows. The differential flows are merely algebraic differences between two alternatives. (There are always at least two alternatives. One is the status quo—i.e., doing nothing.) Exhibit 11–4 shows how the cash flows for each alternative are sketched.

Step 2. Discount the expected cash flows and choose the project with the least cost or the greatest benefit.

Both the total project approach and the differential approach are illustrated in Exhibit 11–4; which one you use is a matter of preference. However, to develop confidence in this area, you should work with both at the start. One approach can serve as proof of the accuracy of the other. In this example, the $8,429 net difference in favor of replacement is the result under either approach.

In any event, the total project approach is preferable for analyzing three or more alternatives simultaneously. After all, the differential approach can only cope with two projects at a time.

When you array the relevant cash flows, be sure to consider the following four types of inflows and outflows:

1. *Initial cash inflows and outflows at time zero.* These cash flows include both outflows for the purchases and installation of equipment and other items required by the new project and either inflows or outflows from disposal of any items that are replaced. In Exhibit 11–4 the $20,000 received from selling the old machine was offset against the $51,000 purchase price of the new machine; the net cash outflow of $31,000 was shown. If the old machine could not be sold, any cost incurred to dismantle and discard it would be *added to* the purchase price of the new machine.

2. *Investments in receivables and inventories.* Investments in receivables, inventories, and intangible assets are basically no different from investments in plant and equipment. In the discounted-cash-flow model, the initial outlays are entered in the sketch of cash flows at time zero. At the end of the useful life of the project, the original outlays for machines may not be recouped at all or may be partially recouped in the amount of the salvage values. In contrast, the entire original investments in receivables and inventories are usually recouped when the project ends. Therefore, all initial investments are typically regarded as outflows at time zero, and their terminal disposal values are regarded as inflows at the end of the project's useful life.

    The example in Exhibit 11–4 required no additional investment in inventory or receivables. However, the expansion of a retail store, for example, entails an additional investment in a building and fixtures *plus* inventories. Such investments would be shown in the format of Exhibit 11–4 as follows (numbers assumed):

	SKETCH OF CASH FLOWS				
End of year	0	1	2	19	20
Investment in building and fixtures	(10)				1
Investment in working capital (inventories)	(6)				6

As the sketch shows, the residual value of the building and fixtures might be small. However, the entire investment in inventories would ordinarily be recouped when the venture was terminated.

The difference between the initial outlay for working capital (mostly receivables and inventories) and the present value of its recovery is the present value of the cost of using working capital in the project. Working capital is constantly revolving in a cycle from cash to inventories to receivables and back to cash throughout the life of the project. But to be sustained, the project requires that money be tied up in the cycle until the project ends.

3. *Future disposal values.* The disposal value at the date of termination of a project is an increase in the cash inflow in the year of disposal. Errors in forecasting terminal disposal values are usually not crucial because the present value is usually small.

4. *Operating cash flows.* The major purpose of most investments is to affect revenues or costs (or both). The cash inflows and outflows associated with most of these effects are easy to identify, but two deserve special mention. First, in relevant-

EXHIBIT 11-4 *(Place a clip on this page for easy reference.)*

Total Project versus Differential Approach to Net Present Value

	PRESENT-VALUE DISCOUNT FACTOR, AT 14%	TOTAL PRESENT VALUE	SKETCH OF CASH FLOWS AT END OF YEAR					
			0	1	2	3	4	5
I. TOTAL PROJECT APPROACH								
A. Replace								
Recurring cash operating costs, using an annuity table*	3.4331	$(102,993)		($30,000)	($30,000)	($30,000)	($30,000)	($30,000)
Disposal value, end of year 5	.5194	1,558						3,000
Initial required investment	1.0000	(31,000)	($31,000)					
Present value of net cash outflows		$(132,435)						
B. Keep								
Recurring cash operating costs, using an annuity table*	3.4331	$(137,324)		($40,000)	($40,000)	($40,000)	($40,000)	($40,000)
Overhaul, end of year 2	.7695	(7,695)			(10,000)			
Disposal value, end of year 5	.5194	4,155						8,000
Present value of net cash outflows		$(140,864)						
Difference in favor of replacement		$ 8,429						
II. INCREMENTAL APPROACH								
A–B. Analysis Confined to Differences								
Recurring cash operating savings, using an annuity table*	3.4331	$ 34,331		$10,000	$10,000	$10,000	$10,000	$10,000
Overhaul avoided, end of year 2	.7695	7,695			$10,000			
Difference in disposal values, end of year 5	.5194	(2,597)						(5,000)
Incremental initial investment	1.0000	(31,000)	($31,000)					
Net present value of replacement		$ 8,429						

* Table 2, page 729.

cost analysis, the only pertinent overhead costs are those that will differ among alternatives. There is need for careful study of the fixed overhead under the available alternatives. In practice, this is an extremely difficult phase of cost analysis, because it is hard to relate the individual costs to any single project. Second, depreciation and book values should be ignored. The cost of assets is recognized by the initial outlay (point one in this section), not by depreciation as computed under accrual accounting.

☐ Complications

The foregoing material has been an *introduction* to the area of capital budgeting. In practice, a variety of factors complicate the analysis, including:

1. *Income taxes*. Comparison between alternatives is best made after considering tax effects, because the tax impact may alter the picture. (The effects of income taxes are considered in Chapter 12 and may be studied now if desired.)
2. *Inflation*. Predictions of cash flows and discount rates should be based on consistent inflation assumptions. This is explained in more detail in Chapter 12.
3. *Mutually exclusive projects*. When the projects are mutually exclusive, so that the acceptance of one automatically entails the rejection of the other (e.g., buying Dodge or Ford trucks), the project that has the largest net present value should be undertaken.
4. *Unequal lives*. What if alternative projects have unequal lives? Comparisons may be made over the useful life of either the longer-lived project or the shorter-lived one. For our purposes, we will use the life of the longer-lived project. To provide comparability, we assume reinvestment in the shorter-lived project at the end of its life and give it credit for any residual value at the time the longer-lived project ends. The important consideration is what would be done in the time interval between the termination dates of the shorter-lived and longer-lived projects.

OTHER MODELS FOR ANALYZING LONG-RANGE DECISIONS

Although the use of discounted-cash-flow models for business decisions has increased steadily over the past four decades, simpler models are also used. Often managers use them in *addition* to DCF analyses.

These models, which we are about to explain, are conceptually inferior to discounted-cash-flow approaches. Then why do we bother studying them? First, because changes in business practice occur slowly. Use of the simpler models is well entrenched in many businesses. Second, because where simpler models such as payback are in use, they should be used properly, even if better models are available. The situation is similar to using a pocket knife instead of a scalpel for removing a person's appendix. If the pocket knife is used by a knowledgeable and skilled surgeon, the chances for success are much better than if it is used by a bumbling layperson. Third, the simpler models might provide some useful information to supplement the DCF analysis.

Of course, as always, the accountant and manager face a cost-and-value-of-information decision when they choose a decision model. Reluctance to use discounted-cash-flow models may be justified if the more familiar payback model or other models lead to the same investment decisions.

One existing technique may be called the emergency-persuasion method. No formal planning is used. Fixed assets are operated until they crumble, product lines are carried until they are obliterated by competition, and requests by a manager for authorization of capital outlays are judged on the basis of past operating performance regardless of its relevance to the decision at hand. These approaches to capital budgeting are examples of the unscientific management that often leads to bankruptcy.

☐ Payback Model

Payback time or **payback period** is the measure of the time it will take to recoup, in the form of cash inflow from operations, the initial dollars of outlay. Assume that $12,000 is spent for a machine with an estimated useful life of eight years. Annual savings of $4,000 in cash outflow are expected from operations. Depreciation is ignored. The payback calculations follow:

$$\text{payback time} = \frac{\text{initial incremental amount invested}}{\text{equal annual incremental } cash \text{ inflow from operations}}$$

$$P = \frac{I}{O} = \frac{\$12,000}{\$4,000} = 3 \text{ years} \tag{1}$$

The payback model merely measures how quickly investment dollars may be recouped; it does *not* measure profitability. This is its major weakness because a shorter payback time does not necessarily mean that one project is preferable to another. On the other hand, it might provide a rough estimate of riskiness.

Assume that an alternative to the $12,000 machine is a $10,000 machine whose operation will also result in a reduction of $4,000 annually in cash outflow. Then

$$P_1 = \frac{\$12,000}{\$4,000} = 3.0 \text{ years}$$

$$P_2 = \frac{\$10,000}{\$4,000} = 2.5 \text{ years}$$

The payback criterion indicates that the $10,000 machine is more desirable. However, one fact about the $10,000 machine has been purposely withheld. What if its useful life is only 2.5 years? Ignoring the impact of compound interest for the moment, the $10,000 machine results in zero benefit, while the $12,000 machine (useful life eight years) generates cash inflows for five years beyond its payback period.

The main objective in investing is profit, not the recapturing of the initial outlay. If a company wants to recover its outlay fast, it need not spend in the first place. Then no waiting time is necessary; the payback time is zero. When a wealthy investor was assured by the promoter of a risky oil venture that he would have his money back within two years, the investor replied, "I already have my money."

The payback approach may also be applied to the data in Exhibit 11–4, page 355. What is the payback time? Applying Equation 1:

$$P = \frac{I}{O} = \frac{\$31,000}{\$10,000} = 3.1 \text{ years}$$

However, the formula can be used with assurance only when there are equal annual cash inflows from operations. In this instance, an additional $10,000 is saved by avoiding an overhaul at the end of the second year. When annual cash inflows are not equal, the payback computation must take a cumulative form—that is, each year's net cash flows are accumulated until the initial investment is recouped:

YEAR	INITIAL INVESTMENT	NET CASH INFLOWS	
		Each Year	Accumulated
0	$31,000	—	—
1	—	$10,000	$10,000
2	—	20,000	30,000
2.1	—	1,000	31,000

The payback time is slightly beyond the second year. Straight-line interpolation within the third year reveals that the final $1,000 needed to recoup the investment would be forthcoming in 2.1 years:

$$2 \text{ years} + \left(\frac{\$1,000}{\$10,000} \times 1 \text{ year} \right) = 2.1 \text{ years}$$

☐ Accounting Rate-of-Return Model

The label for the **accounting rate-of-return** model or method is not uniform. It is also known as the *accrual accounting rate-of-return model* (a more accurate description), the *unadjusted rate-of-return model*, the *financial statement model*, the *book-value model*, the *rate-of-return on assets model*, the *accounting model*, and the *approximate rate-of-return model*. Its computations supposedly dovetail most closely with conventional accounting models of calculating income and required investment.

The equations for the accounting rate of return are:

$$\text{accounting rate of return} = \frac{\text{increase in expected average annual operating income}}{\text{initial increase in required investment}} \qquad (2)$$

$$R = \frac{O - D}{I} \qquad (3)$$

where R is the average annual rate of return on initial additional investment, O is the average annual incremental cash inflow from operations, D is the incremental average annual depreciation, and I is the initial incremental amount invested.

Assume the same facts as in Exhibit 11–1: investment is $6,075, useful life is four years, estimated disposal value is zero, and expected annual cash inflow from operations is $2,000. Annual depreciation would be $6,075 ÷ 4 = $1,518.75, rounded to $1,519. Substitute these values in Equation 3:

$$R = \frac{\$2,000 - \$1,519}{\$6,075} = 7.9\%$$

If the denominator is the "average" investment, which is often assumed for equipment as being the average book value over the useful life, or $6,075 ÷ 2 = $3,037.5, rounded to $3,038, the rate would be doubled:[4]

$$R = \frac{\$2,000 - \$1,519}{\$3,038} = 15.8\%$$

With the original investment in the denominator, the accounting rate-of-return is usually less than the IRR. When the "average" investment is used, the accounting rate-of-return generally exceeds the IRR.

□ Defects of Accounting Rate-of-Return Model

The *accounting rate-of-return* model is based on the familiar financial statements prepared under accrual accounting. Unlike the payback model, the accounting model at least has profitability as an objective. However, it has two major drawbacks.

First, as compared with discounted-cash-flow models, the required investment tends to be understated. The investment base for decision making should include such items as costs of research, sales promotion, and startups, which the accountant usually writes off immediately as expenses.

Second, the accounting model ignores the time value of money. Expected future dollars are unrealistically and erroneously regarded as equal to present dollars. The discounted-cash-flow model explicitly allows for the force of interest and the exact timing of cash flows. In contrast, the accounting model is based on *annual averages*. To illustrate, consider a petroleum company with three potential projects to choose from: an expansion of an existing gasoline station, an investment in an oil well, and the purchase of a new gasoline station. To simplify the calculations, assume a three-year life for each project. Exhibit 11–5 summarizes the comparisons. Note that the accounting rate of return would indicate that all three projects are equally desirable and that the internal rate of return properly discriminates in favor of earlier cash inflows.

Thus the conflict of purposes is highlighted in Exhibit 11–5. The accounting model uses concepts of investment and income that were originally designed for the quite different purpose of accounting for periodic income and

---

[4] The measure of the investment recovered in the example above is $1,519 per year, the amount of the annual depreciation. Consequently, the average investment committed to the project would decline at a rate of $1,519 per year from $6,075 to zero; hence the average investment would be the beginning balance plus the ending balance ($6,075) divided by 2, or $3,038. Note that when the ending balance is not zero, the average investment will *not* be half the initial investment.

EXHIBIT 11–5

Comparison of Accounting Rates of Return and Internal Rates of Return

	EXPANSION OF EXISTING GASOLINE STATION	INVESTMENT IN AN OIL WELL	PURCHASE OF NEW GASOLINE STATION
Initial investment	$ 90,000	$ 90,000	$ 90,000
Cash inflows from operations:			
Year 1	$ 40,000	$ 80,000	$ 20,000
Year 2	40,000	30,000	40,000
Year 3	40,000	10,000	60,000
Totals	$120,000	$120,000	$120,000
Average annual cash inflow	$ 40,000	$ 40,000	$ 40,000
Less: Average annual depreciation ($90,000 ÷ 3)	30,000	30,000	30,000
Increase in average annual net income	$ 10,000	$ 10,000	$ 10,000
Accounting rate of return on initial investment	11.1%	11.1%	11.1%
Internal rate of return, using discounted-cash-flow techniques	16.0%*	23.2%*	13.3%*

* Computed by trial-and-error approaches using Tables 1 and 2, pages 728–729. See the appendix to this chapter for a detailed explanation.

financial position. The resulting accounting rate of return may be far from the real mark.

However, the accounting model usually facilitates follow-up, because the same approach is used in the forecast as is used in the accounts. Yet exceptions to this ideal situation often occur, commonly arising from the inclusion in the forecast of some initial investment items that are not handled in the same manner in the subsequent accounting records. For example, the accounting for trade-ins and disposal values varies considerably. In practice, spot checks are frequently used on key items.

PERFORMANCE EVALUATION

☐ **Potential Conflict**

Many managers are reluctant to accept DCF models as the best way to make capital-budgeting decisions. Their reluctance stems from the wide usage of the accrual accounting model for evaluating performance. That is, managers become frustrated if they are instructed to use a DCF model for making decisions that are evaluated later by a non-DCF model, such as the typical accrual accounting rate-of-return model.

To illustrate, consider the potential conflict that might arise in the example of Exhibit 11–1. Recall that the expected rate of return was 12%, based on an outlay of $6,075 that would generate cash savings of $2,000 for each of four years and no terminal disposal value. Under accrual accounting, using straight-line depreciation, the evaluation of performance for years one through four would be:

	Year 1	Year 2	Year 3	Year 4
Cash operating savings	$2,000	$2,000	$2,000	$2,000
Straight-line depreciation,				
$6,075 ÷ 4	1,519	1,519	1,519	1,519*
Effect on operating income	481	481	481	481
Book value at beginning				
of year	6,075	4,566	3,037	1,518
Accounting rate-of-return	7.9%	10.6%	15.8%	31.7%

* Total depreciation of 4 × $1,519 = $6,076 differs from $6,075 due to rounding error.

Many managers would be inclined against replacing equipment, despite the internal rate of 12%, if their performance were evaluated by accrual accounting models. They might be especially reluctant if they were likely to be transferred to new positions every year or two. This accrual accounting system understates the return in early years.

As Chapter 5 indicated, the reluctance to replace is reinforced if a heavy book loss on old equipment would appear in year 1's accrual income statement (see page 136)—even though such a loss would be irrelevant in a properly constructed decision model.

□ Reconciliation of Conflict

How can the foregoing conflict be reconciled? An obvious solution would be to use the same model for decisions and for evaluating performance. The accrual accounting model is often dominant for evaluating all sorts of performance; that is why many organizations use it for both purposes and do not use a DCF model at all. Critics claim that this nonuse of DCF may lead to many instances of poor capital-budgeting decisions.

Another obvious solution would be to use DCF for both capital-budgeting decisions and the performance evaluation audit, often called a **postaudit.** Several organizations perform such audits on selected capital investments. A major reason for not auditing all capital-budgeting decisions routinely is that most accounting systems are designed to evaluate operating performances of products, departments, divisions, territories, and so on, year by year. In contrast, capital-budgeting decisions frequently deal with individual *projects*, not the collection of projects that are usually being managed simultaneously by divisional or department managers. Top managers may regard the routine gathering of data for individual projects as being too costly.

Some companies have solved the conflict by a dual approach. Managers use both the DCF model and the accrual accounting model at decision-making time. The decision is based on the DCF model, but the performance evaluation is tied back to the accrual accounting model.

The conflicts between the long-standing, pervasive accrual accounting model and various formal decision models represent one of the most serious unsolved problems in the design of management control systems. Top management cannot expect goal congruence if it favors the use of one type of model for decisions and the use of another type for performance evaluation.

SUMMARY

Capital budgeting is long-term planning for proposed capital outlays and their financing. Projects are accepted if their rate of return exceeds a minimum desired rate of return.

Because the discounted-cash-flow model explicitly and automatically weighs the time value of money, it is the best method to use for long-range decisions. The overriding goal is maximum long-run net cash inflows.

The discounted-cash-flow model has two variations: internal rate of return and net present value. Both models take into account the timing of cash flows and are thus superior to other methods.

Risk is present in almost all capital investments. Sensitivity analysis helps to assess the riskiness of a project.

The payback model is a popular approach to capital-spending decisions. It is simple and easily understood, but it neglects profitability.

The accounting rate-of-return model is also widely used in capital budgeting, although it is conceptually inferior to discounted-cash-flow models. It fails to recognize explicitly the time value of money. Instead, the accounting model depends on averaging techniques that may yield inaccurate answers, particularly when cash flows are not uniform through the life of a project.

SUMMARY PROBLEM FOR YOUR REVIEW

☐ Problem

Review the problem and solution shown in Exhibit 11–4, page 355. Conduct a sensitivity analysis as indicated below. Consider each requirement as independent of other requirements.

1. Compute the net present value if the minimum desired rate of return were 20%.

2. Compute the net present value if predicted cash operating costs were $35,000 instead of $30,000, using the 14% discount rate.

3. By how much may the cash operating savings fall before reaching the point of indifference, the point where the net present value of the project is zero, using the original discount rate of 14%?

☐ Solution

1. Either the total project approach or the differential approach could be used. The differential approach would show:

	TOTAL PRESENT VALUE
Recurring cash operating savings, using an annuity table (Table 2):	
2.9906 × $10,000 =	$29,906
Overhaul avoided: .6944 × $10,000 =	6,944
Difference in disposal values:	
.4019 × $5,000 =	(2,010)
Incremental initial investment	(31,000)
Net present value of replacement	$ 3,840
2. Net present value in Exhibit 11–4	$ 8,429
Present value of additional $5,000 annual operating costs,	
3,4331 × $5,000	17,166
New net present value	$ (8,737)

3. Let X = annual cash operating savings and let net present value = 0. Then

$$0 = 3.4331(X) + \$7,695 - \$2,597 - \$31,000$$
$$3.4331X = \$25,902$$
$$X = \$ \ 7,545$$

(Note that the $7,695, $2,597, and $31,000 are at the bottom of Exhibit 11–4.)

If the annual savings fall from $10,000 to $7,545, a decrease of $2,455, the point of indifference will be reached.

An alternative way to obtain the same answer would be to divide the net present value of $8,429 (see bottom of Exhibit 11–4) by 3.4331, obtaining $2,455, the amount of the annual difference in savings that will eliminate the $8,429 of net present value.

HIGHLIGHTS TO REMEMBER

1. Common errors in DCF analysis include
   a. Deducting depreciation from operating cash inflows
   b. Using the wrong present-value table
   c. Incorrectly analyzing investments in working capital (for example, inventories)

2. A serious practical impediment to the adoption of discounted-cash-flow models is the widespread use of conventional accrual models for evaluating performance. Frequently, the optimal decision under discounted cash flow will not produce a good showing in the early years, when performance is computed under conventional accounting methods. For example, heavy depreciation charges and the expensing rather than capitalizing of initial development costs will hurt reported income for the first year.

ACCOUNTING VOCABULARY

Accounting Rate of Return *p. 358*   Capital Budgeting *340*   Cost of Capital *342*
Cutoff Rate *342*   Differential Approach *353*   Discount Rate *342*   Hurdle Rate
342   Internal Rate of Return *344*   Net-Present-Value Method *342*   Payback
Period *357*   Payback Time *357*   Postaudit *361*   Required Rate *342*   Sensitivity
Analysis *351*   Target Rate *342*   Total Project Approach *353*

APPENDIX 11: CALCULATIONS OF INTERNAL RATES OF RETURN

EXPANSION OF EXISTING GASOLINE STATION

(Data are from Exhibit 11–5, p. 360.)

$90,000 = present value of annuity of $40,000 at X percent for three years, or what factor F in the
table of the present values of an annuity will satisfy the following equation:

$90,000 = $40,000 F

F = $90,000 ÷ $40,000 = 2.2500

Now, on the year 3 line of Table 2, page 729, find the column that is
closest to 2.2500. You will find that 2.2500 is extremely close to a rate of return
of 16%—so close that straight-line interpolation is unnecessary between 14%
and 16%. Therefore, the internal rate of return is 16%.

INVESTMENT IN AN OIL WELL

Trial-and-error methods must be used to calculate the rate of return that will
equate the future cash flows with the $90,000 initial investment. As a start,
note that the 16% rate was applicable to a uniform annual cash inflow. But
now use Table 1 (p. 728) because the flows are not uniform, and try a higher
rate, 22%, because you know that the cash inflows are coming in more quickly
than under the uniform inflow:

YEAR	CASH INFLOWS	TRIAL AT 22% Present-Value Factor	TRIAL AT 22% Total Present Value	TRIAL AT 24% Present-Value Factor	TRIAL AT 24% Total Present Value
1	$80,000	.8197	$65,576	.8065	$64,520
2	30,000	.6719	20,157	.6504	19,512
3	10,000	.5507	5,507	.5245	5,245
			$91,240		$89,277

Because $91,240 is greater than $90,000, the true rate must be greater than
22%. Try 24%. Now $89,277 is less than $90,000 so the true rate lies somewhere
between 22% and 24%. It can be approximated by straight-line interpolation:

INTERPOLATION		TOTAL PRESENT VALUES	
22%	$91,240		$91,240
True rate			90,000
24%	89,277		
Difference	$ 1,963		$ 1,240

Therefore:

$$\text{true rate} = 22\% + \frac{1,240}{1,963} \times 2\%$$

$$= 22\% + 1.3\% = 23.3\%$$

PURCHASE OF A NEW GASOLINE STATION

In contrast to the oil-well project, this venture will have slowly increasing cash inflows. The trial rate should be much lower than the 16% rate applicable to the expansion project. Let us try 12%:

YEAR	CASH INFLOWS	TRIAL AT 12%		TRIAL AT 14%	
		Present-Value Factor	Total Present Value	Present-Value Factor	Total Present Value
1	$20,000	.8929	$17,858	.8772	$17,544
2	40,000	.7972	31,888	.7695	30,780
3	60,000	.7118	42,708	.6750	40,500
			$92,454		$88,824

INTERPOLATION		TOTAL PRESENT VALUES	
12%	$92,454		$92,454
True rate			90,000
14%	88,824		
	$ 3,630		$ 2,454

$$\text{true rate} = 12\% + \frac{2,454}{3,630} \times 2\%$$

$$= 12\% + 1.4\% = 13.4\%$$

ASSIGNMENT MATERIAL

Special Note: Ignore income taxes. The effects of income taxes are considered in the next chapter.

FUNDAMENTAL ASSIGNMENT MATERIAL

11–1. **EXERCISES IN COMPOUND INTEREST: ANSWERS SUPPLIED.**[5]   Use the appropriate interest table to compute the following:

    a. It is your sixty-fifth birthday. You plan to work five more years before retiring. Then you want to take $5,000 for a Mediterranean cruise. What lump sum do you have to invest now in order to accumulate the $5,000? Assume that your minimum desired rate of return is:

        (1) 6%, compounded annually.
        (2) 10%, compounded annually.
        (3) 20%, compounded annually.

    b. You want to spend $1,000 on a vacation at the end of each of the next five years. What lump sum do you have to invest now in order to take the five vacations? Assume that your minimum desired rate of return is:

        (1) 6%, compounded annually.
        (2) 10%, compounded annually.
        (3) 20%, compounded annually.

    c. At age sixty, you find that your employer is moving to another location. You receive termination pay of $5,000. You have some savings and wonder whether to retire now.

        (1) If you invest the $5,000 now at 6%, compounded annually, how much money can you withdraw from your account each year so that at the end of five years there will be a zero balance?
        (2) If you invest it at 10%?

    d. At 16%, compounded annually, which of the following plans is more desirable in terms of present values? Show computations to support your answer.

	ANNUAL CASH INFLOWS	
Year	Mining	Farming
1	$100,000	$ 20,000
2	80,000	40,000
3	60,000	60,000
4	40,000	80,000
5	20,000	100,000
	$300,000	$300,000

11–2. **COMPARISON OF CAPITAL-BUDGETING TECHNIQUES.**   St. Joseph Hospital is considering the purchase of a new diagnostic machine for its laboratory at a cost of $20,000. It is expected to save $4,000 in cash operating costs per year. Its estimated useful life is eight years, and it will have zero disposal value.

Required:

    1. What is the payback time?
    2. Compute the net present value if the minimum rate of return desired is 8% compounded annually. Should the hospital buy? Why?
    3. Compute the internal rate of return.
    4. Compute the accounting rate of return on the initial investment. Assume that St. Joseph uses straight-line depreciation.

11–3. **SENSITIVITY ANALYSIS.**   The Midwest Railroad is considering the replacement of an old power jack tamper used in the maintenance of track with a new improved version that should save $5,000 per year in net cash operating costs. The old equipment has zero disposal value, but it could be used for the next 12 years. The predicted useful life of the new equipment is 12 years, and it will cost $25,000.

---

[5] The answers appear at the end of the assignment material for this chapter, page 377.

Required:
1. What is the payback time?
2. Compute the internal rate of return.
3. Management is unsure about the useful life. An optimistic prediction is 20 years; a pessimistic one, 6. What would be the approximate rates of return if the useful lives of both machines were (a) 6 years and (b) 20 years?
4. Suppose that both lives will be 12 years but that the savings will be $3,000 per year instead of $5,000. What would be the rate of return?
5. Suppose that both lives are 12 years, the savings are $5,000 per year, and the minimum desired rate of return is 10% compounded annually. What is the annual cost savings for which the new jack tamper would have an internal rate of return of exactly 10%?

ADDITIONAL ASSIGNMENT MATERIAL

11–4. Capital budgeting has three phases: 1) identification of potential investments, 2) selection of investments, and 3) postaudit of investments. What is the accountant's role in each phase?

11–5. Distinguish among the symbols DCF, NPV, and IRR.

11–6. According to Alexander Pope (1688–1744), "A little learning is a dangerous thing." How might this apply to capital budgeting?

11–7. "The higher the interest rate, the less I worry about errors in predicting terminal values." Do you agree? Explain.

11–8. "Double-counting occurs if depreciation is separately considered in discounted-cash-flow analysis." Do you agree? Explain.

11–9. "Problem solving is project oriented rather than time-period oriented." Explain.

11–10. Why is discounted cash flow a superior method for capital budgeting?

11–11. Why should depreciation be excluded from discounted-cash-flow computations?

11–12. "It is important that a firm use one and only one capital-budgeting model. Using multiple models may cause confusion." Do you agree? Explain.

11–13. "The DCF model assumes certainty and perfect capital markets. Thus, it is impractical to use it in most real-world situations." Do you agree? Explain.

11–14. Can net present value ever be negative? Why?

11–15. "The higher the minimum rate of return desired, the higher the price that a company will be willing to pay for cost-saving equipment." Do you agree? Explain.

11–16. Why should the differential approach to alternatives always lead to the same decision as the total project approach?

11–17. "Discounted-cash-flow approaches will not work if the competing projects have unequal lives." Do you agree? Explain.

11–18. State a rule that can serve as a general guide to capital-budgeting decisions.

11–19. "If discounted-cash-flow approaches are superior to the payback and the accounting rate-of-return methods, why should we bother to learn the others? All it does is confuse things." Answer this contention.

11–20. What is the basic flaw in the payback model?

11–21. Compare the accounting rate-of-return approach and the discounted-cash-flow approach with reference to the time value of money.

11–22. **EXERCISE IN COMPOUND INTEREST.** Xerox Corporation plans to expand its communications business. The company expects to accumulate sufficient cash from its new operations to pay a lump sum of $200 million to Prudential Insurance Company at the end of four years. Prudential will lend money on a promissory note now, will take no payments until the end of four years, and desires 12% interest compounded annually.

1. How much money will Prudential lend Xerox?
2. How much will Xerox owe Prudential at the end of Year 1? At the end of Year 2? Show computations.

11–23. EXERCISE IN COMPOUND INTEREST. Refer to the preceding problem. Suppose Xerox and Prudential agree on a 12% interest rate compounded annually. However, Xerox will pay the $200 million in installments of $50 million annually at the end of *each* of the next four years. How much money will Prudential lend Xerox?

11–24. EXERCISES IN COMPOUND INTEREST.

1. Union bank offers depositors a lump-sum payment of $20,000 six years hence. If you desire an interest rate of 8% compounded annually, how much would you be willing to deposit? At an interest rate of 16%?
2. Repeat the foregoing Requirement 1, but assume that the interest rates are compounded semiannually.

11–25. EXERCISE IN COMPOUND INTEREST. A building contractor has asked your bank for a loan. You are pondering various proposals for repayment:

1. Lump sum of $300,000 four years hence. How much will you lend if your desired rate of return is (a) 12% compounded annually, (b) 24% compounded annually?
2. Repeat Requirement 1 but assume that the interest rates are compounded semiannually.
3. Suppose that the loan is to be paid in full by equal payments of $75,000 at the end of each of the next four years. How much will you lend if your desired rate of return is (a) 12% compounded annually, (b) 24% compounded annually?

11–26. FUTURE VALUES.

1. Suppose that you borrow $15,000 now at 16% interest compounded annually. The borrowed amount plus interest will be repaid in a lump sum at the end of six years. How much must be repaid? Use Table 1 and the basic equation: PV = Future amount × Conversion factor.
2. Assume the same facts as above except that the loan will be repaid in equal installments at the end of each of six years. How much must be repaid each year? Use Table 2 and the basic equation: PV_A = Future annual amounts × Conversion factor.

11–27. DEFERRED ANNUITY EXERCISE. It is your thirty-fifth birthday. On your fortieth birthday, and on three successive birthdays thereafter, you intend to spend exactly $2,000 for a birthday celebration. What lump sum do you have to invest now in order to have the four celebrations? Assume that the money will earn interest, compounded annually, of 8%.

11–28. PRESENT VALUES AND DEFERRED SPORTS SALARIES. Gary Hogeboom, former quarterback for the Dallas Cowboys, signed a 1985 contract that included $6 million in deferred income. The January 13, 1985 issue of *The Dallas Morning News* reported:

☐ The Cowboys will pay Hogeboom $300,000 a year on February 1 from 1994–2013, a total of $6 million. The present value of that money discounted at 12 percent is $600,000–$700,000, a source said.

Do you agree with the present value that the source reported? If not, what is the appropriate present value? Assume that the calculations are made on February 1, 1985.

11–29. RATIONALE OF NPV MODEL. The Paragon Company has a chance to invest $10,000 in a project that is certain to pay $4,500 at the end of each of the next three years. The minimum desired rate of return is 10%.

1. What is the project's net present value?

2. Show that Paragon Company would be equally as well off undertaking the project or having its present value in cash. Do this by calculating the cash available at the end of three years if (a) $10,000 is borrowed at 10%, with interest paid at the end of each year, and the investment is made, or (b) cash equal to the project's NPV is invested at 10% compounded annually for three years. Use the following formats. Year 1 for the first alternative is completed for you.

ALTERNATIVE (a)—INVEST IN PROJECT

Year	(1) Loan Balance at Beginning of Year	(2) Interest at 10% Per Year	(3) (1) + (2) Accumulated Amount at End of Year	(4) Cash for Repayment of Loan	(5) (3) − (4) Loan Balance at End of Year
1	$10,000	$1,000	$11,000	$4,500	$6,500
2					
3					

ALTERNATIVE (b)—KEEP CASH

Year	(1) Investment Balance at Beginning of Year	(2) Interest at 10% Per Year	(3) (1) + (2) Accumulated Amount at End of Year
1			
2			
3			

INTERNAL RATE OF RETURN. Fill in the blanks:

	NUMBER OF YEARS		
	5	10	20
Amount of annual cash inflow*	$ 5,000	$ _____	$20,000
Required initial investment	$18,954	$50,000	$ _____
Internal rate of return	_____ %	16%	20%

* To be received at the end of each year.

INTERNAL RATE AND NPV. Fill in the blanks:

	NUMBER OF YEARS		
	8	18	28
Amount of annual cash inflow*	$ 9,000	$ _____	$12,000
Required initial investment	$ _____	$80,000	$49,879
Internal rate of return	20%	12%	_____ %
Minimum desired rate of return	14%	_____ %	26%
Net present value	$ _____	($26,897)	$ _____

* To be received at the end of each year.

ILLUSTRATION OF TRIAL-AND-ERROR METHOD OF COMPUTING RATE OF RE-
TURN. Study Exhibit 11–2, page 345. Suppose the annual cash inflow will be
$2,300 rather than $2,000.

Required: | What is the internal rate of return?

11–33. **NEW EQUIPMENT.** The Rose Company has offered to sell some new packaging
equipment to the Cobb Company. The list price is $42,000, but Rose has agreed
to accept some old equipment in trade. A trade-in allowance of $6,000 was agreed
upon. The old equipment was carried at a book value of $12,700 and could be
sold outright for $5,000 cash. Cash operating savings are expected to be $5,200
annually for the next 12 years. The minimum desired rate of return is 12%.
The old equipment has a remaining useful life of 12 years. Both the old and
the new equipment will have zero disposal values 12 years from now.

Required: | Should Cobb buy the new equipment? Show your computations, using the net-
present-value method. Ignore income taxes.

11–34. **REPLACEMENT OF EQUIPMENT.** Refer to Problem 5–31, page 147. Assume that
the new equipment will cost $100,000 in cash and that the old machine cost
$81,000 and can be sold now for $16,000 cash.

Required: | 1. Compute the net present value of the replacement alternative, assuming that
the minimum desired rate of return is 10%.
2. What will be the internal rate of return?
3. How long is the payback period on the incremental investment?

11–35. **PRESENT VALUES OF CASH INFLOWS.** Hiramatsu Products has just been established. Operating plans indicate the following expected cash flows:

	OUTFLOWS	INFLOWS
Initial investment now	$210,000	$ —
End of year: One	150,000	200,000
Two	200,000	250,000
Three	250,000	300,000
Four	300,000	380,000
Five	300,000	380,000

Required: | 1. Compute the net present value for all of these cash flows. This should be a
single amount. Use a discount rate of 14%.
2. Is the internal rate of return more than 14% or less than 14%? Why?

11–36. **FIXED AND CURRENT ASSETS; EVALUATION OF PERFORMANCE.** (Alternate is
11–37.) Mercy Hospital has been under pressure to keep costs down. Indeed,
the hospital administrator has been managing various revenue-producing centers
to maximize contributions to the recovery of the operating costs of the hospital
as a whole. The administrator has been considering whether to buy a special-
purpose X-ray machine for $190,000. Its unique characteristics would generate
additional cash operating income of $50,000 per year for the hospital as a whole.

The machine is expected to have a useful life of six years and a terminal
salvage value of $25,000.

The machine is delicate. It requires a constant inventory of various supplies
and spare parts. When these items can no longer be used, they are instantly
replaced, so an investment of $10,000 must be maintained at all times. However,
this investment is fully recoverable at the end of the useful life of the machine.

1. Compute the net present value if the required rate of return is 14%.
2. Compute the internal rate of return (to the nearest whole percentage).
3. Compute the accounting rate of return on (a) the initial investment and (b) the "average" investment.
4. Why might the administrator be reluctant to base her decision on the DCF model?

11–37. **EFFECTS OF CURRENT ASSETS AND RESIDUAL VALUES.** (Alternate is 11–36.) The manager of a department store is considering whether to remodel space that has been devoted to large household appliances. She is thinking of dropping those products and replacing them with expensive high-fashion clothing.

New display fixtures and dressing areas will be needed. They will cost $70,000 and are expected to be useful for five years with a terminal salvage value of $5,000. Additional cash inflows from operations are expected to be $40,000 per year.

To sustain the higher anticipated sales volumes, additional investments in receivables and inventories will be required. An initial investment of $60,000 is needed for these current assets. This level must be maintained steadily. When these activities are terminated, the receivables and inventories will be converted to cash and fully recouped.

The manager has decided to use a five-year planning horizon for this possible use of space. Experience has shown that selling high-fashion clothing is risky, so there is a strong likelihood that the space will be changed at the end of five years.

Required:

1. Compute (a) net present value, using a required rate of 16%, (b) internal rate of return (to the nearest whole percentage), (c) accounting rate of return on the initial investment, and (d) accounting rate of return on the "average" investment.
2. As the store manager, which type of model would you prefer for the purposes of making this decision and of evaluating subsequent performance? Give reasons and compare the principal types of models.

11–38. **CAPITAL BUDGETING WITH UNEVEN CASH FLOWS.** The Stanford University Engineering School is considering the purchase of a special-purpose machine for $30,000. It is expected to have a useful life of three years with no terminal salvage value. The university's controller estimates the following savings in cash operating costs:

YEAR	AMOUNT
1	$13,000
2	13,000
3	12,000

Required:

Compute:

1. Payback period.
2. Net present value if the required rate of return is 14%.
3. Internal rate of return.
4. Accounting rate of return (a) on the initial investment and (b) on the "average" investment.

REPLACING OFFICE EQUIPMENT. Helpline House, a city agency created to help troubled children and teenagers, is considering replacing its present manual NCR bookeeping machines with microcomputers. Recent budget cuts have made the administration very concerned about the rising costs of operations.

To convert to IBM, two operators would have to be sent to school. Required training and remodeling would cost $6,000.

Helpline's three NCR machines were purchased for $6,000 each, five years ago. Their expected life was ten years. Their resale value now is $3,000 each and will be zero in five more years. The total cost of the new IBM hardware, software, and peripheral equipment will be $50,000; it will have zero disposal value in five years.

The three NCR operators are each paid $8 an hour. They usually work a 40-hour week. Machine breakdowns occur monthly on each machine, resulting in repair costs of $50 per month and overtime of 4 hours, at time-and-one-half, per machine per month, to complete the normal monthly workload. Paper, supplies, and so on cost $100 a month for each NCR.

The IBM system will require only two regular operators, on a regular workweek of forty hours each, to do the same work. Rates are $10 an hour, and no overtime is expected. Paper, supplies, and so on will cost $3,300 annually. Maintenance and repairs are fully serviced by IBM for $1,050 annually. (Assume a 52-week year.)

Required:
1. Using discounted-cash-flow techniques, compute the present value of all relevant cash flows, under both alternatives, for the five-year period discounted at 10%, compounded annually.
2. Should Helpline House keep the NCR machines or replace them, if the decision is based solely on the given data?
3. What other considerations might affect the decision?

11–40. **REPLACEMENT DECISION FOR PRINTING COMPANY.** Fujita Printing Company is considering replacement of an offset press with a new, five-color version just introduced by Japanese Electronic Manufacturing, Inc. (JEM). The present press cost $18,000 5 years ago and has an estimated remaining life of 12 years. A year from now the press will require a major overhaul estimated to cost $5,000. It can be sold immediately for $3,500 cash. If not sold within the next three years, it will have no salvage value. In addition, it will cost $1,000 to dismantle and dispose of the press, whenever it is retired.

A new JEM press costs $74,000, including freight, delivery, and setup. It has an estimated life of 12 years; at that time, the mechanical parts are likely to be worn out. However, printing technology is progressing rapidly, and the new press will probably be sold after 7 years to take advantage of newly developed capabilities. The sale price in 7 years (after deducting the cost of dismantling) will be only $5,000.

The new JEM press will turn out higher-quality copies at twice the speed of the old press. One worker operates the current press 40 hours per week and is paid $30,000 (including fringe benefits) per year. The operator would be used productively in other parts of the company for 20 hours per week if the new press is purchased. No increase in business is expected, so the new press would run only 20 hours per week.

The JEM sales rep offers an annual maintenance contract on the new press for $1,000 per year. In addition, the press will require a thorough overhaul at the end of the fourth year at an estimated cost of $7,000.

Records show the annual normal maintenance of the current press to be $1,200. Use of electricity, ink, and other materials does not differ between the machines.

Required:
Should Fujita Printing buy the new JEM press? A 10% rate of return is desired. Compute present values. Ignore income taxes. What subjective factors might influence your decision?

11–41. **DISCOUNTED CASH FLOW, UNEVEN REVENUE STREAM, RELEVANT COSTS.** Mr. Parr, the owner of a nine-hole golf course on the outskirts of a large city, is considering the proposal that this course be illuminated and operated at night. Mr. Parr purchased the course early last year for $75,000. His receipts from operations during the 28-week season were $24,000. Total disbursements for the year, for all purposes, were $15,500.

The required investment in lighting this course is estimated at $20,000. The system will require 75 lamps of 1,000 watts each. Electricity costs 6.4¢ per kilowatt-hour. The expected average hours of operation per night is five. Because of occasional bad weather and the probable curtailment of night operations at the beginning and end of the season, it is estimated that there will be only 130 nights of operation per year. Labor for keeping the course open at night will cost $15 per night. Lamp renewals are estimated at $300 per year; other maintenance and repairs, per year, will amount to 4% of the initial cost of the lighting system. Property taxes on this equipment will be about 2% of its initial cost. It is estimated that the average revenue, per night of operation, will be $90 for the first two years.

Considering the probability of competition from the illumination of other golf courses, Mr. Parr decides that he will not make the investment unless he can make at least 14% per annum on his investment. Because of anticipated competition, revenue is expected to drop to $70 per night for years 3 through 5. It is estimated that the lighting equipment will have a salvage value of $10,000 at the end of the five-year period.

Required:

Using discounted-cash-flow techniques, determine whether Mr. Parr should install the lighting system.

11–42. **MINIMIZING TRANSPORTATION COSTS.** The Harris Company produces industrial and residential lighting fixtures at its manufacturing facility located in Los Angeles. Shipment of company products to an eastern warehouse is presently handled by common carriers at a rate of 25¢ per pound of fixtures. The warehouse is located in Cleveland, 2,500 miles from Los Angeles.

The treasurer of Harris Company is presently considering whether to purchase a truck for transporting products to the eastern warehouse. The following data on the truck are available:

Purchase price	$35,000
Useful life	5 years
Salvage value after 5 years	zero
Capacity of truck	10,000 lb
Cash costs of operating truck	$.90 per mile

The treasurer feels that an investment in this truck is particularly attractive because of his successful negotiation with X Company to back-haul X's products from Cleveland to Los Angeles on every return trip from the warehouse. X has agreed to pay Harris $2,400 per load of X's products hauled from Cleveland to Los Angeles up to and including 100 loads per year.

Harris's marketing manager has estimated that 500,000 pounds of fixtures will have to be shipped to the eastern warehouse each year for the next five years. The truck will be fully loaded on each round trip.

Ignore income taxes.

Required:

1. Assume that Harris requires a minimum rate of return of 20%. Should the truck be purchased? Show computations to support your answer.
2. What is the minimum number of trips that must be guaranteed by the X Company to make the deal acceptable to Harris, based on the foregoing numbers alone?
3. What qualitative factors might influence your decision? Be specific.

11–43. **INVESTMENT IN MACHINE AND WORKING CAPITAL.** The Hoffmann Company has an old Languido grinder with a net disposal value of $10,000 now and $4,000 five years from now. A new Rapido grinder is offered for $60,000 cash or $50,000 with a trade-in. The new grinder will result in an annual operating cash outflow of $40,000 as compared with the old grinder's annual outflow of $50,000. The disposal value of the new grinder five years hence will be $4,000.

Because the new grinder will produce output more rapidly, the average investment in inventories will be $160,000 by using the new grinder instead of $200,000.

The minimum desired rate of return is 20%. The company uses discounted-cash-flow techniques to guide these decisions.

Required: Should the Rapido grinder be acquired? Show your calculations. Company procedures require the computing of the present value of each alternative. The most desirable alternative is the one with the least cost. Assume PV of $1 at 20% for five years is $.40; PV of annuity of $1 at 20% for five years is $3.

11–44. **USES OF WAREHOUSE: REVIEW OF CHAPTERS 5 AND 11.**

a. The Rosenberg Company is currently leasing one of its small warehouses to another company for $3,000 per year, on a month-to-month basis.

b. The estimated sales value of the warehouse is $30,000. This price is likely to remain unchanged indefinitely—even if a contemplated public expressway results in the building's condemnation. The building originally cost $20,000 and is being depreciated at $500 annually. Its net book value is $9,000.

c. The Rosenberg Company is seriously considering converting the warehouse into a retail outlet for selling furniture at ridiculously low discount prices. Such an endeavor would entail remodeling, at a cost of $18,000. The remodeling would be extremely modest because the major attraction would be flimsy furniture at rock-bottom prices. The remodeling can be accomplished over a single weekend.

d. The inventory, cash, and receivables needed to open and sustain the retail outlet would be $70,000. This total is fully recoverable whenever operations terminate.

e. The president, who paid an expressway engineer $1,000 to discover when and where the expressway will be built, is virtually certain that the warehouse will be available for no more than four years. He has asked you to give him an analysis of whether the company should continue to lease the warehouse or convert it to a retail outlet, assuming that the minimum annual rate of return desired is 14% over a four-year planning horizon. Estimated annual operating data, exclusive of depreciation, are:

f. Sales	$200,000
g. Operating expenses	177,000
h. Nonrecurring sales promotion costs at *beginning* of year 1	20,000
i. Nonrecurring termination costs at *end* of year 4	10,000

The president has definitely decided not to sell the warehouse until forced to by condemnation proceedings.

Required: **1.** Show how you would handle the *individual* items on the company's analysis form, which is set up as follows:

ITEM	DESCRIPTION	NET PRESENT VALUE	CASH FLOWS IN YEAR				
			0	1	2	3	4
a.							
b.							
.							
.							
.							
h.							
i.							

Use the following present-value factors: the PV of $1 in year 4 = $.60 and the PV of a 4-year annuity of $1 = $2.90. Ignore income taxes. If you think an item is irrelevant, leave the space blank.

2. After analyzing all the relevant data, compute the net present value. Indicate which course of action, based on the data alone, should be taken.

11–45. **CAFETERIA FACILITIES.** The cafeteria in Scandia Towers, an office building in downtown Stockholm, is open 250 days a year. It offers typical cafeteria-line service. At the noon meal (open to the public), serving-line facilities can accommodate 200 people per hour for the two-hour serving period. The average customer has a 30-minute lunch period. Serving facilities are unable to handle the overflow of noon customers with the result that, daily, 200 dissatisfied customers who do not wish to stand in line choose to eat elsewhere. Projected over a year, this results in a considerable loss to the cafeteria.

To tap this excess demand, the cafeteria is considering two alternatives: (a) installing two vending machines, at a cost of Skr. 50,000 apiece (Skr. means Swedish kroner), or (b) completely revamping present serving-line facilities with new equipment, at a cost of Skr. 800,000. The vending machines and serving-line equipment have a useful life of ten years and will be depreciated on a straight-line basis. The minimum desired rate of return for the cafeteria is 10%. The average sale is Skr. 15, with a contribution margin of 30%. This will remain the same if new serving-line facilities are installed.

Data for alternative *a* (vending machines) are as follows:

Service cost per year is Skr. 3,000; salvage value of each machine at the end of ten years is Skr. 5,000.

Contribution margin is 20%. It is estimated that 60% of the dissatisfied customers will use the vending machines and spend an average of Skr. 15. The estimated salvage value of the present equipment will net Skr. 20,000 at the end of the ten-year period.

Data for alternative *b* (new serving-line facilities) are as follows:

Yearly salary for an extra part-time cashier is Skr. 40,000; salvage value of old equipment is Skr. 50,000; salvage value of new equipment, at the end of ten years, is Skr. 100,000; cost of dismantling old equipment is Skr. 10,000. It is estimated that all the previously dissatisfied customers will use the new facilities.

All other costs are the same under both alternatives and need not be considered.

Required: Using the net-present-value model, which is the better alternative?

11–46. **CASH FLOW PREDICTION, MODEL COMPARISON, AND PRICING.** A consultant to the hotel industry predicted the costs of two types of 300-room hotels in the vicinity of Stamford, Connecticut (*Forbes*, March 12, 1984). A "commercial class" hotel requires an investment of $95,000 per room and an "executive class" requires $125,000. He indicated that the rule-of-thumb in the hotel industry is to charge a nightly room rate of $1 per $1,000 of room building cost. The going rate in the Stamford area is $79 for commercial class rooms and $135 for executive class rooms. Suppose that the annual fixed cost for running a commercial class hotel with 300 rooms is $750,000 and for executive class is $1,000,000; variable costs are $10 per occupied night in commercial class and $15 in executive class. An occupancy rate of 65% is expected for either hotel. The minimum desired rate of return is 14%, compounded annually.

Required:

1. Calculate the net present value, internal rate-of-return, payback time, and accounting rate-of-return for a commercial class hotel and for an executive class hotel. Assume that the economic life of each hotel is 20 years, the costs and prices are not expected to change over the 20 years, and straight-line depreciation is taken over 20 years. Assume a 365-day year.
2. Did you use the going room rate in the Stamford area or the rule of thumb of $1 per $1,000 of building cost for your room rate in answering Requirement 1? Why? Evaluate the rule of thumb presented in the problem.

11–47. MAKE OR BUY, DISCOUNTED CASH FLOW, AND ACCOUNTING RATE OF RETURN. Refer to Problem 5–35, Requirement 1, page 149.

1. Using a net-present-value analysis, which alternative is more attractive? Assume that the minimum rate of return desired is 8%.
2. Using the accounting rate-of-return method, what is the rate of return on the initial investment?

11–48. REPLACEMENT DECISION. Amtrak, a passenger train company subsidized by the U.S. government, has included a dining car on the lone passenger train it operates from Buffalo to Albany, N.Y. Yearly operations of the dining car have shown a consistent loss, which is expected to persist, as follows:

Revenue (in cash)		$200,000
Expenses for food, supplies, etc. (in cash)	$100,000	
Salaries	110,000	210,000
Net loss (ignore depreciation on the dining car itself)		($ 10,000)

The Auto-vend Company has offered to sell automatic vending machines to Amtrak for $22,000, less a $3,000 trade-in allowance on old equipment (which is carried at $3,000 book value, and which can be sold outright for $3,000 cash) now used in the dining car operation. The useful life of the vending equipment is estimated at ten years, with zero scrap value. Experience elsewhere has led executives to predict that the equipment will serve 50% more food than the dining car, but prices will be 50% less, so the new gross receipts will probably be $150,000. The variety and mix of food sold are expected to be the same as for the dining car. A catering company will completely service and supply the machines, paying 10% of gross receipts to the Amtrak company and bearing all costs of food, repairs, and so on. All dining car employees will be discharged immediately. Their termination pay will total $30,000. However, an attendant who has some general knowledge of vending machines will be needed for one shift per day. The annual cost to Amtrak for the attendant will be $14,000.

For political and other reasons, the railroad will definitely not abandon its food service. The old equipment will have zero scrap value at the end of ten years.

1. Compute the net present value, in dollars, of the proposed investment. Assume that Congress has specified that a minimum desired rate of return of 10% be used for these types of investments. For this problem, assume that the PV of $1 at 10% to be received at the end of ten years is $.40 and that the PV of an annuity of $1 at 10% for ten years is $6.00. Ignore income taxes.

2. What would be the minimum amount of annual *revenue* that Amtrak would have to receive from the catering company to justify making the investment? Show computations.

☐ Solutions to Exercises in Compound Interest, Problem 11–1

The general approach to these exercises centers on one fundamental question: Which of the two basic tables am I dealing with? No calculations should be made until after this question is answered with assurance. If you made any errors, it is possible that you used the wrong table.

a. From Table 1, page 728:
   (1) $3,736.50.
   (2) $3,104.50.
   (3) $2,009.50.

The $5,000 is a lum-sum *amount* or *future worth*. You want the present value of that amount:

$$PV = \frac{S}{(1-i)^n}$$

The conversion factors for $n = 5$, $1/(1+i)^5$, for various values of i are on line 5 of Table 1. Substituting:

$PV = \$5,000(.7473) = \$3,736.50$	(1)
$PV = \$5,000(.6209) = \$3,104.50$	(2)
$PV = \$5,000(.4019) = \$2,009.50$	(3)

Note that the higher the interest rate, the lower the present value.

b. From Table 2, page 729:
   (1) $4,212.40.
   (2) $3,790.80.
   (3) $2,990.60.

The $500 withdrawal is an equal annual amount, an annuity. You need to find the present value of an annuity for five years:

$PV_A = $ annual withdrawal $\times$ F   where F is the conversion factor.

Substituting:

$PV_A = \$1,000(4.2124) = \$4,212.40$	(1)
$PV_A = \$1,000(3.7908) = \$3,790.80$	(2)
$PV_A = \$1,000(2.9906) = \$2,990.60$	(3)

c. From Table 2:
   (1) $1,186.97.
   (2) $1,318.98.

You have $5,000, the present value of your contemplated annuity. You must find the annuity that will just exhaust the invested principal in five years.

$$PV_A = \text{annual withdrawal} \times F \qquad (1)$$

$$\$5,000 = \text{annual withdrawal} \times 4.2124$$

$$\text{annual withdrawal} = \$5,000 \div 4.2124$$
$$= \$1,186.97$$

$$\$5,000 = \text{annual withdrawal} \times 3.7908 \qquad (2)$$

$$\text{annual withdrawal} = \$5,000 \div 3.7908$$
$$= \$1,318.98$$

d. From Table 1: Mining is preferable; its present value exceeds that of farming by $215,722 − $177,206 = $38,516. Note that the nearer dollars are more valuable than the distant dollars.

YEAR	PRESENT-VALUE AT 16% FROM TABLE 1	PRESENT-VALUE OF MINING	PRESENT VALUE OF FARMING
1	.8621	$ 86,210	$ 17,242
2	.7432	59,456	29,728
3	.6407	38,442	38,442
4	.5523	22,092	44,184
5	.4761	9,522	47,610
		$215,722	$177,206

Note that all the factors in Table 1, page 728, which measure the present value of a lump sum, are less than one. All factors in Table 2, page 729, that measure the present value of a series of *two or more* payments are greater than one.

Chapter 12

CAPITAL BUDGETING:

TAXES AND INFLATION

LEARNING OBJECTIVES

When you have finished studying this chapter, you should be able to:

1. Analyze a typical income statement to determine the net after-tax cash inflow from operations.
2. Compute the after-tax present values of projects involving straight-line depreciation and ACRS depreciation.
3. Explain the after-tax effect on cash of disposing of assets.
4. Demonstrate how depreciation is analyzed in various capital-budgeting models.
5. Compute the impact of inflation on a capital-budgeting project.

This chapter extends the coverage of the preceding chapter. We are especially concerned with the effect of income taxes on capital-budgeting decisions. However, other topics are also explored, especially how to analyze the effects of inflation.

INCOME TAXES AND CAPITAL BUDGETING

☐ General Characteristics

Income taxes are cash disbursements. Income taxes can influence the *amount* and/or the *timing* of cash flows. Their basic role in capital budgeting is no different from that of any other cash disbursement. However, taxes tend to narrow the cash differences between projects. Cash savings in operations will cause an increase in taxable income and thus a partially offsetting increase in tax outlays. For example, a 60% income tax rate would reduce the net attractiveness of $1 million in cash operating savings to $400,000.

U.S. federal income tax rate on ordinary corporate taxable income below $50,000 currently is 15%. Rates then increase until companies with taxable income over $330,000 pay 34%. These rates are sometimes subject to additional surcharges that may vary from year to year. State income tax rates vary considerably. Therefore, overall corporate income tax rates vary widely.

☐ Effects of Depreciation Deductions

Organizations that pay income taxes generally keep two sets of books—one for reporting to the public and one for reporting to the tax authorities. This is not illegal or immoral; in fact, it is necessary. Tax reporting must follow detailed rules designed to achieve certain social goals. These rules do not lead to financial statements that best measure an organization's financial results and position, so it is more informative to financial statement users if a separate set of rules is used for financial reporting. In this chapter we are concerned with effects on the cash outflows for taxes. Therefore, we focus on the *tax reporting* rules, not those for public financial reporting.

Depreciation often differs between tax and public reporting. Exhibit 12-1 shows the interrelationship of income before taxes, income taxes, and depreciation. Please examine this key exhibit carefully before reading on. Assume that the company has a single fixed asset, equipment, which was purchased for $125,000 cash and has a five-year life. The equipment is used to produce annual sales revenue of $130,000 and expenses (excluding depreciation) of $70,000. The purchase cost of the asset is tax deductible in the form of yearly

EXHIBIT 12-1

Basic Analysis of Income Statement,
Income Taxes, and Cash Flows

TRADITIONAL ANNUAL INCOME STATEMENT

(S)	Sales	$130,000
(E)	Less: Expenses, excluding depreciation	$ 70,000
(D)	Depreciation (straight-line)	25,000
	Total expenses	$ 95,000
	Income before taxes	$ 35,000
(T)	Income taxes @ 60%	21,000
(I)	Net income	$ 14,000

Total after-tax effect on cash is
either S − E − T = $130,000 − $70,000 − $21,000 = $39,000
or I + D = $14,000 + $25,000 = $39,000

ANALYSIS OF THE SAME FACTS FOR CAPITAL BUDGETING

Cash effects of operations:		
(S–E)	Cash inflow from operations: $130,000 − $70,000	$60,000
	Income tax outflow, @ 60%	36,000
	After-tax inflow from operations (excluding depreciation)	$24,000
Effects of depreciation:		
(D)	Straight-line depreciation: $125,000 ÷ 5 = $25,000	
	Income tax savings @ 60%	15,000
	Total after-tax effect on cash	$39,000

depreciation. Depreciation deductions (and similar deductions that are non-cash expenses when deducted) have been called **tax shields** because they protect that amount of income from taxation. However, all allowable expenses, both cash and noncash items, are tax shields because they reduce income and thereby reduce income taxes.

As Exhibit 12–2 shows, the depreciable asset represents a valuable future tax deduction of $125,000. The present value of this deduction depends directly on its specific yearly effects on future income tax payments. Therefore the present value is influenced by the depreciation method selected, the tax rates, and the discount rate.

Exhibit 12–2 shows two methods for analyzing the data for capital budgeting, assuming straight-line depreciation.[1] Both lead to the same final answer, a net present value of $15,587 for the investment in this asset. The choice of analytical method is a matter of personal preference. However, method 2 will be used in this chapter. Why? Because it highlights the impact of the alternative depreciation methods on present values.

The $125,000 investment really buys two streams of cash: (1) net inflows

---

[1] For simplicity, and to underscore the general approach, the *half-year convention* is ignored here. It is explained later in the chapter.

EXHIBIT 12-2 *(Place a clip on this page for easy reference.)*

Impact of Income Taxes on Capital-Budgeting Analysis

Assume: Original cost of equipment, $125,000; 5-year life; zero terminal disposal value; pretax annual cash inflow from operations, $60,000; income tax rate, 60%; required after-tax rate of return, 12%. All items are in dollars except discount factors. The after-tax cash flows are from Exhibit 12-1.

	12% DISCOUNT FACTOR, FROM APPROPRIATE TABLES	TOTAL PRESENT VALUE AT 12%	SKETCH OF AFTER-TAX CASH FLOWS AT END OF YEAR					
			0	1	2	3	4	5
Method 1 (Discount the total annual effects together)								
After-tax effect on cash, excluding depreciation	3.6048	$140,587		39,000	39,000	39,000	39,000	39,000
Investment	1.0000	(125,000)	(125,000)					
Net present value, of the investment		$ 15,587						
Method 2 (Discount two annual effects separately)								
Cash effects of operations, excluding depreciation	3.6048	$ 86,515		24,000	24,000	24,000	24,000	24,000
Cash effects of depreciation: Savings of income taxes	3.6048	54,072		15,000	15,000	15,000	15,000	15,000
Total after-tax effect on cash		$140,587						
Investment	1.0000	(125,000)	(125,000)					
Net present value of the investment		$ 15,587						

from operations plus (2) savings of income tax outflows (which have the same effect in capital budgeting as additions to cash inflows). The choice of depreciation method will not affect the cash inflows from operations. But different depreciation methods will affect the cash outflows for income taxes. That is, a straight-line method will produce one present value of tax savings, and an accelerated method will produce a different present value. Such differences can be pinpointed more easily if method 2 is used.

Tax Deductions, Cash Effects, and Timing

Before proceeding, review the basic relationships just portrayed (in dollars):

LINE	(A) ITEMS USED IN COMPUTING TAXABLE INCOME	(B) CURRENT PRETAX CASH EFFECT	(C) EFFECT ON INCOME TAX CASH OUTFLOWS AT 60%	(B)–(C) NET CASH EFFECT
1. Sales	$130,000	$130,000	$78,000	$52,000
2. Expenses, excluding depreciation	70,000	70,000	42,000	28,000
3. Cash effect of operations	$ 60,000	$ 60,000	$36,000	$24,000
4. Depreciation	25,000	0	15,000	15,000
5. Net cash effects		$ 60,000	$21,000	$39,000
6. Income before income taxes	$ 35,000			
7. Income taxes	21,000			
8. Net income	$ 14,000			

This tabulation highlights why the net cash effects of operations (the items on lines 1, 2, and 3) are computed by multiplying the pretax amounts by (1 − the tax rate), or 1 − .60 = .40. The total effect is the cash flow itself less the tax effect. Each additional $1.00 of sales also adds $.60 of taxes, leaving a net cash inflow of $.40; each additional $1.00 of cash expense reduces taxes by $.60, leaving a net cash outflow of $.40. Thus, the after-tax effect of the $70,000 of *cash* expenses (line 2) is $70,000 × .40 = $28,000. Note that this is a cash *outflow*.

In contrast, the after-tax effects of the *noncash* expenses (depreciation on line 4) are computed by multiplying the tax deduction of $25,000 by the tax rate itself, or $25,000 × .60 = $15,000. Note that this is a cash *inflow*. The total cash effect of a noncash expense is *only* the tax-savings effect.

Throughout the illustrations in this chapter, we assume that all income tax flows occur simultaneously with the pretax cash flows. That is, consider line 3. We are ignoring the likelihood that part or all of the $36,000 tax payments related to the $60,000 pretax cash effects of operations of year 1 may not actually occur until, say, April of year 2.

This assumption of no lags in income tax effects is also largely in accordance with the facts in the real world. Why? Because both individual and corporate taxpayers generally "pay-as-they-go." That is, estimated tax payments are made in installments at least quarterly, not in one lump sum in the subsequent year.

Another assumption throughout this chapter is that the companies in question are profitable. That is, the companies will have enough taxable income from all sources to use all income tax benefits in the situations described.

☐ **Accelerated Depreciation**

Governments have frequently enacted income tax laws that permit accelerated depreciation instead of straight-line depreciation. **Accelerated depreciation** is defined as any pattern of depreciation that writes off depreciable assets more quickly than does ordinary straight-line depreciation. These laws are aimed at encouraging investments in long-lived assets.

An extreme example clearly demonstrates why accelerated depreciation is attractive to investors. Reconsider the facts in Exhibit 12–2. Suppose, as was the case in England, that the entire initial investment can be written off immediately for income tax reporting. Focus on Method 2 to see the rise in net present value from $15,587 to $36,515:

	PRESENT VALUES	
	As in Exhibit 12–2	Complete Write-off Immediately
Cash effects of operations	$ 86,515	$ 86,515
Cash effects of depreciation	54,072	75,000*
Total after-tax effect on cash	140,587	161,515
Investment	(125,000)	(125,000)
Net present value	$ 15,587	$ 36,515

* Assumes that the tax effect occurs simultaneously with the investment at time zero: $125,000 × .60 = $75,000.

In summary, the earlier you can take the depreciation, the greater is the present value of the income tax savings. The total tax savings will be the same regardless of the depreciation method. In the example the tax savings from the depreciation deduction is either .60 × $125,000 = $75,000 in year zero or .60 × $25,000 = $15,000 per year for five years, a total of $75,000. However, the time value of money makes the immediate savings worth more than future savings. The mottoes in income tax planning are: "When there is a legal choice, take the *deduction sooner* rather than later," and "Recognize *taxable income later* rather than sooner."

How much present value gain is achieved by accelerating depreciation? It depends on the rate of return that can be earned on the tax payments that are delayed and the amount by which depreciation can be accelerated. The ultimate acceleration is immediate write-off; at 12% this gained $75,000 − $54,072 = $20,928 in present value over straight-line depreciation in the example.

☐ Accelerated Cost Recovery System (ACRS)

For years, the U.S. income tax laws permitted several forms of accelerated depreciation. But most depreciable assets placed in service after December 31, 1980 have been depreciated for tax purposes using the **Accelerated Cost Recovery System (ACRS)**. The Internal Revenue Code of 1986 identifies six ACRS classes and the assets that belong to each. Examples of assets in each class are shown in Exhibit 12–3.

An asset's ACRS class specifies its "recovery period," which is the number of years over which the acquisition cost is to be depreciated. The recovery periods are generally shorter than the useful lives of the assets. The combination of these short recovery periods with higher depreciation in the early years of an asset's life provides great acceleration of depreciation. However, the exact amount of acceleration to be allowed is often debated by members of Congress, who seem to change the rules almost annually.

☐ Depreciation Methods

ACRS depreciation schedules for three, five, seven, and ten year assets are based on the *double-declining balance (DDB)* method. The DDB method divides 100% by the number of years of ACRS cost recovery, then doubles the resulting rate. For example, the DDB rate for five-year assets is $(100\% \div 5) \times 2 = 40\%$. This percentage is applied to the *undepreciated amount* each year to compute the annual depreciation. Exhibit 12–4 shows that the five-year schedule has depreciation of $40\% \times 100\% = 40\%$ in the first year, $40\% \times (100\% - 40\%) = 24\%$ in the second, $40\% \times (100\% - 40\% - 24\%) = 14.4\%$ in the third, and so on.[2]

Taxpayers can switch to straight-line depreciation on an asset at the time when straight-line depreciation over the remaining recovery years provides more depreciation than continuation of DDB. For a five-year asset the switch comes in the fourth year. The undepreciated amount is $(100\% - 40\% - 24\% - 14.4\%) = 21.6\%$. DDB depreciation would be $40\% \times 21.6\% = 8.64\%$, but straight-line depreciation over each of the two remaining years is $21.6\% \div 2 = 10.8\%$. This switch is incorporated in Exhibit 12–4.

---

[2] The precise timing of the tax savings from depreciation is influenced by some complex provisions of the tax code. One such provision is the **half-year convention,** which treats all assets as if they were placed in service at the midpoint of the year. Half of the first year's depreciation is assigned to the tax year in which the asset was acquired and half to the following tax year, and so on for each year. For example, an asset purchased on the first day of the tax year is allowed only one-half year's depreciation during the asset's first year in service. Why? Because the asset's first year coincides with the tax year of acquisition. An asset purchased on the last day of a tax year has one-and-one-half years of depreciation in its first year in service (that is, the half year allowed for the year of acquisition and the full year for the following year). If assets are acquired uniformly throughout the year, *on average* they will have one full year of depreciation in their first year and in each year thereafter through the end of the recovery period. For simplicity, we will assume that every asset has a full year of depreciation in its first year in service and in each succeeding year of the recovery period, as shown in Exhibit 12–4.

EXHIBIT 12–3

Classifications in Accelerated Cost Recovery System (ACRS)

3-year	Special tools for several specific industries; tractor units for over-the-road.
5-year	Automobiles; trucks; research equipment; computers; machinery and equipment in selected industries.
7-year	Office furniture; railroad cars; machinery and equipment in a majority of industries.
10-year	Water transportation equipment; machinery and equipment in selected industries.
15-year	Most land improvements; machinery and equipment in selected industries.
20-year	Farm buildings; electricity generation and distribution equipment.
27.5-year	Residential rental property.
31.5-year	Nonresidential real property.

EXHIBIT 12–4

Selected Double-Declining Balance Depreciation Schedules*

Year**	3-Year Property	5-Year Property	10-Year Property
1	66.7%	40.0%	20.0%
2	22.2%	24.0%	16.0%
3	11.1%	14.4%	12.8%
4		10.8%	10.2%
5		10.8%	8.2%
6–8			6.6%
9–10			6.5%***

* Includes a switch to straight-line in years 3, 4, and 6, respectively.

** The year refers to a year of the asset's life. This may not correspond to a calendar (or tax) year.

*** Because of rounding errors, this was rounded down to assure that total depreciation is 100%.

The fifteen and twenty year ACRS depreciation schedules are based on the 150%—declining—balance method, in which 100% divided by the number of years of ACRS cost recovery is multiplied by 1.5 rather than doubled. The 27.5-year and 31.5-year schedules are based on straight-line depreciation.

For some companies, accelerated depreciation may not be desirable. After all, a few companies, especially new ones, expect to suffer taxable losses for a series of years. Such companies may prefer to delay as much of their depreciation deductions as is permissible. The tax laws allow such companies to use straight-line depreciation over the recovery period as an alternative to the accelerated ACRS methods.

☐ Present Value of ACRS Depreciation

In capital-budgeting decisions it is often useful to know the present value of the ACRS tax savings. Table 3 in Appendix B, p. 730, provides present values for $1 to be depreciated over double-declining-balance schedules for three, five, seven, and ten year recovery periods and 150%-declining-balance for fifteen and twenty year recovery periods. To find the tax savings, the factors in Table 3 are used as follows:

1. Find the factor from Table 3 for the appropriate recovery period and required rate of return.
2. Multiply the factor by the tax rate to find the tax savings per dollar of investment.
3. Multiply the result by the amount of the investment to find the total tax savings.

For example, consider an investment of $18,000 in five-year ACRS equipment. A 12% after-tax required rate of return and a 40% tax rate produce a tax savings with a present value of .7809 × .40 × $18,000 = $5,622.48.

☐ ACRS and Straight-Line Depreciation

Reconsider the data in Exhibit 12–2, page 382. Suppose the useful life of the equipment is ten years instead of five years, though it qualifies as a five-year property for ACRS cost recovery. It was purchased on July 1, 19X1. The cash inflows from operations, before depreciation, have a present value of 5.6502 × $24,000 = $135,605. (The 5.6502 factor comes from the 12% column and 10-year row, Table 2 in Appendix B, p. 729.) The present value of the tax savings from depreciation depends on the method of depreciation and the recovery period used. The tax savings can be computed independently from the cash effects of operations.

Exhibit 12–5 presents straight-line and ACRS computations of tax savings over five- and ten-year periods. The advantage of ACRS is based on two factors: (1) short recovery period and (2) providing more depreciation in the early years. Both advantages are illustrated in Exhibit 12–5. The present value of the tax savings with ACRS and a five-year recovery period is $58,568. This is $58,568 − $48,218 = $10,350 more than if ACRS had been used with a ten-year recovery period, $58,568 − $54,072 = $4,496 more than if straight-line depreciation had been used over a five-year period, and $58,568 − $42,378 = $16,190 more than straight-line over 10 years. In this case, the major advantage of ACRS comes from using the five-year recovery period in place of the ten-year useful life.

☐ Gains or Losses on Disposal

The impact on income taxes of the disposal of equipment for cash can be summarized as follows, using the data from our example under three different assumptions about cash proceeds and when sale occurs. For simplicity, straight-line depreciation is assumed:

		END OF YEAR (IN DOLLARS)		
		5	**3**	**3**
(a)	Cash proceeds of sale	10,000	70,000	20,000
	Book value: zero and $125,000 − 3($25,000)	0	50,000	50,000
	Gain (loss)	10,000	20,000	(30,000)
	Effect on income taxes at 60%:			
(b)	Tax saving, an inflow effect: .60 × loss			18,000
(c)	Tax paid, an outflow: .60 × gain	(6,000)	(12,000)	
	Total cash inflow at disposal:			
	(a) plus (b)			38,000
	(a) minus (c)	4,000	58,000	

Ponder these calculations. Note especially that the total cash inflow effect of a disposal at a loss is the selling price plus the income tax savings.

Summary Comparison

	ACRS		STRAIGHT-LINE	
	5-Year Recovery Property	10-Year Recovery Property	5-Year Recovery Property	10-Year Recovery Property
Present value of cash effects from operations*	$135,605	$135,605	$135,605	$135,605
Present value of tax savings from depreciation	58,568	48,218	54,072	42,378
Total after-tax present value	$194,173	$183,823	$189,677	$177,983
Original investment	125,000	125,000	125,000	125,000
Net present value of the asset	$ 69,173	$ 58,823	$ 64,677	$ 52,983

* $24,000 × 5.6502 = $135,605. The present value factor is from Appendix B, Table 2, page 729, 12% column and 10-year row.

The often-heard expression, "What the heck, it's deductible," sometimes warps perspective. Even though losses bring income tax savings and gains bring additional income taxes, gains are still more desirable than losses. In the foregoing tabulation, the loss in the last column produces income tax savings of $18,000.[3] Each $1,000 of additional proceeds would reduce the tax

[3] In this case, the old equipment was sold outright. Where there is a trade-in of old equipment for new equipment of like kind, special income tax rules result in the gain or loss being added to, or deducted from, the capitalized value of the new equipment. The gain or loss is not recognized in the year of disposal; instead, it is spread over the life of the new asset as an adjustment of the new depreciation charges.

EXHIBIT 12–5

Effects of Acceleration and Short Recovery Period on Present Values of Tax Savings from Depreciation

Assume same basic data as in Exhibit 12–2, except that useful life is 10 years instead of 5 years.

| | | | | ACRS* | | STRAIGHT LINE | |
	Year	Tax Rate (1)	PV Factor @ 12% (2)	Depreciation (3)	Present Value of Savings (1) × (2) × (3)	Depreciation (4)	Present Value of Savings (1) × (2) × (4)
5-year recovery property:	1	.60	.8929	$50,000	$26,787	$25,000	$13,393
	2	.60	.7972	30,000	14,350	25,000	11,958
	3	.60	.7118	18,000	7,687	25,000	10,677
	4	.60	.6355	13,500	5,148	25,000	9,533
	5	.60	.5674	13,500	4,596	25,000	8,511
	Total present value				$58,568		$54,072
10-year recovery property:	1	.60	.8929	$25,000	$13,393	$12,500	$ 6,697
	2	.60	.7972	20,000	9,566	12,500	5,979
	3	.60	.7118	16,000	6,833	12,500	5,338
	4	.60	.6355	12,750	4,862	12,500	4,766
	5	.60	.5674	10,250	3,490	12,500	4,256
	6	.60	.5066	8,250	2,508	12,500	3,800
	7	.60	.4523	8,250	2,239	12,500	3,393
	8	.60	.4039	8,250	1,999	12,500	3,029
	9	.60	.3606	8,125	1,758	12,500	2,705
	10	.60	.3220	8,125	1,570	12,500	2,415
	Total present value				$48,218		$42,378

* The present value of the tax savings from ACRS depreciation can also be calculated using Table 3 of Appendix B, page 730:

present value = original cost × factor from Table 3 × income tax rate
5-year recovery property: present value = $125,000 × .7809 × .60
= $58,568

10-year recovery property: present value = $125,000 × .6429 × .60
= $48,218

savings by $600, but it would still result in $400 more cash. Suppose that proceeds equal to book value ($50,000) were received. The total cash inflow would be $50,000 instead of $38,000; no tax effect would occur.

☐ Income Tax Complications

In the foregoing illustrations, believe it or not, we deliberately avoided many possible income tax complications. As all taxpaying citizens know, income taxes are affected by many intricacies, including progressive tax rates, loss carrybacks and carryforwards, state income taxes, short- and long-term gains, distinctions between capital assets and other assets, offsets of losses against related gains, exchanges of property of like kind, exempt income, and so forth.[4]

Keep in mind that miscellaneous changes in the tax law occur each year. An example is the **investment tax credit**, which provided a lump-sum reduction in taxes to companies making qualified investments. The credit was equal to a specified percentage of the investment. It was first available in 1962, and since then it has been suspended and reinstated, and the allowable percentage has been changed several times. Most recently it was again suspended. Always check the current tax law before calculating the tax consequences of a decision.

SUMMARY PROBLEM FOR YOUR REVIEW

☐ **Problem One**

Consider the investment opportunity presented in Exhibit 12–2, page 382; original cost of equipment, $125,000; five year economic life; zero terminal salvage value; pretax annual cash inflow from operations, $60,000; income tax rate, 60%; required after-tax rate of return, 12%. Assume that the equipment is 5-year recovery property for ACRS purposes that was acquired on July 1. The net present value (NPV) is:

	PRESENT VALUES (PV)
Cash effects of operations,*	
$60,000 × (1 − .60) × 3.6048	$ 86,515
Cash effects of depreciation on income tax savings using ACRS,†	
$125,000 × .60 × .7809	58,568
Total after-tax effect on cash	$145,083
Investment	125,000
Net present value	$ 20,083

* See Exhibit 12–2, page 382, for details.
† See Exhibit 12–5, page 389, for details.

Required:

Consider each requirement independently.

1. Suppose the equipment was expected to be sold for $20,000 cash immediately after the end of year 5. Compute the net present value of the investment.
2. Ignore the assumption in Requirement 1. Return to the original data. Suppose the economic life of the equipment was eight years rather than five years. Compute the net present value of the investment, assuming accelerated cost recovery is used.

---

[4] For book-length coverage of these and other complications, see *Federal Tax Course* (Englewood Cliffs, N.J.: Prentice-Hall), published annually.

1. Net present value as given		$ 20,083
Cash proceeds of sale	$ 20,000	
Book value	0	
Gain	$ 20,000	
Income taxes at 60%	12,000	
Total after-tax effect on cash	$ 8,000	
PV of $8,000 to be received in		
5 years at 12%, $8,000 × .5674		4,539
NPV of investment		$ 24,622
2. Net present value as given		$ 20,083
Add the present value of $24,000 per year for 8 years:		
Discount factor of 4.9676 × $24,000 =	$119,222	
Deduct the present value of $24,000 per year for 5 years	86,515	
Increase in present value		32,707
Net present value		$ 52,790

The investment would be very attractive. Note especially the relationship between ACRS and the economic useful life of the asset. ACRS specifies lives (or recovery periods) for various types of depreciable assets. The ACRS recovery period is unaffected by the economic useful lives of the assets. Thus a longer useful life for an asset increases operating cash flows without decreasing the present value of the tax savings.

CONFUSION ABOUT DEPRECIATION

The meaning of depreciation and book value is widely misunderstood. Pause and consider their role in decisions. Suppose a bank has some printing equipment with a book value of $30,000, an expected terminal disposal value of zero, a current disposal value of $12,000, and a remaining useful life of three years. For simplicity, assume that straight-line depreciation of $10,000 yearly will be taken.

These data should be examined in perspective, as Exhibit 12–6 indicates. In particular, note that the inputs to the decision model are the predicted income tax effects on cash. Book values and depreciation may be necessary for making *predictions*. By themselves, however, they are not inputs to DCF decision models.

The following points summarize the role of depreciation regarding the replacement of equipment:

1. *Initial investment*. As Chapter 5 explained (p. 132), the amount paid for (and hence depreciation on) old equipment is irrelevant except for its effect on tax cash flows. In contrast, the amount paid for new equipment is relevant because it is an expected future cost that will not be incurred if replacement is rejected.

2. *Do not double count*. The investment in equipment is a one-time outlay at time zero, so it should not be double-counted as an outlay in the form of depreciation. Depreciation by itself is irrelevant; it is not a cash outlay. However, depreciation must be considered when *predicting income tax cash outflows*.

3. *Relation to income tax cash flows*. Relevant quantities were defined in Chapter 4, page 88, as expected future data that will differ among alternatives. Given

EXHIBIT 12–6

Perspective on Book Value and Depreciation

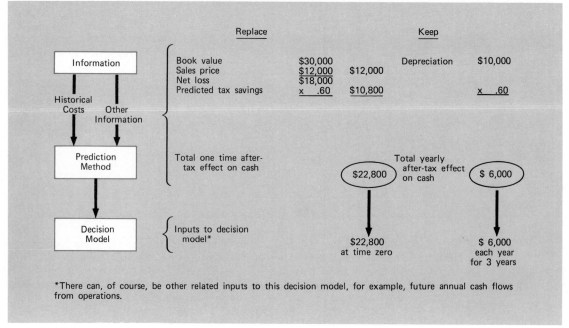

*There can, of course, be other related inputs to this decision model, for example, future annual cash flows from operations.

this definition, book values and past depreciation are irrelevant in all capital-budgeting decision models. The relevant item is the *income tax cash effect*, not the book value or the depreciation. Using the approach in Exhibit 12–6, the book value and depreciation are essential data for the *prediction method*, but the expected future income tax cash disbursements are the relevant data for the decision model.

CAPITAL BUDGETING AND INFLATION

☐ **Watch for Consistency**

Inflation may be defined as the decline in the general purchasing power of the monetary unit. If significant inflation is expected over the life of a project, it should be specifically and consistently analyzed in a capital-budgeting model. Indeed, even a relatively small inflation rate, say, 3%, can have sizable cumulative effects through a series of years.

The key to appropriate consideration of inflation in capital budgeting is *consistent* treatment of the hurdle rate and the predicted cash inflows and outflows. Such consistency can be achieved by including an element for inflation in both the hurdle rate and in the cash inflow and outflow predictions:

1. Market interest rates include an inflation factor. For example, consider a money market account that pays 10% interest. Part of the 10% return compensates an investor for receiving future payments in inflated dollars, that is, in dollars

with less purchasing power than those invested. Therefore, basing the hurdle rate on quoted market rates automatically includes an inflation element in the rate. Such a rate is called a *nominal rate*.

2. Inflation affects many cash inflows and outflows. The predictions used in capital budgeting should include those inflation effects. For example, suppose 1,000 units of a product are expected to be sold in each of the next two years. Assume this year's price is $50 and inflation causes next year's price to be $52.50. This year's predicted cash inflow is 1,000 × $50 = $50,000 and next year's *inflation adjusted* cash inflow is 1,000 × $52.50 = $52,500.

Consider an illustration: purchase cost of equipment, $200,000; useful life, 5 years; zero terminal salvage value; pretax operating cash savings per year, $83,333 (in 19X0 dollars); income tax rate, 40%. For simplicity, ordinary straight-line depreciation of $200,000 ÷ 5 = $40,000 per year is assumed. The after-tax hurdle rate, based on quoted market rates, is 25%. It includes an inflation factor of 10%.

Exhibit 12–7 displays correct and incorrect ways to analyze the effects of inflation. The key words are *internal consistency*. The correct analysis (1) uses a hurdle rate that includes an element attributable to inflation and (2) explicitly adjusts the predicted operating cash flows for the effects of inflation. Note that the correct analysis favors the purchase of the equipment, but the incorrect analysis does not.

The incorrect analysis in Exhibit 12–7 is inherently inconsistent. The predicted cash inflows *exclude* adjustments for inflation. Instead, they are stated in 19X0 dollars. However, the discount rate *includes* an element attributable to inflation. Such an analytical flaw may induce an unwise refusal to purchase.[5]

---

[5] Another correct analysis of inflation uses "real" monetary units (real dollars) exclusively. To be internally consistent, the DCF model would use an inflation-free required rate of return and inflation-free operating cash flows. Using the numbers in Exhibit 12–7, the 25% hurdle rate would be lowered to exclude the 10% expected inflation rate, the $50,000 operating cash savings in 19X0 dollars would be used in 19X1, 19X2, 19X3, and 19X4, and the tax savings due to depreciation would be reduced to 19X0 dollars. Properly used, this type of analysis would lead to the same net present value as the analysis used in Exhibit 12–7. In this case, the inflation-free hurdle rate, also called a *real* rate, would be calculated as follows: (1 + market rate) ÷ (1 + inflation rate) = (1 + inflation-free rate), or 1.25 ÷ 1.10 = 1.13636. The inflation-free rate is 1.13636 − 1 = 13.636%. The net present value can be calculated as follows:

(1) After-tax savings in 19X0 Dollars	(2) Depreciation Tax Savings in 19X0 Dollars*	(3) Total Tax Savings (1) + (2)	(4) PV Factor at 13.636%†	(5) Present Value (3) × (4)
$50,000	$14,545	$64,545	.8800	$ 56,800
50,000	13,223	63,223	.7744	48,960
50,000	12,021	62,021	.6815	42,267
50,000	10,928	60,928	.5997	36,539
50,000	9,935	59,935	.5277	31,628
			Total present value =	$216,194

* $16,000 ÷ 1.10; $16,000 ÷ 1.10²; etc.

† 1 ÷ 1.13636; 1 ÷ 1.13636²; 1 ÷ 1.13636³; etc.

This analysis yields a net present value of $216,194 − $200,000 = $16,194, the same as in Exhibit 12–7 (except for a $2 rounding error).

EXHIBIT 12–7   *(Place a clip on this page for easy reference.)*

Inflation and Capital Budgeting

DESCRIPTION	AT 25% PV Factor	AT 25% Present Value	0	1	2	3	4	5
						SKETCH OF RELEVANT CASH FLOWS (IN DOLLARS)		
End of year								
Correct Analysis (Be sure the discount rate includes an element attributable to inflation and adjust the predicted cash flows for inflationary effects.)								
Cash operating inflows:								
Pretax inflow in 19X0 dollars $83,333								
Income tax effect at 40% 33,333								
After-tax effect on cash $50,000				$55,000*	$60,500	$66,550	$73,205	$80,526
	.8000	$ 44,000						
	.6400	38,720						
	.5120	34,074						
	.4096	29,985						
	.3277	26,388						
Subtotal		$173,167						
Annual depreciation $200,000 ÷ 5 = $40,000 Cash effect of depreciation: savings in income taxes @ 40% = $40,000 × .40 = $16,000	2.6893	43,029		$16,000†	$16,000	$16,000	$16,000	$16,000
Investment in equipment	1.0000	(200,000)	($200,000)					
Net present value		$ 16,196						
Incorrect Analysis (A common error is to adjust the discount rate as above, but *not* adjust the predicted cash inflows.)								
Cash operating inflows after taxes	2.6893	$134,465		$50,000	$50,000	$50,000	$50,000	$50,000
Tax effect of depreciation	2.6893	43,029		16,000	16,000	16,000	16,000	16,000
Investment in equipment	1.0000	(200,000)	($200,000)					
Net present value		$ (22,506)						

* Each year is adjusted for anticipated inflation: $50,000 × 1.10, $50,000 × 1.10^2, $50,000 × 1.10^3, and so on.

† The annual savings in income taxes from depreciation will be unaffected by inflation. Why? Because the income tax deduction must be based on original cost of the asset in 19X0 dollars.

Role of Depreciation

The correct analysis in Exhibit 12–7 shows that the tax effects of depreciation are *not* adjusted for inflation. Why? Because U.S. income tax laws permit a depreciation deduction based on the 19X0 dollars invested, nothing more.

Critics of income tax laws emphasize that capital investment is discouraged by not allowing the adjusting of depreciation deductions for inflationary effects. For instance, the net present value in Exhibit 12–7 would be larger if depreciation were not confined to the $40,000 amount per year. The latter generates a $16,000 saving in 19X1 dollars, then $16,000 in 19X2 dollars, and so forth. Defenders of existing U.S. tax laws assert that capital investment is encouraged in many other ways. The most prominent example is provision for accelerated cost recoveries over lives that are much shorter than the economic lives of the assets.

Improving Predictions and Feedback

The ability to forecast and cope with changing prices is a valuable management skill, especially when inflation is significant. In other words, price variances become more important. Auditing and feedback should help evaluate management's predictive skills.

The adjustment of the operating cash flows in Exhibit 12–7 uses a *general*-price-level index of 10%. However, where feasible use *specific* indexes or tailor-made predictions for price changes in materials, labor, and other items. These predictions may have different percentage changes from year to year.

SUMMARY

Income taxes can have a significant effect on the desirability of an investment. An outlay for a depreciable asset should result in two streams of cash: (a) inflows from operations plus (b) savings of income tax outflows that may be analyzed as additions to cash inflows.

Accelerated depreciation (including the ACRS method) and investment tax credits increase net present value. They have been heavily used by the U.S. Government to encourage investments.

The correct analysis in capital budgeting provides an internally consistent analysis of inflationary aspects. For example, the required rate of return (a) should include an element attributable to anticipated inflation, and (b) predicted operating cash flows should be adjusted for the effects of anticipated inflation.

SUMMARY PROBLEMS FOR YOUR REVIEW

Problem One appeared earlier in this chapter.

Problem Two

Examine the correct analysis in Exhibit 12–7, page 394. Suppose the cash operating inflows persisted for an extra year. Compute the present value of the inflow for the sixth year. Ignore depreciation.

☐ Problem Three

Examine Exhibit 12–5, page 389. Assume an anticipated inflation rate of 12%. How would you change the present values of depreciation under straight line and ACRS to accommodate the inflation rate?

☐ Solution to Problem Two

The cash operating inflow would be $50,000 × 1.10⁶, or $80,526 × 1.10, or $88,579. Its present value would be $88,579 × .2621, the factor from Table 1 (period 6 row, 25% column), or $23,217.

☐ Solution to Problem Three

The straight-line and ACRS computations in Exhibit 12–5 would not be changed. The tax effects of depreciation are unaffected by inflation. U.S. income tax laws permit a deduction based on 19X0 dollars, nothing more.

HIGHLIGHTS TO REMEMBER

1. Managers have an obligation to avoid income taxes. Avoidance is not evasion. *Avoidance* is the use of legal means to minimize tax payments; *evasion* is the use of illegal means. Income tax problems are often exceedingly complex, so qualified counsel should be sought whenever the slightest doubt exists.

2. When income tax rates and required rates of return are high, the attractiveness of immediate deductions heightens. Generally, depreciation deductions should be taken as early as legally permissible.

3. The after-tax impact of operating cash inflows is obtained by multiplying the inflows by 1 minus the tax rate. In contrast, the impact of depreciation on cash flows is obtained by multiplying the depreciation by the tax rate itself.

4. Inflation should be specifically accounted for in a capital-budgeting model. However, expected tax effects of depreciation should not be adjusted because they are unaffected by inflation.

ACCOUNTING VOCABULARY

Accelerated Cost Recovery System (ACRS) *p. 385*   Accelerated Depreciation *384*
Half-year Convention *386*   Inflation *392*   Investment Tax Credit *390*
Tax Shield *381*.

ASSIGNMENT MATERIAL

Special note: Throughout this assignment material, *unless directed otherwise*, assume that

1. All income tax cash flows occur simultaneously with the pretax cash flow.
2. Where ACRS is specified, the straight-line option is *not* chosen.

3. The companies in question will have enough taxable income from other sources to use all income tax benefits from the situations described.
4. There is no investment tax credit.

FUNDAMENTAL ASSIGNMENT MATERIAL

12–1. **STRAIGHT-LINE DEPRECIATION AND PRESENT VALUES.** (Alternate is 12–28.) The president of a machine tool company is considering the purchase of an automated work station. The cost is $400,000, the life is five years, and there is no terminal value. Annual pretax cash inflows from operations would increase by $160,000, the income tax rate is 60%, and the required after-tax rate of return is 14%.

Required:

1. Compute the net present value, assuming straight-line depreciation of $80,000 yearly for tax purposes. Should the equipment be acquired? For simplicity, ignore the half-year convention; that is, take a full year's depreciation each year.
2. Suppose the asset will be fully depreciated at the end of Year 5 but its disposal value will be $40,000. Assume that a full year's depreciation is taken in the fifth year. Should the equipment be acquired? Show computations.
3. Ignore Requirement 2. Suppose the required after-tax rate of return is 10% instead of 14%. Should the equipment be acquired? Show computations.

12–2. **ACRS AND PRESENT VALUES.** (Alternate is 12–29.) The general manager of a fishing company has a chance to purchase a new sonar device for all its vessels at a total cost of $250,000. The ACRS recovery period is five years, and there is no salvage value. Annual pretax cash inflow from operations is $95,000, the economic life of the equipment is five years, there is no terminal salvage value, the income tax rate is 55%, and the after-tax required rate of return is 16%.

Required:

1. Compute the net present value, assuming ACRS basis of accelerated cost recovery. Should the equipment be acquired?
2. Suppose the economic life of the equipment is six years, which means that there will be $95,000 cash inflow from operations in the sixth year. Assume that ACRS is used. Should the equipment be acquired? Show computations.

12–3. **INCOME TAXES AND DISPOSAL OF ASSETS.** (Alternate is 12–30.) Assume that income tax rates are 40%.

1. The book value of an old machine is $20,000. It is to be sold for $6,000 cash. What is the effect of this decision on cash flows, after taxes?
2. The book value of an old machine is $10,000. It is to be sold for $15,000 cash. What is the effect on cash flows, after taxes, of this decision?

12–4. **INFLATION AND CAPITAL BUDGETING.** (Alternate is 12–42.) The head of the mining division of a major conglomerate has proposed investing $250,000 in a mainframe computer. The useful life is only five years with no terminal value. It is a five-year property for ACRS purposes. Labor savings of $125,000 per year (in year zero dollars) are expected from the system. The income tax rate is 55%, the after-tax required rate of return is 25%, which includes an 8% element attributable to inflation.

Required:

1. Compute the net present value of the computer. Use the nominal required rate of return and adjust the cash flows for inflation.
2. Compute the net present value of the computer using the nominal required rate of return without adjusting the cash flows for inflation.
3. Compare your answers in Requirements 1 and 2. Which is correct? Would using the incorrect analysis generally lead to over- or underinvestment?

ADDITIONAL ASSIGNMENT MATERIAL

12-5. Explain why accelerated depreciation methods are superior to straight-line methods for income tax purposes.

12-6. "ACRS does not allow straight-line depreciation." Do you agree? Explain.

12-7. Accelerated depreciation can take many forms. Describe two.

12-8. ACRS provides two types of acceleration. Identify them.

12-9. "The ACRS half-year convention causes assets to be depreciated beyond the lives specified in the ACRS recovery schedules." Do you agree? Explain.

12-10. What are the major influences on the present value of a tax deduction?

12-11. "An investment in equipment really buys two streams of cash." Do you agree? Explain.

12-12. "If income tax rates do not change through the years, my total tax payments will be the same under every depreciation method. Therefore I really do not care what depreciation schedule is permitted." Do you agree? Explain.

12-13. "Immediate disposal of equipment, rather than its continued use, results in a full tax deduction of the undepreciated cost now—rather than having such a deduction spread over future years in the form of annual depreciation." Do you agree? Explain, using the $30,000 book value of old equipment in Exhibit 12-6, page 392, as a basis for your discussion.

12-14. Name some income tax complications that were ignored in the illustrations in this chapter.

12-15. Distinguish between tax avoidance and tax evasion.

12-16. "Tax planning is unimportant because the total income tax bill will be the same in the long run, regardless of short-run maneuvering." Do you agree? Explain.

12-17. Describe how internal consistency is achieved when considering inflation in a capital-budgeting model.

12-18. "Capital investments are always more profitable in inflationary times because the cash inflows from operations generally increase with inflation." Comment on this statement.

12-19. Explain how U.S. tax laws fail to adjust for inflation.

12-20. **ROLE OF DEPRECIATION IN DECISION MODELS.** A student of management accounting complained, "I'm confused about how depreciation relates to decisions. For example, Chapter 5 says that depreciation on old equipment is irrelevant, but depreciation on new equipment is relevant. Chapter 11 said that depreciation was irrelevant in discounted-cash-flow models, but Chapter 12 shows the relevance of depreciation."

Required: | Prepare a careful explanation that will eliminate the student's confusion.

12-21. **DEPRECIATION, INCOME TAXES, CASH FLOWS.** Fill in the unknowns (in thousands of dollars):

(S) Sales	750
(E) Expenses excluding depreciation	550
(D) Depreciation	100
Total expenses	650
Income before income taxes	?
(T) Income taxes at 40%	?
(I) Net income	?
Cash effects of operations:	
Cash inflow from operations	?
Income tax outflow at 40%	?
After-tax inflow from operations	?
Effect of depreciation:	
Depreciation, $100	
Income tax savings	?
Total after-tax effect on cash	160

12–22. DEPRECIATION, INCOME TAXES, CASH FLOWS. Fill in the unknowns (in thousands of dollars):

(S) Sales	?
(E) Expenses excluding depreciation	?
(D) Depreciation	200
Total expenses	900
Income before income taxes	?
(T) Income taxes at 40%	?
(I) Net income	300
Cash effects of operations:	
Cash inflow from operations	?
Income tax outflow at 40%	?
After-tax inflow from operations	?
Effect of depreciation:	
Depreciation, $200	
Income tax savings	?
Total after-tax effect on cash	?

12–23. ACRS RECOVERY PERIODS. Consider the following business assets: (a) a heavy-duty truck, (b) an office word processor, (c) a commercial building, (d) filing cabinets for an office, (e) an electron microscope used in industrial research, and (f) a residential apartment complex. What is the recovery period for each of these assets under the prescribed ACRS method?

12–24. ACRS DEPRECIATION. Airborne Freight Corporation provides overnight delivery of packages throughout the United States. Consider a light-duty van acquired for $20,000 on November 1. Using the prescribed ACRS method, compute the depreciation deduction for tax purposes for the year of purchase and the following year.

12–25. ACRS DEPRECIATION. Puget Sound Ship Builders acquired the following business assets on October 1, 1987: (a) office furniture, $3,000; (b) light truck, $16,000; and (c) tugboat, $25,000. For each asset, compute the depreciation for tax purposes for 1987 and 1988, as prescribed by ACRS.

12–26. ACRS DEPRECIATION. In 1987 the Arnosti Glass Manufacturing Company acquired the following assets and immediately placed them into service:

(1) Special tools (a 3-year ACRS asset) that cost $30,000 on February 1.
(2) A desk-top computer that cost $10,000 on December 15.
(3) Special calibration equipment that was used in research and development and cost $5,000 on July 7.
(4) An office desk that cost $2,000 purchased March 1.

Compute the depreciation for tax purposes, under the prescribed ACRS method in 1987 and 1988.

12–27. ACRS RECOVERY PERIOD. Mississippi Power Company is considering the purchase of some equipment for $1.25 million. The chief financial officer is not sure whether the tax authorities will approve the classification of the equipment as 20-year or 15-year ACRS property. She wants to know how much difference the classification makes. The tax rate is 45%, and the required after-tax rate of return is 14%.

1. Compute the present value of the tax savings if the equipment is classified as 20-year property. As 15-year property.
2. Which classification has the higher present value? by how much?

12–28. STRAIGHT-LINE DEPRECIATION AND PRESENT VALUES. (Alternate is 12–1.) The president of a genetic engineering company is contemplating acquiring some equipment used for research and development. The equipment will cost $150,000 cash and will have a three-year useful life and zero terminal salvage value. Annual pretax cash savings from operations will be $75,000. The income tax rate is 40%, and the required after-tax rate of return is 16%.

1. Compute the net present value, assuming straight-line depreciation of $50,000 yearly for tax purposes.
2. Suppose the asset will be fully depreciated at the end of year 3, but its disposal value will be $18,000. Compute the net present value. Show computations.
3. Ignore Requirement 2. Suppose that the required after-tax rate of return is 12% instead of 16%. Should the equipment be acquired? Show computations.

12–29. ACRS AND PRESENT VALUES. (Alternate is 12–2.) The president of Ohio Valley Electronic Company is considering whether to buy some equipment for the Black River plant. The equipment will cost $1.5 million cash and will have a 10-year useful life and zero terminal salvage value. Annual pretax cash savings from operations will be $370,000. The income tax rate is 40%, and the required after-tax rate of return is 16%.

1. Compute the net present value, using a 7-year ACRS recovery period. Should the equipment be acquired?
2. Suppose the economic life of the equipment is 15 years, which means that there will be $370,000 additional annual cash savings from operations in years 11–15. Assume that a 7-year ACRS recovery period is used. Should the equipment be acquired? Show computations.

12–30. GAINS OR LOSSES ON DISPOSAL. (Alternate is 12–3.) An asset with a book value of $40,000 was sold for cash on January 1, 19X6.

Assume two selling prices: $50,000 and $25,000. For each selling price, prepare a tabulation of the gain or loss, the effect on income taxes, and the total after-tax effect on cash. The applicable income tax rate is 40%.

12–31. INVESTMENT TAX CREDIT. A furniture manufacturing company purchased machinery for $400,000 in late 1985. At that time the company was allowed to take a 10% investment tax credit, but the basis on which ACRS depreciation was taken had to be reduced by one-half of the credit. Investment tax credits are changed by the U.S. Congress almost every year. Remember that an investment tax credit is a direct deduction from taxes equal to the applicable percentage times the cost of the investment. The company has a 16% after-tax required rate of return and a 40% tax rate.

Describe the total effects of the investment tax credit on this investment. Assume the machinery is a five-year property for ACRS purposes, and that ACRS depreciation based on the Internal Revenue Code of 1986 was used. Be specific.

12–32. **TAX INCENTIVES FOR CAPITAL INVESTMENT.** Diamond Vineyards is a successful small winery in California's Napa Valley. The owner, Gino Colucchio, is considering an additional line of business: selling wind-generated electricity to the local utility. California law requires power utilities to purchase windmill electricity. Gino could put windmills on his current land without disturbing the grape crop. A windmill generates 240,000 kilowatt hours annually, and the utility would pay $.05 per kilowatt hour. There are essentially no operating costs.

At the time Gino considered purchasing his first windmill, the cost was $100,000 per windmill. Initially he was discouraged and almost abandoned the idea. But then he learned about three government tax credit programs that applied to investments in windmills. First, a general investment tax credit of 8% could be taken. That is, Diamond's federal income taxes could be immediately reduced by 8% of the cost of the windmill. In addition, windmills qualified for a "business energy credit" of 15%, reducing federal income taxes by another 15% of the cost. Finally, windmills qualified for half of California's 25% solar investment tax credit. This reduced Diamond's California state income tax by 12.5% of the windmill's cost. Despite the tax credits, the full cost can be depreciated.

Assume that windmills are 5-year ACRS property, although the economic life is 20 years. Diamond's required rate of return is 14% after taxes, and the combined federal and state income tax rate is 45%.

Required:
1. Would Gino purchase a windmill without the tax credits? Calculate the net present value.
2. Would Gino purchase a windmill with the tax credits? Calculate the net present value.
3. What is the most that Gino would pay for a windmill, provided the tax credits are available?
4. Evaluate the effect of tax credits on stimulating investment.

12–33. **FOOTBALL COACHING CONTRACT.** (H. Schaefer.) Bo Hays, a successful college football coach, has just signed a "million-dollar-plus" contract to coach a new professional team. The contract is a personal services contract for 5 years with the team's owner, I. M. Rich (if the team is disbanded Bo can still collect from Rich). Under the terms of the contract, Bo will be paid $150,000 cash at the start of the contract plus $150,000 at the end of each of the 5 years. Rich also agrees to buy a $275,000 house that Bo can use rent-free for all 5 years.

Rich earns a substantial income from numerous business ventures. His marginal tax rate is about 60%. Bo's cash salary payments are tax deductible to Rich, as are the depreciation expenses on the house. Rich will depreciate the house over a 27.5-year life with zero salvage value using the straight-line method of depreciation. Rich is certain the house can be sold at the end of 5 years for a price equal to its remaining book value. For simplicity, assume that a full year of ordinary straight-line depreciation of the entire purchase price of the house is permissible each of the five years for tax purposes. There is no investment tax credit on the house.

Required:
1. Determine Rich's yearly after-tax cash outflows under Bo's contract.
2. Given your answers to Requirement 1, calculate the net present value of the costs of Bo's contract to Rich, assuming Rich employs a 10% minimum desired rate of return. Show your calculations clearly and in an orderly fashion. You may round to the nearest thousand dollars.

12–34. **PRESENT VALUE OF AFTER-TAX CASH FLOWS.** Tsumagari Company, an electronics company in Kobe, Japan, is planning to buy new equipment to produce a new product. Estimated data are (monetary amounts are in Japanese yen):

Cash cost of new equipment now	¥400,000
Estimated life in years	10
Terminal salvage value	¥ 50,000
Incremental revenues per year	¥300,000
Incremental expenses per year other than depreciation	¥165,000

Assume a 60% flat rate for income taxes. All revenue and expenses other than depreciation will be received or paid in cash. Use a 14% discount rate. Assume that ordinary straight-line depreciation (ignoring the half-year convention)based on a ten-year useful life is permissible for tax purposes. Also assume that the terminal salvage value will affect the depreciation per year.

Required:

Compute:

1. Depreciation expense per year.
2. Anticipated net income per year.
3. Annual net cash inflow.
4. Payback period.
5. Accounting rate of return on initial investment.
6. Net present value.

12–35. **ACRS AND REPLACEMENT OF EQUIPMENT.** Refer to Problem 5–31, page 147. Assume that income tax rates are 60%. The minimum desired rate of return, after taxes, is 6%. Using the net-present-value technique, show whether the proposed equipment should be purchased. Present your solution on both a total project approach and an incremental approach. For illustrative purposes, assume that the old equipment would have been depreciated on a straight-line basis and the proposed equipment on an ACRS basis of accelerated cost recovery. Assume it is three-year ACRS property.

12–36. **ACRS, RESIDUAL VALUE.** The Gooden Company estimates that it can save $10,000 per year annual operating cash costs for the next five years if it buys a special-purpose machine at a cost of $33,000. Residual value is expected to be $7,000, although no residual value is being provided for in using ACRS (five-year life and accelerated depreciation) for tax purposes. The equipment will be sold at the beginning of the sixth year; for purposes of this analysis assume that the proceeds are received at the end of the fifth year. The minimum desired rate of return, after taxes, is 10%. Assume the income tax rate is 45%.

Required:

1. Using the net-present-value model, show whether the investment is desirable.
2. Suppose the equipment will produce savings for six years instead of five. Residual value is expected to be the same a year later. Using the net-present-value model, show whether the investment is desirable.

12–37. **PURCHASE OF EQUIPMENT.** The O'Neill Company is planning to spend $45,000 for modernized production equipment. It will replace equipment that has zero book value and no salvage value, although the old equipment would last another seven years.

The new equipment will save $13,500 in cash operating costs for each of the next seven years, at which time it will be sold for $3,000. A major overhaul costing $4,000 will occur at the end of the fourth year; the old equipment would require no such overhaul. The entire cost of the overhaul is deductible for tax purposes in the fourth year. The equipment is five-year property for ACRS purposes.

The minimum desired rate of return after taxes is 12%. The applicable income tax rate is 60%.

Compute the after-tax net present value. Is the new equipment a desirable investment?

12–38. MAKE OR BUY AND REPLACEMENT OF EQUIPMENT. Toyland Company was one of the original producers of "transformers." An especially complex part of 'Sect-a-con needs special tools that are not useful for other products. These tools were purchased on November 16, 19X3 for $200,000.

It is now July 1, 19X7. The manager of the Transformer Division, Ramona Ruiz, is contemplating three alternatives. First, she could continue to produce 'Sect-a-con using the current tools; they will last another five years, at which time they would have zero terminal value. Second, she could sell the tools for $30,000 and purchase the parts from an outside supplier for $1.10 each. Third, she could replace the tools with new, more efficient tools costing $180,000.

Ruiz expects to produce 80,000 units of 'Sect-a-con each of the next five years. Manufacturing costs for the part have been as follows, and no change in costs is expected:

Direct material	$ .38
Direct labor	.37
Variable overhead	.17
Fixed overhead*	.45
Total unit cost	$1.37

* Depreciation accounts for two-thirds of the fixed overhead. The balance is for other fixed overhead costs of the factory that require cash outlays, 60% of which would be saved if production of the parts were eliminated.

The outside supplier offered the $1.10 price as a once-only offer. It is unlikely such a low price would be available later. Toyland would also have to guarantee to purchase at least 70,000 parts for each of the next five years.

The new tools that are available would last for five years with a disposal value of $40,000 at the end of five years. Both the old and new tools are five-year ACRS property, and both use the current ACRS schedules. Straight-line depreciation is used for book purposes and ACRS for tax purposes. The sales representative selling the new tools stated, "The new tools will allow direct labor and variable overhead to be reduced by $.21 per unit." Ruiz thinks this estimate is accurate. However, she also knows that a higher quality of materials would be necessary with the new tools. She predicts the following costs with the new tools:

Direct material	$ .40
Direct labor	.25
Variable overhead	.08
Fixed overhead	.60*
Total unit cost	$1.33

* The increase in fixed overhead is caused by depreciation on the new tools.

The company has a 40% marginal tax rate and requires a 12% after-tax rate of return.

1. Calculate the net present value of each of the three alternatives. Recognize all applicable tax implications. Which alternative should Ruiz select?
2. What are some factors besides the net present value that should influence Ruiz's selection?

12–39. MINIMIZING TRANSPORTATION COSTS. The Harris Company produces industrial and residential lighting fixtures at its manufacturing facility in Los Angeles. Shipment of company products to an eastern warehouse is presently handled by common carriers at a rate of 25¢ per pound of fixtures (expressed in year zero dollars). The warehouse is located in Cleveland, 2,500 miles from Los Angeles.

The treasurer of Harris Company is presently considering whether to purchase a truck for transporting products to the eastern warehouse. The following data on the truck are available:

Purchase price	$35,000
Useful life	5 years
Terminal residual value	Zero
Capacity of truck	10,000 lb
Cash costs of operating truck	$.90 per mile
	(expressed in year 1 dollars)

The treasurer feels that an investment in this truck is particularly attractive because of his successful negotiation with X Company to back-haul X's products from Cleveland to Los Angeles on every return trip from the warehouse. X has agreed to pay Harris $2,400 per load of X's products hauled from Cleveland to Los Angeles for as many loads as Harris can accommodate, up to and including 100 loads per year over the next five years.

The Harris marketing manager has estimated that 500,000 pounds of fixtures will have to be shipped to the eastern warehouse each year for the next five years. The truck will be fully loaded on each round trip.

Make the following assumptions:
a. Harris requires a minimum 20% after-tax rate of return, which includes a 10% element attributable to inflation.
b. A 40% tax rate.
c. ACRS based on 5-year cost recovery period.
d. An inflation rate of 10%.

1. Should the truck be purchased? Show computations to support your answer.
2. What qualitative factors might influence your decision? Be specific.

12–40. ACRS AND LOW-INCOME HOUSING. Carver Jackson is a real estate developer who specializes in residential apartments. A complex of 20 run-down apartments has recently come on the market for $155,000. Jackson predicts that after remodeling, the 12 one-bedroom units will rent for $190 per month and the 8 two-bedroom apartments for $220. He budgets 15% of the rental fees for repairs and maintenance. The apartments should last for 30 years if the remodeling is done well. Remodeling costs are $6,000 per apartment. Both purchase price and remodeling costs qualify as 27.5-year ACRS property.

The ACRS schedule assigns an equal amount of depreciation to each of the first 27 years and one-half year to the 28th year. The present value at 10% of $1 of cost recovery spread over the 28 years in this way is .3372.

Jackson does not believe he will keep the apartment complex for its entire 30-year life. Most likely he will sell it just after the end of the tenth year. His predicted sales price is $400,000.

Jackson's after-tax required rate of return is 10%, and his tax rate is 35%.

Should Jackson buy the apartment complex? What is the after-tax net present value? Ignore the investment tax credit and other tax complications such as capital gains.

12–41. **INFLATION AND NONPROFIT INSTITUTION.** Veterans' Hospital is considering the purchase of a photocopying machine for $7,000 on December 31, 19X7, useful life five years, and no residual value. The cash operating savings are expected to be $2,000 annually, measured in 19X7 dollars.

The hurdle rate is 14%, which includes an element attributable to anticipated inflation of 6%.

Use the 14% hurdle rate for Requirements 1 and 2:

1. Compute the net present value of the project without adjusting the cash operating savings for inflation.
2. Repeat Requirement 1, adjusting the cash operating savings upward in accordance with the 6% inflation rate.
3. Compare your results in Requirements 1 and 2. What generalization seems applicable about the analysis of inflation in capital budgeting?

12–42. **SENSITIVITY OF CAPITAL BUDGETING TO INFLATION.** (Alternate is 12–4.) G. Lockwood, the president of a Toronto trucking company, is considering whether to invest $410,000 in new semiautomatic loading equipment that will last five years, have zero scrap value, and generate cash operating savings in labor usage of $160,000 annually, using 19X7 prices and wage rates. It is December 31, 19X7. The minimum desired rate of return is 18% per year after taxes.

1. Compute the net present value of the project. Assume a 40% tax rate and, for simplicity, assume ordinary straight-line depreciation of $410,000 ÷ 5 = $82,000 annually for tax purposes.
2. Lockwood is wondering if the model in Requirement 1 provides a correct analysis of the effects of inflation. She maintains that the 18% rate embodies an element attributable to anticipated inflation. For purposes of this analysis, she assumes that the existing rate of inflation, 10% annually, will persist over the next five years. Repeat Requirement 1, adjusting the cash operating savings upward in accordance with the 10% inflation rate.
3. Which analysis, the one in Requirement 1 or 2, is correct? Why?

12–43. **NOMINAL AND REAL RATES.** The Romano Company is considering the purchase of a labor-saving piece of equipment on January 2, 19X7 for $600,000. The useful life is five years, there is no salvage value, cost savings of $250,000 (in January 1, 19X7 dollars) per year are expected, and the tax rate is 40%. The real (inflation-free) hurdle rate is 10% and the inflation rate is 8%. Therefore, the nominal hurdle rate is 18.8%. The present value factors for 18.8% are:

Year	1	2	3	4	5	Total
Factor	.8418	.7085	.5964	.5020	.4226	3.0713

For simplicity, assume that straight-line depreciation of $600,000 ÷ 5 = $120,000 per year is used for tax purposes with a full year of depreciation each of the five years. Also assume that cash flows occur at the end of each year. For example, the first year's cash saving is 1.08 × $250,000 = $270,000 on December 31, 19X7.

1. Calculate the present value of the investment using the nominal rate, as in Exhibit 12–7, page 394.
2. Calculate the present value of the investment using the real rate, as described in footnote 4, page 393.
3. Compare the present values in Requirements 1 and 2.

12–44. **APPROACHES TO INFLATION.** (CMA, adapted.) Catix Corporation is a division-alized company, and each division has the authority to make capital expenditures up to $200,000 without approval of the corporate headquarters. The corporate controller has determined that the cost of capital for Catix Corporation is 21%. This rate includes an allowance for inflation, which is expected to occur at an average rate of 8% over the next five years. Catix pays income taxes at the rate of 40%.

The Electronics Division of Catix is considering the purchase of an auto-mated assembly and soldering machine for use in the manufacture of its printed circuit boards. The machine would be placed in service in early 1987. The divi-sional controller estimates that if the machine is purchased, two positions will be eliminated yielding a cost savings for wages and employee benefits. However, the machine would require additional supplies, and more power would be required to operate the machine. The cost savings and additional costs in current 1986 prices are as follows:

Wages and employee benefits of the two positions eliminated ($25,000 each)	$50,000
Cost of additional supplies	$ 3,000
Cost of additional power	$10,000

The new machine would be purchased and installed at the end of 1986 at a net cost of $80,000. If purchased, the machine would be depreciated on a straight-line basis at $20,000 per year for both book and tax purposes. The machine will become technologically obsolete in four years and will have no salvage value at that time.

The Electronics Division compensates for inflation in capital expenditure analyses by adjusting the expected cash flows by an estimated price-level index. The adjusted after-tax cash flows are then discounted using the appropriate dis-count rate. The estimated year-end index values for each of the next five years are presented below.

YEAR	YEAR-END PRICE INDEX
1986	1.00
1987	1.08
1988	1.17
1989	1.26
1990	1.36
1991	1.47

The Plastics Division of Catix compensates for inflation in capital expenditure analyses by using a cost of capital (21%) that includes an inflation factor to discount the project cash flows. The Plastics Division recently rejected a project with cash flows and economic life similar to those associated with the machine under consideration by the Electronics Division. The Plastics Division's analysis of the rejected project was as follows:

Net pretax cost savings	$37,000
Less incremental depreciation expenses	20,000
Increase in taxable income	$17,000
Increase in income taxes (40%)	6,800
Increase in after-tax income	$10,200
Add back noncash expense (depreciation)	20,000
Net after-tax annual cash inflow (unadjusted for inflation)	$30,200
Present value of net cash inflows using a minimum required return of 21%	$76,708
Investment required	(80,000)
Net present value	$ (3,292)

All operating revenues and expenditures occur at the end of the year. Appropriate 21% discount factors follow:

	END OF PERIOD				
	1	2	3	4	5
Single payment	.83	.68	.56	.47	.39
Annuity	.83	1.51	2.07	2.54	2.93

Required:

1. Using the price index provided, prepare a schedule showing the net after-tax annual cash flows adjusted for inflation for the automated assembly and soldering machine under consideration by the Electronics Division.
2. Without prejudice to your answer to Requirement 1, assume that the net after-tax annual cash flows adjusted for inflation for the project being considered by the Electronics Division are as follows:

	1987	1988	1989	1990
Net after-tax annual cash flow adjusted for inflation	$30,000	$35,000	$37,000	$40,000

Calculate the net present value for Electronic Division's project that will be meaningful to management.

3. Evaluate the methods used by the Plastics Division and the Electronics Division to compensate for expected inflation in capital expenditure analyses.

Chapter 13

JOB-COSTING SYSTEMS AND OVERHEAD APPLICATION

LEARNING OBJECTIVES

When you have finished studying this chapter, you should be able to:

1. Distinguish between the two fundamental types of product-costing systems: job-order and process.
2. Prepare summary journal entries for the typical transactions of a job-costing system.
3. Compute predetermined factory overhead rates, factory overhead applied to production, and the amounts of over-applied and underapplied factory overhead.
4. Identify the meaning and purpose of normalized overhead rates.
5. Describe the two methods and their rationale for disposing of underapplied and overapplied overhead at the end of a year.
6. Explain an operation or hybrid costing system.

This chapter and the next two show how data may be accumulated within an accounting system and how various alternative methods of applying costs to products affect inventories and income determination. These are essentially scorekeeping tasks. Management makes policy decisions, at one time or another, regarding methods of product costing. Because such decisions affect the way net income will be determined, managers should know the various approaches to product costing. Moreover, as we have seen previously, a knowledge of product-costing techniques will enhance a manager's understanding of product costs, particularly when the latter are used for pricing and evaluating product lines. Keep in mind that *product costing* is separable from *control*. That is, a good planning and control system may be coupled with any of a number of product-costing practices.

This chapter may be studied immediately after Chapter 3 without loss of continuity. Therefore, to begin, review the first two sections of Chapter 3 ("Classifications of Costs" and "Relationships of Income Statements and Balance Sheets") and the Chapter 3 Appendix ("Classification of Labor Costs"). It is not necessary to review the other parts of Chapter 3.

Our focus is on manufacturing costs, because accountants view selling, administrative, and other nonmanufacturing costs as being expenses immediately and therefore totally excludable from costs of *product* for inventory valuation purposes.

DISTINCTION BETWEEN JOB COSTING AND PROCESS COSTING

Recall that Chapter 3 defined *cost objective* as any activity for which a separate measurement of costs is desired. Two principal cost objectives were illustrated: departments and products. Cost-accounting systems have a twofold purpose fulfilled by their day-to-day operations: (1) allocate costs to departments for planning and control, hereafter for brevity's sake often called *control*, and (2) allocate costs to units of product for *product costing*.

Two extremes of product costing are usually termed **job-order costing** and **process costing**. *Job-order* (or *job-cost* or *production-order*) accounting methods are used by companies whose products are readily identified by individual units or batches, each of which receives varying degrees of attention and skill. Industries that commonly use job-order methods include construction, printing, aircraft, furniture, and machinery.

Process costing is most often found in such industries as chemicals, oil, textiles, plastics, paints, flour, canneries, rubber, lumber, food processing, glass, mining, cement, and meat packing. In these there is mass production of like units, which usually pass in continuous fashion through a series of uniform production steps called *operations* or *processes*. This is in contrast to the production of tailor-made or unique goods, such as special-purpose machinery or printing.

The distinction between the job-cost and the process-cost methods centers largely on how product costing is accomplished. Unlike process costing, which deals with great masses of like units and broad averages of unit costs, the essential feature of the job-cost method is the attempt to apply costs to specific jobs, which may consist of either a single physical unit (such as a custom sofa) or a few like units (such as a dozen tables) in a distinct batch or job lot.

The most important point is that product costing is an *averaging* process. The unit cost used for inventory purposes is the result of taking some accumulated cost that has been allocated to production departments and dividing it by some measure of production. The basic distinction between job-order costing and process costing is the breadth of the denominator: in job-order costing, it is small (for example, one painting, 100 advertising circulars, or one special packaging machine); but in process costing, it is large (for example, thousands of pounds, gallons, or board feet).

ILLUSTRATION OF JOB-ORDER COSTING

☐ **Data for Illustration**

This section illustrates the principal aspects of a job-costing system, including the basic records and journal entries. Consider the Martinez Electronics Company, which has a job-order cost system with the following inventories on December 31, 19X1:

Direct materials (12 types)	$110,000
Work in process	—
Finished goods (unsold units from two jobs)	12,000

The following is a summary of events for the year 19X2:

	MACHINING	ASSEMBLY	TOTAL
1. Direct materials purchased on account	—	—	$1,900,000
2. Direct materials requisitioned for manufacturing	$1,000,000	$890,000	1,890,000
3. Direct-labor costs incurred	200,000	190,000	390,000
4a. Factory overhead **incurred**	290,000	102,000	392,000
4b. Factory overhead **applied**	280,000	95,000	375,000
5. Cost of goods completed and transferred to finished-goods inventory	—	—	2,500,000
6a. Sales on account	—	—	4,000,000
6b. Cost of goods sold	—	—	2,480,000

Most of the foregoing data are straightforward and easy to understand. However, the term *factory overhead applied* is being introduced here for the first time. It will be explained later in this chapter.

The accounting for these events will now be explained, step by step.

☐ Basic Records

The bulk of the scorekeeping is a detailed recording and summarization of source documents such as requisitions, work tickets, and invoices. In January 19X2 several jobs were begun. For example, Job 404 was begun and completed. Exhibit 13–1 is the completed *job-cost sheet* or *job order*.

As Exhibit 13–1 illustrates, the job-cost sheet is the basic record for product costing. A file of current job-cost sheets (or similar computer records)

EXHIBIT 13–1

Completed Job Cost Sheet and Sample Source Documents

Job Order No. ___404___

MACHINING DEPARTMENT

Reference	Date	Quantity	Unit Cost	Amount	Summary
Direct materials:					
Type M—					
Various requisitions	Various	900	$2.00	$1,800	
Type N—					
Various requisitions	Various	900	5.00	4,500	$ 6,300
Direct labor:					
Various time tickets	Various	320 hrs	9.00	2,880	2,880
Factory overhead applied		425 mach. hrs	4.00	1,700	1,700
Total machining					$10,880

ASSEMBLY DEPARTMENT

(Entries would be similar to above)					xxx
Total assembly (assumed)					$ 2,000
Total product cost					$12,880

Sample Source Documents

Direct Material Requisition No. ✗✗

Job No. __404__ Date _Jan. 5, 19X2_
Department _Machining_ Account _Work in process_

Description	Quantity	Unit Cost	Amount
	XX	X	XX

Time Ticket No. ✗✗

Job No. __404__ Date _Jan. 7, 19X2_
Department _Machining_ Account _Work in process_
Operation _Drill_

Units: Start _3:00 p.m._ Rate ____
   Worked   10
   Rejected ___—___ Stop _4:15 p.m._ Amount ____
   Completed 10

becomes the subsidiary ledger for the general ledger account, Work-in-Process Inventory, often simply called Work in Process (sometimes abbreviated WIP). As each job begins, a job-cost sheet is prepared. As units are worked on, entries are made on the job-cost sheet. Three classes of costs are applied to the units as they pass through the departments: material requisitions are used to apply costs of direct material, time tickets (also called work tickets) are used to apply costs of direct labor, and *predetermined* overhead rates are used to apply factory overhead to products. The computation of these rates will be described in the next major section of this chapter.

Exhibit 13–2 is an overview of the general flow of costs through a job-order costing system. The top half of the exhibit summarizes the effects of transactions on the key manufacturing accounts in the general ledger. The bottom half shows the key subsidiary ledger records and also indicates the source documents for the major transactions. As you proceed through the detailed explanation of transactions, keep checking each explanation against the overview in Exhibit 13–2.

☐ **Explanation of Transactions**

The following transaction-by-transaction summary analysis will explain how product costing is achieved.

1. Transaction: Direct materials purchased, $1,900,000.

Analysis: The asset Direct-Materials Inventory is increased. The liability Accounts Payable is increased.

Entry: In the journal (explanation omitted):

Direct-materials inventory	1,900,000	
Accounts payable		1,900,000

Post to the ledger:

Direct-Materials Inventory			Accounts Payable	
Bal.	110,000		1.	1,900,000
1.	1,900,000			

2. Transaction: Direct materials requisitioned, $1,890,000.

Analysis: The asset Work in Process (Inventory) is increased. The asset Direct-Materials Inventory is decreased.

Entry: In the journal:

Work in process	1,890,000	
Direct-materials inventory		1,890,000

Post to the ledger:

Direct-Materials Inventory				Work in Process	
Bal.	110,000	2.	1,890,000	2.	1,890,000
1.	1,900,000				
Bal.	120,000				

EXHIBIT 13–2

Job-order Costing, General Flow of Costs (in thousands)

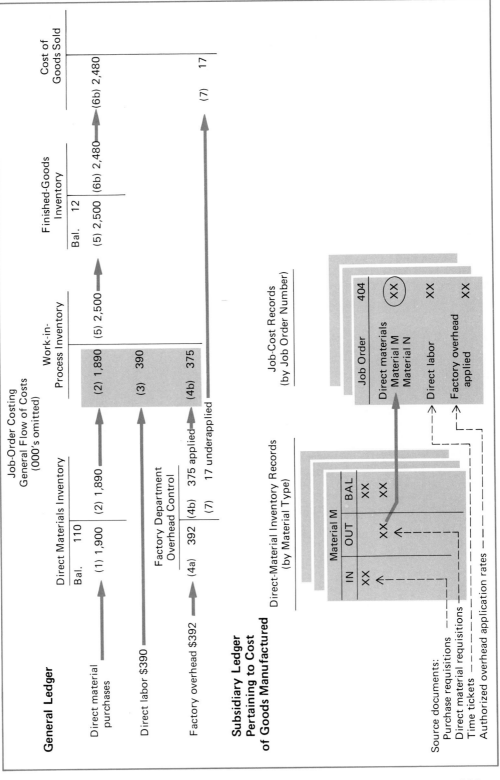

Job-Order Costing
General Flow of Costs
(000's omitted)

General Ledger

Direct Materials Inventory

Bal. 110 | (2) 1,890
(1) 1,900 |

Direct material purchases

Work-in-Process Inventory

(2) 1,890 | (5) 2,500
(3) 390 |
(4b) 375 |

Direct labor $390

Factory Department Overhead Control

(4a) 392 | (4b) 375 applied
| (7) 17 underapplied

Factory overhead $392

Finished-Goods Inventory

Bal. 12 | (6b) 2,480
(5) 2,500 |

Cost of Goods Sold

(6b) 2,480
(7) 17

Subsidiary Ledger Pertaining to Cost of Goods Manufactured

Direct-Material Inventory Records (by Material Type)

Material M

IN	OUT	BAL
XX	XX	XX
	XX	XX

Job-Cost Records (by Job Order Number)

Job Order 404

Job Order

Direct materials
Material M   XX
Material N   XX

Direct labor   XX

Factory overhead applied   XX

Source documents:
Purchase requisitions
Direct material requisitions
Time tickets
Authorized overhead application rates

413

3. Transaction: Direct-labor costs incurred, $390,000.

Analysis: The asset Work in Process (Inventory) is increased. The liability Accrued Payroll is increased.

Entry: In the journal:

Work in process	390,000	
Accrued payroll		390,000

Post to the ledger:

Accrued Payroll			Work in Process		
	3.	390,000	2.	1,890,000	
			3.	390,000	

4a. Transaction: Factory overhead incurred, $392,000.

Analysis: These actual costs are first charged to departmental overhead accounts, which may be regarded as assets until their amounts are later "cleared" or transferred to other accounts. Each department has detailed overhead accounts such as indirect labor, utilities, repairs, depreciation, insurance, and property taxes. These details support a summary factory department overhead control account. The managers are responsible for regulating these costs, item by item. As these costs are charged to the departments, the other accounts affected will be assorted assets and liabilities. Examples include cash, accounts payable, accrued payables, and accumulated depreciation.

Entry: In the journal:

Factory department overhead control	392,000	

Cash, accounts payable, and
      various other balance sheet
      accounts
		392,000

Post to the ledger:

Factory Department Overhead Control		Various Balance Sheet Accounts	
4a.	392,000		4a.	392,000

4b. Transaction: Factory overhead applied, $95,000 + $280,000 = $375,000.

Analysis: The asset Work in Process (Inventory) is increased. The asset Factory Department Overhead Control is decreased. (A fuller explanation occurs later in this chapter.)

Entry: In the journal:

Work in process	375,000	
Factory department overhead control		375,000

Post to the ledger:

Factory Department Overhead Control			Work in Process		
4a.	392,000	4b. 375,000	2.	1,890,000	
			3.	390,000	
			4b.	375,000	

5. Transaction: Cost of goods completed, $2,500,000.

Analysis: The asset Finished Goods (Inventory) is increased. The asset Work in Process (Inventory) is decreased.

Entry: In the journal:

Finished goods	2,500,000	
Work in process		2,500,000

Post to the ledger:

	Work in Process				Finished Goods	
2.	1,890,000	5.	2,500,000	Bal.	12,000	
3.	390,000			5.	2,500,000	
4b.	375,000					
Bal.	155,000					

6a. Transaction: Sales on account, $4,000,000.

    Analysis: The asset Accounts Receivable is increased. The revenue Sales is increased.

    Entry: In the journal:

        Accounts receivable   4,000,000

           Sales   4,000,000

        Post to the ledger:

	Accounts Receivable			Sales	
6a.	4,000,000			6a.	4,000,000

6b. Transaction: Cost of goods sold, $2,480,000.

    Analysis: The expense Cost of Goods Sold is increased. The asset Finished Goods is decreased.

    Entry: In the journal:

        Cost of goods sold   2,480,000

           Finished goods   2,480,000

        Post to the ledger:

	Finished Goods				Cost of Goods Sold	
Bal.	12,000	6b.	2,480,000	6b.	2,480,000	
5.	2,500,000					
Bal.	32,000					

☐ Summary of Transactions

Exhibit 13–2 summarizes the Martinez transactions for the year. The selected accounts from the general ledger focus on how product costing is accomplished. All the inventory accounts are presented. Work in Process receives central attention. The costs of direct material used, direct labor, and factory overhead applied to product are brought into Work in Process. In turn, the costs of completed goods are transferred to Finished Goods. As goods are sold, their costs become expense in the form of Cost of Goods Sold. The year-end accounting for the $17,000 of underapplied overhead is explained later.

APPLICATION OF OVERHEAD TO PRODUCTS

☐ Cost Application

Consider a new term, *cost application*, often called *cost absorption*. Until now the term cost allocation has been used indiscriminately to refer to the identifying or tracing of accumulated costs to *any* cost objective (whether a department or a product). Indeed, *cost allocation* is a general term. However, when costs are allocated to *products*, the process of allocation is frequently called *application* or *absorption*. These latter terms will be used in this chapter. In any event, be alert to obtain the exact meanings of such terms when you encounter them in practice.

☐ Predetermined Overhead Application Rates

To show how factory overhead is applied to jobs, explore the Martinez illustration in more depth.

The following manufacturing overhead budget has been prepared for the coming year, 19X2:

	MACHINING	ASSEMBLY
Indirect labor	$ 75,600	$ 36,800
Supplies	8,400	2,400
Utilities	20,000	7,000
Repairs	10,000	3,000
Factory rent	10,000	6,800
Supervision	32,600	30,400
Depreciation on equipment	114,000	14,400
Insurance, property taxes, etc.	7,200	2,400
	$277,800	$103,200

As products are worked on, factory overhead is applied to the jobs. A predetermined overhead rate is used, computed as follows:

$$\text{overhead application rate} = \frac{\text{total budgeted factory overhead}}{\substack{\text{total budgeted amount of application} \\ \text{base (such as direct-labor costs,} \\ \text{direct-labor-hours, or machine-hours)}}}$$

In our illustration, the overhead rates are as follows:

	YEAR 19X2	
	Machining	Assembly
Budgeted manufacturing overhead	$277,800	$103,200
Budgeted machine-hours	69,450	
Budgeted direct-labor cost		206,400
Predetermined overhead rate, per machine-hour: $277,800 ÷ 69,450 =	$4	
Predetermined overhead rate, per direct-labor dollar: $103,200 ÷ $206,400 =		50%

Note that the overhead rates are predetermined; they are estimates. These rates are then used to apply overhead based on *actual* events. That is, the total overhead applied in our illustration is the result of multiplying *actual* machine-hours or labor dollars by the *budgeted* overhead rates:

Machining: Actual machine-hours of 70,000 × $4 = $280,000
Assembly: Actual direct labor of $190,000 × .50 = 95,000
Total factory overhead applied $375,000

The summary journal entry for the application (entry 4b) is:

| 4b. | Work in process | 375,000 | |
| | Factory department overhead control | | 375,000 |

☐ Choosing the Application Base

Factory overhead is a conglomeration of manufacturing costs that, unlike direct material or direct labor, cannot conveniently be applied on an individual basis. But such overhead is an integral part of a product's total cost. Therefore it is applied in an indirect manner, using a cost-allocation base that is common to all jobs worked on and is the best available index of the product's relative use of, or benefits from, the overhead items. In other words, there should be a strong correlation between the factory overhead incurred and the base chosen for its application, such as machine-hours or direct-labor cost.

In the machining department, two or more machines can often be operated simultaneously by a single direct laborer. Use of machines generates most overhead cost in the machining department, for example, depreciation, repairs. Therefore, machine-hours are the base for application of overhead costs. This necessitates keeping track of the machine-hours used for each job, creating an added data collection cost. Thus, both direct-labor costs and machine-hours must be accumulated for each job.

In contrast, the workers in the assembly department are paid equal hourly rates, so the cost of direct labor is an accurate reflection of the relative attention and effort devoted to various jobs. No separate job records have to be kept of the labor *hours*. All that is needed is to apply the 50% overhead rate to the cost of direct labor already entered on the job-cost sheets. Of course, if the hourly labor rates differ greatly for individuals performing identical tasks, hours of labor, rather than dollars spent for labor, would have to be used as a base. Otherwise, a $9-per-hour worker would cause more overhead applied than an $8-per-hour worker, even though the same time would probably be taken and the same facilities used by each employee for the same work.

Sometimes direct-labor dollars is the best overhead allocation base even if wage rates vary within a department. For example, higher skilled labor may use more costly equipment and have more indirect labor support. Moreover, many factory overhead costs include costly labor fringe benefits such as pensions and payroll taxes. The latter are more closely related to direct-labor dollars than to direct-labor-hours.

No matter which cost allocation bases are chosen, the overhead rates are used day after day throughout the year to cost the various jobs worked on by each department. All overhead is applied to all jobs worked on during the year on the appropriate basis of machine-hours or direct-labor costs of each job. If management predictions are accurate, the total overhead applied to the year's jobs via these predetermined rates should be equal to the total overhead costs actually incurred.

PROBLEMS OF OVERHEAD APPLICATION

☐ Normalized Overhead Rates

Few companies wait until the *actual* factory overhead is finally known before the costs of products are computed. Instead, a *budgeted* or predetermined overhead rate is commonly used because most managements want a close approximation of the cost of different products before the end of a fiscal period. Essentially this need is for pricing, interim income determination, and inventory valuation.

Basically, our illustration has demonstrated the *normal costing* approach. Why? Because an annual average overhead rate is used consistently throughout the year for product costing, without altering it from day to day and from month to month. The resultant "normal" product costs include an average or normalized chunk of overhead.

As actual overhead costs are incurred by departments from month to month, they are charged, in detail, to the departments. These actual costs are accumulated weekly or monthly and are then compared with budgeted costs to obtain budget variances for performance evaluation. This *control* process is completely divorced from the *product-costing* process of applying overhead to specific jobs.

During the year and at year end, the amount incurred will rarely equal the amount applied. This variance between incurred and applied cost can be analyzed. The following are usually contributory causes: poor forecasting; inefficient use of overhead items; price changes in individual overhead items; erratic behavior of individual overhead items (e.g., repairs made only during slack time); calendar variations (e.g., 20 workdays in one month, 22 in the next); and, probably most important, operating at a different level of volume than the level used as a denominator in calculating the predetermined overhead rate (e.g., using 100,000 forecasted direct-labor-hours as the denominator and then actually working only 80,000 hours).

All these peculiarities of overhead are mingled in an annual overhead pool. Thus an annual rate is predetermined and used regardless of the month-to-month peculiarities of specific overhead costs. Such an approach is more defensible than, say, applying the actual overhead for each month, because a *normal* product cost is more useful for decisions, and more representative for inventory-costing purposes, than an "actual" product cost that is distorted by month-to-month fluctuations in production volume and by the erratic behavior of many overhead costs. For example, the employees of a gypsum plant had the privilege of buying company-made items "at cost." It was a joke common among employees to buy "at cost" during high-volume months. Unit costs were then lower under the actual overhead application system in use, whereby overhead rates would fall as volume soared, and vice versa, as shown here:

| | ACTUAL OVERHEAD | | | DIRECT-LABOR-HOURS | ACTUAL OVERHEAD APPLICATION RATE* PER DIRECT-LABOR-HOUR |
	Variable	Fixed	Total		
Peak-volume month	$60,000	$40,000	$100,000	100,000	$1.00
Low-volume month	30,000	40,000	70,000	50,000	1.40

* Divide total overhead by direct-labor hours. Note that the presence of fixed overhead causes the fluctuation in unit costs from $1.00 to $1.40. The variable component is $.60 an hour in both months, but the fixed component is $.40 in the peak-volume month ($40,000 ÷ 100,000) and $.80 in the low-volume month ($40,000 ÷ 50,000).

☐ Disposition of Underapplied or Overapplied Overhead

Our Martinez illustration contained the following data:

Transaction	
4a. Factory overhead incurred	$392,000
4b. Factory overhead applied	375,000
Underapplied factory overhead	$ 17,000

The journal entries led to the following postings:

Factory Department Overhead Control			
4a.	392,000	4b.	375,000
Bal.	17,000		

Total costs of $392,000 must eventually be charged to expense in some way. The $375,000 will become part of the Cost of Goods Sold expense when the products to which it is applied are sold. The remaining $17,000 must also become expense by some method.

When predetermined rates are used, the difference between incurred and applied overhead is typically allowed to accumulate during the year. When the amount applied to product exceeds the amount incurred by the departments, the difference is called **overapplied** or *overabsorbed* **overhead**; when the amount applied is less than incurred, the difference is called **underapplied** or *underabsorbed* **overhead**. At year end, the difference ($17,000 in our illustration) is disposed of in one of two major ways.

Method 1: Immediate Write-off. This is the most widely used approach. The $17,000 is regarded as a reduction in current income by adding the underapplied overhead to the cost of goods sold. (The same logic is followed for overapplied overhead except that the result would be an addition to current income because cost of goods sold would be decreased.)

The theory underlying the direct write-off is that most of the goods worked on have been sold, and a more elaborate method of disposition is not worth the extra trouble. Another justification is that the extra overhead costs represented by underapplied overhead do not qualify as part of ending inventory costs because they do not represent assets. They should be written off because they largely represent inefficiency or the underutilization of available facilities.

The immediate write-off eliminates the $17,000 difference with a simple journal entry, labeled as transaction 7 in Exhibit 13–2:

7.	Cost of goods sold (or a separate charge against revenue)	17,000	
	Factory department overhead control		17,000
	To close ending underapplied overhead directly to cost of goods sold.		

Method 2: Proration Among Inventories. This method prorates underapplied overhead among three accounts. Theoretically, if the objective is to obtain as accurate a cost allocation as possible, all the overhead costs of the individual jobs worked on should be recomputed, using the actual rather than the original predetermined rates. This approach is rarely feasible, so a practical attack is to prorate on the basis of the ending balances in each of three accounts (Work in Process, $155,000; Finished Goods, $32,000; and Cost of Goods Sold, $2,480,000).

	(1)	(2)	(3)
	BALANCE, END OF 19X2*	PRORATION OF UNDERAPPLIED OVERHEAD	ADJUSTED BALANCE END OF 19X2
Work in Process	$ 155,000	155/2,667 × 17,000 = $ 988	$ 155,988
Finished Goods	32,000	32/2,667 × 17,000 = 204	32,204
Cost of Goods Sold	2,480,000	2,480/2,667 × 17,000 = 15,808	2,495,808
	$2,667,000	$17,000	

* See page 415 for details.

The journal entry for the proration follows:

Work in process	988	
Finished goods	204	
Cost of goods sold	15,808	
Factory department overhead control		17,000
To prorate ending underapplied over-		
head among three accounts.		

The amounts prorated to inventories here are not significant. In practical situations, prorating is done only when inventory valuations would be materially affected. Exhibit 13-3 provides a schematic comparison of the two major methods of disposing of underapplied (or overapplied) factory overhead.

EXHIBIT 13–3

Year-end Disposition of Underapplied Factory Overhead
(COGS = Cost of Goods Sold)

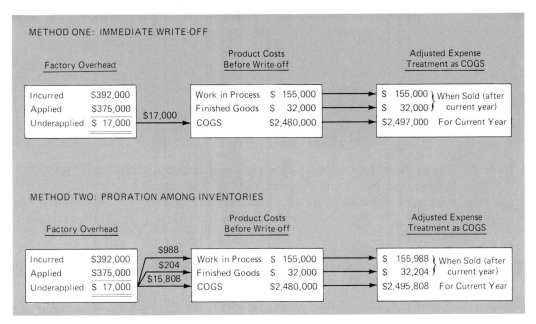

☐ The Use of Variable and Fixed Application Rates

As we have seen, overhead application is the most troublesome aspect of product costing. The presence of fixed costs is the biggest single reason for the costing difficulties. Most companies have made no distinction between variable- and fixed-cost behavior in the design of their accounting systems. For instance, reconsider the development of overhead rates in our illustration. The machining department developed the rate as follows:

$$\text{overhead application rate} = \frac{\text{budgeted total overhead}}{\text{budgeted machine-hours}}$$

$$= \frac{\$277,800}{69,450} = \$4 \text{ per machine-hour}$$

Some companies distinguish between variable overhead and fixed overhead for product costing as well as for control purposes. This distinction could have been made in the machining department. Rent, supervision, depreciation, and insurance would have been considered the fixed portion of the total manufacturing overhead, and two rates could have been developed:

$$\text{variable-overhead application rate} = \frac{\text{budgeted total variable overhead}}{\text{budgeted machine-hours}}$$

$$= \frac{\$114,000}{69,450}$$

$$= \$1.64 \text{ per machine-hour}$$

$$\text{fixed-overhead application rate} = \frac{\text{budgeted total fixed overhead}}{\text{budgeted machine-hours}}$$

$$= \frac{\$163,800}{69,450}$$

$$= \$2.36 \text{ per machine-hour}$$

Such rates can be used for product costing, and distinctions between variable and fixed overhead incurrence can also be made for control purposes.

☐ Application Bases in Future

Throughout the twentieth century, most manufacturers have tended to use broad averages for applying overhead to products. For example, many companies have used a single plantwide overhead rate instead of several departmental rates. Furthermore, few companies have used more than one application base. Survey after survey have indicated that over 90% of the companies use direct-labor dollars or direct-labor-hours as their single application base.

In recent years, manufacturing has become more heavily automated, and overhead has become a much larger proportion of total manufacturing cost. Some companies have seen their factory overhead rates as a percentage of direct-labor cost soar from 25% in the 1940s to 1,000% and higher in the 1980s. Consequently, many more companies are seriously studying whether multiple overhead rates should be adopted for product costing. For example, we can expect to see a machining department have at least two departmental overhead rates. Some overhead will be applied to jobs as a percentage of direct material costs (to apply the overhead costs related to the processing and handling of materials). Other overhead will be applied on the basis of machine hours.

The increasing use of computers and automated production processes has substantially increased the accuracy and decreased the cost of collecting information. As computerized data bases are used more widely, we are likely to see closer identification of the costs of departmental activities with the products that flow through. In some cases, there will be several overhead rates within one department. There might be an overhead rate related to the direct materials of the product, an additional rate related to the direct labor, an additional rate related to metered energy usage, and an additional rate related to machine usage.

In summary, as managers seek more accurate product costing, overhead application solely on the basis of direct-labor-hours or direct labor cost is certain to diminish in popularity.

☐ Actual versus Normal Costing

The overall system we have just described is sometimes called an actual costing system because every effort is made to trace the actual costs, as incurred, to the physical units benefited. However, it is only partly an actual system because the overhead, by definition, cannot be definitely assigned to physical products. Instead, overhead is applied on an average or normalized basis, in order to get representative or normal inventory valuations. Hence we shall label the system a **normal costing** system. The cost of the manufactured product is composed of *actual* direct material, *actual* direct labor, and *normal* applied overhead.

The two job-order costing approaches may be compared as follows:

	ACTUAL COSTING	NORMAL COSTING
Direct materials	Actual	Actual
Direct labor	Actual	Actual
Manufacturing overhead	Actual	Predetermined rates*

* Actual inputs (such as direct-labor-hours or direct-labor costs) multiplied by predetermined overhead rates (computed by dividing total budgeted manufacturing overhead by a budgeted application base such as direct-labor hours).

Under actual costing no overhead would be applied as jobs were worked on. Instead, overhead would be applied only after all overhead costs for the year were known. Then, using an "actual" average rate(s) instead of a predetermined rate(s), costs would be applied to all jobs that had been worked on throughout the year. All costs incurred would be exactly offset by costs applied to the Work-in-Process Inventory. However, increased accuracy would be obtained at the serious sacrifice of timeliness in using costs for measuring operating efficiency, determining selling prices, and producing interim financial statements.

Normal costing has replaced actual costing in many organizations precisely because the latter approach fails to provide costs of products as they are worked on during the year. It is possible to use a normal-costing system plus year-end adjustments to produce final results that closely approximate the results under actual costing. To do so in our illustration, the underapplied overhead is prorated among Work in Process, Finished Goods, and Cost of Goods Sold, as shown earlier in this chapter (Method 2 in Exhibit 13–3).

☐ Product Costing in Service and Nonprofit Organizations

This chapter has concentrated on how to apply costs to manufactured products. However, the job-costing approach is used in nonmanufacturing situations too. The focus shifts from the costs of products to the costs of services. Examples include appliance repair, auto repair, dentistry, auditing, income tax preparation, and medical care. For example, universities have research "projects," airlines have repair and overhaul "jobs," and public accountants have audit "engagements."

To illustrate, consider service industries, such as repairing, consulting, legal, and accounting services. Each customer order is a different job with a special account or order number. Sometimes only costs are traced directly to the job, sometimes only revenue is traced, and sometimes both. For example, automobile repair shops typically have a repair order for each car worked on, with space for allocating materials and labor costs. Customers are permitted to see only a copy showing the retail prices of the materials, parts, and labor billed to their orders. If the repair manager wants cost data, a system may be designed so that the "actual" parts and labor costs of each order are traced to a duplicate copy of the job order. That is why you often see auto mechanics "punching in" and "punching out" their starting and stopping times on "work tickets" as each new order is worked on.

The job-order approach occurs in nonprofit industries too. Costs or revenues may be traced to individual hospital patients, individual social welfare cases, and individual university research projects.

In nonprofit organizations the "product" is usually not called a "job order." Instead, it may be called a program or a class of service. A "program" is an identifiable group of activities that frequently produces outputs in the form of services rather than goods. Examples include a safety program, an education program, a family counseling program. Often many departments work simultaneously on many programs, so the "job-order" costing challenge is to "apply" the various department costs to the various programs. Then wiser management decisions may be made regarding the allocation of limited resources among competing programs.

Although this chapter has focused on product costing, the job order is also used for planning and control purposes. For example, consider an auditing engagement by a public accounting firm. The firm might have a condensed budget for 19X1 as follows:

Revenue	$10,000,000
Direct labor (for professional hours charged to jobs)	2,500,000
Contribution to overhead and operating profit	7,500,000
Overhead (all other costs)	6,500,000
Operating profit	$ 1,000,000

Overhead rate for costing jobs: $6,500,000 ÷ $2,500,000 = 260% of direct labor

Markup rate for pricing jobs: $10,000,000 ÷ $2,500,000 = 400% of direct labor

As each job is budgeted, the expected number of direct professional hours (that is, hours worked directly on the audit by partners, managers, and subordinate accountants) is predicted. The direct-labor cost would be computed by multiplying the hours by the labor cost per hour. Partners' time would be charged to the job at an appropriate cost rate; subordinates would be charged at lower rates.

The overhead cost of the job would be compiled by multiplying the direct-labor cost by the overhead rate.

The budgeted revenue for the job would be compiled by multiplying the direct labor by the markup rate.

The partner in charge of the job would monitor progress by comparing the hours logged to date with the original budget and with the estimated hours remaining on the job. The degree of profitability of each job heavily depends on whether the audit can be accomplished within the budgeted time limits and on whether the target revenue can be collected from the client.

The costs of the job would include direct labor, applied overhead, and direct travel costs (which are usually billed to the client at 100 percent of such costs). The 1980s have been marked by increasing efforts to pinpoint more costs in a direct basis. Compare the alternatives:

ALTERNATIVE 1		ALTERNATIVE 2	
Direct professional labor	xxx	Direct professional labor	xxx
Applied overhead	xxx	Direct support labor, such	
Total costs as a basis for		as secretarial costs	xxx
markup	xxx	Photocopying	xxx
Travel costs	xxx	Phone calls	xxx
Total costs	xxx	Fringe benefits to all	
		direct labor	xxx
		Total direct costs	xxx
		Applied overhead	xxx
		Total costs as a basis for	
		markup	xxx
		Travel costs	xxx
		Total costs	xxx

Alternative 2 would have a lower overhead application rate as a percentage of direct costs. Why? Because many costs that firms formerly regarded as part of overhead, an indirect cost, have been shifted to become direct costs. Alternative 2 is representative of changes throughout manufacturing and service industries. That is, as data processing becomes more economical, more costs than just direct material and direct labor will be classified as direct costs wherever feasible. Alternative 2 provides a more accurate identification of costs to specific jobs. In general, as competition intensifies, managers of all organizations want more accurate costs as guides to pricing and to allocating effort among particular products, services, or customers.

OPERATION OR HYBRID COSTING

Many manufacturers use a combination of job costing and process costing that may be called **operation costing, hybrid costing, or specification costing.** These manufacturers make goods that have some common characteristics plus some individual characteristics. For example, mass producers of clothing may make both high-quality and low-quality goods. Some jackets may be all wool and have many tailoring steps; others may be all polyester and have few tailoring steps. Other examples are woodworking, furniture manufacturing, shoe manufacturing, and electronics manufacturing.

An *operation* may be defined as a standardized production step, method, or technique that is repetitively performed. An *operation costing* system accumulates the cost of direct labor and factory overhead by operation for control purposes. Indeed, these costs are often lumped together as conversion costs for purposes of product costing. That is, direct labor vanishes as a separate major classification. There is no special distinction between direct labor and the other costs of the operation, such as power, repairs, and supplies. A single average unit conversion cost is calculated for the operation. This unit conversion cost is then applied to all physical units passing through the operation. The direct-material costs are applied specifically to the product in a way similar to a job-order costing system. Thus, the product costs are accounted for as follows:

	PRODUCTION ORDERS	
	For 100 Polyester Jackets	For 100 Wool Jackets
Direct materials (actual costs applied)	$2,000	$5,000
Conversion costs (predetermined costs applied on the basis of machine-hours, labor-hours, product units):		
Operation 1	675	675
Operation 2	400	400
Operation 3	—	500
Operation 4	900	900
Operation 5	—	400
Total manufacturing costs applied to products	$3,975	$7,875

The highlight of this hybrid system is the use of some predetermined, budgeted, or estimated costing rate for applying both the direct labor and the factory overhead of each operation. For example, the costs for operation 1 might be budgeted as follows:

$$\text{budgeted application rate for conversion costs} = \frac{\text{conversion costs (that is budgeted direct labor + budgeted factory overhead)}}{\text{machine-hours in operation 1}}$$

$$= \frac{\$180,000 + \$360,000}{20,000} = \$27$$

Suppose that it takes 25 machine-hours to process 100 jackets in operation 1. Then the cost of operation 1 per 100 jackets is $25 \times \$27 = \$675$.

As goods undergo operation 1, conversion costs are applied to them by multiplying the application rate times the machine-hours used in that operation. Any under- or overapplication of operation 1 costs are disposed of at the end of the year in the same manner as underapplied or overapplied factory overhead in job-costing systems.

SUMMARY

Accounting systems should be designed to satisfy control and product-costing purposes simultaneously. Costs are initially charged to department responsibility centers (cost centers); then they are applied to products to get inventory costs for balance sheets and income statements, to guide pricing, and to evaluate product performance.

Product costing is an averaging process. Process costing deals with broad averages and great masses of like units. Job costing deals with narrow averages and a unique unit or a small batch of like units.

Indirect manufacturing costs (factory overhead) are often applied to products using predetermined overhead rates. The rates are computed by dividing total budgeted overhead by a measure of total activity such as expected labor-hours or machine-hours. These rates are usually annual averages. The resulting product costs are normal costs, consisting of actual direct material plus actual direct labor plus applied overhead using predetermined rates.

Operation costing is a combination of job costing and process costing. Direct materials are applied specifically to the product, but direct labor vanishes as a separate classification. The cost of a product is the sum of the direct materials plus an applied conversion cost for each operation undergone.

SUMMARY PROBLEM FOR YOUR REVIEW

□ Problem

Review the Martinez illustration, especially Exhibits 13-2 and 13-3, pages 413-421. Prepare an income statement for 19X2 through the gross profit line. Use the immediate write-off method for overapplied or underapplied overhead.

□ Solution

Exhibit 13-4 recapitulates the final impact of the Martinez illustration on the financial statements. Note how the immediate write-off means that the $17,000 is added to the cost of goods sold.

EXHIBIT 13–4

Relation of Costs to Financial Statements

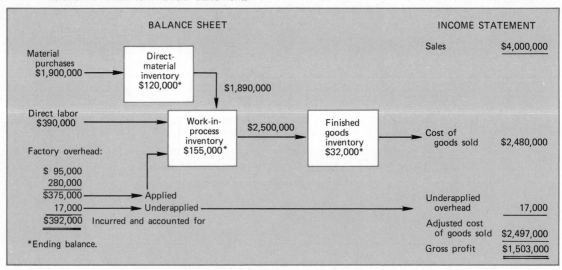

As you study Exhibit 13–4, trace the three major elements of cost (direct material, direct labor, and factory overhead) through the accounts.

HIGHLIGHTS TO REMEMBER

1. This chapter emphasized product costing, which may take various forms. However, every accounting system also has a fundamental control purpose:

CONTROL PURPOSE	PRODUCT-COSTING PURPOSE
Accumulate costs by	Apply costs by
a. Responsibility center	Job-order costing
b. Responsibility center	Process costing
c. Responsibility center	Combinations of job-order and process costing

2. Accounting for overhead is frequently the most difficult aspect of job-order costing. If normalized overhead rates are used, underapplied or overapplied overhead usually cumulates from month to month. The final amount of underapplied or overapplied overhead is typically added to or subtracted from the cost of goods sold at the end of the year.

3. If the amount of underapplied or overapplied overhead is significant, it is prorated over the appropriate inventory accounts as well as cost of goods sold.

ACCOUNTING VOCABULARY

Hybrid Costing *p. 426*   Job Order *411*   Job-order Costing *409*   Normal Costing *423*   Operation Costing *426*   Overapplied Factory Overhead *419*   Process Costing *409*   Specification Costing *426*   Underapplied Factory Overhead *419*

APPENDIX 13: RELATIONSHIPS AMONG SOURCE DOCUMENTS, SUBSIDIARY LEDGERS, AND GENERAL LEDGER

The source documents, such as material requisitions or time tickets, which were illustrated in Exhibit 13–1, are usually made in multiple copies, each being used for a specific task. For example, a materials requisition could be executed by a supervisor in as many as five copies and disposed of as follows:

1. Kept by storekeeper who issues the materials.
2. Used by stores ledger clerk (or a computer) for posting to perpetual inventory cards for materials.
3. Used by job-order cost clerk (or a computer) to post the job-cost sheet (Exhibit 13–1).
4. Used by general ledger clerk as a basis for a summary monthly entry for all of the month's requisitions (Exhibit 13–2).
5. Retained by the supervisor. The requisition can be used as a cross check against the performance reports which show the usage of material.

Of course, machine accounting and computer systems can use a single punched card as a requisition or the data may be entered directly via a computer terminal. Sorting, re-sorting, classifications, reclassifications, summaries, and re-summaries can easily provide any desired information. Because these source documents are the foundation for data accumulation and reports, the importance of accurate initial recording cannot be overemphasized.

Copies of these source documents are used for direct postings to subsidiary ledgers. Sometimes the subsidiary ledgers will contain summarized postings of daily batches of source documents, rather than individual direct postings. Accounting data are most condensed in the general ledger and most detailed on the source documents, as the following listing shows:

ITEM	
Work in process	General ledger (usually monthly totals only)
Job-cost sheets	Subsidiary ledgers (perhaps daily summaries)
Material requisitions or time tickets	Source documents (minute to minute, hour to hour)

The daily scorekeeping duties are accomplished with source documents and subsidiary ledgers. Copies of the source documents are independently summarized and are usually posted to the general ledger only once a month. See entry 2, Exhibit 13–2 (p. 413), where, for convenience, a year was used, rather than a month.

To obtain a bird's-eye view of a system, we have been concentrating on general ledger relationships. However, remember that the general ledger is a very small part of the accountant's daily work. Furthermore, current control is aided by hourly, daily, or weekly flash reports of material, labor, and machine usage. The general ledger itself is a summary device. Reliance on the general ledger for current control is ill-advised because the resulting reports come too late and are often too stale for management control use.

FUNDAMENTAL ASSIGNMENT MATERIAL

13–1. **BASIC JOURNAL ENTRIES.** (Alternate is 13–25.) The Chan Company, a small furniture company, provided you with the following data (in thousands): Inventories, December 31, 19X1:

Direct materials	$22
Work in process	65
Finished goods	75

Summarized transactions for 19X2:

a. Purchases of direct materials	$100
b. Direct materials used	108
c. Direct labor	90
d. Factory overhead incurred	192
e. Factory overhead applied, 180% of direct labor	?
f. Cost of goods completed and transferred to finished goods	325
g. Cost of goods sold	350
h. Sales on account	700

Required:
1. Prepare summary journal entries for 19X2 transactions. Omit explanations.
2. Show the T-accounts for all inventories, Cost of Goods Sold, and Factory Department Overhead Control. Show the ending balances of the inventories. Do not adjust for underapplied or overapplied factory overhead.

13–2. **DISPOSITON OF OVERHEAD.** Refer to the preceding problem (although this problem can be solved independently). All numbers are in thousands. Assume that overhead was underapplied by $30 and that ending inventories for direct materials, work in process, and finished goods were $14, $100, and $50, respectively. Unadjusted cost of goods sold is $350.

Required:
1. Assume that the $30 was written off solely as an adjustment to cost of goods sold. Prepare the journal entry. Omit explanations in this and the next entry.
2. Management has decided to prorate the $30 to the appropriate accounts (using the unadjusted ending balances) instead of writing it off solely as an adjustment of cost of goods sold. Prepare the journal entry. Would the reported gross margin be higher or lower than in Requirement 1? By how much?

ADDITIONAL ASSIGNMENT MATERIAL

13–3. Distinguish between job costing and process costing.

13–4. "The basic distinction between job-order costing and process costing is the breadth of the denominator." Explain.

13–5. "Cost application or absorption is terminology related to the product-costing purpose." Why?

13–6. What are some reasons for differences between the amounts of *incurred* and *applied* overhead?

13–7. Sometimes five copies of a stores requisition are needed. What are their uses?

13–8. "The general ledger entries are only a small part of the accountant's daily work." Explain.

13–9. "Costs of inefficiency cannot be regarded as assets." Explain.

13–10. "Under actual overhead application, unit costs soar as volume increases, and vice versa." Do you agree? Explain.

13–11. "Overhead application is overhead allocation." Do you agree? Explain.

13–12. Describe the subsidiary ledger for work in process in a job-cost system.

13–13. Define *normal costing*.

13–14. What is the best theoretical method of allocating underapplied or overapplied overhead, assuming that the objective is to obtain as accurate a cost application as possible?

13–15. "There should be a strong relationship between the factory overhead incurred and the base chosen for its application." Why?

13–16. State three examples of service industries that use the job-costing approach.

13–17. "As data processing becomes more economical, more costs than just direct material and direct labor will be classified as direct costs wherever feasible." State three examples of such costs.

13–18. "Job costs are accumulated for purposes of inventory valuation and income determination." State two other purposes.

13–19. Why is *operation costing* also called *hybrid costing*?

13–20. Explain the accounting procedures for product costing in a hybrid or operation-costing system.

13–21. "Sometimes direct-labor dollars is the best overhead allocation base even if wage rates vary within a department." Do you agree? Explain.

13–22. **JOB-COST RECORD.** The University of Washington uses job-cost sheets for various research projects in its engineering school. A principal reason for such records is to justify requests for reimbursements of costs on projects sponsored by the federal government.

Consider the following summarized data regarding Project No. 321 conducted by some chemical engineers:

March 3, Direct materials, various metals, $1,500
March 4, Direct materials, various chemicals, $1,100
March 3–7, Direct labor, research assistants, 90 hours
March 5–7, Direct labor, research associates, 50 hours
Research associates receive $25 per hour; assistants, $15. The overhead rate is 80% of direct-labor cost.

Required:

1. Sketch a job-cost sheet. Post all data to the cost sheet. Compute the total cost of the project through March 7.
2. The chemical engineering department has several other research projects that are at various stages of completion. Job-cost sheets are used for all research projects. What general ledger account would summarize the cost of all research projects? Explain how that account is related to the job-cost sheets.

13–23. **DIRECT MATERIALS.** The LM Co. had an ending inventory of direct materials of $50,000. During the year the company had acquired $900,000 of materials and had used $910,000. Compute the beginning inventory.

13–24. **DIRECT MATERIALS.** For each of the following independent cases, fill in the blanks (in thousands of dollars):

	CASES			
	1	2	3	4
Direct-materials inventory, December 31, 19X1	—	6	10	4
Purchased	7	4	6	—
Used	4	3	—	9
Direct-materials inventory, December 31, 19X2	6	—	3	5

13–25. BASIC JOURNAL ENTRIES. (Alternate is 13–1.) The following data (in thousands) summarize the factory operations of the Bensmeier Manufacturing Co. for the year 19X1, its first year in business:

a. Direct materials purchased for cash	$230
b. Direct materials issued and used	220
c. Labor used directly on production	100
d1. Indirect labor	80
d2. Depreciation of plant and equipment	40
d3. Miscellaneous factory overhead (ordinarily would be detailed)	30
e. Overhead applied: 180% of direct labor	?
f. Cost of production completed	450
g. Cost of goods sold	300

Required:
1. Prepare summary journal entries. Omit explanations. For purposes of this problem, combine the items in *d* as "overhead incurred."
2. Show the T-accounts for all inventories, Costs of Goods Sold, and Factory Department Overhead Control. Compute the ending balances of the inventories. Do not adjust for underapplied or overapplied factory overhead.

13–26. ACCOUNTING FOR OVERHEAD, PREDETERMINED RATES. Catherine Electronics Co. uses a predetermined overhead rate in applying overhead to individual job orders on a *machine-hour* basis for Department No. 1 and on a *direct-labor-hour* basis for Department No. 2. At the beginning of 19X4, the company's management made the following budget predictions:

	DEPT. NO. 1	DEPT. NO. 2
Direct-labor-hours	100,000	200,000
Machine-hours	300,000	41,000
Direct-labor cost	$2,200,000	$4,000,000
Factory overhead	$2,400,000	$2,000,000

Cost records of recent months show the following accumulations for Job Order No. 341:

	DEPT. NO. 1	DEPT. NO. 2
Direct-labor cost	$15,400	$ 7,000
Material placed in production	$22,000	$40,000
Machine-hours	2,300	60
Direct-labor-hours	700	350

Required:
1. What is the predetemined overhead *rate* that should be applied in Department No. 1? In Department No. 2?
2. What is the *total overhead* cost of Job Order No. 341?
3. If Job Order No. 341 consists of 1,000 units of product, what is the *unit cost* of this job?
4. At the *end* of 19X4, actual results for the year's operations were as follows:

	DEPT. NO. 1	DEPT. NO. 2
Actual machine-hours	275,000	39,500
Actual direct-labor-hours	105,000	210,000
Actual overhead costs incurred	$2,500,000	$1,900,000

Find the underapplied or overapplied overhead for each department and for the factory as a whole.

JOURNAL ENTRIES FOR OVERHEAD. Consider the following summarized data regarding 19X3:

	BUDGET	ACTUAL
Indirect labor	$ 400,000	$ 360,000
Supplies	40,000	35,000
Repairs	90,000	85,000
Utilities	100,000	110,000
Factory rent	120,000	120,000
Supervision	60,000	63,000
Depreciation, equipment	200,000	200,000
Insurance, property taxes, etc.	40,000	41,000
a. Total factory overhead	$1,050,000	$1,014,000
b. Direct materials used	$1,500,000	$1,410,000
c. Direct labor	$1,000,000	$1,100,000

Required:

Omit explanations for journal entries.

1. Prepare a summary journal entry for the actual overhead incurred for 19X3.
2. Prepare summary journal entries for direct materials used and direct labor.
3. Factory overhead was applied by using a budgeted rate based on budgeted direct-labor costs. Compute the rate. Prepare a summary journal entry for the application of overhead to products.
4. Post the journal entries to the T-accounts for Work in Process and Factory Department Overhead Control.
5. Suppose overapplied or underapplied factory overhead is written off as an adjustment to cost of goods sold. Prepare the journal entry. Post the overhead to the overhead T-account.

13–28. **RELATIONSHIPS AMONG OVERHEAD ITEMS.** Fill in the unknowns:

	Case A	Case B	Case C
Budgeted factory overhead	$4,000,000	?	$2,000,000
Budgeted application base:			
Direct-labor cost	2,500,000		
Direct-labor-hours		400,000	
Machine-hours			400,000
Overhead application rate	?	$8	?

13-29. RELATIONSHIPS AMONG OVERHEAD ITEMS. Fill in the unknowns:

	Case 1	Case 2
a. Budgeted factory overhead	$800,000	$400,000
b. Application base, budgeted direct-labor cost	400,000	?
c. Budgeted factory overhead rate	?	80%
d. Direct-labor cost incurred	360,000	?
e. Factory overhead incurred	710,000	390,000
f. Factory overhead applied	?	?
g. Underapplied (overapplied) factory overhead	?	25,000

13-30. UNDERAPPLIED AND OVERAPPLIED OVERHEAD. Ruiz Medical Supply Corporation applies factory overhead at a rate of $8 per direct-labor-hour. Selected data for 19X3 operations are (in thousands):

	CASE 1	CASE 2
Direct-labor-hours	18	30
Direct-labor-cost	$120	$210
Indirect-labor cost	25	35
Sales commissions	15	10
Depreciation, manufacturing equipment	10	15
Direct-material cost	200	230
Factory fuel costs	12	18
Depreciation, finished-goods warehouse	4	14
Cost of goods sold	380	490
All other factory costs	119	182

Required:

Compute for each case:

1. Factory overhead applied.
2. Total factory overhead incurred.
3. Amount of underapplied or overapplied factory overhead.

13-31. DISPOSITION OF OVERHEAD. Consider the following balances at the end of the year 19X2 (in thousands):

Indirect manufacturing costs incurred	$490
Indirect manufacturing costs applied	544
Work-in-process inventory	100
Finished-goods inventory	200
Cost of goods sold	600

Required:

1. Assume that underapplied or overapplied overhead is regarded as a reduction or addition to current income via adding or deducting the amount from the unadjusted cost of goods sold. What is the adjusted cost of goods sold?
2. Assume that the underapplied or overapplied overhead is prorated among the pertinent accounts in proportion to their ending unadjusted balances. What is the adjusted cost of goods sold?
   For a more detailed examination of the data, see Problem 13-32.
3. By how much would gross profit be affected by adopting the approach in Requirement 2 rather than Requirement 1? Would the gross profit be higher or lower?

13–32. DISPOSITION OF OVERHEAD. A company uses a job-order system. At the end of 19X4 the following balances existed (in millions):

Cost of goods sold	$60
Finished goods	10
Work in process	30
Factory overhead (actual)	50
Factory overhead (applied)	60

Required:

1. Prepare journal entries for two different ways to dispose of the underapplied overhead.
2. Gross profit, before considering the effects in Requirement 1, was $40 million. What is the adjusted gross profit under the two methods demonstrated?

13–33. RELATIONSHIPS OF MANUFACTURING COSTS. (CMA.) Selected data concerning the past fiscal year's operations of the Televans Manufacturing Company are (in thousands):

	INVENTORIES	
	Beginning	Ending
Raw materials	$75	$ 85
Work in process	80	30
Finished goods	90	110
Other data:		
Raw materials used		$326
Total manufacturing costs charged to production during the year (includes raw materials, direct labor, and factory overhead applied at a rate of 60% of direct-labor cost)		686
Cost of goods available for sale		826
Selling and general expenses		25

Required:

Select the best answer for each of the following items:

1. The cost of raw materials purchased during the year amounted to
   a. $411   c. $316   e. None of these
   b. $360   d. $336
2. Direct-labor costs charged to production during the year amounted to
   a. $135   c. $360   e. None of these
   b. $225   d. $216
3. The cost of goods manufactured during the year was
   a. $636   c. $736   e. None of these
   b. $766   d. $716
4. The cost of goods sold during the year was
   a. $736   c. $691   e. None of these
   b. $716   d. $801

13–34. RELATIONSHIP OF SUBSIDIARY AND GENERAL LEDGERS, JOURNAL ENTRIES. The following summarized data are available on three job-cost sheets:

	330		331		332
	March	April	March	April	April
Direct materials	$7,000	$1,500	$9,000	—	$10,000
Direct labor	3,000	1,000	4,000	$2,000	1,500
Factory overhead applied	6,000	?	8,000	?	?

The company's fiscal year ends on April 30. Factory overhead is applied as a percentage of direct-labor cost. The balances in selected accounts on March 31 were direct-materials inventory, $16,000, and finished goods inventory, $15,000.

Job 330 was completed during April and transferred to finished goods. Job 331 was still in process at the end of April, as was Job 332, which had begun on April 24. These were the only jobs worked on during March and April.

Job 330 was sold along with other finished goods by April 30. The total cost of goods sold during April was $28,000. The balance in Cost of Goods Sold on March 31 was $410,000.

Required:
1. Prepare a schedule showing the balance of the work-in-process inventory, March 31. This schedule should show the total costs of each job sheet. Taken together, the job-cost sheets are the subsidiary ledger supporting the general ledger balance of work in process.
2. What is the overhead application rate?
3. Prepare summary general journal entries for all costs added to Work in Process during April. Also prepare an entry for all costs transferred from Work in Process to Finished Goods. Post to the pertinent T-accounts.
4. Prepare a schedule showing the balance of the work-in-process inventory, April 30.

13–35. **STRAIGHTFORWARD JOB COSTING.** The Dunkel Custom Furniture Company has two departments. Data for 19X5 include the following:

Inventories, January 1, 19X5:

Direct materials (30 types)	$100,000
Work in process (in assembly)	60,000
Finished goods	20,000

Manufacturing overhead budget for 19X5:

	MACHINING	ASSEMBLY
Indirect labor	$200,000	$ 400,000
Supplies	40,000	50,000
Utilities	100,000	90,000
Repairs	150,000	100,000
Supervision	100,000	200,000
Factory rent	50,000	50,000
Depreciation on equipment	150,000	100,000
Insurance, property taxes, etc.	50,000	60,000
	$840,000	$1,050,000

Budgeted machine-hours were 84,000; budgeted direct-labor cost in Assembly was $2,100,000. Manufacturing overhead was applied using predetermined rates on the basis of machine-hours in Machining and on the basis of direct-labor cost in Assembly.

Following is a summary of actual events for the year:

	MACHINING	ASSEMBLY	TOTAL
a. Direct materials purchased			$ 1,700,000
b. Direct materials requisitioned	$1,000,000	600,000	1,600,000
c. Direct-labor costs incurred	800,000	2,600,000	3,400,000
d1. Factory overhead incurred	1,000,000	1,000,000	2,000,000
d2. Factory overhead applied	800,000	?	?
e. Cost of goods completed	—	—	7,110,000
f1. Sales	—	—	12,000,000
f2. Cost of goods sold	—	—	7,100,000

The ending work in process (all in Assembly) was $50,000.

Required:

1. Compute the predetermined overhead rates.
2. Compute the amount of the machine-hours actually worked.
3. Compute the amount of factory overhead applied in the Assembly Department.
4. Prepare general journal entries for transactions *a* through *f*. Work solely with the total amounts, not the details for Machining and Assembly. Explanations are not required. Show data in thousands of dollars. Present T-accounts, including ending inventory balances, for direct materials, work in process, and finished goods.
5. Prepare a partial income statement similar to the one illustrated in Exhibit 13–4, p. 428. Overapplied or underapplied overhead is written off as an adjustment of current cost of goods sold.

13–36. COMPARISON OF OVERHEAD ACCOUNTING FOR CONTROL AND FOR PRODUCT COSTING. The Faston Company has an overhead rate of $3 per direct-labor hour, based on expected variable overhead of $100,000 per year, expected fixed overhead of $200,000 per year, and expected direct-labor-hours of 100,000 per year.

Data for the year's operations follow:

	DIRECT-LABOR-HOURS USED	OVERHEAD COSTS INCURRED*
First six months	60,000	$168,000
Last six months	36,000	136,000

* Fixed costs incurred were exactly equal to budgeted amounts throughout the year.

1. What is the underapplied or overapplied overhead for each six-month period? Label your answer as underapplied or overapplied.
2. Explain *briefly* (not over 50 words for each part) the probable reasons for the exact figures attributable to the causes you cite.

13–37. FINDING UNKNOWNS. (Alternate is 13–38.) The Brindisi Company has the following balances on December 31, 19X7. All amounts are in millions:

Factory overhead applied	$180
Cost of goods sold	400
Factory overhead incurred	200
Direct-materials inventory	50
Finished-goods inventory	40
Work-in-process inventory	90

The cost of goods completed was $380. The cost of direct materials requisitioned for production during 19X7 was $170. The cost of direct materials purchased was $190. Factory overhead was applied to production at a rate of 180% of direct-labor cost.

Required: Compute the beginning inventory balances of direct materials, work in process, and finished goods. *Hint*: Use T-accounts. These computations can be made without considering any possible adjustments for overapplied or underapplied overhead.

13–38. **FINDING UNKNOWNS.** (Alternate is 13–37.) The Heger Company has the following balances (in millions) as of December 31, 19X8:

Work-in-process inventory	$ 27
Finished-goods inventory	130
Direct-materials inventory	80
Factory overhead incurred	150
Factory overhead applied at 150% of	
direct-labor cost	120
Cost of goods sold	300

The cost of direct materials purchased during 19X8 was $230. The cost of direct materials requisitioned for production during 19X8 was $200. The cost of goods completed was $404, all in millions.

Required: Before considering any year-end adjustments for overapplied or underapplied overhead, compute the beginning inventory balances of direct materials, work in process, and finished goods.

13–39. **ONE OR TWO APPLICATION RATES.** The Epstein Co. in Geneva, Switzerland, has the following 19X2 budget for its two departments in Swiss francs (SF):

	MACHINING	FINISHING	TOTAL
Direct labor	SF 300,000	SF 700,000	SF 1,000,000
Factory overhead	SF 900,000	SF 700,000	SF 1,600,000
Machine-hours	60,000	20,000	80,000

In the past, the company has used a single plantwide overhead application rate based on direct-labor cost. However, as products have multiplied and as competition has intensified, the president has questioned the accuracy of the profits or losses shown on various products. He knows that changes in costs are more heavily affected by machine-hours in the first department and by direct-labor costs in the second department.

The president has given you the following data regarding two jobs:

	JOB	
	361	362
Machining		
Direct materials	SF 3,000	SF 3,000
Direct labor	SF 2,000	SF 1,000
Machine-hours	1,000	80
Finishing		
Direct labor	SF 1,000	SF 2,000
Machine-hours	100	100

1. Compute six factory overhead application rates, three based on direct-labor cost and three based on machine-hours for machining, finishing, and for the plant as a whole.
2. Use the application rates to compute the total costs of Job 361 and 362 as follows: (a) plantwide rate based on direct-labor cost and (b) machining based on machine-hours and finishing based on direct-labor cost.
3. Evaluate your answers in Requirement 2. Which set of job costs do you prefer? Why?

13–40. NONPROFIT JOB COSTING. Job-order costing is usually identified with manufacturing companies. However, service industries and nonprofit organizations also use the method. Suppose a social service agency has a cost-accounting system that tracks cost by department (for example, family counseling, general welfare, and foster children) and by case. In this way, the manager of the agency is better able to determine how her limited resources (mostly professional social workers) should be allocated. Furthermore, her interchanges with her superiors and various politicians are more fruitful when she can cite the costs of various types of cases.

The condensed line-item budget for the general welfare department of the agency for 19X6 showed:

Professional salaries:			
Level 12	6 @ $32,000 =	$192,000	
Level 10	18 @ $24,000 =	432,000	
Level 8	30 @ $16,000 =	480,000	$1,104,000
Other costs			441,600
Total costs			$1,545,600

For costing various cases, the manager favored using a single overhead application rate based on the ratio of total overhead to direct labor. The latter was defined as those professional salaries assigned to specific cases.

The professional workers filled out a weekly "case time" report, which approximated the hours spent for each case.

The instructions on the report were: "Indicate how much time (in hours) you spent on each case. Unassigned time should be listed separately." About 20% of available time was unassigned to specific cases. It was used for professional development (for example, continuing education programs). "Unassigned time" became a part of "overhead," as distinguished from the direct labor.

1. Compute the "overhead rate" as a percentage of direct labor (that is, the assignable professional salaries).
2. Suppose that last week a welfare case, Client No. 462, required two hours of Level 12 time, four hours of Level 10 time, and nine hours of Level 8 time. How much job cost should be allocated to Client No. 462 for the week? Assume that all professional employees work a 1,650-hour year.

13–41. CHOOSING OVERHEAD APPLICATION BASES IN ACCOUNTING FIRM. The managing partner of an accounting firm is considering the desirability of tracing more costs to jobs than just direct labor. In this way, the firm will be better able to justify billings to clients.

Last year's costs were:

Direct professional labor	$ 8,000,000
Overhead	16,000,000
Total costs	$24,000,000

The following costs were included in overhead:

Computer time	$1,600,000
Secretarial costs	1,400,000
Photocopying	300,000
Fringe benefits to direct labor	1,600,000
Phone call time with clients	
(estimated but not tabulated)	1,100,000
Total direct costs	$6,000,000

The firm's data processing techniques now make it feasible to document and trace these costs to individuual jobs.

In December, as an experiment the partner had arranged to trace these costs to six audit engagements. Two job records showed the following:

	Engagement	
	412	418
Direct professional labor	$10,000	$10,000
Fringe benefits to direct labor	2,000	2,000
Phone call time with clients	1,000	400
Computer time	3,000	500
Secretarial costs	2,500	1,000
Photocopying	500	100
Total direct costs	$19,000	$14,000

Required:

1. Compute the overhead application rate based on last year's costs.
2. Suppose last year's costs were reclassified so that $6 million would be regarded as direct costs instead of overhead. Compute the overhead application rate as a percentage of direct labor and as a percentage of total direct costs.
3. Using the three rates computed in Requirements 1 and 2, compute the total costs of engagements 412 and 418.
4. Suppose that client billing was based on a 20% markup of total job costs. Compute the billings that would be forthcoming in Requirement 3.
5. Which method of job costing and overhead application do you favor? Explain.

13–42. **BASIC OPERATION COSTING.** Strykalski Co. manufactures a variety of bookcases. The company's manufacturing operations and costs applied to products for April were:

	CUTTING	ASSEMBLY	FINISHING
Direct labor	$40,000	$20,000	$80,000
Factory overhead	80,000	30,000	80,000

Three styles of bookcases were produced in April. The quantities and direct material cost were:

STYLE	QUANTITY	DIRECT MATERIALS
Standard	5,000	$100,000
Deluxe	3,000	120,000
Unfinished	2,000	40,000

The unfinished bookcases, as the name implies, had no finishing operations whatsoever.

Required:
1. Tabulate the total conversion costs of each operation, the total units produced, and the conversion cost per unit.
2. Tabulate the total costs, the units produced, and the cost per unit.

13–43. OPERATION COSTING WITH ENDING WORK IN PROCESS. O'Brien Co. uses three operations in sequence to make television sets. Consider the following:

	PRODUCTION ORDERS	
	For 1,000 Standard- Quality Sets	For 1,000 Better- Quality Sets
Direct materials (actual costs applied)	$40,000	$90,000
Conversion costs (predetermined costs applied on the basis of machine hours used):		
Operation 1	20,000	20,000
Operation 2	?	?
Operation 3	—	10,000
Total manufacturing costs applied	$?	$?

Required:
1. Operation 2 was highly automated. Product costs depended on a budgeted application rate for conversion costs based on machine-hours. The budgeted costs for 19X2 were $100,000 direct labor and $440,000 factory overhead. Budgeted machine-hours were 18,000. Each set required 6 minutes of time in Operation 2. Compute the costs of processing 1,000 sets in Operation 2.
2. Compute the total manufacturing costs of 1,000 sets and the cost per standard-quality set and per better-quality set.
3. Suppose at the end of the year that 500 standard-quality sets were in process through Operation 1 only and 600 better-quality sets were in process through Operation 2 only. Compute the cost of the ending work-in-process inventory. Assume that no direct materials are applied in Operation 2, but that $10,000 of additional direct materials are applied to each 1,000 sets processed in Operation 3.

13–44. APPENDIX 13 PROBLEM: SOURCE DOCUMENTS. Refer to Problem 13–25. For each journal entry, indicate (a) the most likely name for the source documents that would authorize the entry and (b) how the subsidiary ledgers, if any, would be affected.

13–45. APPENDIX 13 PROBLEM: SOURCE DOCUMENTS. Refer to Problem 13–1. For each journal entry, indicate (a) the most likely name for the source documents that would authorize the entry and (b) how the subsidiary ledgers, if any, would be affected.

13–46. RECONSTRUCTION OF TRANSACTIONS. (This problem is more challenging than the others in this chapter.)

You are asked to bring the following incomplete accounts of a plant acquired in a merger up to date through January 31, 19X2. Also consider the data that appear after the T-accounts.

Direct-Materials Inventory		Accrued Factory Payroll	
12/31/X1 Balance 30,000			1/31/X2 Balance 3,000

Work-in-Process		Factory Department Overhead Control	
		Total January charges 57,000	

Finished Goods		Cost of Goods Sold	
12/31/X1 Balance 20,000			

Additional Information

(1) The overhead is applied using a predetermined rate that is set every December by forecasting the following year's overhead and relating it to forecast direct-labor costs. The budget for 19X2 called for $400,000 of direct labor and $600,000 of factory overhead.

(2) The only job unfinished on January 31, 19X2, was No. 419, on which total labor charges were $2,000 (125 direct-labor-hours), and total direct-material charges were $19,000.

(3) Total materials placed into production during January totaled $120,000.

(4) Cost of goods completed during January was $200,000.

(5) January 31 balances of direct materials totaled $15,000.

(6) Finished-goods inventory as of January 31 was $40,000.

(7) All factory workers earn the same rate of pay. Direct-labor hours for January totaled 2,500. Indirect labor and supervision totaled $10,000.

(8) The gross factory payroll paid on January paydays totaled $52,000. Ignore withholdings.

(9) All "actual" factory overhead incurred during January has already been posted.

Required:

a. Direct materials purchased during January.
b. Cost of goods sold during January.
c. Direct-labor costs incurred during January.
d. Overhead applied during January.
e. Balance, Accrued Factory Payroll, December 31, 19X1.
f. Balance, Work in Process, December 31, 19X1.
g. Balance, Work in Process, January 31, 19X2.
h. Overapplied or underapplied overhead for January.

Chapter 14

PROCESS-COSTING SYSTEMS

LEARNING OBJECTIVES

When you have finished studying this chapter, you should be able to:

1. Explain the basic ideas underlying process costing, particularly the expression of output in terms of **equivalent units**.

2. Demonstrate how the presence of beginning inventories affects the computations of unit costs under the first-in, first-out and weighted-average methods.

3. Compute costs and prepare journal entries for the principal transactions in a process-costing system.

Cost-accounting systems fulfill two major purposes by their day-to-day operations: (1) they allocate costs to departments for *planning and control*, and (2) they apply costs to units of product for *product costing*. Other chapters deal with planning and control. This chapter concentrates on a basic type of product costing called *process costing*.

THIS CHAPTER MAY BE STUDIED IMMEDIATELY AFTER EITHER CHAPTER 3 OR CHAPTER 13. THE THREE MAJOR PARTS OF THIS CHAPTER MAY BE STUDIED INDEPENDENTLY. PART ONE INTRODUCES PROCESS COSTING. THE NEXT TWO PARTS EXPLORE THE SUBJECT IN MORE DEPTH.

☐ PART ONE: Introduction to Process Costing

NATURE OF PROCESS COSTING

The preceding chapter emphasized that all product costing uses averaging to determine costs per unit of production. The average unit cost may be relatively narrow, as in the production of a particular printing order in job-order costing. In contrast, the average may be relatively broad, as in the production of aspirin in process costing. *Process costing* is a system that applies costs to like products that are usually mass produced in continuous fashion through a series of production steps.

The principal difference between job costing and process costing arises from the type of products that are the cost objectives. Job-order costing is found in industries such as printing, construction, and furniture manufacturing, where each unit or batch (job) of product tends to be unique and easily identifiable. Process costing is found where there is mass production through a sequence of several processes, such as mixing and cooking. Examples include chemicals, flour, glass, and paint.

Exhibit 14–1 shows the major differences between job-order costing and process costing. Several work-in-process accounts are used in process costing. As goods move from process to process, their costs are transferred accordingly.

The process-costing approach is less concerned with distinguishing among individual units of product. Instead, accumulated costs for a period, say, a month, are divided by quantities produced during that period to get broad, average unit costs. Process costing may be adopted in nonmanufacturing activities as well as in manufacturing activities. Examples include dividing the costs of giving state automobile driver's license tests by the number of tests given and dividing the costs of an X-ray department by the number of X-rays processed.

EXHIBIT 14–1

Comparison of Job-Order and Process Costing

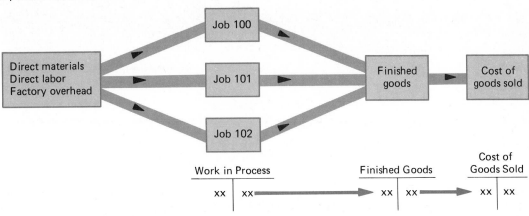

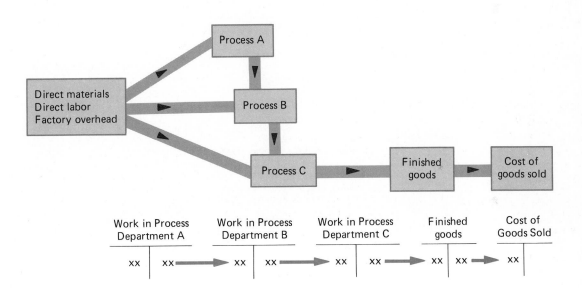

Process costing systems are usually simpler and less expensive than job-order costing. Individual jobs do not exist. There are no job-cost sheets. The unit cost for inventory purposes is calculated by accumulating the costs of each processing department and dividing the total cost by an appropriate measure of output. For instance, the accumulated cost of a cooking department may be divided by the number of items processed.

The relationships of the inventory accounts are (in millions):

Work in Process—Cooking				Work in Process—Freezing		
Direct materials	14	Transfer cost of goods completed to next department		Cost transferred in from		Transfer cost of goods completed to finished
Direct labor	4					
Factory overhead	8		24 →	Cooking	24	goods 26
	26			Additional costs	3	
					27	
Ending inventory	2					
				Ending inventory	1	

The journal entries are similar to those for the job-order costing system. That is, direct materials, direct labor, and factory overhead are accounted for as before. However, now there is more than a single Work-in-Process account for all units being manufactured. There are two or more Work-in-Process accounts, one for each processing department. The foregoing data would be journalized as follows:

1.	Work in process—Cooking	14	
	Direct materials inventory		14
	To record direct materials used.		
2.	Work in process—Cooking	4	
	Accrued payroll		4
	To record direct labor.		
3.	Work in process—Cooking	8	
	Factory overhead		8
	To record factory overhead applied to product.		
4.	Work in process—Freezing	24	
	Work in process—Cooking		24
	To transfer goods from the cooking process.		
5.	Work in process—Freezing	3	
	Accrued payroll		1
	Factory overhead		2
	To record direct labor and factory overhead applied to product.		
6.	Finished goods	26	
	Work in process—Freezing		26
	To transfer goods from the freezing process.		

□ **Physical Units and Equivalent Units (Steps 1 and 2)**

Consider another illustration. Suppose a toy company buys wood as its direct material for its Forming Department. The department processes one type of toy. The toys are transferred to the Finishing Department, where hand shaping and metal are added.

Suppose the Forming Department manufactured 25,000 units during April. The department's April costs were:

Direct materials		$ 70,000
Conversion costs		
Direct labor	$10,625	
Factory overhead	31,875	42,500
Costs to account for		$112,500

The unit cost of goods completed would simply be $112,500 ÷ 25,000 = $4.50. An itemization would show:

Direct materials, $70,000 ÷ 25,000	$2.80
Conversion costs, $42,500 ÷ 25,000	1.70
Unit cost of a whole completed unit	$4.50

Suppose not all 25,000 units were completed during April. How should each department calculate the cost of goods transferred and the cost of goods remaining in the ending work-in-process inventory? This is the major product-costing problem. If an identical amount of work is done on each unit, the solution is easy. But what if the units in the ending inventory are only partially processed? Then the product costing system must distinguish between the fully processed units and the partially processed units.

Five key steps in process cost accounting will be described:

Step 1: Summarize the flow of physical units.
Step 2: Calculate output in terms of equivalent units.
Step 3: Summarize the total costs to account for, which are the total debits in Work in Process (that is, the costs applied to Work in Process).
Step 4: Calculate unit costs.
Step 5: Apply costs to units completed and to units in the ending work in process.

The major difficulty in process costing is applying costs to partially completed products, the units in process at the end of a period. For example, now suppose 5,000 units were still in process at the end of April; only 20,000 were started and fully completed. All direct materials had been placed in process, but on the average only 25% of the conversion costs had been applied to the 5,000 units.

How should the output for April be described? Not as 25,000 units. Instead, the output was 20,000 fully completed units and 5,000 partially completed units. A partially completed unit is not a perfect substitute for a fully completed unit. Accordingly, output is usually stated in equivalent units, not physical units.

Equivalent units are used to measure the output in terms of the quantities of each of the factors of production applied thereto. That is, an equivalent

EXHIBIT 14-2

Forming Department
Output in Equivalent Units
For the Month Ended April 30, 19X1

| | (STEP 1) | (STEP 2) EQUIVALENT UNITS | |
FLOW OF PRODUCTION	PHYSICAL UNITS	Direct Materials	Conversion Costs
Started and completed	20,000	20,000	20,000
Work in process, ending inventory	5,000	5,000	1,250*
Work done to date	25,000	25,000	21,250

* 5,000 physical units × .25 degree of completion of conversion costs.

unit is regarded as the collection of inputs (work applications) necessary to produce one complete physical unit of product. In our example, Exhibit 14-2 shows that the output would be measured as 25,000 equivalent units of direct-materials cost and 21,250 equivalent units of conversion costs.

Measures in equivalent units extend beyond manufacturing situations. Such measures are a favorite way of expressing workloads in terms of a common denominator. For example, radiology departments measure their output in terms of weight units. Various X-ray procedures are ranked in terms of the time, supplies, and related costs devoted to each. A simple chest X-ray may receive a weight of one. But a skull X-ray may receive a weight of three because it uses three times the resources as a procedure with a weight of one. Another example is the expression by universities of students enrolled in terms of full-time enrollment equivalents.

☐ Calculation of Product Costs (Steps 3, 4, and 5)

In process costing, costs are often divided into only two main classifications: direct materials and conversion costs. The latter are all manufacturing costs other than direct materials. Direct labor is usually not a major part of total costs, so it is combined with factory overhead costs (such as the costs of energy, repairs, and material handling) as a major classification called conversion costs.

Exhibit 14-3 is a production-cost report. It shows Steps 3, 4, and 5. Step 3 summarizes the total costs to account for (that is, the total costs in, or debits to, Work in Process—Forming). Step 4 obtains unit costs by dividing total costs by the appropriate measures of equivalent units. The unit cost of a completed unit is $2.80 + $2.00 = $4.80. Why is the unit cost $4.80 instead of the $4.50 calculated earlier in this chapter (p. 447)? Because the $42,500 conversion cost is spread over 21,250 units instead of 25,000 units. Step 5 then uses these unit costs to apply costs to products.

EXHIBIT 14–3

Forming Department
Production Cost Report
For the Month Ended April 30, 19X1

		DIRECT MATERIALS	CONVERSION COSTS
(Step 3)	Costs to account for ($112,500)		
	Direct materials	$70,000	
	Conversion costs		$42,500
(Step 4)	Divide by equivalent units	25,000	21,250
	Unit costs	$2.80	$2.00
(Step 5)	Application of costs:		
	To units completed and transferred to the Finishing Department, 20,000 × ($2.80 + $2.00) or 20,000 × $4.80		$ 96,000
	To units not completed and still in Forming work in process:		
	Direct materials, 5,000 × $2.80 =	$14,000	
	Conversion costs, 1,250 × $2.00 =	2,500	16,500
	Total costs accounted for		$112,500

☐ **Journal Entries**

The summarized journal entries for the data in our illustration follow:

1.	Work in process—Forming		70,000	
	Direct-materials inventory			70,000
	Materials added to production in April.			
2.	Work in process—Forming		10,625	
	Accrued payroll			10,625
	Direct labor in April.			
3.	Work in process—Forming		31,875	
	Factory overhead			31,875
	Factory overhead applied in April.			
4.	Work in process—Finishing		96,000	
	Work in process—Forming			96,000
	Cost of goods completed and transferred in April from Forming to Assembly.			

The key T-account would show:

Work in Process—Forming			
1. Direct materials	70,000	4. Transferred out to Finishing	96,000
2. Direct labor	10,625		
3. Factory overhead	31,875		
	112,500		
Bal. April 30	16,500		

SUMMARY PROBLEM FOR YOUR REVIEW

☐ Problem One

Compute for process A in a candy factory the cost of work completed and the cost of the ending inventory of work in process:

Units:
   Started and completed, 30,000 units
   Ending work in process, 10,000 units, 100% completed for materials but 60% completed for conversion costs.

Costs:
   Total, $81,600; materials, $60,000; conversion, $21,600

☐ Solution One

| | (STEP 1) PHYSICAL | (STEP 2) EQUIVALENT UNITS | |
FLOW OF PRODUCTION	UNITS	Direct Materials	Conversion
Started and completed	30,000	30,000	30,000
Ending work in process	10,000	10,000*	6,000*
Work done to date	40,000	40,000	36,000

* 10,000 × 100% = 10,000; 10,000 × 60% = 6,000.

		DIRECT MATERIALS	CONVERSION COSTS
(Step 3)	Costs to account for ($81,600)	$60,000	$21,600
(Step 4)	Divide by equivalent units	40,000	36,000
	Unit costs	$1.50	$0.60
(Step 5)	Application of costs:		
	Completed and transferred,		
	30,000 × ($1.50 + $0.60)		$63,000
	Ending work in process:		
	Materials, 10,000 × $1.50	$15,000	
	Conversion, 6,000 × $0.60	3,600	18,600
	Total costs accounted for		$81,600

☐ PART TWO: Effects of Beginning Inventories

When beginning inventories are present, product costing becomes more complicated. Change our illustration. Suppose there had been 3,000 units in work in process on March 31. All direct materials had been placed in process, but on the average only 40% of the conversion costs had been applied to the 3,000 units.

```
Units:
  Work in process, March 31, 3,000 units, 100% completed for materials
    but only 40% completed for conversion costs
  Units started in April, 22,000
  Units completed during April, 20,000
  Work in process, April 30, 5,000 units, 100% completed for materials but
    only 25% completed for conversion costs

Costs:
  Work in process, March 31:
    Direct materials                            $7,500
    Conversion costs                             2,125          $  9,625
  Direct materials added during April                            70,000
  Conversion costs added during April                            42,500
    Total costs to account for                                 $122,125
```

The total costs to account for include the $9,625 of beginning inventory in addition to the $112,500 added during April.

Two widely described inventory methods will be discussed: the weighted-average method and the first-in, first-out method. The five-step approach is recommended for both methods.

WEIGHTED-AVERAGE METHOD

The weighted-average (WA) method has been called a "rollback" method. Why? Because the averaging includes (1) all work done in the current period plus (2) the work done in the preceding period on the current period's beginning inventory of work in process.

Exhibit 14–4 shows the first two steps, the computation of physical units

EXHIBIT 14–4

Forming Department
Output in Equivalent Units
For the Month Ended April 30, 19X1
(Weighted-Average Method)

| | | (STEP 2) EQUIVALENT UNITS | |
| | (STEP 1) | | |
FLOW OF PRODUCTION	PHYSICAL UNITS	Direct Materials	Conversion Costs
Work in process, March 31	3,000 (40%)*		
Started in April	22,000		
To account for	25,000		
Completed and transferred out during current period	20,000	20,000	20,000
Work in process, April 30	5,000 (25%)*	5,000	1,250†
Units accounted for	25,000		
Work done to date		25,000	21,250

* Degrees of completion for conversion costs at the dates of inventories.
† .25 × 5,000 = 1,250.

and equivalent units. Note that this illustration differs from the previous illustration in only one major respect, the presence of beginning work in process. The total equivalent units completed and in ending work in process are unaffected by the relative amounts of work done *during* April and *before* April. The computation of equivalent units ignores whether all 25,000 units to account for came from beginning work in process, or all were started in April, or some combination thereof. Thus, both Exhibits 14–2 and 14–4 show the total work done to date, 25,000 equivalent units of direct materials and 21,250 units of conversion costs.

Exhibit 14–5 presents a production cost report. Again, the total costs to account for, the unit costs, and the total costs of units transferred out and in ending work in process will be the same as in Exhibit 14–3. Why? Because the equivalent units for work done to date, which is the divisor for unit costs, is unaffected by whether all work was done in April or some before April on the March 31 inventory of work in process.

Why is the term *weighted-average* method used to describe this method? Primarily because the unit costs used for applying costs to products are affected by the *total costs incurred to date*, regardless of whether those costs were incurred during or before April. The unit costs in Exhibit 14–5 are higher than those in Exhibit 14–3. Why? Because the equivalent units are the same, but the total costs include the costs incurred before April as well as those costs added during April.

EXHIBIT 14–5

Forming Department
Production Cost Report
For the Month Ended April 30, 19X1
(Weighted-Average Method)

		TOTALS	Direct Materials	Conversion Costs
			DETAILS	
(Step 3)	Work in process, March 31	$ 9,625	$ 7,500	$ 2,125
	Current costs added	112,500	70,000	42,500
	Total costs to account for	$122,125	$77,500	$44,625
(Step 4)	Divisor, equivalent units			
	for work done to date		25,000	21,250
	Unit costs (weighted averages)		$3.10	$2.10
(Step 5)	Application of costs:			
	Completed and transferred			
	(20,000 units)	$104,000	20,000 ($3.10 + $2.10)	
	Work in process, April 30:			
	Direct materials	15,500	5,000 ($3.10)	
	Conversion costs	2,625		1,250* ($2.10)
	Total work in process	18,125		
	Total costs accounted for	$122,125		

* Equivalent units of work done. For more details, see Exhibit 14–4.

Ponder what has happened so far in this chapter:

1. In the first simple example, we assumed no beginning or ending inventories of work in process. Thus, when the $112,500 of costs incurred during April were applied to the 25,000 units worked on and fully completed during April, the unit cost (p. 447) was $2.80 + $1.70 = $4.50.
2. However, in the next example, we assumed that some of the units were not fully completed by the end of the month. This reduced the equivalent units and thus increased the unit cost (Exhibit 14–3, p. 449) to $2.80 + $2.00 = $4.80.
3. Then, in this latest example, we assumed that some of the units had also been worked on before April. The costs of that work are carried in work-in-process inventory, March 31. The addition of these costs (with no change in the equivalent units) increased the unit cost of work completed in April to $3.10 + $2.10 = $5.20.

FIRST-IN, FIRST-OUT METHOD

The first-in, first-out (FIFO) method sharply distinguishes the current work done from the previous work done on the beginning inventory of work in process. The calculation of equivalent units is confined to the work done in the current period, April in this illustration.

Exhibit 14–6 presents steps 1 and 2. The easiest way to compute equiva-

EXHIBIT 14–6

Forming Department
Output in Equivalent Units
For the Month Ended April 30, 19X1
(FIFO Method)

Same as Exhibit 14–4 FLOW OF PRODUCTION	(STEP 1) PHYSICAL UNITS	(STEP 2) EQUIVALENT UNITS	
		Direct Materials	Conversion Costs
Work in process, March 31	3,000 (40%)*		
Started in April	22,000		
To account for	25,000		
Completed and transferred out	20,000	20,000	20,000
Work in process, April 30	5,000 (25%)*	5,000	1,250†
Units accounted for	25,000		
Work done to date		25,000	21,250
Less: Old equivalent units for work done on beginning work in process in previous periods		3,000‡	1,200§
Work done in current period only		22,000	20,050

* Degree of completion for conversion costs at the dates of inventories.
† $5,000 \times .25 = 1,250$.
‡ $3,000 \times 1.00 = 3,000$.
§ $3,000 \times .40 = 1,200$.

lent units under the FIFO method is, first, compute the work done to date. Exhibit 14–6 shows these computations, which are exactly the same as in Exhibit 14–4. Second, deduct the work done *before* the current period. The remainder is the work done *during* the current period, which is the key to computing the unit costs by the FIFO method.

FIFO is really a small step in the direction of job-order costing. Why? Because FIFO recognizes a distinct batch of production each time period, whereas the weighted-average method does not. The divisor equivalent units for computing a unit cost are the equivalent units of current work done only.

Exhibit 14–7 is the production-cost report. It presents steps 3, 4, and 5. The $9,625 beginning inventory balance is kept separate from current costs. The calculations of equivalent unit costs are confined to costs added in April only.

The bottom half of Exhibit 14–7 shows two ways to compute the costs of goods completed and transferred out. The first and faster way is to compute

EXHIBIT 14–7

Forming Department
Production Cost Report
For the Month Ended April 30, 19X1
(FIFO Method)

		TOTALS	DETAILS Direct Materials	DETAILS Conversion Costs
(Step 3)	Work in process, March 31	$ 9,625	(work done before April)	
	Current costs added	112,500	$70,000	$42,500
	Total costs to account for	$122,125		
(Step 4)	Divisor, equivalent units of work done in April only		22,000	20,050
	Unit costs (for FIFO basis)		$3.1818	$2.1197
(Step 5)	Application of costs Work in process, April 30:			
	Direct materials	$ 15,909	5,000 ($3.1818)	
	Conversion costs	2,650		1,250* ($2.1197)
	Total work in process (5,000 units)	18,559		
	Completed and transferred out (20,000 units), $122,125 − $18,559	103,566†		
	Total costs accounted for	$122,125		

* Equivalent units of work done. See Exhibit 14–6 for more details.

† Check: Work in process, March 31	$ 9,625
Additional costs to complete, conversion costs of 60% of 3,000 × $2.1197 =	3,815
Started and completed, 22,000 − 5,000 = 17,000; 17,000 × ($3.1818 + $2.1197) =	90,126
Total cost transferred	$103,566

Unit cost transferred, $103,566 ÷ 20,000 = $5.1783

the $18,559 ending work in process and then deduct it from the $122,125 total costs to account for, obtaining $103,566. As a check on accuracy, it is advisable to use a second way; compute the cost of goods transferred in the detailed manner displayed in the footnote in Exhibit 14–7.

DIFFERENCES BETWEEN FIFO AND WEIGHTED-AVERAGE METHODS

The key difference between the FIFO and weighted-average computation is equivalent units:

> FIFO—Equivalent units are the work done in the current period only.
> Weighted-average—Equivalent units are the work done to date, including the earlier work done on the current period's beginning inventory of work in process.

In turn, differences in equivalent units lead to differences in unit costs. Accordingly, there are differences in costs applied to goods completed and still in process. In our example:

	WEIGHTED AVERAGE*	FIFO†
Cost of goods transferred out	$104,000	$103,566
Ending work in process	18,125	18,559
Total costs accounted for	$122,125	$122,125

* From Exhibit 14–5, page 452.
† From Exhibit 14–7, page 454.

In this example, the FIFO ending inventory is higher than the weighted-average inventory by only $434, or 2.4% ($434 ÷ $18,125 = 2.4%). The difference is attributable to variations in current unit costs of direct materials and conversion costs for March and for April. The unit cost of the work done in April only was $3.1818 + $2.1197 = $5.3015, as shown in Exhibit 14–7. In contrast, Exhibit 14–5 shows the weighted-average unit cost of $3.10 + $2.10 = $5.20. Therefore, the FIFO method results in a larger work-in-process inventory, April 30, and a smaller April cost of goods transferred out.

Ordinarily, the difference in unit costs under the weighted-average and FIFO methods would be even less significant than the small difference illustrated here. Fluctuations in unit costs from month to month in process costing are usually caused by volatile materials prices, not conversion costs.

The FIFO method involves more detailed computations than the weighted-average method. That is why FIFO is almost never used in practice in process costing *for product-costing purposes*. However, the FIFO *equivalent units* for current work done is essential *for planning and control purposes*. Why? Consider our example. The FIFO computations of equivalent units help managers to measure the efficiency of April performance independently from

March performance. Thus, budgets or standards for each month's departmental costs can be compared against actual results in light of the actual work done during any given month.

SUMMARY PROBLEM FOR YOUR REVIEW

☐ **Problem Two**

Compute for Process I in a food processing plant the cost of work completed and the cost of the ending inventory of work in process. Assume (1) weighted-average (WA) method and (2) FIFO method.

Units:		
Beginning work in process, 5,000 units, 100% completed for materials, 40% completed for conversion costs		
Started during month, 28,000 units		
Completed during month, 31,000 units		
Ending work in process, 2,000 units, 100% completed for materials, 50% for conversion costs		
Costs:		
Beginning work in process:		
Direct materials	$8,060	
Conversion costs	1,300	$ 9,360
Direct materials added in current month		41,440
Conversion costs added in current month		14,700
Total cost to account for		$65,500

☐ **Solution Two**

	(STEP 1)	(STEP 2) EQUIVALENT UNITS	
FLOW OF PRODUCTION	PHYSICAL UNITS	Material	Conversion Costs
Completed and transferred out	31,000	31,000	31,000
Ending work in process	2,000	2,000*	1,000*
1. Equivalent units, weighted-average	33,000	33,000	32,000
Less: Beginning work in process	5,000	5,000†	2,000†
2. Equivalent units, FIFO	28,000	28,000	30,000

* $2,000 \times 100\% = 2,000$; $2,000 \times 50\% = 1,000$.
† $5,000 \times 100\% = 5,000$; $5,000 \times 40\% = 2,000$.

1.

WEIGHTED-AVERAGE METHOD	TOTAL COST	DIRECT MATERIALS	CONVERSION COSTS
Beginning work in process	$ 9,360	$ 8,060	$ 1,300
Current costs added	56,140	41,440	14,700
Total cost to account for	$65,500	$49,500	$16,000
Equivalent units, weighted-average		33,000	32,000
Unit costs, weighted-average	$2.00	$1.50	$0.50
Transferred out, 31,000 × $2.00	$62,000		
Ending work in process:			
Direct materials	$ 3,000	2,000 ($1.50)	
Conversion cost	500		1,000 ($.50)
Total work in process	$ 3,500		
Total costs accounted for	$65,500		

2.

FIFO METHOD	TOTAL COST	DIRECT MATERIALS	CONVERSION COSTS
Beginning work in process	$ 9,360	(work done before month)	
Current costs added	56,140	41,440	14,700
Total costs to account for	$65,500		
Equivalent units, FIFO		28,000	30,000
Unit costs, FIFO	$1.97	$1.48	$0.49
Ending work in process			
Direct materials	$ 2,960	2,000 ($1.48)	
Conversion cost	490		1,000 ($.49)
Total work in process	$ 3,450		
Transferred out, $65,500 − $3,450	62,050*		
Total costs accounted for	$65,500		

* Check:

Beginning work in process	$ 9,360
Costs to complete, 60% × 5,000 × $.49	1,470
Started and completed,	
(31,000 − 5,000) ($1.48 + $.49)	51,220
Total cost transferred	$62,050

Unit cost transferred, $62,050 ÷ 31,000 = $2.00161

□ PART THREE: Accounting in Subsequent Process

A process subsequent to the initial manufacturing process provides a more thorough picture of process costing. For example, consider the Finishing Department, which processes the formed toys through the addition of hand shaping and metal. Although various materials might be added at various stages of finishing, for simplicity here, suppose all additional materials are added at the end of the process.

The following is a summary of the April operations in the Finishing Department:

Units:
  Work in process, March 31, 5,000 units, 60% completed for conversion costs
  Units transferred in during April, 20,000
  Units completed during April, 21,000
  Work in process, April 30, 4,000 units, 30% completed for conversion costs

Costs:

Work in process, March 31 (transferred-in costs, $17,750; conversion costs $7,250)	$ 25,000
Transferred-in costs from Forming during April	104,000*
Direct materials added during April	23,100
Conversion costs added during April	38,400
Total costs to account for	$190,500

* Assume the weighted-average method was used in the Forming Department.

These facts will be used to demonstrate the weighted-average method and the FIFO method of process costing. As before, the five-step procedure will be followed.

WEIGHTED-AVERAGE METHOD

Study Exhibit 14–8 regarding the Finishing Department. The exhibit shows the initial two steps that analyze physical flows and calculate equivalent units. Direct-material costs have zero degrees of completion regarding beginning and ending work-in-process inventories. Remember that, in this example, materials are introduced at the *end* of the process. In contrast, the equivalent units for transferred-in costs are always fully completed at each of the inventory dates; they are introduced at the *beginning* of the process.

EXHIBIT 14–8

Finishing Department
Output in Equivalent Units
For the Month Ended April 30, 19X1
(Weighted-Average Method)

FLOW OF PRODUCTION	(STEP 1) PHYSICAL UNITS	(STEP 2) EQUIVALENT UNITS		
		Transferred-in Costs	Direct Materials	Conversion Costs
Work in process, March 31	5,000 (60%)*			
Transferred in	20,000			
To account for	25,000			
Completed and transferred out during current period	21,000	21,000	21,000	21,000
Work in process, April 30	4,000 (30%)*	4,000	—	1,200†
Units accounted for	25,000			
Work done to date		25,000	21,000	22,200

* Degrees of completion for conversion costs at the dates of inventories.
† 4,000 × .30 = 1,200.

EXHIBIT 14–9

Finishing Department
Production Cost Report
For the Month Ended April 30, 19X1
(Weighted-Average Method)

	FLOW OF PRODUCTION	TOTALS	Transferred-in Costs	Direct Materials	Conversion Costs
				DETAILS	
	Work in process, March 31	$ 25,000	$ 17,750	$ —	$ 7,250
	Current costs added	165,500	104,000	23,100	38,400
(Step 3)	Total costs to account for	$190,500	$121,750	$23,100	$45,650
(Step 4)	Divisor, equivalent units for work done to date		25,000	21,000	22,200
	Unit costs (weighted averages)	$8.0263	$4.87	$1.10	$2.0563
(Step 5)	Application of costs: Completed and transferred out, 21,000 × $8.0263	$168,552	[21,000 × ($4.87 + $1.10 + $2.0563)]		
	Work in process, ending inventory, 4,000:				
	Transferred-in costs	$ 19,480	4,000 ($4.87)		
	Direct materials	—			
	Conversion costs	2,468			1,200* ($2.0563)
	Work in process, April 30	21,948			
	Total costs accounted for	$190,500			

* 4,000 × .30 = 1,200.

Consider the nature of **transferred-in costs** (or **previous department costs**). They are costs incurred in a previous department that have been received by a subsequent department. They are similar but not identical to any additional direct-materials costs added in the subsequent department. Therefore, the Finishing Department's calculations must provide separately for transferred-in costs.

Exhibit 14–9 is a production-cost report. It shows steps 3, 4, and 5. It presents the total costs to account for. Equivalent unit costs are computed and then applied to the units completed and in ending WIP.

Examine Exhibit 14–9 closely and note the following points: (1) The weighted-average method, unlike the FIFO method, necessitates the subdivision of the costs of beginning work in process into its components. (2) In this way, these components can be added to the current costs to obtain a combined amount for each cost element: transferred-in costs, direct materials, and conversion costs. (3) Thus, the unit costs of each cost element will be weighted averages.

Production cost reports may also be presented in briefer form. For example, the data in Exhibits 14–8 and 14–9 could be the supporting computations for a summary production-cost report. The latter would really be a formal presentation of the effects on the Work in Process—Finishing account:

	PHYSICAL UNITS	TOTAL COSTS
Work in process, March 31	5,000	$ 25,000
Current costs added	20,000	157,500
To account for	25,000	$182,500
Completed and transferred out	21,000	$161,832
Work in process, April 30	4,000	20,668
Work accounted for	25,000	$182,500

FIRST-IN, FIRST-OUT METHOD

Consider the FIFO method. Exhibit 14–10 presents the first two steps. Exhibit 14–11, the production cost report, shows steps 3, 4, and 5. The underlying approaches to computations remain the same for departments beyond the first department. The only difference is the category of transferred-in costs, which must not be overlooked.

Exhibit 14–11 again shows how the divisor equivalent units for FIFO differ from the divisor equivalent units for the weighted-average method. FIFO uses equivalent units for work done in the current period only.

EXHIBIT 14–10

Finishing Department
Output in Equivalent Units
For the Month Ended April 30, 19X1
(FIFO Method)

Same as Exhibit 14–8 FLOW OF PRODUCTION	(STEP 1) PHYSICAL UNITS	(STEP 2) EQUIVALENT UNITS Transferred-in Costs	Direct Materials	Conversion Costs
Work in process, March 31	5,000 (60%)*			
Transferred in	20,000			
To account for	25,000			
Completed and transferred out during current period	21,000	21,000	21,000	21,000
Work in process, April 30	4,000 (30%)*	4,000	—	1,200†
Units accounted for	25,000			
Work done to date		25,000	21,000	22,200
Less: Old equivalent units for work done on beginning work in process in previous periods		5,000‡	0	3,000§
Work done in current period only		20,000	21,000	19,200

* Degrees of completion for conversion costs at the dates of inventories.
† 4,000 × .30 = 1,200.
‡ 5,000 × 1.00 = 5,000.
§ 5,000 × .60 = 3,000.

EXHIBIT 14–11

Finishing Department
Production Cost Report
For the Month Ended April 30, 19X1
(FIFO Method)

| | | | DETAILS | |
	TOTALS	Transferred-in Costs	Direct Materials	Conversion Costs
(Step 3) Work in process, March 31	$ 25,000	(work done before April)		
Current costs added	165,500	$104,000	$23,100	$38,400
Total costs to account for	$190,500			
(Step 4) Divisor, equivalent units		20,000	21,000	19,200
Unit costs of work done during April only	$8.30	$5.20	$1.10	$2.00
(Step 5) Application of costs:				
Work in process, April 30:				
Transferred-in costs	$ 20,800	4,000 ($5.20)		
Direct materials	—		—	
Conversion costs	2,400			1,200* ($2.00)
Total work in process (4,000 units)	23,200			
Completed and transferred out (21,000 units), $190,500 − $23,200	167,300†			
Total costs accounted for	$190,500			

* Equivalent units of work done. See Exhibit 14–10 for details.

† Check:

Work in process, March 31	$ 25,000
Additional costs to complete:	
Direct materials, 5,000 × $1.10 =	5,500
Conversion costs, 5,000 × .40 × $2.00	4,000
Started and completed 21,000 − 5,000 = 16,000; 16,000 × $8.30	132,800
Total cost of goods completed and transferred	$167,300

Unit cost transferred, $167,300 ÷ 21,000 = $7.9667

In a series of departmental transfers, each department is regarded as a distinct accounting entity. All costs tranferred out during a given period are carried at one unit cost by the next department. For example, Exhibit 14–11 used FIFO to compute the total cost of goods completed and transferred. But note that the next department (or Finished-Goods inventory) would carry the goods transferred at a single average unit cost ($7.9667 in this illustration) as a matter of convenience. That is, examine footnote † in Exhibit 14–11. The Finishing Department's beginning inventory, whose costs were accounted for separately under the FIFO method, is mingled with the goods started and completed in computing the $7.9667 unit cost of goods transferred.

JOURNAL ENTRIES

A complete set of summarized journal entries for the two departments follows. The entries assume that the weighted-average method has been used, and that the inventory in the Forming Department was $9,625.

1.	Work in process—Forming		70,000	
	Direct-materials inventory			70,000
	Materials added to production in April.			
2.	Work in process—Forming		10,625	
	Accrued payroll			10,625
	Direct labor in April.			
3.	Work in process—Forming		31,875	
	Factory overhead			31,875
	Factory overhead applied in April.			
4.	Work in process—Finishing		104,000	
	Work in process—Forming			104,000
	Cost of goods completed and transferred in April from Forming to Assembly.			
5.	Work in process—Finishing		23,100	
	Direct-materials inventory			23,100
	Materials added to production in April.			
6.	Work in process—Finishing		12,800	
	Accrued payroll			12,800
	Direct labor in April.			
7.	Work in process—Finishing		25,600	
	Factory overhead			25,600
	Factory overhead applied in April.			
8.	Finished goods inventory		168,552	
	Work in process—Finishing			168,552
	Cost of goods completed and transferred in April from Finishing to finished goods inventory.			

The key T-accounts now show:

Work in Process—Forming				Work in Process—Finishing				Finished-Goods Inventory		
3/31 Bal.	9,625			3/31 Bal.	25,000					
1.	70,000	4.	104,000	4.	104,000	8.	168,552	8.	168,552	
2.	10,625			5.	23,100					
3.	31,875			6.	12,800					
	122,125			7.	25,600					
					190,500					
4/30 Bal.	18,125			4/30 Bal.	21,948					

SUMMARY PROBLEMS FOR YOUR REVIEW

The following facts will be used for three problems.

Consider a Finishing Department that processes formed toys through the addition of hand shaping and metal. For simplicity assume that all additional materials are added at the end of the process.

The April operations in the Finishing Department were:

```
Units:
  Work in process, March 31, 5,000 units, 80% completed for
    conversion costs
  Units transferred in during April, 20,000
  Units completed during April, 21,000
  Work in process, April 30, 4,000 units, 40% completed for
    conversion costs
Costs:
  Work in process, March 31
    ($29,000 transferred-in costs,
      $9,060 conversion costs)                              $ 38,060
  Transferred-in costs from Forming during April              96,000
  Direct materials added during April                         25,200
  Conversion costs added during April                         38,400
    Total costs to account for                              $197,660
```

Problem Three

Compute the equivalent units for direct materials and conversion costs. Assume the (1) weighted-average method and (2) the FIFO method.

Problem Four

Assume the weighted-average method for the Finishing Department. Prepare (1) a schedule of output in equivalent units and (2) a production-cost report. Headings for the exhibits may be omitted.

Problem Five

Assume the FIFO method for the Finishing Department. Compute the unit costs for applying April costs to products.

Solution Three

	DIRECT MATERIALS	CONVERSION COSTS
Completed and transferred out during April	21,000	21,000
Work in process, April 30	0	1,600*
(1) Work done to date (for weighted-average method)	21,000	22,600
Less: Old equivalent units for work done on beginning work in process in previous periods	0	4,000†
(2) Work done in April only (for FIFO method)	21,000	18,600

* 40% of 4,000 = 1,600.

† 80% of 5,000 = 4,000.

☐ Solution Four

1.

FLOW OF PRODUCTION	PHYSICAL UNITS	Transferred-in Costs	Direct Materials	Conversion Costs
		EQUIVALENT UNITS		
Work in process, March 31	5,000 (80%)*			
Transferred in	20,000			
To account for	25,000			
Completed and transferred out during current period	21,000	21,000	21,000	21,000
Work in process, April 30	4,000 (40%)*	4,000	—	1,600†
Units accounted for	25,000			
Work done to date		25,000	21,000	22,600

* Degrees of completion for conversion costs at the dates of inventories.
† 4,000 × .40 = 1,600

2.

FLOW OF PRODUCTION	TOTALS	Transferred-in Costs	Direct Materials	Conversion Costs
		DETAILS		
Work in process, March 31	$ 38,060	$ 29,000	$ —	$ 9,060
Current costs added	159,600	96,000	25,200	38,400
Total costs to account for	$197,660	$125,000	$25,200	$47,460
Divisor, equivalent units for work done to date		25,000	21,000	22,600
Unit costs	$8.30	$5.00	$1.20	$2.10
Application of costs: Completed and transferred out, 21,000 × $8.30	$174,300			
Work in process, ending inventory, 4,000:				
Transferred in costs	20,000	4,000 ($5.00)		
Direct materials	—			
Conversion costs	3,360			1,600 ($2.10)
Work in process, April 30	23,360			
Total costs accounted for	$197,660			

☐ Solution Five

	TRANSFERRED-IN COSTS	DIRECT MATERIALS	CONVERSION COSTS
Current costs added	$96,000	$25,200	$38,400
Divide by equivalent units for work done in April	20,000*	21,000†	18,600†
Unit costs	$4.80	$1.20	$2.0645

* Units transferred in during April.
† Calculations are in Solution Three.

ADDITIONAL FEATURES OF PROCESS COSTING

This chapter's illustrations plus almost all process-cost problems blithely mention various degrees of completion for inventories in process. The accuracy of these estimates depends on the care and skill of the estimator and the nature of the process. Estimating the degree of completion is usually easier for materials than for conversion costs. The conversion sequence usually consists of a number of standard operations or a standard number of hours, days, weeks, or months for mixing, heating, cooling, aging, curing, and so forth. Thus the degree of completion for conversion costs depends on what proportion of the total effort needed to complete one unit or one batch has been devoted to units still in process. In industries where no exact estimate is possible, or, as in textiles, where vast quantities in process prohibit costly physical estimates, all work in process in every department is assumed to be one-third or one-half or two-thirds complete. In other cases, continuous processing entails little change of work-in-process levels from month to month. Consequently, in such cases, work in process is safely ignored, and monthly production costs are assigned solely to goods completed.

Process costing is often marked by significant shrinkage, evaporation, spoilage, and waste. As a general rule, the costs of the related units are separately identified. If deemed as being within normal limits, such costs are allocated to the good units produced. If abnormal spoilage occurs, such costs are written off as a separate expense (loss) of the current period instead of being allocated to the good units. A detailed explanation of these topics is beyond the scope of this introduction to process costing.

SUMMARY

Process costing is used for inventory costing when there is continuous mass production of like units. The key concept in process costing is that of equivalent units, the expression of output during a given period in terms of doses or amounts of work applied thereto.

Five basic steps may be used in solving process-cost problems. Process costing is complicated by varying amounts of cost factors, by the presence of beginning inventories, and by the presence of costs transferred in from prior departments.

Two widely advocated process-costing techniques are known as the *weighted-average* and *first-in, first-out* methods.

HIGHLIGHTS TO REMEMBER

1. This introduction to process costing has concentrated on general approaches. The FIFO method has been explored primarily to illustrate how the equivalent units for the current period provide the key measures of the work accomplished during a given period (April in our examples). This type of measurement is used widely for planning and controlling materials and labor, especially when linked with the standard-costing systems described in Chapter 7. The weighted-average method has been covered primarily because it is

widely used in practice for product-costing purposes, as distinguished from planning and control purposes.

The practice of expressing work in terms of equivalent whole units is widespread in both manufacturing and nonmanufacturing situations. For example, universities measure the number of part-time students attending night courses in terms of full-time equivalents.

Regarding Part Three of the chapter, avoid these common pitfalls:

a. Transferred-in costs from previous departments should be included in your calculations. Such costs should be treated as if they were another kind of material cost, because each department is treated as a separate entity. In other words, when successive departments are involved, transferred goods from one department become all or a part of the raw materials of the next department, although they are called *transferred-in costs*, not raw materials.

b. In calculating costs to be transferred on a first-in, first-out basis, do not overlook the costs attached at the beginning of the period to goods that were in process but are now included in the goods transferred. For example, do not overlook the $25,000 in Exhibit 14–11, page 461.

c. Unit costs may fluctuate between periods. Therefore, transferred goods may contain batches accumulated at different unit costs (see point b). These goods, when transferred to the next department, are typically valued by that next department at *one* average unit cost.

ACCOUNTING VOCABULARY

Equivalent Units *p. 447*   Previous Department Costs *459*   Transferred-in Costs *459*

FUNDAMENTAL ASSIGNMENT MATERIAL

14–1. **COVERAGE OF PART ONE OF CHAPTER.**   (Alternates are 14–8 and 14–9.) Chan Company produces transistor radios in large quantities. The manufacturing costs for the Assembly Department during March were:

Direct materials added		$ 80,000
Conversion costs:		
Direct labor	$25,760	
Factory overhead applied	38,640	64,400
Assembly costs to account for		$144,400

There was no beginning inventory of work in process. Suppose that work on 10,000 radios was begun during January, but that only 8,000 radios were fully completed and transferred to the Finishing Department. All the parts had been made or placed in process, but only 60% of the labor had been completed for each of the 2,000 radios in the ending inventory.

Required:

1. Compute the equivalent units and unit costs for March.
2. Compute the costs of units completed and transferred to the Finishing Department. Also compute the cost of the ending work in process. (For journal entries, see Problem 14–14.)

14-2. **COVERAGE OF PART TWO OF CHAPTER.** (Alternate is 14–28.) The Gustavo Company has a fabricating process for cotton textiles. Material is introduced at the beginning of the process in Department A. Conversion costs are applied uniformly throughout the process. As the process is completed, goods are immediately transferred to a finishing process in Department B. Data for the month of April 19X1 follow:

Work in process, beginning inventory completed for materials, but only 40% completed for conversion costs, $64,400 (materials, $51,000; conversion costs, $13,400)	10,000 units, 100%
Units started during April	60,000
Units completed during April	30,000
Work in process, ending inventory completed for materials, but only 60% completed for conversion costs	40,000 units, 100%
Direct materials added during April	$600,000
Conversion costs added during April	$100,000

Production was inefficient in March. In April severe material price increases occurred. Demand was increasing, so the company began to increase its inventories.

Required:

Compute the cost of goods transferred out of the department during April. Compute the cost of the ending inventory of work in process. Prepare a production-cost report or a similar orderly tabulation of your work. Assume weighted-average product costing. (For the FIFO method and journal entries, see Problems 14–31 and 14–32.)

14-3. **COVERAGE OF PART THREE OF CHAPTER.** (Alternate is 14–41.) The Gustavo Company has a fabricating process for cotton textiles. Material is introduced at the *beginning* of the process in Department A. As the process is completed, goods are immediately transferred to a finishing process in Department B. Additional material is added at the *end* of the process in Department B. Conversion costs are applied uniformly through both processes. Data for B for April follow.

Work in process, beginning inventory completed for conversion costs, $221,850 (transferred-in costs, $189,000; conversion costs, $32,850)	15,000 units, 30%
Units started during April	30,000
Units completed during April	39,000
Work in process, ending inventory	6,000, 50% completed for conversion costs
Transferred-in costs from Department A during April	$342,000
Material cost added during April	$ 54,600
Conversion costs added during April	$168,750

Required:

Compute the cost of goods transferred out of the department during April. Compute the cost of the ending inventory of work in process. Prepare a production-cost report or a similar orderly tabulation of your work. Assume weighted-average product costing. (For the FIFO method, see Problem 14–40.)

ADDITIONAL ASSIGNMENT MATERIAL FOR PART ONE

14–4. Give three examples of industries where process-costing systems are probably used.

14–5. Give three examples of nonprofit organizations where process-costing systems are probably used.

14–6. Give three examples of equivalent units in various organizations.

14–7. "There are five key steps in process cost accounting." What are they?

14–8. **STRAIGHTFORWARD COMPUTATIONS.** (Alternates are 14–1 and 14–9.) The Ramirez Company produces parts for television sets in large quantities. For simplicity, focus on an Assembly Department. Assume that there was no beginning work in process. One million units were started during the year. Direct materials used were $890,000; conversion costs were $285,000, consisting of $171,000 of direct labor and $114,000 of factory overhead.

All the direct materials had been placed in process, but on the average only half of the conversion costs had been completed for each of the 100,000 units still in process at the end of the year.

Required:

Prepare a tabulation or tabulations of the flow of production in physical units, the equivalent units, the unit costs, and the application of costs to units transferred to the Finishing Department.

14–9. **STRAIGHTFORWARD COMPUTATIONS.** (Alternates are 14–1 and 14–8.) A department produces textile products. All direct materials are introduced at the start of the process. Conversion costs are incurred uniformly throughout the process.

In May there was no beginning inventory. Units started, completed, and transferred, 400,000. Units in process, May 31, 80,000. Each unit in ending work in process was 75% converted. Costs incurred during May: direct materials, $3,360,000; conversion costs, $920,000.

Required:

1. Compute the total work done in equivalent units and the unit cost for May.
2. Compute the cost of units completed and transferred. Also compute the cost of units in ending work in process.

14–10. **NONPROFIT PROCESS COSTING.** The California State Franchise Tax Board must process millions of income tax returns yearly. Because of negative votes by the citizens, the tax board must work with fewer personnel than it did before. To find ways to improve productivity, some work-measurement experts have been closely observing the processing of tax returns.

When the taxpayer sends in his or her return, documents such as checks and withholding statements are compared with the data on the return. Other inspections of the return are also conducted. Although the processing time taken depends on the complexity of the return, the expected time allowed is based on an "average" return.

Assume that 1.2 million returns were received on April 15. On April 23, the work-measurement experts found that all processing steps had been fully completed on 40 percent of the returns. However, 60 percent still had to be submitted for final inspection.

Required:

1. The final inspection process represents 25 percent of the complete processing time. Compute the total work done in terms of equivalent units.
2. Various materials and supplies amounting to $144,000 were consumed in processing the returns (punched cards, inspection check sheets, clips, staples, and so on). For these calculations, materials and supplies are regarded as direct materials. The conversion costs were $3,060,000. Compute the unit costs of materials and supplies and of conversion.
3. Compute the cost of tax returns still in process.

14–11. UNEVEN FLOW. A one-department company manufactured basic hand-held calculators. Various materials were added at various stages of the process. The outer back shell and the carrying case, which represented 10% of the total material cost, were added at the final step of the assembly process. All other materials were considered to be "in process" by the time the calculator reached a 50% stage of completion.

Ninety-one thousand calculators were started in production during 19X1. At year-end, 5,000 calculators were in various stages of completion, but all of them were beyond the 50% stage and on the average they were regarded as being 70% completed for conversion costs.

The following costs were incurred during the year: direct materials, $181,000; conversion costs, $268,500.

Required:
1. Prepare a schedule of physical units, equivalent units, and unit costs.
2. Tabulate the cost of goods completed and the cost of ending work in process.

14–12. TWO MATERIALS. The following data pertain to the mixing department for November:

Units:	
Work in process, October 31	0
Units started	50,000
Completed and transferred to finishing department	35,000
Costs:	
Material M	$250,000
Material N	$105,000
Conversion costs	$ 82,000

Material M is introduced at the start of the process, while material N is added when the product reaches an 80% stage of completion. Conversion costs are incurred uniformly throughout the process.

The ending work in process is 40% completed for conversion costs.

Required:
1. Compute the equivalent units and unit costs for November.
2. Compute the total cost of units completed and transferred to finished goods. Also compute the cost of the ending work in process.

14–13. MATERIALS AND CARTONS. A London company manufactures and sells small portable fans. Business is booming because, to save on costs of electricity, many households are using fans instead of air conditioners. Various materials are added at various stages in the Assembly Department. Costs are accounted for on a process-cost basis. The end of the process involves conducting a final inspection and adding a cardboard carton.

The final inspection requires 5% of the total processing time. All materials besides the carton are added by the time the fans reach an 80% stage of completion of conversion.

There were no beginning inventories. One hundred thousand fans were started in production during 19X3. At the end of the year, which was not a busy time, 4,000 fans were in various stages of completion. All of the ending units in work in process were at the 95% stage. They awaited final inspection and being placed in cartons.

Total direct materials consumed in production, except for cartons, cost £1.5 million. Cartons used cost £172,800. Total conversion costs were £798,400.

Required:
1. Present a schedule of physical units, equivalent units, and unit costs of direct materials, cartons, and conversion costs.
2. Present a summary of the cost of goods completed and the cost of ending work in process.

14-14. **JOURNAL ENTRIES.** Refer to the data in Problem 14-1. Prepare summary journal entries for the use of direct materials, direct labor, and factory overhead applied. Also prepare a journal entry for the transfer of goods completed and transferred. Show the postings to the Work in Process account.

14-15. **JOURNAL ENTRIES.** Refer to the data in Problem 14-8. Prepare summary journal entries for the use of direct materials, direct labor, and factory overhead applied. Also prepare a journal entry for the transfer of goods completed and transferred. Show the postings to the Work in Process—Assembly Department account.

ADDITIONAL ASSIGNMENT MATERIAL FOR PART TWO

14-16. Identify the major distinction between the first two and the final three steps of the five major steps in accounting for process costs.

14-17. Present an equation that describes the physical flow in process costing.

14-18. Why is "work done in the current period only" a key measurement of equivalent units?

14-19. "The beginning inventory is regarded as if it were a batch of goods separate and distinct from the goods started *and* completed by a process during the current period." What method of process costing is being described?

14-20. "Equivalent units are the work done to date." What method of process costing is being described?

14-21. "Ordinarily, the differences in unit costs under FIFO and weighted-average methods are insignificant." Do you agree? Explain.

14-22. **PHYSICAL UNITS.** Fill in the unknowns in physical units:

| | CASE | |
FLOW OF PRODUCTION	A	B
Work in process, beginning inventory	1,000	4,000
Started	6,000	?
Completed and transferred	?	8,000
Work in process, ending inventory	3,000	2,000

14-23. **MULTIPLE CHOICE.** The Ace Company had computed the physical flow (of physical units) for Department A, for the month of April, as follows:

Units completed:	
From work in process on April 1	10,000
From April production	30,000
	40,000

Materials are added at the beginning of the process. Units of work in process at April 30 were 8,000. The work in process at April 1 was 80% complete as to conversion costs and the work in process at April 30 was 60% complete as to conversion costs. What are the equivalent units of production for the month of April using the FIFO method? Choose one of the following combinations:

	MATERIALS	CONVERSION COSTS
a.	38,000	36,800
b.	38,000	38,000
c.	48,000	44,800
d.	48,000	48,000

14–24. **EQUIVALENT UNITS.** Fill in the unknowns:

FLOW OF PRODUCTION IN UNITS	(STEP 1) PHYSICAL UNITS	(STEP 2) EQUIVALENT UNITS Direct Materials	Conversion Costs
Work in process, beginning inventory	20,000*		
Started	70,000		
To account for	90,000		
Completed and transferred out	?	?	?
Work in process, ending inventory	5,000†	?	?
Accounted for	90,000		
Work done to date		?	?
Less: Old equivalent units for work done on beginning work in process in previous periods		?	?
Work done in current period only (FIFO method)		?	?

* Degree of completion: direct materials, 60%; conversion costs, 30%.
† Degree of completion: direct materials, 70%; conversion costs, 80%.

14–25. **COMPUTE EQUIVALENT UNITS.** Consider the following data for June:

	PHYSICAL UNITS
Started in June	50,000
Completed in June	45,000
Ending inventory, work in process	15,000
Beginning inventory, work in process	10,000

The beginning inventory was 60% complete regarding materials and 20% complete regarding conversion costs. The ending inventory was 40% complete regarding materials and 80% complete regarding conversion costs.

Required:

Prepare a schedule of equivalent units for the work done to date and the work done during June only.

14–26. **FIFO AND UNIT MATERIAL COSTS.** The Morales Company uses the FIFO process-cost method. Consider the following for March:

Beginning inventory, 20,000 units, 60% completed regarding materials, which cost $100,000

Units completed, 75,000

Cost of materials placed in process during March, $396,000

Ending inventory, 10,000 units, 30% completed regarding materials

Required: Compute the material cost per equivalent unit for the work done in March only. No units were lost or spoiled.

14–27. **FIFO Method, Conversion Cost.** Given the following information, compute the unit conversion cost for the month of June for the Paton Company, using the FIFO process-cost method. Show details of your calculation.

(1) Units completed, 30,000
(2) Conversion cost in beginning inventory, $7,500
(3) Beginning inventory, 5,000 units with 40% of conversion cost
(4) Ending inventory, 10,000 units with 60% of conversion cost
(5) Conversion costs put into production in June, $136,000

14–28. **Weighted-Average Process-Costing Method.** (Alternate is 14–2.) The Nifty Paint Co. uses a process-cost system. Materials are added at the beginning of a particular process and conversion costs are incurred uniformly. Work in process at the beginning is assumed 50% complete; at the end, 40%. One gallon of material makes 1 gallon of product. Data follow:

Beginning inventory	900 gal
Direct materials added	12,100 gal
Ending inventory	400 gal
Conversion costs incurred	$18,465
Cost of direct materials added	$52,030
Conversion costs, beginning inventory	$1,951
Cost of direct materials, beginning inventory	$2,570

Required: Use the weighted-average method. Prepare a schedule of output in equivalent units and a schedule of application of costs to products. Show the cost of goods completed and of ending work in process. (For the FIFO method and journal entries, see the next two problems.)

14–29. **FIFO Computations.** Refer to the preceding problem. Using FIFO, repeat the requirements.

14–30. **Journal Entries.** Refer to the data in Problem 14–28. Prepare summary journal entries for the use of direct materials and conversion costs. Also prepare a journal entry for the transfer of goods completed, assuming that the goods are transferred from Department A to Department B.

14–31. **FIFO Method.** Refer to Problem 14–2. Using FIFO costing, repeat the requirements.

14–32. **Journal Entries.** Refer to the data in Problem 14–2. Prepare summary journal entries for the use of direct materials and conversion costs. Also prepare a journal entry for the transfer of the goods completed and transferred from Department A to Department B.

14–33. "Transferred-in costs are those incurred in the preceding period." Do you agree? Explain.

14–34. Why should the accountant distinguish between *transferred-in costs* and *new material costs* for a particular department?

14–35. "The FIFO method should really be called the modified FIFO or departmental FIFO method." Do you agree? Explain.

14–36. "The total conversion costs are divided by the equivalent units for the work done to date." Does this quotation describe the weighted-average method or does it describe FIFO?

14–37. Under what conditions can significant amounts of work in process be safely ignored in process costing?

14–38. Describe the general approach to process costing followed when significant spoilage occurs.

14–39. "Transferred-in costs may be regarded as if they were another type of material costs." Do you agree? Explain.

14–40. FIFO METHOD. Refer to Problem 14–3. Repeat the requirements, using FIFO.

14–41. WEIGHTED-AVERAGE METHOD. (Alternate is 14–3.) A company has two processes. Material is introduced at the *beginning* of the process in Department A, but no material is added in Department B, which is the Finishing Department. Conversion costs are applied uniformly throughout both processes. As the process in Department A is completed, goods are immediately transferred to Department B; as goods are completed in Department B, they are transferred to Finished Goods.

Simplified data for Department B for the month of November are:

Work in process, beginning inventory	300 units
	⅓ completed, $5,530
	(transferred-in-costs,
	$4,680; conversion
	costs, $850)
Units started during November	?
Units completed during November	500
Work in process, ending inventory	300, ⅔ completed
Cost transferred in from Department A	
during November	$7,000
Conversion costs added during	
November	$3,000

Required:
1. Prepare a schedule showing the computation of output in equivalent units for November. Use the weighted-average method.
2. Prepare a schedule of the total costs of units completed and transferred to finished goods and the total costs of the ending work in process. (For the FIFO method, see the next problem.)

14–42. FIFO METHOD. Refer to the preceding problem. Repeat the requirements using FIFO.

14–43. FIFO AND WEIGHTED-AVERAGE. Consider these April data for Department B:

	PHYSICAL UNITS	EQUIVALENT UNITS Transferred in	Materials	Conversion
Work in process, beginning	?			
Started	?			
To account for	20,000			
Completed and transferred out				
From beginning inventory	?	?	?	?
Started and completed				
currently	9,000	?	?	?
Work in process, ending	5,000	?	?	?
Accounted for	?			
Work done during April only		?	?	?
Work done before April on the				
beginning inventory		?	?	?
Work done to date		?	?	?

Materials are added at the beginning of the process in Department B. Conversion costs are incurred uniformly throughout the process. At the inventory dates, the beginning inventory was 50% converted and the ending inventory was 20% converted.

Required:

1. Fill in the unknowns.
2. Suppose that Department B March conversion costs associated with the April beginning inventory were $7,600 and current conversion costs in April for all production were $26,000. Compute the appropriate unit conversion costs under the (a) FIFO method and (b) weighted-average method.
3. Suppose that current transferred-in costs during April were $112,000. The March transferred-in costs associated with the April beginning inventory were $42,000. Compute the appropriate unit transferred-in costs under the (a) FIFO method and (b) weighted-average method.

Chapter 15

OVERHEAD APPLICATION: DIRECT AND ABSORPTION COSTING

LEARNING OBJECTIVES

When you have finished studying this chapter, you should be able to:

1. Identify the basic feature that distinguishes the direct-costing approach from the absorption-costing approach.
2. Construct an income statement, using each of the two product-costing approaches.
3. Identify the nature of the production volume variance, compute it, and state how it should appear in the income statement.
4. Identify the two methods for disposing of the standard cost variances at the end of a year and give the rationale for each.
5. Identify the differences among the three alternative cost bases of an absorption-costing system: actual, normal, and standard.
6. Analyze and compare all the major variances in a standard absorption-costing system (Appendix 15A).
7. Prepare journal entries for a standard absorption-costing system (Appendix 15B).

The preceding two chapters concentrated on how an accounting system accumulates costs by departments and *applies* costs to the products or services that are produced by those departments. This chapter[1] concentrates on two major variations of product costing. We use a standard product-costing system here for illustrative purposes. However, these variations can be used in nonstandard product-costing systems too.

DIRECT VERSUS ABSORPTION COSTING

☐ Accounting for Fixed Manufacturing Overhead

Two major methods of product costing are compared in this chapter: *direct costing* (the contribution approach) and *absorption costing* (the functional, full-costing, or traditional approach). These methods differ in only one conceptual respect: fixed manufacturing overhead is excluded from the cost of products under direct costing but is included in the cost of products under absorption costing. In other words, direct costing signifies that fixed factory overhead is not inventoried. In contrast, absorption costing indicates that inventory values include fixed factory overhead.

Direct costing is more accurately called *variable* or *marginal costing*, because it applies only the *variable* production costs to the product. As Exhibit 15–1 shows, fixed manufacturing overhead (fixed factory overhead) is regarded as an expired cost to be immediately charged against sales—not as an unexpired cost to be held back as inventory and charged against sales later as a part of cost of goods sold.

The term "direct" costing is widely used, but "variable" costing is a more accurate description. Why? Because, as Exhibit 15–1 shows, the "direct"-costing approach to the inventorying of costs is not confined to only "direct" materials and labor; it also includes an "indirect" cost—the *variable* manufacturing overhead. Such terminological confusion is unfortunate but apparently unavoidable in a field such as management accounting, where new analytical ideas or approaches arise in isolated fashion. Newly coined terms, which may not be accurately descriptive, often become embedded too deeply to be supplanted later.

---

[1] Chapter 15 contains sufficient product-costing information to understand the issues raised. Therefore, it may be studied without having studied Chapters 13 and 14. However, Chapter 3 (particularly the first half, which is worth reviewing now) and Chapter 7 should be studied before undertaking Chapter 15. This book was written to permit the utmost flexibility. In particular, many instructors may prefer to follow Chapter 3 with Chapter 13 and then follow Chapter 7 with Chapter 15.

EXHIBIT 15–1

Comparison of Flow of Costs

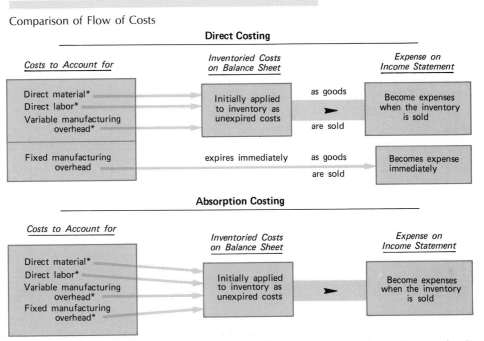

Direct Costing

Costs to Account for	Inventoried Costs on Balance Sheet		Expense on Income Statement
Direct material* Direct labor* Variable manufacturing overhead*	Initially applied to inventory as unexpired costs	as goods ▶ are sold	Become expenses when the inventory is sold
Fixed manufacturing overhead	expires immediately	as goods are sold	Becomes expense immediately

Absorption Costing

Costs to Account for	Inventoried Costs on Balance Sheet		Expense on Income Statement
Direct material* Direct labor* Variable manufacturing overhead* Fixed manufacturing overhead*	Initially applied to inventory as unexpired costs	▶	Become expenses when the inventory is sold

* As goods are manufactured, the costs are "applied" to inventory usually via the use of unit costs.

Take a moment to reflect on Exhibit 15–1. Also, reexamine Exhibit 3–3, page 66, which provides an overview of income statement and balance sheet relationships.

Absorption costing is more widely used than direct costing. However the growing use of the contribution approach in performance measurement and cost analysis has led to increasing use of direct costing for internal-reporting purposes. Over half of the major firms in the United States use direct costing for some internal reporting, and nearly a quarter use it as the primary internal format. In contrast, neither the public accounting profession nor the Internal Revenue Service approves of direct costing for external-reporting or tax purposes. Therefore, all firms use absorption costing for their reports to shareholders and tax authorities.

Until the last decade or two, use of direct costing for internal reporting was expensive. It requires information to be processed two ways, one for external reporting and one for internal reporting. The increasing use and decreasing cost of computers has reduced the added cost of a direct-costing system. Most managers no longer face the question of whether to invest in a separate direct-costing *system*. Rather, they simply choose a direct-costing or absorption-costing *format* for reports. Many well-designed accounting systems used today can produce either format.

□ Facts for Illustration

To make these ideas more concrete, consider the following example. The Greenberg Company had the following standard costs for 19X7 and 19X8:

BASIC PRODUCTION DATA AT STANDARD COST	
Direct material	$1.30
Direct labor	1.50
Variable manufacturing overhead	.20
Standard variable costs per unit	$3.00

Fixed manufacturing overhead (fixed factory overhead) was budgeted at $150,000. Expected production in each year was 150,000 units. Sales price, $5 per unit.

Selling and administrative expense is assumed for simplicity to be all fixed at $65,000 yearly, except for sales commissions at 5% of dollar sales. Actual product quantities were:

	19X7	19X8
In units:		
Opening inventory	—	30,000
Production	170,000	140,000
Sales	140,000	160,000
Ending inventory	30,000	10,000

There were no variances from the standard variable manufacturing costs, and fixed manufacturing overhead incurred was exactly $150,000 per year.

Required:
1. Prepare income statements for 19X7 and 19X8 under direct costing.
2. Prepare income statements for 19X7 and 19X8 under absorption costing.
3. Show a reconciliation of the difference in operating income for 19X7, 19X8, and the two years as a whole.

The solution to this problem will be explained, step by step, in subsequent sections. The solution to Requirement 1 is in Exhibit 15–2, to Requirement 2 in Exhibit 15–3, and to Requirement 3 in Exhibit 15–4.

□ Direct-Costing Method

The solution to Requirement 1 is shown in Exhibit 15–2. It has a familiar contribution-approach format, the same format introduced in Chapter 3. The only new characteristic of Exhibit 15–2 is the presence of a detailed calculation of cost of goods sold, which is affected by changes in the beginning and ending inventories. (In contrast, the income statements in Chapters 3 through 7 assumed that there were no changes in the beginning and ending inventories.)

EXHIBIT 15–2 Direct Costing

GREENBERG COMPANY
Comparative Income Statements (in thousands of dollars)
For the Years 19X7 and 19X8
(Data are in text)

		19X7		19X8	
Sales, 140,000 and 160,000 units, respectively	(1)		$700		$800
Variable expenses:					
Variable manufacturing cost of goods sold					
Opening inventory, at standard variable costs of $3		$ —		$ 90	
Add: Variable cost of goods manufactured					
at standard, 170,000 and 140,000 units,					
respectively		510		420	
Available for sale, 170,000 units in each year		$510		$510	
Deduct: Ending inventory, at standard					
variable cost of $3		90*		30†	
Variable manufacturing cost of goods sold		$420		$480	
Variable selling expenses, at 5% of dollar sales		35		40	
Total variable expenses	(2)		455		520
Contribution margin	(3) = (1) − (2)		$245		$280
Fixed expenses:					
Fixed factory overhead		150		150	
Fixed selling and administrative expenses		65		65	
Total fixed expenses	(4)		215		215
Operating income	(3) − (4)		$ 30		$ 65

* 30,000 units × $3 = $90,000.
† 10,000 units × $3 = $30,000.

The costs of the product are accounted for by applying all *variable* manu-facturing costs to the goods produced at a rate of $3 per unit; thus inventories are valued at standard variable costs. In contrast, fixed manufacturing costs are not applied to any products but are regarded as expenses in the period they are incurred.

Again, before reading on, please trace the facts from the illustrative problem to the presentation in Exhibit 15–2, step by step.

☐ Absorption-Costing Method

The standard absorption-costing framework is shown in Exhibit 15–3. It differs from the direct costing format in three ways:

1. The unit product cost used for computing cost of goods sold is $4, not $3. Why? Because fixed manufacturing overhead of $1 is added to the $3 variable manufac-turing cost. The $1 of fixed manufacturing overhead applied to each unit is the **fixed overhead rate**. It is determined by dividing the budgeted fixed overhead by a denominator volume, usually the expected production for the budget period:

$$\text{fixed overhead rate} = \frac{\text{budgeted fixed overhead}}{\text{denominator volume}} = \frac{\$150,000}{150,000 \text{ units}} = \$1$$

EXHIBIT 15–3   Absorption Costing

GREENBERG COMPANY
Comparative Income Statements (in thousands of dollars)
For the Years 19X7 and 19X8
(Data are in text)

	19X7		19X8	
Sales		700		800
Cost of goods sold:				
Opening inventory, at standard absorption cost of $4*	—		120	
Cost of goods manufactured at standard of $4	680		560	
Available for sale	680		680	
Deduct: Ending inventory at standard absorption cost of $4	120		40	
Cost of goods sold, at standard		560		640
Gross profit at standard		140		160
Production-volume variance†		20 F		10 U
Gross margin or gross profit, at "actual"		160		150
Selling and administrative expenses		100		105
Operating income		60		45

* Variable cost $3
   Fixed cost ($150,000 ÷ 150,000)   1
   Standard absorption cost $4

† Computation of production-volume variance based on denominator volume of 150,000 units:

19X7	$20,000 F	(170,000 − 150,000) × $1
19X8	10,000 U	(150,000 − 140,000) × $1
Two years together	$10,000 F	(310,000 − 300,000) × $1

U = Unfavorable. F = Favorable.

2. Fixed factory overhead does not appear as a separate line in an absorption-costing income statement. Instead, the fixed factory overhead is included in two places: as part of the cost of goods sold and as a *production-volume variance*.[2] A production-volume variance (which is explained further on pages 483–484) appears whenever actual production deviates from the denominator volume used in computing the fixed manufacturing overhead rate:

production-volume variance = (actual volume − denominator volume) ×
fixed overhead rate

3. The format for an absorption-costing income statement separates costs into the major categories of *manufacturing* and *nonmanufacturing*. In contrast, a direct-costing income statement separates costs into the major categories of *fixed* and *variable*. In an absorption-costing statement, revenue less *manufacturing* cost (both fixed and variable) is *gross profit* or *gross margin*. In a direct-costing state-

---

[2] The *production-volume variance* is usually called simply the **volume variance** in practice. Other equivalent terms are *activity variance* and *capacity variance*. The term *production-volume variance* is favored here because it is a more precise description of the fundamental nature of the variance.

ment, revenue less all *variable* costs (both manufacturing and nonmanufacturing) is the *contribution margin*:

DIRECT COSTING		ABSORPTION COSTING	
Revenue	aa	Revenue	aa
All variable costs	(bb)	All manufacturing cost	
Contribution margin	cc	of goods sold	(ww)
All fixed costs	(dd)	Gross margin	xx
Operating income	ee	All nonmanufacturing costs	(yy)
		Operating income	zz

All three differences between direct- and absorption-costing formats arise solely because direct-costing treats fixed manufacturing overhead differently than does absorption costing. Subsequent sections will explain further how fixed factory overhead is accounted for in an absorption-costing system.

FIXED OVERHEAD AND ABSORPTION COSTS OF PRODUCT

☐ Variable and Fixed Unit Costs

A graphical presentation compares (1) the costs in the flexible budget used for departmental budgeting and control purposes with (2) the costs applied to products under an absorption-costing system. Even though absorption-costing systems rarely split factory overhead into variable and fixed components, we do so here to stress the underlying assumptions. For *variable* costs, the graphs are:

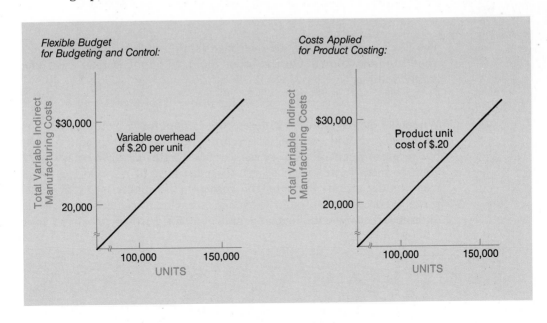

The two graphs are identical. The expected variable overhead costs from the flexible budget are the same as the variable overhead costs applied to the products. Both *budgeted* and *applied* variable overhead are $.20 per unit. Each time 1,000 additional units are produced, we expect to incur an additional $200 of variable overhead, and $200 of variable overhead cost is added to the inventory account for the items. The variable costs used for budgeting and control are the same as those used for product costing.

In contrast, the graph for *applied fixed overhead costs* differs from the flexible budget:

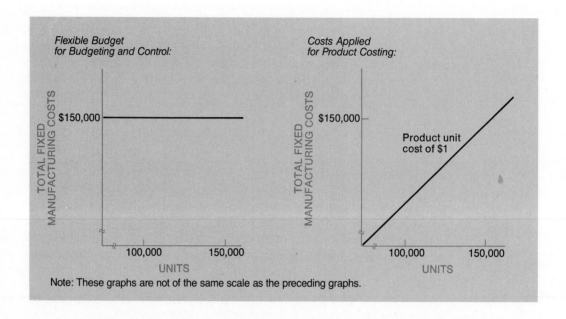

The flexible budget for fixed overhead is a lump-sum budgeted amount; it is unaffected by volume. On the other hand, the applied fixed cost depends on actual volume:

fixed cost applied = actual volume × fixed overhead rate

Whenever actual volume differs from denominator volume, the costs used for budgeting and control differ from those used for product costing. The budgeting and control purpose regards fixed costs in a straightforward manner, viewing them in accordance with their actual cost behavior pattern. In contrast, as the graphs indicate, the absorption product-costing approach views these fixed costs as though they had a variable-cost behavior pattern. The difference between applied and budgeted fixed overhead is the production-volume variance.

☐ Nature of Production-Volume Variance

The **production-volume variance** can be calculated in two ways:[3]

production-volume variance = applied fixed overhead − budgeted fixed overhead

or

production-volume variance = (actual volume − denominator volume) × fixed overhead rate

A production-volume variance arises when the actual production volume achieved does not coincide with the volume used as a denominator for computing the fixed overhead rate for product-costing purposes:

1. When denominator production volume and actual production volume are identical, there is no production-volume variance.
2. When actual volume is less than denominator volume, the production-volume variance is unfavorable because usage of facilities is less than expected. It is measured in Exhibit 15–3 for 19X8 as follows:

   (denominator volume − actual volume)
   × budgeted fixed-overhead rate = production-volume variance

   (150,000 hours − 140,000 hours) × $1 = $10,000 U

   or

   budget minus applied = production-volume variance
   $150,000 − $140,000 = $10,000 U

3. Where actual volume exceeds denominator volume, as was the case in 19X7, the production-volume variance is favorable because it indicates better than expected use of facilities:

   production-volume variance = (150,000 units − 170,000 units) × $1 = $20,000 F

The production-volume variance is the conventional measure of the cost of departing from the level of activity originally used to set the fixed overhead rate.[4] Most companies consider production-volume variances to be beyond

---

[3] Both formulas are correct. To see this, recall that

$$\text{fixed overhead rate} = \frac{\text{budgeted fixed overhead}}{\text{denominator volume}}$$

Multiplying both sides by denominator volume yields:

budgeted fixed overhead = denominator volume × fixed overhead rate

Now we can calculate the production-volume variance:

production-volume variance = applied fixed overhead − budgeted fixed overhead
= (actual volume × fixed overhead rate) − (denominator volume × fixed overhead rate)
= (actual volume − denominator volume) × fixed overhead rate

[4] Do not confuse the production-volume variance described here with the sales-volume variance described in Chapter 7. The production-volume variance arises because of the peculiarities of historical-cost accounting for fixed overhead in an absorption-cost system. In contrast, the sales-volume variance in Chapter 7 is an entirely separate measure. It aims at estimating

immediate control, although sometimes a manager responsible for volume has to do some explaining or investigating. Sometimes failure to reach the denominator volume is caused by idleness due to disappointing total sales, poor production scheduling, unusual machine breakdowns, shortages of skilled workers, strikes, storms, and the like.

There is no production-volume variance for variable overhead. The concept of production-volume variance arises for fixed overhead because of the conflict between accounting for control (by flexible budgets) and accounting for product costing (by application rates). Note again that the fixed-overhead budget serves the control purpose, whereas the development of a product-costing rate results in the treatment of fixed overhead as if it were a variable cost.

Above all, we should recognize that fixed costs are simply not divisible as variable costs are; they come in big chunks, and they are related to the provision of big chunks of production or sales capability rather than to the production or sale of a single unit of product.

☐ Selecting the Denominator Level

The fixed overhead rate in an absorption-costing framework depends on the volume level chosen as the denominator in the computation; the higher the level of volume, the lower the rate.

The selection of an appropriate denominator level is a matter of judgment. Management usually desires a single representative standard fixed cost for a unit of product to apply over a period of at least one year, despite month-to-month changes in production volume. Therefore, the predicted total fixed cost and the denominator volume used in calculating the fixed overhead rate should cover at least a one-year period. Most managers favor using the budgeted annual volume as the denominator; others favor using some longer-run (three- to five-year) approximation of "normal" activity; and others favor using maximum or full capacity (often called **practical capacity**).

Although fixed-overhead rates are often important for product costing and long-run pricing, such rates have limited significance for control purposes. At the lower levels of supervision, almost no fixed costs are under direct control; even at higher levels of supervision, many fixed costs are uncontrollable in the short run within wide ranges of anticipated activity.

☐ Actual, Normal, and Standard Costing

Overhead variances are not restricted to standard costing systems. Many companies apply *actual* direct materials and actual direct labor costs to products or services but use *standards* for applying overhead. Such a procedure is

---

the effects on profit of deviating from a static master budget. It is the budgeted unit contribution margin multiplied by the difference between the master (static) budgeted sales in units and the actual sales in units.

called **normal costing.** The following chart compares normal costing with two other basic ways for applying costs by the absorption-costing method:

	ACTUAL COSTING	NORMAL COSTING	STANDARD COSTING
Direct materials	Actual costs	Actual	Budgeted prices × standard inputs allowed for actual output achieved
Direct labor	Actual	Actual	
Variable factory overhead	Actual	Budgeted rates × actual inputs	
Fixed factory overhead			

The same chart without fixed factory overhead would compare these same three basic ways of applying costs by the direct-costing method.

Both normal absorption costing and standard absorption costing generate production volume variances. In addition, normal and standard costing methods produce all other overhead variances under both direct and absorption formats.

RECONCILIATION OF DIRECT COSTING AND ABSORPTION COSTING

Exhibit 15–4 contains a reconciliation of the operating incomes shown in Exhibits 15–2 and 15–3. The difference can be explained in a shortcut way by multiplying the fixed-overhead product-costing rate by the *change* in the total units in the beginning and ending inventories. Consider 19X8: the change in units was 20,000, so the difference in net income would be 20,000 units multiplied by $1.00 = $20,000.

The difference in income also equals the difference in fixed costs. Exhibit 15–5 shows that the fixed costs for 19X8 under direct costing were $150,000. Under absorption costing, fixed costs appear in two places: cost of goods sold and production-volume variance. Note that $30,000 of fixed costs incurred before 19X8 were held over in the beginning inventory. During 19X8, $140,000 of fixed costs were added to inventory, and $10,000 was still lodged in the ending inventory of 19X8. Thus, the fixed cost included in cost of goods sold for 19X8 was $30,000 + $140,000 − $10,000 = $160,000. In addition, the production-volume variance is $10,000, unfavorable. The total fixed cost charged as 19X8 expenses under absorption costing is $170,000, or $20,000 more than the $150,000 charged under direct costing. Therefore, 19X8 direct-costing income is higher by $20,000.

Remember that it is the relationship between sales and production that determines the difference between direct-costing and absorption-costing income. Whenever sales exceed production, that is, when inventory decreases, direct-costing income is greater than absorption-costing income.

EXHIBIT 15–4

Reconciliation of Operating Income Under Direct Costing
and Absorption Costing

	19X7	19X8	TOGETHER
Operating income under			
Absorption costing (see Exhibit 15–3, p. 480)	$60,000	$ 45,000	$105,000
Direct costing (see Exhibit 15–2, p. 479)	30,000	65,000	95,000
Difference to be explained	$30,000	$–20,000	$ 10,000
The difference can be reconciled by			
multiplying the fixed-overhead			
rate by the **change** in the total			
inventory units:			
Fixed-overhead rate	$1	$1	$1
Change in inventory units:			
Opening inventory	—	30,000	—
Ending inventory	30,000	10,000	10,000
Change	30,000	–20,000	10,000
Difference in operating income explained	$30,000	$–20,000	$ 10,000

EXHIBIT 15–5

Tracing Fixed Manufacturing Costs During 19X8
(Data are from Exhibits 15–2 and 15–3)

		INVENTORY		EXPENSE
Direct Costing				
No fixed overhead carried over from 19X7				
Fixed overhead actually incurred in 19X8	$150,000 ———————————————————→			$150,000
Absorption Costing		UNITS	DOLLARS	
Fixed overhead in beginning inventory	$ 30,000	30,000	$ 30,000	
Fixed overhead incurred in 19X8	150,000			
To account for:	$180,000			
Applied to product, 140,000 @ $1		140,000	140,000	
Available for sale		170,000	$170,000	
Contained in standard cost of goods sold	$160,000	160,000	160,000 ——→	$160,000
In ending inventory	10,000	10,000	$ 10,000	
Not applied, so becomes unfavorable				
production-volume variance	10,000 ——————————————————→			10,000
Fixed factory overhead charged				
against 19X8 operations				$170,000
Accounted for, as above	$180,000			
Difference in operating income				
occurs because $170,000 expires				
rather than $150,000				$ 20,000

So far, our example has deliberately ignored the possibility of any variance except the production-volume variance, which arises solely because of the desire for an application rate for fixed overhead in an absorption-costing situation (and the resultant likelihood that the chosen denominator level will differ from the actual production level achieved). It is the only variance that does not appear on both direct- and absorption-costing income statements.

Now we will introduce other variances that were explained in Chapter 7. Assume some additional facts for 19X8 (the second of the two years covered by our example):

Flexible-budget variances:	
Direct material	None
Direct labor	$34,000 U
Variable factory overhead	$ 3,000 U
Fixed factory overhead	$ 7,000 U
Supporting data (used to compute the above variances as shown in Appendix 15A):	
Standard direct-labor-hours allowed for 140,000 units of output produced	35,000
Standard direct-labor rate per hour	$6.00
Actual direct-labor-hours of inputs	40,000
Actual direct-labor rate per hour	$6.10
Variable manufacturing overhead actually incurred	$31,000
Fixed manufacturing overhead actually incurred	$157,000

As Chapter 7 explains, flexible-budget variances may arise for both variable overhead and fixed overhead. Consider the following:

	ACTUAL AMOUNTS	FLEXIBLE-BUDGET AMOUNTS	FLEXIBLE-BUDGET VARIANCES
Variable factory overhead	$ 31,000	$ 28,000	$3,000
Fixed factory overhead	157,000	150,000	7,000

The relationship between the fixed overhead flexible-budget variance and the production-volume variance is shown in Exhibit 15–6. The difference between the actual fixed overhead and that applied to products is the underapplied (or overapplied) overhead. It has two components: (1) production-volume variance and (2) fixed overhead flexible-budget variance (also called the *fixed overhead spending variance* or simply *fixed overhead budget variance*).

All variances other than the production-volume variance are essentially flexible-budget variances. They measure components of the differences between actual amounts and the flexible-budget amounts for the output achieved. Flexible budgets are primarily designed to assist planning and control rather than product costing. The production-volume variance is not a flexible-budget variance. It is designed to aid product costing.

EXHIBIT 15–6

Fixed Overhead Variances for 19X8 (Data are from Exhibit 15–3)

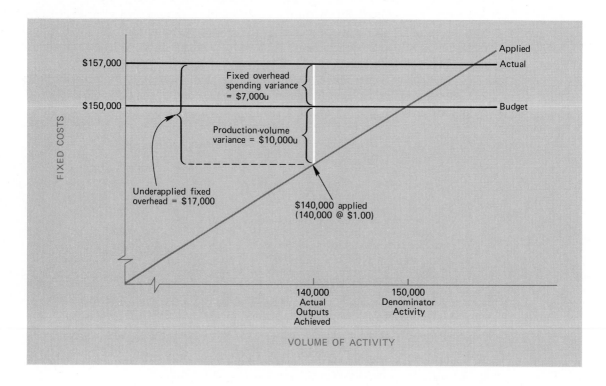

Exhibit 15–7 contains the income statement under absorption costing that incorporates these new facts. These new variances hurt income by $44,000 because, like the production-volume variance, they are all charged against income in 19X8. When variances are favorable, they increase operating income.

DISPOSITION OF STANDARD COST VARIANCES

The advocates of standard costing contend that variances are by and large subject to current control. This is particularly true when the standards are viewed as being currently attainable. Therefore, variances are not inventoriable and should be considered as adjustments to the income of the period instead of being added to inventories. In this way, inventory valuations will be more representative of desirable and attainable costs.

The countervailing view favors assigning the variances to the inventories and cost of goods sold related to the production during the period the variances arose. This is often called **prorating** the variances. Prorating makes inventory valuations more representative of the "*actual*" costs incurred to obtain the products. In practice, unless the variances are deemed significant in amount,

EXHIBIT 15–7

Absorption Costing
Modification of Exhibit 15–3 for 19X8
(Additional facts are in text)

		(IN THOUSANDS)
Sales, 160,000 at $5		$800
Opening inventory at standard, 30,000 at $4	$120	
Cost of goods manufactured at standard, 140,000 at $4	560	
Available for sale, 170,000 at $4	$680	
Deduct ending inventory at standard, 10,000 at $4	40	
Cost of goods sold at standard, 160,000 at $4		640
Gross profit at standard		$160
Flexible-budget variances, both unfavorable:		
Variable manufacturing costs ($34,000 + $3,000)	$ 37	
Fixed factory overhead	7	
Production-volume variance (arises only because of		
fixed overhead), unfavorable	10	
Total variances		54
Gross profit at "actual"		$106
Selling and administrative expenses		105
Operating income		$ 1

they are usually not prorated because the managers who use standard cost systems favor the views in the preceding paragraph.

Therefore, in practice, variances are typically regarded as adjustments to current income. The form of the disposition is unimportant. Exhibit 15–7 shows the variances as a component of the computation of gross profit at "actual." The variances could appear instead as a completely separate section elsewhere in the income statement. This helps to distinguish between product costing (that is, the cost of goods sold, at standard) and loss recognition (unfavorable variances are "lost" or "expired" costs because they represent waste and inefficiency thereby not qualifying as inventoriable costs. That is, waste is not an asset.)

SUMMARY

Standard cost-accounting systems are usually designed to satisfy *control* and *product-costing* purposes simultaneously. Many varieties of product costing are in use. For years, manufacturing companies have regularly used absorption costing, which includes fixed factory overhead as a part of the cost of product based on some predetermined application rate (variances are not inventoried). In contrast, direct costing, which is more accurately called *variable costing*, charges fixed factory overhead to the period immediately—that is, fixed overhead is altogether excluded from inventories. Absorption costing continues to be much more widely used than direct costing, although the growing use of the contribution approach in performance measurement has led to increasing use of direct costing for internal purposes.

The production-volume variance is linked with absorption costing, not direct costing. It arises from the conflict between the control-budget purpose and the product-costing purpose of cost accounting. The production-volume variance is measured by the predetermined fixed overhead rate multiplied by the difference between denominator production volume and actual production volume.

SUMMARY PROBLEM FOR YOUR REVIEW

☐ Problem

1. Reconsider Exhibits 15–2 and 15–3, pages 479 and 480. Suppose production in 19X8 was 145,000 units instead of 140,000 units, but sales were 160,000 units. Assume that the net variances for all variable manufacturing costs were $37,000, unfavorable. Regard these variances as adjustments to standard cost of goods sold. Also assume that actual fixed costs were $157,000. Prepare income statements for 19X8 under direct costing and under absorption costing.
2. Explain why operating income was different under direct costing and absorption costing. Show your calculations.
3. Without regard to Requirement 1, would direct costing or absorption costing give a manager more leeway in influencing short-run operating income through production-scheduling decisions? Why?

☐ Solution

1. See Exhibits 15–8 and 15–9. Note that the ending inventory will be 15,000 units instead of 10,000 units.

EXHIBIT 15–8

GREENBERG COMPANY
Income Statement (Direct Costing)
For the Year 19X8
(in thousands of dollars)

Sales		$800
Opening inventory, at variable standard cost of $3	$ 90	
Add: Variable cost of goods manufactured	435	
Available for sale	$525	
Deduct: Ending inventory, at variable standard cost of $3	45	
Variable cost of goods sold, at standard	$480	
Net flexible-budget variances for all variable costs, unfavorable	37	
Variable cost of goods sold, at actual	$517	
Variable selling expenses, at 5% of dollar sales	40	
Total variable costs charged against sales		557
Contribution margin		$243
Fixed factory overhead	$157*	
Fixed selling and administrative expenses	65	
Total fixed expenses		222
Operating income		$ 21†

* This could be shown in two lines, $150,000 budget plus $7,000 variance.

† The difference between this and the $65,000 operating income in Exhibit 15–2 occurs because of the $37,000 unfavorable variable-cost variances and the $7,000 unfavorable fixed-cost flexible-budget variance.

EXHIBIT 15-9

GREENBERG COMPANY
Income Statement (Absorption Costing)
For the Year 19X8
(in thousands of dollars)

Sales		$800
Opening inventory, at standard cost of $4	$120	
Cost of goods manufactured, at standard	580	
Available for sale	$700	
Deduct: Ending inventory, at standard	60	
Cost of goods sold, at standard	$640	
Net flexible-budget variances for all variable		
manufacturing costs, unfavorable	$37	
Fixed factory overhead flexible-budget		
variance, unfavorable	7	
Production-volume variance, unfavorable	5*	
Total variances	49	
Cost of goods sold, at actual		689†
Gross profit, at "actual"		$111
Selling and administrative expenses:		
Variable	40	
Fixed	65	105
Operating income		$ 6‡

* Production-volume variance is $1 × (150,000 denominator volume − 145,000 actual production).

† This format differs slightly from Exhibit 15–7, page 489. The difference is deliberate; it illustrates that the formats of income statements are not rigid.

‡ Compare this result with the $1,000 operating income in Exhibit 15–7. The *only* difference is traceable to the *production* of 145,000 units instead of 140,000 units, resulting in an unfavorable production-volume variance of $5,000 instead of $10,000.

2. Decline in inventory levels is 30,000 − 15,000, or 15,000 units. The fixed overhead rate per unit in absorption costing is $1. Therefore, $15,000 more fixed overhead was charged against operations under absorption costing than under direct costing. The direct-costing statement shows fixed factory overhead of $157,000, whereas the absorption-costing statement includes fixed factory overhead in three places: $160,000 in cost of goods sold, $7,000 U in fixed factory overhead flexible-budget variance, and $5,000 U as a production-volume variance, for a total of $172,000. Generally, when inventories decline, absorption costing will show less income than will direct costing; when inventories rise, absorption costing will show more income than direct costing.

3. Some version of absorption costing will give a manager more leeway in influencing operating income via production scheduling. Operating income will fluctuate in harmony with changes in net sales under direct costing, but it is influenced by both production and sales under absorption costing. For example, compare the direct costing in Exhibits 15–2 and 15–8. As the second note to Exhibit 15–8 indicates, the operating income may be affected by assorted variances (but not the production-volume variance) under direct costing, but production scheduling per se will have no effect on operating income. On the other hand, compare the operating income of Exhibits 15–7 and 15–9.

As the third note to Exhibit 15–9 explains, production scheduling as well as sales influence operating income. Production was 145,000 rather than 140,000 units. So $5,000 of fixed overhead became a part of ending inventory (an asset) instead of part of the production-volume variance (an expense)—that is, the production-volume variance is $5,000 lower and the ending inventory contains $5,000 more fixed overhead in Exhibit 15–9 than in Exhibit 15–7. The manager adds $1 to 19X8 operating income with each unit of production under absorption costing, even if the unit is not sold.

HIGHLIGHTS TO REMEMBER

1. Standard costing uses budgeted product costs for direct material, direct labor, and factory overhead. If the standards are currently attainable, the variances are not inventoried. Instead, they are directly charged or credited to current operations.
2. Normal costing uses actual product costs for direct material and direct labor and budgeted

EXHIBIT 15–10

Comparative Income Effects

	DIRECT COSTING	ABSORPTION COSTING	COMMENTS
1. Fixed factory overhead inventoried?	No	Yes	Basic theoretical question of when a cost should become an expense.
2. Production-volume variance?	No	Yes	Choice of denominator volume affects measurement of operating income under absorption costing.
3. Treatment of other variances?	Same	Same	Underscores the fact that the basic difference is the accounting for fixed factory overhead, not the accounting for variable factory overhead.
4. Classifications between variable and fixed costs are routinely made?	Yes	No	However, absorption cost can be modified to obtain subclassifications of variable and fixed costs, if desired.
5. Usual effects of changes in inventory levels on operating income:			Differences are attributable to timing of the transformation of fixed factory overhead into expense.
Production = sales	Equal	Equal	
Production > sales	Lower*	Higher†	
Production < sales	Higher	Lower	
6. Cost-volume-profit relationships	Tied to sales	Tied to production *and* sales	Management control benefit: Effects of changes in volume on operating income are easier to understand under variable costing.

* That is, lower than absorption costing.
† That is, higher than direct costing.

product costs for overhead. Overhead variances, but not direct-labor and direct-materials variances, can occur.

3. Exhibit 15–10 summarizes the effects that direct costing and absorption costing have on income.

ACCOUNTING VOCABULARY

Fixed Overhead Rate *479*   Normal Costing *485*   Practical Capacity *484*
Production-Volume Variance *483*   Prorating *488*   Volume Variance *480*.

APPENDIX 15A: COMPARISONS OF PRODUCTION-VOLUME VARIANCES WITH OTHER VARIANCES

PRODUCTION-VOLUME VARIANCE IS UNIQUE

The only new variance introduced in this chapter is the production-volume variance, which arises because fixed-overhead accounting must serve two masters: the *control-budget* purpose and the *product-costing* purpose. Let us examine these variances in perspective by using the approach originally demonstrated in Exhibit 7–6, page 202. The results of the approach are in Exhibit 15–11, which deserves your careful study, particularly the two notes. Please ponder the exhibit before reading on.

Exhibit 15–12 provides a graphical comparison of the variable and fixed overhead costs that were analyzed in Exhibit 15–11. Note how the control-budget line and the product-costing line (the applied line) are superimposed in the graph for variable overhead but differ in the graph for fixed overhead.

Underapplied or overapplied overhead is always the difference between the actual overhead incurred and the overhead applied. An analysis may then be made:

$$\text{underapplied overhead} = \text{flexible budget variance} + \text{production-volume variance}$$

$$\text{for variable overhead} = \$3,000 + 0 = \$3,000$$

$$\text{for fixed overhead} = \$7,000 + \$10,000 = \$17,000$$

LOST-CONTRIBUTION MARGINS

Finally, what is the economic significance of unit fixed costs? Unlike variable costs total fixed costs do not change in the short run as production or sales fluctuate. Management would obtain a better measure of the cost of underutilization of physical facilities by trying to approximate the related lost-contribution margins instead of the related historical fixed costs. Fixed-cost incurrence often involves lump-sum outlays based on a pattern of expected recoupment. But ineffective utilization of existing facilities has no bearing on the amount of fixed costs currently incurred. The economic effects of the inability to reach target volume levels are often directly measured by lost-contribution margins, even if these have to be approximated. The historical-cost approach fails to emphasize the distinction between *fixed-cost incurrence*, on the one

EXHIBIT 15-11

Analysis of Variances
(Data are from text for 19X8)

	(A) COST INCURRED: ACTUAL INPUTS × ACTUAL PRICE	(B) FLEXIBLE BUDGET BASED ON ACTUAL INPUTS	(C) FLEXIBLE BUDGET BASED ON ACTUAL OUTPUTS ACHIEVED	(D) PRODUCT COSTING: APPLIED TO PRODUCT
Direct labor:	$40,000 \times \$6.10 =$ $244,000	$40,000 \times \$6 =$ $240,000	$(35,000 \times \$6$ or $140,000 \times \$1.50) =$ $210,000^*$	$(35,000 \times \$6$ or $140,000 \times \$1.50) =$ $210,000^*$
	$40,000 \times (\$6.10 - \$6)$ = price variance, $4,000 U	$5,000 \times \$6 =$ efficiency variance, $30,000 U	Never a variance	
		Flexible-budget variance, $34,000 U		Never a variance
Variable factory overhead:	(given) $31,000	$40,000 \times \$.80 =$ $32,000	$(35,000 \times \$.80$ or $140,000 \times \$.20) =$ $28,000^*$	$28,000^*$
		Spending variance, $1,000 F	$5,000 \times \$.80 =$ efficiency variance, $4,000 U	Never a variance
		Flexible-budget variance, $3,000 U		Never a variance
			Underapplied overhead, $3,000 U	
Fixed factory overhead:	$157,000	Lump sum $150,000	Lump sum $150,000†	$140,000 \times \$1.00 =$ $140,000
		Spending variance, $7,000 U	Never a variance	Production-volume variance, $10,000 U
		Flexible-budget variance, $7,000 U	Production-volume variance, $10,000 U	
			Underapplied overhead, $17,000 U	

U = Unfavorable, F = Favorable.

* Note especially that the flexible budget for variable costs rises and falls in direct proportion to production. Note also that the control-budget purpose and the product-costing purpose harmonize completely; the total costs in the flexible budget will always agree with the standard variable costs applied to product because they are based on standard costs per unit multiplied by units produced.

† In contrast with variable costs, the flexible budget total for fixed costs will always be the same regardless of the units produced. However, the control-budget purpose and the product-costing purpose conflict; whenever actual production differs from denominator production, the standard costs applied to product will differ from the flexible budget. This difference is the production-volume variance. In this case, the production-volume variance may be computed by multiplying the $1 rate times the difference between the 150,000 denominator volume and the 140,000 units of output achieved.

EXHIBIT 15–12

Comparison of Control and Product-Costing Purposes, Variable Overhead and Fixed Overhead
(not to scale)

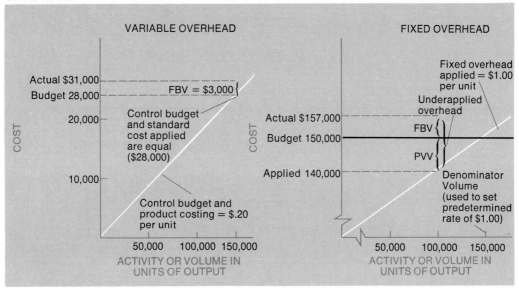

FBV = Flexible-budget variance.
PVV = Production-volume variance.

hand, and the objective of *maximizing the total contribution margin*, on the other hand. These are separable management problems, and the utilization of existing capacity is more closely related to the latter.

For instance, the production-volume variance for 19X8 in our example was computed at $10,000 by multiplying a unit fixed cost of $1 by the 10,000-unit difference between the 150,000 units of denominator activity and 140,000 units produced. This $10,000 figure may be helpful in the sense that management is alerted in some crude way to the probable costs of failure to produce 150,000 units. But the more relevant information is the lost contribution margins that pertain to the 10,000 units. This information may not be so easy to obtain. The lost contribution margins may be zero in those cases where there are no opportunities to obtain any contribution margin from alternative uses of available capacity; in other cases, however, the lost-contribution margins may be substantial. For example, if demand is high, the breakdown of key equipment may cost a company many thousands of dollars in lost contribution margins. Unfortunately, in these cases, existing accounting systems would show production-volume variances based on the unitized fixed costs and entirely ignore any lost contribution margins.

APPENDIX 15B: ILLUSTRATION OF STANDARD ABSORPTION-COSTING SYSTEM

This illustration presents the journal entries that would accompany a standard absorption-costing system such as that described in this chapter.

The Delar Company began business on January 2, 19X1. Its executives were experienced in the industry and had a standard cost system installed from the outset.

Overhead rates were established based on an expected activity (volume) level of 25,000 standard direct-labor-hours. Note that volume is measured by standard direct-labor-hours allowed for any given output of product; it is not measured by the actual direct-labor-hours of input. The rates were computed as follows:

$$\text{variable rate} = \frac{\text{budgeted variable factory overhead}}{\text{expected volume}} = \frac{\$50,000}{25,000} = \$2$$

$$\text{fixed rate} = \frac{\text{budgeted fixed factory overhead}}{\text{expected volume}} = \frac{\$150,000}{25,000} = \$6$$

A summary of results follows:

RELATED TO JOURNAL ENTRY NUMBER		
1.	Direct material purchased: 100,000 lbs. at $.95, $95,000	
2.	Pounds of direct material used: 90,000	
	Standard allowances per unit of finished output:	
	Direct materials: 1 lb. @ $1	$1.00
3.	Direct labor: .25 hr. @ $12	3.00
4.	Variable factory overhead: .25 hr. @ $2	f6 .50
	Variable factory costs	$4.50
5.	Fixed factory overhead: .25 hr. @ $6	1.50
	Total standard cost per unit	$6.00
3.	Direct labor incurred: 21,250 hours @ $12.20, or $259,250	
4,5.	Factory overhead incurred: variable, $42,000; fixed, $150,000	
6.	Production in units: 80,000	
7.	Sales in units: 60,000	

Try to prepare your own journal entries before studying those in Exhibit 15–13. Note that all inventories are carried at standard unit costs, not actual unit costs.

Variances are usually measured as early as possible. Purchase price variances for direct materials are identified upon purchase and efficiency variances upon withdrawal for production. Direct-labor variances are usually measured as production occurs. Overhead variances are typically computed monthly. However, they may not be isolated formally in the ledger accounts until the end of the year, as follows:

Variable factory-overhead budget variance	2,000	
Fixed factory-overhead production-volume variance	30,000	
Factory department overhead control		32,000
Underapplied overhead:		
Variable: $42,000 − $40,000 = $2,000		
Fixed: $150,000 − (.25)(80,000)($6) = $30,000		

Note how this entry reduces the balance in Factory Department Overhead Control to zero.

The attained volume of .25 × 80,000 units = 20,000 hours was 5,000 hours below the budgeted hours selected as the denominator volume. This discrepancy caused a production-volume variance of $30,000 (5,000 hours × $6), the difference between the *budgeted* and the *applied* fixed factory overhead.

EXHIBIT 15–13

Standard Absorption-Costing System
Journal Entries

1.	Direct-materials inventory	100,000	
	Direct-material purchase price variance		5,000
	Accounts payable		95,000
	($.95 − $1.00) × $100,000 lbs. = − $5,000		
2.	Work in process	80,000	
	Direct-material efficiency variance	10,000	
	Direct-materials inventory		90,000
	(90,000 − 80,000) × $1 = $10,000		
3.	Work in process	240,000	
	Direct-labor price variance	4,250	
	Direct-labor efficiency variance	15,000	
	Accrued payroll or cash		259,250
	21,250 × ($12.20 − $12.00) = $4,250		
	[21,250 − (.25 × 80,000)] × $12 = $15,000		
4a.	Factory department overhead control	42,000	
	Accounts payable and other accounts		42,000
4b.	Work in process	40,000	
	Factory department overhead control		40,000
	(.25 × 80,000 units) × $2 = $40,000		
5a.	Factory department overhead control	150,000	
	Accounts payable and other accounts		150,000
5b.	Work in process	120,000	
	Factory department overhead control		120,000
	(.25 × 80,000 units) × $6 = $120,000		
6.	Finished goods	480,000	
	Work in process		480,000
	80,000 units × $6 = $480,000		
7.	Cost of goods sold	360,000	
	Finished goods		360,000
	60,000 units × $6 = $360,000		

The variance accounts are temporary income statement accounts. The journal entry that disposes of all variances to income summary follows:

Income summary	56,250	
Direct-material purchase price variance	5,000	
Direct-material efficiency variance		10,000
Direct-labor price variance		4,250
Direct-labor efficiency variance		15,000
Variable factory-overhead variance		2,000
Fixed factory-overhead variance		30,000
To adjust income for all variances.		

ASSIGNMENT MATERIAL

☐ **Fundamental Assignment Material**

15–1. **COMPARISON OF DIRECT COSTING AND ABSORPTION COSTING.** (Alternate is 15–14.) Arlington Boat Company produced 110 sailboats during 19X7 and sold 100 at $10,000 each. Costs for 19X7 were

Direct material used	$210,000
Direct labor	400,000
Variable manufacturing overhead	50,000
Fixed manufacturing overhead	220,000
Selling and administrative expenses (all fixed)	90,000

There were no beginning inventories or work-in-progress inventories, but ending direct-material inventory was $100,000. There were no cost variances.

Required:
1. What is the ending finished-goods inventory under absorption-costing procedures?
2. What is the ending finished-goods inventory under direct-costing procedures?
3. Would income be higher or lower under direct costing? By how much? Why?

15–2. **COMPARISON OF ABSORPTION AND DIRECT COSTING.** (Alternate is 15–15.) The following simplified income statement for Nguyen Company is based on direct costing. Assume that the denominator volume for absorption costing in 19X5 and 19X6 was 1,300 units and that total fixed costs were identical in 19X5 and 19X6. There is no beginning or ending work in process.

NGUYEN COMPANY
Income Statement
For the Year Ended December 31, 19X6

Sales, 1,180 units at $10		$11,800
Deduct variable costs:		
Beginning inventory, 130 units at $7	$ 910	
Variable manufacturing cost of goods manufactured, 1,100 units at $7	7,700	
Variable manufacturing cost of goods available for sale	$8,610	
Ending inventory, 50 units at $7	350	
Variable manufacturing cost of goods sold	$8,260	
Variable selling and administrative expenses	400	
Total variable costs		8,660
Contribution margin		$ 3,140
Deduct fixed costs:		
Fixed factory overhead at budget	$2,600	
Fixed selling and administrative expenses	500	
Total fixed costs		3,100
Operating income		$ 40

Required:
1. Prepare an income statement based on absorption costing. Assume that actual fixed costs were equal to budgeted fixed costs.
2. Explain the difference in operating income between absorption costing and direct costing. Be specific.

□ Additional Assignment Material

15–3. Why is it artificial to unitize fixed costs?

15–4. "The fixed cost per unit is directly affected by the denominator selected." Do you agree? Explain.

15–5. Why do advocates of currently attainable standard costs as a method for product costing claim that it is conceptually superior to actual costing?

15–6. "Direct costing means that only direct material and direct labor are inventoried." Do you agree? Why?

15–7. "The dollar amount of the production-volume variance depends on what activity level was chosen to determine the application rate." Explain.

15–8. "Absorption costing regards more categories of costs as product costs." Explain. Be specific.

15–9. "An increasing number of companies are using direct costing in their corporate annual reports." Do you agree? Explain.

15–10. Why is there no production-volume variance for direct labor?

15–11. How is fixed overhead applied to product?

15–12. The Internal Revenue Service requires proration of any significant variances for tax reporting. Why do you suppose the IRS requires proration?

15–13. **SIMPLE COMPARISON OF DIRECT AND ABSORPTION COSTING.** Beltline Software Company began business on January 1, 19X5, with assets of $250,000 cash and equities of $250,000 capital stock. In 19X5 it manufactured some inventory at a cost of $125,000, including $25,000 for rent and other fixed overhead for the programmers' facilities. In 19X6 it manufactured nothing and sold half of its inventory for $80,000 cash. In 19X7 it manufactured nothing and sold the remaining half for another $80,000 cash. It had no fixed expenses in 19X6 or 19X7.

There are no other transactions of any kind. Ignore income taxes.

Required: | Prepare an ending balance sheet plus an income statement for 19X5, 19X6, and 19X7 under (1) absorption costing and (2) direct costing (variable costing).

15–14. **COMPARISON OF DIRECT COSTING AND ABSORPTION COSTING.** (Alternate is 15–1.) From the following information pertaining to a year's operations, answer the questions below:

Units sold	5,000
Units produced	6,000
Fixed manufacturing overhead	$ 7,200
Variable manufacturing overhead	1,500
Selling and administrative expenses (all fixed)	2,500
Direct labor	11,000
Direct material used	9,100
Beginning inventories	0
Contribution margin	10,400
Direct-material inventory, end	1,800
There are no work-in-process inventories.	

Required: | 1. What is the ending finished-goods inventory cost under traditional costing procedures (absorption costing)?
2. What is the ending finished-goods inventory cost under variable-costing procedures (direct costing)?
3. Does absorption costing or direct costing show higher operating income? by how much?

15–15. COMPARING DIRECT COSTING AND ABSORPTION COSTING. (Alternate is 15–2.) Simple numbers are used in this problem to highlight the concepts covered in the chapter.

Assume that the ABC Company produces one product that sells for $5. ABC uses a standard cost system. Total standard variable costs of production are $2 per unit, fixed manufacturing costs are $1,500 per year, and selling and administrative expenses are $300 per year, all fixed. Denominator volume is 1,000 units per year.

Required:

1. For each of the following nine combinations of sales and production (*in units*) for 19X6 prepare condensed income statements under direct costing and under absorption costing.

	(1)	(2)	(3)	(4)	(5)	(6)	(7)	(8)	(9)
Sales	600	800	1,000	800	1,000	1,200	1,000	1,200	1,400
Production	800	800	800	1,000	1,000	1,000	1,200	1,200	1,200

Use the following formats:

Direct Costing		Absorption Costing	
Revenue	$ aa	Revenue	$ aa
Cost of goods sold	(bb)	Cost of goods sold	(uu)
Contribution margin	$ cc	Gross profit at standard	$ vv
Fixed manufacturing costs	(dd)	Favorable (unfavorable)	
Fixed selling and admin-		production volume	
istrative expenses	(ee)	variance	ww
		Gross profit at "actual"	$ xx
		Selling and administrative	
		expenses	(yy)
Operating income	$ ff	Operating income	$ zz

2. a. In which of the nine combinations is direct-costing income greater than absorption-costing income? In which is it lower? The same?
b. In which of the nine combinations is the production-volume variance unfavorable? favorable?
c. How much profit is added by selling one more unit under direct costing? under absorption costing?
d. How much profit is added by producing one more unit under direct costing? under absorption costing?
e. Suppose sales, rather than production, is the critical factor in determining the success of ABC Company. Which format, direct costing or absorption costing, provides the better measure of performance?

15–16. COMPARISONS OVER FOUR YEARS. The E Corporation began business on January 1, 19X7, to produce and sell a single product. Reported operating income figures under both absorption and direct (variable) costing for the first four years of operation are:

YEAR	DIRECT COSTING	ABSORPTION COSTING
19X6	$40,000	$40,000
19X7	20,000	50,000
19X8	60,000	40,000
19X9	60,000	50,000

Standard production costs per unit, sales prices, overhead rates, and denominator volume levels were the same in each year. There were no underapplied or overapplied overhead costs and no variances in any year. All nonmanufacturing expenses were fixed, and there were no nonmanufacturing cost variances in any year.

Required: In what year(s) did "units produced" equal "units sold"?

In what year(s) did "units produced" exceed "units sold"?

What is the dollar amount of the December 31, 19X9, finished-goods inventory? (Give absorption-costing value.)

What is the difference between "units produced" and "units sold" in 19X7, if you know that the absorption-costing fixed-manufacturing-overhead application rate is $2 per unit? (Give answer in units.)

15–17. **DIRECT AND ABSORPTION COSTING.** The Schaefer Company sold 20,000 units at $24 each during 19X7. Production data follow:

Actual production	24,000 units
Denominator activity	30,000 units
Manufacturing costs incurred:	
Variable	$240,000
Fixed	120,000
Nonmanufacturing costs incurred:	
Variable	$ 60,000
Fixed	56,000

Required: 1. Determine operating income for 19X7, assuming the firm uses the direct-costing approach to product costing. (Do not prepare a statement.)

2. Assume that (a) there is *no* January 1, 19X7, inventory, (b) *no* variances are allocated to inventory, and (c) the firm uses a "full-absorption" approach to product costing. Compute (a) the cost assigned to December 31, 19X7, inventory and (b) operating income for the year ended December 31, 19X7. (Do not prepare a statement.)

15–18. **ALL-FIXED COSTS.** (Suggested by Raymond P. Marple.) The Marple Company has built a massive water-desalting factory next to an ocean. The factory is completely automated. It has its own source of power, light, heat, and so on. The salt water costs nothing. All producing and other operating costs are fixed; they do not vary with output because the volume is governed by adjusting a few dials on a control panel. The employees have flat annual salaries.

The desalted water is not sold to household consumers. It has a special taste that appeals to local breweries, distilleries, and soft-drink manufacturers. The price, 10¢ per gallon, is expected to remain unchanged for quite some time.

The following are data regarding the first two years of operations:

| | IN GALLONS | | COSTS (ALL FIXED) | |
	Sales	Production	Manufacturing	Other
19X1	5,000,000	10,000,000	$450,000	$100,000
19X2	5,000,000	0	450,000	100,000

Orders can be processed in four hours, so management decided, in early 19X2, to gear production strictly to sales.

Required:

1. Prepare three-column income statements for 19X1, for 19X2, and for the two years together using (a) direct costing and (b) absorption costing.
2. What is the break-even point under (a) direct costing and (b) absorption costing?
3. What inventory costs would be carried on the balance sheets on December 31, 19X1 and 19X2, under each method?
4. Comment on your answers in Requirements 1 and 2. Which costing method appears more useful?

15–19. **SEMIFIXED COSTS.** The McFarland Company differs from the Marple Company (described in Problem 15–18) in only one respect: it has both variable and fixed manufacturing costs. Its variable costs are $.025 per gallon, and its fixed manufacturing costs are $225,000 per year.

Required:

1. Using the same data as in the preceding problem, except for the change in production-cost behavior, prepare three-column income statements for 19X1, for 19X2, and for the two years together using (a) direct costing and (b) absorption costing.
2. Why did McFarland earn a profit for the two-year period while Marple suffered a loss?
3. What inventory costs would be carried on the balance sheets on December 31, 19X1 and 19X2, under each method?

15–20. **EXTENSION OF CHAPTER ILLUSTRATION.** Reconsider Exhibits 15–2 and 15–3, pages 479 and 480. Suppose that in 19X8 production was 160,000 units instead of 140,000 units, and sales were 150,000 units. Assume the following variable-cost variances:

Material price variance	17,000 U
Labor efficiency variance	7,500 U
Variable overhead efficiency variance	1,000 U

All other variable-cost variances are zero. Also assume that actual fixed manufacturing costs were $165,000.

Required:

1. Prepare income statements for 19X5 under direct costing and under absorption costing. Use a format similar to Exhibits 15–8 and 15–9, pages 490–491.
2. Explain why operating income was different under direct costing and absorption costing. Show your calculations.

15–21. **ABSORPTION AND DIRECT COSTING.** Standard costs for Espinoza Company for 19X7 and 19X8 are:

Direct materials	$22
Direct labor	14
Variable factory overhead	3
Fixed factory overhead	9
Standard variable costs per unit	$48

Actual data for the two years were:

	19X7	19X8
Units of finished goods:		
Opening inventory	—	3,000
Production	13,000	10,000
Sales	10,000	11,000
Ending inventory	3,000	2,000

Fixed factory overhead was budgeted at $108,000 per year. The denominator volume was 12,000 units, so the fixed overhead rate was $108,000 ÷ 12,000 = $9 per unit.

Budgeted sales price was $70 per unit. Selling and administrative expenses were budgeted at variable, $7 *per unit sold*, and fixed, $80,000 per month.

Assume that there were absolutely no variances from any standard variable costs or budgeted selling prices or budgeted fixed costs in 19X7.

There were no beginning or ending inventories of work in process.

Required:
1. For 19X7, prepare income statements based on standard direct (variable) costing and standard absorption costing. (The next problem deals with 19X8.)
2. Explain why operating income differs between direct costing and absorption costing. Be specific.

15–22. **ABSORPTION AND DIRECT COSTING.** Assume the same facts as in the preceding problem. In addition, consider the following actual data for 19X8.

Direct materials	$268,000
Direct labor	151,600
Variable factory overhead	32,500
Fixed factory overhead	104,000
Selling and administrative costs:	
Variable	80,400
Fixed	80,000
Sales	780,000

Required:
1. For 19X8, prepare income statements based on standard direct (variable) costing and standard absorption costing. Arrange your income statements in the following general format:
    Sales (at standard or budgeted prices)
    Cost of goods sold (at standard costs)
    Gross profit at standard
    Selling and administrative costs (at standard)
    Operating income before variances
    Variances (list in detail)
    Operating income
2. Explain why operating income differs between direct costing and absorption costing. Be specific.

15–23. **FUNDAMENTALS OF OVERHEAD VARIANCES.** The McKinney Company is installing an absorption standard cost system and a flexible overhead budget. Standard costs have recently been developed for its only product. Overhead rates are as follows:

Variable overhead, 6 hours at $2	$12
Fixed overhead, 6 hours at $3	18
Standard overhead per unit of finished product	$30

Denominator activity (expected activity) is 12,000 standard direct-labors hours per month. The fixed overhead rate for product costing is not changed from month to month.

Required:

1. Calculate the budgeted fixed overhead.
2. Graph the following for volume from zero to 15,000 hours:
   a. Budgeted variable overhead.
   b. Variable overhead applied to product.
3. Graph the following for volume from zero to 15,000 hours:
   a. Budgeted fixed overhead.
   b. Fixed overhead applied to product.
4. Assume that 10,000 standard direct-labor-hours are allowed for the output achieved during October. Actual variable overhead of $21,400 was incurred; actual fixed overhead amounted to $37,600. Calculate the
   a. Fixed-overhead flexible-budget variance.
   b. Fixed-overhead production-volume variance.
   c. Variable overhead flexible-budget variance.
5. Assume that 12,500 standard direct-labor-hours are allowed for the output achieved during November. Actual overhead incurred amounted to $59,800, $37,800 of which was fixed. Calculate the
   a. Fixed-overhead flexible-budget variance.
   b. Fixed-overhead production-volume variance.
   c. Variable overhead flexible-budget variance.

15–24. **FIXED OVERHEAD AND PRACTICAL CAPACITY.** The expected volume of a paper-making plant of Scott Paper Company was 34,335 hours per month. Practical capacity was 45,780 hours per month. The standard hours allowed for the actual output achieved in January were 40,320. The budgeted fixed factory overhead items were:

Supervision	$ 29,875
Indirect labor	177,125
Depreciation, equipment	242,115
Depreciation, factory building	37,035
Insurance	10,040
Property taxes	18,835
Total	$515,025

Because of unanticipated scheduling difficulties and the need for more indirect labor, the actual fixed factory overhead was $537,260.

Required:

1. Using practical capacity as the denominator for applying fixed factory overhead, prepare a summary analysis of fixed-overhead variances for January.
2. Using expected activity as the denominator for applying fixed factory overhead, prepare a summary analysis of fixed-overhead variances for January.
3. Explain why some of your variances in Requirements 1 and 2 are the same and why some differ.

15–25. **SELECTING A DENOMINATOR LEVEL.** Rosella Donato is a consultant to Lake Michigan Manufacturing Company (LMMC). She is helping to install a standard cost system for 19X5. For product-costing purposes, the system must apply fixed factory costs to products manufactured. She has decided that the fixed-overhead rate should be based on direct-labor-hours, but she is uncertain about the appropriate denominator volume. LMMC has grown rapidly; it has added production capacity approximately every four years. The last addition was completed in early 19X5, and the total capacity is now 7,500,000 labor-hours per year. Donato predicts the following operating levels (in direct-labor-hours, DLH) through 19X9:

YEAR	CAPACITY USED
19X5	6,750,000 DLH
19X6	7,000,000 DLH
19X7	7,250,000 DLH
19X8	7,500,000 DLH
19X9	7,750,000 DLH

The current plan is to add another 1,000,000 direct-labor-hours of capacity in early 19X9.

Donato has identified three alternatives for the denominator volume:
(1) Predicted volume for the year in question.
(2) Average volume over the four years of the current production setup.
(3) Practical (or full) capacity.

Required:

1. Suppose annual fixed factory overhead is expected to be $9,750,000 through 19X8. For simplicity, assume no inflation. Calculate the fixed overhead rates (to the nearest cent) for 19X6, 19X7, and 19X8 using each of the three alternative denominator volumes.
2. Provide a brief description of the effect of using each method of computing the denominator volume.
3. Which method do you prefer? Why?

15–26. **EXTENSION OF APPENDIX 15A ILLUSTRATION.** Study the format of the analysis of variances in Exhibit 15–11, p. 494. Suppose production is 156,000 units. Also assume:

Standard direct-labor-hours allowed per unit produced	.25
Standard direct-labor rate per hour	$6.00
Actual direct-labor-hours of input	42,000
Actual direct-labor rate per hour	$6.10
Variable manufacturing overhead actually incurred	$33,000
Fixed manufacturing overhead actually incurred	$157,000

Required:

Prepare an analysis of variances similar to that shown in Exhibit 15–11.

15–27. **ANALYSIS OF OPERATING RESULTS.** (CMA, adapted.) Northwest Gear, a wholly owned subsidiary of Itak, Inc., produces and sells three main product lines. The company employs a standard cost-accounting system for record-keeping purposes.

At the beginning of 19X7, the president of Northwest Gear presented the budget to the parent company and accepted a commitment to contribute $15,800 to Guardian's consolidated profit in 19X7. The president has been confident that the year's profit would exceed budget target, since the monthly sales reports that he has been receiving have shown that sales for the year will exceed budget by 10%. The president is both disturbed and confused when the controller presents the following adjusted forecast as of November 30, 19X7, indicating that profit will be 11% under budget:

NORTHWEST GEAR
Forecasts of Operating Results

	FORECASTS AS OF	
	1/1/X7	11/30/X7
Sales	$341,000	$375,100
Cost of sales at standard	285,000*	313,500
Gross margin at standard	$ 56,000	$ 61,600
Over- (under-) absorbed fixed manufacturing overhead		(6,000)
Actual gross margin	$ 56,000	$ 55,600
Selling expenses	$ 13,400	$ 14,740
Administrative expenses	26,800	26,800
Total operating expenses	$ 40,200	$ 41,540
Earnings before tax	$ 15,800	$ 14,060

* Includes fixed manufacturing overhead of $30,000.

There have been no sales price changes or product-mix shifts since the 1/1/X7 forecast. The only cost variance on the income statement is the underabsorbed manufacturing overhead. This arose because the company produced only 16,000 standard machine-hours (budgeted machine-hours were 20,000) during 19X7 as a result of a shortage of raw materials while its principal supplier was closed by a strike. Fortunately, Northwest Gear's finished-goods inventory was large enough to fill all sales orders received.

Required:

1. Analyze and explain why the profit has declined in spite of increased sales and good control over costs. Show computations.
2. What plan, if any, could Northwest Gear adopt during December to improve its reported profit at year-end? Explain your answer.
3. Illustrate and explain how Northwest Gear could adopt an alternative internal cost-reporting procedure that would avoid the confusing effect of the present procedure. Show the revised forecasts under your alternative.
4. Would the alternative procedure described in Requirement 3 be acceptable to Itak, Inc., for financial-reporting purposes? Explain.

15–28. **STANDARD ABSORPTION AND STANDARD DIRECT COSTING.** A division of Recreation Equipment Company (REC) produces tents and has the following results for a certain year. All variances are written off as additions to (or deductions from) the standard cost of goods sold. Find the unknowns, designated by letters.

Sales: 100,000 units, at $43	$4,300,000
Net variance for standard variable manufacturing costs	$41,000 unfavorable
Variable standard cost of goods manufactured	$20 per unit
Variable selling and administrative expenses	$4 per unit
Fixed selling and administrative expenses	$950,000
Fixed manufacturing overhead	$250,000
Maximum capacity per year	125,000 units
Denominator volume for year	100,000 units
Beginning inventory of finished goods	15,000 units
Ending inventory of finished goods	25,000 units
Beginning inventory: direct-costing basis	a
Contribution margin	b
Operating income: direct-costing basis	c
Beginning inventory: absorption-costing basis	d
Gross margin	e
Operating income: absorption-costing basis	f

15–29. **FILL IN THE BLANKS.** Study Appendix 15A. Consider these data:

	FACTORY OVERHEAD	
	Fixed	Variable
Actual incurred	$5,400	$11,000
Budget for standard hours allowed for output achieved	5,000	9,000
Applied	4,700	9,000
Budget for actual hours of input	5,000	9,900

From the above information fill in the blanks:

The flexible-budget variance is $_____	Fixed $_____
	Variable $_____
The production-volume variance is $_____	Fixed $_____
	Variable $_____
The spending variance is $_____	Fixed $_____
	Variable $_____
The efficiency variance is $_____	Fixed $_____
	Variable $_____

Mark your variances "F" for favorable and "U" for unfavorable.

15–30. **FILL IN THE BLANKS.** Study Appendix 15A. Consider the following data regarding factory overhead:

	VARIABLE	FIXED
Budget for actual hours of input	$7,600	$3,800
Applied	8,000	4,000
Budget for standard hours allowed for actual output achieved	?	?
Actual incurred	8,400	3,750

Required:

Using the above data, fill in the blanks below. Use "F" for favorable or "U" for unfavorable for each variance.

	TOTAL OVERHEAD	VARIABLE	FIXED
1. Spending variance	_____	_____	_____
2. Efficiency variance	_____	_____	_____
3. Production-volume variance	_____	_____	_____
4. Flexible-budget variance	_____	_____	_____
5. Underapplied overhead	_____	_____	_____

15–31. **STRAIGHTFORWARD PROBLEM ON STANDARD COST SYSTEM.** Study Appendix 15A. Longview Foundry, Inc., uses flexible budgets and a standard cost system. The month's data for a department follow:

```
Direct-labor costs incurred, 11,000 hours, $127,600
Variable overhead costs incurred, $28,500
Fixed-overhead budget variance, $1,500 favorable
Finished units produced, 2,000
Fixed-overhead costs incurred, $40,000
Variable overhead applied at $2.70 per hour
Standard direct-labor cost, $12 per hour
Denominator production per month, 2,500 units
Standard direct-labor-hours per finished unit, 5
```

Required: | Prepare an analysis of all variances (similar to Exhibit 15–11, p. 494).

15–32. **STRAIGHTFORWARD PROBLEM ON STANDARD COST SYSTEM.** Study Appendix 15A. The Hong Kong Company uses a standard cost system. The month's data regarding its single product follow:

```
Fixed-overhead costs incurred, $6,150
Variable overhead applied at $.90 per hour
Standard direct-labor cost, $4 per hour
Denominator production per month, 2,500 units
Standard direct-labor-hours per finished unit, 5
Direct-labor costs incurred, 11,000 hours, $41,800
Variable overhead costs incurred, $9,500
Fixed-overhead budget variance, $100, favorable
Finished units produced, 2,000
```

Required: | Prepare an analysis of all variances (similar to Exhibit 15–11, p. 494).

15–33. **JOURNAL ENTRIES.** Study Appendix 15B. Refer to the data in Problem 15–31. Prepare journal entries for direct labor, variable overhead, and fixed overhead. Include the recognition of all variances in your entries. Omit explanations.

15–34. **JOURNAL ENTRIES.** Study Appendix 15B. Refer to the data in Problem 15–32. Prepare journal entries for direct labor, variable overhead, and fixed overhead. Include the recognition of all variances in your entries. Omit explanations.

15–35. **DISPOSITION OF VARIANCES.** In January 19X7 General Diversified, Inc., started a division for making "acrobots." Management hoped that these toys would be the new fad of 19X7. During 19X7 it produced 150,000 acrobots. Financial results were as follows:

```
Sales: 90,000 units @ $24
Direct labor at standard: 150,000 × $7 = $1,050,000
Direct-labor variances: $47,000 U
Direct material at standard: 150,000 × $5 = $750,000
Direct-material variances: $13,000 U
Overhead incurred @ standard: 150,000 × $3 = $450,000
Overhead variances: $5,000 F
```

General Diversified allows divisions to choose one of two methods of accounting for variances:
(1) Direct charge to income.
(2) Proration to the production of the period. Method 2 requires variances to be spread equally over the units produced during the period.

1. Calculate the division's operating income (a) using method 1 and (b) using method 2. Assume no selling and administrative expenses.
2. Calculate ending inventory value (a) using method 1 and (b) using method 2. Note that there was no beginning inventory.
3. What is the major argument in support of each method?

15–36. **COMPARING THE PERFORMANCE OF TWO PLANTS.** In 1984 an Italian shoe manufacturer decided to take advantage of the strong position of the dollar and began exporting shoes to the United States. Two plants, one in Naples and one in Florence, were built to make the shoes. By selling shoes to importers for an average of L.88,000 (that is, 88,000 Italian lira, or about $50), managers had predicted a contribution margin of L.35,200 per pair. Each plant would break even at a volume of 10,000 pairs of shoes. The two plants were given considerable autonomy, but they were expected to report profitable operations at the end of each year.

In January 1986, the company president, Anthony Carpetto, received the following information for 1985:

	NAPLES	FLORENCE
Sales	L. 880,000,000	L. 880,000,000
Cost of goods sold	528,000,000	844,800,000
Gross margin	L. 352,000,000	L. 35,200,000
Administrative costs (fixed)	35,200,000	35,200,000
Operating income	L. 316,800,000	L. 0
Production	20,000,000 pairs	10,000,000 pairs
Variances (included in cost of goods sold)	L. 316,800,000 F	0

F = Favorable. U = Unfavorable.

Carpetto was puzzled by the wide disparity in operating income despite the same sales volume for each plant. He was particularly concerned about the relative profitability of the plants. The dollar was losing strength, and demand in the United States for Italian shoes was declining. One plant might have to be closed. "Put the Florence plant on notice that shutdown could come at any time," Carpetto instructed you, his controller.

Reconstruct the given income statements in as much detail as possible. Then explain in detail why the income statements differ, and clarify this situation confronting the president. Assume that there are no price or efficiency variances.

15–37. **INVENTORY MEASURES, PRODUCTION SCHEDULING, AND EVALUATING DIVISIONAL PERFORMANCE.** The Dore Company stresses competition between the heads of its various divisions, and it rewards stellar performance with year-end bonuses that vary between 5% and 10% of division net operating income (before considering the bonus or income taxes). The divisional managers have great discretion in setting production schedules.

Division Y produces and sells a product for which there is a long-standing demand but which can have marked seasonal and year-to-year fluctuations. On November 30, 19X2, Robert Smith, the Division Y manager, is preparing a production schedule for December. The following data are available for January 1 through November 30:

Beginning inventory, January 1, in units	10,000
Sales price, per unit	$500
Total fixed costs incurred for manufacturing	$11,000,000
Total fixed costs: other (not inventoriable)	$11,000,000
Total variable costs for manufacturing	$22,000,000
Total other variable costs (fluctuate with units sold)	$5,000,000
Units produced	110,000
Units sold	100,000
Variances	None

Production in October and November was 10,000 units each month. Practical capacity is 12,000 units per month. Maximum available storage space for inventory is 25,000 units. The sales outlook, for December through February, is 6,000 units monthly. To retain a core of key employees, monthly production cannot be scheduled at less than 4,000 units without special permission from the president. Inventory is never to be less than 10,000 units.

The denominator used for applying fixed factory overhead is regarded as 120,000 units annually. The company uses a standard absorption-costing system. All variances are disposed of at year-end as an adjustment to standard cost of goods sold.

Required:

1. Given the restrictions as stated, and assuming that the manager wants to maximize the company's net income for 19X2:
   a. How many units should be scheduled for production in December?
   b. What net operating income will be reported for 19X2 as a whole, assuming that the implied cost behavior patterns will continue in December as they did throughout the year to date? Show your computations.
   c. If December production is scheduled at 4,000 units, what would reported net income be?
2. Assume that standard direct costing is used rather than standard absorption costing:
   a. What would net income for 19X2 be, assuming that the December production schedule is the one in Requirement 1, part (a)?
   b. Assuming that December production was 4,000 units?
   c. Reconcile the net incomes in this requirement with those in Requirement 1.
3. From the viewpoint of the long-run interests of the company as a whole, what production schedule should the division manager set? Explain fully. Include in your explanation a comparison of the motivating influence of absorption and direct costing in this situation.
4. Assume standard absorption costing. The manager wants to maximize his after-income-tax performance over the long run. Given the data at the beginning of the problem, assume that income tax rates will be halved in 19X3. Assume also that year-end write-offs of variances are acceptable for income tax purposes. How many units should be scheduled for production in December? Why?

15–38. PERFORMANCE EVALUATION. The Larson Company is a small flour milling company in the Midwest. Everett Larson became president in 19X6. He is concerned with the ability of his production manager to control costs. To aid his evaluation, Larson set up a standard cost system.

Standard costs were based on 19X6 costs in several categories. Each 19X6 cost was divided by 1,740,000 cwt, the volume of 19X6 production, to determine a standard for 19X7 (cwt. means hundredweight, or 100 pounds):

	19X6 Cost (in thousands)	19X7 Standard per hundredweight
Direct materials	$2,262	$1.30
Direct labor	1,218	.70
Variable overhead	2,088	1.20
Fixed overhead	3,132	1.80
Total	$8,700	$5.00

At the end of 19X7, Larson compared actual results to the standards he established. Production was 1,580,000 cwt, and variances were as follows:

	ACTUAL	STANDARD	VARIANCE
Direct materials	$2,240	$2,054	$186 U
Direct labor	1,094	1,106	12 F
Variable overhead	1,892	1,896	4 F
Fixed overhead	3,130	2,844	286 U
Total	$8,356	$7,900	$456 U

Larson was not surprised by the unfavorable variance in direct materials. After all, wheat prices in 19X7 averaged 10% above those in 19X6. But he was disturbed by the lack of control of fixed overhead. He called in the production manager and demanded an explanation.

Required:

1. Prepare an explanation for the large unfavorable fixed overhead variance.
2. Discuss the appropriateness of using one year's costs as the next year's standards.

Chapter 16

QUANTITATIVE TECHNIQUES USED IN MANAGEMENT ACCOUNTING

LEARNING OBJECTIVES

When you have finished studying this chapter, you should be able to:

1. Distinguish between making decisions under certainty and making decisions under uncertainty.
2. Construct a decision table involving probabilities and compute the expected value of each action.
3. Use standard deviation and expected value to compute the coefficient of variation, and indicate how it can measure the relative degrees of risk among alternatives.
4. Compute the expected value of perfect information.
5. Develop the equations and inequalities for a linear-programming solution.
6. Interpret the optimal solution to a linear-programming model, including an explanation of shadow prices.
7. Determine the economic order quantity (EOQ), the safety stock, and the reorder point in a simple inventory situation.

Because the branches of knowledge overlap, it is always an oversimplification to specify where the field of accounting starts and where it ends. Some accountants believe that accounting should restrict itself to scorekeeping, the compilation of financial history. Others feel that if accountants do not move quickly to assimilate a working knowledge of computer technology and assorted mathematical techniques, their attention-directing and problem-solving functions will be seized by the expanding field of management science.

We need not be concerned with the controversy over what accounting is and what it is not. Regardless of its label, the subject matter of this chapter affects management planning and control and is therefore important to accountants and to managers.

Management processes are continually changing. In profit-seeking and nonprofit organizations, in service and manufacturing industries, in large firms and small, managers are using increasingly sophisticated methods. To provide useful information, accountants must keep abreast of the changes in management methods. If a manager uses a quantitative model, the accountant must understand it well enough to provide relevant information. Even more important, accountants are still considered the top quantitative experts in most organizations. As such, they must provide leadership in choosing new methods that promise better ways of accomplishing objectives.

Accountants should know how mathematical models may improve planning and control. Methods of processing information and making decisions that were appropriate in "smokestack" industries may not apply to "high-tech" firms. Cost systems developed for manufacturing firms may not provide relevant information in service industries.

The computer revolution, especially the ready availability of personal computers, has put quantitative techniques at managers' fingertips. A few years ago, the study of quantitative techniques was an option for accountants. Now it's a necessity.

This chapter is a survey. Technical competence in any of the areas mentioned can be achieved only by thorough specialized study. We shall explore decision theory and uncertainty, linear-programming models, and inventory-control models.

The accountant often provides a majority of the data for these decision models. An understanding of the nature of decision models should directly affect how the accountant designs a formal information system.

DECISION THEORY AND UNCERTAINTY

☐ **Formal Decision Models**

A **model** is a simplified description of a device, system, or situation. It includes the factors and interrelationships most important to the user of the model; those of least importance are omitted. Every model requires a trade-off between simplicity and realism. A model car for a three-year-old child differs greatly from a model of the same car used by the automobile company's designers.

Accounting systems and financial reports are models of an organization. Of course, they exclude a great deal of information about the organization. They focus on certain key factors, ones that are useful for many decisions. However, the accountant's model is not helpful in all decisions.

Managers often use decision models expressed in mathematical terms. A decision model distills raw data into a form useful to managers in choosing among alternative courses of action. The careful use of decision models supplements hunches and implicit rules of thumb with explicit assumptions and criteria.

Sometimes decision models replace managers as decision makers. Examples are inventory models and production scheduling models where the output from the model can be implemented without human intervention. More often, a decision model quantifies many factors in a situation and produces a suggested decision. A manager then considers the output of the model together with other information to make a final decision. In these cases the decision model quantifies and summarizes part, but not all, of the useful data.

Mathematical decision models have been criticized because they oversimplify and ignore important factors. By their nature, such models are simplified. But an intelligent manager who knows both the limitations and strengths of a decision model can use it to aid in decision making. Many examples of successful applications can be cited. For example, inventory-control and linear-programming models are widely used. The test of success is not whether mathematical models lead to perfect decisions, but whether such models lead to better decisions than via alternative techniques. How is this test applied? Sometimes it is difficult, but conceptually the test is to compare the net financial impact (after deducting the cost of accumulating the information used in the decision) of the decision generated by the mathematical model versus the net financial impact of the decision generated by other techniques. In other words, the relative attractiveness of using mathematical decision models is again subject to the cost-benefit test.

☐ **Decision Theory**

Decision theory is a complex, somewhat ill-defined body of knowledge developed by statisticians, mathematicians, economists, and psychologists that tries to prescribe how decisions should be made and to describe systematically which variables affect choices. The basic approach of decision theory has the following characteristics:

1. *An objective that can be quantified.* This objective can take many forms. Most often, it is expressed as a maximization (or minimization) of some form of profit (or cost). This quantification is often called a **choice criterion** or an **objective function**. This objective function is used to evaluate the courses of action and to provide a basis for choosing the best alternative.
2. *A set of the alternative courses of action under explicit consideration.* This set of *actions* should be collectively exhaustive and mutually exclusive.[1]
3. *A set of all relevant **events** (sometimes called **states** or **states of nature**) that can occur.* This set should also be collectively exhaustive and mutually exclusive. Therefore one and only one of the states will actually occur.
4. *A set of **probabilities** that describes the likelihood of occurrence for each event.*
5. *A set of **outcomes** (often called **payoffs**) that measure the consequences of the various possible actions in terms of the objective function.* Outcomes depend on the specific course of action taken and the specific event that occurs.

☐ Decision Tables

An example may clarify the essential ingredients of a formal model. Suppose that a decision maker has only two possible courses of action regarding the quality-control aspects of a project: accept a unit of product or reject the unit of product. The decision maker also predicts that only two events can affect the outcomes: either the product unit conforms to the quality standards, or it does not conform. The combination of actions, events, and outcomes can be presented in a **decision table** (also called **payoff table**):

ALTERNATIVE ACTIONS	ALTERNATIVE EVENTS AND OUTCOMES	
	Conform	Nonconform
Accept	$12[1]	$2[2]
Reject	$ 7[3]	$7[4]

Note: The number references in this table relate to the corresponding numbers in the list that follows.

The outcomes in this example are the dollar contributions to profit; they are assumed to take the pattern shown here because:

1. Acceptance and conformance should produce the normal contribution to profit.
2. Acceptance and nonconformance eventually results in expensive rework after the product is processed through later stages, so the profit contribution is lower.
3. Rejection and conformance results in immediate unnecessary rework that reduces the normal profit contribution.
4. Rejection and nonconformance results in the same immediate necessary rework described in item 3.

The payoff table includes three of the five ingredients of the formal model: actions, events, and outcomes. The other two ingredients are the probabilities

---

[1] "Collectively exhaustive" means that *all* possible actions are included. "Mutually exclusive" means that no two actions can both be undertaken.

and the choice criterion. Assume that the probability of conform is 0.6 and that of nonconform is 0.4. Assume also that the choice criterion is to maximize the expected value of the outcome, the contribution to profit. The decision table can now be expanded:

	EVENTS		
	Conform	Nonconform	
PROBABILITY OF EVENT	0.6	0.4	EXPECTED VALUE OF CONTRIBUTION
ACTIONS			
Accept	$12 outcome	$2 outcome	$8
Reject	$ 7 outcome	$7 outcome	$7

Given this model, the decision maker would always accept the product, because the expected value of the outcome is larger for Accept than for Reject. Let $\overline{A}$ = the "average" or expected value,[2] then:

if accept, $\overline{A} = \$12(0.6) + \$2(0.4) = \$7.20 + \$.80 = \$8$

if reject, $\overline{A} = \$7(0.6) + \$7(0.4) = \$4.20 + \$2.80 = \$7$

As you can see, an expected value is simply a weighted average using the probability of each event to weight the outcomes for each action. (Incidentally, $\overline{A}$ is pronounced *A-bar*.)

☐ Decisions Under Certainty

Decisions are frequently classified as those made under certainty and those made under uncertainty. Certainty exists when there is absolutely no doubt about which event will occur and when there is a single outcome for each possible action. The decision table would appear as follows (data assumed):

	EVENT
	Conform
PROBABILITY OF EVENT	1.0
ACTIONS	
Accept	$12 outcome
Reject	$ 7 outcome

---

[2] An expected value is an arithmetic mean, a weighted average using the probabilities as weights. The formula is:

$$\overline{A} = \sum_{x=1}^{n} A_x P_x$$

where A_x is the outcome or payoff or cost or cash flow for the xth possible event or state of nature, P_x is the probability of occurrence of that outcome, $\overline{A}$ is the expected value of the outcome, x is the identity of each event, and n is the number of events, and Σ signifies summation.

Note that there is only one column in this decision table because there is only one possible event. The decision obviously consists of choosing the action that will produce the better outcome. However, decisions under certainty are not *always* obvious. There are often countless alternative actions, each of which may offer a different outcome. The problem, then, is finding the best one. For example, the problem of allocating 20 different job orders to 20 different machines, any one of which could do the job, can involve literally *billions* of different combinations. Each way of assigning these jobs is another possible action. The payoff table would have only one outcome *column* because the costs of production using the various machines are assumed to be known; however, it would have nearly 2½ quintillion *rows*. This demonstrates that decision making under certainty can be more than just a trivial problem.

When an outcome is certain for a particular (or given) action, the prediction is a single point with no dispersion on either side. There is a 100% chance of occurrence if the action is taken; in other words, the probability is 1.0. For example, the expected cash inflow on an action, buying a federal Treasury note, might be, say, $4,000 for next year. This might be graphed as follows:

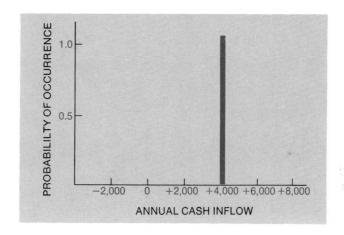

☐ Decisions Under Uncertainty

Of course, decision makers must frequently contend with uncertainty rather than certainty; they face a number of possible events, given a particular course of action. They must assign a probability to each event. Situations differ in the degree of objectivity by which probabilities are assigned.

The probabilities may be assigned with a high degree of objectivity.[3] That is, if decision makers know the probability of occurrence of each of a number of events, their assignment of probabilities is "objective" because of

---

[3] This is sometimes called decision making under risk, as distinguished from decision making under uncertainty. The distinction between risk and uncertainty in the current literature and in practice is so blurred that the terms are used interchangeably here.

mathematical proofs or the compilation of historical evidence. For example, the probability of obtaining a head in the toss of a symmetrical coin is 0.5; that of drawing a particular playing card from a well-shuffled deck, 1/52. In a business, the probability of having a specified percentage of spoiled units may be assigned with great confidence, which is based on production experience with thousands of units.

If decision makers have no basis in past experience or in mathematical proofs for assigning the probabilities of occurrence of the various events, they must resort to the *subjective* assignment of probabilities. For example, the probability of the success or failure of a new product may have to be assessed without the help of any related experience. This assignment is subjective because no two individuals assessing a situation will necessarily assign the same probabilities. Even if executives are virtually certain about the *range* of possible events or possible outcomes, they may differ about the likelihoods of various possibilities within that range.

The concept of uncertainty can be illustrated by considering two proposed investment projects, each with a one-year useful life. The manager has carefully considered the risks and has subjectively determined the following discrete probability distribution of expected cash flows for the next year:

PROJECT 1		PROJECT 2	
Probability	Cash Inflow	Probability	Cash Inflow
0.10	$3,000	0.10	$2,000
0.20	3,500	0.25	3,000
0.40	4,000	0.30	4,000
0.20	4,500	0.25	5,000
0.10	5,000	0.10	6,000

☐ Expected Value and Standard Deviation

Exhibit 16–1 shows a graphical comparison of the probability distributions. The usual approach to this problem is to compute an **expected value** for each probability distribution.

The expected values of the cash inflows from Projects 1 and 2 are both $4,000:

$$\overline{A} \text{ (Project 1)} = 0.1(3,000) + 0.2(3,500) + 0.4(4,000) + 0.2(4,500) + 0.1(5,000)$$
$$= \$4,000$$

$$\overline{A} \text{ (Project 2)} = 0.1(2,000) + 0.25(3,000) + 0.3(4,000) + 0.25(5,000) + 0.1(6,000)$$
$$= \$4,000$$

Incidentally, the expected value of the cash inflow from the federal Treasury note discussed on page 517 is also $4,000:

$$\overline{A} \text{ (Treasury note)} = 1.0(4,000) = \$4,000$$

Note that mere comparison of these $4,000 expected values is an oversimplification. These three single figures are not strictly comparable; one represents certainty, whereas the other two represent the expected values over

EXHIBIT 16–1

Comparison of Probability Distributions

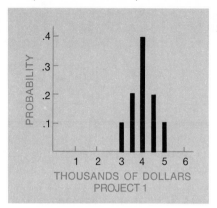

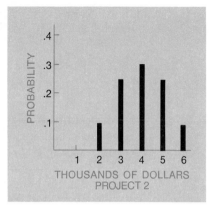

PROJECT 1 — THOUSANDS OF DOLLARS

PROJECT 2 — THOUSANDS OF DOLLARS

a range of possible outcomes. Decision makers must explicitly or implicitly (by "feel" or hunch) recognize that they are comparing figures that are really representations of probability distributions; otherwise, the reporting of the expected value alone may mislead them.[4]

To give the decision maker more information, the accountant could provide the complete probability distribution for each proposal. However, often that course means flooding the manager with too many data for convenient comprehension. Therefore a middle ground is often used. A summary measure of the underlying dispersion is supplied. The most common measure of the dispersion of a probability distribution for a single variable is the **standard deviation**—the square root of the mean of the squared deviations from the expected value. The standard deviation is denoted by σ, which is *sigma*, the lowercase Greek letter for s:

$$\sigma = \sqrt{\sum_{x=1}^{n} (A_x - \overline{A})^2 P_x}$$

The standard deviation for Project 1 is smaller than that for Project 2:

for Project 1: $\sigma_1 = [0.1(3,000 - 4,000)^2 + 0.2(3,500 - 4,000)^2$
$+ 0.4(4,000 - 4,000)^2 + 0.2(4,500 - 4,000)^2$
$+ 0.1(5,000 - 4,000)^2]^{1/2}$
$= [300,000]^{1/2} = \$548$

for Project 2: $\sigma_2 = [0.1(2,000 - 4,000)^2 + 0.25(3,000 - 4,000)^2$
$+ 0.3(4,000 - 4,000)^2 + 0.25(5,000 - 4,000)^2$
$+ 0.1(6,000 - 4,000)^2]^{1/2}$
$= [1,300,000]^{1/2} = \$1,140$

for the Treasury note: $\sigma_T = \sqrt{1.0(4,000 - 4,000)^2} = 0$

---

[4] For example, how would you feel about choosing between the following two investments? First, invest \$10 today with a probability of 1.0 of obtaining \$11 in two days. Second, invest \$10 today with a probability of 0.5 of obtaining \$22 in two days and 0.5 of obtaining \$0. The expected value is \$11 in both cases.

A measure of relative dispersion is the *coefficient of variation,* which is the standard deviation divided by expected value. The coefficient for Project 2 is $1,140 \div 4,000 = 0.29$; for Project 1 it is $548 \div 4,000 = 0.14$; and for the Treasury note it is $0 \div 4,000 = 0$. Therefore, because the coefficient is a relative measure of risk or uncertainty, Project 2 is said to have a greater degree of risk than Project 1, which, in turn, has a greater degree of risk than the Treasury note.

☐ The Accountant and Uncertainty

Many accounting practitioners and managers shudder at the notion of using subjective probabilities to quantify things that are supposedly "intangible" or "unmeasurable" or "qualitative" or "unquantifiable." However, their position is weak, simply because decisions *do* have to be made. The attempts by statisticians, mathematicians, and modern accountants to measure the unmeasurable is an old and natural chore that scientists have performed for centuries. The use of subjective probabilities merely formalizes the intuitive judgments and hunches that managers so often use. It forces decision makers to expose and evaluate what they may have done unconsciously for years.

Many statisticians and accountants favor presenting the entire probability distribution directly to the decision maker. Others first divide the information into a threefold classification of optimistic, middle, and pessimistic categories. Still others provide summary measures of dispersion, such as the standard deviation or the coefficient of variation. In any event, we are likely to see increasing recognition of uncertainty and probability distributions in accounting reports. In this way, the information will portray underlying phenomena in a more realistic fashion instead of as if there were only a world of certainty.

☐ Example of General Approach to Uncertainty

An example of the general approach to dealing with uncertainty may clarify some of the preceding ideas.

☐ Problem

Once a day, a retailer stocks units (bags) of fresh pastries; each costs 40¢ and sells for $1. The retailer never reduces his price; leftovers are given to a nearby church. He estimates characteristics as follows:

DEMAND	PROBABILITY
0	0.05
1	0.20
2	0.40
3	0.25
4	0.10
5 or more	0.00
	1.00

The retailer wants to know how many units he should stock to maximize expected profits. Try to solve before consulting the solution that follows:

□ Solution

The profit per unit sold is 60¢; the loss per unit unsold is 40¢. All the alternatives may be assessed in the following *decision table*:

	EVENTS: DEMAND OF					
	0	1	2	3	4	EXPECTED
PROBABILITY OF EVENT	0.05	0.20	0.40	0.25	0.10	VALUE
ACTIONS: **UNITS PURCHASED**						
0	$ 0	$ 0	$ 0	$ 0	$ 0	$ 0
1	− .40	.60	.60	.60	.60	.55
2	− .80	.20	1.20	1.20	1.20	.90
3	−1.20	−.20	.80	1.80	1.80	.85
4	−1.60	−.60	.40*	1.40	2.40	.55

As shown in an earlier section, the computation of expected value ($\bar{A}$) for each action is affected by the probability weights and the outcome associated with each combination of actions and events:

$$\bar{A} \text{ (Stock 1)} = 0.05(-.40) + 0.20(.60) + 0.40(.60) + 0.25(.60) + 0.10(.60)$$
$$= \$.55$$

$$\bar{A} \text{ (Stock 2)} = 0.05(-.80) + 0.20(.20) + 0.40(1.20) + 0.25(1.20) + 0.10(1.20)$$
$$= \$.90$$

and so on.

To maximize expected value, the retailer should stock two units ($\bar{A}$ = $.90).

□ Obtaining Additional Information

Sometimes executives are hesitant about making a particular decision. They want more information before making a final choice. Some additional information is nearly always obtainable—at a price. Consider a popular technique for computing the maximum amount that should be paid for such additional information. The general idea is to compute the expected value under ideal circumstances—that is, circumstances that would permit the retailer to predict, with absolute certainty, the number of units to be sold on any given day.

The basic decision is whether to purchase advance revelation *without knowing what the revelation will be*. Exhibit 16–2 presents a decision table with perfect information. The expected value of the decision *with* perfect

EXHIBIT 16–2

Decision Table with Perfect Information

| | EVENTS: DEMAND OF | | | | | |
PROBABILITY OF EVENT	0 0.05	1 0.20	2 0.40	3 0.25	4 0.10	EXPECTED VALUE
ACTIONS: **UNITS PURCHASED**						
0	$0					$ 0
1		$.60				.12
2			$1.20			.48
3				$1.80		.45
4					$2.40	.24
Total expected value						$1.29

information is the sum of the best outcome for each event multiplied by its probability:

$$\overline{A} \text{ (perfect information)} = 0.05(0) + 0.20(.60) + 0.40(1.20)$$
$$+ 0.25(1.80) + 0.10(2.40) = \$1.29$$

In Exhibit 16–2, it is assumed that the retailer will never err in his forecasts and that demand will fluctuate from zero to four exactly as indicated by the probabilities. The maximum day-in, day-out average profit is $1.29. Consequently, the most the retailer should be willing to pay for perfect advance information would be the difference between:

Expected value *with* perfect information	$1.29
Expected value *with* existing information	.90
Expected value *of* perfect information	$ .39

In the real world, of course, the retailer would not pay 39¢ because no amount of additional information is likely to provide perfect knowledge. But businesses often obtain additional knowledge through sampling, and sampling costs money. The executive needs a method (1) for assessing the probable benefits, in relation to its cost, of additional information from sampling, and (2) for determining the best sample size. In the present example, no sampling technique would be attractive if its daily cost equaled or exceeded the 39¢ ceiling price.

☐ Good Decisions and Bad Outcomes

Always distinguish between a good decision and a good outcome. One can exist without the other. By definition, uncertainty rules out guaranteeing that the best outcome will be obtained. Thus it is possible that "bad luck" will produce unfavorable consequences even when "good" decisions have occurred.

Consider the following example. Suppose you are offered a gamble for a mere $1, a fair coin toss where heads you win, tails you lose. You will win $20 if the event is heads, but you will lose $1 if the event is tails. As a rational decision maker, you proceed through the logical phases: gathering information, assessing consequences, and making a choice. You accept the bet. The coin is tossed. You lose. From your viewpoint, this was a bad outcome but a good decision. From your opponent's viewpoint, it was a good outcome but a bad decision.

A decision can only be made on the basis of information available at the time of the decision. Hindsight is often flawless, but a bad outcome does not necessarily mean that it flowed from a bad decision. A good decision increases the chances of a good outcome but does not guarantee it.

LINEAR-PROGRAMMING MODELS

☐ Characteristics

Linear programming is a potent mathematical approach to a group of management problems that contain many interacting variables and that basically involve the allocation of limited resources in such a way as to increase profit or decrease cost. There are nearly always limiting factors or scarce resources that are restrictions, restraints, or constraints on available alternatives. Linear programming has been applied to a vast number of decisions, such as machine scheduling, product mix, raw-material mix, scheduling flight crews, production routing, shipping schedules, transportation routes, blending gasoline, blending sausage ingredients, and designing transformers. In general, linear programming is the standard technique for combining materials, labor, and facilities to best advantage when all the relationships are approximately linear and many combinations are possible.

Note that linear programming is a decision model under conditions of *certainty*, where constraints affect the allocation of resources among competing uses. That is, the model analyzes a total list of actions whose outcomes are known with certainty and chooses the combination of actions that will maximize profit or minimize cost.

☐ The Techniques, the Accountant, and the Manager

All of us are familiar with linear equations (e.g., $X + Y = 9$). We also know that simultaneous linear equations with two or three unknowns become progressively more difficult to solve with only pencil and paper. Linear programming essentially involves (1) constructing a set of simultaneous linear equations, which represent the model of the problem and which include many variables, and (2) solving the equations with the help of a computer.

The formulation of the equations—that is, the building of the model—

is far more challenging than the mechanics of the solution. The model aims at being a valid and accurate portrayal of the problem. Computer programs can then generate a solution from the equations you prepare.

As a minimum, accountants and executives should be able to recognize the types of problems in their organizations that are most susceptible to analysis by linear programming. They should be able to help in the construction of the model (i.e., in specifying the variables, objective function, and the constraints). Ideally, they should understand the mathematics and should be able to talk comfortably with the operations researchers who are attempting to express their problem mathematically. However, the position taken here is that the accountant and the manager should concentrate on formulating the model and *analyzing* the solution and not worry about the technical intricacies of *obtaining* the solution. The latter may be delegated to the mathematicians; the feasibility and advisability of delegating the former is highly doubtful.

☐ Illustration of Product Mix

In Chapter 4, pages 103–105, you learned about producing the product with the largest contribution margin per unit of limiting factor. This simple rule works when only one resource is in short supply. But what can you do if there are two or more limiting factors? Linear programming is a method for determining the mix of products that best uses the available resources.

> Consider the following illustration: machine 1 is available for 24 hours, and machine 2 is available for 20 hours, for the processing of two products. Product X has a contribution margin of $2 per liter; product Y, $1 per kilogram. These products must be sold in such combination that the number of liters of X must be equal to or less than the number of kilograms of Y. A liter of X requires 6 hours of time on machine 1 and 10 hours of time on machine 2. A kilogram of Y requires 4 hours of time on machine 1 only. What daily production combination will produce the maximum contribution to profit?

The linear-programming approach may be divided into three phases.

1. Formulate the model.
2. Solve the model.
3. Analyze the solution.

Phases 1 and 3 are especially important to accountants. Phase 2 is routine and is nearly always performed by a computer.

1. MODEL FORMULATION. There are three parts to a linear-programming model: the variables, the objective function, and the constraints. In a product-mix linear program, the quantity produced of each product is represented by a *variable*, and the solution identifies an optimal quantity for each variable. Let X be the number of liters of Product X produced and Y the number of kilograms of Product Y.

The *objective* of a linear-programming model is usually to maximize the total contribution margin or to minimize costs. The first row in our linear-programming model, the objective function, indicates that we seek the product combination that maximizes total contribution margin:

$$1. \quad \text{max. } \$2X + \$1Y$$

This is the objective function.

There are generally three types of *constraints* in a product-mix linear programming model:

a. Limiting factor constraints—there is one such constraint for each limiting factor. Row 2 is the constraint for machine 1 and row 3 for machine 2.

$$2. \quad 6X + 4Y \leq 24$$
$$3. \quad 10X \quad\;\; \leq 20$$

b. Sales constraints—these might include restrictions on either total sales of a product or on the product mix of sales. They may be imposed by market demand or by management policies. Row 4 indicates that the number of liters of X must not exceed the number of kilograms of Y; it is the only sales constraint.

$$4. \quad X - Y \leq 0$$

c. Nonnegativity constraints—each variable is forced to be positive because negative production is impossible. Rows 5 and 6 represent these constraints; often they are assumed rather than being stated explicitly.

$$5. \quad X \geq 0$$
$$6. \quad Y \geq 0$$

2. MODEL SOLUTION. A computer is needed to solve nearly all practical linear-programming models. Why? Because even moderately sized models could take days, or even months, to solve by hand. Because our simple example has only two variables, we can use graphical methods to demonstrate the procedure used to solve linear programming problems. You should regard the graphical approach as an illustration only; do not expect to use it to solve most practical linear-programming problems.

The solution procedure begins by identifying *feasible* solutions. To be feasible, a combination of variables must satisfy all the constraints—it must be technically possible. In Exhibit 16–3 a line represents each constraint, and the arrows show the feasible side. For example, only combinations of X and Y to the lower left of the machine 1 constaint are feasible. The nonshaded area in Exhibit 16–3 contains the feasible region of X and Y values.

Next, the feasible solution that best satisfies the objective function is identified. Each dashed line in Exhibit 16–3 includes all combinations of X and Y that produce a given contribution to profit. For example, the dashed line on the lower left shows all combinations of X and Y that have a contribution of $2. The dashed line farthest up and to the right that still touches the feasible region represents the largest possible contribution. This line will always go through a corner of the feasible region. The optimal solution is $X = 2$ and $Y = 3$, the corner where the machine 1 constraint inter-

EXHIBIT 16–3

Linear Programming: Graphic Solution

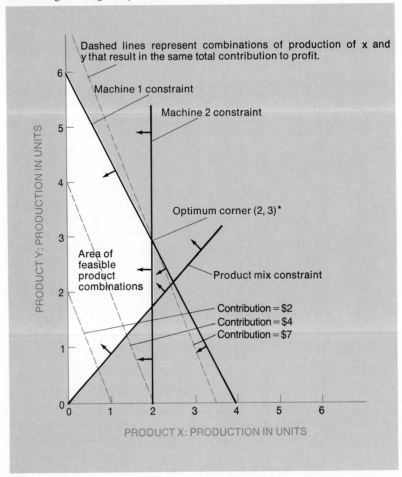

sects with the machine 2 constraint. The total contribution is $(2 \times \$2) + (3 \times \$1) = \$7$.

Computer programs for solving linear programming models exploit the fact that the best solution must lie at a corner of the feasible region. They use the *simplex* method, which identifies the best solution by systematically examining corner solutions. A condensed solution produced by LINDO, a popular linear-programming package available on mainframe and personal computers, is shown in Exhibit 16–4. The first line gives the largest feasible contribution margin, \$7. The next section lists the optimal solution, $X = 2$ and $Y = 3$. The rest of the exhibit will be explained later.

3. SOLUTION ANALYSIS. A computer solution to a linear programming model provides more than the optimal solution. You can perform *sensitivity analysis*

EXHIBIT 16–4

LINDO Solution to Linear Programming Example

OBJECTIVE FUNCTION VALUE		
1	7.000	
VARIABLE	VALUE	
X	2.00000	
Y	3.00000	
ROW	SLACK	DUAL PRICES
2	0.00000	0.25000
3	0.00000	0.05000
4	1.00000	0.00000

on the solution. Sensitivity analysis answers the question, "How would the optimal solution change if some part of the linear programming model changes?" We often are uneasy about some estimates used in the model, such as contribution margins or constraint coefficients. How critical are these estimates to the solution? If the optimal decision does not change over a large range for a particular estimate, the manager should pay nothing for a more refined measure of that item. We may also want information about what would happen to the solution if we deliberately changed part of the model. For example, we might obtain a larger amount of one of the limiting resources. The effects of *small* increases or decreases in resources are shown by shadow prices. In most situations, determining the effects of large changes in resources requires additional analysis.

Shadow prices, also called **dual prices**, provide useful information for sensitivity analysis. Each constraint has a related shadow price. The shadow price answers "what if" questions about the constraint. It indicates how much the objective function will increase if one more unit of the limiting resource is available or decrease if there is one less unit. *What if* one more hour is available on machine 2? *What if* there were one less hour available on machine 1? A shadow price is essentially the *opportunity* cost of the limiting resource.

The condensed LINDO solution presented in Exhibit 16–4 gives two items of information about each constraint (except the nonnegativity constraints). The *slack* indicates whether the resource represented by the constraint is really a *limiting* resource. If slack is zero, the optimal production plan uses all of the available supply of the resource. The constraint is *binding*. In this case, obtaining more of the resource could be worthwhile; the dual price (or shadow price) shows how worthwhile. If you can purchase more of the resource at a price less than the shadow price, you should do so.[5] One more hour on

---

[5] This statement assumes that the resource had no variable cost. If the resource has a variable cost, the shadow price is the amount *above the variable cost* that you should be willing to pay for the resource. For example, if direct labor was paid $10 per hour but there was an upper limit on the amount of labor available, a $2 shadow price on the labor constraint means that up to $10 + $2 = $12 could be paid for additional labor.

machine 1 is worth $.25; similarly, if one less hour were available on machine 1, the contribution would *decrease* by $.25. (Note that row 2 is the constraint on machine 1.)

If the slack is positive, the resource is not limiting production. The constraint is not binding. Other factors dominate. You would not pay for any more of a resource that has slack; therefore, its dual price is zero. In the illustration, the constraint that X be less than Y is not binding. No advantage is gained by allowing X to be greater than Y.

Shadow prices are only one example of useful information from the solution of a linear programming model. However, further exploration is left to courses in quantitative methods, management science, or operations research.

INVENTORY PLANNING AND CONTROL MODELS

□ Characteristics

Comprehensive inventory planning and control systems have been successfully installed in many companies. The major objective of inventory management is to discover and maintain the optimum level of investment in the inventory. Inventories may be too high or too low. If too high, there are unnecessary carrying costs and risks of obsolescence. If too low, production may be disrupted or sales permanently lost. The best inventory level is that which minimizes the total costs associated with inventory.

The purchase costs or the manufacturing costs of the inventory (that is, the acquisition costs) would usually be irrelevant to the inventory-control decisions considered here, because we assume that the total annual quantity required would be the same for the various alternatives. Exhibit 16–5 shows

EXHIBIT 16–5

Some Relevant Costs of Inventories

> ### COSTS OF ORDERING
>
> 1. Preparing purchase or production orders
> 2. Receiving (unloading, unpacking, inspecting)
> 3. Processing all related documents
> 4. Extra purchasing or transportation costs for frequent orders*
> 5. Extra costs of numerous small production runs, overtime, setups, and training
>
> plus
>
> ### COSTS OF CARRYING
>
> 1. Foregone return on capital invested in inventory†
> 2. Risk of obsolescence and deterioration
> 3. Storage-space costs
> 4. Personal property taxes on inventory
> 5. Insurance on inventory

* Includes foregone purchase or transportation discounts that would be available on larger orders.

† Average inventory investment times the desired rate of return; these costs do not appear explicitly in conventional accounting records.

the main relevant costs that must be considered, the costs of *ordering* the inventory plus the costs of *carrying* it.

The two significant cost items tend to offset one another. As orders decrease in frequency and grow in size, the total relevant costs of carrying the inventory, including interest, rise, but the total costs of ordering, delivery, and so on, decrease; and vice versa.

How Much to Order?

The two main questions in inventory control are how much to order at a time and when to order. A key factor in inventory policy is computing the best size of either a normal purchase order for raw materials or a shop order for a production run. This optimum size is called the **economic order quantity** (EOQ) or **economic lot size**, the size that will result in minimum total annual costs of the item in question. Consider this example:

Problem

A refrigerator manufacturer buys certain steel shelving in sets from outside suppliers at $4 per set. Total annual needs are 5,000 sets at a rate of 20 sets per working day. The following cost data are available:

Desired annual return on inventory investment,	
10% × $4	$.40
Rent, insurance, taxes, per unit per year	.10
Carrying costs per unit per year	$ .50
Costs per purchase order:	
Clerical costs, stationery, postage, telephone, etc.	$10.00

What is the economic order quantity?

Solution

Exhibit 16–6 shows tables of total relevant costs under various alternatives. The column with the least cost indicates the economic order quantity.

Exhibit 16–6 shows minimum costs at two levels, 400 and 500 units. The next step would be to see if costs are lower somewhere between 400 and 500 units, say, at 450 units:

Average inventory, 225 × $.50	$113	Carrying costs
Number of orders (5,000/450), 11.1 × $10 =	111	Purchase order costs
	$224	Total relevant costs

The dollar differences here are extremely small, but the approach is important. The same approach is shown in graphic form in Exhibit 16–7.

EXHIBIT 16–6

Annualized Relevant Costs of Various Standard Orders
(250 working days)

E	Order size	50	100	200	400	500	600	800	1,000	5,000
E/2	Average inventory in units*	25	50	100	200	250	300	400	500	2,500
A/E	Number of purchase orders†	100	50	25	12.5	10	8.3	6.3	5	1
S(E/2)	Annual carrying cost @ $.50	$ 13	$ 25	$ 50	$100	$125	$150	$200	$ 250	$1,250
P(A/E)	Average purchase-order cost @ $10	1,000	500	250	125	100	83	63	50	10
C	Total annual relevant costs	$1,013	$525	$300	$225	$225	$233	$263	$ 300	$1,260

Least cost

E = Order size
A = Annual quantity used in units
S = Annual cost of carrying one unit in stock one year
P = Cost of placing a purchase order
C = Total annual relevant costs

* Assume that stock is zero when each order arrives. (Even if a certain minimum inventory were assumed, it has no bearing on the choice here as long as the minimum is the same for each alternative.) Therefore the average inventory relevant to the problem will be one-half the order quantity. For example, if 600 units are purchased, the inventory on arrival will contain 600. It will gradually diminish until no units are on hand. The average inventory would be 300; the carrying cost, $.50 × 300, or $150.

† Number to meet the total annual need for 5,000 sets: 5,000 ÷ order size.

☐ Order-Size Formula

The graphic approach has been expressed as a formula (derived via calculus):

$$E = \sqrt{\frac{2AP}{S}}$$

where E = order size, A = annual quantity used in units, P = cost of placing an order, and S = annual cost of carrying one unit in stock for one year.
Substituting:

$$E = \sqrt{\frac{2(5,000)(\$10)}{\$.50}} = \sqrt{\frac{\$100,000}{\$.50}} = \sqrt{200,000}$$

$$E = 447, \text{ the economic order quantity}$$

As we may expect, the order size gets larger as the annual quantity used (A) or the cost of placing an order (P) gets larger or as the annual cost of carrying one unit (S) gets smaller.

EXHIBIT 16–7

Graphic Solution of Economic Order Quantity

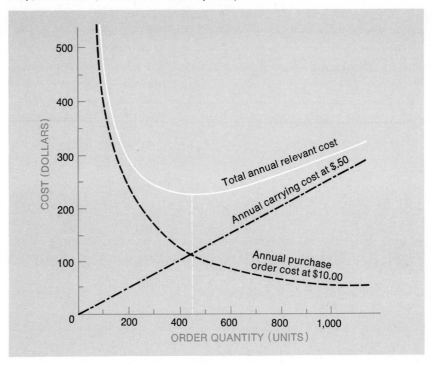

☐ When to Order?

Although we have seen how to compute economic order quantity, we have not yet considered another key decision: When to order? This question is easy to answer only if we know the **lead time**, the time interval between placing an order and receiving delivery, know the EOQ, and are *certain* of demand during lead time. The graph in Exhibit 16–8 will clarify the relationships among the following facts:

Economic order quantity	447 sets of steel shelving
Lead time	2 weeks
Average usage	100 sets per week

Exhibit 16–8, Part A, shows that the *reorder point*—the quantity level that automatically triggers a new order—depends on expected usage during the lead time; that is, if shelving is being used at a rate of 100 sets per week and the lead time is two weeks, a new order will be placed when the inventory level reaches 200 sets.

EXHIBIT 16–8

Demand in Relation to Inventory Levels

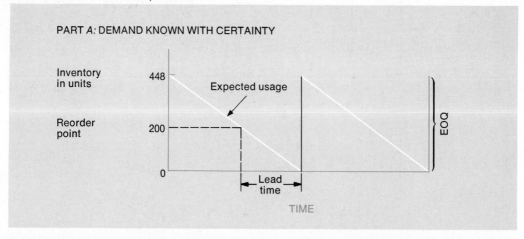

PART A: DEMAND KNOWN WITH CERTAINTY

Inventory in units — 448 — Expected usage

Reorder point — 200

0

Lead time

TIME

EOQ

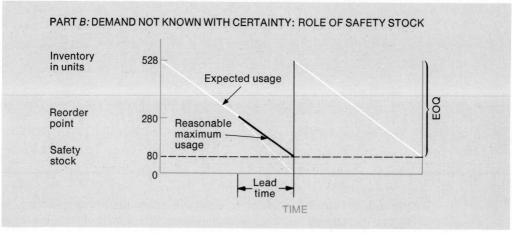

PART B: DEMAND NOT KNOWN WITH CERTAINTY: ROLE OF SAFETY STOCK

Inventory in units — 528 — Expected usage

Reorder point — 280 — Reasonable maximum usage

Safety stock — 80

0

Lead time

TIME

EOQ

☐ Minimum Inventory: Safety Allowance

Our previous example assumed that 100 sets would be used per week—a demand pattern that was known with certainty. Businesses are seldom blessed with such accurate forecasting; instead, demand may fluctuate from day to day, from week to week, or from month to month. Thus the company will run out of stock if there are sudden spurts in usage beyond 100 per week, delays in processing orders, or delivery delays. Obviously then, nearly all companies must provide for some **safety stock**—some minimum or buffer inventory as a cushion against reasonable expected maximum usage. The appropriate level of safety stock depends on the cost of running out of inventory versus the carrying cost of the safety stock.

Part B of Exhibit 16–8 is based on the same facts as Part A, except that usage varies between 60 and 140 sets per week. If it is very costly to run out of inventory, the safety stock might be, say, 80 sets (excess usage of 40 sets per week multiplied by two weeks). The reorder point is commonly computed as safety stock plus the average usage during the lead time.

The foregoing discussion of inventory control revolved around the so-called two-bin or constant-order-quantity system: When inventory levels recede to X, then order Y. Another widely used model is the constant-order-cycle system. For example, every month, review the inventory level on hand and order enough to bring the quantity on hand and on order up to some predetermined level of units. The reorder date is fixed, and the quantity ordered depends on the usage since the previous order and the outlook during the lead time. Demand forecasts and seasonal patterns should also be considered in specifying the size of orders during the year.

□ MRP and Just-in-Time Inventory Systems

In the 1970s and early 1980s many firms implemented **Material Requirements Planning (MRP)** systems to tie their inventory policies to their production scheduling. An MRP system specifies a production plan to meet a given output schedule. It then determines what materials and subcomponents are required for the production and when they are needed. From this, purchasing schedules and subcomponent manufacturing schedules are set. A model to determine optimal lot sizes, such as the EOQ model discussed here, is an important part of an MRP system.

During the 1980s many managers became concerned that inventory carrying costs were too high. This concern arose primarily because Japanese competitors seemed to have lower inventory costs. Many firms in Japan use **just-in-time inventory systems**, often called *Kanban* systems for continuous processing operations. A just-in-time system minimizes inventories by arranging to have materials and subcomponents arrive just as they are needed—no sooner and no later. This requires materials and subcomponents to be ordered and received in small batches—or, in the extreme, continuously at the same rate as they are needed for production. If there are large ordering costs, or if setup costs for manufacturing subcomponents are great, a just-in-time system is expensive. A major side effect of installing a just-in-time system is increased attention to reducing ordering and setup costs. Many firms have been remarkably successful in accomplishing this. Examples include Hewlett-Packard and Toyota.

In summary, both MRP and just-in-time systems tie inventory policy to production scheduling. MRP is more successful in a batch production environment, just-in-time in a continuous environment. MRP can be considered a "push" system; inventory is acquired and pushed through the system. Just-in-time is a "pull" system; inventory is not acquired until production needs it (that is, pulls it in). If a batch environment can be easily made into a continuous environment, inventory costs might be saved with a just-in-time system.

SUMMARY

Mathematical decision models are increasingly being used because they replace or supplement hunches with explicit assumptions and criteria. As these decision models become more widely used, accounting reports for decision making will tend to give more formal, explicit recognition of uncertainty. For example, the reporting of probability distributions for some revenues and costs is more likely.

Accountants often provide inputs to assorted decision models, such as linear-programming models and inventory control models. Therefore both accountants and managers need to understand the uses and limitations of the models.

SUMMARY PROBLEM FOR YOUR REVIEW

☐ Problem

Review this chapter's examples on statistical probability theory, page 520, linear programming, page 524, and inventory control, page 529, by trying to solve them before studying their solutions.

HIGHLIGHTS TO REMEMBER

1. Accountants generally report and analyze by using single sets of numbers to depict future and past events, as if we were in a world of certainty. The explicit use of probability distributions often helps remind us that we face an uncertain world.

2. Distinguish between good decisions and good outcomes. A good decision can produce either a good or a bad outcome. Similarly, a good outcome can result from a bad decision. However, the best protection against a bad outcome is a good decision. As Damon Runyon observed: "The race is not always to the swift, nor the battle to the strong—but that's the way to bet."

3. A linear-programming model is useful in product-mix decisions. In addition to identifying an optimal solution, it provides information for sensitivity analysis.

4. Inventory models minimize the sum of carrying costs and ordering or setup costs. Just-in-time systems have focused attention on reducing ordering and setup costs, thereby decreasing inventory levels.

ACCOUNTING VOCABULARY

Choice Criterion *p. 515*   Decision Table *515*   Dual Price *527*   Economic Lot Size *529*   Economic Order Quantity *529*   Events *515*   Expected Value *518*   Just-in-Time Systems *533*   Lead Time *531*   Linear Programming *523*   Material Requirement Planning (MRP) Systems *533*   Model *514*   Objective Function *515*   Outcomes *515*   Payoffs *515*   Payoff Table *515*   Probabilities *515*   Safety Stock *532*   Shadow Price *527*   Standard Deviation *519*   States *515*   States of Nature *515*.

FUNDAMENTAL ASSIGNMENT MATERIAL

16–1. **INFLUENCE OF UNCERTAINTY OF FORECASTS.** The figures used in many examples and problems in this and other textbooks are subject to uncertainty. For simplicity, the expected future amounts of sales, direct material, direct labor, and other operating costs are presented as if they were errorless predictions. For instance, this textbook and others might state that a facilities rearrangement "should result in cash operating savings of $X per year." Suppose some industrial engineers have prepared three estimates of savings for next year:

EVENT	PERCENTAGE CHANCE OF OCCURRENCE	SAVINGS
Pessimistic	10%	$2,000
Most likely	60	3,000
Optimistic	30	4,000

Required: 1. Calculate the expected-value of savings.
2. Why does the expected value differ from the "most likely" savings?

16–2. **EXPECTED VALUES AND PERFECT INFORMATION.** The captain of a commercial salmon fishing boat had to decide where to fish. He has three possible locations, and the wind affects what he will catch in each one.

PLACE	POUNDS OF FISH IF WIND IS FROM THE			
	North	East	West	South
Rolling Bay	140	80	60	20
Miller Point	50	40	190	50
Murden Cove	30	50	80	160

On a typical day this time of the year the wind is from the north 30% of the time, from the east 10%, from the west 40%, and from the south, 20%.

Required: 1. Without further information, calculate the expected pounds of fish for each location. Where should the captain fish?
2. Suppose the captain has a chance to obtain a flawless weather report, one that always correctly predicts the direction of the wind. If salmon sells wholesale for $2.50 per pound, what is the most the captain should spend for the weather forecast?

16–3. **LINEAR PROGRAMMING.** A company manufactures two kinds of precision tools, C (cheap) and E (expensive). The contribution margin of C is $4 per unit, while E's contribution margin per unit is $5. The tools are produced in three operations: machining, assembling, and finishing. The following is the average time, in hours, required for each tool:

	MACHINING	ASSEMBLING	FINISHING
C	1	5	3
E	2	4	2
Maximum time available for each operation	700	1,700	850

Assume that the time available can be allocated to either type of tool. Express the relationships as inequalities. Using graphic analysis, show which product mix will result in the maximum total contribution margin.

16–4. **EOQ AND REORDER POINT.** The Boeing Company purchases many parts for its aircraft from subcontractors. Suppose you were the manager in charge of purchasing passenger seats for commercial airplanes. Because Boeing signs contracts well in advance of the scheduled delivery of aircraft, the annual demand for seats can be predicted very accurately and is level throughout the year. For 19X8, 26,000 seats will be required.

The subcontractor supplying seats, Cascade Supply, produces them in batches. Because they incur a setup cost each time a new batch is produced, you have agreed to a contract paying $17,592 per batch plus $100 per seat. Each time a batch of seats is received it costs $2,100 to reorganize the warehouse for the shipment.

Annual carrying costs per seat in inventory are:

Desired return on inventory investment	$13
Rent, insurance, and taxes on inventory	3
Total carrying costs per unit per year	$16

Required:
1. What is the economic order quantity?
2. Suppose you desire a safety stock of 2,000 seats and lead time to receive shipment after an order is placed is 2 weeks. What level should the inventory reach before you order? Assume a 52-week year.

ADDITIONAL ASSIGNMENT MATERIAL

16–5. "The management accountant must be technically competent in computer technology and modern mathematics." Do you agree? Explain.

16–6. "I'm not certain what uncertainty is." Explain *uncertainty* briefly.

16–7. Consider the following probability distribution:

DAILY SALES EVENT IN UNITS	PROBABILITY
1,000	0.1
1,500	0.5
2,000	0.2
2,500	0.1
3,000	0.1
	1.0

A student commented: "If a manager has perfect information, she will always sell 3,000 units." Do you agree? Explain.

16–8. What is a decision table?

16–9. Which of the following are linear equations?

$$x + y + 4z + 6a = 8c + 4m$$

$$x^2 = y$$

$$x^2 - y = 4$$

$$4c = 27$$

16–10. What is the minimum competence in linear programming that managers should have?

16–11. How is the shadow price in linear programming useful to managers?

16–12. What are the principal costs of having too much inventory? Too little inventory?

16–13. "The safety stock is the average amount of inventory used during lead time." Do you agree? Explain.

16–14. "If demand and lead time were known with certainty, no safety stock would be needed." Do you agree? Explain.

16–15. "Lead time is the interval between placing an order and using the inventory." Do you agree? Explain.

16–16. "The major objective of inventory management is to minimize cash outlays for inventories." Do you agree? Explain.

16–17. **LONG-DISTANCE PHONE CALLS.** A memorandum from the president of Stanford University contained the following:

☐ As of October 20 the placement of person-to-person telephone calls from the University extensions will cease; rather, you are asked to place station-to-station calls instead. . . . We anticipate that this change in policy will save over $30,000 per year in toll charges.

You will be interested to know that for the same cost approximately two station-to-station calls can be made for each person-to-person call. Further, a sampling of Stanford users indicates that there is the probability of 50% that a station-to-station call will be successfully completed the first time.

Required: Using the data given, compute the annual Stanford long-distance phone bill for person-to-person calls before the new policy took effect. In all cases, assume that two station-to-station calls will obtain the desired person.

16–18. **PROBABILITIES: AUTOMATIC OR SEMIAUTOMATIC EQUIPMENT.** Jamestown Industrial Products Company plans to produce a new product. Two types of production equipment are being considered. The more costly equipment will result in lower labor and related variable costs:

EQUIPMENT	TOTAL ORIGINAL COST	VARIABLE COSTS, PER UNIT OF PRODUCT
Semiautomatic	$40,000	$4.50
Automatic	95,000	3.50

Marketing executives believe that this unique product will be salable only over the next year. Neither piece of equipment would have a salvage value at the end of a year. Their best estimate of potential sales at $6 per unit follows:

TOTAL UNITS	PROBABILITY
30,000	0.2
50,000	0.4
60,000	0.2
70,000	0.2

Prepare an analysis to indicate the best course of action.

16–19. PROBABILITIES AND MULTIPLE CHOICE. (CMA, adapted.) Select the best answer for each of the accompanying items. Show computations where applicable.

The ARC Radio Company is trying to decide whether or not to introduce as a new product a wrist "radiowatch" designed for shortwave reception of exact time as broadcast by the National Bureau of Standards. The "radiowatch" would be priced at $60, which is exactly twice the variable cost per unit to manufacture and sell it. The incremental fixed costs necessitated by introducing this new product would amount to $240,000 per year. Subjective estimates of the probable demand for the product are shown in the following probability distribution:

ANNUAL DEMAND	PROBABILITY
6,000 units	0.2
8,000 units	0.2
10,000 units	0.2
12,000 units	0.2
14,000 units	0.1
16,000 units	0.1

(1) The expected value of demand for the new product is (**a**) 11,100 units, (**b**) 10,200 units, (**c**) 9,000 units, (**d**) 10,600 units, (**e**) 9,800 units.

(2) The probability that the introduction of this new product will not increase the company's profit is (**a**) 0.00, (**b**) 0.04, (**c**) 0.40, (**d**) 0.50, (**e**) 0.60.

16–20. COMPUTATION OF EXPECTED VALUE. (CMA, adapted.) The Unimat Company manufactures a unique thermostat that yields dramatic cost savings from effective climatic control of large buildings. The efficiency of the thermostat depends on the quality of a specialized thermocoupler. These thermocouplers are purchased from Houston Controls Company for $15 each.

Since early 19X6, an average of 10% of the thermocouplers purchased from Houston Controls have not met Unimat's quality requirements. The number of unusable thermocouplers has ranged from 5% to 25% of the total number purchased and has resulted in failures to meet production schedules. In addition, Unimat has incurred additional costs to replace the defective units because the rejection rate of the units is within the range agreed upon in the contract.

Unimat is considering a proposal to manufacture the thermocouplers. The company has the facilities and equipment to produce the components. The engineering department has designed a manufacturing system that will produce the thermocouplers with a defective rate of 4% of the number of units produced. Defective units are not identified until the end of the production process. The following schedule presents the engineers' estimates of the probabilities that different levels of variable manufacturing cost per thermocoupler will be incurred under this system. Additional annual fixed costs incurred by Unimat if it manufactures the thermocoupler will amount to $32,500.

ESTIMATED VARIABLE MANUFACTURING COST PER GOOD THERMOCOUPLER UNIT	PROBABILITY OF OCCURRENCE
$10	10%
12	30
14	40
16	20
	100%

Unimat Company will need 18,000 good thermocouplers to meet its annual demand requirements.

Required: Prepare an expected value analysis to determine whether Unimat Company should manufacture the thermocouplers.

16–21. NET PRESENT VALUES, PROBABILITIES, AND CAPITAL BUDGETING. At a board of directors' meeting of a large diversified company, a director raised the question of the profitability of a communications satellite to be launched in three years. The project began two years ago. The president stated that $10 million had been invested in the project in each of the previous years and that an equal amount must be invested in each of the next three years. There would be no income from the project until the total investment was completed. The probability of receiving $4 million cash inflow from operations at the end of the first year after completion would be 0.8; the probability of receiving $8 million at the end of the second year after completion would be 0.7; the probability of receiving $15 million at the end of the third year after completion would be 0.6; the probability of receiving $30 million at the end of each of the following seven years would be 0.5. In each year, if the given cash inflow is not received, the cash inflow is zero.

This company expects a minimum rate of return of 10% on investments.

Required: As a director, would you have approved of this project when it was first undertaken? Support your answer with figures, using the net-present-value approach.

16–22. INVENTORY LEVELS AND SALES FORECASTING. Each day an owner of a sidewalk stand stocks toll house cookies, which cost 30¢ and sell for 50¢ each. Leftovers are given to a nearby hospital. Demand characteristics are:

DEMAND	PROBABILITY
Less than 20	0.00
20	0.10
21	0.40
22	0.30
23	0.20
24 or more	0.00

Required:
1. How many units should be stocked to maximize expected operating income? Show your computations.
2. If the owner of the stand were clairvoyant, so that she could perfectly forecast the demand each day and stock the exact number of cookies needed, what would be her expected operating income per day? What is the maximum price that she should be willing to pay for perfect information?

16–23. EXPECTED VALUE AND INFORMATION. James Wilson runs a newspaper stand. He buys copies of *The New York Times* for $.60 (including shipping) and sells them for $1.00. Daily demand varies, but a condensed analysis of the past 100 days shows the following sales:

NO. OF DAYS	NO. OF NEWSPAPERS SOLD
10	140
20	160
25	180
45	200

Wilson has been buying 200 copies each day. Papers only come in bundles of 20. He estimates that on 25 days he could have sold 220 papers if he had them.

Required:
1. What is the expected demand for copies of *The New York Times*? The standard deviation?
2. What is Mr. Wilson's expected profit when he purchases 200 copies? When he purchases 180 copies?
3. What is the most Mr. Wilson would pay each day to learn the demand before he orders papers?

16–24. **EVALUATION OF DEGREE OF RISK: STANDARD DEVIATION AND COEFFICIENT OF VARIATION.** Suppose you manage a travel agency. You are trying to choose between two types of computer equipment. Model L is new on the market, and model P is the industry standard. Each computer promises labor savings; probability distributions are as follows:

COMPUTER L		COMPUTER P	
Probability	Labor Savings	Probability	Labor Savings
0.10	$1,000	0.10	$2,000
0.25	3,000	0.25	3,000
0.30	5,000	0.30	4,000
0.25	7,000	0.25	5,000
0.10	9,000	0.10	6,000

Required:
1. For each proposal, compute (a) the expected value of the labor savings, (b) the standard deviation, and (c) the coefficient of variation.
2. Which computer has the greater degree of risk? Why?

16–25. **EXPECTED VALUE, STANDARD DEVIATION, AND RISK.** Suppose the Van Horne Company is planning to invest in a common stock for one year. An investigation of the expected dividends and expected market price has been conducted. The probability distribution of expected returns for the year, as a percentage, is:

PROBABILITY OF OCCURRENCE	POSSIBLE RETURN
0.05	.284
0.10	.224
0.20	.160
0.30	.100
0.20	.040
0.10	−.024
0.05	−.084

Required:
1. Compute the expected value of possible returns, the standard deviation of the probability distribution, and the coefficient of variation.
2. Van Horne could also earn 6% for certain on federal bonds. What are the standard deviation and the coefficient of variation of such an investment?
3. Relate the computations in Requirement 1 with those in Requirement 2. That is, what role does the coefficient of variation play in determining the relative attractiveness of various investments?

16–26. PROBABILITIES AND COSTS OF REWORK VERSUS COSTS OF SETUP. Bruxelles Fabricators has an automatic machine ready and set to make a production run of 2,000 parts. For simplicity, only four events are assumed possible:

FAULTY PARTS	PROBABILITY
30	0.6
200	0.2
600	0.1
900	0.1

The incremental cost of reworking a faulty part is BFr 1.2. (BFr means Belgian Francs.) An expert mechanic can check the setting. He can, without fail, bring the faulty parts down to 30, but this is time consuming and costs BFr 150 per setting.

Should the setting be checked?

16–27. COST AND VALUE OF INFORMATION. An oil-well driller, Mr. Barnes, is thinking of investing $50,000 in an oil-well lease. He estimates the probability of finding a producing well as 0.2. Such a discovery would result in a net gain of $200,000 ($250,000 revenue − $50,000 cost). The probability of not getting any oil, resulting in the complete loss of the $50,000, is 0.8.

Required:

1. What is the net expected value of investing?
2. Mr. Barnes desires more information because of the vast uncertainty and the large costs of making a wrong decision. There will be an unrecoverable $50,000 outlay if no oil is found; there will be a $200,000 opportunity cost if he does not invest and the oil is really there. What is the most he should be willing to pay for perfect information regarding the presence or absence of oil? Explain.

16–28. FORMULATION OF A LINEAR-PROGRAMMING MODEL. Bayhill Manufacturing Company produces three products, A, B, and C. Forecasts from the sales staff show that a maximum of 130,000 units of product A can be sold at $20, 50,000 of B at $10, and 50,000 of C at $30. Costs for the products are:

	A	B	C
Direct material	$ 7.00	$3.75	$16.60
Direct labor	2.00	1.00	3.50
Variable overhead	1.00	.50	1.75
Fixed overhead	4.00	2.00	7.00
Selling and administrative (all variable)	1.50	.75	2.25
Total cost	$15.50	$8.00	$31.10

Bayhill has two departments—machining and assembly. Both have limited capacity (measured by machine-hours) and cannot be expanded within the coming year. Production rates are as follows:

	A	B	C
Machining	2 per hour	4 per hour	3 per hour
Assembly	4 per hour	8 per hour	1⅓ per hour

Machining has 67,000 machine-hours available, Assembly has 63,000.

The sales manager of Bayhill contends that it is critical to maintain a full product line and supply all three products to a base of loyal customers. She indicates that at least 80,000 units of A, 32,000 units of B, and 12,000 units of C must be produced to accomplish this.

Suppose that you are assigned to determine what quantities of each product to produce.

Required: Formulate this problem as a linear-programming model. Be sure to include (1) the objective function and (2) all constraints.

16–29. **FUNDAMENTAL APPROACH OF LINEAR PROGRAMMING.** A company has two departments, machining and finishing. The company's two products require processing in each of two departments. Data follow:

| | CONTRIBUTION MARGIN PER | DAILY CAPACITY IN UNITS | |
PRODUCT	UNIT	Department 1: Machining	Department 2: Finishing
A	$2.00	200	120
B	2.50	100	200

Severe shortages of material for Product B will limit its production to a maximum of 90 per day.

Required: How many units of each product should be produced to obtain the maximum net income? Show the basic relationships as inequalities. Solve by using graphical analysis.

16–30. **PRODUCTION SCHEDULING AND LINEAR PROGRAMMING.** A factory can produce either Product A or Product B. Machine 1 can produce 15 units of B or 20 units of A per hour. Machine 2 can produce 20 units of B or 12 units of A per hour. Machine 1 has a maximum capacity of 10,000 hours, and Machine 2 a maximum capacity of 8,000 hours.

Product A has a unit contribution margin of 20¢; B, 16¢. There is an unlimited demand for either product; however, both products must be produced together through each machine in a combination such that the quantity of B is at least 20% of the quantity of A.

Required: Which combination of products should be produced? Solve by graphic analysis. Express all relationships as inequalities.

16–31. **LINEAR-PROGRAMMING MODEL FOR PRODUCT MIX.** (CMA, adapted). Jenlock Mill Company produces two grades of interior plywood from fir and pine lumber. The fir and pine lumber can be sold as saw lumber or used in the plywood.

To produce the plywood, thin layers of wood are peeled from the logs in panels, the panels are glued together to form plywood sheets, and then dried. The peeler can peel enough panels from logs to produce 300,000 sheets of plywood in a month. The dryers have a capacity of 1,200,000 minutes for the month. The amount of lumber used and the drying time required for each sheet of plywood by grade is:

	GRADE A PLYWOOD SHEETS	GRADE B PLYWOOD SHEETS
Fir (in board feet)	18	15
Pine (in board feet)	12	15
Drying time (in minutes)	4	6

The only restriction on the production of fir and pine lumber is the capacity of the mill saws to cut the logs into boards. These saws have a capacity of 500,000 board feet per month regardless of species.

Jenlock has the following quantities of lumber available for July production:

Fir	2,700,000 board feet
Pine	3,000,000 board feet

The contribution margins for each type of output are as follows:

Fir lumber	$ .20 per board foot
Pine lumber	$ .10 per board foot
Grade A plywood	$2.25 per sheet
Grade B plywood	$1.80 per sheet

The demand in July for plywood is expected to be a maximum of 80,000 sheets for grade A and a maximum of 100,000 sheets for Grade B. There are no demand restrictions on pine and fir lumber.

Jenlock Mill Company uses a linear programming model to determine the production quantities of each product. The correct formulation of the linear programming model is presented below followed by a condensed LINPRO solution. The variables are defined as follows:

F = board feet of fir lumber to be sold
P = board feet of pine lumber to be sold
A = number of sheets of Grade A plywood to be sold
B = number of sheets of Grade B plywood to be sold

The formulation is:

Maximize: .20F + .10P + 2.25A + 1.80B

$$
\begin{array}{rcrcrcrcl}
F & & & + & 18A & + & 15B & \leq & 2{,}700{,}000 \\
& & P & + & 12A & + & 15B & \leq & 3{,}000{,}000 \\
& & & & A & + & B & \leq & 300{,}000 \\
& & & & 4A & + & 6B & \leq & 1{,}200{,}000 \\
F & + & P & & & & & \leq & 500{,}000 \\
\\
& & & & A & & & \leq & 80{,}000 \\
& & & & & & B & \leq & 100{,}000
\end{array}
$$

The solution is:

OBJECTIVE FUNCTION VALUE		
1	$381,200	
VARIABLE	VALUE	
F	0	
P	500,000	
A	80,000	
B	84,000	
ROW	SLACK	DUAL PRICES
2	0	.12
3	280,000	0
4	136,000	0
5	376,000	0
6	0	.10
7	0	.09
8	16,000	0

Required:

1. Provide a brief explanation of each of the eight rows of the problem formulation.
2. How much fir, pine, Grade A plywood, and Grade B plywood should Jenlock Mill Company produce? What is the total contribution margin from this product mix?
3. Will Jenlock Mill Company use all its resources to their capacities during July if it follows the linear-programming solution? If not, what resources and how much of each remain unused?
4. Suppose additional mill saw capacity were available at $.08 per board foot. Should additional capacity be acquired? By how much will the total contribution change if one additional board foot of capacity were acquired?

16–32. **ECONOMIC ORDER QUANTITY.** (CMA, adapted) Colonial Furniture Company manufactures a line of inexpensive home furnishings. Colonial executives estimate the demand for Williamsburg oak chairs, one of the company's products, at 6,000 units. The chairs sell for $80 apiece. The costs relating to the chairs are estimated to be as follows for 19X7:

(1) Standard manufacturing cost per chair—$50
(2) Costs to initiate a production run—$300
(3) Annual cost of carrying the chair in inventory—20% of standard manufacturing cost

In prior years, Colonial has scheduled the production for the chairs in two equal production runs. Suppose the company just became aware of the economic order quantity (EOQ) model.

Required:

Calculate the expected annual cost savings Colonial Furniture Company could experience if it employed the economic order quantity model to determine the number of production runs that should be initiated during the year for the manufacture of the Williamsburg oak chairs.

16–33. **INVENTORY CONTROL AND TELEVISION TUBES.** The Nemmers Company assembles private-brand television sets for a retail chain, under a contract requiring delivery of 100 sets per day for each of 250 business days per year. Each set requires a picture tube, which Nemmers buys outside for $20 each. The tubes are loaded on trucks at the supplier's factory door and are then delivered by a trucking service at a charge of $100 per trip, regardless of the size of the shipment. The cost of storing the tubes (including the desired rate of return on the investment) is $2 per tube per year. Because production is stable throughout the year, the average inventory is one-half the size of the truck lot. Tabulate the relevant annual cost of various truck-lot sizes at 5, 10, 15, 25, 50, and 250 trips per year. Show your results graphically. (Note that the $20 unit cost of tubes is common to all alternatives and hence may be ignored.)

16–34. **REORDER POINT.** A university uses 50 tons of coal per year to heat its buildings. The university orders 5 tons at a time. Lead time for the order is 5 days, and the safety stock is a 3-day supply. Usage is assumed to be constant over a 360-day year. Calculate the reorder point.

16–35. **EOQ AND REORDER POINT.** (CMA, adapted.) SaPane company is a regional distributor of automobile window glass. With the introduction of the new subcompact car models and the expected high level of consumer demand, management wants to determine the total inventory cost associated with maintaining an optimal supply of replacement windshields for the new subcompact cars introduced by each of the three major manufacturers. SaPane expects a daily demand for 36 windshields. The purchase price of each windshield is $50.

Other costs associated with ordering and maintaining an inventory of these windshields are as follows:

(1) The historical ordering costs incurred in the Purchase Order Department for placing and processing orders is:

YEAR	ORDERS PLACED AND PROCESSED	TOTAL ORDERING COSTS
1984	20	$12,300
1985	55	12,475
1986	100	12,700

Management expects the ordering costs to increase 16% over the amounts and rates experienced the last three years.

(2) The windshield manufacturer charges SaPane a $75 shipping fee per order.

(3) A clerk in the Receiving Department receives, inspects, and secures the windshields as they arrive from the manufacturer. This activity requires 8 hours per order received. This clerk has no other responsibilities and is paid at the rate of $9 per hour. Related variable overhead costs in this department are $2.50 per labor-hour.

(4) Additional warehouse space will have to be rented to store the new windshields. Space can be rented as needed in a public warehouse at an estimated cost of $2,500 per year plus $5.35 per windshield.

(5) Taxes and fire insurance on the inventory are $1.15 per windshield.

(6) The desired rate of return on the investment in inventory is 21% of the purchase price.

Six working days are required from the time the order is placed with the manufacturer until it is received. SaPane uses a 300-day work year when making economic order quantity computations.

Required:

Calculate the following values for SaPane Company.

1. The value for ordering cost that should be used in the EOQ formula.
2. The value for storage cost that should be used in the EOQ formula.
3. The economic order quantity.
4. The reorder point in units.

16–36. **INVENTORY POLICY.** (CMA.) Breakon, Inc., manufactures and distributes machine tools. The tools are assembled from approximately 2,000 components manufactured by the company. For several years the production schedule called for one production run of each component each month. This schedule has resulted in a high inventory turnover rate of 4.0 times but requires 12 setups for each component every year. (Inventory turnover is cost of goods sold divided by average inventory.) In a normal year $3,500 of cost is incurred for each component to produce the number of units sold. The company has been successful in not letting the year-end inventory drop below $100 for each component.

The production manager recommends that the company gradually switch to a schedule of producing the annual needs of each component in one yearly production run. He believes this would reduce costs because only one setup cost would be incurred each year for every component rather than 12. At the present time the costs for each setup are $36. Estimated annual costs associated with carrying inventory, per $1 of inventory value, are: property tax, 4%; insurance, 2%; and storage cost, 20%. The firm estimates its cost of capital to be 10% after taxes and pays income taxes at 40% of taxable income.

Required:

1. If Breakon converts to the "once-a-year" production schedule for its components, calculate the total investment released or additional investment required once the changeover is completed.
2. If Breakon converts to the "once-a-year" production schedule, calculate the after-tax savings or added expenses once the changeover is completed.
3. What factors other than those referred to in Requirements 1 and 2 should be considered in reaching a decision to change the production policy?
4. Do your calculations support a change to the proposed policy? Explain your answer.

Chapter 17

BASIC ACCOUNTING: CONCEPTS, TECHNIQUES, AND CONVENTIONS

LEARNING OBJECTIVES

When you have finished studying this chapter, you should be able to:

1. Identify the meanings and interrelationships of the principal elements of financial statements: assets, liabilities, owners' equity, revenues, expenses, dividends, and others.
2. Analyze typical business transactions to determine their effects on the principal elements of financial statements.
3. Distinguish between the accrual basis of accounting and the cash basis of accounting.
4. Select relevant items from a set of data and assemble them into a balance sheet, an income statement, and a statement of retained income.
5. Distinguish between the reporting of corporate owners' equity and the reporting of owners' equity for partnerships and sole proprietorships.
6. Identify the generally accepted accounting principles and the main conventions that underlie financial reporting for external purposes.

This chapter introduces the accounting process to individuals with little or no background in accounting and to those who want a review of some fundamental ideas.[1] We shall become acquainted with some vocabulary and with what financial statements say and do not say. Knowing what financial statements do *not* communicate is just as important as knowing what they do communicate. We shall be concerned mainly with how to measure the managers' custodial or stewardship responsibilities for the resources entrusted to them. This is basically a scorekeeping task.

This chapter covers the fundamentals without employing some of the bookkeeping techniques (for example, ledger accounts) and language (for example, debit and credit) that are commonplace in accounting. However, the chapter appendixes probe the ideas of the chapter in greater depth, using a more technical approach.

We consider the essence of profit-making activities and how the accountant portrays them. As we examine what the accountant does, we shall introduce the relevant concepts and conventions. Although the major focus will be on profit-seeking organizations, the main ideas also apply to nonprofit organizations. Moreover, managers of the latter usually have personal investments in profit-seeking organizations or must interact with businesses in some way.

ENTITIES AND ACCOUNTING TRANSACTIONS

Managers, investors, and other interested groups usually want the answers to two important questions about an organization: How well did the organization perform for a given period of time? and Where does the organization stand at a given point in time? The accountant answers these questions with two major financial statements: an **income statement** and a **balance sheet**. To obtain these statements, accountants continually record the history of an organization. Through the **financial accounting** process, the accountant accumulates, analyzes, quantifies, classifies, summarizes, and reports the seemingly countless events and their effects on the **entity**. An *entity* is a specific area of accountability, a clear-cut boundary for reporting. The entity concept is important because accounting usually focuses on the financial impact of events as they affect a particular entity. An example of an entity is a university, which also encompasses many smaller entities such as the School of Law and the School of Engineering.

---

[1] The aim of this section of the book (Chapters 17–20) is to provide an overview of an area that has come to be known as financial accounting. Thus, readers of the authors' companion volume, *Introduction to Financial Accounting*, will find that these chapters provide a review rather than new material. For expanded coverage, see *Introduction to Financial Accounting*.

In terms of their financial impact on economies throughout the world, **corporations** are the principal form of entity. *Corporations* are organizations created by individual state laws. The owners are identified as stockholders (also called shareholders). When approved by the state, the corporation becomes a separate entity, an "artificial person" that conducts its business completely apart from its owners.

The accounting process focuses upon **transactions**. A *transaction* is any event that affects the financial position of an entity and requires recording. Through the years, many concepts, conventions, and rules have been developed regarding what events are to be recorded as *accounting transactions* and how their financial impact is measured. These concepts will be introduced gradually over the remaining chapters.

FINANCIAL STATEMENTS

Financial statements are summarized reports of accounting transactions. They can apply to any point in time and to any span of time.

An efficient way to learn about accounting is to study a specific illustration. Suppose Retailer No. 1 began business as a corporation on March 1. An opening balance sheet (more accurately called **statement of financial position** or **statement of financial condition**) follows:

RETAILER NO. 1
Balance Sheet (Statement of Financial Position)
As of March 1, 19X1

ASSETS		EQUITIES	
Cash	$100,000	Paid-in capital	$100,000

The balance sheet is a photograph of financial status at an instant of time. It has two counterbalancing sections—assets and equities. **Assets** are economic resources that are expected to benefit future activities. **Equities** are the claims against, or interests in, the assets.

The accountant conceives of the balance sheet as an equation:

$$\text{assets} = \text{equities}$$

The equities side of this fundamental equation is often divided as follows:

$$\text{assets} = \text{liabilities} + \text{owners' equity}$$

The **liabilities** are the entity's economic obligations to nonowners. The **owners' equity** is the excess of the assets over the liabilities. For a corporation, the owners' equity is called **stockholders' equity**. In turn, the stockholders' equity is composed of the ownership claim against, or interest in, the total assets arising from any paid-in investment (**paid-in capital**), plus the ownership claim arising as a result of profitable operations (**retained income** or **retained earnings**).

Consider a summary of the *transactions* that occurred in March:

1. Initial invesment by owners, $100,000 cash.
2. Acquisition of inventory for $75,000 cash.
3. Acquisition of inventory for $35,000 on open account. A purchase (or a sale) on open account is an agreement whereby the buyer pays cash some time after the date of sale, often in 30 days. Amounts owed on open accounts are usually called **accounts payable**, liabilities of the purchasing entity.
4. Merchandise carried in inventory at a cost of $100,000 was sold on open account for $120,000. These open customer accounts are called **accounts receivable**, assets of the selling entity.
5. Cash collections of accounts receivable, $30,000.
6. Cash payments of accounts payable, $10,000.
7. On March 1, $3,000 cash was disbursed for store rent for March, April, and May. Rent is $1,000 per month, payable quarterly in advance, beginning March 1.

Note that these are indeed *summarized* transactions. For example, all the sales will not take place at once, nor will purchases of inventory, collections from customers, or disbursements to suppliers. A vast number of repetitive transactions occur in practice, and specialized data collection techniques are used to measure their effects on the entity.

The foregoing transactions can be analyzed using the balance sheet equation, as shown in Exhibit 17–1. Explanations of Exhibit 17–1 follow:

Transaction 1, the initial investment by owners, has been explained previously. Note, in this illustration, that paid-in capital represents the claim arising from the owners' total initial investment in the corporation.[2]

Transactions 2 and 3, the purchases of inventory, are steps toward the ultimate goal—the earning of a profit. But stockholders' equity is unaffected. That is, no profit is recorded until a sale is made.

Transaction 4 is the sale of $100,000 of inventory for $120,000. Two things happen simultaneously: a new asset, Accounts Receivable, is acquired (4a) in exchange for the giving up of Inventory (4b), and Stockholders' equity is increased by the amount of the asset received ($120,000) and decreased by the amount of the asset given up ($100,000).

Transaction 5, cash collections of accounts receivable, are examples of events that have no impact on stockholders' equity. Collections are merely the transformation of one asset (Accounts Receivable) into another (Cash).

Transaction 6, cash payments of accounts payable, also do not affect stockholders' equity—they affect assets and liabilities only. In general, collections from customers and payments to suppliers of the *principal* amounts

---

[2] Stock certificates usually bear some nominal "par or stated value" that is far below the actual cash invested. For example, the par or stated value of the certificates might be only $10,000; if so, the formal recording of an ownership claim arising from the investment might be split between two subparts, one for $10,000 "capital stock, at par" and another for $90,000 "paid-in capital in excess of par value of capital stock." See the next chapter for additional discussion, page 607.

EXHIBIT 17–1 *(Put a clip on this page for easy reference.)*

RETAILER NO. 1
Analysis of Transactions (in dollars)
For March 19X1

	ASSETS				=		EQUITIES	
						Liabilities +	Stockholders' Equity	
		Accounts		Prepaid		Accounts	Paid-in	Retained
Transactions	Cash	+ Receivable	+ Inventory	+ Rent	=	= Payable	+ Capital +	Income
1. Initial investment	+100,000				=		+100,000	
2. Acquire inventory for cash	− 75,000		+ 75,000		=			
3. Acquire inventory for credit			+ 35,000		=	+35,000		
4a. Sales on credit		+120,000			=			+120,000 (revenue)
4b. Cost of inventory sold			− 100,000		=			−100,000 (expense)
5. Collect from customers	+ 30,000	− 30,000			=			
6. Pay accounts of suppliers	− 10,000				=	−10,000		
7a. Pay rent in advance	− 3,000			+3,000	=			
7b. Recognize expiration of rental services				−1,000	=			− 1,000 (expense)
Balance, 3/31/X1	+ 42,000	+ 90,000	+ 10,000	+2,000	=	+25,000	+100,000	+ 19,000
	144,000						144,000	

of debt have no direct impact on stockholders' equity. Of course, as will be seen in a subsequent section, *interest* on debt does affect stockholders' equity as an item of expense.

Transaction 7, the cash disbursement for rent, is made to acquire the right to use store facilities for the next three months. At March 1, the $3,000 measures the future benefit from these services, so the asset *Prepaid Rent* is created (7*a*). *Assets* are defined as economic resources. They are not confined to items that you can see or touch, such as cash or inventory. Assets also include legal rights to future services such as the use of facilities.

Transaction 7*b* recognizes that one-third of the rental services have expired during March, so the asset is reduced and stockholders' equity is also reduced by $1,000 as rent expense for March. This recognition of rent *expense* means that $1,000 of the asset Prepaid Rent has been "used up" (or has flowed out of the entity) in the conduct of operations during March.

For simplicity, we have assumed no expenses other than *cost of goods sold* and *rent*. The accountant would ordinarily prepare at least two financial statements: the balance sheet and the income statement.

RETAILER NO. 1
Income Statement
For the Month Ended March 31, 19X1

Sales (revenue)		$120,000
Expenses:		
Cost of goods sold	$100,000	
Rent	1,000	
Total expenses		101,000
Net income		$ 19,000

RETAILER NO. 1
Balance Sheet
March 31, 19X1

ASSETS		LIABILITIES AND STOCKHOLDERS' EQUITY		
Cash	$ 42,000	Liabilities: Accounts payable		$ 25,000
Accounts receivable	90,000	Stockholders' equity:		
Inventory	10,000	Paid-in capital	$100,000	
Prepaid rent	2,000	Retained income	19,000	119,000
Total	$144,000	Total		$144,000

RELATIONSHIP OF BALANCE SHEET AND INCOME STATEMENT

The income statement has measured the operating performance of the corporation by matching its accomplishments (revenue from customers, which usually is called *sales*) and its efforts (*cost of goods sold* and other expenses). The balance sheet shows the financial position at an instant of time, but the income statement measures performance for a span of time, whether it be a month, a quarter, or longer. The income statement is the major link between balance sheets:

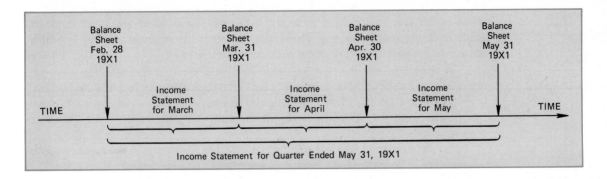

Examine the changes in stockholders' equity in Exhibit 17-1. The accountant records **revenue** and **expense** so that they represent increases (revenues) and decreases (expenses) in the owners' claims. At the end of a given period, these items are summarized in the form of an income statement. The heading of a balance sheet indicates a single date. The heading of an income statement indicates a specific period of time. The balance sheet is a photograph; the income statement is a motion picture.

Each item in a financial statement is frequently called an **account,** so that term will occasionally be used in the rest of this book. In the above example, the outflows of assets are represented by decreases in the Inventory and Prepaid Rent accounts and corresponding decreases in stockholders' equity in the form of Cost of Goods Sold and Rent Expense. Expense accounts are basically negative elements of stockholders' equity. Similarly, the Sales (revenue) account is a positive element of stockholders' equity.

REVENUES AND EXPENSES

Review transaction 4. As Exhibit 17-1 shows, this transaction has two phases, a revenue phase (4a) and an expense phase (4b) (dollar signs omitted):

DESCRIPTION OF TRANSACTIONS	ASSETS	=	EQUITIES
Balances after Transaction 3 in Exhibit 17-1	135,000 =		135,000
4a. Sales on account (inflow)	Accounts receivable +120,000 =	Stockholders' equity +120,000	
4b. Cost of inventory sold (outflow)	Inventory −100,000 =	Stockholders' equity −100,000	
Balances, after Transaction 4	155,000 =		155,000

Transaction 4a illustrates the realization of *revenue*. *Revenues* are generally gross increases in assets from delivering goods or services. To be **realized** (that is, formally recognized in the accounting records as revenue earned during the current period), revenue must ordinarily meet three tests. First, the goods or services must be fully rendered (for example, delivery to customers). Second, an exchange of resources evidenced by a market transaction must occur (for example, the buyer pays or promises to pay cash and the seller delivers merchandise). Third, the collectibility of the asset (for example, an account receivable) must be reasonably assured.

Transaction 4b illustrates the incurrence of an expense. *Expenses* are generally gross decreases in assets from delivering goods or services.

Transactions 4a and 4b also illustrate the fundamental meaning of **profits** or **earnings** or **income**, which can simply be defined as the excess of revenues over expenses.

As the Retained Income column in Exhibit 17–1 shows, increases in revenues increase stockholders' equity. In contrast, increases in expenses decrease stockholders' equity. So expenses are negative stockholders' equity accounts.

Transactions 2 and 3 were purchases of merchandise inventory. They were steps toward the ultimate goal—the earning of a profit. But by themselves purchases earn no profit; remember that stockholders' equity was unaffected by the inventory acquisitions in transactions 2 and 3. That is, no profit is realized until a sale is actually made to customers.

Transaction 4 is the $120,000 sale on open account of inventory that had cost $100,000. Two things happen simultaneously: a $120,000 inflow of assets in the form of accounts receivable (4a) in exchange for a $100,000 outflow of assets in the form of inventory (4b). Liabilities are completely unaffected, so owners' equity rises by $120,000 − $100,000, or $20,000.

Users of financial statements desire an answer to the question, How well did the organization perform for a given period of time? The income statement helps answer this question. For Retailer No. 1, there has been a change in stockholders' equity attributable solely to operations. This change is measured by the revenue and expenses for the specific period.

THE ANALYTICAL POWER OF THE BALANCE SHEET EQUATION

As you study Exhibit 17–1, consider how accountants use the fundamental balance sheet equation as their framework for analyzing and reporting the effects of transactions:

$$\text{assets (A)} = \text{liabilities (L)} + \text{stockholders' equity (SE)} \tag{1}$$

SE equals original ownership claim plus the increase in ownership claim because of profitable operations. That is, *SE* equals the claim arising from paid-in capital plus the claim arising from retained income. Therefore,

$$\text{A} = \text{L} + \text{paid-in capital} + \text{retained income} \tag{2}$$

But, in our illustration, Retained Income equals Revenue minus Expenses. Therefore,

Revenue and *Expense accounts* are nothing more than subdivisions of stockholders' equity—temporary stockholders' equity accounts. Their purpose is to summarize the volume of sales and the various expenses, so that management is kept informed of the reasons for the continual increases and decreases in stockholders' equity in the course of ordinary operations. In this way comparisons can be made, standards or goals can be set, and control can be better exercised.

The entire accounting system is based on the simple balance sheet equation. As you know, equations in general possess enormous analytical potential because of the dual algebraic manipulations that they permit. The equation is always kept in balance because of the duality feature.

Exhibit 17–1 illustrates the dual nature of the accountant's analysis. For each transaction, the equation is *always* kept in balance. If the items affected are confined to one side of the equation, you will find the total amount added equal to the total amount subtracted on that side. If the items affected are on both sides, then equal amounts are simultaneously added or subtracted on each side.

The striking feature of the balance sheet equation is its universal applicability. No transaction has ever been conceived, no matter how simple or complex, that cannot be analyzed via the equation. The top technical partners in the world's largest professional accounting firms, when confronted with the most intricate transactions of multinational companies, will inevitably discuss and think about their analyses in terms of the balance sheet equation. The partners focus on its major components: assets, liabilities, and owners' equity (including the explanations of changes in owners' equity that most often take the form of revenues and expenses).

ACCRUAL BASIS AND CASH BASIS

The process of determining income and financial position is anchored to the **accrual basis** of accounting, as distinguished from the **cash basis**. In accrual accounting, the impact of events on assets and equities is recognized in the time periods when services are rendered or used, regardless of when the related cash is paid or received. That is, revenue is recognized as it is *earned*, and expenses are recognized as they are *incurred*—not when cash changes hands. For example, Transaction 4a in Exhibit 17–1, page 551, recognizes revenue when sales are made on credit. Similarly, Transactions 4b and 7b show that expenses are recognized as efforts are expended or services used to obtain the revenue. Therefore, income is affected by measurements of noncash resources and obligations. The accrual basis is the principal conceptual framework for matching accomplishments (revenue) with efforts (expenses).

If the **cash basis** of accounting were used instead of the accrual basis, the recognition of revenue and expense would depend on the timing of various cash receipts and disbursements. In our Retailer No. 1 example, the March income statement would contain the following:

Revenue (cash collected from customers)		$ 30,000
Expenses:		
Cash disbursed for merchandise ($75,000 in Transaction 2 plus $10,000 in Transaction 6)	$85,000	
Cash disbursement for rent	3,000	
Total expenses		88,000
Net loss		−$58,000

The March 31 balance sheet would have:

Cash	$42,000	Paid-in capital	$100,000
		Retained income	−58,000
		Stockholders' equity	$ 42,000

The major deficiency of the cash basis of accounting is apparent from this example: it ignores the impact on net income and financial position of the liability for accounts payable and the impact of such very real assets as accounts receivable, inventory, and prepaid rent.

Despite the incompleteness of the cash basis of accounting, it is used widely by individuals when they measure their income for personal income tax purposes. For this limited purpose, the cash basis often gives a good approximation of what might also be reported on the accrual basis. Long ago, however, accountants and managers found cash-basis financial statements, such as the foregoing, to be unsatisfactory as a measure of both performance and position. Now more than 95% of all business is conducted on a credit basis; cash receipts and disbursements are not the critical transactions as far as the recognition of revenue and expense is concerned. Thus the accrual basis evolved in response to a desire for a more complete, and therefore more accurate, report of the financial impact of various events.

ADJUSTMENTS TO THE ACCOUNTS

To measure income under the accrual basis, the accountant uses **adjustments** at the end of each reporting period. *Adjustments* (also called *adjusting the books*, *adjusting entries*, *adjusting the accounts*) may be defined as the key final process that ensures the assignment of financial effects of transactions to the appropriate time periods. Thus adjustments are made at periodic intervals, that is, just before the computation of ending balances when the financial statements are about to be prepared.

Adjustments refine the accountant's accuracy and provide a more complete and significant measure of efforts, accomplishments, and financial position. They are an essential part of accrual accounting.

Earlier a *transaction* was defined as any economic event that should be recorded by the accountant. Note that this definition is *not* confined to market transactions, which are actual exchanges of goods and services between the entity and another party. For instance, the losses of assets from fire or theft are also transactions even though no market exchange occurs.

Adjustments are a special category of transactions. The principal adjustments may be classified into four types:

  I. Expiration of Unexpired Costs
  II. Realization (Earning) of Unearned Revenues
  III. Accrual of Unrecorded Expenses
  IV. Accrual of Unrecorded Revenues

These types will be explained in this and later sections.

As we shall see, all of these adjustments have an important common characteristic. They reflect **implicit transactions**, in contrast to the **explicit transactions** that trigger nearly all day-to-day routine entries.

To illustrate, entries for credit sales, credit purchases, cash received on account, and cash disbursed on account are supported by explicit evidence. This evidence is usually in the form of **source documents** (for example, sales slips, purchase invoices, employee time records). On the other hand, adjustments for unpaid wages, prepaid rent, interest owed, and the like, are prepared from special schedules or memorandums that recognize events (like the passage of time) that are temporarily ignored in day-to-day recording procedures.

Assets frequently expire because of the passage of time. This first type of adjustment was illustrated in Exhibit 17–1 by the recognition of rent expense in transaction 7*b*.

Other examples of adjusting for asset expirations include the writeoffs to expense of such assets as Office Supplies Inventory, Advertising Supplies Inventory, and Prepaid Fire Insurance. The other three types of adjustments are discussed later in this chapter.

☐ **The Measurement of Expenses: Assets Expire**

Transactions 4*b* and 7*b* demonstrate how assets may be viewed as bundles of economic services awaiting future use or expiration. It is helpful to think of assets, other than cash and receivables, as prepaid or stored costs (for example, inventories or plant assets) that are carried forward to future periods rather than immediately charged against revenue:

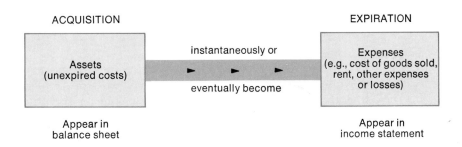

Expenses are used-up assets. Thus assets are **unexpired costs** held back from the expense stream and carried in the balance sheet to await expiration in future periods. When costs expire, accountants often say they are *written off* to expense.

The analysis of the inventory and rent transactions in Exhibit 17–1 maintains this distinction of acquisition and expiration. The unexpired costs of inventory and prepaid rent are assets until they are used up and become expenses.

Sometimes services are acquired and used almost instantaneously. Examples are advertising services, interest services (the cost of money, which is a service), miscellaneous supplies, and sales salaries and commissions. Conceptually, these costs should, at least momentarily, be viewed as assets upon acquisition before being written off as expenses. For example, suppose there was an eighth transaction in Exhibit 17–1, whereby newspaper advertising was acquired for $1,000 cash. To abide by the acquisition-expiration sequence, the transaction might be analyzed in two phases:

	ASSETS			= LIABILITIES +	STOCKHOLDERS' EQUITY	
Trans-action	Cash +	Other Assets +	Unexpired Advertising =		Paid-in Capital +	Retained Income
8a.	−1,000		+1,000	=		
8b.			−1,000	=		−1,000 (expense)

Frequently, services are acquired and used up so quickly that accountants do not bother recording an asset such as Unexpired Advertising or Prepaid Rent for them. Instead, a shortcut is taken:

Trans-action	Cash + Other Assets	= Liabilities + Paid-in Capital +	Retained Income
8 (a) and (b) together	−1,000	=	−1,000 (expense)

Making the entry in two steps instead of one may seem cumbersome, and it is—from a practical bookkeeping viewpoint. But our purpose is not to learn how to be efficient bookkeepers. We want an orderly way of thinking about what the manager does. The manager acquires goods and services, not expenses per se. These goods and services become expenses as they are used in obtaining revenue.

When does an unexpired cost expire and become an expense? Sometimes this question is not easily answered. For example, some accountants believe that research and development costs should be accounted for as unexpired costs (often found on balance sheets as "Deferred Research and Development

Costs") and written off (amortized) in some systematic manner over a period of years. But the regulators of financial accounting in the United States have ruled that such costs have vague future benefits that are difficult to measure reliably. Thus, research costs must be written off as expenses immediately; hence, research costs should never appear in balance sheets.

☐ Depreciation

To keep the expense-adjustment illustration simple, until now we have deliberately ignored the accounting for long-lived assets such as equipment. Suppose Retailer No. 1 had acquired some store equipment for $14,000 on March 1. Equipment is really a bundle of services that will have a limited useful life. Accountants usually predict the length of the useful life, predict the ultimate disposal value, and allocate the *cost* of the equipment to the years of its useful life in some systematic way. This process is called the recording of **depreciation** expense; it applies to physical assets such as buildings, equipment, furniture, and fixtures owned by the entity. Land is not subject to depreciation.

The most popular depreciation method is the *straight-line method*. Suppose the predicted life of the equipment is ten years, and the estimated terminal disposal value is $2,000:

$$\text{straight-line depreciation expense} = \frac{\text{original cost} - \text{estimated terminal disposal value}}{\text{years of useful life}}$$

$$= \frac{\$14,000 - \$2,000}{10}$$

$$= \$1,200 \text{ per year, or } \$100 \text{ per month}$$

More will be said about depreciation in subsequent chapters. *But no matter how much is said, the essence of the general concept of expense should be clear by now.* The purchases and uses of goods and services (for example, inventories, rent, equipment) ordinarily consist of two basic steps: (1) the *acquisition* of the *assets* (transactions 2, 3, and 7a) and (2) the *expiration* of the assets as *expenses* (transactions 4b and 7b). When these assets expire, the total assets and owners' equity are decreased. When sales to customers bring new assets to the business, its total assets and owners' equity are increased. Expense accounts are basically negative elements of stockholders' equity. Similarly, revenue accounts are basically positive elements of stockholders' equity.

Earlier we examined the basic distinctions between the accrual basis and cash basis of accounting. There are various reasonable interpretations of the meaning of *cash basis*. For example, the Internal Revenue Service has a set of such interpretations. For our purposes, we use a "strict" and "extreme" interpretation, as explained earlier. In contrast, in practice the cash basis is almost always modified. How? It provides for the spreading of the cost of depreciable assets to expenses over more than just one year. In other words, in practice depreciation expense exists under both the accrual and the cash basis of accounting.

This is an unusually long chapter, so pause. If you have never studied account-ing before, or if you studied it long ago, do not proceed until you have solved the following problem. There are no shortcuts. Pushing a pencil is an absolute necessity for becoming comfortable with accounting concepts. The cost-benefit test will easily be met; your gain in knowledge will exceed your investment of time.

Another suggestion is to do the work on your own. In particular, do not ask for help from any professional accountants if they introduce any new terms beyond those already covered. For example, the technical terms of debits, credits, and ledger accounts will only confuse, not clarify, at this stage. Instead, scrutinize Exhibit 17–1, page 551. Note how the balance sheet equation is affected by each transaction. Then do the review problem that follows.

SUMMARY PROBLEM FOR YOUR REVIEW

□ **Problem One**

The Retailer No. 1 transactions for March were analyzed early in this chapter. The balance sheet showed the following balances as of March 31, 19X1:

	ASSETS	EQUITIES
Cash	$ 42,000	
Accounts receivable	90,000	
Inventory	10,000	
Prepaid rent	2,000	
Accounts payable		$ 25,000
Paid-in capital		100,000
Retained income		19,000
	$144,000	$144,000

The following is a summary of the transactions that occurred during the next month, April:

(1) Cash collections of accounts receivable, $88,000.
(2) Cash payments of accounts payable, $24,000.
(3) Acquisitions of inventory on open account, $80,000.
(4) Merchandise carried in inventory at a cost of $70,000 was sold on open account for $85,000.
(5) Adjustment for recognition of rent expense for April.
(6) Some customers paid $3,000 in advance for merchandise that they ordered but is not expected in inventory until mid-May. (What asset must rise? Does this transaction increase liabilities or stockholders' equity?)
(7) Total wages of $6,000 (which were ignored for simplicity in March) were paid on four Fridays in April. These payments for employee services were recognized by increasing Wages Expense and decreasing Cash.
(8) Wages of $2,000 were incurred near the end of April, but the employees had not been paid as of April 30. Accordingly, the accountant increased Wages Expense and increased a liability, Accrued Wages Payable.

EXHIBIT 17–2   *(Place a clip on this page for easy reference.)*

RETAILER NO. 1
Analysis of Transactions (in dollars)
For April 19X1

	ASSETS				=	EQUITIES — Liabilities			Stockholders' Equity	
Transaction	Cash	Accounts Receivable	Inventory	Prepaid Rent	=	Accounts Payable	Accrued Wages Payable	Unearned Sales Revenue*	Paid-in Capital	Retained Income
Bal. 3/31/X1	+42,000	+90,000	+10,000	+2,000	=	+25,000			+100,000	+19,000
1.	+88,000	−88,000			=					
2.	−24,000				=	−24,000				
3.			+80,000		=	+80,000				
4a.		+85,000			=					+85,000 (revenue)
4b.			−70,000		=					− 70,000 (expense)
5.				−1,000	=					− 1,000 (expense)
6.	+3,000				=			+3,000*		
7.	−6,000				=					− 6,000 (expense)
8.					=		+2,000			− 2,000 (expense)
9.	−18,000				=					−18,000 (dividend)
4/30/X1	+85,000	+87,000	+20,000	+1,000	=	+81,000	+2,000	+3,000	+100,000	+ 7,000
	193,000				=	193,000				

* Some managers and accountants would call this account "Customer Deposits" or "Advances from Customers" or "Deferred Sales Revenue" or "Unrealized Sales Revenue."

561

(9) Cash dividends declared by the board of directors and disbursed to stockholders on April 29 equaled $18,000. (What account besides Cash is affected?) As will be explained on page 568, Cash and Retained Income are each decreased by $18,000.

Required:

1. Using the *accrual basis* of accounting, prepare an analysis of transactions, employing the equation approach demonstrated in Exhibit 17–1. To have plenty of room for new accounts, put your analysis sideways.
2. Prepare a balance sheet as of April 30, 19X1, and an income statement for the month of April. Also prepare a new report, the Statement of Retained Income, which should show the beginning balance, followed by a description of any major changes, and end with the balance as of April 30, 19X1.
3. Using the *cash basis* of accounting, prepare an income statement for April. Compare the net income with that computed in Requirement 2. Which net income figure do you prefer as a measure of the economic performance for April? Why?

Entries 6 through 9 and the statement of retained income have not been explained. However, as a learning step, try to respond to the requirements here anyway. Explanations follow almost immediately.

☐ Solution to Problem One

Part 1. ANALYSIS OF TRANSACTIONS. The answer is in Exhibit 17–2. The first five transactions are straightforward extensions or repetitions of the March transactions. But the rest of the transactions are new. They are discussed in the sections that follow the solutions to the second and third parts of this problem.

Part 2. PREPARATION OF FINANCIAL STATEMENTS. See Exhibits 17–3, 17–4, and 17–5. The first two of these exhibits show financial statements already described in this chapter: the balance sheet and the income statement. Exhibit 17–5 presents a new statement, the *Statement of Retained Income*, which is merely a formal presentation of the changes in retained income during the reporting period. It starts with the beginning balance, adds net income for the period in question, and deducts cash dividends to arrive at the ending balance. Frequently, this statement is tacked on to the bottom of an income statement. If so, the result is a *combined* statement of income and statement of retained income.

EXHIBIT 17–3

RETAILER NO. 1
Balance Sheet
As of April 30, 19X1

ASSETS		EQUITIES		
Cash	$ 85,000	Liabilities:		
Accounts receivable	87,000	Accounts payable	$ 81,000	
Inventory	20,000	Accrued wages		
Prepaid rent	1,000	payable	2,000	
		Unearned sales		
		revenue	3,000	$ 86,000
		Stockholders' equity:		
		Paid-in capital	$100,000	
		Retained income	7,000	107,000
Total assets	$193,000	Total equities		$193,000

EXHIBIT 17–4

RETAILER NO. 1
Income Statement (Multiple-Step)*
For the Month Ended April 30, 19X1

Sales		$85,000
Cost of goods sold		70,000
Gross profit		$15,000
Operating expenses:		
Rent	$1,000	
Wages	8,000	9,000
Net income		$ 6,000

* A **"single step" statement** would not draw the gross profit figure but would merely list all the expenses—including cost of goods sold—and deduct the total from sales. **Gross profit** is defined as the excess of sales over the cost of the inventory that was sold. It is sometimes called **gross margin**.

EXHIBIT 17–5

RETAILER NO. 1
Statement of Retained Income
For the Month Ended April 30, 19X1

Retained income, March 31, 19X1	$19,000
Net income for April	6,000
Total	$25,000
Dividends	18,000
Retained income, April 30, 19X1	$ 7,000

Part 3. CASH-BASIS INCOME STATEMENT. See Exhibit 17–6. The net income is $61,000 on the cash basis, but only $6,000 on the accrual basis. Accountants prefer the accrual basis because it provides a more complete and precise measurement of economic performance, a better matching of accomplishments with efforts. For example, the timing of disbursements to reduce accounts payable obviously is less closely related to April's sales than is the cost of inventory that was sold in April.

EXHIBIT 17–6

RETAILER NO. 1
Income Statement (Cash Basis)
For the Month Ended April 30, 19X1

Sales (collections from customers, including advance payments)		$91,000
Expenses:		
Disbursements for merchandise	$24,000	
Wages	6,000	30,000
Net income		$61,000

ACCOUNTING FOR UNEARNED REVENUE

Transaction 6 is $3,000 collected in advance from customers for merchandise they ordered. This transaction is an example of **unearned revenue**, sometimes called **deferred revenue**, which is a liability because the retailer is obligated to deliver the goods ordered or to refund the money if the goods are not delivered. Some managers might prefer to call this account *advances from customers*, or *customer deposits*, instead of *unearned sales revenue*, but it is an unearned revenue account no matter what its label. That is, it is revenue collected in advance that has not been earned as yet. Advance collections of rent and magazine subscriptions are other examples.

Sometimes it is easier to see how accountants analyze transactions by visualizing the financial positions of both parties to a contract. For instance, for the rent transaction of March 1 compare the financial impact on Retailer No. 1 with the impact on the landlord who received the rental payment:

	RETAILER NO. 1			LANDLORD		
	A =	L +	SE	A =	L +	SE
					Unearned	
		Prepaid	Rent		Rent	Rent
	Cash	Rent	Expense	Cash	Revenue	Revenue
1. Prepayment	−3,000 =	+3,000		+3,000 =	+3,000	
2. March expiration		= −1,000	−1,000		= −1,000	+1,000
3. April expiration		= −1,000	−1,000		= −1,000	+1,000

You are already familiar with the Retailer No. 1 analysis. The $1,000 monthly entries for Retailer No. 1 are examples of the first type of adjustments, the expiration of unexpired costs.

Study the transactions from the viewpoint of the owner of the rental property. The first transaction recognizes *unearned revenue*, which is a *liability* because the lessor is obligated to deliver the rental services (or to refund the money if the services are not delivered).

The two types of adjustments on page 565 are really mirror images of each other. If one party to a contract has a prepaid expense, the other has unearned revenue. A similar analysis could be conducted for, say, a three-year fire insurance policy or a three-year magazine subscription. The buyer recognizes a prepaid expense (asset) and uses adjustments to spread the initial cost to expense over the useful life of the services. In turn, the seller, such as a magazine publisher, must initially recognize its liability, Unearned Subscription Revenue. The *unearned* revenue is then systematically recognized as *earned* revenue as magazines are delivered throughout the life of the subscription. The diagrams below show that explicit cash transactions in such situations are initially recognized as balance sheet items and are later transformed into income statement items via periodic adjustments:

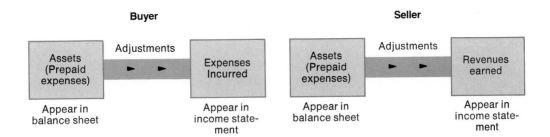

Buyer			
Assets (Prepaid expenses)	Adjustments ► ►	Expenses Incurred	
Appear in balance sheet		Appear in income statement	

Seller			
Assets (Prepaid expenses)	Adjustments ► ►	Revenues earned	
Appear in balance sheet		Appear in income statement	

You have now seen how two types of adjustments might occur: (1) expiration of unexpired costs and (2) realization (earning) of unearned revenues. Next we consider the third type of adjustment: accrual of unrecorded expenses, as illustrated by wages.

ACCRUAL OF UNRECORDED EXPENSES (WAGES)

An entity usually "incurs" an expense and "accrues" a debt or liability during a given period even though no explicit transaction occurs. Examples are wages of employees and interest on borrowed money. The liabilities grow as the clock ticks or as some services are continuously acquired and used, so they are said to **accrue** (accumulate).

It is awkward and unnecessary to make hourly, daily, or even weekly formal recordings in the accounts for many accruals. Consequently, adjustments are made to bring each expense (and corresponding liability) account up to date just before the formal financial statements are prepared.

☐ Accounting for Payment of Wages

Consider wages. Most companies pay their employees at predetermined times. Here is a sample calendar for April:

APRIL						
S	M	T	W	T	F	S
	1	2	3	4	5	6
7	8	9	10	11	12	13
14	15	16	17	18	19	20
21	22	23	24	25	26	27
28	29	30				

Suppose Retailer No. 1 pays its employees each Friday for services rendered during that week. For example, wages paid on April 26 would be compensation for the week ended April 26. The cumulative total wages paid on the Fridays during April were $6,000. Although day-to-day and week-to-week procedures may differ from entity to entity, a popular way to account for wages expense is the shortcut procedure described earlier for goods and services that are routinely consumed in the period of their purchase:

	ASSETS (A) = LIABILITIES (L) + STOCKHOLDERS' EQUITY (SE)		
	Cash		Wages Expense
7. Routine entry for explicit transactions	−6,000	=	−6,000

Accounting for Accrual of Wages

The company expanded its work force on April 29. Even if the work force had not expanded, an accrual would be necessary. Assume that, in addition to the $6,000 already paid, Retailer No. 1 owes $2,000 for employee services rendered during the last two days of April. The employees will not be paid for these services until the next regular weekly payday, May 3. No matter how simple or complex a set of accounting procedures may be in a particular entity, periodic adjustments ensure that the financial statements adhere to accrual accounting. The tabulation that follows repeats entry 7 for convenience and then adds entry 8:

	A	=	L	+	SE
	Cash		Accrued Wages Payable		Wages Expense
7. Routine entry for explicit transactions	−6,000	=			−6,000
8. Adjustment for implicit transaction, the accrual of unrecorded wages		=	+2,000		−2,000
Total effects	−6,000	=	+2,000		−8,000

Entry 8 is the first example in this book of the impact of the analytical shortcut that bypasses the asset account and produces an expense that is offset by an increase in a liability. Conceptually, entries 7 and 8 could each be subdivided into the asset acquisition–asset expiration sequence, but this two-step sequence is not generally used in practice for such expenses that represent the immediate consumption of services.

Accrued expenses arise when payment *follows* the rendering of services; prepaid expenses arise when payment *precedes* the service. Other examples of accrued expenses include sales commissions, property taxes, income taxes, and interest on borrowed money. Interest is rent paid for the use of money, just as rent is paid for the use of buildings or automobiles. The interest accumulates (accrues) as time unfolds, regardless of when the actual cash for interest is paid.

ACCRUAL OF UNRECORDED REVENUES

The final type of adjustment, which is not illustrated in the "Summary Problem for Your Review," is the realization of revenues that have been earned but not yet recorded as such in the accounts. It is the mirror image of the accrual of unrecorded expenses. Consider a financial institution that lends cash to Retailer No. 1 on a three-month promissory note for $50,000 with interest at 1.5% per month payable at maturity. The following tabulation shows the mirror-image effect of the adjustment for interest at the end of the first month (.015 × $50,000 = $750):

FINANCIAL INSTITUTION, THE LENDER			RETAILER NO. 1, THE BORROWER		
A	= L +	SE	A =	L +	SE
Accrued Interest Receivable		Interest Revenue		Accrued Interest Payable	Interest Expense
+750	=	+750		= +750	−750

To recapitulate, Exhibit 17–7 summarizes the four major types of the adjustments needed to implement the accrual basis of accounting.

EXHIBIT 17–7

Four Major types of Accounting Adjustments Before Preparation of Financial Statements

	Expense	Revenue
Payment precedes recognition of expense or revenue	I Expiration of unexpired cost. *Illustration*: The write-off of prepaid rent as rent expense (Exhibit 17–2, p. 561, entry 5)	II Realization (earning) of unearned revenues. *Illustration*: The mirror image of type I, whereby the landlord recognizes rent revenue and decreases unearned rent revenue (rent collected in advance)
Recognition of expense or revenue precedes payment	III Accrual of unrecorded expenses. *Illustration*: Wage expense for wages earned by employees but not yet paid (Exhibit 17–2, entry 8)	IV Accrual of unrecorded revenues. *Illustration*: Interest revenue earned but not yet collected by a financial institution.

DIVIDENDS AND RETAINED INCOME

☐ Dividends Are Not Expenses

As transaction 9, Exhibit 17–4, and Exhibit 17–5 (pp. 562–563) show, cash dividends are not expenses like rent and wages. They should not be deducted from revenues because dividends are not directly related to the generation of sales or the conduct of operations. Cash dividends are distributions of assets to stockholders that reduce retained income. The ability to pay dividends is fundamentally caused by profitable operations. Retained income increases as profits accumulate and decreases as dividends occur.

The entire right-hand side of the balance sheet can be thought of as claims against the total assets. The liabilities are the claims of creditors. The stockholders' equity represents the claims of owners arising out of their initial investment (paid-in capital) and subsequent profitable operations (retained income). **Retained income** is also called **retained earnings, undistributed earnings**, or **reinvested earnings**. As a company grows, this account can soar enormously if dividends are not paid. Retained income can easily be the largest stockholders' equity account.

☐ Retained Income Is Not Cash

Retained income is *not* a pot of cash that is awaiting distribution to stockholders. Consider the following illustration:

Step 1. Assume an opening balance sheet of:

Cash	$100	Paid-in capital	$100

Step 2. Purchase inventory for $50 cash. The balance sheet now reads:

Cash	$ 50	Paid-in capital	$100
Inventory	50		
	$100		

Steps 1 and 2 demonstrate a fundamental point. Ownership equity is an undivided claim against the total assets (in the aggregate). For example, half the shareholders do not have a specific claim on cash, and the other half do not have a specific claim on inventory. Instead, all the shareholders have an undivided claim against (or, if you prefer, an undivided interest in) all the assets.

Step 3. Now sell the inventory for $80. Inventory is reduced to zero, and cash is increased to $50 + $80 = $130:

Cash	$130	Paid-in capital	$100
		Retained income	30
		Total equities	$130

At this stage, the retained income might be related to a $30 increase in cash. But the $30 in retained income connotes only a *general* claim against *total* assets. This may be clarified by the transaction that follows.

Step 4. Purchase equipment and inventory, in the amounts of $70 and $50, respectively. Now cash is $130 − $70 − $50 = $10:

Cash	$ 10	Paid-in capital	$100
Inventory	50	Retained income	30
Equipment	70		
Total assets	$130	Total equities	$130

To what assets is the $30 in retained income related? Is it linked to Cash, to Inventory, or to Equipment? The answer is indeterminate. This example helps to explain the nature of the Retained Income account. It is a *claim*, not a pot of gold. Retained income is increased by profitable operations, but the cash inflow from sales is an increment in assets (see step 3). When the cash inflow takes place, management will use the cash, most often to buy more inventory or equipment (step 4). Retained income is a *general* claim against, or undivided interest in, *total* assets, *not* a specific claim against cash or against any other particular asset.[3]

As stated above, **dividends** are distributions of assets that reduce ownership claims. The cash assets that are disbursed typically arose from profitable operations. Thus dividends or withdrawals are often spoken of as "distributions of profits" or "distributions of retained income." Dividends are often erroneously described as being "paid *out of* retained income." In reality, cash dividends are distributions of assets and liquidate a portion of the ownership claim. The distribution is made possible by profitable operations.

The amount of cash dividends declared by the board of directors of a company depends on many factors, the least important of which is usually the balance in Retained Income. Although profitable operations are generally essential, dividend policy is also influenced by the company's cash position and future needs for cash to pay debts or to purchase additional assets. It is also influenced by whether the company is committed to a stable dividend policy or to a policy that normally ties dividends to fluctuations in net income.

[3] A term that is virtually archaic, **earned surplus**, is sometimes still found in stockholders' equity sections. Fortunately, its use is fading fast. Earned surplus is an interchangeable term for retained income. The trouble with the term is that *surplus* is misleading. It connotes something superfluous or unessential or left over; therefore, consequent misunderstandings of the term might be expected. As the example shows, earned surplus (retained income) is not an asset, nor does it represent an unnecessary ownership interest.

Under a stable policy, dividends may be paid consistently even if a company encounters a few years of little or no net income.

PROPRIETORSHIPS AND PARTNERSHIPS

The owners' equity section of the balance sheet can be affected by four basic types of transactions: (1) investments, (2) withdrawals, (3) revenues, and (4) expenses.

ASSETS = LIABILITIES +		OWNERS' EQUITY
	− Owners' withdrawals (e.g., corporate cash dividends)	+ Owners' investments
	− Expenses	+ Revenues

The basic accounting concepts that underlie the owners' equity are unchanged regardless of whether ownership takes the form of a corporation, sole proprietorship, or partnership. However, in **proprietorships** and **partnerships**, distinctions between paid-in capital (that is, the investments by owners) and retained income are rarely made. Compare the possibilities for Retailer No. 1 as of April 30:

OWNERS' EQUITY FOR A CORPORATION

Stockholders' equity:		
Captial stock (paid-in capital)	$100,000	
Retained income	7,000	
Total stockholders' equity		$107,000

OWNERS' EQUITY FOR A SOLE PROPRIETORSHIP

Alice Walsh, capital	$107,000

OWNERS' EQUITY FOR A PARTNERSHIP

Susan Zingler, capital	$ 53,500
John Martin, capital	53,500
Total partners' equity	$107,000

In contrast to corporations, sole proprietorships and partnerships are not legally required to account separately for paid-in capital (that is, proceeds from issuances of capital stock) and for retained income. Instead, they typically accumulate a single amount for each owner's original investments, subsequent investments, share of net income, and withdrawals. In the case of a sole proprietorship, then, the owner's equity will consist of a lone capital account.

Other terms for owners' equity are **equity capital** and **net worth**. The latter term is fading (the faster, the better). Net worth is a poor term because it implies that the owners' equity is a measure of the "current value" of the business. The total owners' equity is a measure of the ownership claim against the total assets, but it does not necessarily yield an accurate approximation of what some outsider is willing to pay for such an ownership interest. The selling price of a business depends on future profit projections that may not have any direct relationship to the existing assets or equities of the entity as measured by its accounting records.

NONPROFIT ORGANIZATIONS

The examples in this chapter have focused on profit-seeking organizations, but balance sheets and income statements are also used by nonprofit organizations. For example, hospitals and universities have income statements, although they are called *statements of revenue and expense*. The "bottom line" is frequently called "excess of revenue over expense" rather than "net income."

The basic concepts of assets, liabilities, revenue, and expense are applicable to all organizations, whether they be utilities, symphony orchestras, private, public, American, Asian, and so forth. However, some nonprofit organizations have been slow to adopt several ideas that are widespread in progressive companies. For example, in many governmental organizations the accrual basis of accounting has not replaced the cash basis. This has hampered the evaluation of the performance of such organizations.

GENERALLY ACCEPTED ACCOUNTING PRINCIPLES

☐ "Principles" Is a Misnomer

The financial statements of publicly held corporations and many other corporations are subject to an **independent audit** that forms the basis for a professional accounting firm's opinion, typically including the following key phrasing:

☐ In our opinion, the accompanying financial statements present fairly the financial position of the ABC Company at December 31, 19X1, and the results of its operations for the year then ended, in conformity with generally accepted accounting principles applied on a basis consistent with that of the preceding year.

We will explore the meaning of such key phrases as "present fairly" and "generally accepted accounting principles." An accounting firm must conduct an audit before it can render the foregoing opinion. Such an *audit* is an "examination" or in-depth inspection that is made in accordance with generally accepted auditing standards (which have been developed primarily by the American Institute of Certified Public Accountants). This examination includes miscellaneous tests of the accounting records, internal control systems, and other auditing procedures as deemed necessary. The examination culminates with the rendering of the accountant's **independent opinion**. This opinion (sometimes called **certificate**) is the accountant's testimony that *management's* financial statements are in conformity with generally accepted accounting principles.

The auditor's opinion, usually appearing at the end of annual reports prepared for stockholders and other external users, is often mistakenly relied on as an infallible guarantee of financial truth. Somehow accounting is thought to be an exact science, perhaps because of the aura of precision that financial statements possess. But accounting is more art than science. The financial reports may appear accurate because of their neatly integrated numbers, but they are the results of a complex measurement process that rests on a huge bundle of assumptions and conventions called **generally accepted accounting principles (GAAP).**

What are these generally accepted accounting principles? This technical term covers much territory. It includes both broad concepts or guidelines and detailed practices. It includes all conventions, rules, and procedures that together make up accepted accounting practice at any given time.

Accounting principles become "generally accepted" by agreement. Such agreement is not influenced solely by formal logical analysis. Experience, custom, usage, and practical necessity contribute to the set of principles. Accordingly, it might be better to call them *conventions*, because principles connote that they are the product of airtight logic.

☐ FASB, APB, and SEC

Every technical area seems to have regulatory bodies or professional associations whose names are often abbreviated. Accounting is no exception.

During the 1970s and 1980s, American generally accepted accounting principles have been most heavily influenced by the **Financial Accounting Standards Board (FASB)** and its predecessor body, the **Accounting Principles Board (APB)**. The FASB consists of seven qualified individuals who work full time. The board is supported by a large staff and an annual $10 million budget.

The board is an independent creature of the private sector and is financially supported by various professional accounting associations (such as the leading organization of the auditors, the American Institute of Certified Public Accountants, the AICPA). Many of the **APB Opinions** and **FASB Statements** will be referred to in succeeding chapters of this book.

The U.S. Congress has designated the **Securities and Exchange Commission (SEC)** as holding the ultimate responsibility for specifying the generally accepted accounting principles for companies whose stock is held by the general investing public. However, the SEC has informally delegated much rule-making power to the FASB. This public sector–private sector relationship may be sketched as follows:

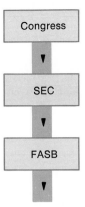

Issues pronouncements on various accounting issues. These pronouncements govern the preparation of typical financial statements.

Independent auditing firms (**Certified Public Accountants**) issue opinions concerning the fairness of financial statements prepared for external use (for example, corporate annual reports). These auditors are required to see that the statements do not depart from the FASB Statements and the APB Opinions.

Reconsider the three-tiered structure above. Note that Congress can overrule both the SEC and the FASB, and the SEC can overrule the FASB. Such undermining of the FASB occurs rarely, but pressure is exerted on all three tiers by corporations if they think an impending pronouncement is "wrong." Hence the setting of accounting principles is a complex process involving heavy interactions among the affected parties: public regulators (Congress and SEC), private regulators (FASB), companies, the public accounting profession, representatives of investors, and other interested groups.

In sum, the public body (the SEC) has informally delegated much rule-making power regarding accounting theory to the private body (the FASB). The FASB issues pronouncements on various accounting issues. Independent auditing firms, which render opinions concerning the fairness of corporate financial statements prepared for external use, are required to see that corporate statements do not depart from these pronouncements.

THREE MEASUREMENT CONVENTIONS

Three broad measurement or valuation conventions (principles) establish the basis for implementing accrual accounting: *realization* (when to recognize revenue), *matching* and *cost recovery* (when to recognize expense), and the *stable monetary unit* (what unit of measure to use).

☐ Realization

The first broad measurement or valuation convention, **realization**, was discussed earlier in this chapter in the section "Revenues and Expenses." In general, revenue is realized when the goods or services in question are delivered to customers. For further discussion, review p. 554.

☐ Matching and Cost Recovery

Generally accepted accounting principles are based on the concepts of accrual accounting described earlier in this chapter. You may often encounter a favorite buzzword in accounting: **matching**. The process of matching is the relating of accomplishments or revenues (as measured by the selling prices of goods and services delivered) and efforts or expenses (as measured by the cost of goods and services used) to a *particular period* for which a measurement of income is desired. In short, matching is a short description of the accrual basis for measuring income.

The heart of recognizing expense is the **"cost recovery"** concept. That is, assets such as inventories, prepayments, and equipment are carried forward as assets because their costs are expected to be recovered in the form of cash inflows (or reduced cash outflows) in future periods. At the end of each period, the accountant (especially the outside auditor at the end of each year) carefully examines the evidence to be assured that these assets—these unexpired costs—should not be written off as an expense of the current period. For instance, in our chapter example, prepaid rent of $2,000 was carried forward as an asset as of March 31 because the accountant is virtually certain that it represents a future benefit. Why? Because without the prepayment, cash outflows of $2,000 would have to be made for April and May. So the presence of the prepayment is a benefit in the sense that future cash outflows will be reduced by $2,000. Furthermore, future revenue (sales) will be high enough to ensure the recovery of the $2,000.

☐ Stable Monetary Unit

The monetary unit (for example, the dollar in the United States, Canada, Australia, New Zealand, and elsewhere) is the principal means for measuring assets and equities. It is the common denominator for quantifying the effects of a wide variety of transactions. Accountants record, classify, summarize, and report in terms of the dollar, franc, pound, mark, or other monetary unit.

Such measurement assumes that the principal counter—the dollar, for example—is an unchanging yardstick. Yet we all know that a 1988 dollar does not have the same purchasing power as a 1978 or 1968 dollar. Therefore accounting statements that include different dollars must be interpreted and compared with full consciousness of the limitations of the basic measurement unit. (For an expanded discussion, see Chapter 20.)

Accountants have been extensively criticized for not making explicit and formal adjustments to remedy the defects of their measuring unit. In the face of this, some accountants maintain that price-level adjustments would lessen objectivity and would add to the general confusion. They claim that the price-level problem has been exaggerated, and that the adjustments would not significantly affect the vast bulk of corporate statements because most accounts are in current or nearly current dollars.

On the other hand, inflation has been steady and its effects are sometimes surprisingly pervasive. We can expect to see continuing experimentation with reporting that measures the effects of changes in the general economywide price level and in the prices of specific assets. The most troublesome aspect, however, is how to interpret the results after they are measured. Investors and managers are accustomed to the conventional statements. The intelligent interpretation of statements adjusted for changes in the price level will require extensive changes in the habits of users.

The body of generally accepted accounting principles contains more than just the measurement conventions just discussed. Other major concepts include going concern, objectivity, materiality, and cost benefit. These are discussed in the first appendix to this chapter.

SUMMARY

An underlying structure of concepts, techniques, and conventions provides a basis for accounting practice. The three major measurement conventions are realization, matching, and stable monetary unit. The accrual basis is the heart of accounting, whereby revenues are recognized as earned and expenses as incurred rather than as related cash is received or disbursed.

At the end of each accounting period, adjustments must be made so that financial statements may be presented on a full-fledged accrual basis. The major adjustments are for (1) the expiration of unexpired costs, (2) realization (earning) of unearned revenues, (3) accrual of unrecorded expenses, and (4) accrual of unrecorded revenues.

Income statements usually appear in single-step, condensed form in published annual reports and in multiple-step, detailed form in the reports used within an organization.

SUMMARY PROBLEM FOR YOUR REVIEW

(Problem One appeared earlier in this chapter, page 560.)

☐ **Problem Two**

The following interpretations and remarks are sometimes encountered with regard to financial statements. Do you agree or disagree? Explain fully.

1. "If I purchase 100 shares of the outstanding common stock of General Motors Corporation (or Retailer No. 1), I invest my money directly in that corporation. General Motors must record that transaction."
2. "Sales show the cash coming in from customers and the various expenses show the cash going out for goods and services. The difference is net income."
3. Consider the following recent accounts of Delta, a leading U.S. airline:

Paid-in capital	$ 199,371,000
Retained earnings	824,280,000
Total stockholders' equity	$1,023,651,000

A shareholder commented, "Why can't that big airline pay higher wages and dividends too. It can use its hundreds of millions of dollars of retained earnings to do so."

4. "The total Delta stockholders' equity measures the amount that the shareholders would get today if the corporation were liquidated."

5. "Conservatism is desirable because investors will be misled if the financial report is too rosy."

☐ Solution to Problem Two

1. Money is invested directly in a corporation only upon original issuance of the stock by the corporation. For example, 100,000 shares of stock may be issued at $80 per share, bringing in $8 million to the corporation. This is a transaction between the corporation and the stockholders. It affects the corporate financial position:

Cash	$8,000,000	Stockholders' equity	$8,000,000

In turn, 100 shares of that stock may be sold by an original stockholder (A) to another individual (B) for $130 per share. This is a private transaction; no cash comes to the corporation. Of course, the corporation records the fact that 100 shares originally owned by A are now owned by B, but the corporate financial position is unchanged. Accounting focuses on the business entity; the private dealings of the owners have no direct effect on the financial position of the entity and hence are unrecorded except for detailed records of the owners' identities.

2. Cash receipts and disbursements are not the fundamental basis for the accounting recognition of revenues and expenses. Credit, not cash, lubricates the economy. Therefore, if services or goods have been rendered to a customer, a legal claim to cash in the form of a receivable is deemed sufficient justification for recognizing revenue; similarly, if services or goods have been used up, a legal obligation in the form of a payable is justification for recognizing expense.

   This approach to the measurement of net income is known as the accrual basis. Revenue is recognized as it is earned by (a) goods or services rendered, (b) an exchange in a market transaction, and (c) the assurance of the collectibility of the asset received. Expenses or losses are recognized when goods or services are used up in the obtaining of revenue (or when such goods or services cannot justifiably be carried forward as an asset because they have no potential future benefit). The expenses and losses are deducted from the revenue, and the result of this matching process is net income, the net increase in stockholders' equity from the conduct of operations.

3. As the chapter indicated, retained earnings is not cash. It is a stockholders' equity account that represents the accumulated increase in ownership claims because of profitable operations. This claim or interest may be partially liquidated by the payment of cash dividends, but a growing company will reinvest cash in sustaining the added investments in receivables, inventories, plant, equipment, and other assets so necessary for expansion. As a result, the ownership claims reflected by retained earnings may become "permanent" in the sense that, as a practical matter, they will never be liquidated as long as the company remains a going concern.

   This linking of retained earnings and cash is only one example of erroneous interpretation. As a general rule, there is no direct relationship between the individual items on the two sides of the balance sheet. For example, Delta's cash was less than $46 million on the above balance sheet date when its retained earnings exceeded $800 million.

4. Stockholders' equity is a difference, the excess of assets over liabilities. If the assets were carried in the accounting records at their liquidating value today, and the liabilities were carried at the exact amounts needed for their extinguishment, the remark would be true. But such valuations would be coincidental because assets are customarily carried at *historical cost* expressed in an unchanging monetary unit. Intervening changes in markets and general price levels in inflationary times may mean that the assets are woefully understated. Investors may make a critical error if they think that balance sheets indicate current values.

Furthermore, the "market values" for publicly owned shares are usually determined by daily trading conducted in the financial marketplaces such as the New York Stock Exchange. These values are affected by numerous factors, including the *expectations* of (a) price appreciation and (b) cash flows in the form of dividends. The focus is on the future; the present and the past are examined as clues to what may be forthcoming. Therefore the present stockholders' equity is usually of only incidental concern.

For example, the above stockholders' equity was $1,023,651,000 ÷ 39,761,154 shares, or $26 per share. During a year of low profits, Delta's market price per common share fluctuated between $22 and $36.

5. Conservatism is an entrenched practice among accountants, and it is also favored by many managers and investors. However, it has some ramifications that should be remembered. Conservatism will result in fast write-offs of assets with consequent lower balance sheet values and lower net incomes. But later years may show higher net incomes because of the heavier write-offs in early years.

So being conservative has some long-run countereffects because, for any asset, early fast write-offs will lighten expenses in later years. This countervailing effect is especially noteworthy when a company is having trouble making any net income. In such cases, the tendency is to wipe the slate clean by massive write-offs that result in an enormous net loss for a particular year. Without such asset write-offs to burden future years, the prospects brighten for reporting future net profits rather than net losses.

Conservatism has another boomerang effect. The understatement of assets and net income may prompt anxious stockholders to sell their shares when they should hold them. A dreary picture may be every bit as misleading as a rosy one.

HIGHLIGHTS TO REMEMBER

1. *Balance sheet* is a widely used term, but it is not as descriptive as its newer substitute terms: *statement of financial position* or *statement of financial condition*.

2. Other than cash and receivables, assets may be regarded as unexpired, prepaid, or stored costs (for example, inventory or equipment) that are carried forward to future periods rather than being immediately offset against revenue as expenses of the current period.

3. Revenues and expenses are components of stockholders' equity. Revenues increase stockholders' equity; expenses decrease stockholders' equity.

4. Dividends are not expenses.

5. In accrual accounting, an expense is often not accompanied by an immediate cash disbursement. That is, *expense* should not be confused with the term *cash disbursement*.

6. In accrual accounting, revenue is often not accompanied by an immediate cash receipt. That is, *revenue* should not be confused with the term *cash receipt*.

7. Frequently, accounting adjustments are clarified when they are seen as mirror images by looking at both sides of the adjustment simultaneously. For example, (a) the expiration of unexpired costs (the tenant's rent expense) is accompanied by (b) the realization (earning) of unearned revenues (the landlord's rent revenue).

8. Similarly, (a) the accrual of unrecorded expenses (a borrower's interest expense) is accompanied by (b) the accrual of unrecorded revenues (a lender's interest revenue).

9. If you have had little or no exposure to accounting, you should solve at least the "Summary Problems for Your Review" before proceeding to the next chapter. To read about basic accounting concepts is not enough. Work some problems too—the more, the better.

ACCOUNTING VOCABULARY

More new terms were introduced in this chapter (and its appendixes) than in any other, so be sure that you understand the following:

Account *p. 553*   Accounting Principles Board (APB) *572*   Accounts Payable *550* Accounts Receivable *550*   Accrual Basis *555*   Accrue *565*   Adjusting Entries *556* Adjustments *556*   APB Opinions *572*   Assets *549*   Balance Sheet *548* Capital *571*   Cash Basis *555*   Certificate *572*   Certified Public Accountant *573* Continuity Convention *579*   Corporation *549*   Cost-Benefit Criterion *580*   Cost of Goods Sold *552*   Credit *582*   Debit *582*   Deferred Credit *564*   Deferred Income *564*   Deferred Revenue *564*   Depreciation *559*   Dividends *569*   Earned Surplus *569*   Earnings *554*   Entity *548*   Equities *549*   Equity Capital *571* Expense *553*   Expired Costs *558*   Explicit Transactions *557*   FASB Statements *572* Financial Accounting *548*   Financial Accounting Standards Board (FASB) *572* Generally Accepted Accounting Principles (GAAP) *572*   Going Concern Convention *578*   Gross Margin *563*   Gross Profit *563*   Implicit Transactions *557* Income *554*   Income Statement *548*   Independent Audit *571*   Independent Opinion *572*   Ledger *582*   Liabilities *549*   Matching and Cost Recovery *574* Materiality *579*   Net Worth *571*   Objectivity *579*   Owners' Equity *549*   Paid-in Capital *549*   Partnership *570*   Profits *554*   Proprietorship *570*   Realization *554* Reinvested Earnings *568*   Retained Earnings *550*   Retained Income *550* Revenue *553*   Securities and Exchange Commission (SEC) *572*   Single-step Income Statement *563*   Source Documents *557*   Statement of Financial Condition *549* Statement of Financial Position *549*   Stockholders' Equity *549*   Transaction *549* Undistributed Earnings *568*   Unearned Revenue *564*   Unexpired Costs *558* Verifiability *579*

APPENDIX 17A: ADDITIONAL ACCOUNTING CONCEPTS

This appendix describes the following concepts, which are prominent parts of the body of generally accepted accounting principles: going concern or continuity, objectivity or verifiability, materiality, and cost-benefit.

THE GOING CONCERN OR CONTINUITY CONVENTION

Many accountants would regard **going concern** as a fact of life rather than as a convention or assumption. To view an entity as a going concern is to assume that it will continue indefinitely or at least that it will not be liquidated in the near future. This notion implies that existing *resources*, such as plant assets, *will be used* to fulfill the general purposes of a continuing entity *rather than sold* in tomorrow's real estate or equipment markets. It also implies that existing liabilities will be paid at maturity in an orderly manner.

Suppose a piece of specialized equipment was acquired a few days ago for $10,000. Sudden price increases then occurred. The equipment would now cost $12,000 to replace. However, because of heavy dismantling and moving costs, the equipment would net only $7,000 if it were sold. The going concern convention is often cited as the justification for adhering to acquisition cost ($10,000 in this example) as the primary basis for valuing assets such as inventories, land, buildings, and equipment. Some critics of these accounting practices believe that such valuations are not as informative as their replacement cost ($12,000) or their realizable values upon sale ($7,000). Defenders of using $10,000 as an appropriate asset valuation argue that a going concern will generally use the asset as originally intended. Therefore the acquisition cost is the preferable basis for accountability and evaluation of performance. Hence other values are not germane because replacement or disposal will not occur en masse as of the balance sheet date.

The opposite view to this going concern or **continuity convention** is an immediate-liquidation assumption, whereby all items on a balance sheet are valued at the amounts appropriate if the assets were to be sold for cash in piecemeal fashion within a few days or months. This liquidation approach to valuation is usually used only when the entity is in severe, near-bankrupt straits.

OBJECTIVITY OR VERIFIABILITY

Users want assurance that the numbers in the financial statements are not fabricated by management or by accountants in order to mislead or to falsify the financial position and performance. Consequently, accountants seek and prize **objectivity** as one of their principal strengths and regard it as an essential characteristic of measurement. Objectivity results in accuracy that is supported by convincing evidence that can be verified by independent accountants. It is a relative rather than an absolute concept. Some measurements can be extremely objective (such as cash in a cash register) in the sense that the same measurement would be produced by each of a dozen CPAs. But there are gradations of objectivity. A dozen CPAs are less likely to arrive at the same balances for receivables, inventories, plant and equipment, and miscellaneous assets. Yet they strive for measurement rules that will produce results that are subject to independent check. That is why accountants are generally satisfied with existing tests of realization; requiring an exchange to occur before revenue is realized helps ensure **verifiability**.

Many critics of existing accounting practices want to trade objectivity (accuracy) for what they conceive as more relevant or valid information. For example, the accounting literature is peppered with suggestions that accounting should attempt to measure "economic income," even though objectivity may be lessened. This particular suggestion often involves introducing asset valuations at replacement costs when these are higher than historical costs. The accounting profession has generally rejected these suggestions, even when reliable replacement price quotations are available, because no evidence short of a bona fide sale is regarded as sufficient to justify income recognition. However, inflation during the past 15 years has led to experimentation with the use of replacement costs and other versions of current values for external purposes. (See Chapter 20 for a fuller discussion.)

MATERIALITY

Because accounting is a practical art, the practitioner often tempers accounting reports by applying the convention of **materiality**. Many outlays that theoretically should be recorded as assets are immediately written off as expenses because of their lack of significance. For example, many corporations have a rule that requires the immediate write-off to expense of all outlays under a specified minimum of, say, $100, regardless of the useful life of the asset acquired. In such a case, coat hangers may be acquired that may last indefinitely but may never appear in the balance sheet as assets. The resulting $100 understatement of assets and stockholders' equity would be too trivial to worry about.

When is an item material? There will probably never be a universal clear-cut answer. What is trivial to General Motors may be material to Joe's Tavern. An item is material if it is sufficiently large so that its omission or misstatement would tend to mislead the user of the financial statements under consideration. A working rule is that an item is material if its proper accounting would probably affect the decision of a knowledgeable user. In sum, materiality is an important convention. But it is difficult to use anything other than prudent judgment to tell whether an item is material.

COST-BENEFIT

Accounting systems vary in complexity from the minimum crude records kept to satisfy governmental authorities to the sophisticated budgeting and feedback schemes that are at the heart of management planning and controlling. As a system is changed, its potential benefits should exceed its additional costs. Often the benefits are difficult to measure, but this **cost-benefit criterion** at least implicitly underlies the decisions about the design of accounting systems. The reluctance to adopt suggestions for new ways of measuring financial position and performance is frequently because of inertia, but it is often because the apparent benefits do not exceed the obvious costs of gathering and interpreting the information.

ROOM FOR JUDGMENT

Accounting is commonly misunderstood as being a precise discipline that produces exact measurements of a company's financial position and performance. As a result, many individuals regard accountants as little more than mechanical tabulators who grind out financial reports after processing an imposing amount of detail in accordance with stringent predetermined rules. Although accountants take methodical steps with masses of data, their rules of measurement allow much room for judgment. Managers and accountants who exercise this judgment have more influence on financial reporting than is commonly believed. These judgments are guided by the basic concepts, techniques, and conventions called generally accepted accounting principles (GAAP). Examples of the latter include the basic concepts just discussed. Their meaning will become clearer as these concepts are applied in future chapters.

APPENDIX 17B: USING LEDGER ACCOUNTS

This chapter offered some insight into the overall approach of the accountant to the measuring of economic activity. This appendix focuses on some of the main techniques that the accountant would use to analyze the illustrated transactions in the chapter.

THE ACCOUNT

To begin, consider how the accountant would record the Retailer No. 1 transactions that were introduced in the chapter. Exhibit 17–1 (p. 551) showed their effects on the elements of the balance sheet equation:

	A		=	L	+	SE
	Cash	Inventory	=	Accounts Payable		Paid-in Capital
1. Initial investment by owners	+100,000		=			+100,000
2. Acquire inventory for cash	−75,000	+75,000	=			
3. Acquire inventory on credit		+35,000	=	+35,000		

This balance sheet equation approach emphasizes the concepts, but it can obviously become unwieldy if many transactions occur. You can readily see that changes in the balance sheet equation can occur many times daily. In large businesses, such as in a department store, hundreds or thousands of repetitive transactions occur hourly. In practice, **ledger accounts** must be used to keep track of how these multitudes of transactions affect each particular asset, liability, revenue, expense, and so forth. The accounts used here are simplified versions of those used in practice. They are called T-accounts because they take the form of the capital letter T. The above transactions would be shown in T-accounts as follows:

| ASSETS | = | LIABILITIES + STOCKHOLDERS' EQUITY |

Cash

Increases		Decreases	
(1)	100,000	(2)	75,000
Bal.	25,000		

Accounts Payable

Decreases		Increases	
		(3)	35,000

Inventory

Increases		Decreases	
(2)	75,000		
(3)	35,000		
Bal.	110,000		

Paid-in Capital

Decreases		Increases	
		(1)	100,000

The above entries were made in accordance with the rules of a *double-entry system*, whereby at least two accounts are affected by each transaction. Asset accounts have left-side balances. They are increased by entries on the left side and decreased by entries on the right side.

Liabilities and stockholders' equity accounts have right-side balances. They are increased by entries on the right side and decreased by entries on the left side.

The format of the T-account eliminates the use of negative numbers. Any entry that reduces an account balance is *added* to the side of the account that *decreases* the account balance.

Each T-account summarizes the changes in a particular asset or equity. Each transaction is keyed in some way, such as by the numbering used in this illustration or by date or both. This keying facilitates the rechecking (auditing) process by aiding the tracing of transactions to original sources. A balance of an account is computed by deducting the smaller total amount from the larger. Accounts exist to keep an up-to-date summary of the changes in specific assets and equities.

A balance sheet can be prepared anytime if the accounts are up to date. The necessary information is tabulated in the accounts. For example, the balance sheet after the first three transactions would contain:

	ASSETS		EQUITIES	
Cash	$ 25,000	Liabilities:		
Inventory	110,000	Accounts payable		$ 35,000
		Stockholders' equity:		
		Paid-in capital		100,000
Total assets	$135,000	Total equities		$135,000

GENERAL LEDGER

Exhibit 17–8 is the *general ledger* of Retailer No. 1. The *general ledger* is defined as the group of accounts that supports the accounts shown in the major financial statements.[4] Exhibit 17–8 is merely a recasting of the facts that were analyzed in Exhibit 17–1. Study Exhibit 17–8 by comparing its analysis of each transaction against its corresponding analysis in Exhibit 17–1, page 551.

DEBITS AND CREDITS

The balance sheet equation has often been mentioned in this chapter. Recall:

$$A = L + \text{paid-in capital} \tag{1}$$

$$A = L + \text{paid-in capital} + \text{retained income} \tag{2}$$

$$A = L + \text{paid-in capital} + \text{revenue} - \text{expense} \tag{3}$$

The accountant often talks about entries in a technical way:

Transposing,

$$A + \text{expenses} = L + \text{paid-in capital} + \text{revenue} \tag{4}$$

Finally,

$$\text{left} = \text{right}$$
$$\text{debit} = \text{credit} \tag{5}$$

Debit means one thing and one thing only—"left side of an account" (not "bad," "something coming," etc.). **Credit** means one thing and one thing only—"right side of an account" (not "good," "something owed," etc.). The word *charge* is often used instead of *debit*, but no single word is used as a synonym for *credit*.

---

[4] The general ledger is usually supported by various *subsidiary ledgers*, which provide details for several accounts in the general ledger. For instance, an accounts receivable subsidiary ledger would contain a separate account for each credit customer. The accounts receivable balance that appears in the Sears balance sheet is in a single account in the Sears general ledger. However, that lone balance is buttressed by detailed individual accounts receivable with millions of credit customers. You can readily visualize how some accounts in general ledgers might have subsidiary ledgers supported by sub-subsidiary ledgers, and so on. Thus a subsidiary accounts receivable ledger might be subdivided alphabetically into Customers A–D, E–H, and so forth.

EXHIBIT 17-8

General Ledger of RETAILER NO. 1

1. Initial investment
2. Acquire inventory for cash
3. Acquire inventory on credit
4a. Sales on credit
4b. Cost of inventory sold
5. Collect from customers
6. Pay accounts of suppliers
7a. Pay rent in advance
7b. Recognize expiration of rental services

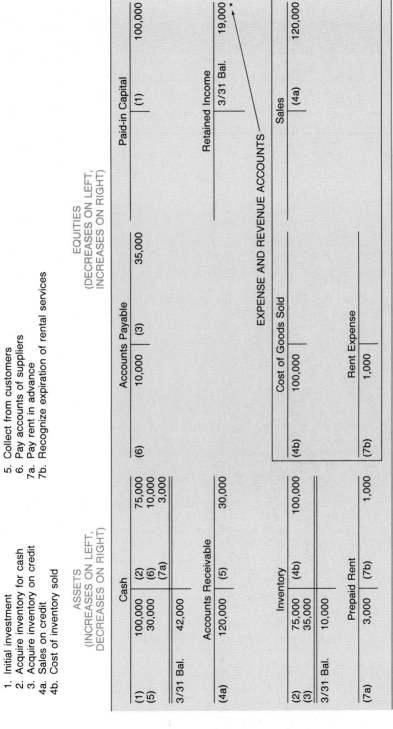

*The details of the revenue and expense accounts appear in the income statement. Their net effect is then transferred to a single account, Retained Income, in the balance sheet.

Note: An ending balance should be drawn for each account, but all balances are not shown here because some can be computed easily by inspection.

For example, if you asked an accountant what entry to make for transaction 4b, the answer would be: "I would debit (or charge) Cost of Goods Sold for $100,000; and I would credit Inventory for $100,000." Note that the total dollar amount of the debits (entries on the left side of the account(s) affected) will *always* equal the total dollar amount of credits (entries on the right side of the account(s) affected) because the whole accounting system is based on an equation. The symmetry and power of this analytical debit-credit technique is indeed impressive.

Assets are traditionally carried as left-side balances. Why do assets and expenses both carry debit balances? They carry left-side balances for different reasons. *Expenses are temporary stockholders' equity accounts. Decreases in stockholders' equity are entered on the left side of the accounts because they offset the normal (i.e., right-side) stockholders' equity balances. Because expenses decrease stockholders' equity, they are carried as left-side balances.*

To recapitulate:

ASSETS		=	LIABILITIES		+	STOCKHOLDERS' EQUITY	
Increase	Decrease		Decrease	Increase		Decrease	Increase
+	−		−	+		−	+
debit	credit		debit	credit		debit	credit
left	right		left	right		left	right

Because revenues increase stockholders' equity, they are recorded as credits. Because expenses decrease stockholders' equity, they are recorded as debits.

You have just seen an example of *double-entry* accounting, so named because at least two accounts are *always* affected in each transaction.

THE STRANGE DEBIT-CREDIT LANGUAGE

Beginners in the study of accounting are frequently confused by the words *debit* and *credit*. Perhaps the best way to minimize confusion is to ask what words would be used as substitutes? *Left* would be used instead of debit, and *right* would be used instead of credit.

The words *debit* and *credit* have a Latin origin. They were used centuries ago when double-entry bookkeeping was introduced by Paciolo, an Italian monk. Even though *left* and *right* are more descriptive words, *debit* and *credit* are too deeply entrenched to avoid.

Debit and credit are used as verbs, adjectives, or nouns. That is, "debit $1,000 to cash and credit $1,000 to accounts receivable" are examples of uses as verbs, meaning that $1,000 should be placed on the left side of the cash account and on the right side of the accounts receivable account. Similarly, if "a debit is made to cash" or "cash has a debit balance of $12,000," the *debit* is a noun or adjective that describes the status of a particular account. Thus debit and credit are short words that are packed with meaning.

In our everyday conversation we sometimes use the words *debits* and *credits* in a general sense that may completely diverge from their technical accounting uses. For instance, we may give praise by saying "She deserves plenty of credit for her good deed" or "That misplay is a debit on his ledger." When you study accounting, forget these general uses and misuses of the words. Merely think right (or left).

Consider how the words *debit* and *credit* appear on the bank statement or credit card statement of your account. For example *credit balance* in your checking account means that the bank owes you money. That is, a right-hand (credit) balance indicates a liability of the bank to you.

ASSIGNMENT MATERIAL

The assignment material for each remaining chapter is divided as follows:
   Fundamental Assignment Material
      General Coverage
      Understanding Published Financial Reports
   Additional Assignment Material
      General Coverage
      Understanding Published Financial Reports
The "General Coverage" subgroups focus on concepts and procedures that are applicable to a wide variety of specific settings. Many instructors believe that these "traditional" types of questions, exercises, and problems have proved their educational value over many years of use in introductory textbooks.

The "Understanding Published Financial Reports" subgroups focus on real-life situations. They have the same basic aims as the "General Coverage" subgroups. Indeed, some instructors may confine their assignments to the "Understanding Published Financial Reports" subgroups. The distinctive characteristic of the latter subgroups is the use of actual companies and news events to enhance the student's interest in accounting. Many students and instructors get more satisfaction out of a course that frequently uses actual situations as a means of learning accounting methods and concepts.

FUNDAMENTAL ASSIGNMENT MATERIAL

☐ **General Coverage**

17–1. **BALANCE SHEET EQUATION.** (Alternate is 17–4.) Find the unknowns (in thousands), showing computations to support your answers. Consider each case independently.

	CASE		
	1	2	3
Assets, beginning of period	$ 80	$ C	$ G
Assets, end of period	90	290	F
Liabilities, beginning of period	C	100	95
Liabilities, end of period	G	G	85
Paid-in capital, beginning of period	10	20	E
Paid-in capital, end of period	F	F	75
Retained income, beginning of period	25	70	90
Retained income, end of period	E	E	100
Revenues	100	D	300
Expenses	85	180	260
Net income	D	30	C
Dividends	–0–	10	D
Additional investment by stockholders	–0–	40	25

17–2. ANALYSIS OF TRANSACTIONS, PREPARATION OF STATEMENTS. (Alternates are Problems 17–5 and 17–30.) The Dorian Company was incorporated on March 1, 19X1. Dorian had six holders of common stock. Alice Dorian, who was the president and chief executive officer, held 60 percent of the shares. The company rented space in department stores and specialized in selling costume jewelry. Dorian's first venture was in the Goliath Department Store.

The following events occurred during March.

(1) The company was incorporated. Common stockholders invested $80,000 cash.

(2) Purchased merchandise inventory for cash, $50,000.

(3) Purchased merchandise inventory on open account, $10,000.

(4) Merchandise carried in inventory at a cost of $35,000 was sold for cash for $20,000 and on open account for $60,000, a grand total of $80,000. Dorian (not Goliath) carries and collects these accounts receivable.

(5) Collection of the above accounts receivable, $12,000.

(6) Payments of accounts payable, $6,000. See Transaction 3.

(7) Special display equipment and fixtures were acquired on March 1 for $21,000. Their expected useful life was 21 months, with no terminal scrap value. Straight-line depreciation was adopted. This equipment was removable. Dorian paid $5,000 as a down payment and signed a promissory note for $16,000.

(8) On March 1, Dorian signed a rental agreement with Goliath. The agreement called for a flat $3,000 per month, payable quarterly in advance. Therefore Dorian paid $9,000 cash on March 1.

(9) The rental agreement also called for a payment of 10% of all sales. This payment is in addition to the flat $3,000 per month. In this way, Goliath would share in any success of the venture and be compensated for general services such as cleaning and utilities. This payment was to be made in cash on the last day of each month as soon as the sales for the month were tabulated. The March payment was made on time.

(10) Wages, salaries, and sales commissions were all paid in cash for all earnings by employees. The amount was $32,000.

(11) Depreciation expense was recognized. See Transaction 7.

(12) The expiration of an appropriate amount of prepaid rental services was recognized. See Transaction 8.

Required:

1. Prepare an analysis of Dorian Company's transactions, employing the equation approach demonstrated in Exhibit 17–1. Two additional columns will be needed: Equipment and Fixtures, Notes Payable. Show all amounts in thousands.

2. Prepare a balance sheet as of March 31, 19X1, and an income statement for the month of March. Ignore income taxes.

3. Given these sparse facts, analyze Dorian's performance for March and its financial position as of March 31, 19X1.

17–3. COMPARISON OF CASH VERSUS ACCRUAL BASIS. Refer to the preceding problem. Prepare an income statement on the cash basis for March. Compare it with the income statement on the accrual basis. Which basis provides a better measure of economic performance? Why?

☐ Understanding Published Financial Reports

17–4. BALANCE SHEET EQUATION. (Alternate is 17–1.) H. J. Heinz Corporation is a large processor and marketer of food products, including Heinz, Star-Kist, and Ore-Ida brands. Its actual terminology and actual data (in millions of dollars) follow for its fiscal year ended May 1, 1986:

Assets, beginning of period	$2,343
Assets, end of period	E
Liabilities, beginning of period	A
Liabilities, end of period	1,244
Paid-in capital, beginning of period	165
Paid-in capital, end of period	D
Retained earnings, beginning of period	956
Retained earnings, end of period	C
Revenues	4,048
Costs and expenses	B
Net earnings	266
Dividends	106
Additional investments by stockholders	1

Required: | Find the unknowns (in millions), showing computations to support your answers.

17-5. ANALYSIS OF TRANSACTIONS, PREPARATION OF STATEMENTS. (Alternates are 17-2 and 17-30.) La-Z-Boy Chair Company manufactures and sells popular furniture. The company's actual condensed balance sheet data, April 30, 1985, follow (in millions):

Cash	$ 19	Accounts payable	$ 16
Accounts receivable	90	Other liabilities	48
Inventories	28	Paid-in capital	10
Prepaid expenses	3		
Property, plant, and equipment	53	Retained earnings	119
Total	$193	Total	$193

The following summarizes some major transactions during May 1985 (in millions):
(1) Furniture carried in inventory at a cost of $3 was sold for cash of $2 and on open account for $6, a grand total of $8.
(2) Acquired inventory on account, $5.
(3) Collected receivables, $3.
(4) On May 2, used $3 cash to prepay some rent and insurance.
(5) Payments on accounts payable (for inventories), $2.
(6) Paid selling and administrative expenses in cash, $1.
(7) Of the $3 of prepaid expenses, April 30, rent and insurance expired in May, amounting to a total of $1.
(8) Depreciation expense of $1 was recognized for May.

Required: | 1. Prepare an analysis of La-Z-Boy's transactions, employing the equation approach demonstrated in Exhibit 17-1, page 551. Show all amounts in millions. (For simplicity, only a few major transactions are illustrated here.)
2. Prepare a statement of earnings for the month ended May 31, 1985, and a balance sheet, May 31, 1985. Ignore income taxes.

17-6. CASH BASIS VERSUS ACCRUAL BASIS. Refer to the preceding problem. Prepare a statement of earnings on the cash basis for May. Compare it with the earnings statement on the accrual basis. Which basis provides a better measure of economic performance? Why?

BASIC ACCOUNTING: CONCEPTS, TECHNIQUES, AND CONVENTIONS

ADDITIONAL ASSIGNMENT MATERIAL

☐ **General Coverage**

17–7. Give at least two synonymous terms for each of the following: *balance sheet*; *income statement*; *assets*.

17–8. Give at least three other terms for *retained earnings*.

17–9. Criticize: "As a stockholder, I have a right to more dividends. You have millions stashed away in retained earnings. It's about time that you let the true owners get their hands on that pot of gold."

17–10. Criticize: "Dividends are distributions of profits."

17–11. Explain why advertising should be viewed as an asset upon acquisition.

17–12. Give five examples of accounting entities.

17–13. Define *going concern*.

17–14. What is the major criticism of using the dollar as the principal accounting measure?

17–15. What does the accountant mean by *objectivity*?

17–16. Criticize: "Assets are things of value owned by the entity."

17–17. Criticize: "Net income is the difference in the ownership capital account balances at two points in time."

17–18. Distinguish between the accrual basis and the cash basis.

17–19. How do adjusting entries differ from routine entries?

17–20. Why is it better to refer to the *costs*, rather than *values*, of assets such as plant or inventories?

17–21. If gross profit is 60%, express the relationship of cost of goods sold to gross profit in percentage terms.

17–22. What is the role of cost-benefit (economic feasibility) in the development of accounting principles?

17–23. TRUE OR FALSE. Use *T* or *F* to indicate whether each of the following statements is true or false.

(1) The cash balance is the best evidence of stockholders' equity.
(2) From a single balance sheet, you can find stockholders' equity for a period of time but not for a specific day.
(3) It is not possible to determine change in the condition of a business from a single balance sheet.
(4) Retained Earnings should be accounted for as an asset item.
(5) Cash should be classified as a stockholders' equity item.
(6) Machinery used in the business should be recorded at replacement cost.

17–24. NATURE OF RETAINED INCOME. This is an exercise on the relationships among assets, liabilities, and ownership equities. The numbers are small, but the underlying concepts are large.

(1) Assume an opening balance sheet of:

Cash	$1,000	Paid-in capital	$1,000

(2) Purchase inventory for $600 cash. Prepare a balance sheet. A heading is unnecessary in this and subsequent requirements.
(3) Sell the entire inventory for $850 cash. Prepare a balance sheet. Where is the retained income in terms of relationships within the balance sheet? That is, what is the meaning of the retained income? Explain in your own words.

(4) Buy inventory for $400 cash and equipment for $700 cash. Prepare a balance sheet. Where is the retained income in terms of relationships within the balance sheet? That is, what is the meaning of the retained income? Explain in your own words.

(5) Buy inventory for $300 on open account. Prepare a balance sheet. Where is the retained income and account payable in terms of the relationships within the balance sheet? That is, what is the meaning of the account payable and the retained income? Explain in your own words.

17–25. INCOME STATEMENT. Here is a statement of an automobile dealer:

O'REILLY TOYOTA, INC.
Statement of Profit and Loss
December 31, 19X3

Revenues		
Sales	$1,100,000	
Increase in market value of land and building	200,000	$1,300,000
Deduct expenses:		
Advertising	$ 100,000	
Sales commissions	60,000	
Utilities	20,000	
Wages	150,000	
Dividends	100,000	
Cost of cars purchased	700,000	1,130,000
Net profit		$ 170,000

Required: | List and describe any shortcomings of this statement.

17–26. CUSTOMER AND AIRLINE. The Levitz Furniture Company decided to hold a managers' meeting in Hawaii in February. To take advantage of special fares, Levitz purchased airline tickets in advance from United Airlines at a total cost of $90,000. These were acquired on December 1 for cash.

Required: | Using the balance sheet equation format, analyze the impact of the December payment and the February travel on the financial position of both Levitz and United.

17–27. TENANT AND LANDLORD. The Ace Hardware Company, a retail hardware store, pays quarterly rent on its store at the beginning of each quarter. The rent per quarter is $9,000. The owner of the building in which the store is located is the Rouse Corporation.

Required: | Using the balance sheet equation format, analyze the effects of the following on the tenant's and the landlord's financial position:

1. Ace Hardware pays $9,000 rent on July 1.
2. Adjustment for July.
3. Adjustment for August.
4. Adjustment for September.

17–28. FIND UNKNOWNS. The following data pertain to the Elway Corporation. Total assets at January 1, 19X1, were $90,000; at December 31, 19X1, $120,000. During 19X1, sales were $200,000, cash dividends were $4,000, and operating expenses (exclusive of cost of goods sold) were $50,000. Total liabilities at December 31, 19X1, were $55,000; at January 1, 19X1, $40,000. There was no additional capital paid in during 19X1.

Required: (These need not be computed in any particular order.)

1. Stockholders' equity, January 1, 19X1
2. Net income for 19X1
3. Cost of goods sold for 19X1

17–29. BALANCE SHEET EQUATION: SOLVING FOR UNKNOWNS. Compute the unknowns (V, W, X, Y, Z) in each of the individual cases, Columns A through G.

GIVEN	A	B	C	D	E	F	G
Assets at beginning of period		$ 9,000				Z	$ 8,200
Assets at end of period		12,000					9,600
Liabilities at beginning of period		6,000				$12,000	4,000
Liabilities at end of period		Y					6,000
Stockholders' equity at beginning of period	$7,000	X				V	X
Stockholders' equity at end of period	X	5,000				10,000	W
Sales			X		$15,000	14,000	20,000
Inventory at beginning of period				$ 8,000	6,000	Y	
Inventory at end of period				6,000	7,000	7,000	
Purchases of inventory				11,000	9,000	6,000	
Gross profit			2,000		Y	6,000	V
Cost of goods sold*			7,000	X	X	X	Z
Other expenses					4,000	4,000	5,000
Net profit	3,000	Z			Z	W	Y
Dividends	1,000	–0–				1,500	400
Additional investments by stockholders						5,000	–0–

* Note that Cost of goods sold = Beginning inventory + Purchases − Ending inventory.

17–30. FUNDAMENTAL TRANSACTION ANALYSIS AND PREPARATION OF STATEMENTS. (Alternates are 17–2 and 17–5, but this is longer.) Three women who were college classmates have decided to pool a variety of work experiences by opening a woman's clothing store. The business has been incorporated as Sartorial Choice, Inc. The following transactions occurred during April.

(1) On April 1, 19X1, each woman invested $9,000 in cash in exchange for 1,000 shares of stock each.
(2) The corporation quickly acquired $50,000 in inventory, half of which had to be paid for in cash. The other half was acquired on open accounts that were payable after 30 days.
(3) A store was rented for $500 monthly. A lease was signed for one year on

April 1. The first two months' rent were paid in advance. Other payments were to be made on the second of each month.

(4) Advertising during April was purchased on open account for $3,000 from a newspaper owned by one of the stockholders. Additional advertising services of $6,000 were acquired for cash.

(5) Sales were $65,000. The average markup above the cost of the merchandise was two-thirds of cost. Eighty percent of the sales were on open account.

(6) Wages and salaries incurred in April amounted to $11,000, of which $5,000 was paid.

(7) Miscellaneous services paid for in cash were $1,410.

(8) On April 1, fixtures and equipment were purchased for $6,000 with a down payment of $1,000 plus a $5,000 note payable in one year.

(9) See transaction 8 and make the April 30 adjustment for interest expense *accrued* at 9.6%. (The interest is not *due* until the note matures.)

(10) See transaction 8 and make the April 30 adjustment for depreciation expense on a straight-line basis. The estimated life of the fixtures and equipment is ten years with no expected terminal scrap value. Straight-line depreciation here would be $6,000 ÷ 10 years = $600 per year, or $50 per month.

(11) Cash dividends of $300 were declared and disbursed to stockholders on April 29.

Required:

1. Using the accrual basis of accounting, prepare an analysis of transactions, employing the equation approach demonstrated in Exhibit 17–1. Place your analysis sideways; to save space, use abbreviated headings. Work slowly. Use the following headings: Cash, Accounts Receivable, Inventory, Prepaid Rent, Fixtures and Equipment, Accounts Payable, Notes Payable, Accrued Wages Payable, Accrued Interest Payable, Paid-in Capital, and Retained Income. Exhibit 17–1 is on page 551.

2. Prepare a balance sheet and a multiple-step income statement. Also prepare a statement of retained income.

3. What advice would you give the owners based on the information compiled in the financial statements?

17–31. **DEBITS AND CREDITS.** Study Appendix 17B. Determine for the following transactions whether the account *named in parentheses* is to be debited or credited.

(1) Sold merchandise (Merchandise Inventory), $1,000.

(2) Paid Johnson Associates $3,000 owed them (Accounts Payable).

(3) Bought merchandise on account (Merchandise Inventory), $2,000.

(4) Received cash from customers on accounts due (Accounts Receivable), $1,000.

(5) Bought merchandise on open account (Accounts Payable), $5,000.

(6) Borrowed money from a bank (Notes Payable), $10,000.

17–32. **TRUE OR FALSE.** Study Appendix 17B. Use *T* or *F* to indicate whether each of the following statements is true or false.

(1) Debit entries must always be recorded on the left.

(2) Decreases in accounts must be shown on the debit side.

(3) Both increases in liabilities and decreases in assets should be entered on the right.

(4) Money borrowed from the bank should be credited to Cash and debited to Notes Payable.

(5) Purchase of inventory on account should be credited to Inventory and debited to Accounts Payable.

(6) Decreases in liability accounts should be recorded on the right.

(7) Increases in asset accounts must always be entered on the left.

(8) Increases in stockholders' equity always should be entered as credits.

(9) Equipment purchases for cash should be debited to Equipment and credited to Cash.

(10) Asset credits should be on the right and liability credits on the left.

(11) Payments on mortgages should be debited to Cash and credited to Mortgages Payable. Mortgages are long-term debts.

17–33. **USING T-ACCOUNTS.** Study Appendix 17B. Refer to Problem 17–2. Make entries for March in T-accounts. Key your entries and check to see that the ending balances agree with the financial statements.

17–34. **USING T-ACCOUNTS.** Study Appendix 17B. Refer to Problem One of the "Summary Problems for Your Review." The transactions are analyzed in Exhibit 17–2. Make entries in T-accounts and check to see that the ending balances agree with the financial statements in Exhibits 17–3, 17–4, 17–5 on page 563.

17–35. **T-ACCOUNTS.** Study Appendix 17B. Refer to Problem 17–30. Use T-accounts to present an analysis of April transactions. Key your entries and check to see that the ending balances agree with the financial statements.

17–36. **MEASURING INCOME FOR TAX AND OTHER PURPOSES.** The following are the summarized transactions of Dr. Cristina Faragher, a dentist, for 19X7, her first year in practice.

(1) Acquired equipment and furniture for $50,000. Its expected useful life is five years. Straight-line depreciation will be used, assuming zero terminal disposal value.

(2) Fees collected, $80,000. These fees included $2,000 paid in advance by some patients on December 31, 19X7.

(3) Rent is paid at the rate of $500 monthly, payable on the twenty-fifth of each month for the following month. Total disbursements during 19X7 for rent were $6,500.

(4) Fees billed but uncollected, December 31, 19X7, $15,000.

(5) Utilities expense paid in cash, $600. Additional utility bills unpaid at December 31, 19X7, $100.

(6) Salaries expense of dental assistant and secretary, $16,000 paid in cash. In addition, $1,000 was earned but unpaid on December 31, 19X7.

Dr. Faragher may elect either the cash basis or the accrual basis of measuring income for income tax purposes, provided that she uses it consistently in subsequent years. Under either alternative, the original cost of the equipment and furniture must be written off over its five-year useful life rather than being regarded as a lump-sum expense in the first year.

Required:
1. Prepare a comparative income statement on both the cash and accrual bases, using one column for each basis.
2. Which basis do you prefer as a measure of Dr. Faragher's performance? Why? What is the justification for the government's allowing the use of the cash basis for income tax purposes?

☐ Understanding Published Financial Reports

17–37. **BALANCE SHEET EFFECTS.** The Bank of America showed the following items (among others) on its balance sheet at December 31, 19X1:

Cash	$ 947,000,000
Total deposits	$6,383,000,000

Required:
1. Suppose you made a deposit of $1,000 in the bank. How would each of the bank's assets and equities be affected? How much would each of your personal assets and equities be affected? Be specific.

2. Suppose a savings and loan association makes an $800,000 loan to a local hospital for remodeling. What would be the effect on each of the association's assets and equities immediately after the loan is made? Be specific.

3. Suppose you borrowed $10,000 from the Household Finance Company on a personal loan. How would such a transaction affect each of your personal assets and equities?

17–38. PREPARE BALANCE SHEET. Crown Zellerbach Company is a large producer of timber, wood products, pulp, and paper. A recent annual report included the following balance sheet items at December 31 (in thousands of dollars):

Various notes payable	$ 563,213
Cash	(1)
Total shareholders' equity	(2)
Total liabilities	(3)
Accounts receivable	230,370
Capital stock	140,061
Inventories	305,609
Accounts payable	138,211
Properties	1,151,742
Additional shareholders' equity	822,380
Other assets	272,820
Other liabilities	299,844
Total assets	1,963,709

Required:

Prepare a condensed balance sheet, including amounts for

1. Cash. What do you think of its relative size?
2. Total shareholders' equity.
3. Total liabilities.

17–39. NET INCOME AND RETAINED INCOME. McDonald's Corporation is a well-known fast-food restaurant company. The following data are from a recent annual report (in thousands):

McDonald's Corporation

Retained earnings, end of year	$2,146,736	Dividends	$ 70,006
Revenues	3,414,798	General administrative and selling expenses	380,014
Interest expense	122,019	Depreciation	178,133
Income tax expense	318,400	Retained earnings beginning of year	1,817,653
Food and paper	949,422		
Wages and salaries	540,801	Other operating expenses	458,447
Rent	78,473		

Required:

1. Prepare (a) an income statement and (b) a statement of retained income for the year.
2. Comment briefly on the relative size of the cash dividend.

17–40. THE CASE OF THE PRESIDENT'S WEALTH. This is a classic case in accounting. From the *Chicago Tribune*, August 20, 1964:

☐ Accountants acting on President Johnson's orders today reported his family wealth totaled $3,484,098.

The statement of capital, arrived at through conservative procedures of evaluation, contrasted with a recent estimate published by *Life* magazine, which put the total at 14 million dollars.

The family fortune, which is held in trust while the Johnsons are in the White House, was set forth in terms of book values. The figures represent original cost rather than current market values on what the holdings would be worth if sold now.

Announced by the White House press office, but turned over to reporters by a national accounting firm at their Washington branch office, the financial statement apparently was intended to still a flow of quasi-official and unofficial estimates of the Johnson fortune. . . .

ASSETS	
Cash	$ 132,547
Bonds	398,540
Interest in Texas Broadcasting Corp.	2,543,838
Ranch properties and other real estate	525,791
Other assets, including insurance policies	82,054
Total assets	$3,682,770

LIABILITIES AND CAPITAL	
Note payable on real estate holding, 5% due 1971	$ 150,000
Accounts payable, accrued interest, and income taxes	48,672
Total liabilities	$ 198,672
Capital	$3,484,098

The report apportions the capital among the family, with $378,081 credited to the President; $2,126,298 to his wife Claudia T., who uses the name Lady Bird; $490,141 to their daughter Lynda Bird; and $489,578 to their daughter Luci Baines.

The statement said the family holdings—under the names of the President, his wife, and his two daughters, Lynda Bird and Luci Baines—had increased from $737,730 on January 1, 1954, a year after Johnson became Democratic leader of the Senate, to $3,484,098 on July 31 this year, a gain of $2,746,368. . . .

A covering letter addressed to Johnson said the statement was made "in conformity with generally accepted accounting principles applied on a consistent basis."

By far the largest part of the fortune was listed as the Johnsons' interest in the Texas Broadcasting Corporation, carried on the books as worth $2,543,838.

The accountants stated that this valuation was arrived at on the basis of the cost of the stock when the Johnsons bought control of the debt-ridden radio station between 1943 and 1947, plus accumulated earnings ploughed back as equity, less 25 percent capital gains tax.[5]

---

[5] You need not be concerned about the details of this method of accounting until you study Chapter 19. In brief, when an investor holds a large enough stake in a corporation, such investment is accounted for at its acquisition cost plus the investor's pro-rata share of the investee's net income (or net loss) minus the investor's share of dividends. For example, suppose the Texas Broadcasting Company earned $100,000 in a given year and Johnson owned 100% of the company. In this situation, the Johnson financial statements would show an increase in Interest in Texas Broadcasting Corp. of $100,000 less the $25,000 income tax that would become payable upon disposition of the investment. (Today's accountants would prefer to increase the Investment account by the full $100,000 and the liabilities by $25,000. See the Carter financial statements.)

Editorial, *Chicago Tribune*, August 22, 1964:

☐ An accounting firm acting on Mr. Johnson's instructions and employing what it termed "generally accepted auditing standards" has released a statement putting the current worth of the Lyndon Johnson family at a little less than 3½ million dollars. . . .

Dean Burch, chairman of the Republican National Committee, has remarked that the method used to list the Johnson assets was comparable to placing the value of Manhattan Island at $24, the price at which it was purchased from the Indians. The Johnson accounting firm conceded that its report was "not intended to indicate the values that might be realized if the investment were sold."

In fact, it would be interesting to observe the response of the Johnson family if a syndicate of investors were to offer to take Texas Broadcasting off the family's hands at double the publicly reported worth of the operation. . . .

Required:
1. Evaluate the criticisms, making special reference to fundamental accounting concepts or "principles."
2. The financial statements of President and Mrs. Carter are shown in an accompanying exhibit. Do you prefer the approach taken by the Carter statements as compared with the Johnson statements? Explain.

Perry, Chambliss, Sheppard and Thompson
Certified Public Accountants
Americus, Georgia
JAMES EARL CARTER, JR. AND ROSALYNN CARTER
STATEMENT OF ASSETS AND LIABILITIES
DECEMBER 31, 1977
(UNAUDITED)

ASSETS

	COST BASIS	ESTIMATED CURRENT VALUE
Cash	$204,979.04	$204,979.04
Cash Value of Life Insurance	45,506.88	45,506.88
U.S. Savings Bonds, Series E	1,425.00	1,550.94
Loan Receivable	50,000.00	50,000.00
Overpayment of 1977 Income Taxes	51,121.27	51,121.27
Personal Assets Trust—Note 3	151,097.87	557,717.11
Residence, Plains, Georgia	45,000.00	54,090.00
Lots in Plains, Georgia	1,100.00	3,155.00
Automobile	4,550.75	2,737.50
Total Assets	$554,780.81	$970,857.74

LIABILITIES

	COST BASIS	ESTIMATED CURRENT VALUE
Miscellaneous Accounts Payable, Estimated	$ 1,500.00	$ 1,500.00
Provision for Possible Income Taxes on Unrealized Asset Appreciation—Note 4	0	174,000.00
Total Liabilities	$ 1,500.00	$175,500.00
Excess of Assets over Liabilities	$553,280.81	$795,357.74

NOTES TO FINANCIAL STATEMENTS

NOTE 1: Estimated market values of real estate are 100% of the fair market values as determined by county tax assessors except as to certain assets held in the personal assets trust, which are stated at book value.

NOTE 2: This statement excludes campaign fund assets and liabilities.

NOTE 3: The interest in Carter's Warehouse partnership, the capital stock of Carter's Farms, Inc., the remainder interest in certain real estate and securities and a commercial lot in Plains, Georgia, were transferred to a personal assets trust in January, 1977. The primary purpose of the trust is to isolate the President from those of his assets which are most likely to be affected by actions of the federal government. The President was responsible as a general partner for obligations of the partnership before his partnership interest was transferred to the trust. The transfer to the trust did not affect such responsibility.

NOTE 4: If the market values of the assets were realized, income taxes would be payable at an uncertain rate. A provision for such income taxes has been made at rates in effect for 1977.

NOTE 5: The amounts in the accompanying statements are based principally upon the accrual basis method of accounting.

Chapter 18

UNDERSTANDING CORPORATE

ANNUAL REPORTS—PART ONE

LEARNING OBJECTIVES

When you have finished studying this chapter, you should be able to:

1. Identify the meanings and relationships of the main types of items in the balance sheet of a corporation.
2. Measure the financial effects of various transactions.
3. Distinguish between reserves and funds in the financial statements.
4. Identify the meanings and relationships of the principal elements in the income statement of a corporation.
5. Identify the meanings and relationships of the elements in the statement of retained earnings.
6. Prepare the statement of changes in financial position.
7. Identify the relationship of depreciation to the statement of changes in financial position and indicate the effects of depreciation on income taxes, cash, and working capital.

Accounting is often called the language of business. It is a language with a special vocabulary aimed at conveying the financial story of organizations. To understand corporate annual reports, you must learn at least the fundamentals of the language. This chapter presents the basic meanings of many terms and relationships used in the financial statements found in annual reports.

Accounting is commonly misunderstood as being a precise discipline that produces exact measurements of a company's financial position and performance. As a result, many individuals regard accountants as little more than mechanical tabulators who grind out financial reports after processing an imposing amount of detail in accordance with stringent predetermined rules. Although accountants do take methodical steps with masses of data, their rules of measurement allow much room for judgment. Managers and accountants who exercise this judgment have more influence on financial reporting than is commonly believed.

This chapter extends the discussion of the financial statements in the preceding chapter. It also introduces the Statement of Changes in Financial Position. Additional coverage (including investments in subsidiaries, consolidated statements, financial ratios, accounting for inventories, and accounting for inflation) will be found in the final two chapters of this book.

CLASSIFIED BALANCE SHEET

Exhibit 18–1 is a classified balance sheet for Chesebrough-Pond's Inc., maker of such products as Ragu Spaghetti sauces, Vaseline petroleum jelly, and Prince tennis racquets. There are five main sections: current assets, noncurrent assets, current liabilities, noncurrent liabilities, and shareholders' equity. Be sure to locate each of these items in Exhibit 18–1 when you read the description of the item in the following pages.

☐ **Current Assets**

Current assets are cash plus assets that are reasonably expected to be converted to cash or sold or consumed during the normal operating cycle. They are the assets directly involved in the operating cycle, including cash; temporary investments in marketable securities; receivables of nearly all kinds, including installment accounts and notes receivable if they conform to normal industry practice and terms; inventories; and prepaid expenses.

Most organizations exist to provide goods or services to those who want them. Whether they are profit seeking or not, they typically follow a similar,

EXHIBIT 18–1 *(Place a clip on this page for easy reference.)*

CHESEBROUGH-POND'S INC.
Balance Sheet

(IN THOUSANDS)	DECEMBER 31 1984	DECEMBER 31 1983
Assets		
Current assets		
Cash and short-term investments	$ 100,566	$ 88,014
Accounts receivable	365,054	335,516
Inventories	502,894	396,515
Prepaid expenses	37,931	30,566
Total current assets	1,006,445	850,611
Noncurrent assets		
Property, plant, and equipment		
At cost	508,748	399,209
Less: Accumulated depreciation	179,426	157,365
Net property, plant, and equipment	329,322	241,844
Goodwill and trademarks	58,451	38,897
Investments and other assets	53,092	40,558
Total noncurrent assets	440,865	321,229
Total assets	$1,447,310	$1,171,910
Liabilities and Shareholders' Equity		
Current liabilities		
Notes payable	$ 265,952	$ 130,408
Accounts payable and accrued liabilities	208,649	168,277
Income taxes payable	28,810	30,751
Current portion of long-term debt	3,516	10,852
Total current liabilities	506,927	340,288
Noncurrent liabilities		
Long-term debt	243,929	131,784
Other noncurrent liabilities	44,148	32,923
Deferred income taxes	26,689	16,970
Total noncurrent liabilities	314,766	181,677
Total liabilities	821,693	521,965
Shareholders' equity		
Common stock	36,180	36,112
Additional paid-in capital	96,331	95,079
Retained earnings	659,152	606,834
Foreign currency translation adjustment	(89,892)	(67,408)
	701,771	670,617
Less: Treasury stock, at cost	76,154	20,672
Total shareholders' equity	625,617	649,945
Total liabilities and shareholders' equity	$1,447,310	$1,171,910

somewhat rhythmic, pattern of economic activity. An **operating cycle** (also called a **working-capital cycle** or *cash cycle* or *earnings cycle*) is the time span during which cash is spent to acquire goods and services that are used to produce the organization's output, which in turn is sold to customers, who in turn pay for their purchases with cash. Consider a retail business. Its operating cycle is illustrated in the following diagram (figures assumed):

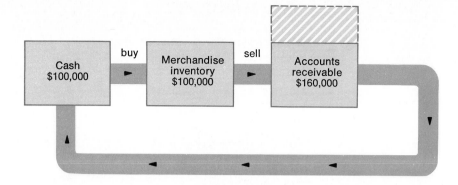

The box for Accounts Receivable (amounts owed to the business by customers) is larger than the other two boxes because the objective is to sell goods at a price higher than acquisition cost. Retailers and nearly all other businesses buy goods and services and perform acts (such as placing them in a convenient location or changing their form) that merit selling prices that they expect will yield a profit. The total amount of profit earned during a particular period depends on the excess of the selling prices over the costs of the goods and additional expenses and on the speed of the operating cycle.

Accountants sometimes assume that an operating cycle is one year. But several operating cycles may occur during one year. In contrast, some businesses need more than one year to complete a single cycle. The distillery, tobacco, and lumber industries are examples. Inventories in such industries are nevertheless regarded as current assets. Similarly, installment accounts and notes receivable are typically classified as current assets even though they will not be fully collected within one year.

Some comments on specific kinds of current assets follow:

Cash consists of bank deposits in checking accounts plus money on hand. Incidentally, visualize how a deposit would be accounted for by a bank. Its cash will increase and its liabilities increase in the form of "Deposits," which are really "Deposits Payable."

Short-term investments represent an investment of excess cash not needed immediately.[1] The idea is to get earnings on otherwise idle cash. The money is typically invested in securities that are highly liquid (easily convertible into cash) and that have relatively stable prices, such as short-term notes or government bonds. These securities are usually shown at cost or market price, whichever is lower. The market price is disclosed parenthetically if it is above cost.

Accounts receivable is the total amount owed to the company by its customers. Because some accounts will ultimately be uncollectible, the total is reduced by an allowance or provision for doubtful accounts (that is, possible "bad debts" arising from credit extended to customers who do not pay). The difference represents the net amount that will probably be collected.

---

[1] Short-term investments are frequently called *marketable securities*, but this is a misnomer. Strictly speaking, marketable securities may be held for either a short-term or a long-term purpose. Short-term investments should be distinguished from *long-term investments* in the capital stock or bonds of other companies. The latter are noncurrent assets.

EXHIBIT 18–2

CHESEBROUGH-POND'S INC.
Footnote 5 to the 1984 Financial Statements

5. Property, Plant, and Equipment (in thousands)

	1984	1983
Land	$ 12,013	$ 9,844
Buildings and building improvements	142,008	114,598
Machinery and equipment	317,619	247,170
Leasehold improvements	21,584	16,726
Construction-in-progress	15,524	10,871
	$508,748	$399,209
Less: Accumulated depreciation	179,426	157,365
Net property, plant, and equipment	$329,322	$241,844

Included are property, plant, and equipment relative to capital leases (in thousands) of:

	1984	1983
Cost	$ 39,415	$ 28,368
Less: Accumulated depreciation	10,057	8,424
Net property, plant, and equipment	$ 29,358	$ 19,944

Inventories consist of merchandise, finished products of manufacturers, goods in the process of being manufactured, and raw materials. These are frequently carried at cost or market (defined as replacement cost), whichever is lower. Cost of manufactured products normally is composed of raw material plus the costs of its conversion (direct labor and manufacturing overhead) into a finished product.

Determining the cost of inventories is not always as easy as it may seem at first glance. When the total cost of goods purchased or produced by a company is measured, how should it be allocated between the goods sold (an expense) and the goods still on hand (an asset)? This is easy if the products are readily identifiable, like the cars of an automobile dealer or the expensive merchandise of a jewelry store. Advanced data processing systems have made such specific identification possible for more and more organizations. But it is still expensive to have an elaborate identification system for goods that are purchased and sold in vast numbers and variety. Chapter 20 discusses the assumptions that are made to simplify inventory measurement.

Prepaid expenses are usually unimportant in relation to other assets. They are short-term prepayments or advance payments to suppliers. Examples are prepayment of rent and insurance premiums for coverage over the coming operating cycle. They belong in current assets because if they were not present, more cash would be needed to conduct current operations.[2]

☐ Property, Plant, and Equipment

Property, plant, and equipment are sometimes called **fixed assets** or plant assets. Because they are physical items that can be seen and touched, they are often called **tangible assets**. Details about property, plant, and equipment are usually found in a footnote to the financial statements. See Exhibit 18–2. Footnotes are an integral part of the financial statements. They contain explanations for the summary figures that appear in the statements.

Land is typically accounted for as a separate item and is carried indefinitely at its original cost.

Plant and equipment are initially recorded at cost: the invoice amount, plus freight and installation, less cash discounts. The major difficulties of measurement center on the choice of a pattern of *depreciation*—that is, the allocation of the original cost to the particular periods or products that benefit from the use of the assets.

Remember that depreciation is a process of allocation of the original cost of acquisition; it is not a process of valuation in the ordinary sense of the term. The usual balance sheet presentation does *not* show replacement cost, resale value, or the price changes since acquisition. The accounting for the latter is discussed in Chapter 20.

The amount of original cost to be allocated over the total useful life of the asset as depreciation is the difference between the total acquisition cost and the estimated **residual value** (also called **terminal disposal value** or **salvage value**). The depreciation allocation to each year may be made on the basis of time or service. The estimate of useful life, which is an important factor in determining the yearly allocation of depreciation, is influenced by estimates of physical wear and tear, technological change, and economic obsolescence. Thus, the useful life is usually less than the physical life.

There are three general methods of depreciation. By far the most common is *straight-line*, used for at least some assets by over 90% of all organizations. A small number of firms use either *accelerated* or *units-of-production* methods for some assets. (Most firms use accelerated depreciation in their financial statements prepared for the Internal Revenue Service. This is discussed later in the chapter.) The straight-line method allocates the same cost to each year of an asset's useful life. Accelerated methods allocate more of the cost to the early years and less to the later years. The units-of-production method allocates cost based on the amount of production rather than the passage of time.

---

[2] Sometimes prepaid expenses are lumped with **deferred charges** as a single amount, *prepaid expenses and deferred charges*, that appears at the bottom of the current asset classification or at the bottom of all the assets as an "other asset." Deferred charges are like prepaid expenses, but they have longer-term benefits. For example, the costs of relocating a mass of employees to a different geographical area or the costs of rearranging an assembly line may be carried forward as deferred charges and written off as expense over a three- to five-year period.

Suppose equipment with an estimated useful life of four years is acquired for $41,000. Its estimated residual value is $1,000. Exhibit 18–3 shows how the asset would be displayed in the balance sheet if a straight-line method of depreciation were used. The annual depreciation expense that would appear on the income statement each of the four years would be:

$$\frac{\text{original cost} - \text{estimated residual value}}{\text{years of useful life}}$$

$$= \frac{\$41,000 - \$1,000}{4} = \$10,000 \text{ per year}$$

In Exhibit 18–1 or 18–2 the original cost of fixed assets on the 1984 balance sheet is $508,748,000. There is **accumulated depreciation** of $179,426,000, the amount previously charged as depreciation expense, so the net property, plant, and equipment at December 31, 1984 is $508,748,000 − $179,426,000 = $329,322,000.

☐ Depreciation Is Not Cash

Depreciation is the part of an asset that has been used up. It is gone. It is not a pool of cash set aside to replace the asset. Professor William A. Paton, a leading scholar in accounting, once compared depreciation with a boy's eating of a jelly-filled doughnut (the original cost, $41,000). The boy is so eager to taste the jelly that he licks it and creates a hole in the center of the doughnut (the depreciation of $10,000 in year 1). He continues his attack on the doughnut, and the hole enlarges. The hole is the *accumulated depreciation*, the total amount eaten. The *net book value* or *carrying amount* of the asset, the part remaining, diminishes as the hole gradually becomes larger throughout the useful life of the doughnut. At the end of the useful life, the *book value* consists of the original doughnut ($41,000) less its gaping hole ($40,000), leaving a crumbly $1,000.

EXHIBIT 18–3

Straight-Line Depreciation*
(figures assumed)

	BALANCES AT END OF YEAR			
	1	2	3	4
Plant and equipment (at original acquisition cost)	$41,000	$41,000	$41,000	$41,000
Less: Accumulated depreciation (the portion of original cost that has already been charged to operations as expense)	10,000	20,000	30,000	40,000
Net book value (the portion of original cost that will be charged to future operations as expense)	$31,000	$21,000	$11,000	$ 1,000

* Other patterns of depreciation are discussed later in this chapter.

If you remember that accumulated depreciation is like a hole in a doughnut, you will be less likely to fall into the trap of those who think that accumulated depreciation is a sum of cash being accumulated for the replacement of plant assets.

If a company decides to accumulate specific cash for the replacement of assets, such cash is an asset that should be specifically labeled as a cash *fund* for replacement and expansion. Holiday Inns, Inc., had such a fund, calling it a *capital construction fund*. Such funds are quite rare because most companies can earn better returns by investing any available cash in ordinary operations rather than in special funds. Typically, companies will use or acquire cash for the replacement and expansion of plant assets only as specific needs arise.

Leasehold improvements are included in property, plant, and equipment (see Exhibit 18–2). Such improvements may be made by a lessee (tenant) who invests in painting, decorating, fixtures, and air-conditioning equipment that cannot be removed from the premises when a lease expires. The costs of leasehold improvements are written off in the same manner as depreciation; however, their periodic write-off is called *amortization*.

Natural resources such as mineral deposits are not illustrated here, but they are typically grouped with plant assets. Their original cost is written off in the form of *depletion* as the resources are used. For example, a coal mine may cost $10 million and originally contain an estimated 5 million tons. The depletion rate would be $2 per ton. If 500,000 tons were mined during the first year, depletion would be $1 million for that year; if 300,000 tons were mined the second year, depletion would be $600,000; and so forth until the entire $10 million has been charged as depletion expense.

The property, plant, and equipment account also contains an amount for capitalized leases (see Exhibit 18–2). Long-term leases that are considered to be essentially the same as purchases are accounted for by the lessee (tenant) as if the resources were purchased. An example is a 10-year lease of a machine with ownership passing to the lessee at the end of the lease. The present value of the lease payments is recorded as an asset and is depreciated as if it were the purchase price. Exhibit 18–2 shows an original cost of $39,415,000 and accumulated depreciation of $10,057,000 at the end of 1984.

Long-term investments include long-term holdings of securities of other firms. Accounting for intercorporate investments is discussed in detail in Chapter 19, pages 639–654.

☐ **Intangible Assets**

Tangible assets can be physically observed. In contrast, **intangible assets** are a class of *long-lived assets* that are not physical in nature. They are rights to expected future benefits deriving from their acquisition and continued possession. Examples are goodwill, franchises, patents, trademarks, and copyrights. In Exhibit 18–1 goodwill and trademarks total $58,451,000 at December 31, 1984.

Goodwill, which is discussed in more detail in the next chapter, is defined as the excess of the cost of an acquired company over the sum of the fair market values of its identifiable individual assets less the liabilities. For example, suppose Company A acquires Company B at a cost to A of $10 million and can assign only $9 million to various identifiable assets such as receivables, plant, and patents less liabilities assumed by the buyer; the remainder, $1 million, is goodwill. Identifiable intangible assets, such as franchises and patents, may be acquired singly, but goodwill cannot be acquired separately from a related business. This excess of the purchase price over the fair market value is called "goodwill" or "purchased goodwill" or, more accurately, "excess of cost over fair value of net identifiable assets of businesses acquired."

The accounting for goodwill illustrates how an *exchange* transaction is a basic concept of accounting. After all, there are many owners who could obtain a premium price for their companies. But such goodwill is never recorded. Only the goodwill arising from an *actual acquisition* with arm's-length bargaining should be shown as an asset on the purchaser's records.

For shareholder-reporting purposes, goodwill must be amortized, generally in a straight-line manner, over the periods benefited. The longest allowed amortization period is 40 years. The shortest amortization period is not specified, but a lump-sum write-off on acquisition is forbidden.

☐ Historical Thrust Toward Conservatism

Many managers and accountants insist that some intangible assets have unlimited lives. Nevertheless, the attitude of the regulatory bodies toward accounting for intangible assets has become increasingly conservative. For example, before 1970, the amortization of goodwill, trademarks, and franchises with indefinite useful lives was not mandatory. But in 1970 the Accounting Principles Board ruled that the values of all intangible assets eventually disappear, thus making amortization mandatory.

Before 1975, many companies regarded research and development costs as assets. Research costs were treated as deferred charges to future operations and were amortized over the years of expected benefit, usually three to six years. In 1975 the FASB banned deferral and required write-off of these costs as incurred. The FASB admitted that research and development costs may generate many long-term benefits, but the general high degree of uncertainty about the extent and measurement of future benefits led to conservative accounting in the form of immediate write-off.

☐ Liabilities

Current liabilities are existing debts that fall due within the coming year or within the normal operating cycle if longer than a year. Turn again to Exhibit 18–1. *Notes payable* are short-term debt backed by formal promissory notes held by a bank or business creditors. *Accounts payable* are amounts owed to suppliers who extended credit for purchases on open account. These purchases are ordinarily supported by signatures on purchase orders or similar business documents. *Accrued liabilities* or *accrued expenses payable* are recognized for wages, salaries, interest, and similar items. The accountant recognizes expenses as they occur in relation to the operations of a given time period regardless of when they are paid for in cash. *Income taxes payable* is a special accrued expense of enough magnitude to warrant a separate classification. The *current portion of long-term debt* shows the payments due within the next year on bonds and other long-term debt.

Some companies also list *unearned revenue*, also called deferred revenue. This occurs when cash is received before the related goods or services are delivered. For example, *Time* magazine has such an account because it is obligated to send magazines to subscribers with prepaid subscriptions.

Long-term liabilities are existing debts that fall due beyond one year. Exhibit 18–4 presents details on the long-term debts of Chesebrough-Pond's; only the total appears on the balance sheet in Exhibit 18–1. Note that all such debt is listed in total, and the payments due in the next year are deducted and listed as current liabilities. There are many kinds of long-term liabilities; the most basic types are discussed in the following paragraphs.

Secured debt provides debtholders with first claim on specified assets. Mortgage bonds are an example of secured debt. If the company is unable to meet its regular obligations on the bonds, the specified assets may be sold and the proceeds used to liquidate the obligations to the bondholders. Chesebrough-Pond's shows no secured debt.

Unsecured debt consists of **debentures,** bonds, notes, or loans, which are formal certificates of indebtedness that are accompanied by a promise to pay interest at a specified annual rate. Unsecured debtholders are general creditors, who have a general claim against total assets rather than a specific claim against particular assets.

Leases that are essentially purchases entail the recording of an asset (described earlier in this chapter) and a liability for the contracted payments. The liability is usually called *obligations under capital leases*.

EXHIBIT 18–4

CHESEBROUGH-POND'S INC.
Footnote 8 to the 1984 Financial Statements

8. Long-Term Debt (in thousands)

	December 31	
	1984	1983
Bank loans	$ 99,375	$ —
10⅝% notes due July 1990	69,104	69,087
Obligations under capital leases	26,782	21,464
Term loans	12,184	10,110
Other	40,000	41,975
	$247,445	$142,636
Less: Current portion	3,516	10,852
Total	$243,929	$131,784

Many companies issue debt that is *convertible* into common stock. Convertibility allows bondholders to participate in a company's success. Suppose convertible bonds are issued for $1,000 when the stock price is $22, with a provision that each bond can be converted into 40 common shares. If the stock price increases by 50% to $33 a share, the bondholder could exchange the $1,000 bond for 40 shares worth 40 × $33 = $1,320.

Subordinated *bonds* or *debentures* are like any long-term debt except that the bondholders are junior to the other creditors in exercising claims against assets. *Senior* debt is the opposite. If a company cannot meet its regular obligations, secured debtholders are paid first, followed by senior debtholders.

The final item listed with long-term liabilities is *deferred income taxes*. This is a rather technical and controversial item that arises because the financial statements used for reporting to shareholders differ legitimately from those used for reporting to the income tax authorities. Appendix 18 provides more details about deferred taxes.

□ Stockholders' Equity

Stockholders' equity (also called *owners' equity* or *capital* or *net worth*) as an overall class is the total residual interest in the business. It is a balance sheet difference, the excess of total assets over total liabilities. There may be many subclasses. It arises from two main sources: (1) contributed or paid-in capital and (2) retained income.

Paid-in capital typically comes from owners who invest in the business in exchange for stock certificates, which are issued as evidence of stockholder rights. Capital stock can be divided into two major classes, *common stock* and *preferred stock*. Some companies have several categories of each, all with a variety of different attributes.

All companies have **common stock.** It has no predetermined rate of dividends and is the last to obtain a share in the assets when the corporation is dissolved. Common shares usually have voting power in the management of the corporation. Common stock is usually the riskiest investment in a corporation, being unattractive in dire times but attractive in prosperous times because, unlike other stocks, there is no limit to the stockholder's potential participation in earnings.

Exhibit 18–1 shows that Chesebrough-Pond's Inc. has only common stock. However, about 40% of the major companies in the United States also have **preferred stock**. It typically has some priority over other shares regarding dividends or the distribution of assets upon liquidation. For example, suppose the preferred stock annual dividend is $5 per share. These dividends must be paid in full before any dividends are paid to any other classes of stock. Preferred shareholders do not ordinarily have voting privileges regarding the management of the corporation.

Stock frequently has a designated **par** or **legal** or **stated** value that is printed on the face of the certificate. For preferred stock (and bonds), par is a basis for designating the amount of dividends or interest. Many preferred stocks have $100 par values; therefore a 9%, $100-par preferred stock would carry a $9 annual dividend. Similarly, an 8% *bond* usually means that the investor is entitled to annual interest of $80 because most bonds have par values of $1,000. However, for common stock, par value has no practical importance. Historically, the par amount of common stock was intended only to measure the maximum legal liability of the stockholder in case the corporation could not pay its debts. Currently, par is set at a nominal amount (for example, $1) in relation to the market value of the stock upon issuance (for example, $70). It is generally illegal for a corporation to sell an original issue of its common stock below par. Shareholders typically have **limited liability,** which means that creditors cannot seek payment from them as individuals if the corporation itself cannot pay its debts.

Paid-in capital in excess of par is the excess received over the par or stated or legal value of the shares issued. This amount is also frequently called *additional paid-in capital*, as in Exhibit 18–1. Common shares are almost always issued at a price substantially greater than par. Suppose that all outstanding common shares of Chesebrough-Pond's Inc. had been issued for cash. The cumulative balance sheet effect at December 31, 1984, would be:

Cash	$132,511,000	Common stock, par value	$ 36,180,000
		Additional paid-in-capital	96,331,000
		Stockholders' equity	$132,511,000

Retained earnings, also called *retained income*, is the increase in stockholders' equity caused by profitable operations. It was explained more fully in Chapter 17. Retained earnings is the dominant item of stockholders' equity for most companies. For instance, as of January 1, 1986, R. J. Reynolds Industries had common stockholders' equity of $4,796 million, of which $4,357 million was retained income.

The *foreign currency translation adjustment* exists for companies with foreign operations. It arises from changes in the exchange rate between the dollar and the foreign currency. Further details are beyond the scope of this book.

Treasury stock is a corporation's issued stock that has subsequently been repurchased by the company and is being held for a specific purpose. Such repurchase is a decrease in ownership claims. It should therefore appear on a balance sheet as a deduction from total stockholders' equity. The stock is not retired; it is only held temporarily "in the treasury" to be distributed later, possibly as a part of an employee stock purchase plan or as an executive bonus or for use in an acquisition of another company. Cash dividends are not paid on shares held in the treasury; cash dividends are distributed only to the shares outstanding (in the hands of stockholders), and treasury stock is not outstanding stock. Treasury stock is usually of minor significance in the financial picture of a corporation.

☐ Reserves and Funds

Accountants occasionally use the term *reserve* in their reports. To a layperson, reserve normally means setting aside a specific amount of cash or securities for a special purpose such as vacations, illness, and birthday gifts. Accountants *never* use the word *reserve* to describe such an amount; instead they call such assets a **fund**. For example, a *pension fund* is cash or other highly liquid assets segregated for meeting the pension obligations. Similarly, a *sinking fund* is usually cash or securities segregated for meeting obligations on bonded debt. Holidays Inns, Inc., has a *construction fund* for building new hotels.

The word **reserve** is on the wane, but it is used frequently enough to warrant an acquaintance with its three broad meanings in accounting:

1. *Retained income reserve.* A restriction of intent or authority to *declare* dividends, denoted by a specific subdivision of retained income. The term *appropriated* or *restricted* is better terminology than reserve. Examples are reserves for contingencies (which can refer to any possible *future* losses from such miscellany as foreign devaluations of currency, lawsuits, and natural disasters) and reserves for self-insurance (which refer to possible *future* losses from fires or other casualty losses). This reserve is *not* a reduction of total retained income; it is merely an earmarking or subdividing of part of retained income.

2. *Asset valuation.* An offset to an asset. Examples: reserves for depreciation, depletion, uncollectible accounts, or reduction of inventory or investments to market value. "Allowance for . . ." is much better terminology.

3. *Liability.* An estimate of a definite liability of indefinite or uncertain amount. Examples: reserves for income taxes, warranties, pensions, and vacation pay. "Estimated liability for . . ." is much better terminology. An example of a liability reserve was provided in an annual report of Pitney-Bowes, Inc. (the major manufacturer of postage meters). It contained the following liability account: Reserve for Future Windup Costs of Discontinued Operations.

INCOME STATEMENT

☐ Use of Subtotals

Most investors are vitally concerned about a company's ability to produce long-run earnings and dividends. In this regard, income statements are more important than balance sheets. Revenue is shown first; this represents the total sales value of products delivered and services rendered to customers. Expenses are then listed and deducted. The statement can take one of two major forms: single-step or multiple-step. The single-step statement merely lists all expenses without drawing subtotals, whereas the multiple-step statement contains one or more subtotals. Exhibit 18–5 illustrates the two most common subtotals: *gross profit* and *income from operations*.

Subtotals highlight significant relationships. As explained in the preceding chapter, sometimes cost of goods sold is deducted from sales to show gross profit or gross margin. This indicates the size of the margin above merchandise costs—an important statistic for many managers and analysts.

Depreciation expense, selling expenses, and administrative expenses are often grouped as "operating expenses" and deducted from the gross profit to obtain *operating income*, which is also called *operating profit*. (Of course, cost of goods sold is also an operating expense. Why? Because it is also deducted from sales revenue to obtain "operating income.")

☐ **Operating and Financial Management**

Operating income is a popular subtotal because of the oft-made distinction between operating management and financial management. *Operating management* is mainly concerned with the major day-to-day activities that generate sales revenue (that is, using a given set of resources). In contrast, *financial management* is mainly concerned with where to get cash and how to use cash for the benefit of the entity (that is, obtaining and investing the needed capital). Examples of questions of financial management include: How much cash should be held in checking accounts? Should we pay a dividend? Should we borrow or issue common stock? The best managements perform both operating management and financial management superbly. However, many managers are better operating managers than financial managers, or vice versa.

Because interest income and expense are usually a result of financial rather than operating decisions, they often appear as separate items after operating income. In this way, comparisons of operating income between years and between companies are facilitated. Some companies make heavy use of debt, which causes high interest expenses, whereas other companies incur little debt and interest expenses. Other nonoperating items might include gains or losses from foreign exchange transactions or from disposals of fixed assets.

☐ **Income, Earnings, Profits**

Although this book tends to use *income* most often, the terms *income*, *earnings*, and *profits* are often used as synonyms. The income statement is also called the *statement of earnings*, the *statement of profit and loss*, and the *P & L statement*. Most companies, as illustrated in Exhibits 18–5 and 18–6, will use net *income* on their income statements but the term "earnings" is becoming increasingly popular because it has a preferable image. *Earnings* apparently implies compensation for honest work, whereas *income* or *profit* evidently inspires cartoonists to portray managers as greedy, evil-looking individuals.

The term *net income* is the popular "bottom line"—the residual after deducting *all* expenses, including income taxes. The term "net" is seldom used for any subtotals that precede the calculation of net income; instead, the subtotals are called "income." Thus the appropriate term is "operating income" or "income from operations," not "net operating income."

Income taxes are often a prominent expense and are not merely listed with operating expenses. Instead, income taxes are usually deducted as a separate item immediately before net income. This expense is often called "provision for income taxes," as in Exhibit 18–5.

EXHIBIT 18–5

CHESEBROUGH-PONDS INC.
Statement of Income (in thousands except per share data)

| | December 31 | |
	1984	1983
Net sales	$1,857,330	$1,685,417
Cost of products sold	935,098	806,980
Gross Profit	$ 922,232	$ 878,437
Selling, advertising, and administrative expenses	694,398	647,116
Income from operations	$ 227,834	$ 231,321
Other income (expense):		
Interest expense	(56,871)	(32,632)
Interest income	17,122	11,752
Miscellaneous, net	6,291	4,973
Total other income (expense)	$ (33,458)	$ (15,907)
Income before provision for income taxes	194,376	215,414
Provision for income taxes	74,847	87,536
Net income	$ 119,529	$ 127,878
Earnings per share	$3.40*	$3.58*

* Computation of earnings per share

	1984	1983
Net income	$119,529,000	$127,878,000
Divided by average common shares outstanding	35,132,000	35,768,000
Earnings per share	$3.40	$3.58

Income statements conclude with disclosure of *earnings per share*. Exhibit 18–5 illustrates this as the net income divided by the average number of common shares outstanding during the year.

EXHIBIT 18–6

CHESEBROUGH-POND'S INC.
Statement of Retained Earnings
For the Year Ended December 31, 1984
(in thousands of dollars)

Retained earnings, December 31, 1983	$606,834
Net income (Exhibit 18–5)	119,529
Total	726,363
Deduct: Dividends on common stock	67,211
Retained earnings, December 31, 1984	$659,152

STATEMENT OF RETAINED EARNINGS

The analysis of the changes in retained earnings is frequently placed in a separate statement, the **statement of retained earnings**, also called **statement of retained income**. As Exhibit 18–6 demonstrates, the major reasons for change in retained earnings are dividends and net income. Note especially that dividends are *not* expenses; they are not deductions in computing net income, as Chapter 17 explained in more detail. (This is a long chapter. Solve problems one through four, pages 623–624, before proceeding.)

STATEMENT OF CHANGES IN FINANCIAL POSITION

☐ **Concept of Changes Statement**

A **statement of changes in financial position** must be presented as a basic financial statement in corporate annual reports. Before becoming required in 1971, the statement was most widely known as a **statement of sources and applications of funds**. The FASB is considering a proposal that, among other things, renames it *Statement of Cash Flows*. For brevity in the ensuing discussion, we will frequently call it a **changes statement**. Many accountants call it a **funds statement;** the term is convenient, but not descriptive.

The major purpose of the statement of changes in financial position is to provide a detailed presentation of the results of financial management, as distinguished from operating management. The changes statement summarizes the financing and investing activities of the enterprise. The statement shows directly information that readers of financial reports could otherwise obtain only by makeshift analysis and interpretation of published balance sheets and statements of income and retained earnings.

Balance sheets are statements of financial position, whereas changes statements are obviously statements of *changes* in financial position. Balance sheets show the status at a day in time. In contrast, changes statements, income statements, and statements of retained earnings cover periods of time; they provide the explanations of why the balance sheet items have changed. This linkage may be depicted as shown in the accompanying diagram:

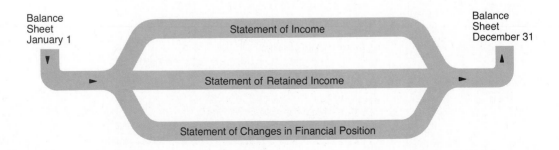

The statement of changes in financial position was devised to provide the reader with a glimpse of where the resources came from during the year and where they have gone.

☐ Focus on Working Capital

The fundamental approach is simple: (1) list activities that increased resources (*sources*) and those that decreased resources (*uses*), and (2) separate the changes caused by operations from those caused by financing and investment activities. Two definitions of *resources* are commonly used: working capital and cash.

A popular approach is to view the changes statement as an explanation of working capital changes. A focus on working capital provides a perspective on the entire natural operating cycle rather than just one part thereof (such as cash). A cash focus is discussed on pages 619–622.

Accountants define **working capital** as the excess of current assets over current liabilities. Pure, unrestricted cash is working capital in its finest sense. However, *working capital* is broader than *cash* alone. It is a "net" concept; that is, it is the *difference* between a particular category of assets and the related category of liabilities.

As used in a statement of changes in financial position, working capital is a residual concept, a relatively abstract idea. You cannot borrow it or spend it. Working capital, sometimes called net current assets, is akin to net assets (which equals stockholders' equity). The only difference is that working capital is confined to current assets minus current liabilities, whereas stockholders' equity encompasses all assets minus all liabilities.

☐ Typical Sources and Uses

Most changes statements have displayed the sources and uses of working capital, as follows:

> *Sources of working capital (or working capital provided):*
> Operations (excess of revenue over charges against revenue requiring working capital)
> Sale of noncurrent assets (plant, equipment, long-term investments in securities)
> Issuance of long-term debt
> Issuance of capital stock
> *Uses of working capital (or working capital applied):*
> Declaration of cash dividends
> Purchase of noncurrent assets (plant, equipment, long-term investments in securities)
> Reduction of long-term debt
> Repurchase of outstanding capital stock

Financial analysts have cited the following useful information as being revealed by a changes statement: the major sources from which working capital has been obtained (that is, profitable operations, borrowing, sale of capital stock); clues as to the financial management habits of the executives (that is, management attitudes toward spending and financing); the proportion of working capital applied to plant, dividends, debt retirement, and so forth; indications of the impact of working capital flows upon future dividend-paying probabilities; and an indication of the company's trend toward general financial strength or weakness.

☐ Example of Changes Statement

Changes statements can appear complex at first glance because so many different formats are used. However, the basic ideas are straightforward. Generally, as an example will show, accountants build the changes statement from the changes in balance sheet items, together with a few additional facts.

Consider the condensed 1985 financial statements of La-Z-Boy Chair Company, maker of a variety of furniture, including its well-known La-Z-Boy reclining chairs:

LA-Z-BOY COMPANY
Statement of Income
For the Year Ended April 30, 1985
(in millions)

Sales		$283
Deduct: Expenses requiring working capital	$256	
Depreciation	5	261
Net income		$ 22

LA-Z-BOY COMPANY
Balance Sheets
(in millions)

ASSETS	April 30 1985	April 30 1984	Increases (Decreases)	LIABILITIES AND OWNERS' EQUITY	April 30 1985	April 30 1984	Increases (Decreases)
Current assets:				Current liabilities	$ 34	$ 29	$ 5
Cash	$ 9	$ 16	$ (7)	Long-term liabilities	12	13	(1)
Accounts receivable	91	77	14	Total liabilities	$ 46	$ 42	$ 4
Inventories	31	27	4	Stockholders' equity	135	116	19
Total current assets	$131	$120	$11	Total liabilities and			
Property, plant, and				stockholders' equity	$181	$158	$23
equipment	50	38	12				
Total assets	$181	$158	$23				

In fiscal 1985 the company retired long-term debt of $1 million and issued capital stock for cash of $3 million. Cash dividends were $6 million. New equipment was acquired for $21 million, and old equipment was sold for cash equal to its book value of $4 million.

Because the changes statement explains the causes for the change in working capital, the first step is to compute the amount of the change (which represents the net effect, in millions):

	APRIL 30	
	1985	1984
Current assets	$131	$120
Current liabilities	34	29
Working capital	$ 97	$ 91
Net increase in working capital, $97 − $91		$6

Exhibit 18–7 illustrates how this computation is usually shown in detail in the second part of the changes statement in the section called *changes in components of working capital*.

The statement in Exhibit 18–7 gives a direct picture of where the working capital came from and where it has gone. In this instance, the excess of sources over uses increased working capital by $6 million. Without the statement of changes, the readers of the annual report would have to conduct their own analysis of the balance sheets, income statement, and statement of retained earnings to get a grasp of the impact of financial management decisions.

☐ Preparing a Changes Statement

The changes statement in Exhibit 18–7 has two major categories: *sources* (increases in working capital) and *uses* (decreases in working capital). You can prepare such a changes statement in six steps:

Step 1. Prepare a schedule of changes in the components of working capital. (See the second section of Exhibit 18–7.) The total change is the amount to be explained by the sources and uses of working capital listed on the changes statement.

Step 2. Calculate working capital provided by operations. (See Schedule A in Exhibit 18–7.) This is the first item listed under sources of working capital, $27 million for La-Z-Boy. The next section gives further details.

Step 3. Determine other sources and uses of working capital by gathering additional information (given in this case). In an actual case the keys are (a) to know the typical sources and uses and (b) to search systematically for them through the annual report. Nonoperating sources and uses generally arise from financing and investment activities.

Step 4. If all the necessary information is not directly available, analyze changes in all balance sheet items *except* current assets and current liabilities. The following rule will help to determine whether such changes are sources or uses:

EXHIBIT 18–7

LA-Z-BOY COMPANY
Statement of Changes in Financial Position
For the Year Ended April 30, 1985
(in millions)

SOURCES AND USES OF WORKING CAPITAL

Sources	
Working capital provided by operations	
(from Schedule A below)	$27
Disposal of plant and equipment	4
Issuance of additional capital stock	3
Total sources	$34
Uses	
Repayment of long-term debt	$ 1
Declaration of cash dividends	6
Acquisition of plant and equipment	21
Total uses	$28
Increase in working capital	$ 6

CHANGES IN COMPONENTS OF WORKING CAPITAL

	April 30 1985	April 30 1984	Increase (Decrease) in Working Capital
Current assets			
Cash	$ 9	$ 16	$ (7)
Accounts receivable	91	77	14
Inventories	31	27	4
Total current assets	$131	$120	$11
Current liabilities	34	29	(5)
Working capital	$ 97	$ 91	
Increase in working capital			$ 6

SCHEDULE A
WORKING CAPITAL PROVIDED BY OPERATIONS

First alternative presentation (using addback method):	
Net income (from income statement)	$ 22
Add: Charges against income not requiring working capital:	
Depreciation	5
Working capital provided by operations	$ 27
Second alternative presentation (using the straightforward method):*	
Sales	$283
Deduct: All expenses requiring working capital (detailed)	256
Working capital provided by operations	$ 27

* Although the straightforward method is frequently easier to understand, the addback method is used almost exclusively in annual reports. Be sure you see why each method produces the same figure, $27 million.

Sources of working capital	Uses of working capital
Increases in long-term liabilities or stockholders' equity	Decreases in long-term liabilities or stockholders' equity
Decreases in noncurrent assets	Increases in noncurrent assets

Consider La-Z-Boy Company. Three noncurrent accounts need to be analyzed: property, plant, and equipment; long-term liabilities; and stockholders' equity.

a. The $12 million increase in property, plant, and equipment is explained by three items in the changes statement—assets acquired, asset dispositions, and depreciation expense during the period (in millions):

$$\text{net increase} = \text{acquisitions} - \text{disposals} - \text{depreciation expense}$$

$$\$12 \quad = \quad \$21 \quad - \quad \$4 \quad - \quad \$5$$

If information about any one of the three items is unavailable, it can be calculated using the foregoing equation.

b. La-Z-Boy Company used working capital to retire long-term liabilities, decreasing both working capital and long-term liabilities by $1 million.

c. The $19 million increase in stockholders' equity was caused by three factors—issuance of common stock, net income, and dividends (in millions):

$$\text{net increase} = \text{new issuance} + \text{net income} - \text{dividends}$$

$$\$19 \quad = \quad \$3 \quad + \quad \$22 \quad - \quad \$6$$

Step 5. The difference between the total sources and uses is the net change in working capital. This change must agree with the amount calculated in Step 1, a $6 million increase for La-Z-Boy Company.

Step 6. Major investment and financing activities must be included in the changes statement even though working capital is unaffected. For example, consider the acquisition of a building in exchange for the issuance of capital stock. The changes statement would show the issuance of capital stock as a source of working capital, *as if* cash had been received. The acquisition of the building would be a use of working capital, *as if* the cash had been immediately spent for the building. La-Z-Boy Company did not have such transactions in 1985.

□ Working Capital Provided by Operations

The first major item in the sources section is **working capital provided by operations**. Sales to customers are almost always *the* major source of working capital. Correspondingly, outlays for cost of goods sold and operating expenses are almost always *the* major uses of working capital. The excess of sales over all the expenses requiring working capital is, by definition, the working capital provided by operations.

There are two ways to compute the amount of this item: the *addback method* and the *straightforward method*. Both are shown in Schedule A of Exhibit 18–7. Because it is easier to understand, please initially consider the **straightforward method**, which directly computes working capital provided by operations as shown in the second alternative presentation in Schedule A: sales of $283 million minus expenses of $256 million equals working capital provided by operations, $27 million. It is sometimes called the *direct method*.

An alternative, often convenient, way to compute working capital provided by operations is to begin with net income. Then adjust for those items that entered the computation of net income but did not affect working capital. This is called the **addback method** (or **indirect method**). The two methods can be compared as follows (in millions):

Sales	$283	A	
Deduct: Expenses requiring working capital	256	B	Straightforward Method
Working capital provided by operations (A − B)	$ 27	C	
Deduct: Expenses not requiring working capital, depreciation	5	D	
Net income (C − D)	$ 22	E	
Add: Expenses not requiring working capital, depreciation	5	D	Addback Method
Working capital provided by operations (E + D = A − B)	$ 27	C	

Notice that depreciation of $5 million was subtracted from working capital provided by operations to calculate net income. Therefore, $5 million must be added back to net income to measure working capital provided by operations.

As the footnote to Schedule A of Exhibit 18–7 indicates, the first alternative presentation, here called the *addback method*, is used almost exclusively in annual reports even though it may require a bit more effort to understand. The usual presentation would omit Schedule A and include its content in the body of the changes statement as follows (in millions):

Sources:	
Net income	$22
Add: Charges not requiring working capital: depreciation	5
Working capital provided by operations	$27
Other sources:	
Disposal of plant and equipment	4
Issuance of additional capital stock	3
Total sources	$34

If the addback method is somewhat more difficult to fathom, why is it used so heavily? There are two main reasons besides the unsatisfying reason: "Because we've always done it that way." First, beginning with net income shows the important link with the income statement. Second, the straightforward method (which begins with sales) can require a detailed listing of expenses that is cumbersome and duplicates much of what is already contained in the income statement. The addback method is really a shortcut computation of the target number, working capital provided by operations.

☐ Role of Depreciation

The most crucial aspect of a changes statement is how *depreciation* and other expenses that do not require working capital relate to the flow of working capital. There is widespread misunderstanding of the role of depreciation in financial reporting, so let us examine this point in detail.

Accountants view depreciation as an allocation of historical cost to expense. Therefore depreciation expense does not entail a current outflow of cash, which is the prime form of working capital. Consider again the comparison of the straightforward and addback methods on page 618. Net income is a residual; by itself, it provides no working capital. Instead of beginning with the Sales total and working down (A − B = C on page 618), accountants usually start with Net Income and add back all charges not requiring working capital (E + D = C, or $22 million + $5 million = $27 million on p. 618).

Unfortunately, the use of this shortcut method may at first glance create an erroneous impression that depreciation is, by itself, a source of working capital. If that were really true, a corporation could merely double or triple its bookkeeping entry for depreciation expense when working capital was badly needed! What would happen? Working capital provided by operations would be unaffected. Suppose that depreciation for La-Z-Boy Company were doubled (in millions):

Sales	$283
Less: All expenses requiring working capital (detailed)	256
Working capital provided by operations	$ 27
Less: Depreciation (2 × $5)	10
Net income	$ 17

The doubling affects depreciation *and* net income, but it has no direct influence on working capital provided by operations, which, of course, still amounts to $27 million, the sum of net income and depreciation.

FOCUS ON CASH

☐ Computing Cash Provided by Operations

During the 1980s users of financial statements became increasingly concerned with companies' ability to pay debts. To focus on debt-paying ability, a changes statement that emphasizes changes in *cash* became popular and soon may be required by the FASB. Differences between cash-basis and working capital-basis changes statements are more of form than substance.

Since 1984 a majority of the largest firms in the United States have presented a changes statement that focuses on cash. There are many possible ways to focus on cash rather than working capital. Most companies simply adjust the working capital from operations to show cash from operations and list other sources and uses the same as in a working capital-basis statement. Compare Exhibits 18–8 and 18–7 (p. 616). The only substantive difference is the addition of a section, "Add decreases and deduct increases in noncash working capital," on the cash-basis changes statement in Exhibit 18–8.

The increases in accounts receivable and inventories mean that operating cash has been invested therein, so the resulting cash provided by operations declined. For example, cash provided by operations is diminished by the immediate reinvestment of cash collections in the expansion of inventory.

On the other hand, increases in current liabilities such as trade accounts payable, short-term bank loans, and various accruals have favorable effects

EXHIBIT 18–8

LA-Z-BOY COMPANY
Statement of Changes in Financial Position (Cash)
For the Year Ended April 30, 1985
(in millions)

SOURCES AND USES OF CASH

Sources:	
Net income	$22
Add: Charges not requiring	
working capital: Depreciation	5
Working capital provided	
by operations	$27
Add decreases and deduct	
increases in noncash	
working capital:*	
Accounts receivable	(14)
Inventories	(4)
Current liabilities	5
Cash provided by operations†	$14
Disposal of plant and equipment	4
Issuance of additional capital	
stock	3
Total sources	$21
Uses:	
Acquisition of plant and	
equipment	$21
Repayment of long-term debt	1
Payment of cash dividends	6
Total uses	$28
Decrease in cash	$ (7)
Cash, April 30, 1984	16
Cash, April 30, 1985	$ 9

* Add increases in current liabilities and decreases in current assets; deduct increases in current assets and decreases in current liabilities.

† Frequently called *cash flow from operations* or just plain *cash flow*.

on operating cash. For example, cash provided by operations is increased by a 90-day bank loan, and drains on cash are postponed when suppliers give credit instead of demanding immediate payment.

In a nutshell, when cash is tied up in inventories, it cannot be used to pay creditors. Therefore, when inventories go up, cash provided by operations goes down. In contrast, when a company has fewer receivables and more payables, it has more cash.

Some typical adjustments to convert from working capital provided by operations to cash provided by operations are:

> *Add*:
>   Increases in current liabilities
>   Decreases in noncash current assets
> *Deduct*:
>   Decreases in current liabilities
>   Increases in noncash current assets

When resources are defined as cash rather than as working capital, changes in noncash working capital become part of what *explains* the changes in resources, and only cash is left *to be explained*. In essence, the last two lines of Exhibit 18–8 (beginning and ending cash balance) serve the same function as the schedule of changes in components of working capital did in the working capital–basis statement. They confirm that the activities in the body of the statement did indeed explain the change in resources.

□ Cash Flow

Rampant inflation in the late 1970s and early 1980s engendered many criticisms of the historical cost/nominal dollar accrual measures of income and financial position. One response, as Chapter 20 describes, has been supplementary disclosures using constant dollars and current costs. Another response has been a more intense focus on cash provided by operations and a major shift toward focusing on cash rather than working capital in the statement of changes in financial position. Synonyms have arisen for *cash provided by operations*, most notably **cash flow**, which is shortened nomenclature for *cash flow from operations*. These terms are used interchangeably, but *cash flow* is used most frequently. The importance of cash flow was stressed by Harold Williams, the former chairman of the Securities and Exchange Commission quoted in *Forbes*: "If I had to make a forced choice between having earnings information and having cash flow information, today I would take cash flow information."

Some companies like to stress a *cash-flow-per-share* figure (or a working-capital-generated-per-share figure) and provide it in addition to the required earnings-per-share figure. Cash flow per share and working capital provided by operations per share are sometimes erroneously used as synonyms. Net income is an attempt to summarize management performance. Cash flow or working capital provided by operations gives an incomplete picture of that performance because it ignores noncash expenses that are just as important as cash expenses for judging overall company performance. Moreover, such reported cash flows per share say nothing about the funds needed for replacement and expansion of facilities, thus seeming to imply that the entire per-share cash flows from operations may be available for cash dividends. Because they give an incomplete picture, cash-flow-per-share figures can be quite misleading. They should be interpreted cautiously.

DEPRECIATION, INCOME TAXES, AND WORKING CAPITAL

A major objective of this chapter is to pinpoint the relationships among depreciation expense, income tax expense, cash as a major item of working capital, and accumulated depreciation. Too often, these relationships are confused. For instance, the business press frequently contains misleading quotations such as the following: "We plan to invest $3.75 million over the next year. Of that, $2 million will come from depreciation and amortization and $1.75 million from a bond issue." Accountants quarrel with such phrasing because depreciation is not itself a direct source of cash, as we saw earlier in this chapter.

To encourage investment in plant and equipment, federal income tax laws permit faster write-offs for depreciation than straight-line. These faster write-offs, called *accelerated depreciation*, take a variety of forms. For example, for most plant and equipment placed in service after 1980, the U.S. income tax laws specify an *Accelerated Cost Recovery System (ACRS)*. In essence, ACRS bases depreciation deductions on arbitrary "recovery" periods that are usually shorter than estimated useful lives. Terminal values are ignored. Moreover, ACRS spreads the depreciation deductions so that higher amounts are taken in the earlier years than in the later years of the prescribed lives.

Depreciation is a deductible noncash expense for income tax purposes. Hence the higher the depreciation allowed to be deducted in any given year, the lower the taxable income and the cash disbursements for income taxes. In short, if depreciation expense is higher, more cash is conserved and kept for various uses. Therefore, compared with the straight-line method, accelerated depreciation methods result in a higher cash balance *after* income tax. Compare an accelerated method with the straight-line method, using assumed numbers. In this case, assume that the ACRS schedules provide a $28,000 deduction instead of the $17,000 deduction under straight-line depreciation:

		STRAIGHT-LINE DEPRECIATION	ACCELERATED DEPRECIATION
(C)	Income before depreciation	$60,000	$60,000
	Depreciation deduction on income tax return	17,000	28,000
	Income before income taxes	$43,000	$32,000
(T)	Income taxes @ 40%	17,200	12,800
	Net income	$25,800	$19,200
	Net after-tax working capital provided by operations:		
C − T:	$60,000 − $17,200	$42,800	
	$60,000 − $12,800		$47,200

Some strange results occur here. The reported net income is *lower* under accelerated depreciation than under straight-line depreciation, but the cash balance is *higher*. Thus, suppose managers were forced to use one depreciation method for all purposes. Managers who are concerned about reported net income to shareholders may prefer straight-line to accelerated depreciation. This dilemma is not faced by managers in the United States, where straight-line depreciation is often used for shareholder purposes while accelerated depreciation is used for income tax purposes.

There is only one source of working capital provided by operations: *sales to customers*. As our example shows, the effect of more depreciation on cash or working capital is *indirect*: it reduces income taxes by 40% of the extra depreciation deduction of $11,000, or $4,400. Therefore accelerated depreciation keeps more cash in the business for a longer span of time because of the postponement of disbursements for income taxes.

Consider the account for accumulated depreciation. No cash is there. It is a reduction in an asset, a hole in the doughnut, regardless of whether income tax rates are zero, 20%, or 90%.

SUMMARY

This chapter explained the meaning of the account titles most often found in the major financial statements. Accountants have narrow meanings for many of their terms, including *funds*, *reserves*, *working capital*, *depreciation*, and others. In particular, the term *depreciation* is misunderstood. Unless these terms are clear, the user is likely to misinterpret financial reports.

Statements of changes in financial position, also (less accurately) called *funds statements*, are increasing in importance because they yield direct insights into the financial management policies of a company. They also directly explain why a company with high net income may nevertheless be unable to pay dividends because of the weight of other financial commitments such as plant expansion or retirement of debt.

SUMMARY PROBLEMS FOR YOUR REVIEW

☐ **Problem One**

"The book value of plant assets is the amount that would be spent today for their replacement." Do you agree? Explain.

☐ **Problem Two**

On December 31, 19X1, a magazine publishing company receives $300,000 in cash for three-year subscriptions. This is regarded as unearned revenue. Show the balances in that account at December 31, 19X2, 19X3, and 19X4. How much revenue would be earned in each of those three years?

☐ Problem Three

"A reserve for depreciation provides cash for the replacement of fixed assets." Do you agree? Explain.

☐ Problem Four

"A reserve for contingencies is cash earmarked for use in case of losses on lawsuits or fires." Do you agree? Explain.

☐ Problem Five

Examine Exhibits 18–7 (p. 616) and 18–8 (p. 620). Explain why La-Z-Boy Company's cash decreased by $7 million (as shown in Exhibit 18–8) but working capital increased by $6 million (as shown in Exhibit 18–7).

☐ Solution to Problem One

Net book value of the plant assets is the result of deducting accumulated depreciation from original cost. This process does not attempt to capture all the technological and economic events that may affect replacement value. Consequently, there is little likelihood that net book value will approximate replacement cost.

☐ Solution to Problem Two

The balance in unearned revenue would decline at the rate of $100,000 yearly; $100,000 would be recognized as earned revenue in each of three years.

☐ Solution to Problem Three

Reserve for depreciation is a synonym for *accumulated depreciation*. It is a reduction in an asset, an offset to or deduction from original cost. It is a "hole in a doughnut" and in no way represents a direct stockpile of cash for replacement.

☐ Solution to Problem Four

Reserve for contingencies is a retained income reserve, a formal restriction of intent or authority to *declare* dividends, often made voluntarily by a board of directors. Its purpose is to warn stockholders that future dividend possibilities are constrained by future possible events that might bear sad economic consequences.

Often restrictions of authority to *declare* dividends are the result of legal agreements with bondholders or other creditors who do not want resources paid to shareholders in the form of dividends until creditor claims are met.

☐ Solution to Problem Five

Most of the items in the cash-basis changes statement, Exhibit 18–8, are identical to items in the working capital-basis changes statement, Exhibit 18–7. Both statements include working capital from operations ($27 million), other sources of cash or working capital ($4 million + $3 million), and total uses ($21 million + $1 million + $6 million). These items completely explain the $6 million increase in working capital:

working capital from operations + other sources − other uses = increase in working capital
$$\$27 + (\$4 + \$3) - (\$21 + \$1 + \$6) = \$6$$

Exhibits 18–8 and 18–7 differ because the cash-basis changes statement includes increases and decreases in *noncash working capital* accounts whereas the working capital-basis statement does not. Therefore, the difference between changes in cash and changes in working capital can be explained by changes in noncash working capital. Cash was used to increase accounts receivable by $14 million and inventories by $4 million. Cash was made available by a $5 million increase in current liabilities. These three changes affect cash but not working capital:

increase in cash = increase in working capital − increase in accounts receivable
− increase in inventories + increase in current liabilities

$$-\$7 = +\$6 - \$14 - \$4 + \$5$$

HIGHLIGHTS TO REMEMBER

1. Traditionally, accountants have accounted for *costs* (measured by historical outlays) rather than *values* (measured by what might be paid or received for individual assets at the current date).
2. For a given year, the accrual basis of accounting will produce different measures of income than the cash basis.
3. Most controversies in accounting center on when revenue is earned or when costs expire and become expenses. In particular, many disputes arise over how and when the costs of inventories and equipment should be released as expenses.
4. Pinpoint the relationships of depreciation to cash. Moreover, "generally accepted accounting principles" pertain mainly to reports to shareholders. In contrast, reports to income tax authorities must be in accord with laws and regulations.

ACCOUNTING VOCABULARY

Accumulated Depreciation *p.* 603   Addback Method *618*   Cash Flow *621*   Changes Statement *612*   Common Stock *607*   Current Assets *598*   Current Liabilities *605*   Debentures *606*   Deferred Charges *602*   Fixed Assets *602*   Fund *609*   Funds Statement *612*   Goodwill *604*   Intangible Assets *604*   Legal Value *607*   Limited Liability *608*   Long-Term Liabilities *606*   Operating Cycle *599*   Par Value *607*   Preferred Stock *607*   Reserve *609*   Residual Value *602*   Salvage Value *602*   Stated Value *607*   Statement of Changes in Financial Position *612*   Statement of Retained Earnings *612*   Statement of Retained Income *612*   Statement of Sources and Applications of Funds *612*   Straightforward Method *617*   Subordinated *607*   Tangible Assets *602*   Terminal Disposal Value *602*   Treasury Stock *608*   Working Capital *613*   Working Capital Cycle *599*   Working Capital Provided by Operations *617*

APPENDIX 18: SHAREHOLDER REPORTING, INCOME TAX REPORTING, AND DEFERRED TAXES

Reports to stockholders must abide by "generally accepted accounting principles (GAAP)." In contrast, reports to income tax authorities must abide by the income tax rules and regulations. These rules comply with GAAP in many respects, but they frequently diverge. Therefore there is nothing immoral or unethical about "keeping two sets of records." In fact, it is necessary.

Keep in mind that the income tax laws are patchworks that often are designed to give taxpayers special incentives for making investments. For example, tax authorities in some countries have permitted taxpayers to write off the full cost of new equipment as expense in the year acquired. Although such a total write-off may be permitted for income tax purposes, it is not permitted for shareholder reporting purposes.

Major differences between GAAP and the U.S. tax laws are found in accounting for amortization and depreciation. For example, consider how the accounting for perpetual franchises, trademarks, and goodwill differs. Their acquisition costs must be amortized for shareholder reporting. However, the Internal Revenue Service will not allow amortization because such assets have indefinite useful lives. Tax reporting and shareholder reporting are *required* to differ.

Depreciation causes the largest differences between tax and shareholder reporting in the United States. Most companies use straight-line depreciation for reporting to shareholders. Why? Managers believe that it best matches expenses with revenues. But companies use accelerated depreciation for tax reporting. Why? It postpones (or

EXHIBIT 18–9

Illustration of Deferred Taxes

	19X5	19X6	Total
Income Statement for Tax Purposes			
Revenue	$100,000	$100,000	200,000
Expenses, except depreciation	80,000	80,000	160,000
Depreciation	20,000	0	20,000
Operating income	$ 0	$ 20,000	$ 20,000
Taxes payable @ 40%	$ 0	$ 8,000	$ 8,000
Income Statement for Shareholder Reporting			
Revenue	$100,000	$100,000	$200,000
Expenses, except depreciation	80,000	80,000	160,000
Depreciation	10,000	10,000	20,000
Operating income	$ 10,000	$ 10,000	$ 20,000
Less income taxes:			
Paid or payable almost immediately	0	8,000	8,000
Deferred	4,000	(4,000)	0
Net income	$ 6,000	$ 6,000	$ 12,000

	DECEMBER 31	
	19X5	19X6
Balance sheet effect		
Liability: Deferred income taxes	$4,000	$0

defers) tax payments. Congress provided this deferral opportunity to motivate companies to increase their investment.

For reporting to shareholders, accountants must match income tax expense with the revenues and expenses that caused the taxes. When revenues and expenses on the statement to tax authorities differ from the revenues and expenses on the shareholders' report, deferred taxes can arise.

Consider a simple example. The total depreciation on a company's only asset over a two-year period, 19X5–19X6, was $20,000. Revenue was $100,000 each year, expenses (other than depreciation) were $80,000, and the tax rate was 40%. For tax purposes, the entire $20,000 of depreciation was charged as an expense in 19X5; for shareholder reporting, $10,000 was charged each year. Such differences in timing of expenses are completely legitimate.

Exhibit 18–9 illustrates tax deferral. Total operating income over the two years was $20,000, and total taxes were $8,000. According to the tax law, all $20,000 of operating income and $8,000 of taxes applied to 19X6. In contrast, for financial reporting, half of the operating income was recognized each year; therefore, half of the taxes should be recognized each year. $4,000 of taxes were related to 19X5 revenues and expenses, but the *payment* was postponed (*deferred*) to 19X6. A $4,000 *expense* for deferred taxes was included on the 19X5 financial reporting income statement, and the obligation for future payment of the tax was listed with the liabilities on the balance sheet. In 19X6 $4,000 of tax *expense* was again related to the revenues and expenses of the period. However, the tax *payment* was $8,000. The payment covers the $4,000 expense for 19X6 and pays off the $4,000 of taxes deferred from 19X5.

FUNDAMENTAL ASSIGNMENT MATERIAL

☐ General Coverage

Note: Instructors who prefer to focus on cash rather than working capital may wish to assign one or more of Problems 18–2, 18–54, and 18–55.

18–1. **CHANGES STATEMENT.** (Alternate is 18–51.) The Redondo Company has the following balance sheets (in millions):

	AS OF DECEMBER 31			AS OF DECEMBER 31	
	19X7	19X6		19X7	19X6
Current assets (detailed)	$ 90	$ 80	Current liabilities (detailed)	$ 50	$ 45
Fixed assets (net of depreciation)	65	40	Long-term debt	5	—
Goodwill	5	10	Stockholders' equity	105	85
	$160	$130		$160	$130

Net income in 19X7 was $26 million. Cash dividends paid were $6 million. Depreciation was $7 million. Half the goodwill was amortized. Fixed assets of $32 million were purchased.

Required: | Prepare a statement of changes in financial position using a focus on working capital.

18–2. PREPARE A CASH-BASIS CHANGES STATEMENT. (Problem 18–53 is an extension of this problem.) Galvez Company had net income of $80,000 on sales of $990,000 in 19X3. The statement of changes in financial position for 19X3 was (in thousands):

SOURCES AND USES OF WORKING CAPITAL		
Sources		
Working capital provided by operations		$200
Issuance of additional capital stock		400
Total sources		$600
Uses		
Redemption of long-term debt	$400	
Acquisition of plant and equipment	300	
Payment of cash dividends	100	
Total uses		800
Decrease in working capital		$(200)

CHANGES IN COMPONENTS OF WORKING CAPITAL

	DECEMBER		Increase (Decrease) in Working
	19X3	19X2	Capital
Current assets			
Cash	$ 20	$ 60	$ (40)
Accounts receivable	240	150	90
Inventories	450	350	100
Total current assets	$710	$560	$ 150
Current liabilities			
Accounts payable	$560	$300	$(260)
Accrued payables	100	10	(90)
Total current liabilities	$660	$310	$(350)
Working capital	$ 50	$250	
Decrease in working capital			$(200)

Required: | Prepare a statement of changes in financial position that focuses on cash. Point out the differences between your cash-basis statement and the given working capital-basis statement.

18–3. DEPRECIATION AND WORKING CAPITAL. Delahanty Company has the following data for 19X5: all expenses requiring working capital, $630,000; depreciation, $80,000; sales, $910,000. Ignore income taxes.

Required: | Compute working capital provided by operations and net income. Assume that depreciation is tripled. Compute working capital provided by operations and net income.

18–4. BALANCE SHEET FORMAT. Georgia-Pacific Corporation, one of the world's largest forest products companies, lists the following approximate balances on its balance sheet for January 1, 1986 (in millions):

Land, buildings, machinery, and equipment, at cost	$4,741
Common stock	83
Cash	62
Commercial paper and other short-term notes payable	104
Preferred stock	156
Receivables	569
Prepaid expenses	26
Accumulated depreciation	(2,135)
Accounts payable	276
Additional paid-in capital	1,004
Inventories	634
Other assets	165
Accrued compensation, interest, and other payables	320
Timber and timberlands, net	804
Deferred income taxes	606
Long-term debt	1,257
Retained earnings	?

Required: Prepare a balance sheet in proper form for Georgia-Pacific. Include the proper amount for retained earnings.

18–5. **CASH AND WORKING CAPITAL PROVIDED BY OPERATIONS.** The 1985 annual report of Knight-Ridder Newspapers, Inc. included the following items in its consolidated statement of changes in financial position (in thousands):

Net increase in noncash working capital	$ 23,083
Decrease in cash	17,374
Cash provided by operations	220,113
Dividends paid to stockholders	46,077

Required: Compute the working capital provided by operations.

ADDITIONAL ASSIGNMENT MATERIAL

☐ General Coverage

18–6. "The operating cycle for a company is one year." Do you agree? Why?

18–7. Why is the term *marketable securities* a misnomer?

18–8. Why should short-term prepaid expenses be classified as current assets?

18–9. Enumerate the items most commonly classified as current assets.

18–10. "Sometimes 100 shares of stock should be classified as current assets and sometimes not." Explain.

18–11. "Accumulated depreciation is a hole in a doughtnut." Explain.

18–12. "Accumulated depreciation is a sum of cash being accumulated for the replacement of fixed assets." Do you agree? Explain.

18–13. "Most companies use straight-line depreciation, but they should use accelerated depreciation." Criticize this quote.

18–14. Criticize: "Depreciation is the loss in value of a fixed asset over a given span of time."

18–15. What factors influence the estimate of useful life in depreciation accounting?

18–16. "Accountants sometimes are too concerned with physical objects or contractual rights." Explain.

18–17. "Goodwill may have nothing to do with the personality of the manager or employees." Do you agree? Explain.

18–18. Why are intangible assets and deferred charges usually swiftly amortized?

18–19. "Asset valuation reserves are created by charges to stockholders' equity." Do you agree? Explain.

18–20. "ACRS helps conserve cash." Do you agree? Explain.

18–21. What are the three major types of reserves?

18–22. What is a subordinated debenture?

18–23. What is the role of a par value of stock or bonds?

18–24. "Common shareholders have limited liability." Explain.

18–25. "Treasury stock is negative stockholders' equity." Do you agree? Explain.

18–26. "The statement of changes in financial position, more recently called the statement of sources and uses of funds, is an optional statement included by most companies in their annual reports." Do you agree? Explain.

18–27. The changes statement that focuses on cash is becoming more popular. Why?

18–28. Name the three types of activities summarized in the changes statement.

18–29. "The schedule of changes in components of working capital is an integral part of the statement of changes in financial position." Do you agree? Explain.

18–30. Why is the addback method used so much in practice?

18–31. "Cash flow per share (or working capital provided by operations per share) can be downright misleading." Why?

18–32. What are the major sources of working capital? Applications?

18–33. What types of insights are provided by a changes statement?

18–34. What is working capital?

18–35. What are some examples of expenses and losses not affecting working capital?

18–36. What are the two major ways of computing working capital provided by operations?

18–37. "The ordinary purchase of inventory has no effect on working capital." Why?

18–38. "Net losses lead to decreases in working capital." Do you agree? Explain.

18–39. "Depreciation is usually a big source of working capital." Do you agree? Explain.

18–40. What are some weaknesses of the idea that funds are working capital?

18–41. Give the two common definitions of *funds* in changes statements.

18–42. What is the major difference between a statement of changes in financial position that focuses on cash and a statement that focuses on working capital?

18–43. An asset with a book value of $80,000 was sold for $100,000. The gain of $20,000 was included in income. Correct the following sources section of the changes statement:

Sources:	
Net income	$250,000
Plus: Depreciation	70,000
Working capital provided by operations	$320,000
Proceeds from sale of equipment	100,000
Total sources	$420,000

18–44. Indicate whether each of the following is a source of working capital, a use of working capital, or neither:
(a) Sale of a machine for $15,000
(b) Retire $75,000 of long-term debt
(c) Depreciation of $18,000
(d) Purchase land for $120,000
(e) Issue capital stock for $70,000
(f) Receive payment of $5,000 on accounts receivable
(g) Pay $20,000 of cash dividends
(h) Pay $7,000 of accounts payable
(i) Purchase treasury shares for $4,000

18–45. Consider the nine transactions in Problem 18–44. Indicate whether each is a source of *cash*, a use of *cash*, or neither.

18–46. What are the effects on working capital flows of the following transaction: The purchase of fixed assets at a cost of $150,000, of inventories at a cost of $200,000, and of receivables at a cost of $50,000, paid for by the assumption of a $70,000 mortgage on the fixed assets and the giving of a 90-day promissory note for $330,000.

18–47. The net income of the LaCrosse Company was $1.2 million. Included on the income statement are the following:

Uninsured loss of inventory, by flood (classified as a part of operating expenses)	$320,000
Gain on the sale of equipment	200,000
Dividend income	10,000
Interest income, including $5,000 not yet received	20,000
Amortization of patents	50,000
Depreciation	360,000

Compute the working capital provided by operations, assuming that interest and dividend income are a part of operating income.

18–48. "The presence of a deferred tax account on the liabilities side of the balance sheet means that cumulative tax payments have exceeded the cumulative tax expense charged on financial reports to shareholders." Do you agree?

18–49. BALANCE SHEET CLASSIFICATION OF RESERVES AND FUNDS. Designate whether each of the following is essentially an asset account (A), asset valuation account (AV), liability account (L), or retained earnings account (R):
(1) Reserve for sinking fund
(2) Reserve for vacation pay
(3) Reserve for possible future losses in foreign operations
(4) Sinking fund for retirement of bonds
(5) Reserve for employees' bonuses
(6) Reserve for purchases of other companies
(7) Construction fund
(8) Reserve for impending economic recession
(9) Reserve for replacement of facilities at higher price levels
(10) Reserve to reduce investments from cost to market value

18–50. MEANING OF BOOK VALUE. The Bavarian Properties Company purchased an office building near Munich 20 years ago for 1 million Deutsche marks (DM), DM 200,000 of which was attributable to land. The mortgage has been fully paid. The current balance sheet follows:

			Stockholders'	
Cash		DM 400,000	equity	DM 760,000
Land		200,000		
Building at cost	DM 800,000			
Accumulated depreciation	640,000			
Book value		160,000		
Total assets		DM 760,000		

The company is about to borrow DM 1.8 million on a first mortgage to modernize and expand the building. This amounts to 60% of the combined appraised value of the land and building before the modernization and expansion.

Required: Prepare a balance sheet after the loan is made and the building is expanded and modernized but before any further depreciation is charged. Comment on its significance.

18–51. CHANGES STATEMENT AND ANALYSIS OF GROWTH. (Alternate is 18–1.) The Aztec Company has the following balance sheets (in millions):

	DECEMBER 31			DECEMBER 31	
	19X7	19X6		19X7	19X6
Current assets:			Current liabilities		
Cash	$ 3	$ 10	(detailed)	$105	$ 30
Receivables, net	60	30	Long-term debt	150	—
Inventories	100	50	Stockholders' equity	208	160
Total current assets	$163	$ 90			
Plant assets (net of accumulated depreciation)	300	100	Total liabilities and		
Total assets	$463	$190	stockholders' equities	$463	$190

Net income for 19x7 was $54 million. Cash dividends paid were $6 million. Depreciation was $20 million. Fixed assets were purchased for $220 million, $150 million of which was financed via the issuance of long-term debt outright for cash.

Renee Alvarez, the president and majority stockholder, was a superb operating executive. She was imaginative and aggressive in marketing and ingenious and creative in production. But she had little patience with financial matters. After examining the most recent balance sheet and income statement she muttered, "We've enjoyed ten years of steady growth; 19X7 was our most profitable ever. Despite such profitability, we're in the worst cash position in our history. Just look at those current liabilities in relation to our available cash! This whole picture of the more you make, the poorer you get just does not make sense. These statements must be cockeyed."

Required:
1. Prepare a statement of changes in financial position (sources and applications of working capital).
2. Using the changes statement and other information, write a short memorandum to Alvarez, explaining why there is such a squeeze on cash.

18–52. PREPARE CHANGES STATEMENT. The Friedlander Co. has assembled the accompanying balance sheet and income statement and reconciliation of retained earnings for 19X9.

Balance Sheet
December 31
(in millions)

	19X9	19X8	CHANGE
Assets			
Cash	$ 10	$ 25	$(15)
Accounts receivable	40	28	12
Inventory	70	50	20
Prepaid general expenses	4	3	1
Plant assets, net	202	150	52
	$326	$256	$ 70
Liabilities and shareholders' equity			
Accounts payable for merchandise	$ 74	$ 60	$ 14
Accrued property tax payable	3	2	1
Mortgage payable	50	—	50
Capital stock	100	100	—
Retained earnings	99	94	5
	$326	$256	$ 70

FRIEDLANDER CO.
Income Statement and Reconciliation of Retained Earnings
For the Year Ended December 31, 19X9 (in millions)

Sales			$250
Less: Cost of goods sold			
Inventory, Dec. 31, 19X8		$ 50	
Purchases		160	
Cost of goods available for sale		$210	
Inventory, Dec. 31, 19X9		70	140
Gross profit			$110
Less: Other expenses			
General expense		$ 51	
Depreciation		40	
Property taxes		10	101
Net income			$ 9
Dividends			4
Net income retained			$ 5
Retained earnings, Dec. 31, 19X8			94
Retained earnings, Dec. 31, 19X9			$ 99

On December 30, 19X9, Friedlander paid $42 million in cash and signed a $50 million mortgage on a new plant acquired to expand operations. Because net income was $9 million, the highest in the company's history, Sidney Friedlander, the chief executive officer, was distressed by the company's extremely low cash balance.

Required:
1. Prepare a statement of changes in financial position that focuses on working capital. You may wish to use Exhibit 18–7, page 616, as a guide. However, incorporate the First Alternative Presentation (as illustrated there in Schedule A) in the body of your changes statement. That is, the sources section should begin with net income.
2. Redo the sources section (only) in Requirement 1 by incorporating the Second Alternative Presentation (as illustrated in Schedule A of Exhibit 18–7, page

616) in the body of your changes statement. That is, the body of the sources section should begin with sales.

3. What is revealed by the statement of changes in financial position? Does it help you reduce Mr. Friedlander's distress? Why?

4. Briefly explain to Mr. Friedlander why cash has decreased even though working capital has increased and net income was $9 million.

18–53. **INTERPRET A CHANGES STATEMENT.** Refer to the facts in Problem 18–2.

Required:

1. Prepare two alternative presentations of a supporting schedule of working capital provided by operations.

2. Prepare a short memorandum summarizing the information contained in the changes statement. Present information about operations, financing activities, and investment activities.

18–54. **FOCUS ON CASH.** Refer to the facts in Problem 18–51. Prepare a statement of changes in financial position (cash). Then briefly explain to Alvarez why cash has decreased even though net income was $54 million.

18–55. **FOCUS ON CASH.** Refer to the facts in Problem 18–52. Prepare a statement of changes in financial position (cash). Then briefly explain to Friedlander why cash has decreased even though working capital has risen by $3 million and net income was $9 million.

☐ **Understanding Published Financial Reports**

18–56. **VARIOUS INTANGIBLE ASSETS.** Consider the following:

a. (i) Dow Chemical Company's annual report indicated that research and development expenditures were $507 million during 1984. How did this amount affect operating income, which was $848 million? (ii) Suppose the entire $507 million arose from outlays for patents acquired from various outside parties on December 30, 1984. What would be the operating income for 1984? (iii) How would the Dow balance sheet, December 31, 1984, be affected by (ii)?

b. On December 30, 1986, American Telephone & Telegraph Company (AT&T) acquired new patents on some communications equipment for $10 million. Technology changes quickly. The equipment's useful life is expected to be 5 years rather than the 17-year life of the patent. What will be the amortization for 1987?

c. Hilton Hotels has an account classified under assets in its balance sheet called pre-opening costs. A footnote said that these costs "are charged to income over a three-year period after the opening date." Suppose that expenditures for pre-opening costs in 1986 were $2,000,000 and the pre-opening costs account balance on December 31, 1986, was $1,840,000 and 1985, $2,390,000. What amount was amortized for 1986?

d. The Gannett Co., Inc., publisher of many newspapers including *USA Today*, purchased radio stations KKBQ-AM and FM in Houston and WDAE-AM in Tampa in 1984 for a total of $41 million. A footnote in the 1984 annual report stated that goodwill is "amortized over a period of 40 years." Assume that both purchases were on January 2 and that Gannett could assign only $33 million to identifiable individual assets. What is the minimum amount of amortization of goodwill for 1984? Could the entire amount be written off in 1984? Explain.

18–57. **VARIOUS LIABILITIES.** For each of the following items, indicate how the financial statements will be affected. Identify the affected accounts specifically.

(1) Whirlpool Corporation sells electric appliances, including automatic washing machines. Experience in recent years has indicated that warranty costs average 3.2% of sales. Sales of washing machines for October were $3 million.

Cash disbursements and obligations for warranty service on washing machines during October totaled $81,000.

(2) Pepsi-Cola Company of New York gets cash deposits for its returnable bottles. In August it received $100,000 cash and disbursed $89,000 for bottles returned.

(3) The Chase Manhattan Bank received a $1,200 savings deposit on April 1. On June 30 it recognized interest thereon at an annual rate of 5%. On July 1 the depositor closed her account with the bank.

(4) The Shubert Theater sold for $100,000 cash a "season's series" of tickets in advance of December 31 for four plays, each to be held in successive months beginning in January. (a) What is the effect on the balance sheet, December 31? (b) What is the effect on the balance sheet, January 31?

18–58. **AIRPLANE CRASH.** Recently, a DC-10 airplane owned by American Airlines crashed. It had been purchased for $18 million but was carried on American's books at $10.8 million. The plane's replacement cost, reflected in the insurance payment, was $37 million.

A news story reported: "American Airlines reported yesterday second-quarter earnings jumped 117.1 percent over those a year earlier. The quarter's profits included a $24.3 million after-tax gain from the proceeds of insurance."

Required:

1. Prepare an analysis of the facts, including the acquisition of a new airplane. Use the format of the balance sheet equation. Because of various complications, the applicable income tax was relatively small.

2. Do you think a casualty should generate a reported gain? Why?

18–59. **DEPRECIATION, INCOME TAXES, AND CASH FLOW.** The annual report of Emery Air Freight showed some balances, December 31, 1984, in the following way (in thousands):

Aircraft	$ 85,061
Other property and equipment	144,778
	$229,839
Less: Accumulated depreciation	64,360
	$165,479

The cash balance was $12,478,000.

Depreciation expense during 1984 was $23,901,000. The condensed income statement follows (in thousands):

Revenues	$817,789
Expenses (including depreciation)	753,494
Operating income	$ 64,295

For purposes of this problem, assume that all revenues and expenses, excluding depreciation, are for cash.

Required:

1. Emery used straight-line depreciation. Suppose accelerated depreciation had been $33,901,000 instead of $23,901,000. Operating income would be decreased by $10,000,000. Assume zero income taxes. Fill in the blanks in the accompanying table (in thousands of dollars).

2. Repeat Requirement 1, but assume an income tax rate of 40%. Assume also that Emery uses the same depreciation method for reporting to shareholders and to the income tax authorities.

3. Compare your answers in Requirements 1 and 2. Does depreciation provide cash? Explain as precisely as possible.

| | 1. ZERO INCOME TAXES | | 2. 40% INCOME TAXES | |
	Straight-Line Depreciation	Accelerated Depreciation	Straight-Line Depreciation	Accelerated Depreciation
Revenues	$?	$?	$?	$?
Cash operating expenses	?	?	?	?
Cash provided by operations before income taxes	?	?	?	?
Depreciation expense	?	?	?	?
Operating income	?	?	?	?
Income tax expense	?	?	?	?
Net income	$?	$?	$?	$?
Supplementary analysis:				
Cash provided by operations before income taxes	$?	$?	$?	$?
Income tax expense	?	?	?	?
Net cash provided by operations	$?	$?	$?	$?

4. Assume that Emery had used straight-line depreciation for reporting to shareholders and to income tax authorities. Indicate the change (increase or decrease and amount) in the following balances if Emery had used accelerated depreciation instead of straight-line: cash, accumulated depreciation, operating income, retained income. What would be the new balances in cash and accumulated depreciation?

5. Refer to Requirement 1. Suppose depreciation were increased by an extra $5 million under both the straight-line and the accelerated method. How would cash be affected? Be specific.

18–60. **VALUATION OF INTANGIBLE ASSETS OF FOOTBALL TEAM.** New owners acquired the Los Angeles Rams football team for $7.2 million. They valued the contracts of their 40 players at a total of $3.5 million, the franchise at $3.6 million, and other assets at $100,000. For income tax purposes, the Rams amortized the $3.5 million over five years; therefore they took a tax deduction of $700,000 annually.

The Internal Revenue Service challenged the deductions. It maintained that only $300,000 of the $7.2 million purchase price was attributable to the player contracts and that the $3.2 million of the $3.5 million in dispute should be attributed to the league franchise rights. Such franchise rights are regarded by the Internal Revenue Service as a valuable asset with an indefinite future life; therefore, no amortization is permitted for tax-reporting purposes.

Suppose the operating income for each of the five years (before any amortization) was $1 million.

Required:

1. Consider the reporting to the Internal Revenue Service. Tabulate a comparison of annual operating income (after amortization) according to two approaches (a) the Rams and (b) the IRS. What is the difference in annual operating income?
2. Consider the reporting to shareholders. Reports to shareholders by American companies do not have to adhere to the same basis used for income tax purposes. The Rams had been using a 5-year life for player contracts and a 40-year life for the league franchise rights. Tabulate a comparison of operating income (after amortization) using (a) this initial approach and (b) the approach whereby only $300,000 would have been attributed to player contracts. What is the difference in annual operating income?

3. Comment on the results in Requirements 1 and 2. Which alternative do you think provides the most informative report of operating results? Why? Prior to 1970, many companies did not amortize intangible assets.

18–61. **INTERPRETING A CHANGES STATEMENT.** Marantz Company, Inc., maker of recording and playback equipment, had a net loss of $2,584,000 for the nine months ended September 30, 1985. The following statement of changes in financial position was included in the quarterly report (in thousands):

	NINE MONTHS ENDED SEPTEMBER 30, 1985
Applications of working capital	
Absorbed by operations	$2,325
Reduction of long-term debt	96
Additions to property and equipment	77
Total applications	$2,498
Sources of working capital	
Sales of property and equipment	0
Decrease in other assets	42
Total sources	$ 42
Decrease in working capital	$2,456

During the first nine months of 1985, cash increased from $1,185,000 to $1,451,000 and property and equipment decreased from $1,740,000 to $1,558,000.

Required:

1. Calculate the charges against income in the first nine months of 1985 that did not require working capital.
2. Explain the $182,000 decrease in property and equipment.
3. Explain how cash could increase by $266,000 while working capital decreased by $2,456,000.

Chapter 19

UNDERSTANDING CORPORATE ANNUAL REPORTS—PART TWO

LEARNING OBJECTIVES

After studying this chapter, you should be able to:

1. Contrast accounting for investments using the equity method and the cost method.
2. Explain the basic ideas and methods used in the preparation of consolidated financial statements.
3. Describe how goodwill arises and is accounted for.
4. Explain and illustrate a variety of popular financial ratios.
5. Identify the major implications that "efficient" stock markets have for accounting.

This chapter continues the discussion of corporate annual reporting begun in the preceding chapter. Part One covers intercorporate investments, including consolidated statements and goodwill. Part Two covers the analysis of financial statements. *Either part may be studied independently, depending on your specific interest.*

☐ PART ONE INTERCORPORATE INVESTMENTS, INCLUDING CONSOLIDATIONS

EQUITY METHOD FOR INTERCORPORATE INVESTMENTS

Investments in the equity securities of one company by another company are accounted for in one of three different ways: cost method, equity method, or consolidation. Choice among the three depends on the type of relationship between the "investor" and the "investee." For example, the ordinary stockholder is a passive investor who follows the **cost method** whereby the initial investment is recorded at cost and dividends are recorded as income when received.

U.S. companies must use the *equity method* instead of the cost method if the investor exerts a "significant influence" over the operating and financial policies of an investee. Such influence can exist even when the investor holds 50% or less of the outstanding voting stock. The **equity method** accounts for the investment at the acquisition cost adjusted for the investor's share of dividends and earnings or losses of the investee subsequent to the date of investment. Accordingly, the carrying amount of the investment is increased by the investor's share of investee's earnings. The carrying amount is reduced by dividends received from the investee and by the investor's share of investee's losses. The equity method is generally used for a 20% through 50% interest because such a level of ownership is regarded as a presumption that the investor has the ability to exert significant influence, whereas the cost method is generally used to account for interests of less than 20%. The treatment of an interest in excess of 50% is explained in the following section, "Consolidated Financial Statements."

Compare the cost and equity methods. Suppose Company A acquires 40% of the voting stock of Company B for $80 million. In Year 1, B has a net income of $30 million and pays cash dividends of $10 million. A's 40% shares would be $12 million and $4 million, respectively. The balance sheet equation of A would be affected as follows:

	EQUITY METHOD				COST METHOD			
	ASSETS		= EQUITIES		ASSETS		= EQUITIES	
	Cash	Investments	Liab.	Stk. Eq.	Cash	Investments	Liab.	Stk. Eq.
1. Acquisition	−80	+80	=		−80	+80	=	
2. Net income of B		+12	=	+12	No entry and no effect			
3. Dividends from B	+4	−4	=	___	+4	___	=	+4
Effects for year	−76	+88	=	+12	−76	+80	=	+4

The investment account will have a net increase of $8 million for the year. The dividend will increase the cash account by $4 million.

The investment account will be unaffected. The dividend will increase the cash account by $4 million.

Under the equity method, income is recognized by A as it is earned by B rather than when dividends are received. Cash dividends do not affect net income; they increase Cash and decrease the Investment balance. In a sense, A's "claim" on B grows by its share of B's net income. The dividend is a partial liquidation of A's "claim." The receipt of a dividend is similar to the collection of an account receivable. The revenue from a sale of merchandise on account is recognized when the receivable is created; to include the collection also as revenue would be double-counting. Similarly, it would be double-counting to include the $4 million of dividends as income after the $12 million of income is already recognized as it is earned.

The major justification for using the equity method instead of the cost method is that it more appropriately recognizes increases or decreases in the economic resources underlying the investments. Further, the cost method may allow management of the investor company to unduly influence its own reported net income. How? Under the cost method, the reported net income of the investor is directly affected by the dividend policies of the investee, over which the investor might have significant influence. Under the equity method, A's reported net income could not be influenced by the manipulation of B's dividend policies.

Sears, the world's largest retailer of general merchandise, holds ownership in several companies. An example is Sears's 23% interest in Roper Corporation, a manufacturer of household appliances. Sears must use the equity method in accounting for such investments because an ownership interest in excess of 20% is presumed to be evidence of ability to exert significant influence.

CONSOLIDATED FINANCIAL STATEMENTS

U.S. companies having substantial ownership of other companies must issue *consolidated financial statements*, which are explained in this section. A reader cannot hope to understand a corporate annual report without understanding the basic assumptions underlying consolidations. Consolidated financial statements have been required for many years in the United States. Worldwide use has grown rapidly in recent years.

A publicly held business is typically composed of two or more separate legal entities that constitute a single overall economic unit. This is almost always a parent-subsidiary relationship where one corporation (the parent) owns more than 50% of the outstanding voting shares of another corporation (the **subsidiary**).

Why have subsidiaries? Why not have the corporation take the form of a single legal entity? The reasons include limiting the liabilities in a risky venture, saving income taxes, conforming with government regulations with respect to a part of the business, doing business in a foreign country, and expanding in an orderly way. For example, there are often tax advantages in acquiring the capital stock of a going concern rather than its individual assets.

Consolidated statements combine the financial positions and earnings reports of the parent company with those of various subsidiaries into an overall report as if they were a single entity. The aim is to give the readers a better perspective than could be obtained by their examining a large number of separate reports of individual companies.

☐ The Acquisition

When parent and subsidiary financial statements are consolidated, double-counting of assets and equities must be avoided via "intercompany eliminations." Suppose Company P (parent) acquired a 100% voting interest in S (subsidiary) for $213 million cash at the beginning of the year.[1] Their balance sheet accounts are analyzed in the equation form below. Investment in S is presented in the first column because it is a focal point in this chapter, not because it appears first in actual balance sheets. Figures in this and subsequent tables are in millions of dollars:

	ASSETS		= LIABILITIES +		STOCKHOLDERS' EQUITY
	Investment + in S	Cash and Other = Assets	Accounts Payable, Etc.	+	Stockholders' Equity
P's accounts, Jan. 1:					
Before acquisition		650 =	200	+	450
Acquisition of S	+213	−213 =			
S's accounts, Jan. 1		400 =	187	+	213
Intercompany eliminations	−213	=			−213
Consolidated, Jan. 1	0 +	837 =	387	+	450

[1] In this example, the purchase price equals the Stockholders' Equity of the acquired company. The preparation of consolidated statements in situations where these two amounts differ is discussed later, in the section "Accounting for Goodwill," pages 651–653.

Note that the $213 million is paid to the *former owners* of S as private investors. The $213 million is *not* an addition to the existing assets and stockholders' equity of S. *That is, the books of S are completely unaffected by P's initial investment and P's subsequent accounting thereof.* S is not dissolved; it lives on as a separate legal entity.

Each legal entity has its individual set of books; the consolidated entity does not keep a separate set of books. Instead, working papers are used to prepare the consolidated statements. A *consolidated* balance sheet reports *all* assets and liabilities of *both* the parent and the subsidiary.

Suppose a consolidated balance sheet were prepared immediately after the acquisition. The consolidated statement shows the details of *all* assets and liabilities of *both* the parent and the subsidiary. The *Investment in S* account on P's books is the evidence of an ownership interest, which is held by P but is really composed of all of the assets and liabilities of S. The consolidated statements cannot show both the evidence of interest *plus* the detailed underlying assets and liabilities. So this double-counting is avoided by eliminating the reciprocal evidence of ownership present in two places: (1) the Investment in S on P's books and (2) the Stockholders' Equity on S's books.

In summary, if the $213 million elimination of the reciprocal accounts did not occur, there would be a double-counting in the consolidated statement:

ENTITY	TYPES OF RECORDS
P	Parent books.
+ S	Subsidiary books.
= Preliminary consolidated report	No separate books, but periodically P and S assets and liabilities are added together via work sheets.
− E	"Eliminating entries" to remove double-counting
= Consolidated report to investors	

☐ After Acquisition

Long-term investments in equity securities, such as this investment in S, are carried in the *investor's* balance sheet by the equity method, the same method of accounting for an unconsolidated ownership interest of 20% through 50%, as previously described. Suppose S has a net income of $50 million for the year. If the parent company were reporting alone, it would account for the net income of its subsidiary by increasing its Investment in S account and its Stockholders' Equity account (in the form of Retained Earnings) by 100% of $50 million.

The income statements for the year would contain (numbers in millions assumed):

	P	S	CONSOLIDATED
Sales	$900	$300	$1,200
Expenses	800	250	1,050
Operating income	$100	$ 50	$ 150
Pro-rata share (100%) of subsidiary net income	50	—	
Net income	$150	$ 50	

P's parent-company–only income statement would show its own sales and expenses plus its pro-rata share of S's net income (as the equity method requires).

Reflect on the changes in P's accounts, S's accounts, and the consolidated accounts (in millions of dollars):

	ASSETS		= LIABILITIES +	STOCKHOLDERS' EQUITY
	Investment + In S	Cash and Other = Assets	Accounts Payable, + Etc.	Stockholders' Equity
P's accounts:				
Beginning of year	213 +	437 =	200 +	450
Operating income		+100 =		+100*
Share of S income	+50	=		+50*
End of year	263 +	537 =	200 +	600
S's accounts:				
Beginning of year		400 =	187 +	213
Net income		+50 =		+50*
End of year		450 =	187 +	263
Intercompany eliminations	−263	=		−263
Consolidated, end of year	0 +	987 =	387 +	600

* Changes in the retained earnings portion of stockholders' equity.

Review at this point to see that consolidated statements are the summation of the individual accounts of two or more separate legal entities. They are prepared periodically via worksheets. The consolidated entity does not have a separate continuous set of books like the legal entities. Moreover, a consolidated income statement is merely the summation of the revenues and expenses of the separate legal entities being consolidated after eliminating double-counting.[2] The income statement for P shows a $150 million net income; for S, a $50 million net income; for consolidated, a $150 million net income.

---

[2] An example of double-counting is sales by P to S (or by S to P). A consolidated income statement should not include the sale when P sells the item to S and again when S sells it to an outsider. Suppose that P bought an item for $1,000 and sold it to S for $1,200. P recognized revenue of $1,200, cost of goods sold of $1,000, and income of $200. S recorded an inventory item of $1,200. In consolidation, this transaction must be eliminated. After adding together the individual accounts of P and S, you must deduct $1,200 from revenue, $1,000 from cost of goods sold, and $200 from inventory. This eliminates the $200 of income that P recognized and reduces inventory to the original $1,000 that P paid for the item.

A consolidated balance sheet often includes an account on the equities side called **Outside Stockholders' Interest in Subsidiaries**, often also termed simply **Minority Interests**. It arises because the consolidated balance sheet is a combination of all the assets and liabilities of a subsidiary. If the parent owns, for example, 90% of the subsidiary stock, then outsiders to the consolidated group own the other 10%. The account Outside Stockholders' Interest in Subsidiaries is a measure of this minority interest. The following diagram shows the area encompassed by the consolidated statements; it includes all the subsidiary assets, item by item. The creation of an account for minority interests, in effect, corrects this overstatement. The remainder, after deducting minority interests, is P's total ownership interest.

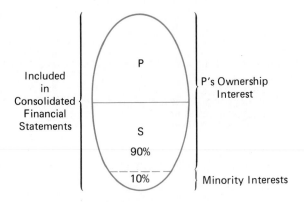

The next table, using the basic figures of the previous example, shows the overall approach to a consolidated balance sheet immediately after the acquisition. P owns 90% of the stock of S for a cost of 0.90 × $213, or $192 million. The minority interest is 10%, or $21 million. (All dollar amounts are rounded to the nearest million.)

	ASSETS		= LIABILITIES +	STOCKHOLDERS' EQUITY	
	Investment + In S	Cash and Other Assets	= Accounts Payable, Etc.	+ Minority Interest	+ Stockholders' Equity
P's accounts, Jan. 1: Before acquisition		650	= 200		+ 450
Acquisition of 90% of S	+192	−192	=		
S's accounts, Jan. 1		400	= 187		+ 213
Intercompany eliminations	−192		=	+21	−213
Consolidated, Jan. 1	0	+ 858	= 387	+ 21	+ 450

Again, suppose S has a net income of $50 million for the year. The same basic procedures are followed by P and by S regardless of whether S is 100% owned or 90% owned. However, the presence of a minority interest changes the *consolidated* income statement slightly, as follows:

	P	S	CONSOLIDATED
Sales	$900	$300	$1,200
Expenses	800	250	1,050
Operating income	$100	$ 50	$ 150
Pro-rata share (90%) of subsidiary net income	45	—	
Net income	$145	$ 50	
Outside interest (10%) in subsidiaries' net income (minority interest in income)			5
Net income to consolidated entity			$ 145

Consolidated balance sheets at the end of the year would also be affected, as follows:

	ASSETS		= LIABILITIES +	STOCKHOLDERS' EQUITY	
	Investment + In S	Cash and Other Assets =	Accounts Payable, Etc.	+ Minority Interest	+ Stockholders' Equity
P's accounts:					
Beginning of year, before acquisition		650 =	200	+	450
Acquisition	192	−192 =			
Operating income		+100 =			+100
Share of S income	+45	=			+45
End of year	237 +	558 =	200	+	595
S's accounts:					
Beginning of year		400 =	187	+	213
Net income		+50 =			+50
End of year	+	450 =	187	+	263
Intercompany eliminations	−237	=		+26*	−263
Consolidated, end of year	0 +	1,008 =	387	+ 26 +	595

* Beginning minority interest plus minority interest in net income: 21 + (0.10 × 50) = 21 + 5 = 26.

As indicated in the table, the entry to consolidate the statements eliminates $263 of stockholders' equity (on S books) and $237 of investment in S (on P books). The $26 difference is the minority interest (on consolidated statements). Thus the minority interest can be regarded as identifying the interest of those shareholders who own the 10% of the *subsidiary* stockholders' equity that is not eliminated by consolidation.

PERSPECTIVE ON CONSOLIDATED STATEMENTS

☐ Consolidated Subsidiaries

Exhibits 19–1 and 19–2 provide an overall look at how balance sheets and income statements appear in corporate annual reports. The circled items ① and ② in the exhibits deserve special mention:

① The headings indicate that these are *consolidated* financial statements.

② On balance sheets, the minority interest typically appears just above the stockholders' equity section, as Exhibit 19–1 shows. On income statements, the minority interest in net income is deducted as if it were an expense of the consolidated entity, as Exhibit 19–2 demonstrates. It generally follows all other expenses. Sometimes you will find minority interest before income taxes and sometimes after. Note that minority interest is a claim of outside stockholders' interest in a *consolidated subsidiary* company. Note also that minority interests arise only in conjunction with *consolidated* financial statements.

To help understanding, consider the following hypothetical relationships that exist for Goliath Corporation, which for more realism could be viewed as a simplified version of General Motors:

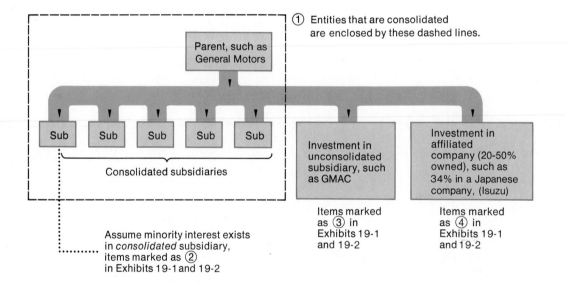

① Entities that are consolidated are enclosed by these dashed lines.

Parent, such as General Motors

Sub Sub Sub Sub Sub

Consolidated subsidiaries

Assume minority interest exists in *consolidated* subsidiary, items marked as ② in Exhibits 19-1 and 19-2

Investment in unconsolidated subsidiary, such as GMAC

Items marked as ③ in Exhibits 19-1 and 19-2

Investment in affiliated company (20-50% owned), such as 34% in a Japanese company, (Isuzu)

Items marked as ④ in Exhibits 19-1 and 19-2

☐ Unconsolidated Subsidiaries

We have already seen how the equity method is used on a parent company's books to account for its investment in subsidiaries. Most often, such investment accounts are eliminated when consolidated statements are prepared, as was just illustrated. Sometimes there is justification for not consolidating one or two subsidiaries with businesses totally different from the parent and other subsidiaries. Examples are a manufacturer's subsidiary finance companies

EXHIBIT 19–1   *(Place a clip on this page for easy reference.)*

GOLIATH CORPORATION
Consolidated Balance Sheets
As of December 31
(In millions of dollars)

ASSETS

	19X3	19X2	CHANGE
Current assets:			
Cash	$ 90	$ 56	
Short-term investments in debt securities at cost (which approximates market value)	—	28	
Accounts receivable (less allowance for doubtful accounts of $2,000,000 and $2,100,000 at their respective dates)	91	95	
Inventories at average cost	120	130	
Total current assets	301	309	(8)
Investments in unconsolidated subsidiaries	63	55	8
Investments in affiliated companies	10	9	1
Property, plant, and equipment:			
Land at original cost	50	39	11
Plant and equipment: 19X3 / 19X2	$192	$135	
Original cost	$192	$135	
Accumulated depreciation	126	112	
Net plant and equipment	66	23	
Total property, plant, and equipment	116	62	57
Other assets:			
Franchises and trademarks	15	16	
Deferred charges and prepayments	3	4	
Total other assets	18	20	(2)
Total assets	$508	$455	53

EQUITIES

	19X3	19X2	CHANGE
Current liabilities:			
Accounts payable	$100	$ 84	
Notes payable	10	—	
Accrued expenses payable	32	22	
Accrued income taxes payable	34	38	
Total current liabilities	176	144	32
Long-term liabilities:			
First mortgage bonds, 5% interest, due Dec. 31, 19X6	25	25	
Subordinated debentures, 6% interest, due Dec. 31, 19X9	30	20	
Total long-term liabilities	55	45	10
Deferred income*	12	9.3	2.7
Outside stockholders' interest in consolidated subsidiaries (minority interests)	6	5.7	0.3
Total liabilities	249	204	
Stockholders' equity:			
Preferred stock, 100,000 shares, $30 part†	3	3	
Common stock, 1,000,000 shares, $1 par	1	1	
Paid-in capital in excess of par	55	55	
Retained earnings	200	192	
Total stockholders' equity	259	251	8
Total equities	$508	$455	53

* Advances from customers on long-term contracts. Other examples are collections for rent and subscriptions, which often are classified as current liabilities.

† Dividend rate is $5 per share; each share is convertible into two shares of common stock. The shares were originally issued for $100. The excess over par is included in "paid-in capital in excess of par." Liquidating value is $100 per share.

EXHIBIT 19–2

GOLIATH CORPORATION

① Consolidated Income Statements
For the year ended December 31
(000's omitted)

	19X3	19X2
Net sales and other operating revenue	$499,000	$599,100
Cost of goods sold and operating expenses, exclusive of depreciation	468,750	554,550
Depreciation	14,000	11,000
Total operating expenses	482,750	565,550
Operating income	16,250	33,550
④ Equity in earnings of affiliates	1,000	900
③ Equity in earnings of unconsolidated subsidiary	8,000	10,000
Total income before interest expense and income taxes	25,250	44,450
Interest expense	2,450	2,450
Income before income taxes	22,800	42,000
Income taxes	12,000	21,900
Income before minority interests	10,800	20,100
② Outside stockholders' interest (minority interests) in consolidated subsidiaries' net income	300	600
Net consolidated income to Goliath Corporation*	10,500	19,500
Preferred dividends	500	500
Net income to Goliath Corporation common stock	$ 10,000	$ 19,000
Earnings per share of common stock: On shares outstanding (1,000,000 shares)	$10.00†	$19.00
Assuming full dilution, reflecting conversion of all convertible securities (1,200,000 shares)	$8.75‡	$16.25

* This is the total figure in dollars that the accountant traditionally labels net income. It is reported accordingly in the financial press.

† This is the figure most widely quoted by the investment community: $10,000,000 ÷ 1,000,000 = $10.00; $19,000,000 ÷ 1,000,000 = $19.00.

‡ Computed, respectively: $10,500,000 ÷ 1,200,000 = $8.75; $19,500,000 ÷ 1,200,000 = $16.25.

and insurance companies. For instance, a consolidated statement of General Motors (GM) and its finance company subsidiary, General Motors Acceptance Corporation (GMAC), would produce a meaningless hodgepodge, so the interest in GMAC is shown as an Investment on the GM consolidated balance sheet, even though the GM interest is 100%. A separate set of GMAC statements is included in the GM annual report.

Investments in domestic unconsolidated subsidiaries are carried via the equity method. The parent's income statement includes its share of unconsolidated subsidiary net income. This income usually appears as a separate item in the consolidated income statement (see ③ in Exhibit 19–2). Note also that the beginning balance of the Investment account in Exhibit 19–1 (see ③) was $55 million. It has risen by $8 million for the year because of the consolidated enterprise's share in the unconsolidated subsidiary net income.

Exhibits 19–1 and 19–2 indicate that the unconsolidated subsidiary did not declare dividends during 19X3. But suppose the parent received $6 million in dividends. The equity method would have the following effects:

Original investment	$55	
Share of subsidiary net income	8 →	Same as now appears in the
Balance	$63	income statement in
Dividends received	6	Exhibit 19–2
Balance, December 31, 19X3	$57	

The $6 million dividend would not appear in the income statement because it would represent a double-counting. Instead, it is regarded as a partial liquidation of the $63 million ownership "claim" as measured in the Investment account. Thus net income of the subsidiary increases this claim and dividends reduce this claim.

Investments in foreign subsidiaries are sometimes carried at cost because of a long-standing reluctance to recognize gains prior to the receipt of a corresponding amount of funds from the foreign subsidiaries. This conservative approach is an outgrowth of many unhappy experiences with wars, expropriations of assets, devaluations of currencies, and currency restrictions.

☐ Investments in Affiliates

As described earlier in the chapter, investments in equity securities that represent 20% to 50% ownership are usually accounted for under the equity method. These investments are frequently called **Investments in Affiliates** or **Investments in Associates**. For example, see the items marked as ④ in Exhibits 19–1 and 19–2. General Motors would account for its 34% investment in Isuzu in this manner. Exhibit 19–1 shows how the Investment account in the balance sheet has risen by the pro-rata share of the current earnings of affiliates, the $1 million shown in the income statement in Exhibit 19–2.

RECAPITULATION OF INVESTMENTS IN EQUITY SECURITIES

Exhibit 19–3 summarizes all the relationships depicted in the preceding exhibits. Take a few moments to review Exhibits 19–1 and 19–2 in conjunction with Exhibit 19–3. In particular, note that minority interests arise only in conjunction with *consolidated* subsidiaries. Why? Because consolidated balance sheets and income statements aggregate 100% of the detailed assets, liabilities, sales, and expenses of the subsidiary companies. Thus, if a minority interest were not recognized, the stockholders' equity and net income of the consolidated enterprise would be overstated.

In contrast, minority interests do not arise in connection with the accounting for investments in *unconsolidated* subsidiaries or investments in affiliated companies. Why? Because no detailed assets, liabilities, revenues,

EXHIBIT 19-3

Summary of Equity Method and Consolidations

ITEM IN EXHIBITS 19-1 AND 19-2	PERCENTAGE OF OWNERSHIP	TYPE OF ACCOUNTING	BALANCE SHEET EFFECTS	INCOME STATEMENT EFFECTS
①	100%	Consolidation	Individual assets, individual liabilities added together	Individual revenues, individual expenses added together
②	Greater than 50% and less than 100%	Consolidation	Same as 1, but recognition given to minority interest in liability section	Same as 1, but recognition given to minority interest near bottom of statement when consolidated net income is computed
③	Greater than 50% up to 100%, but subsidiary in totally different business, so not consolidated	Equity method	Investment carried at cost plus pro-rata share of subsidiary earnings less dividends received	Equity in earnings of *unconsolidated subsidiary* shown on one line as addition to income
④	20% to and including 50%	Equity method	Same as 3	Same as 3, often called equity in earnings of *affiliated or associated* companies

650

and expenses of the unconsolidated subsidiaries or affiliated companies are included in the consolidated statements. The investor's interests in these companies have been recognized on a pro-rata basis only.

As we have seen, the accounting for investments *in voting stock* depends on the nature of the investment:

1. Except for those subsidiaries in insurance and finance activities, investments that represent more than a 50% ownership interest are usually consolidated. A subsidiary is a corporation controlled by another corporation. The usual condition for control is ownership of a majority (more than 50%) of the outstanding voting stock.

2. **a.** If the subsidiary is not consolidated, it is carried by the parent under the equity method, which is cost at date of acquisition adjusted for the investor's share of the earnings or losses of the investee subsequent to the date of investment. Dividends received from the investee reduce the carrying amount of the investment.

   b. The equity method is also generally used for a 20% through 50% interest because such a level of ownership is regarded as a presumption that the owner has the ability to exert significant influence.

   c. Investments in corporate joint ventures should also be accounted for under the equity method. "Corporate joint ventures" are corporations owned and operated by a small group of businesses (the "joint venturers") as a separate business or project for the mutual benefit of the members of the group. Joint ventures are common in the petroleum and construction industries.

3. Marketable *equity* securities held as *short-term investments* are generally carried at the lower of cost or market value.[3] These investments are typically passive in the sense that the investor exerts no significant influence on the investee.

ACCOUNTING FOR GOODWILL

☐ **Purchased Goodwill**

The major example on consolidated financial statements assumed that the acquisition cost of Company S by Company P was equal to the amount of the stockholders' equity, or the *book value*, of Company S. However, the total purchase price paid by P often exceeds the book values of the assets acquired. In fact, the purchase price also often exceeds the sum of the fair market values (current values) of the identifiable individual assets less the liabilities. Such excess of purchase price over fair market value is called *goodwill* or "purchased goodwill" or, more accurately, "excess of cost over fair value of net identifiable assets of businesses acquired." Recall that Chapter 18 discusses the nature of goodwill on pages 604–605.

To see the impact of goodwill on the consolidated statements, refer to our initial example on consolidations, where there was an acquisition of a

---

[3] FASB Statement No. 12, "Accounting for Certain Marketable Securities," requires that a portfolio of securities (rather than each security as an individual investment) should be stated at the lower of cost or market. If the investment is classified as a current asset, any write-downs to market should affect current net income. If the investment is a noncurrent asset, the write-down shall be recorded directly in the stockholders' equity section of the balance sheet as a separate valuation account and not as a component of the determination of net income.

100% interest in S by P for $213 million. Suppose that the price were $40 million higher, or a total of $253 million cash. For simplicity, assume that the fair values of the individual assets of S are equal to their book values. The balance sheets immediately after the acquisition are:

	ASSETS		= LIABILITIES +		STOCKHOLDERS' EQUITY
	Investment In S	+ Cash and Other Assets =	Accounts Payable, Etc.	+	Stockholders' Equity
P's accounts:					
Before acquisition		650 =	200	+	450
Acquisition	+253	−253 =			
S's accounts		400 =	187	+	213
Intercompany eliminations	−213	=			−213
Consolidated	40*	+ 797 =	387	+	450

* The $40 million "goodwill" would appear in the consolidated balance sheet as a separate intangible asset account. It often is shown as the final item in a listing of assets. It is usually amortized in a straight-line manner as an expense in the consolidated income statement over a span of no greater than forty years.

☐ Fair Values of Individual Assets

If the book values of the individual assets of S are not equal to their fair values, the usual procedures are:

1. S continues as a going concern and keeps its accounts on the same basis as before.
2. P records its investment at its acquisition cost (the agreed purchase price).
3. For consolidated reporting purposes, the excess of the acquisition cost over the book values of S is identified with the individual assets, item by item. (In effect, they are revalued at the current market prices prevailing when P acquired S.) Any *remaining excess* that cannot be identified is labeled as purchased goodwill.

Suppose that the fair value of the assets of S (e.g., machinery and equipment) exceeded their book value by $30 million in our example. The balance sheets immediately after acquisition would be the same as above, with a single exception. The $40 million goodwill would now be only $10 million. The remaining $30 million would appear in the consolidated balance sheet as an integral part of the individual assets. That is, S's equipment would be shown at $30 million higher in the consolidated balance sheet than the carrying amount on S's books. Similarly, the depreciation expense on the consolidated income statement would be higher. For instance, if the equipment had five years of useful life remaining, the straight-line depreciation would be $30 ÷ 5, or $6 million higher per year.

As in the preceding tabulation, the $10 million "goodwill" would appear in the consolidated balance sheet as a separate intangible asset account.

Goodwill is frequently misunderstood. The layperson often thinks of goodwill as being the friendly attitude of the neighborhood store manager. But goodwill has many aspects that some observers have divided into causes (sources) and effects (fruits). A purchaser may be willing to pay more than the current values of the individual assets received because the acquired company is able to generate abnormally high earnings (the effects, or fruits). The causes of this excess earning power may be traceable to personalities, skills, locations, operating methods, and so forth. For example, a purchaser may be willing to pay extra (the fruits) because excess earnings can be forthcoming from

1. Saving in time and costs by purchasing a corporation having a share of the market in a type of business or in a geographical area where the acquiring corporation planned expansion
2. Excellent general management skills or a unique product line
3. Potential efficiency by combination, rearrangement, or elimination of duplicate facilities and administration

Of course, "goodwill" is originally generated internally. For example, a happy combination of advertising, research, management talent, and timing may give a particular company a dominant market position (the cause) for which another company is willing to pay dearly (the fruit). This ability to command a premium price for the total business is goodwill. Nevertheless, such goodwill should never be recorded by the selling company. Therefore the *only* goodwill generally recognized as an asset is that identified when one company is purchased by another. The consolidated company must then show in its financial statements the purchased goodwill.

SUMMARY

Nearly all corporate annual reports contain consolidated financial statements, as well as "investment" accounts of various sorts. Acquiring a fundamental understanding of accounting for intercorporate investments is therefore essential for intelligent usage of financial reports.

SUMMARY PROBLEM FOR YOUR REVIEW

☐ Problem One

1. Review the section on minority interests, pages 644–645. Suppose P purchases 60% of the stock of S for a cost of 0.60 × $213, or $128 million. The total assets of P consist of this $128 million plus $522 million of other assets, a total of $650 million. The assets, liabilities, and shareholders' equity of S are unchanged from the amounts given in the example on page 641. Prepare an analysis showing what amounts would appear in a consolidated balance sheet immediately after the acquisition.
2. Suppose S has a net income of $50 million for the year, and P has an operating income of $100 million. Other details are described in the example on page 643. Prepare an analysis showing what amounts would appear in a consolidated income statement and year-end balance sheet.

☐ **Solution to Problem One**

1.

	ASSETS		= LIABILITIES +	STOCKHOLDERS' EQUITY	
	Investment In S	+ Cash and Other Assets =	Accounts Payable, Etc. =	Minority + Interest +	Stockholders' Equity
P's accounts, Jan. 1: Before acquisition		650 =	200	+	450
Acquisition of 60% of S	+128	−128 =			
S's accounts, Jan. 1		400 =	187	+	213
Intercompany eliminations	−128	=		+85	−213
Consolidated, Jan. 1	0 +	922 =	387	+ 85 +	450

2.

	P	S	CONSOLIDATED
Sales	$900	$300	$1,200
Expenses	800	250	1,050
Operating income	$100	$ 50	$ 150
Pro-rata share (60%) of unconsolidated subsidiary net income	30	—	
Net income	$130	$ 50	
Outside interest (40%) in consolidated subsidiary net income (minority interest in income)			20
Net income to consolidated entity			$ 130

	ASSETS		= LIABILITIES +	STOCKHOLDERS' EQUITY	
	Investment In S	+ Cash and Other Assets =	Accounts Payable, Etc. =	Minority + Interest +	Stockholders' Equity
P's accounts: Beginning of year, before acquisition		650 =	200	+	450
Acquisition	128	−128 =			
Operating income		+100 =			+100
Share of S income	+ 30	=			+ 30
End of year	158	622 =	200	+	580
S's accounts: Beginning of year		400 =	187	+	213
Net income		+ 50 =			+ 50
End of year		450 =	187	+	263
Intercompany eliminations	−158	=		+105*	−263
Consolidated, end of year	0 +	1,072 =	387	105 +	580

* 85 beginning of year + 0.40(50) = 85 + 20 = 105.

HIGHLIGHTS TO REMEMBER

1. Exhibits 19–1 and 19–2, pages 647 and 648, summarize the accounting for intercorporate investments. Note how the equity method is applied. The $8 million increase in the Investments account is attributable to the pro-rata share of the *unconsolidated* subsidiary net income shown in Exhibit 19–2.
2. Exhibits 19–1 and 19–2 also display minority interests. Consider the $300,000 increase (Exhibit 19–1) in Outside Stockholders' Interest in Consolidated Subsidiaries. It represents the minority shareholders' interest in the income of *consolidated* subsidiaries, as indicated in the income statement in Exhibit 19–2.
3. Exhibit 19–3, page 650, summarizes the accounting for long-term investments in equity securities. Please review it before you try to solve any problems in these categories.

ACCOUNTING VOCABULARY

Consolidated Statements *p. 641*   Cost Method for Investments *639*   Equity Method *639*   Investments in Affiliates *649*   Investments in Associates *649*   Minority Interests *644*   Outside Stockholders' Interest in Subsidiaries *644*   Subsidiary *641*

☐ PART TWO Analysis of Financial Statements

OBJECTIVE OF ANALYSIS

The primary uses of financial statements are evaluating past performance and predicting future performance. Both of these uses are facilitated by *comparisons*. The ultimate effect of analyzing statements is usually some financial *decision*. After comparing financial statements to past statements, to those of similar organizations, or to industry averages, the analyst will *predict* how the organization will fare. The analyst will then *decide* to buy, sell, or hold the common stock (or lend or not lend).

The financial statements of International Business Machines Corporation (IBM) in Exhibits 19–4 through 19–6 will be the focus of our extended illustration of the computation of financial ratios. The statements are slightly modified for illustrative purposes. Both managers and investors find ratios helpful for comparing and predicting. The managers and the financial community (such as bank officers and stockholders) want clues to help evaluate the operating and financial outlook for an entity. For example, extenders of credit want assurance of being paid in full and on time. Where the amounts lent are significant, the creditor often will ask the debtor for a set of budgeted financial statements. A *budget* or *pro forma statement* is a carefully formulated expression of predicted results, including a schedule of the amounts and timing of cash repayments. For example, a set of budgeted financial statements is one

EXHIBIT 19–4

IBM CORPORATION
Balance Sheet
(in millions)

	DECEMBER 31		
	1984		1983
Assets			
Current assets:			
Cash and marketable securities	$ 4,400		$ 5,500
Accounts receivable	8,100		6,200
Inventories	6,600		4,400
Prepaid expenses	1,300		1,200
Total current assets		$20,400	$17,300
Long-term assets:*			
Plant, property, and equipment, original cost	$29,300		$29,200
Deduct: Accumulated depreciation	13,000		13,000
Plant, property, and equipment, net		16,300	16,200
Long-term investments		6,100	4,000
Total assets		$42,800	$37,500
Liabilities and stockholders' equity			
Current liabilities:			
Accounts and loans payable	$ 2,400		$ 1,800
Taxes payable	2,700		3,200
Wages and benefits payable	2,200		2,100
Deferred sales revenue	300		400
Other accrued expenses	2,000		1,700
Total current liabilities		$ 9,600	$ 9,200
Long-term debt		3,300	2,700
Other liabilities		3,400	2,400
Total liabilities		$16,300	$14,300
Stockholders' equity:			
Paid-in capital**	$ 6,000		$ 5,800
Retained earnings	23,500		19,500
Translation adjustments	(3,000)		(2,100)
Total shareholders' equity		26,500	23,200
Total liabilities and shareholders' equity		$42,800	$37,500

* This caption is frequently omitted. Instead, the long-term assets are merely listed as separate items following the current assets.

** Details are often shown in a supplementary statement or in footnotes. For IBM, there were 622 million shares outstanding at the end of 1984 at $1.25 par value: 622 million × $1.25 = $766 million. Additional paid-in capital was $5,234 million. In 1983 there were 608 million shares, $1.25 × 608 = $760 million par value of paid-in capital, and $5,040 million of additional paid-in capital.

EXHIBIT 19–5

IBM CORPORATION
Statement of Income
(in millions except earnings per share)

	FOR THE YEAR ENDED DECEMBER 31			
	1984		1983	
Revenue:				
Sales	$29,700		$23,300	
Services	9,600		7,700	
Rentals	6,600		9,200	
		$45,900		$40,200
Cost of goods sold:				
Cost of sales	12,400		9,700	
Cost of services	4,300		3,400	
Cost of rentals	2,200		3,100	
		18,900		16,200
Gross profit		$27,000		$24,000
Other operating expenses:				
Selling, general, and administrative	11,500		10,700	
Research, development, and engineering	4,200	15,700	3,600	14,300
Operating income		11,300		9,700
Other expenses (revenue)*		(400)		(300)
Earnings before taxes		11,700		10,000
Provision for income taxes		5,000		4,500
Net income		$ 6,700		$ 5,500
Earnings per share†		$ 10.77		$ 9.05

* Primarily interest expense and interest revenue. Revenue exceeds expense both years.

† Dividends per share, $4.34 and $3.78, respectively. Publicly held companies must show earnings per share on the face of the income statement, but it is not necessary to show dividends per share. Average shares outstanding are 622 million in 1984 and 608 million in 1983.

EXHIBIT 19–6

IBM CORPORATION
Statement of Retained Earnings
(in millions)

	FOR THE YEAR ENDED DECEMBER 31	
	1984	1983
Retained earnings, beginning of year	$19,500	$16,300
Add: Net income	6,700	5,500
Total	26,200	21,800
Deduct: Dividends declared	2,700	2,300
Retained earnings, end of year	$23,500	$19,500

of the first things a banker will request from an entrepreneur proposing a new business. Even established companies such as IBM usually need to provide pro forma statements to assure creditors that the company will pay back the amounts borrowed.

USES OF RATIOS

In addition to obtaining a budget, the supplier of large amounts of credit will inevitably conduct further analysis. Moreover, many lenders do not extend large amounts of credit to a single entity, so they do not probe deeply enough to obtain budgets. There are many indirect ways to make judgments. History is examined. Performances are compared. Industry standards or rules of thumb are employed.

Our illustrative analysis focuses on one company and one or two years. This is sufficient as a start, but other firms in the industry and a series of years should be examined to get a better perspective. That is why annual reports typically contain a table of comparative statistics for five or ten years.

Above all, recognize that by itself a ratio is of limited use. There must be a standard for comparison—a history, a similar entity, an industry, a budget (or similar target).

☐ Component Percentages

The income statement and the balance sheet are often analyzed by **component percentages** (see Exhibit 19–7). In this way, the statements are made comparable through time and among companies inside and outside an industry.

The income statement percentages are usually based on sales = 100%. IBM seems very profitable, but such percentages would have more meaning when compared with the *budgeted* performance for the current year (not shown here). Both the gross margin rate and net income percentage seem high. However, averages for these items vary greatly by industry. Comparison with other similar firms or industry averages is necessary to interpret the rates fully. Changes between one year and the next can reveal important information. IBM's net income increased from 14% to 15%, despite a decrease in gross margin. The main reason for the income increase was a decrease in the selling, general, and administrative costs from 27% to 25% of sales. Note that those costs increased from $10,700 million to $11,500 million, only a 7% increase, while sales increased by 14%.

Corporate annual reports to the public must contain a section that is usually labeled *management's discussion and analysis*. This section concentrates on explaining the major changes in the income statement, changes in liquidity and capital resources, and the impact of inflation. The focus is on a comparison of one year with the next. For example, IBM's annual report had four pages of detailed discussions, including

☐   Total revenue from sales grew to $29.7 billion, an increase of 27.5 percent. . . .
Total revenue from rentals, primarily risk leases, declined by 28.3 percent, a

EXHIBIT 19–7

IBM CORPORATION
Component Percentages
(in millions except percentages)

	FOR THE YEAR ENDED DECEMBER 31			
STATEMENT OF INCOME	1984		1983	
Sales	$45,900*	100%	$40,200	100%
Cost of goods sold	18,900	41%	16,200	40
Gross profit (or gross margin)	$27,000	59	$24,000	60
Selling, general, and administrative	$11,500	25	$10,700	27
Research, development, and engineering	4,200	9	3,600	9
Operating expenses	$15,700	34	$14,300	36
Operating income	$11,300	25	$ 9,700	24
Other revenue and expense	(400)	(1)	(300)	(1)
Income before income taxes	$11,700	26	$10,000	25
Income tax expense	5,000	11	4,500	11
Net income	$ 6,700	15%	$ 5,500	14%

	DECEMBER 31			
BALANCE SHEET	1984		1983	
Current assets	$20,400	48%	$17,300	46%
Plant, property, and equipment, net	16,300	38	16,200	43
Long-term investments	6,100	14	4,000	11
Total assets	$42,800	100%	$37,500	100%
Current liabilities	$ 9,600	22%	$ 9,200	24%
Long-term liabilities	6,700	16	5,100	14
Total liabilities	$16,300	38%	$14,300	38%
Stockholders' equity	26,500	62	23,200	62
Total equities	$42,800	100%	$37,500	100%
Working capital	$10,800		$ 8,100	

* Note the use of dollar signs in columns of numbers. Frequently, they are used at the top and bottom only and not for every subtotal. Their use by companies depends on the preference of management.

trend that has been apparent since 1982. Management expects this trend to continue. . . . The total gross profit margin was down slightly. As rental revenue, with its higher than average profit margin, becomes a smaller contributor to total revenue the overall gross profit margin will tend to be lower than in prior periods.

The balance sheet percentages are usually based on total assets = 100%. See Exhibit 19–7. The most notable feature of the balance sheet percentages is the shift in assets from plant, property, and equipment to current assets and long-term investments. Liabilities have been shifted from current to long-term. The result is a strengthening of IBM's short-term liquidity. Working capital, that is, current assets less current liabilities, increased 33%, from

EXHIBIT 19–8

Some Typical Financial Ratios

TYPICAL NAME OF RATIO	NUMERATOR	DENOMINATOR	USING APPROPRIATE IBM NUMBERS APPLIED TO DECEMBER 31 OF YEAR	
			1984	1983
Short-term ratios:				
Current ratio	Current assets	Current liabilities	20,400 ÷ 9,600 = 2.1	17,300 ÷ 9,200 = 1.9
Inventory turnover	Cost of goods sold	Average inventory at cost†	18,900 ÷ ½(6,600 + 4,400) = 3.4	16,200 ÷ ½(4,400 + 3,500) = 4.1
Average collection period in days	Average accounts receivable† × 365	Sales on account	[½(8,100 + 6,200) × 365] ÷ 45,900 = 57 days*	[½(6,200 + 5,400) × 365] ÷ 40,200 = 53 days
Debt-to-equity ratios:				
Current debt to equity	Current liabilities	Stockholders' equity	9,600 ÷ 26,500 = 36.2%	9,200 ÷ 23,200 = 39.7%
Total debt to equity	Total liabilities	Stockholders' equity	16,300 ÷ 26,500 = 61.5%	14,300 ÷ 23,200 = 61.6%
Profitability ratios:				
Gross profit rate or percentage	Gross profit or gross margin	Sales	27,000 ÷ 45,900 = 58.8%	24,000 ÷ 40,200 = 59.7%
Return on sales	Net income	Sales	6,700 ÷ 45,900 = 14.6%	5,500 ÷ 40,200 = 13.7%
Return on stock-holders' equity	Net income	Average stock-holders' equity†	6,700 ÷ ½(26,500 + 23,200) = 27.0%	5,500 ÷ ½(23,200 + 20,000) = 25.5%
Earnings per share	Net income less dividends on pre-ferred stock, if any	Average common shares outstanding	6,700 ÷ 622 = $10.77	5,500 ÷ 608 = $9.05
Price-earnings	Market price of com-mon share‡	Earnings per share	123 ÷ 10.77 = 11.4	122 ÷ 9.05 = 13.5
Dividend ratios:				
Dividend-yield	Dividends per com-mon share	Market price of com-mon share‡	4.34 ÷ 123 = 3.5%	3.78 ÷ 122 = 3.1%
Dividend-payout	Dividends per com-mon share	Earnings per share	4.34 ÷ 10.77 = 40.3%	3.78 ÷ 9.05 = 41.8%

* This may be easier to see as follows:

Average receivables = ½(8,100 + 6,200) = 7,150

Average receivables as a percentage of annual sales = 7,150 ÷ 45,900 = 15.58%

Average collection period = 15.58% × 365 days = 57 days

† Relevant 1982 amounts are: accounts receivable, $5,400 million; inventory, $3,500 million; and stockholders' equity, $20,000 million.

‡ Market price: December 31, 1984, $123; December 31, 1983, $122.

$8,100 million to $10,800 million. Total assets increased by only 14%, $37,500 million to $42,800 million, over the same period.

☐ Industry Statistics and Typical Ratios

Exhibit 19–8 shows how some typical ratios are computed. As you can readily imagine, various combinations of financial ratios are possible. In any event, one of the most popular uses of such ratios is comparison with similar companies.

Dun & Bradstreet, a financial services firm, informs its subscribers of the creditworthiness of thousands of companies. The firm also regularly compiles many ratios of the companies it monitors. Consider each ratio in Exhibit 19–8 in relation to the industry statistics. For example, some of the Dun & Bradstreet ratios from financial statements of 408 electronic computer equipment companies are:

	CURRENT RATIO	CURRENT DEBT TO STOCK-HOLDERS' EQUITY	TOTAL DEBT TO STOCK-HOLDERS' EQUITY	RETURN ON SALES	RETURN ON STOCK-HOLDERS' EQUITY
	(Times)	(Percent)	(Percent)	(Percent)	(Percent)
Four hundred eight companies:					
Upper quartile*	4.6	19.5	28.8	10.3	23.7
Median	2.7	42.4	73.9	5.2	12.7
Lower quartile	1.6	103.8	153.1	1.3	1.3
IBM†	2.1	36.2	61.5	14.6	27.0

* The individual ratios are ranked from best to worst. The middle figure is the median. The figure halfway between the median and the best is the upper quartile. Similarly, the figure halfway between the median and the worst is the lower quartile.

† Ratios are from Exhibit 19–8. Consult that exhibit for an explanation of the components of each ratio.

☐ Discussion of Individual Ratios

The current ratio is a widely used statistic. Other things being equal, the higher the current ratio, the more assurance the creditor has about being paid in full and on time. As Exhibit 19–8 shows, IBM's current ratio of 2.1 has increased from 1.9 but is still well below the industry median of 2.7.

The next two ratios in Exhibit 19–8 are not available from Dun & Bradstreet on an industry-comparable basis. Still, the inventory turnover and the average collection period are closely watched signals. Deteriorations through time in these ratios help to alert managers to problem areas. For example, a decrease in inventory turnover may suggest slower-moving (or even unsalable) merchandise or a worsening coordination of the buying and selling functions. An increase in the average collection period of receivables may indicate increasing acceptance of poor credit risks or less energetic collection efforts.

Whether the inventory turnover of 3.4 and the average collection period of 57 days are "fast" or "slow" depends on past performance and the performance of similar companies. Both ratios are slightly less favorable than they were a year earlier.

Note how the average collection period is affected by sales *on account*. The computation in Exhibit 19–8 assumes that all sales are credit sales. However, if we relax our assumption, the 57-day period would rise markedly. For example, if half the sales were for cash, the average collection period for accounts receivable would change from 57 to 114 days:

$$\frac{\frac{1}{2}(8,100 + 6,200) \times 365}{\frac{1}{2}(45,900)} = 114 \text{ days}$$

Ratios of debt to equity are shown in the second and third columns of the Dun & Bradstreet tabulation. Both creditors and shareholders watch these ratios to judge the degree of risk of insolvency and of stability of profits. Typically, companies with heavy debt in relation to ownership capital are in greater danger of suffering net losses or even insolvency when business conditions sour. Why? Because revenues and many expenses decline, but interest expenses and maturity dates do not change. IBM's ratios of 36.2% and 61.5% are better than their medians for the industry; they reflect greater stability of profits and lower risk or uncertainty concerning the company's ability to pay its debts on time.

The final two columns in the Dun & Bradstreet tabulation are examples of profitability ratios. Managers and investors study the ratios of net income to sales and gross profit to sales as indicators of *operating success*. To owners, however, the ultimate measure of *overall accomplishment* is the rate of return on their invested capital. Hence the final column displays the ratio of net income to stockholders' equity. IBM's rate of return is splendid. The opportunities to make more handsome returns than 27% after income taxes are rare.

To summarize, in comparison with the Dun & Bradstreet ratios, IBM's current ratio is unimpressive, but its profit ratios are outstanding. Its debt management ratios are better than the medians. All in all, IBM's operating and financial performance seem excellent. The main question raised by the ratio analysis is whether IBM can meet the current portion of its long-term debt without disrupting its normal operations.

☐ Earnings and Dividends

Every analyst has a favorite set of ratios, but one is so popular that it dwarfs all others: *earnings per share of common stock (EPS)*. This is the only ratio that is required as a part of the body of financial statements of publicly held corporations. The EPS must be presented on the face of the income statement.

Exhibit 19–8 shows how EPS is computed, as well as how three other popular ratios are calculated: price-earnings, dividend-yield, and dividend-payout. These ratios are especially useful to investors in the common stock of the company.

An important measure of overall accomplishment is the rate of return on invested capital:

$$\text{rate of return on investment} = \frac{\text{income}}{\text{invested capital}} \qquad (1)$$

On the surface, this measure is straightforward, but its ingredients may differ according to the purpose it is to serve. What is invested capital, the denominator of the ratio? What income figure is appropriate?

The measurement of operating performance (i.e., how profitably assets are employed) should not be influenced by the management's financial decisions (i.e., how assets are obtained). Operating performance is best measured by operating rate of return on average total assets:

$$\frac{\text{pretax operating rate}}{\text{of return on total assets}} = \frac{\text{operating income}}{\text{average total assets available}} \qquad (2)$$

The right-hand side of Equation 2 consists, in turn, of two important ratios:

$$\frac{\text{operating income}}{\text{average total assets available}} = \frac{\text{operating income}}{\text{sales}} \times \frac{\text{sales}}{\text{average total assets available}} \qquad (3)$$

Using Exhibits 19–4 and 19–5, we can compute the following 1984 results for IBM:

$$\frac{\$11,300}{\frac{1}{2}(\$42,800 + \$37,500)} = \frac{\$11,300}{\$45,900} \times \frac{\$45,900}{\$40,150}$$

The right-hand terms in Equation 3 are often called the *operating margin percentage on sales* and the *total asset turnover*, respectively. Equation 3 may be reexpressed:

$$\text{pretax operating rate of return on total assets} = \text{operating margin percentage on sales}$$
$$\times \text{total asset turnover} \qquad (4)$$
$$= 24.6\% \times 1.143 \text{ times} = 28.1\%$$

If ratios are used to evaluate operating performance, they should exclude extraordinary items because they are regarded as nonrecurring items that do not reflect normal performance.

A scrutiny of Equation 4 shows that there are two basic factors in profit making: operating margin percentages and turnover. An improvement in either will, by itself, increase the rate of return on total assets.

The ratios used can also be computed on the basis of figures after taxes. However, the peculiarities of the income tax laws may sometimes distort results—for example, the tax rate may change, or losses carried back or forward might eliminate the tax in certain years.

Many more ratios could be computed. For example, Standard & Poor's Corporation sells a COMPUSTAT service, which via computer can provide financial and statistical information for thousands of companies. The information includes 22 income statement items, 19 balance sheet items, and a variety of financial ratios for up to 20 past years.

EFFICIENT MARKETS AND INVESTOR DECISIONS

Much recent research in accounting and finance has concentrated on whether the stock markets are "efficient." An **efficient capital market** is one in which market prices "fully reflect" all information available at a given time. Therefore, searching for "underpriced" securities in such a market would be fruitless unless an investor has information that is not generally available. If the real-world markets are indeed efficient, a relatively inactive portfolio approach would be an appropriate investment strategy for most investors. The hallmarks of the approach are risk control, high diversification, and low turnover of securities. The role of accounting information would mainly be in identifying the different degrees of risk among various stocks.

Research in finance and accounting during the past 20 years reinforced the idea that financial ratios and other data such as reported earnings provide inputs to predictions of such economic phenomena as financial failure or earnings growth. Furthermore, many ratios are used simultaneously rather than one at a time for such predictions. Above all, the research showed that accounting reports are only one source of information and that in the aggregate the market is not fooled by companies that choose the least conservative accounting policies. In sum, the market as a whole sees through any attempts by companies to gain favor through the choice of accounting policies that tend to boost immediate income. Thus there is evidence that the stock markets may indeed be "efficient," at least in their reflection of accounting data.

Suppose you are the chief executive officer of Company A. Reported earnings are $4 per share and the stock price is $40. You are contemplating changing your method of depreciation for investor-reporting purposes from accelerated to straight-line. Your competitors use straight-line. You think the Company A stock price unjustifiably suffers in comparison to other companies in the same industry.

If straight-line depreciation is adopted by Company A, reported earnings will be $5 instead of $4 per share. Would the stock price rise accordingly from $40 to $50? No. The empirical research on these issues indicates that the stock price would remain at about $40.

The chief executive's beliefs as shown in the foregoing example are shared by many managers, who essentially adhere to an extremely narrow view of the role of an income statement. Such a "bottom-line" mentality is slowly, surely, and sensibly falling into disrepute. At the risk of unfair exaggeration, the view is summarized as follows:

1. The income statement is the sole (or at least the primary) source of information about a company.
2. Lenders and shareholders invest in a company because of its reported earnings. For instance, the higher the reported earnings per share, the higher the stock price, and the easier it is to raise capital.

Basically, these arguments assume that investors can be misled by how reported earnings are measured. But there is considerable evidence that securities markets are not fooled with respect to accounting changes that are devoid of economic substance (that have no effect on cash flows). Why? Because the change generally reveals no new information, so no significant change in stock price is likely.

The research described above concentrates on the effects of accounting on investors *in the aggregate*. Individual investors vary in how they analyze financial statements. One by one, individual users must either incur the costs of conducting careful analyses or delegate that chore to professional analysts. In any event, intelligent analysis cannot be accomplished without an understanding of the assumptions and limitations of financial statements, including the presence of various alternative accounting methods.

SUMMARY

Ratios aid the intelligent analysis of financial statements. They are used as a basis of evaluation, comparison, and prediction. The rate of return on invested capital is a very popular means of comparing performance.

SUMMARY PROBLEM FOR YOUR REVIEW

Problem One appeared earlier in this chapter.

☐ Problem Two

Examine Exhibits 19–4 and 19–5, pages 656–657. Assume some new data in place of certain old data for the December 31, 1984, balance sheet (in millions):

	OLD DATA	NEW DATA
Accounts receivable	$ 8,100	$10,500
Inventories	6,600	9,800
Total current assets	20,400	26,000
Paid-in capital	6,000	9,000
Total stockholders' equity	26,500	29,500

Required:

Compute the following ratios applicable to December 31, 1984, or to the year 1984, as appropriate: current ratio, inventory turnover, average collection period, working capital, and return on stockholders' equity. Compare this new set of ratios with the old set of ratios. Are the new ratios more desirable? Explain.

☐ Solution to Problem Two

All the ratios would be affected.

$$\text{current ratio} = \frac{\text{current assets}}{\text{current liabilities}}$$

$$= \frac{\$26,000}{\$9,600} = 2.7 \text{ instead of } 2.1$$

$$\text{inventory turnover} = \frac{\text{cost of goods sold}}{\text{average inventory}}$$
$$= \frac{\$18,900}{\frac{1}{2}(\$9,800 + \$4,400)}$$
$$= \frac{\$18,900}{\$7,100} = 2.7 \text{ times instead of 3.4 times.}$$

$$\frac{\text{average collection}}{\text{period}} = \frac{\text{average accounts receivable}}{\text{sales on account}} \times 365$$
$$= \frac{\frac{1}{2}(\$10,500 + \$6,200)}{\$45,900} \times 365$$
$$= \frac{\$8,350 \times 365}{\$45,900} = 66 \text{ days instead of 57 days}$$

Working capital is current assets minus current liabilities, which is $26,000 − $9,600 = $16,400 instead of $10,800.

$$\frac{\text{return on}}{\text{stockholders' equity}} = \frac{\text{net income}}{\text{average stockholders' equity}}$$
$$= \frac{\$6,700}{\frac{1}{2}(\$29,500 + \$23,200)}$$
$$= 25.4\% \text{ instead of } 27.0\%$$

The new set of ratios has good news and bad news. The goods news is that the company would appear to be slightly more liquid (a current ratio of 2.7 instead of 2.1) and to have more working capital ($16,400 instead of $10,800). The bad news is that the inventory turnover, the average collection period, and the rate of return on stockholders' equity are less attractive.

HIGHLIGHTS TO REMEMBER

1. Earnings per share is the only financial ratio that is required to be shown in the financial reports of publicly held corporations.
2. Recent research has indicated that capital markets are "efficient" in the sense that investors in the aggregate are not fooled by companies that try to look good by choosing less conservative accounting policies. Accounting is a major source of information, but it is not the sole source.

ACCOUNTING VOCABULARY

For various financial ratios, see Exhibit 19–8, page 660. Also become familiar with:

Component Percentages *p. 658*   Efficient Capital Market *664*

FUNDAMENTAL ASSIGNMENT MATERIAL

Special Note: Problems relating to Part One of the chapter are presented first in each subgrouping of the assignment material.

19-1. COST OR EQUITY METHOD. (Alternate is 19–6.) Suppose General Motors acquired 25% of the voting stock of Indiana Tire Co. for $400 million cash. In year 1, Indiana Tire had a net income of $360 million and paid a cash dividend of $200 million.

Required:

Using the equity and the cost methods, show the effects of the three transactions on the accounts of General Motors. Use the balance sheet equation format.

19-2. CONSOLIDATED FINANCIAL STATEMENTS. (Alternate is 19–7.) Company P acquired a 100% voting interest in Company S for $110 million cash at the beginning of the year. Immediately before the business combination, each company had the following condensed balance sheet accounts (in millions):

	P	S
Cash and other assets	$600	$200
Accounts payable, etc.	$250	$ 90
Stockholders' equity	350	110
Total equities	$600	$200

Required:

1. Prepare a tabulation of the consolidated balance sheet accounts immediately after the acquisition. Use the balance sheet equation format.
2. Suppose that P and S have the following results for the year:

	P	S
Sales	$700	$400
Expenses	550	360

Prepare income statements for the year for P, S, and the consolidated entity.

3. Present the effects of the operations for the year on P's accounts and on S's accounts, using the balance sheet equation. Also tabulate the consolidated balance sheet accounts at the end of the year. Assume that liabilities are unchanged.
4. Suppose S paid a cash dividend of $30 million. What accounts in Requirement 3 would be affected and by how much?

19-3. MINORITY INTERESTS. This extends the preceding problem. However, this problem is self-contained because all the facts are reproduced below. Company P acquired a 70% voting interest in Company S for $77 million cash at the beginning of the year. Immediately before the business combination, each company had the following condensed balance sheet accounts (in millions):

	P	S
Cash and other assets	$600	$200
Accounts payable, etc.	$250	$ 90
Stockholders' equity	350	110
Total equities	$600	$200

Required:

1. Prepare a tabulation of the consolidated balance sheet accounts immediately after the acquisition. Use the balance sheet equation format.
2. Suppose P and S have the following results for the year:

	P	S
Sales	$700	$400
Expenses	550	360

Prepare income statements for the year for P, S, and the consolidated entity.

3. Using the balance sheet equation format, present the effects of the operations for the year on P's accounts and S's accounts. Also tabulate consolidated balance sheet accounts at the end of the year. Assume that liabilities are unchanged.

4. Suppose S paid a cash dividend of $30 million. What accounts in Requirement 3 would be affected and by how much?

19–4. **GOODWILL AND CONSOLIDATIONS.** This extends 19–2. However, this problem is self-contained because all the facts are reproduced below. Company P acquired a 100 percent voting interest in Company S for $170 million cash at the beginning of the year. Immediately before the business combination, each company had the following condensed balance sheet accounts (in millions):

	P	S
Cash and other assets	$600	$200
Accounts payable, etc.	$250	$ 90
Stockholders' equity	350	110
Total equities	$600	$200

Assume that the fair values of the individual assets of S were equal to their book values.

Required:

1. Prepare a tabulation of the consolidated balance sheet accounts immediately after the acquisition. Use the balance sheet equation format.

2. If goodwill is going to be amortized over 40 years, how much was amortized for the first year? If over 5 years, how much was amortized for the first year?

3. Suppose the book values of S's individual assets are equal to their fair market values except for equipment. The net book value of equipment is $30 million and its fair market value is $70 million. The equipment has a remaining useful life of four years. Straight-line depreciation is used.

   a. Describe how the consolidated balance sheet accounts immediately after the acquisition would differ from those in Requirement 1. Be specific as to accounts and amounts.

   b. By how much will consolidated income differ in comparison with the consolidated income that would be reported in Requirement 2? Assume amortization of goodwill over a 40-year period.

19–5. **RATE-OF-RETURN COMPUTATIONS.**

   a. Gregory Company reported a 10% operating margin on sales, an 8% pretax operating return on total assets, and $400 million of total assets. Compute the (i) operating income, (ii) total sales, and (iii) total asset turnover.

   b. Hopper Foods Corporation reported $800 million of sales, $24 million of operating income, and a total asset turnover of 5 times. Compute the (i) total assets, (ii) operating margin percentage on sales, and (iii) pretax operating return on total assets.

19–6. EQUITY METHOD. (Alternate is 19–1.) Sears acquired one-third of the voting stock of Whirlpool Company for $25 million cash. In year 1, Whirlpool had a net income of $21 million and paid cash dividends of $12 million.

Required: Prepare a tabulation that compares the equity method and the cost method of accounting for Sears's investment in Whirlpool. Show the effects on the balance sheet equation under each method. What is the year-end balance in the Investment in Whirlpool account under the equity method? Under the cost method?

19–7. CONSOLIDATED FINANCIAL STATEMENTS. (Alternate is 19–2.) Consider the purchase of Heublein (maker of Smirnoff Vodka and Inglenook wines) by R. J. Reynolds, a major food, beverage, and tobacco company (Del Monte, Canada Dry, Sunkist, and Winston). The purchase price was $1.4 billion. Assume that a 100% interest was acquired.

The balance sheet accounts immediately after the transaction were approximately (in millions):

	R. J. Reynolds	Heublein
Investment in Heublein	$1,400	—
Cash and other assets	6,900	$1,800
Total assets	$8,300	$1,800
Liabilities	4,400	400
Shareholders' equity	3,900	1,400
Total equities	$8,300	$1,800

Required:
1. Using the balance sheet equation format, prepare a tabulation of the consolidated balance sheet accounts immediately after the acquisition.
2. Suppose Heublein had sales of $2,000 million and expenses of $1,900 million for the year. R. J. Reynolds had sales of $9,400 million and expenses of $8,600 million. Prepare income statements for R. J. Reynolds, for Heublein, and for the consolidated company. Assume that neither R. J. Reynolds nor Heublein sold items to the other.
3. Using the balance sheet equation, present the effects of the operations for the year on the accounts of Heublein and R. J. Reynolds. Also tabulate the consolidated balance sheet accounts at the end of the year. Assume that liabilities are unchanged.
4. Suppose Heublein paid a cash dividend of $50 million. What accounts in Requirement 3 would be affected and by how much?

19–8. INVESTMENTS IN EQUITY SECURITIES. Barris Industries, producer of television shows, including "The Gong Show," "The Dating Game," and "The Newlywed Game," holds a 32% interest in Ply*Gem. This investment is recorded on the 1984 balance sheet at $6,542,000, comprising a significant part of the $18,353,000 total assets of Barris.

Ply*Gem's net income for fiscal 1984 was $3,117,000, and at the end of fiscal 1984 Barris's "accumulated equity in undistributed earnings, after consideration of dividends received of $253,000, amounted to $769,000."

Required:
1. How much did Barris Industries pay for its shares of Ply*Gem?
2. Suppose that Ply*Gem paid 25% of its 1984 net income in cash dividends.
   a. By how much did Barris's investment in subsidiaries account change during 1984 as a result of its interest in Ply*Gem?

b. How much income did Barris recognize from its investment in Ply*Gem in 1984?

3. Indicate briefly how the following three classes of investments should be accounted for: (a) greater than 50% interest, (b) 20% through 50% interest, and (c) less than 20% interest.

19–9. **EQUITY METHOD OF ACCOUNTING FOR UNCONSOLIDATED SUBSIDIARIES.** Trans World Airlines owns 100% of Hilton International Company. The airline and hotel operations are now being reported on a consolidated basis. However, in past years the hotel operations were not consolidated with the airline operations for financial-reporting purposes. The following data are extracted from the TWA 1972 annual report (in millions):

	12/31/72	12/31/71
From statement of income:		
Income from airline operations (detailed)	$ (5.3)	
Income from hotel operations (on one line)	8.8	
Net income for the year	$ 3.5	
From balance sheet:		
Investments: Equity in Hilton International	$47.0	$38.2

Required:

If Hilton International had paid cash dividends of $4.1 million in 1972, how would the payment have affected TWA net income for the year? How would it have affected the investment balance at December 31, 1972?

19–10. **INCOME RATIOS AND ASSET TURNOVER.** A semiannual report to the stockholders of Texaco included the following comments on earnings:

☐ On an annualized basis, net income represented an 8.9% return on average total assets of approximately $27.3 billion and an 18.9% return on average stockholders' equity. . . . Net income per gallon on all petroleum products sold worldwide averaged 3.6 cents. Net income was 4 cents on each dollar of revenue.

Required:

Using only this information, compute the (1) total asset turnover, (2) net income, (3) total revenues, (4) average stockholders' equity, and (5) gallons of petroleum products sold.

ADDITIONAL ASSIGNMENT MATERIAL

☐ **General Coverage**

19–11. What is the equity method?

19–12. Contrast the cost method and the equity method.

19–13. "The lower-of-cost-or-market rule is applied to short-term investments in marketable equity securities." Do you agree? Explain.

19–14. "The equity method is usually used for long-term investments." Do you think this is appropriate? Explain.

19–15. Distinguish between control of a company and significant influence over a company.

19–16. What criterion is used to determine whether a parent-subsidiary relationship exists?

19–17. Why have subsidiaries? Why not have the corporation take the form of a single legal entity?

19–18. "A consolidated financial statement simply adds together the separate accounts of a parent company and its subsidiaries." Do you agree? Explain.

19–19. What is a minority interest?

19–20. When is there justification for not consolidating subsidiaries in accounting reports?

19–21. "A consolidated balance sheet can contain an asset, Investment in Unconsolidated Subsidiary." Do you agree that this is appropriate? Explain.

19–22. "Goodwill is the excess of purchase price over the book values of the individual assets acquired." Do you agree? Explain.

19–23. "It is better to write off goodwill immediately, even though it can be amortized over 40 years." Do you agree? Why?

19–24. "A company can carry some investments in unconsolidated subsidiaries at cost." Under what circumstances is this a correct statement?

19–25. Is return on sales a good measure of a company's performance?

19–26. Suppose the president of your company wanted to switch depreciation methods to increase reported net income: "Our stock price is 10% below what I think it should be; changing depreciation method will increase income by 10%, thus getting our share price up to its proper level." How would you respond?

19–27. **PURCHASED GOODWILL.** Consider the following balance sheets (in millions):

	COMPANY A	COMPANY B
Cash	$ 750	$ 80
Inventories	360	70
Plant assets, net	360	60
Total assets	$1,470	$210
Common stock and paid-in surplus	$ 470	$120
Retained income	1,000	90
Total equities	$1,470	$210

A paid $300 million to B stockholders for all their stock. The "fair value" of the plant assets of B is $150 million. The fair value of cash and inventories is equal to their carrying amounts. A and B continued to keep separate books.

Required:
1. Prepare a tabulation showing the balance sheets of A, of B, Intercompany Eliminations, and Consolidated immediately after the acquisition.
2. Suppose that only $90 million rather than $150 million of the total purchase price of $300 million could be logically assigned to the plant assets. How would the consolidated accounts be affected?
3. Refer to the facts in Requirement 1. Suppose A had paid $324 million rather than $300 million. State how your tabulation in Requirement 1 would change.

19–28. **AMORTIZATION AND DEPRECIATION.** Refer to the preceding problem, Requirement 3. Suppose a year passes, and A and B generate individual net incomes of $90 million and $40 million, respectively. The latter is after a deduction by B of $12 million of straight-line depreciation. Compute the consolidated net income if goodwill is amortized (1) over 40 years and (2) over 10 years. Ignore income taxes.

19–29. **ALLOCATING TOTAL PURCHASE PRICE TO ASSETS.** Two entities had the following balance sheet accounts as of December 31, 19X1 (in millions):

	GREYMONT	PARADELT		GREYMONT	PARADELT
Cash and			Current liabilities	$ 50	$ 20
receivables	$ 30	$ 22	Common stock	100	10
Inventories	120	3	Retained income	150	90
Plant assets, net	150	95	Total equities	$300	$120
Total assets	$300	$120			
Net income for					
19X1	$ 19	$ 4			

On January 4, 19X2, these entities combined. Greymont issued $180 million of its shares (at market value) in exchange for all the shares of Paradelt, a motion picture division of a large company. The inventory of films acquired through the combination had been fully amortized on Paradelt's books.

During 19X2, Paradelt received revenue of $21 million from the rental of films from its inventory.

Greymont earned $20 million on its other operations (that is, excluding Paradelt) during 19X2. Paradelt broke even on its other operations (that is, excluding the film rental contracts) during 19X2.

Required:

1. Prepare a consolidated balance sheet for the combined company immediately after the combination on a purchase basis. Assume that $80 million of the purchase price was assigned to the inventory of films.

2. Prepare a comparison of Greymont's net income between 19X1 and 19X2 where 25% of the cost of the film inventories would be properly matched against the revenue from the film rentals. What would be the net income for 19X2 if the $80 million were assigned to goodwill rather than to the library of films, and goodwill were amortized over 40 years?

19–30. **CONSOLIDATED FINANCIAL STATEMENTS.** The Parent Company owns 80% of the common stock of Company S-1 and 60% of the common stock of Company S-2. The balances as of December 31, 19X8, in the condensed accounts follow (in thousands):

	PARENT	S-1	S-2
Sales	$510,000	$80,000	$210,000
Investment in subsidiaries*	71,000	—	—
Other assets	129,000	90,000	30,000
Liabilities to creditors	100,000	20,000	5,000
Expenses	490,000	90,000	195,000
Stockholders' equity, including			
current net income	100,000	70,000	25,000

* Carried at equity in subsidiaries.

Required:

Prepare a consolidated balance sheet as of December 31, 19X8 and a consolidated income statement for 19X8.

19–31. **PREPARE CONSOLIDATED FINANCIAL STATEMENTS.** From the following data, prepare a consolidated balance sheet and an income statement of the Schiff Corporation. All data are in millions and pertain to December 31, 19X7 or to operations for 19X7:

Paid-in capital in excess of par	$102
Interest expense	25
Retained income	198
Accrued income taxes payable	20
Investments in unconsolidated subsidiaries (which are two insurance companies)	70
Cost of goods sold and operating expenses, exclusive of depreciation and amortization	640
Subordinated debentures, 11% interest, due December 31, 19X9	100
Outside stockholders' interest in consolidated subsidiaries' net income	20
Goodwill	100
Net sales and other operating revenue	890
Investments in affiliated companies	30
Common stock, 10,000,000 shares, $1 par	10
Depreciation and amortization	20
Accounts payable	210
Equity in earnings of unconsolidated subsidiary	14
Cash	30
First-mortgage bonds, 10% interest, due December 31, 19Y3	80
Property, plant, and equipment, net	120
Preferred stock, 2,000,000 shares, $50 par, dividend rate is $5 per share, each share is convertible into one share of common stock	100
Short-term investments at cost, which approximates current market	40
Income tax expense	90
Accounts receivable, net	180
Outside stockholders' interest in subsidiaries (minority interests)	90
Inventories at average cost	340
Dividends declared and paid on preferred stock	10
Equity in earnings of affiliated companies	6

19–32. **FINANCIAL RATIOS.** The annual reports of Solbakken Møbler, a Norwegian furniture company, included the following selected data (in millions):

	19X6	19X5	19X4
Annual amounts:			
Net income	Nkr.100*	Nkr. 60	Nkr. 25
Gross margin on sales	525	380	200
Cost of goods sold	975	620	300
Operating expenses	380	295	165
Income tax expense	45	25	10
Dividends declared	30	15	5
End-of-year amounts:			
Long-term assets	Nkr.250	Nkr.220	Nkr.180
Long-term debt	80	65	40
Current liabilities	70	55	35
Cash	10	5	10
Accounts receivable	95	70	40
Merchandise inventory	125	85	60
Paid-in capital	205	205	205
Retained income	125	55	10

* Nkr. is Norwegian kroner. In recent years the exchange rate has varied between six and nine Nkr. per dollar.

During each of the three years, there were outstanding 10 million shares of capital stock, all common. Assume that all sales were on account and that the applicable market prices per share of stock were Nkr.30 for 19X5 and Nkr.40 for 19X6.

Required:

1. Compute each of the following for each of the last two years, 19X5 and 19X6:
   a. Rate of return on sales
   b. Rate of return on stockholders' equity
   c. Inventory turnover
   d. Current ratio
   e. Ratio of total debt to stockholders' equity
   f. Ratio of current debt to stockholders' equity
   g. Gross profit rate
   h. Average collection period for accounts receivable
   i. Price-earnings ratio
   j. Dividend-payout percentage
   k. Dividend yield

2. Answer yes or no to each of these questions and indicate which of the computations in requirement 1 support your answer:
   a. Has the merchandise become more salable?
   b. Is there a decrease in the effectiveness of collection efforts?
   c. Has gross margin rate improved?
   d. Has the rate of return on sales deteriorated?
   e. Has the rate of return on owners' investment increased?
   f. Are dividends relatively more generous?
   g. Have the risks of insolvency changed significantly?
   h. Has the market price of the stock become cheaper relative to earnings?
   i. Have business operations improved?
   j. Has there been a worsening of the company's ability to pay current debts on time?
   k. Has there been a decline in the cash return on the market value of the capital stock?
   l. Did the collectibility of the receivables improve?

3. Basing your observations on only the available data and the ratios you computed, prepare some brief comments on the company's operations and financial changes during the three years.

☐ Understanding Published Financial Reports

19–33. CLASSIFICATION ON BALANCE SHEET. The following accounts appeared in the annual report of the Jewel Companies, Inc.:

(1) Accumulated earnings—reserved for self-insured losses and general contingencies
(2) Long-term indebtedness, due within one year
(3) Investments: minority interest in foreign affiliates (at cost)
(4) Prepaid expenses and supplies
(5) Dividends payable
(6) Treasury stock at cost

Required: Indicate in detail in which section of the balance sheet each account should appear.

19–34. MEANING OF ACCOUNT DESCRIPTIONS. The following account descriptions were found in two annual reports:

Du Pont: Minority interests in earnings of consolidated subsidiaries
Minority interests in consolidated subsidiaries

Philip Morris: Investments in unconsolidated subsidiaries and affiliates
Equity in net earnings of unconsolidated subsidiaries and affiliates

In your own words, explain what each type of account represents. Indicate whether the item appears on the balance sheet or the income statement.

19–35. MEANING OF ACCOUNT DESCRIPTIONS. The following account descriptions were found in various annual reports:

Montgomery Ward: Net earnings of subsidiaries not consolidated
Tenneco: Equity in undistributed earnings of 50% owned companies
St. Regis Paper: Equity in net earnings of subsidiaries not consolidated and associated companies

In your own words, explain what each type of account represents. Also indicate whether the item appears on the balance sheet or the income statement.

19–36. EFFECTS OF TRANSACTIONS UNDER THE EQUITY METHOD. Pioneer Hi-Bred International, maker of seed corn and other farm products, has 19 foreign subsidiaries that are not consolidated. They are accounted for by the equity method. Pioneer's balance sheet showed (in thousands):

	AUGUST 31	
	1985	1984
Equity in unconsolidated subsidiaries	$49,809	$31,667

The last three lines of Pioneer's income statement were (in thousands):

	1985
Equity in net income of unconsolidated subsidiaries	$ 7,748
Net income	$102,592
Earnings per share	$3.21

During fiscal 1985 Pioneer invested an additional $10,394,000 in the subsidiaries.

Required:

1. What was the total amount of dividends paid by the subsidiaries to Pioneer in 1985?
2. Some foreign subsidiaries can be accounted for using the cost method instead of the equity method. What would Pioneer's 1985 net income have been if it had accounted for its unconsolidated subsidiaries using the cost method?
3. What would Pioneer's 1985 earnings per share have been if the cost method had been used?

19–37. CONSOLIDATIONS IN JAPAN. A few years ago Japan's finance ministry issued a directive requiring the 600 largest Japanese companies to produce consolidated financial statements. The previous practice had been to use parent-company-only statements. A story in *Business Week* said: "Financial observers hope that the move will help end the tradition-honored Japanese practice of 'window dressing' the parent company financial results by shoving losses onto hapless subsidiaries, whose red ink was seldom revealed. . . . When companies needed to show a bigger profit, they would sell their product to subsidiaries at an inflated price. . . . Or the parent company charged a higher rent to a subsidiary company using its building."

Required: Could a parent company follow the quoted practices and achieve window dressing in its parent-only financial statements if it used the equity method of accounting for its intercorporate investments? The cost method? Explain.

19–38. **INCOME RATIOS AND ASSET TURNOVER.** Thrifty Corporation operates over 500 Thrifty Drug and Discount stores in the western United States. Its 1985 annual report to stockholders included the following data:

Net income	$31,891,000
Total assets:	
Beginning of year	445,483,000
End of year	504,571,000
Net income as a percent of:	
Total revenue	2.27%
Average stockholders' equity	21.9%

Required: Using only the data given, compute the (1) net income percent of average assets, (2) total revenues, (3) average stockholders' equity, and (4) asset turnover (using two different approaches).

19–39. **FINANCIAL RATIOS.** W. R. Grace & Co. is a diversified worldwide enterprise consisting of chemicals, energy production, retailing, restaurants, and other businesses. Its 1984 income statement and balance sheet are shown in Exhibit 19–9.

Required:
1. Prepare an income statement showing component percentages.
2. Calculate the following financial ratios:
   a. Current ratio
   b. Inventory turnover (1983 inventory was $897.5 million)
   c. Total debt to equity
   d. Gross profit rate
   e. Return on stockholders' equity (1983 stockholders' equity was $2,182.3 million)
   f. Price-earnings (the December 31, 1984 market price was $39.75 per share)
   g. Dividend-yield (1984 dividends were $2.80 per share)
3. What additional information would help interpret the percentages and ratios you calculated?

EXHIBIT 19–9

W. R. GRACE & CO.
Income Statement and Balance Sheet
For the year ended December 31, 1984
(in millions)

INCOME STATEMENT

Sales	$6,727.8
Cost of goods sold	4,344.4
Gross margin	$2,383.4
Selling and administrative expenses	1,539.9
Other operating expenses	324.8
Operating income	$ 518.7
Interest expense, net	114.2
Research and development	78.6
Income before taxes	$ 325.9
Income taxes	130.3
Net income	$ 195.6
Earnings per share	$4.02

BALANCE SHEET

Current assets:			**Current liabilities:**	
Cash	$ 156.8		Accounts and loans payable	$ 813.9
Accounts receivable	652.5		Other current liabilities	346.1
Inventories	1,044.3			
Other current assets	57.0		Total current liabilities	$1,160.0
Total current assets	$1,910.6		Long-term debt	1,970.6
Properties and equipment, net	2,704.2		Total liabilities	$3,130.6
Investments in affiliated companies	275.8		Shareholders' equity	2,197.4
Other long-term assets	437.4			$5,328.0
	$5,328.0			

Chapter 20

DIFFICULTIES IN MEASURING
NET INCOME

LEARNING OBJECTIVES

After studying this chapter, you should be able to:

1. Explain the differences between various inventory methods, especially FIFO and LIFO, and their effects on the measurements of assets and net income.

2. Describe the major differences between financial capital and physical capital.

3. Explain and illustrate four different ways of measuring income: (a) historical cost/nominal dollars, (b) current cost/nominal dollars, (c) historical cost/constant dollars, and (d) current cost/constant dollars.

4. Explain the difference between monetary and nonmonetary items (Appendix 20).

5. Compute general purchasing-power gains and losses (Appendix 20).

The income statement summarizes the performance of an entity over a specified period of time. This chapter focuses on how choices among alternative accounting methods affect the measurement of income. The focus is on the assumptions and limitations of generally accepted accounting methods.

The two major parts of this chapter examine the controversial effects on income of (1) the principal inventory methods and (2) various measurements of changes in price levels. Each major part may be studied independently. There are, of course, many other controversial topics in accounting, including, for example, accounting for long-term leases, pensions, deferred income taxes, and foreign currency translation. However, space limitations preclude our coverage of these topics.

Above all, recognize that all these controversial topics illustrate a central question that managers and accountants must confront: How should income be measured?

☐ PART ONE Principal Inventory Methods

FOUR MAJOR METHODS

Each period, accountants must divide product costs between cost of goods sold and cost of items remaining in ending inventory. Various inventory methods accomplish this division. If unit prices and costs did not fluctuate, all inventory methods would show identical results. But prices change, and these changes raise central issues regarding cost of goods sold (income measurement) and inventories (asset measurement). Four principal inventory methods have been generally accepted in the United States: specific identification, weighted average, FIFO, and LIFO. Each will be explained and compared.

As a preview of the remainder of this section, consider the following simple example of the choices facing management. A new vendor of a cola drink at the fairgrounds bought one can on Monday for 30 cents, a second can on Tuesday for 40 cents, and a third can on Wednesday for 56 cents. He then sold one can on Thursday for 90 cents. What was his gross profit? His ending inventory? Answer these questions in your own mind before reading on.

Exhibit 20–1 provides a quick glimpse of the nature of the generally accepted methods. Their underlying assumptions will be explained shortly. As you can readily see, the vendor's choice of an inventory method can often significantly affect gross profit (and hence net income) and his ending inventory valuation for balance sheet purposes.

EXHIBIT 20–1

Comparison of Inventory Methods for Cola Vendor
Income Statement for the Period Monday Through Thursday
(all monetary amounts are in cents)

| | (1) SPECIFIC IDENTIFICATION | | | (2) | (3) | (4) |
	(1A)	(1B)	(1C)	FIFO	LIFO	WEIGHTED AVERAGE
Sales	90	90	90	90	90	90
Deduct cost of goods sold:						
1 30¢ (Monday) unit	30			30		
1 40¢ (Tuesday) unit		40				
1 56¢ (Wednesday) unit			56		56	
1 weighted average unit, (30 + 40 + 56) ÷ 3	—	—	—	—	—	42
Gross profit for Monday through Thursday	60	50	34	60	34	48
Computation of cost of goods sold:*						
Beginning inventory	0	0	0	0	0	0
Add purchases, 3 units (30 + 40 + 56)	126	126	126	126	126	126
Cost of goods available for sale	126	126	126	126	126	126
Less: Ending inventory, 2 units						
40 + 56	96			96		
30 + 56		86				
30 + 40			70		70	
2 × (126 ÷ 3) = 2 × 42	—	—	—	—	—	84
Cost of goods sold, Monday through Thursday	30	40	56	30	56	42

* This part of the exhibit is based on a **periodic inventory system**. Such a system computes cost of goods sold by deducting the ending inventory, determined by a physical count, from the sum of beginning inventory and purchases during the period. In contrast, a **perpetual inventory system** keeps a running, continuous record that tracks inventories and the cost of goods sold on a day-to-day basis.

1. SPECIFIC IDENTIFICATION (COLUMN 1). This method concentrates on the *physical* linking of the *particular* items sold. If the vendor reached for the Monday can instead of the Wednesday can, the *same inventory method* would show different results. Thus Exhibit 20–1 indicates that gross profit for operations of Monday through Thursday could be 60 cents, 50 cents, or 34 cents, depending on the particular can handed to the customer. Obviously, this method permits great latitude for measuring results in any given period. The next three methods do not trace the actual physical flow of goods except by coincidence.

2. FIRST-IN, FIRST-OUT (FIFO) (COLUMN 2). This method assumes that the stock acquired earliest is sold (used up) first. Thus the Monday unit is deemed to have been sold regardless of the actual physical unit delivered. In times of rising prices, FIFO usually shows the largest gross profit (60 cents in Exhibit 20–1).

3. LAST-IN, FIRST-OUT (LIFO) (COLUMN 3). This method assumes that the stock acquired most recently is sold (used up) first. Thus the Wednesday unit is deemed to have been sold regardless of the actual physical unit delivered. In times of rising prices, LIFO generally shows the lowest gross profit (34 cents in Exhibit 20–1).

4. WEIGHTED-AVERAGE COST (COLUMN 4). This method assumes that all items available for sale during the period are best represented by a weighted-average cost. Exhibit 20–1 shows the calculations. The weighted-average method usually produces a gross profit between that obtained under FIFO and LIFO (48 cents as compared with 60 cents and 34 cents in Exhibit 20–1).

INVENTORIES AND MATCHING

This illustration shows why theoretical and practical disputes easily arise regarding the "best" inventory method. As Exhibit 20–2 demonstrates, the four inventory methods have four separate cost-flow assumptions. When identical goods are purchased at different times and at different prices, accountants face a "matching" problem. The choice of an inventory method is an attempt to adhere to the basic concept of matching and cost recovery that was introduced in Chapter 17. The difficulty is not with "matching" as an *abstract* idea; instead, disputes arise regarding how to *apply* it. Thus more than one inventory method has evolved, and the four methods illustrated in Exhibits 20–1 and 20–2 have all become accepted as a part of the body of generally accepted accounting principles.

EXHIBIT 20–2

Diagram of Inventory Methods
(Data are from Exhibit 20–1; monetary amounts are in cents)

Beginning inventory	+	Merchandise purchases	=	Cost of goods available for sale
0	+	126	=	126

Cost of goods available for sale	−	Cost of goods sold	=	Ending inventory
1 @ 30				
1 @ 40				
1 @ 56				

126	−	30 or 40 or 56	=	96 or 86 or 70	Specific identification
	−	30	=	96	FIFO
	−	56	=	70	LIFO
	−	42	=	84	Weighted average

ESSENCE OF FIFO

Accountants and managers tend to develop strong feelings regarding the comparative merits of FIFO and LIFO. Adherents of FIFO maintain that it is the most practical way to reflect what operating managers actually do. That is, most managers deliberately attempt to move their merchandise on a first-in, first-out basis. This approach avoids spoilage, obsolescence, and the like. Thus the inventory flow assumption underlying FIFO corresponds most closely with the actual physical flows of inventory items in most businesses. Many managers would prefer the specific identification method but find it too costly to apply. Such managers often choose FIFO as the best practical approximation. Furthermore, the asset balance for inventories is a close approximation of the "actual" dollars invested, because the inventory is carried at the most recent purchase prices paid. Such prices are not likely to differ much from current prices at the balance sheet date. Consequently, its proponents maintain that FIFO properly meets the objectives of both the income statement and the balance sheet.

ESSENCE OF LIFO

LIFO is used by over 65% of major U.S. companies for at least part of their inventories. Adherents of LIFO are usually critical of FIFO because of the latter's effects on income when prices are rising. They claim that FIFO-based income is deceiving in the sense that some of the corresponding increase in net assets is merely an "inventory profit." That is, an "inventory profit" is fictitious because for a going concern, part of it is needed for replenishing the inventory. Consequently, it is not profit in the layperson's sense of the term; it does not indicate an amount that is entirely available to pay dividends. For instance, consider our cola vendor:

	FIFO	LIFO
Sales, one unit on Thursday	90¢	90¢
Cost of goods sold	30	56
Gross profit	60¢	34¢

The proponent of LIFO would claim that FIFO "overstates" profits (the "inventory profit") by 60 cents − 34 cents = 26 cents. Suppose replacement prices stay at 56 cents. The vendor will need 30 cents + 26 cents = 56 cents, not merely the 30 cents reported as FIFO cost of goods sold, to replace the unit sold.

Advocates of LIFO also stress that in times of rising prices, there may be greater pressure from stockholders to pay unjustified higher cash dividends under FIFO than LIFO. In the above example, the payment of a cash dividend of 60 cents by a vendor using FIFO would result in his not having enough cash to replenish his inventory. He would have only 90 cents − 60 cents = 30 cents. In contrast, LIFO would be more likely to conserve cash to the extent that less cash dividends would be paid if less income is reported. The vendor would have 90 cents − 34 cents = 56 cents available for replenishing inventory (if he paid a cash dividend of 34 cents, ignoring the effects of other expenses).

CRITICISMS OF LIFO

Critics of LIFO point to absurd balance sheet valuations. Under LIFO, older and older prices, and hence less useful inventory values, are reported, especially if physical stocks grow through the years. In contrast, under FIFO, the balance sheet tends to contain current prices and values.

Another criticism of LIFO is that, unlike FIFO, it permits management to influence immediate net income by the *timing of purchases*. For instance, if prices are rising and a company desires, for income tax or other reasons, to report less income in a given year, managers may be inclined to buy a large amount of inventory near the end of the year. That is, managers may accelerate the replacement of inventory that would normally not occur until early in the next year.

Consider an example. Suppose in our illustration that acquisition prices had increased from 56 cents on Wednesday to 61 cents on Thursday, the day of the sale of one unit. Suppose one more unit was acquired on Thursday for 61 cents. How would net income be affected under FIFO? under LIFO?

There would be no effect on cost of goods sold or gross profit under FIFO, although the balance sheet would show ending inventory as 61 cents higher. In contrast, LIFO would show a 5-cent higher cost of goods sold and a 5-cent lower gross profit:

| | LIFO | |
	As in Exhibit 20-1	If One More Unit Acquired
Sales	90¢	90¢
Cost of goods sold	56	61
Gross profit	34¢	29¢
Ending inventory:		
First layer, Monday	30¢	30¢
Second layer, Tuesday	40¢	40¢
Third layer, Wednesday		56¢
	70¢	126¢

Thus a 34 cents gross profit may be transformed into a 29 cents gross profit merely because of a change in the timing and amount of merchandise *acquired*, not because of any change in *sales*.

The second part of the preceding tabulation uses the word *layer*. As the term implies, a **LIFO layer** (also called **LIFO increment** or **LIFO pool**) is an identifiable addition to inventory. As a company grows, the LIFO layers tend to pile on one another as the years go by. Thus many LIFO companies will show inventories that may have ancient layers (going back to 1940 in some instances). The reported LIFO values may therefore be far below what FIFO values might otherwise show.

Suppose the physical quantity of inventory falls below its level of recent periods. What amounts are charged as cost of goods sold? The old LIFO inventory values! The most recent layers are charged first, but if the physical inventory decreases enough, very old and low costs might comprise cost of goods sold, causing reported income to soar. Income under LIFO, which is generally lower than under FIFO, can suddenly become much higher when inventory is depleted.

IMPORTANCE OF INCOME TAXES

The accounting literature is full of fancy theoretical arguments that support LIFO. For example, some accountants maintain that LIFO shows the "real" impact of inflation on cost of goods sold more clearly than FIFO. But there is one—and only one—dominant reason why more and more U.S. companies have adopted LIFO. *Income taxes*! LIFO is acceptable for income tax purposes. Furthermore, the Internal Revenue Code requires that if LIFO is used for income tax purposes, it must also be used for financial-reporting purposes. If prices persistently rise, and if inventory quantities are maintained so that LIFO layers bearing "old" prices are not used up, current taxable income will be less under LIFO than FIFO. Consequently, income taxes will be postponed. Intelligent financial management would therefore be tempted to adopt LIFO. Indeed, some observers maintain that executives are guilty of serious mismanagement by not adopting LIFO when FIFO produces significantly higher taxable income.

TYRANNY OF REPORTED EARNINGS

The accrual accounting model has survived many tests through time. It is here to stay. Nevertheless, as useful as it is for evaluating performance, its limitations should never be overlooked. For example, net income (or earnings per share) is *only one* measure of performance. Even though this "bottom line" is important, it is sometimes overemphasized in the minds of management. It may lead to decisions that boost current reported net income but may not be in the best long-run interests of the stockholders. Thus managers may slash advertising, maintenance, and research expenses to bolster 19X7 earnings. But such "economy measures" can produce some unfavorable results: reduction in share of the customer market, poorer condition of equipment, and lack of new products, all of which may have devastating effects on earnings in 19X8, 19X9, and thereafter.

Similarly, managers may be reluctant to switch to LIFO from FIFO because reported income will be less. There is widespread but mistaken belief that the stock market can be fooled by the reported net income numbers. In the long run, the wealth of the shareholders is usually enhanced by decisions that postpone income tax disbursements even though reported net income may be lower.

The accompanying table summarizes the choices faced by many top managers:

INVENTORY METHOD	ACTUAL CASH POSITION	REPORTED NET INCOME
FIFO	Lower	Higher
LIFO	Higher	Lower

The dilemma should generally be solved in favor of LIFO. Then the company would have a greater ability to meet the dividend expectations of stockholders or other cash demands. Why? Because the company will have a better cash position despite lower reported net income.

SUMMARY

Four major inventory methods are in use: specific identification, weighted-average, FIFO, and LIFO. When prices are rising, less income is generally shown by LIFO than FIFO.

LIFO is popular in the United States because it offers income tax advantages that become most pronounced during times of steady or rising inventories combined with rising prices. Note that even when inventories are declining, *cumulative* taxable income is always less under LIFO than FIFO because the inventory valuation is less and the cumulative cost of goods sold is higher.

SUMMARY PROBLEMS FOR YOUR REVIEW

☐ **Problem One**

Refer to Exhibit 20–1, page 680. Suppose the remaining two cans were sold on Friday for 90 cents each. All other data are unchanged.

Required:

1. Compute (a) the gross profit for Friday and (b) the gross profit for the week, Monday through Friday, under FIFO and under LIFO.
2. Assume the same facts as in Requirement 1 except that the vendor purchased one additional can of cola on Friday for 65 cents. Compute Friday's gross profit under FIFO and under LIFO.

☐ **Problem Two**

"When prices are rising, FIFO results in fool's profits because more resources are needed to maintain operations than previously." Do you agree? Explain.

1. The cost of goods sold on Friday is equal to Thursday's ending inventory from Exhibit 20–1. Notice that the gross profit for the life of the entity is the same under FIFO or LIFO. The inventory method affects only the timing of the profit. (All answers are in cents.)

		FIFO		LIFO
Sales		180		180
Cost of goods sold:				
Beginning inventory				
(from Exhibit 20–1)	96		70	
Purchases	0		0	
Cost of goods available				
for sale	96		70	
Ending inventory	0		0	
Cost of goods sold		96		70
a. Gross profit, Friday		84		110
Gross profit, Monday through				
Thursday (from Exhibit 20–1)		60		34
b. Gross profit, Monday				
through Friday		144		144

2. Note how the late purchase affects LIFO gross profit but not FIFO gross profit:

		FIFO		LIFO
Sales		180		180
Cost of goods sold:				
Beginning inventory				
(from Exhibit 20–1)	96		70	
Purchases	65		65	
Cost of goods available				
for sale	161		135	
Ending inventory*	65		30	
Cost of goods sold		96		105
Gross profit, Friday		84		75

* Friday unit for FIFO and Monday unit for LIFO.

□ **Solution to Problem Two**

The merit of this position depends on the concept of income favored. LIFO gives a better measure of "distributable" income than FIFO. Recall the cola example in the chapter. The gross profit under FIFO was 60¢ and under LIFO was 34¢. The 60¢ − 34¢ = 26¢ difference is a fool's profit because it must be reinvested to maintain the same inventory level as previously. Therefore the 26¢ cannot be distributed as a cash dividend without reducing the current level of operations.

The following table summarizes differences between FIFO and LIFO:

INVENTORY METHOD	INCOME STATEMENT: MEASUREMENT OF COST OF GOODS SOLD	BALANCE SHEET: MEASUREMENT OF INVENTORY ASSET
FIFO	Distant from current replacement cost	Near current replacement cost
LIFO	Near current replacement cost	Distant from current replacement cost

ACCOUNTING VOCABULARY

First-in, First-out (FIFO) *p. 680*   Last-in, First-out (LIFO) *680*   LIFO Increment *683*   LIFO Layer *683*   LIFO Pool *683*   Periodic Inventory System *680*   Perpetual Inventory System *680*   Specific Identification *680*   Weighted-Average Cost *681*

☐ PART TWO Changing Prices and Income Measurement

The measurement of income is easily the most controversial subject in accounting. The remainder of this chapter focuses on how inflation (or more generally, changing prices) affects the income statement. An appendix explores the problems of accounting for inflation in more depth, although still at an introductory level.

COMPLAINTS ABOUT HISTORICAL COST

Accountants traditionally have maintained that net income is a return *on* the capital invested by shareholders. Suppose an amount equal to the net income of a period is returned to the shareholders as dividends. In the absence of inflation, such a payment leaves the shareholders' invested capital at the end of the period equal to the beginning capital. However, when prices change, this relationship between income and capital is altered. In times of generally rising prices, paying dividends equal to net income, as conventionally measured, usually amounts to paying out some capital itself as well as the return on capital.

A pet theme of politicians and others often is the "unconscionable" or "obscene" profits reported by American companies. In turn, many business executives insist that our traditional historical-cost basis for measuring income produces misleading results, especially during a time of rising prices. Some managers have complained that the reported profits for most years in the past two decades have been so badly overstated that income taxes have been unfairly levied. In many cases, invested capital, rather than earned income, has been taxed.

The industries with huge investments in plant and equipment claim that their profits are badly misstated by generally accepted accounting principles. For instance, consider NYNEX, a company that emerged from the breakup of the Bell System. NYNEX reported 1985 net income of $1,095 million, which would have been a net loss of $82 million if depreciation had been adjusted for inflation.

Managers also find historical cost information inadequate for many internal decisions. Some companies have routinely used inflation-adjusted reports for internal reporting purposes. For example, FMC Corporation, a multinational machinery, vehicle, and chemical producer, has used such information since 1980.

INCOME OR CAPITAL

Before presenting alternatives to historical-cost accounting, we first concentrate on various concepts of income and capital. At first glance, the concept of income seems straightforward. Income is increase in wealth. But what is wealth? It is capital. But what is capital? An endless chain of similar questions can be constructed. The heart of the issue is the distinction between invested capital and income. The time-honored interpretation is that invested capital is a *financial* concept (rather than a *physical* concept). The focus is on the potential profitability of the money invested, no matter what types of inventory, equipment, or other resources have been acquired.

Financial resources (capital) are invested with the expectation of an eventual return *of* that capital together with additional amounts representing the return *on* that capital. Controversies have arisen regarding whether the financial resources generated by the invested capital qualify as returns *of* or *on* capital.

The Financial Accounting Standards Board distinguishes between financial and physical capital maintenance concepts in Statement No. 33, "Financial Reporting and Changing Prices":

☐ Capital is maintained when revenues are at least equal to all costs and expenses. The appropriate measurement of costs and expenses depends on the concept of capital maintenance adopted.

Consider an example where a company begins with owners' investment (capital) of $1,000, which is used immediately to purchase inventory. The inventory is sold a year later for $1,500. The cost of replacing the inventory has risen to $1,200.

	FINANCIAL CAPITAL MAINTENANCE	PHYSICAL CAPITAL MAINTENANCE
Sales	$1,500	$1,500
Cost of goods sold	1,000	1,200
Income	$ 500	$ 300

Most accountants and managers believe that income emerges after financial resources are recovered, a concept called **financial capital maintenance**. Because the $1,000 capital has been recovered, $500 is the measure of income.

On the other hand, some accountants believe that income emerges only after recovering an amount that allows physical operating capability to be maintained, called **physical capital maintenance**. Because $1,200 is the current cost of inventory (cost of maintaining physical capability) at the date of sale, $300 is the measure of income.

MEASUREMENT ALTERNATIVES UNDER CHANGING PRICES

Study the four definitions in this paragraph; they are critical to understanding inflation accounting. **Nominal dollars** are dollar measurements that are not restated for fluctuations in the general purchasing power of the monetary unit, whereas **constant dollars** are nominal dollars restated in terms of current purchasing power. The **historical cost** of an asset is the amount originally paid to acquire it; the **current cost** of an asset is generally the cost to replace it. Traditional accounting uses *nominal* (rather than constant) dollars and *historical* (rather than current) costs. Such accounting has almost exclusively dominated financial reporting throughout this century. Using historical costs implies maintenance of *financial* capital; current costs imply *physical* capital maintenance.

Two approaches, which can be applied separately or in combination, address problems caused by inflation: (1) constant-dollar disclosures account for *general* changes in the purchasing power of the dollar, and (2) current-cost disclosures account for changes in *specific* prices. The two approaches create the following four alternatives for measuring income:

	Historical Cost	Current Cost
Nominal Dollars	Historical cost/ nominal dollars	Current cost/ nominal dollars
Constant Dollars	Historical cost/ constant dollars	Current cost/ constant dollars

The G Company situation described next is used to compare various concepts of income and capital. The four basic methods of income measurement are presented. G Company has the following comparative balance sheets at December 31 (based on historical costs in nominal dollars):

	19X1	19X2
Cash	$ 0	$10,500
Inventory, 400 and 100 units, respectively	8,000	2,000
Total assets	$8,000	$12,500
Original paid-in capital	$8,000	$ 8,000
Retained income	—	4,500
Stockholders' equity	$8,000	$12,500

The company had acquired all 400 units of inventory at $20 per unit (total of $8,000) on December 31, 19X1 and had held the units until December 31, 19X2. Three hundred units were sold for $35 per unit (total of $10,500 cash) on December 31, 19X2. The replacement cost of the inventory at that date was $30 per unit. The general-price-level index was 100 on December 31, 19X1, and 110 on December 31, 19X2. Assume that these are the only transactions. Ignore income taxes.

Historical Cost/Nominal Dollars

Exhibit 20–3 is the basis for the explanations that follow in the next several pages. The first set of financial statements in Exhibit 20–3 shows the time-honored method that uses historical cost/nominal dollars (Method 1). Basically, this method measures invested capital in nominal dollars. It is the most popular approach to income measurement and is commonly called the historical-cost method. Operating income (equals net income in this case) is the excess of realized revenue ($10,500 in 19X2) over the "not restated" historical costs of assets used in obtaining that revenue. As we have already seen, when the conventional accrual basis of accounting is used, an exchange transaction is ordinarily necessary before revenues (and resulting incomes) are deemed to be realized. Thus, no income generally appears until the asset is sold; intervening price fluctuations are ignored.

Current Cost/Nominal Dollars

The second set of financial statements in Exhibit 20–3 illustrates a **current-cost method** that has especially strong advocates in the United Kingdom and Australia (Method 2). This method uses current cost/nominal dollars. In general, the current cost of an asset is the cost to replace it. The focus is on income from continuing operations. This model emphasizes that operating income should be "distributable" income. That is, G Company could pay divi-

EXHIBIT 20-3 *(Put a clip on this page for easy reference)*

Four Major Methods to Measure Income and Capital
(in dollars)

| | NOMINAL DOLLARS*| | | | CONSTANT DOLLARS* | | | |
| | (METHOD 1) | | (METHOD 2) | | (METHOD 3) | | (METHOD 4) | |
	Historical Cost		Current Cost		Historical Cost		Current Cost	
Balance sheets as of December 31	19X1	19X2	19X1	19X2	19X1	19X2	19X1	19X2
Cash	—	10,500	—	10,500	—	10,500	—	10,500
Inventory, 400 and 100 units, respectively	8,000	2,000[b]	8,000	3,000[c]	8,800[e]	2,200[e]	8,800[e]	3,000[c]
Total assets	8,000	12,500	8,000	13,500	8,800	12,700	8,800	13,500
Original paid-in capital	8,000	8,000	8,000	8,000	8,800[f]	8,800[f]	8,800[f]	8,800[f]
Retained income (confined to income from continuing operations)		4,500		1,500		3,900		1,500
Revaluation equity (accumulated holding gains)				4,000				3,200
Total equities	8,000	12,500	8,000	13,500	8,800	12,700	8,800	13,500
Income Statements for 19X2								
Sales, 300 units @ $35		10,500		10,500		10,500		10,500
Cost of goods sold, 300 units		6,000[b]		9,000[c]		6,600[e]		9,000[c]
Income from continuing operations (to retained income)		4,500		1,500		3,900		1,500
Holding gains:[a]								
on 300 units sold				3,000[d]				2,400[g]
on 100 units unsold				1,000[d]				800[g]
Total holding gains[a] (to revaluation equity)				4,000				3,200

* Nominal dollars are not restated for a general price index, whereas constant dollars are restated.

[a] Many advocates of this current cost method favor showing these gains in a completely separate statement of holding gains rather than as a part of the income statement. Others favor including some or all of these gains as a part of income for the year; see Appendix 20 for further discussion.

[b] 100 × $20, [c] 100 × $30, [d] 300 × ($30 − $20), [e] 110/100 × $8,000, [f] 110/100 × $8,000.
   300 × $20.   300 × $30.   100 × ($30 − $20).   110/100 × $2,000,
                                110/100 × $6,000.

[g] $9,000 − restated cost of $6,600 = $2,400 $3,000 − restated cost of $2,200 = $800
   or   or
   300 × ($30 − 110% of $20) = $2,400.   100 × ($30 − 110% of $20) = $800.

dends in an amount of only $1,500, leaving enough assets to allow for replacement of the inventory that has just been sold.

Critics of the historical-cost approach claim that the $4,500 measure of income from continuing operations is misleading because it inaccurately reflects (it overstates) the net increment in distributable assets. If a $4,500 dividend were paid, the company would be less able to continue operations at the same level as before. The $3,000 difference between the two operating incomes ($4,500 − $1,500 = $3,000) is frequently referred to as an "inventory profit" or an "inflated profit." Why? Because $9,000 instead of $6,000 is now necessary to replace the 300 units sold (300 × the increase in price from $20 to $30 equals the $3,000 difference).

☐ Holding Gains and Physical Capital

The current-cost method stresses a separation between *income from continuing operations*, which is defined as the excess of revenue over the current costs of the assets consumed in obtaining that revenue, and **holding gains** (or **losses**), which are increases (or decreases) in the replacement costs of the assets held during the current period. Accountants differ sharply on how to account for holding gains. The "correct" accounting depends on distinctions between capital and income. That is, income cannot occur until invested capital is "recovered" or "maintained." The issue of capital versus income is concretely illustrated in Exhibit 20–3. The advocates of a physical concept of capital maintenance claim that *all* holding gains (both those gains related to the units sold and the gains related to the units unsold) should be excluded from income and become a part of revalued capital, called **revaluation equity**. That is, for a going concern no income can result unless the physical capital devoted to operations during the current period can be replaced.

For simplicity, income taxes are ignored in Exhibit 20–3. The historical cost/nominal dollar method (Method 1) is the only acceptable method for reporting on income tax returns in English-speaking countries. As Appendix 20 discusses in more detail, many managers of heavy industries such as steel and aluminum claim that their capital is being taxed under the historical-cost/nominal-dollar method. These managers maintain that taxes should be levied only on *income from continuing operations*, as computed under the current-cost/nominal-dollar method (Method 2).

☐ Historical Cost/Constant Dollars

Method 3 of Exhibit 20–3 shows the results of applying general index numbers to historical costs. Essentially, the income measurements in each year are restated in terms of *constant dollars* (possessing the same general purchasing power of the current year) instead of the *nominal dollars* (possessing different general purchasing power of various years).

The fundamental reasoning underlying the Method 3 approach goes to the heart of the measurement theory itself. Additions or subtractions must use a *common measuring unit*, be it dollars, francs, meters, ounces, or any chosen measure.

Consider the objections to Method 1. Deducting 6,000 19X1 dollars from 10,500 19X2 dollars to obtain $4,500 is akin to deducting 60 *centimeters* from 105 *meters* and calling the result 45. Grade-school tests are marked wrong when such nonsensical arithmetic is discovered, but accountants have been paid well for years for performing similar arithmetic.

Method 3, historical cost/constant dollars, shows how to remedy the foregoing objections. General indexes may be used to restate the amounts of historical cost/nominal dollar Method 1. Examples of such indexes are the Gross National Product Implicit Price Deflator and the Consumer Price Index for All Urban Consumers (CPI). Anyone who has lived long enough to be able to read this book is aware that the purchasing power of the dollar is unstable. Index numbers are used to gauge the relationship between current conditions and some norm or base condition (which is assigned the index number of 100). For our purpose, a **general price index** compares the average price of a group of goods and services at one date with the average price of a similar group at another date. A price index is an average. It does not measure the behavior of the individual component prices. Some individual prices may move in one direction and some in another. The general consumer price level may soar while the prices of eggs and chickens decline.

Do not confuse *general* indexes, which are used in constant-dollar accounting, with *specific* indexes. The two have entirely different purposes. Sometimes **specific price indexes** are used as a means of approximating the *current costs* of particular assets or types of assets. That is, companies have found specialized indexes to be good enough to get approximations of current costs. This avoids the hiring of professional appraisers or the employing of other expensive means of valuation. For example, Inland Steel uses the Engineering News Record Construction Cost Index to value most of its property, plant, and equipment for purposes of using the current-cost method.

☐ Maintaining Invested Capital

The historical-cost/constant-dollar approach (Method 3) is *not* a fundamental departure from historical costs. Instead, it maintains that all historical costs to be matched against revenue should be restated on some constant-dollar basis so that all revenues and all expenses can be expressed in dollars of the same (usually current) purchasing power. The restated figures *are historical costs* expressed in constant dollars via the use of a general price index.

The *current* dollar is typically employed because users of financial statements tend to think in such terms instead of in terms of old dollars with significantly different purchasing power. The original units in inventory would be updated on each year's balance sheet along with their effect on stockholders' equity. For example, the December 31, 19X1, balance sheet would be restated for comparative purposes on December 31, 19X2:

	NOT RESTATED COST	MULTIPLIER	RESTATED COST
Inventory	$8,000	110/100	$8,800
Original paid-in capital	8,000	110/100	8,800

To extend the illustration, suppose all the inventory was held for two full years. The general price index rose from 110 to 132 during 19X3. The December 31, 19X2 balance sheet items would be restated for comparative purposes on December 31, 19X3:

	RESTATED COST 12/31/X2	MULTIPLIER	RESTATED COST 12/31/X3
Inventory	$8,800	132/110	$10,560*
Original paid-in capital	8,800	132/110	10,560*

* The same result could be tied to the year of acquisition:
Inventory $8,000 × 132/100 = $10,560
Original paid-in capital $8,000 × 132/100 = $10,560

The restated amount is just that—a restatement of original *cost* in terms of current dollars—not a gain in any sense. Therefore this approach should *not* be labeled as an adoption of "current-cost" accounting. Using this approach, if the specific current cost of the inventory goes up or down, the restated cost is unaffected.

The restated historical-cost approach harmonizes with the concept of *maintaining the general purchasing power* of the invested capital (a *financial* concept of capital maintenance) in total rather than maintaining "specific invested capital," item by item. More will be said about this distinction after we examine Method 4.

☐ **Current Cost/Constant Dollars**

Method 4 of Exhibit 20–3 shows the results of applying general index numbers to current costs. As the footnotes of the exhibit explain in more detail, the nominal gains reported under Method 2 are adjusted so that only gains in constant dollars are reported. For example, suppose you buy 100 units on December 31, 19X1 for $2,000 cash. If the current replacement cost of your inventory at December 31, 19X2 is $3,000 but the general price index has risen from 100 to 110, your nominal gain is $1,000, but your "real" gain in constant dollars in 19X2 is only $800: the $3,000 current cost minus the restated historical cost of $2,000 × 1.10 = $2,200.

Suppose the 100 units are held throughout 19X3. The general price index rises from 110 to 132. The replacement cost rises from $30 to $34, a nominal holding gain for 19X3 of $4 × 100 = $400. However, the current-cost/constant-dollar approach (Method 3) would report a real holding loss:

Current cost, restated, December 31, 19X2:	
$3,000 × 132/110	$3,600
Current cost, December 31, 19X3, 100 × $34	3,400
Holding loss	$ 200

Many theorists disagree on the relative merits of historical-cost approaches versus miscellaneous versions of current-cost approaches to income measurement. But there is general agreement among the theorists that restatements in constant dollars would be an improvement (ignoring practical barriers), because otherwise income includes illusory gains caused by using an unstable measuring unit.

FASB PRESENTATION

During the late 1970s, soaring inflation raised questions about the usefulness of historical-cost/nominal-dollar statements. Accountants in many countries struggled with the problem of measuring the current cost of assets.

After extensive public hearings, the Financial Accounting Standards Board issued Statement No. 33, "Financial Reporting and Changing Prices," in 1979. The statement applies to public companies that have either (1) inventories and property, plant, and equipment (before deducting accumulated depreciation) amounting to more than $125 million or (2) total assets amounting to more than $1 billion (after deducting accumulated depreciation). No changes must be made in the *primary* financial statements. All information required by Statement No. 33 is to be presented as *supplementary* schedules in published annual reports. Statement No. 33 is experimental, but in 1985, the FASB committed to requiring the supplementary reports for at least several more years. Appendix 20 has a fuller description of the FASB requirements.

Exhibit 20–4 recasts the income statement in Exhibit 20–3 in accordance with the FASB preferences. The general premise of the bottom part of Exhibit 20–4 is that changes in the current values of assets should be divided into

EXHIBIT 20–4

Recasting of Exhibit 20-3
(To reflect FASB preferences per FASB Statement No. 33)
Statement of Income from Continuing Operations Adjusted for Changing Prices
For the Year Ended December 31, 19X2

	AS REPORTED IN THE PRIMARY STATEMENTS	ADJUSTED FOR CHANGES IN SPECIFIC PRICES (CURRENT COSTS)
Sales, 300 units @ $35	$10,500	$10,500
Cost of goods sold, 300 units	6,000	9,000
Income from continuing operations	$ 4,500	$ 1,500
Increase in specific prices (current cost) of inventories held during the year: 400 units × ($30 − $20)		$ 4,000
Less: Effect of increase in general price level: 10% × 400 × $20		800
Excess of increase in specific prices over increase in the general price level		$ 3,200

two parts: (1) an increase due to general inflation and (2) an increase or de-crease arising because specific prices change at a rate other than the inflation rate. Suppose the inventory value had increased by $800. The company would have just kept pace with inflation. The additional $3,200 increase in the cur-rent cost of the specific assets shows that the company's assets are increasing in value considerably faster than inflation.

Compare Exhibits 20–4 and 20–3:

1. The FASB avoids using the term *holding gain*. Instead, it uses verbose descrip-tions of the final three numbers in Exhibit 20–4. Why? Probably because accoun-tants and managers continue to disagree about whether all, some, or none of the holding gains are really "net income." Note too that in both exhibits these numbers are reported but are not added to income from continuing operations.
2. Exhibit 20–4 is similar to the Method 4 format used in Exhibit 20–3, current cost/constant dollar. In a sense, the statement does double duty. Its first four rows provide all the current cost data that were shown for Method 2 in Exhibit 20–3 ($10,500, $9,000, $1,500, and $4,000). Then it subtracts the $800 increase associated with general inflation from the total $4,000 increase to get the holding gain that represents a real increase in the value of the company. The only infor-mation in Exhibit 20–3 that is not reported in Exhibit 20–4 is the cost of goods sold (and therefore operating income) on a historical-cost/constant-dollar basis (Method 3).

As recently as 1983, current-cost earnings averaged only 28% of the familiar historical cost numbers. However, because of the decline in the rate of inflation, average current-cost earnings are now over half of historical-cost earnings. But the difference varies greatly by company. The 1985 current-cost earnings were 95% of historical-cost earnings for General Motors and only 25% for American Telephone and Telegraph. Both U.S. Steel and Alcoa reported positive 1985 net income, but would have reported losses if they had used current costs.

SUMMARY

The matching of historical costs with revenue is the generally accepted means of measuring net income. But basing such computations on some version of current costs has been proposed as a better gauge of the distinctions between income (the return *on* capital) and capital maintenance (the return *of* capital).

General price indexes are used to adjust historical costs so that all expenses are measured in current dollars of the same purchasing power. Such adjustments do not represent a departure from historical cost. In contrast, specific price indexes are often used to implement the current-cost approach to measuring income and capital.

SUMMARY PROBLEM FOR YOUR REVIEW

Problems One and Two appeared earlier in this chapter.

☐ Problem Three

In 1967 a parcel of land, call it parcel 1, was purchased for $1,200. An identical parcel, 2, was purchased today for $3,600. The general-price-level index has risen from 100 in 1967 to 300 now. Fill in the blanks in the table below.

PARCEL	(1) HISTORICAL COST MEASURED IN 1967 PURCHASING POWER	(2) HISTORICAL COST MEASURED IN CURRENT PURCHASING POWER	(3) HISTORICAL COST AS ORIGINALLY MEASURED
1			
2			
Total	_____	_____	_____

1. Compare the figures in the three columns. Which total presents a nonsense result. Why?
2. Does the write-up of parcel 1 in column 2 result in a gain? Why?
3. Assume that these parcels are the only assets of the business. There are no liabilities. Prepare a balance sheet for each of the three columns.

☐ Solution to Problem Three

PARCEL	(1) HISTORICAL COST MEASURED IN 1967 PURCHASING POWER	(2) HISTORICAL COST MEASURED IN CURRENT PURCHASING POWER	(3) HISTORICAL COST AS ORIGINALLY MEASURED
1	$1,200	$3,600	$1,200
2	1,200	3,600	3,600
Total	$2,400	$7,200	$4,800

1. The addition in column 3 produces a nonsense result. In contrast, the other sums are the results of applying a standard unit of measure. The computations in columns 1 and 2 are illustrations of a restatement of historical cost in terms of a common dollar, a standard unit of measure. Such computations have been frequently called adjustments for changes in the general price level. Whether the restatement is made using the 1967 dollar or the current dollar is a matter of personal preference; columns 1 and 2 yield equivalent results. Restatement in terms of the current dollar (column 2) is most popular because the current dollar has more meaning than the old dollar to the reader of the financial statements.
2. The mere restatement of identical assets in terms of different but equivalent measuring units cannot be regarded as a gain. Expressing parcel 1 as $1,200 in column 1 and $3,600 in column 2 is like expressing parcel 1 in terms of, say, either 1,200 square yards or 9 × 1,200 = 10,800 square feet. Surely, the "write-up" from 1,200 square yards to 10,800 square feet is not a gain; it is merely another way of measuring the same asset. The 1,200 square yards and the 10,800 square feet are equivalent; they are different ways of describing the same asset. That is basically what general-price-level accounting is all about. It says you cannot measure one plot of land in square yards and another in square feet and

add them together before converting to some common measure. Unfortunately, column 3 fails to perform such a conversion before adding the two parcels together; hence the total is internally inconsistent.

3. The balance sheets would be:

	(1)	(2)	(3)
Land	$2,400	$7,200	$4,800
Paid-in capital	$2,400	$7,200	$4,800

Note that (1) is expressed in 1967 dollars, (2) is in current dollars, and (3) is a mixture of 1967 and current dollars.

HIGHLIGHTS TO REMEMBER

Restatements in constant dollars can be applied to both the historical-cost and the current-cost basis of income measurement, as Methods 3 and 4 illustrate. Avoid the misconception that the choices are among the first three methods only. In fact, many advocates of the current-cost/constant-dollar method insist it provides the most useful approximation of net income. In any event, any measurement of income should be based on constant dollars.

When inflation accounting is discussed, accountants and managers frequently confuse and blur the various concepts of income just covered. Highlights of Exhibit 20–3, page 691 include:

1. The choice among accounting measures is often expressed as either historical-cost accounting or general-price-level accounting or current-cost (specific-price-level) accounting. But this is an inaccurate statement of choices.

2. A correct statement would be that there are four major concepts. Nominal dollars may be combined with either historical cost (Method 1) or current cost (Method 2). In addition, general-price-level (constant-dollar) accounting may be combined with either historical-cost accounting (Method 3) or current-cost accounting (Method 4).

3. Method 3, the historical-cost/constant-dollar method, is *not* concerned with current-cost concepts of income, whatever their strengths and weaknesses.

4. The current-cost Methods 2 and 4 for measuring income from operations are based on *physical* rather than *financial* concepts of maintenance of invested capital.

5. Write-ups of nonmonetary assets (inventory in this example) under Method 3 do *not* result in the recognition of gains. They are restatements of *costs* in dollars of equivalent purchasing power. See Appendix 20 for a discussion of the distinction between monetary and nonmonetary assets, as well as other aspects of inflation accounting.

ACCOUNTING VOCABULARY

Constant Dollars *p.* 689   Current Cost 689   Current-Cost Method 690   Financial Capital Maintenance 689   General Price Index 693   Historical Cost 689   Holding Gains (or Losses) 692   Monetary Item 701   Nominal Dollars 689   Physical Capital Maintenance 689   Revaluation Equity 692   Specific Price Index 693

APPENDIX 20: MORE ON INFLATION ACCOUNTING

This appendix extends the discussion in the body of the chapter, emphasizing current-cost depreciation and monetary items. Special attention is given to the FASB requirements regarding these topics.

MEANING OF CURRENT COST

Current cost is the most popular term for describing the fundamental basis for valuing the inventory as shown for Method 2 in Exhibit 20–3. However, it is a general term having several variations. Be on guard as to its meaning in a particular situation. As illustrated in Exhibit 20–3, the current-cost method stresses that income cannot emerge until deducting the current (or reproduction) cost of replenishing the item at today's prices. The regulatory authorities in most of the English-speaking countries have proposed that the current-cost approach be based on replacement costs. In most instances, *replacement cost* means today's cost of obtaining a similar asset that *would produce the same expected cash flows as the existing asset*. For a particular company, these replacement costs would be obtained via price quotations, specific appraisals, or specific indexes for material or construction.

The FASB uses current replacement cost as its dominant requirement for measuring current cost. However, sometimes the replacement cost of a particular asset exceeds its *recoverable amount*. For example, some equipment or inventory may be obsolete. *Recoverable amount* is defined as (1) the net realizable value of an asset that is about to be sold or (2) the net present value of expected cash flows (called *value in use*) of an asset that is not about to be sold. *Net realizable value* is the amount of cash (or its equivalent) expected to be derived from sale of an asset, net of costs required to be incurred as a result of the sale. In sum, the FASB rule is current cost or lower recoverable amount.

PROPERTY, PLANT, AND EQUIPMENT

The general idea of current cost is the same for equipment as for inventories. Nevertheless, the application of the idea is more difficult. An illustration will help to clarify the issues. Extending the example in Exhibit 20–3, suppose that on January 2, 19X3, $5,000 of the $10,500 cash was used to buy sales equipment. The equipment was being fully depreciated over a five-year life on a straight-line basis. The replacement cost of the equipment (new) at the end of 19X3 was $8,000. The general price index was 110 at the end of 19X2 and 132 at the end of 19X3. Exhibit 20–5 shows the effects and why manufacturers of heavy goods would like the IRS to adopt the current-cost approach. That is, the manufacturers would want depreciation expense of $1,600 to be deductible for income tax purposes. At the same time, the "holding gain" of $3,000 should not be subject to tax because it represents capital maintenance rather than income.

Current-cost depreciation is computed by multiplying the depreciation percentage based on useful life ($1 \div 5$ years $= 20\%$) by the new *gross* carrying amount at current cost: $0.20 \times \$8,000 = \$1,600$.

The holding gain in Method 2 (current cost/nominal dollars) is computed by multiplying the percentage increase in gross carrying amount for the year (from $5,000 to $8,000 is a 60% increase) by the beginning *net* carrying amount at current cost: $0.60 \times \$5,000 = \$3,000$.

Pursuing the example for one more year, suppose the replacement cost of the equipment (new) at the end of 19X4 was $12,000. The percentage increase in gross

EXHIBIT 20–5

Relation of Depreciation to Four Methods of Measuring Income
(in dollars)

19x3	NOMINAL DOLLARS (METHOD 1) Historical Cost Jan. 2	Dec. 31	(METHOD 2) Current Cost Jan. 2	Dec. 31	CONSTANT DOLLARS (METHOD 3) Historical Cost Jan. 2	Dec. 31	(METHOD 4) Current Cost Jan. 2	Dec. 31
Balance Sheet Accounts								
Equipment	5,000	5,000	5,000	8,000	6,000ᵈ	6,000	6,000	8,000
Accumulated depreciation	—	1,000	—	1,600	—	1,200	—	1,600
Net carrying amount	5,000	4,000	5,000	6,400	6,000	4,800	6,000	6,400
Income Statement Effects								
Depreciation expense		1,000ᵃ		1,600ᵇ		1,200ᵉ		1,600
Holding gain, equipment		—		3,000ᶜ		—		2,000ᶠ

ᵃ .20 × 5,000. ᶜ .60 × 5,000. ᵉ .20 × 6,000.
ᵇ .20 × 8,000. ᵈ $^{132}/_{110}$ × 5,000. ᶠ 8,000 − 6,000.

carrying amount would be 50% (from $8,000 to $12,000). Method 2 (current cost/ nominal dollars) would show the following effects on the 19X4 income statement:

1. Restate the beginning asset value into end-of-year dollars, recognizing a holding gain:

Holding gain, equipment = percentage price increase × the beginning net carrying amount at beginning-of-year current cost = 0.50 × $6,400 = $3,200.

2. Calculate depreciation based on the restated (end-of-year) value of the asset:

Depreciation expense = depreciation percentage × gross carrying amount at end-of-year current cost = 0.20 × $12,000 = $2,400.

Computations of holding gains can rapidly become complex. For instance, this introductory explanation has avoided such intricacies as (1) using average current cost for the year rather than end-of-year current cost as a basis for depreciation and (2) restating current costs through a series of years in constant dollars. The basic concepts are unchanged, but the arithmetic is tedious.

Income tax laws in the English-speaking countries have been changed to permit accelerated write-offs of the historical costs of depreciable assets. However, no departures from historical-cost methods have been permitted. Managers of companies having large investments in inventories and property, plant, and equipment generally favor the adoption of a current-cost approach to measuring taxable income. Why? Because in times of rising prices, cost of goods sold and depreciation are higher based on current costs than on historical costs. Therefore, taxable income would be less and income tax outflows would be less—as long as no holding gains are subject to taxes.[1]

---

[1] If taxes were levied as indicated, the capital-goods industries would have relatively lower incomes subject to tax than other industries. However, keep in mind that a country usually has the same target *total* income taxes to be generated by the corporate sector. If the taxable

Annual reports frequently contain complaints about high income tax rates. Comparative effective income tax rates are often tabulated to demonstrate striking differences. For example, NYNEX showed 1985 effective income tax rates of 41.2% of earnings before taxes based on historical cost/nominal dollars (as reported to the IRS) and 111.6% based on current cost.

GENERAL PURCHASING POWER GAINS AND LOSSES

We now turn to constant-dollar accounting. First, we compare Methods 1 (historical cost/nominal dollar) and 2 (historical cost/constant dollar) from Exhibit 20–3, page 691. Then the addition of constant-dollar effects to current-cost statements will be briefly discussed.

☐ Monetary Items

A **monetary item** is a claim receivable or payable in a specified number of dollars; the claim remains fixed regardless of changes in either specific or general price levels. Examples are cash, accounts receivable, accounts payable, and bonds payable. In contrast, nonmonetary items have prices that can vary. Examples are inventory, land, equipment, and liabilities for product warranties.

The distinction between monetary and nonmonetary assets is the key to understanding the impact of constant-dollar accounting on income measurement and stockholders' equity. Reconsider the facts depicted in Exhibit 20–3 except that we extend matters throughout 19X3. Suppose the inventory was not replaced. Instead, the $10,500 cash received on December 31, 19X2, was held throughout 19X3 in a noninterest-bearing checking account. Furthermore, assume that the 100 units of inventory on December 31, 19X2, were held throughout 19X3 and remained unsold on December 31, 19X3. The general-price-level index rose from 110 to 132 during 19X3. The familiar historical-cost/nominal-dollar (Method 1) statement would be:

	19X2	19X3
Balance Sheets as of December 31		
Cash	$10,500	$10,500
Inventory	2,000	2,000
Total assets	$12,500	$12,500
Original paid-in capital	$ 8,000	$ 8,000
Retained income	4,500	4,500
Total stockholders' equity	$12,500	$12,500
Income Statement for 19X3		
None (no revenue or expenses)		

Before reading on, reflect on the intuitive meaning of holding cash during a time of inflation. The holder of cash or claims to cash gets burned by inflation. In contrast, the debtor benefits from inflation because the debtor can pay creditors with a fixed amount of dollars that have less current purchasing power than when the debt was originally contracted.

---

income of all corporations declined, all income tax *rates* would undoubtedly be raised so as to produce the same *total* tax collections as before. Thus a replacement-cost basis may redistribute the tax burden among companies so that capital-goods industries pay less total tax. But the chances are high that the overall percentage rate would increase, so that the tax savings in capital-goods industries would be offset by tax increases in other industries.

How do we measure the economic effects of holding cash during inflation? Using the basic historical-cost/constant-dollar method in Exhibit 20–3, let us restate in constant dollars, using 19X3 dollars. Because the general-price-level index rose from 110 to 132, the restatements would be as follows:

	19X2	19X3
Balance Sheets as of December 31		
Cash: 132/110 × 10,500 19X2 dollars	$12,600	$10,500
Inventory: 132/100 × 2,000 19X1 dollars	2,640	2,640
Total assets	$15,240	$13,140
Original paid-in capital:		
132/100 × 8,000 19X1 dollars	$10,560	$10,560
Retained income	4,680[a]	4,680
Revaluation equity	—	(2,100)[b]
Total stockholders' equity	$15,240	$13,140
Income Statement for 19X3		
Holding gain (loss) on monetary item		$ (2,100)

[a] $15,240 − $10,560.   [b] $12,600 − $10,500.

The cash balance is not restated in 19X3 because it is already measured in 19X3 dollars. The formal constant-dollar income statement, assuming no operating activities, would consist of the lone item as in the foregoing table: holding loss on monetary item, $2,100. The monetary item in this case is cash; its loss of purchasing power is $12,600 − $10,500 = $2,100. In turn, stockholders' equity would be reduced by $2,100, as shown by the amount of the revaluation equity.

The label "holding loss" on the monetary item is not used by FASB No. 33. Instead, the following nomenclature is favored: gain (loss) from decline in purchasing power of net monetary items. By using such labels, the FASB tries to dampen the controversy regarding whether holding gains are really a part of net income. For this reason, the accompanying tables include holding gains and losses in revaluation equity rather than in retained income.

☐ Nonmonetary Items

Before reading on, reflect on the intuitive meaning of holding a nonmonetary asset during a time of inflation. Assets in the form of physical things have prices that can fluctuate and thus, unlike cash, offer more protection against the risks of inflation.

The purchasing power of cash fluctuates. A 19X2 cash balance of $10,500 needs to grow to $12,600 during 19X3 to maintain purchasing power. If it stays at $10,500, $2,100 of purchasing power in 19X3 dollars is lost. In contrast, the purchasing power of the amount paid for an asset does not change. The $2,000 of 19X1 dollars paid for inventory can be measured with different yardsticks, for example, 19X3 dollars, but the purchasing power always remains the same. In 19X3, this purchasing power is expressed as (132 ÷ 100) × $2,000 = $2,640. The $640 increase in inventory is not a gain; it simply arises because a new yardstick is being used.

In summary, the purchasing power paid for a nonmonetary asset is fixed, but measurements of this amount depend on which year's dollar is used to measure it. The purchasing power of monetary assets, on the other hand, can vary. Therefore, holding monetary assets and liabilities can create gains or losses in purchasing power.

As of the end of 19X2, the $10,500 cash balance represented the equivalent of $12,600 in terms of 19X3 purchasing power, but at the end of 19X3 it is worth only $10,500. In contrast, the $2,000 historical investment in inventory, which does not represent a fixed monetary claim, represented $2,640 in terms of *19X3 purchasing power*; its purchasing power has not been eroded. The inventory is *restated* to an amount of $2,640. But the $2,640 investment in inventory is unaffected by changes in the general-price-level index during 19X3.

Two difficulties and subtleties of constant-dollar accounting deserve emphasis here. First, all past balance sheets are restated in today's dollars. Second, the balance sheet changes are computed among the *monetary* items to produce purchasing power gains or losses. No such gains or losses will ever appear for nonmonetary items. For example, suppose the $10,500 cash had been immediately reinvested in 300 more units of inventory. How would the constant-dollar statements be affected? No purchasing power loss or gain would have occurred in 19X3:

	DECEMBER 31, 19X2	DECEMBER 31, 19X3
Inventory (instead of cash)		
132/110 × $10,500	$12,600	$12,600
Inventory (as before)	2,640	2,640
Total assets	$15,240	$15,240
Original capital	$10,560	$10,560
Retained income	4,680	4,680
Total stockholders' equity	$15,240	$15,240

Many accountants and managers confuse these restatements of *historical-cost* statements with current-cost notions of income. However, these constant-dollar statements (Method 3 in Exhibit 20–3) adhere to historical cost. The aim is to see whether the *general* purchasing power of the original invested capital has been maintained. Hence, whether *specific* inventory prices have gone up, down, or sideways is of no concern.

In sum, constant-dollar accounting will modify historical-cost statements in two major ways. First, historical costs are restated in constant dollars. Second, purchasing-power gains and losses arising from holding monetary assets and monetary liabilities will be recognized.

Note that holding gains on monetary items are linked with constant-dollar accounting. They do not exist under nominal-dollar accounting. Holding gains on non-monetary items are associated exclusively with "current-cost" accounting and are not an integral part of "historical-cost" accounting.

Finally, constant-dollar accounting may be linked with *either* historical-cost statements or current-cost statements. Thus the $2,100 holding loss on the monetary item just computed would also appear under the current-cost/constant-dollar method as well as the historical-cost/constant-dollar method of Exhibit 20–3.

Constant-dollar adjustments also divide current-cost holding gains into two categories: (1) changes in asset values that result from using a new yardstick for measuring the values and (2) increases (or decreases) in asset values caused by changes in the specific asset values that differ from general changes in purchasing power. For example, the holding gain of $4,000 in column 2 of Exhibit 20–3 represents an increase of inventory value from $20 × 400 = $8,000 in 19X1 dollars to $30 × 400 = $12,000 in 19X2 dollars. The general price index increased 10% in 19X2, making the $8,000 in 19X1 dollars equal to 1.1 × $8,000 = $8,800 in 19X2 dollars. Therefore, of the apparent $4,000 holding gain in column 2, $800 is because of a change in yardstick; only $3,200 is a true increase in value.

SUMMARY PROBLEM FOR YOUR REVIEW

The first three problems appeared earlier in this chapter.

Problem Four

You purchased a parcel of land ten years ago for $40,000 when the general-price-level index was 90. You also placed $40,000 cash in a safety deposit box. The general-price-level index is now 135. A local real estate appraiser maintains that you could obtain $220,000 for the land today.

Required:

1. Prepare a four-column tabulation of the holding gain (loss) on the monetary item and holding gain (loss) on the nonmonetary item for the ten-year period. The four methods of measurement to be shown are historical cost/nominal dollar, current cost/nominal dollar, historical cost/constant dollar, and current cost/constant dollar.
2. Prepare a summary of the four methods. For each method:
   a. Specify whether a financial or a physical concept of capital maintenance is used for determining income from continuing operations.
   b. Does the method explicitly identify holding gains (losses) on monetary items, frequently called gains (losses) in general purchasing power? Answer *yes* or *no* here and in Requirements c, d, and e.
   c. Does the method explicitly identify holding gains (losses) on nonmonetary items?
   d. Does the method use general price indexes such as the Consumer Price Index?
   e. Does the method use specific price indexes such as a construction index?
3. Of the four methods, which do you prefer as the most accurate measure of income? Why?

Solution to Problem Four

1. All amounts are in thousands of dollars.

	MEASUREMENT METHOD			
	(1) Historical Cost/ Nominal Dollars	(2) Current Cost/ Nominal Dollars	(3) Historical Cost/ Constant Dollars	(4) Current Cost/ Constant Dollars
Holding loss on monetary item, commonly called loss in general purchasing power	—	—	(20)[a]	(20)[a]
Holding gain on nonmonetary item	—	180[b]	—	160[c]
Total	—	180	(20)	140

[a] Cash held today, expressed in current purchasing power = 40
Cash held ten years ago, expressed in current purchasing
power = $40 \times (135/90)$ = 60
Holding loss (20)

[b] Current value of 220 − historical cost of 40 = 180.

[c] Current value − restated historical cost
= $220 - 40 \times (135/90) = 220 - 60 = 160$

2. The relationships among the four methods are shown in the following table:

	MEASUREMENT METHOD			
	(1) Historical Cost/ Nominal Dollars	(2) Current Cost/ Nominal Dollars	(3) Historical Cost/ Constant Dollars	(4) Current Cost/ Constant Dollars
a. Concept of capital maintenance for determining income from continuing operations	Financial	Physical	Financial	Physical
Explicit identification of holding gains:				
b. On monetary items	No	No	Yes	Yes
c. On nonmonetary items	No*	Yes	No	Yes
d. Use of general price indexes	No	No	Yes	Yes
e. Use of specific price indexes	No	Yes	No	Yes

* Recognizes losses, not gains, under lower-of-cost or market valuations, which are most often applicable in accounting for inventories and marketable equity securities.

3. Accountants and others have been unable to agree on which method (or model) provides the "most accurate" measure of income. Those who favor Method 1 maintain that no income emerges until an actual sale occurs. Those who favor Method 2 assert that there has been an overall increase in wealth of $180,000 and that the actual sale of land is an incidental factor. Those who favor Method 3 essentially favor the historical-cost approach to measuring income but believe that gains or losses on monetary items are actually realized by mere holding.

Economists tend to favor Method 4 as the most comprehensive way of calibrating an entity's income because it aims at measuring changes in overall command over goods and services, measured in constant purchasing power.

Economists have frequently distinguished between "real" and "nominal" income and capital. The historical-cost method has been severely criticized because it uses a "nominal" measure in the form of unrestated dollars rather than a "real" measure in the form of restated dollars with constant purchasing power. Adherents of the current-cost/constant-dollar model insist that no income can emerge without the maintenance of real capital, that is, nominal capital restated in terms of constant purchasing power.

Essentially, the FASB has avoided answering the tough question that professors and others have debated for years: If you must pick a single number as a measure of net income, which would you choose? As mentioned earlier, the FASB requires disclosures in accordance with Method 1 for primary financial statements and Method 4 for supplementary information. However, the holding gains under Method 4 are merely reported; they are *not* added to income from continuing operations. In short, the FASB has decided to provide an array of income measurements that may be useful. The user of financial statements can then select the numbers that seem most helpful.

As an example of different views as to what really constitutes income, some accountants maintain that a holding gain on a monetary liability is really an adjustment to interest expense. Why? Because lenders raise interest rates to compensate for expected inflation. Therefore the interest expense component of income from continuing operations should be reduced by the holding gain. Following this theory often boosts income considerably. For instance, Puget Sound Power and Light's supplementary disclosures for 1984 included the following current cost/constant dollar information (in millions):

Income from continuing operations	$44.5
Gain attributable to holding net monetary liabilities	36.0
Income including gain attributable to holding net monetary liabilities	$80.5

The $80.5 million is 80% higher than the $44.5 million income from continuing operations. Over the five years 1980 through 1984, Puget Power's holding gain on net monetary liabilities *exceeded* its operating income by an average of over $12 million per year.

FUNDAMENTAL ASSIGNMENT MATERIAL

Special Note: Problems relating to Part One of the chapter are presented first in each subgrouping of the assignment material. For coverage of the basic ideas of inflation accounting, Problem 20–2 is especially recommended; for a closer but still fundamental look, Problem 20–40 is especially recommended.

☐ **General Coverage**

20–1. **LIFO, FIFO, CASH EFFECTS.** Schreuder Company had sales revenue of $432,000 in 19X2 for a line of hardware supplies. The company uses a periodic inventory system. Pertinent data for 19X2 included:

Inventory, December 31, 19X1	16,000 units @ $6	$ 96,000
January purchases	25,000 units @ $7	175,000
July purchases	28,000 units @ $8	224,000
Sales for the year	36,000 units	

Required:
1. Prepare a statement of gross margin for 19X2. Use columns, one assuming LIFO and one assuming FIFO.
2. Assume a 40% income tax rate. Suppose all transactions are for cash. Which inventory method results in more cash for Schreuder Company? By how much?

20–2. **FOUR VERSIONS OF INCOME AND CAPITAL.** Zenith Supplies, Inc., has the following comparative balance sheets as of December 31 (based on historical costs in nominal dollars):

	19X4	19X5
Cash	$ —	$6,000
Inventory, 50 and 20 units, respectively	5,000	1,000
Total assets	$5,000	$7,000
Paid-in capital	$5,000	$5,000
Retained income	—	2,000
Stockholders' equity	$5,000	$7,000

The Consumer Price Index was 320 on December 31, 19X4, and 368 on December 31, 19X5. The company had acquired 50 units of inventory on December 31, 19X4, for $100 each and had held them throughout 19X5. Forty units were sold on December 31, 19X5, for $150 cash each. The replacement cost of the inventory at that date was $120 per unit. Assume that these are the only transactions. Ignore income taxes.

Required:

Use four sets of columns to prepare comparative balance sheets as of December 31, 19X4 and 19X5, and income statements for 19X5 under (1) historical cost/nominal dollars, (2) current cost/nominal dollars, (3) historical cost/constant dollars, and (4) current cost/constant dollars.

□ Understanding Published Financial Reports

20–3. **COMPARISON OF INVENTORY METHODS.** Sperry Corporation is a producer of electronic systems for information processing, aerospace, and defense. The following actual data and descriptions are from the company's fiscal 1985 annual report (in millions):

	MARCH 31	
	1985	1984
Inventories	$1,567.1	$1,180.2

A footnote states: "Inventories are valued at the lower of cost or market, cost generally representing average cost."

The income statement for the fiscal year ended March 31, 1985, included (in millions):

Net sales of products	$4,159.3
Cost of sales of products	2,906.6

Assume that Sperry used the periodic inventory system. Suppose its Univac division had the accompanying data regarding the use of its computer parts that it acquires and resells to customers for maintaining equipment:

Data for Problem 20–3
(dollars are *not* in millions)

	UNITS	TOTAL
Inventory (March 31, 1984)	100	$ 400
Purchase (May 20, 1984)	200	1,000
Sales, June 17 (at $9 per unit)	150	
Purchase (September 25, 1984)	140	840
Sales, February 7, 1985 (at $10 per unit)	160	

Required:

1. For these computer parts only, prepare a tabulation of the cost-of-goods-sold section of the income statement for the year ended March 31, 1985. Support your computations. Round totals to the nearest dollar. Show your tabulation for four different inventory methods: (a) FIFO, (b) LIFO, (c) weighted-average, and (d) specific identification.

For Requirement d, assume that the purchase of May 20 was identified with the sale of June 17. Also assume that the purchase of September 25 was identified with the sale of February 7; the additional units sold were identified with the beginning inventory.

2. By how much would income taxes differ if Sperry used (a) LIFO instead of FIFO for this inventory item? (b) LIFO instead of weighted average? Assume a 40% tax rate.

20–4. **EFFECTS OF LATE PURCHASES.** Refer to the preceding problem. Suppose Sperry acquired 60 extra units at $7 each on March 29, 1985, a total of $420. How would gross margin and income taxes be affected under FIFO? That is, compare FIFO results before and after the purchase of 60 extra units. Under LIFO? That is, compare LIFO results before and after the purchase of 60 extra units. Show computations and explain.

20–5. **FASB FORMAT FOR REPORTING ON CHANGING PRICES.** Transamerica Corporation, a large diversified company, reported 1984 operating income of $151 million on sales of $5,399 million. After adjusting for changes in specific prices (current costs), operating income was $107 million. Three other accounts reported were (in millions):

Excess of increase in specific prices over increase in general price level	$23
Effect of increase in general price level	$64
Increase in specific prices of inventories and property and equipment held during the year	$87

Required:

Prepare a current-cost income statement using the FASB format as illustrated by Exhibit 20–4, page 695. Place all expenses in a single category, so that sales − expenses = operating income.

ADDITIONAL ASSIGNMENT MATERIAL

☐ **General Coverage**

20–6. "There is a single dominant reason why more and more companies have adopted LIFO." What is the reason?

20–7. "Purchases of inventory at the end of a fiscal period can have a direct effect on income under LIFO." Do you agree? Explain.

20–8. "An inventory profit is a fictitious profit." Do you agree? Explain.

20–9. LIFO produces absurd inventory valuations. Why?

20–10. Distinguish between the physical and the financial concepts of maintenance of invested capital.

20–11. What are the two major approaches to recognizing changing prices in measuring income?

20–12. Enumerate four ways to measure income.

20–13. "The choice among accounting measures of income is often expressed as either historical-cost accounting or general-price-level accounting or current-cost accounting." Do you agree? Explain.

20–14. Explain how net income is measured under the current-cost approach.

20–15. What is *distributable income*?

20–16. What is the common meaning of *current cost*?

20–17. "Net realizable value and replacement cost are generally equal." Do you agree? Explain.

20–18. Why do managers in heavy industries such as steel favor the current-cost concept for income tax purposes?

20–19. "General-price-level accounting is a loose way of achieving replacement-cost income accounting." Do you agree? Explain.

20–20. Explain what a general price index represents.

20–21. Distinguish between general indexes and specific indexes.

20–22. "Specific indexes are used in nominal-dollar accounting but not in constant-dollar accounting." Do you agree? Explain.

20–23. "All holding gains should be excluded from income." What is the major logic behind this statement?

20–24. What are three basic positions regarding whether holding gains are income?

20–25. "A holding gain can be recognized but unrealized." Do you agree? Explain.

20–26. "A holding gain may simultaneously be a holding loss." Do you agree? Explain.

20–27. "Because of pressure from the SEC, the FASB issued a revolutionary statement in 1979 abandoning the historical-cost method of income measurement and replacing it with a current-cost method." Do you agree? Explain.

20–28. "Holding gains on nonmonetary items are not recognized in historical-cost/ constant-dollar accounting." Do you agree? Explain.

20–29. "The debtor benefits from inflation." Why?

20–30. "Constant-dollar accounting modifies historical-cost accounting in two major ways." Describe the two ways.

20–31. Net monetary position is the relationship of current assets to current liabilities." Do you agree? Explain.

20–32. What is the argument for departing from the use of historical cost as a basis of recording depreciation of fixed assets?

20–33. **LIFO AND FIFO.** The inventory of the Lakeland Gravel Company on June 30 shows 1,000 tons at $9 per ton. A physical inventory on July 31 shows a total of 1,200 tons on hand. Revenue from sales of gravel for July totals $45,000. The following purchases were made during July:

July 8	2,000 tons @ $10 per ton
July 13	500 tons @ $11 per ton
July 22	600 tons @ $12 per ton

Required:

1. Compute the inventory cost, as of July 31, using (a) LIFO and (b) FIFO.
2. Compute the gross profit, using each method.

20–34. **LIFO, FIFO, PURCHASE DECISIONS, AND EARNINGS PER SHARE.** Suppose a company with 1 million shares of common stock outstanding has had the following transactions during 19X1, its first year in business:

Sales:	1,000,000 units @ $5
Purchases:	800,000 units @ $2
	300,000 units @ $3

The current income tax rate is a flat 50%; the rate next year is expected to be 40%. Prices on inventory are not expected to decline next year.

It is December 20, and as the president, you are trying to decide whether you should buy the 600,000 units you need for inventory now or early next year. The current price is $4 per unit. Prices on inventory are expected to remain stable; in any event, no decline in prices is anticipated.

You have not chosen an inventory method as yet, but you will pick either LIFO or FIFO.

Other expenses for the year will be $1.4 million.

1. Using LIFO, prepare a comparative income statement assuming the 600,000 units (a) are not purchased, (b) are purchased. The statement should end with reported earnings per share.
2. Repeat Requirement 1, using FIFO.
3. Comment on the results obtained. What method would you choose? Why? Be specific.
4. Suppose that in Year 2 the tax rate drops to 40%, prices remain stable, 1 million units are sold at $5, enough units are purchased at $4 so that the ending inventory will be 700,000 units, and other expenses are reduced to $800,000.
   a. Prepare a comparative income statement for the second year showing the impact of each of the four alternatives in requirements 1 and 2 on net income and earnings per share for the second year.
   b. Explain any difference in net income that you encounter among the four alternatives.
   c. Why is there a difference in ending inventory values under LIFO even though the same amount of physical inventory is in stock?
   d. What is the total cash outflow for income taxes for the two years together under the four alternatives?
   e. Would you change your answer in Requirement 3 now that you have completed Requirement 4? Why?

20–35. **LIFO, FIFO, PRICES RISING AND FALLING.** The Suarez Company has a periodic inventory system. Inventory on December 31, 19X1, consisted of 10,000 units at $10 = $100,000. Purchases during 19X2 were 15,000 units. Sales were 14,000 units for sales revenue of $20 per unit.

Prepare a four-column comparative statement of gross margin for 19X2:

1. Assume that purchases were at $12 per unit. Assume FIFO and then LIFO (columns 1 and 2).
2. Assume that purchases were at $8 per unit. Assume FIFO and then LIFO (columns 3 and 4).
3. Assume an income tax rate of 40%. Suppose that all transactions are for cash.
   a. Which inventory method in Requirement 1 results in more cash for Suarez Company? By how much?
   b. Which inventory method in Requirement 2 results in more cash for Suarez Company? By how much?

20–36. **FIFO AND LIFO.** Two divisions of General Diversified, Inc., are in the scrap metal warehousing business, the Newark Division on the East Coast and the Sacramento Division in the West. The manager of each division receives a bonus based on the division's pretax income. The divisions are about the same size and in 19X6 coincidentally encountered seemingly identical operating situations. However, their accounting systems differ; Newark uses FIFO and Sacramento uses LIFO.

Both divisions reported the following data for 19X6:

Beginning inventory, 10,000 tons @ $50 per ton	$ 500,000
Purchase, February 15, 19X6, 20,000 tons @ $70 per ton	1,400,000
Purchase, October 6, 19X6, 30,000 tons @ $90 per ton	2,700,000
Sales, 45,000 tons @ $100 per ton	4,500,000
Other expenses (in addition to cost of goods sold but excluding income taxes)	710,000

The income tax rate is 55%.

Required:

1. Compute net income for the year for each division. Show your calculations.
2. Which division had the better performance for the year? Which accounting system would you prefer if you were manager of one of the divisions? Why? Explain fully. Include your estimate of the overall effect of these events on the cash balance of each division, assuming that all transactions during 19X6 were direct receipts or disbursements of cash.

20–37. **EFFECTS OF LIFO AND FIFO.** (Adapted from a problem originated by George H. Sorter.) The New Delhi Trading Company is starting in business on December 31, 19X0. In each *half year*, from 19X1 through 19X4, it expects to purchase 1,000 units and sell 500 units for the amounts listed below. In 19X5, it expects to purchase no units and sell 4,000 units for the amount indicated below. Monetary amounts are in thousands of rupees (R).

	19X1	19X2	19X3	19X4	19X5
Purchases:					
First 6 months	R 2,000	R 4,000	R 6,000	R 6,000	R 0
Second 6 months	4,000	9,000	6,000	8,000	0
Total	R 6,000	R13,000	R12,000	R14,000	R 0
Sales (at selling price)	R10,000	R10,000	R10,000	R10,000	R40,000

Assume that there are no costs or expenses other than those shown. The income tax rate is 60%, and taxes for each year are payable on December 31 of that year. New Delhi Trading Company is trying to decide whether to use FIFO or LIFO throughout the five-year period.

Required:

1. What was net income under FIFO for each of the five years? Under LIFO? Show calculations.
2. Explain briefly which method, LIFO or FIFO, seems more advantageous, and why.

20–38. **YEAR-END PURCHASES AND LIFO.** A company engaged in the manufacture and sale of jewelry maintained an inventory of gold for use in its business. The company used LIFO for the gold content of its products.

On the final day of its fiscal year, the company bought 10,000 ounces of gold at $400 per ounce. Had the purchase not been made, the company would have penetrated its LIFO layers for 8,000 ounces of gold acquired at $260 per ounce.

The applicable income tax rate is 40%.

Required:

1. Compute the effect of the year-end purchase on the income taxes of the fiscal year.
2. On the second day of the next fiscal year, the company resold the 10,000 ounces of gold to its suppliers. What do you think the Internal Revenue Service should do if it discovers this resale, if anything? Explain.

20–39. **MEANING OF GENERAL INDEX APPLICATIONS AND CHOICE OF BASE YEAR.** VanDyke Company acquired land in mid-1967 for $3 million. In mid-1987 it acquired a substantially identical parcel of land for $7 million. Suppose the general-price-level index annual averages were:

1987–300.0	1977–150.0	1967–90.0

DIFFICULTIES IN MEASURING NET INCOME

711

Required:

1. In four columns, show the computations of the total cost of the two parcels of land expressed in (a) costs as traditionally recorded, (b) dollars of 1987 purchasing power, (c) 1977 purchasing power, and (d) 1967 purchasing power.
2. Explain the meaning of the figures that you computed in Requirement 1.

20–40. **CONCEPTS OF INCOME.** Suppose you are in the business of investing in land and holding it for resale. On December 31, 19X2, a parcel of land has a historical cost of $100,000 and a current value (measured via use of a specific price index) of $400,000; the general price level had tripled since the land was acquired. Suppose also that the land is sold on December 31, 19X3, for $460,000. The general price level rose by 5% during 19X3.

Required:

1. Prepare a tabulation of income from continuing operations and holding gains for 19X3, using the four methods illustrated in Exhibit 20–3, page 691.
2. In your own words, explain the meaning of the results, giving special attention to what income represents.

ASSIGNMENT MATERIAL FOR APPENDIX 20

20–41. **MONETARY AND NONMONETARY ITEMS.** Westwood Company began business on December 31, 19X1, with the following balance sheet. The assets were held throughout 19X2, when the general-price-level index rose from 120 to 144. The familiar historical-cost/nominal-dollar statements would be:

	19X1	19X2
Balance sheets as of December 31:		
Cash	$100,000	$100,000
Land	60,000	60,000
Total assets	$160,000	$160,000
Paid-in capital	$160,000	$160,000

Required:

1. Using the historical-cost/constant-dollar approach, prepare comparative balance sheets and an income statement. Ignore interest and income taxes.
2. Repeat Requirement 1. However, assume that a long-term note payable was issued for $50,000 on December 31, 19X1 and that paid-in capital was therefore $160,000 − $50,000 = $110,000.

20–42. **MONETARY ITEMS.** Suppose Rio Company has Cr$1.5 million cash, which it had acquired at the end of 19X3. (Cr$ is the abbreviation for Brazilian cruzeiro.) Rio held the cash in a safety deposit box through the end of 19X4. The general-price-level index was 200 on December 31, 19X3 and 500 on December 31, 19X4.

Required:

1. Fill in the blanks for the cash held in the safety box:

	(1) MEASURED IN 12/31/X3 PURCHASING POWER	(2) MEASURED IN 12/31/X4 PURCHASING POWER	(3) AS CONVENTIONALLY MEASURED
Cash balance, December 31, 19X3			
Cash balance, December 31, 19X4			
Purchasing power loss from holding monetary item			

2. Suppose the company had purchased land for Cr$1.5 million cash on December 31, 19X3, and held the land throughout 19X4. Prepare a similar tabulation for the land balance except that the final line would refer to a "nonmonetary" rather than a "monetary" item.

20–43. **MONETARY VERSUS NONMONETARY ASSETS.** Kowalski Company owns land acquired for $150,000 one year ago when the general price index was 100. It also owns $150,000 of government bonds acquired at the same time. The index today is 110. Operating expenses and operating revenues, including interest income, resulted in net income (and an increase of cash) of $6,000 measured in historical-cost/nominal-dollar terms. Assume that all income and expense transactions occurred yesterday. The Kowalski Company has no other assets and no liabilities. Its cash balance one year ago was zero.

Required: 1. Prepare comparative balance sheets for the two instants of time plus an income statement summary based on the historical-cost/nominal-dollar method. Then prepare such statements using the historical-cost/constant-dollar method.
2. This is a more important requirement. In your own words, explain the meaning of the historical-cost/constant-dollar statements. Why should the holding of a monetary asset generate a monetary loss while the holding of land causes neither a loss nor a gain?

20–44. **COMPREHENSIVE REVIEW OF APPENDIX.** A company has the following comparative balance sheets at December 31 (based on historical cost in nominal dollars):

	19X1	19X2
Cash	$2,000	$3,400
Inventory, 20 units and 10 units, respectively	2,000	1,000
Total assets	$4,000	$4,400
Original capital	$4,000	$4,000
Retained income	—	400
Stockholders' equity	$4,000	$4,400
General-price-level index	160	176

The company had acquired all the inventory at $100 per unit on December 31, 19X1, and had held the inventory throughout 19X2; ten units were sold for $140 cash each on December 31, 19X2. The replacement cost of the inventory at that date was $125 per unit.

Note: If you are going to solve the next problem too, ignore the requirements of this problem and proceed directly to the more comprehensive problem that follows.

Required: Prepare a four-column tabulation of income statements: (1) historical cost/nominal dollars, (2) current cost/nominal dollars, (3) historical cost/constant dollars, and (4) current cost/constant dollars. Also show beginning and ending balance sheet accounts for each of the four columns. For example, the preceding accounts accompany column 1.

20–45. **EXTENSION OF APPENDIX PROBLEM.** Suppose in the preceding problem that sales equipment had been purchased on December 31, 19X1, for $2,000 cash provided by an extra $2,000 of capital. The equipment was being fully depreciated over a ten-year life on a straight-line basis. The replacement cost of the equipment (new) at the end of 19X2 was $3,000.

Prepare a four-column tabulation in the same manner described in the requirement to the preceding problem.

20–46. SWITCH FROM LIFO TO FIFO. This is a classic problem. Effective January 1, 1970, Chrysler Corporation adopted the FIFO method for inventories previously valued by the LIFO method. The 1970 annual report stated: "This . . . makes the financial statements with respect to inventory valuation comparable with those of the other United States automobile manufacturers."
The Wall Street Journal reported:

☐ The change improved Chrysler's 1970 financial results several ways. Besides narrowing the 1970 loss by $20 million it improved Chrysler's working capital.

The change helped Chrysler's balance sheet by boosting inventories, and thus current assets, by $150 million at the end of 1970 over what they would have been under LIFO. As Chrysler's profit has collapsed over the last two years and its financial position tightened, auto analysts have eyed warily Chrysler's shrinking ratio of current assets to current liabilities.

Chrysler's short-term debt stood at $374 million at year-end, down from $477 million a year earlier but up slightly from $370 million on September 30. Chrysler's cash and marketable securities shrank during the year to $156.4 million at year-end, down from $309.3 million a year earlier and $220 million on Sept. 30.

To get the improvements in its balance sheet and results, however, Chrysler paid a price. Roger Helder, vice president and comptroller, said Chrysler owed the government $53 million in tax savings it accumulated by using the LIFO method since it switched from FIFO in 1957. The major advantage of LIFO is that it holds down profit and thus tax liabilities. The other three major auto makers stayed on the FIFO method. Mr. Helder said Chrysler now has to pay back that $53 million to the government over 20 years, which will boost Chrysler's tax bills about $3 million year.

Required: Given the content of this text chapter, do you think the Chrysler decision to switch from LIFO to FIFO was beneficial to its stockholders? Explain, being as specific and using as many data as you can.

20–47. LIFO AND INVENTORY REDUCTIONS. During the early and middle 1980s, many companies reduced their inventory levels. Some reductions came in response to decreasing demand and some because better inventory management systems were installed. Such reductions led to writing off old inventory layers by companies using LIFO.

Crane Company, a diversified manufacturer of engineered products for industry, wrote off old LIFO layers in 1982, 1983, and 1984. Operating profit was $50.6 million, $25.6 million, and $9.1 million in 1984, 1983, and 1982, respectively. A footnote to Crane's 1984 financial statements stated: "Inventories . . . were reduced as a result of continuing low market demand. The effect [of LIFO inventory reductions] on continuing operations was a reduction in cost in 1984, 1983, and 1982 of approximately $2,000,000, $8,000,000, and $13,000,000, respectively.

Required: Suppose Crane had bought just enough additional inventory each of the three years to avoid inventory reductions and the consequent writing off of old LIFO inventory layers. What would Crane's operating profit have been in each of the three years? Comment on the effect of LIFO in situations such as Crane's.

20–48. EFFECT OF LIFO. Georgia-Pacific, one of the world's largest forest products companies, uses LIFO for over 40% of its inventories and weighted-average cost for the rest.

The total inventory value at the end of 1985 was $634 million. If the weighted-average method had been used for all inventories, the value would have been $105 million higher.

During 1985 the inventory decreased by $64 million. If the weighted-average method had been used for all inventories, the value would have decreased by $95 million. Operating income for 1985 was $290 million.

Required:

Suppose the weighted-average method had always been used for all inventories. Calculate Georgia-Pacific's operating income for 1985. By how much would the cumulative operating income for all years through 1985 differ from that reported? Would it be more or less than the reported amount?

20–49. **EFFECTS OF GENERAL VERSUS SPECIFIC PRICE CHANGES.** The following data are from the annual reports of Gannett Co., owner of 120 newspapers, Zayre Corp., operator of over 290 discount stores, and Goodyear Tire and Rubber Company, respectively (in millions):

	Gannett	Zayre	Goodyear
Increase in specific prices of assets held during the year	$45.8	$ 24.9	$ (4.7)
Less: Effect of increase in general price level	37.5	55.5	252.0
Excess of increase in specific prices over increase in the general price level	$ 8.3	$(30.6)	$(256.7)

Required:

Compare and contrast the relationship between changes in the general price level and changes in the prices of specific assets of each of the three companies.

20–50. **REPLACEMENT COSTS.** (P. Griffin.) This problem does not require knowledge of Appendix 20. Accompanying this problem are excerpts from an annual report of Barber-Ellis of Canada, Limited. Note 1 to the financial report includes the following passage:

☐ The current replacement costs of inventories and of property, plant, and equipment are shown on the balance sheet, and earnings are determined by matching current costs with current revenues. Adjustments of the historical cost of physical assets to their current replacement cost are considered as restatements of shareholders' equity and are shown on the balance sheet under "Revaluation Surplus."

Since this is the first year that the company has prepared current replacement cost financial statements, comparative figures are not available.

Required:

From information in the balance sheet, statement of earnings and retained earnings, and statement of revaluation surplus, determine as of the end of the year:

1. Current replacement cost "Inventories."
2. Current replacement cost "Property, Plant, and Equipment."
3. Current replacement cost "Accumulated Depreciation."
4. Current replacement cost "Total Assets."
5. Current replacement cost "Retained Earnings."

Also determine the following income statement items:

6. Current replacement cost "Cost of Products Sold."
7. Current replacement cost "Net Earnings."

Finally:

8. Explain in words the nature of the difference between the current-replacement-cost "Net Earnings" and the historical-cost "Net Earnings."

BARBER-ELLIS OF CANADA, LIMITED

CURRENT REPLACEMENT COST BALANCE SHEET
END OF THE YEAR

Assets	CURRENT REPLACEMENT COST	HISTORICAL COST
Current:		
Cash	$ 29,783	$ 29,783
Accounts receivable	12,074,945	12,074,945
Inventories	(1)	10,117,804
Prepaid expenses	249,545	249,545
Current assets	$22,721,077	$22,472,077
Property, plant, and equipment	(2)	11,261,927
Accumulated depreciation	(3)	(5,817,772)
Unamortized excess of purchase price of subsidiaries over fair value of net assets acquired	—	816,067
Total assets	$ (4)	$28,732,299

Liabilities	CURRENT REPLACEMENT COST	HISTORICAL COST
Current:		
Bank indebtedness	$ 7,573,983	$ 7,573,983
Accounts payable and accrued liabilities	4,109,189	4,109,189
Income taxes	1,296,693	1,296,693
Dividends, preference shares	700	700
Current portion of long-term debt	486,650	486,650
Current liabilities	$13,467,215	$13,467,215
Deferred income taxes	278,362	278,362
Long-term debt (Note 1)	4,133,650	4,133,650
Total liabilities	$17,879,227	$17,879,227
Shareholders' equity		
Capital stock		
Contributed surplus	$ 565,705	$ 565,705
Retained earnings	45,000	45,000
Revaluation surplus	(5)	10,242,367
	4,319,204	—
Total equities	$ (4)	$28,732,299

CURRENT REPLACEMENT COST STATEMENT OF EARNINGS AND RETAINED EARNINGS

	CURRENT REPLACEMENT COST	HISTORICAL COST
Net sales	$69,058,300	$69,058,300
Cost of products sold	$ (6)	$50,389,580
Selling, general, and administration	10,705,281	10,705,281
Depreciation and amortization	1,095,567	786,969
Interest, long-term debt	381,884	381,884
Interest, current	590,284	590,284
Cost and expenses	$	$62,853,998
Earnings before income taxes	$	$ 6,204,302
Provision for income taxes	2,927,442	2,927,442
Net earnings	$ (7)	$ 3,276,860
Retained earnings, beginning of year	7,939,344	7,939,344
Subtotal	$	$11,216,204
Adjustment of prior years' depreciation on current replacement cost of plant and equipment	$ 1,948,116	—
Dividends	973,837	973,837
Retained earnings, end of year	$	$10,242,367
Earnings per share:		
Basic	$ 4.30	$ 7.09
Fully diluted	4.22	6.96

STATEMENT OF REVALUATION SURPLUS

Revaluation of physical assets to reflect current end-of-year replacement cost:	
Inventories	$ 249,000
Property, plant, and equipment	3,902,271
Excess of purchase price over fair value of assets acquired	(816,067)
Revaluation of cost of products sold during the year	
Portion of earnings determined on historical cost basis which are required to replace inventory sold at the current cost in effect at the date of sale	984,000
Revaluation surplus, end of the year	$4,319,204

Report on Supplementary Financial Statements

To the Shareholders,
Barber-Ellis of Canada, Limited

In conjunction with our examination of and report on the financial statements of Barber-Ellis of Canada, Limited, we have also examined the accompanying supplementary financial statements which have been prepared on a current replacement cost basis.

Uniform criteria for the preparation and presentation of such supplementary financial information have not yet been established and accordingly, acceptable alternatives are available as to their nature and content. In our opinion, however, the accounting basis described in the notes to the supplementary financial statements has been applied as stated and is appropriate in these circumstances.

Touche Ross & Co.
Chartered Accountants

Toronto, Ontario

20–51. **HOLDING GAINS ON MONETARY AND NONMONETARY ITEMS.** (Study Appendix 20. This problem is more difficult than the other problems.) Refer to the data in the preceding problem. The following information is available.

Items from the historical-cost beginning-of-the-year balance sheet of Barber-Ellis:

Cash: $25,200
Long-term debt: $4,133,650
General-price-level index:
 Beginning of the year: 140
 End of the year: 154
 Average for the year: 147

For all constant dollar calculations, use the end-of-year dollar.

Required:

1. Assume that long-term debt did not change during the year. Calculate the purchasing power gain or loss associated with long-term debt (a monetary item). Label it as a gain or loss.
2. Calculate the purchasing power gain or loss associated with cash and label it as a gain or loss. You may assume that a $4,583 increase in cash occurred uniformly throughout the year.
3. Assume that Barber-Ellis purchased *all* of its inventory on December 31 of the preceding year (no other purchases prior to or subsequent to that date). Also assume that goods were sold continuously throughout the year. What are the following numbers?
   a. Holding gain on inventory, using the current-cost/nominal-dollar model
   b. Holding gain on inventory *net* of inflation (that is, based on the current-cost/constant-dollar model)

Appendix A

RECOMMENDED READINGS

The following readings will aid readers who want to pursue some topics in more depth than is possible in this book. There is a hazard in compiling a group of recommended readings. Inevitably, some worthwhile books or periodicals are omitted. Moreover, such a list cannot include books published subsequent to the compilation date. The list is not comprehensive, but it suggests many excellent readings.

PERIODICALS

Professional and academic journals are typically available in university libraries. The following professional journals include articles on the application of management accounting:

Management Accounting. Published by the National Association of Accountants; many articles on actual applications by individual organizations.
FE: The Magazine for Financial Executives. Formerly *Financial Executive*; published by the Financial Executives Institute; emphasizes general policy issues for accounting and finance executives.
Cost and Management. Published by The Society of Management Accountants of Canada; includes much practice-oriented research in management accounting.
Managerial Planning. Published by the Planning Executives Institute; a journal designed for business planners.
Journal of Accountancy. Published by the American Institute of CPAs; emphasizes financial accounting and is directed at the practicing CPA.
Harvard Business Review. Published by Harvard Business School; directed to general managers, but contains excellent articles on applications of management accounting.
Accounting Horizons. A new journal, published by the American Accounting Association, stressing current, practice-oriented articles in all areas of accounting.
GAO Review. Covers managerial accounting issues of interest to the General Accounting Office of the U.S. Government.
Business Week, *Forbes*, *Fortune*, *The Wall Street Journal*. Popular publications that cover a variety of business and economics topics; often their articles relate to management accounting.

Academic journals that cover all accounting topics at a more theoretical level include *The Accounting Review*, the research publication of the American Accounting Association, and *Journal of Accounting Research*, published at the University of Chicago. *Accounting, Organizations and Society*, a British journal, publishes much research on behavioral aspects of management accounting.

BOOKS IN MANAGEMENT ACCOUNTING

Most of the topics in this text are covered in more detail in the many books entitled *Cost Accounting*, including *Cost Accounting: A Managerial Emphasis* by C. T. Horngren and G. Foster (Prentice-Hall, 1987). You can find more advanced coverage in *Advanced Managerial Accounting* by R. S. Kaplan (Prentice-Hall, 1982) and R. Magee, *Advanced Cost Accounting* (Harper & Row, 1986).

The Financial Executives Institute, 10 Madison Avenue, P.O. Box 1938, Morristown, NJ 07960, and the National Association of Accountants, 10 Paragon Drive, P.O. Box 433, Montvale, NJ 07645-0433, have long lists of accounting research publications.

Readings books and handbooks provide information about many managerial accounting topics. Some such books published since 1980 are:

BELL, J., ed., *Accounting Control Systems: A Behavioral and Technical Integration*. New York: Markus Wiener, 1983.

BULLOCH, J., D. KELLER, AND L. VLASHO, eds., *Accountants' Cost Handbook*, 3rd ed. New York: John Wiley, 1983.

CHENALL, R., G. HARRISON, AND D. WATSON, eds., *Organizational Context of Management Accounting*. Boston: Pitman, 1981.

COOPER, D., R. SCAPENS, AND J. ARNOLD, eds., *Management Accounting Research and Practice*. London: The Institute of Cost and Management Accountants, 1983.

DAVIDSON, S., AND R. L. WEIL, eds., *Handbook of Modern Accounting*. New York: McGraw-Hill, 1983.

RAPPAPORT, ALFRED, ed., *Information for Decision Making*, 3rd ed. Englewood Cliffs, NJ: Prentice-Hall, 1982.

ROSEN, L. S., ed., *Topics in Management Accounting*. Toronto: McGraw-Hill, 1984.

THOMAS, W., ed., *Readings in Cost Accounting, Budgeting and Control*, 6th ed. Cincinnati: South-Western Publishing, 1983.

Books of cases provide examples of managerial accounting topics from real organizations:

BARRETT, M. E., AND W. J. BRUNS, JR., *Case Problems in Management Accounting*. Homewood, IL: Richard D. Irwin, 1985.

CAPLAN, E. H., AND J. E. CHAMPOUX, *Cases in Management Accounting: Context and Behavior*. New York: National Association of Accountants, 1978.

ROTCH, W., AND B. ALLEN, *Cases in Management Accounting and Control Systems*. Richmond, VA: Robert F. Dame, 1982.

SHANK, J., *Contemporary Managerial Accounting: A Casebook*. Englewood Cliffs, NJ: Prentice-Hall, 1981.

Many books discuss management accounting in nonprofit organizations, especially in health care. Four examples are:

ANTHONY, R. N., AND D. YOUNG, *Management Control in Nonprofit Organizations*, 3rd ed. Homewood, IL.: Richard D. Irwin, 1984.

RAMANATHAN, K. V., *Management Control in Nonprofit Organizations*. New York: John Wiley, 1982.

SCHAFER, E. L., AND M. E. GOCKE, *Management Accounting for Health Maintenance Organizations*. Denver: Center for Research in Ambulatory Health Care Administration, 1984.

Suver, J. D., and B. R. Neumann, *Management Accounting for Healthcare Organizations*. Oak Brook, IL: Healthcare Financial Management Association, 1981.

Management control systems, the topic of Chapters 6–10, can be explored further in a number of books, including:

Anthony, R. N., J. Dearden, and N. Bedford, *Management Control Systems*. Homewood, IL: Richard D. Irwin, 1984. A popular textbook that includes many cases.

Arrow, K. J., *The Limits of Organization*. New York: W. W. Norton, 1974. A readable classic by the Nobel laureate.

Benke, R., and J. D. Edwards, *Transfer Pricing: Techniques and Uses*. New York: National Association of Accountants, 1980.

Eccles, Robert G., *The Transfer Pricing Problem: A Theory for Practice*. Lexington, MA: Lexington Books, 1985.

Emmanuel, C., and D. Otley, *Accounting for Management Control*. Berkshire, England: Van Nostrand Reinhold (UK), 1985.

Euske, K., *Management Control: Planning, Control, Measurement, and Evaluation*. Reading, MA: Addison-Wesley, 1984.

Lorange, P., *Corporate Planning: An Executive Viewpoint*. Englewood Cliffs, NJ: Prentice-Hall, 1980.

Maciariello, J. A., *Management Control Systems*. Englewood Cliffs, NJ: Prentice-Hall, 1984.

Mautz, R. K., and J. Winjum, *Criteria for Management Control Systems*. New York: Financial Executives Institute, 1981. Focus on internal control.

Merchant, K., *Control in Business Organizations*. Boston: Pitman, 1984.

Solomons, D., *Divisional Performance: Measurement and Control*. New York: Markus Wiener, 1983. A reprint of a 1965 classic that is still relevant.

Vancil, R. F., *Decentralization: Managerial Ambiguity by Design*. Homewood, IL: Dow Jones-Irwin, 1979.

A few other books on various managerial accounting topics are:

Bierman, H., Jr., C. Bonini, and W. Haseman, *Quantitative Analysis for Business Decisions*, 5th ed. Homewood, IL: Richard D. Irwin, 1977. Good background for Chapter 16.

Bierman, H., Jr., and S. Smidt, *The Capital Budgeting Decision*, 5th ed. New York: Macmillan, 1980. Expands the capital budgeting discussion in Chapters 11–12.

Demski, J. S., *Information Analysis*, 2nd ed. Reading, MA: Addison-Wesley, 1980. A rigorous theoretical discussion of the value of information.

Fremgen, J. M., and S. S. Liao, *The Allocation of Corporate Indirect Costs*. New York: National Association of Accountants, 1981.

Holmes, J. R., G. H. Lander, M. A. Tipgos, and M. G. Wallace, Jr., *Profile of the Management Accountant*. New York: National Association of Accountants, 1982.

Klemstine, C. F., and M. Maher, *Management Accounting Research: A Review and Annotated Bibliography*. New York: Garland, 1985.

Seed, A. H., III, *The Impact of Inflation on Internal Planning and Control*. New York: National Association of Accountants, 1981.

Wilson, J., and J. Campbell, *Controllership: The Work of the Managerial Accountant*, 3rd ed. New York: John Wiley, 1981.

BOOKS IN FINANCIAL ACCOUNTING

This book's companion volume, *Introduction to Financial Accounting*, provides an expansion of the financial accounting material (Chapters 17–20). A more detailed coverage of the topics can be found in books entitled *Intermediate Accounting*, including those by P. Danos and E. Imhoff (Prentice-Hall, 1983) and D. E. Keiso and J. J. Weygandt (Wiley, 1986).

Opinions of the Accounting Principles Board are available from the American Institute of CPAs, 1211 Avenue of the Americas, New York, N.Y., 10036. The institute also has a series of research studies on a variety of topics. The pronouncements of the Financial Accounting Standards Board are available from the board's offices, High Ridge Park, Stamford, Conn., 06905.

Financial accounting has such an extensive literature that it is impossible to provide a short list of books that adequately covers the field. However, we will mention four books that cover a wide range of issues. For a perspective on the large firms practicing accounting, see two books by M. Stevens, *The Big Eight* and *The Accounting Wars* (Macmillan, 1981 and 1985, respectively). Research relating financial reporting to the capital markets is summarized in T. R. Dyckman and D. Morse, *Efficient Capital Markets and Accounting: A Critical Analysis* (Prentice-Hall, 1981). Application of this research to financial statement analysis is provided in G. Foster, *Financial Statement Analysis* (Prentice-Hall, 1986).

FUNDAMENTALS OF COMPOUND INTEREST AND THE USE OF PRESENT-VALUE TABLES

NATURE OF INTEREST

Interest is the cost of using money. It is the rental charge for cash, just as rental charges are often made for the use of automobiles or boats.

Interest does not always entail an outlay of cash. The concept of interest applies to ownership funds as well as to borrowed funds. The reason why interest must be considered on *all* funds in use, regardless of their source, is that the selection of one alternative necessarily commits funds that could otherwise be invested in some other opportunity. The measure of the interest in such cases is the return foregone by rejecting the alternative use. For instance, a wholly owned home or business asset is not cost-free. The funds so invested could alternatively be invested in government bonds or in some other venture. The measure of this opportunity cost depends on what alternative incomes are available.

Newspapers often contain advertisements of financial institutions citing interest rates that are "compounded." This appendix explains compound interest, including the use of present-value tables.

Simple interest is calculated by multiplying an interest rate by an unchanging principal amount. In contrast, *compound interest* is calculated by multiplying an interest rate by a principal amount that is changed each interest period by the previously accumulated (unpaid) interest. The accumulated interest is added to the principal to become the principal for the new period. For example, suppose you deposited $10,000 in a financial institution that promised to pay 10% interest per annum. You then let the amount accumulate for three years before withdrawing the full balance of the deposit. The *simple-interest* deposit would accumulate to $13,000 at the end of three years:

	PRINCIPAL	SIMPLE INTEREST	BALANCE, END OF YEAR
Year 1	$10,000	$10,000 × 0.10 = $1,000	$11,000
Year 2	10,000	10,000 × 0.10 = 1,000	12,000
Year 3	10,000	10,000 × 0.10 = 1,000	13,000

Compound interest provides interest on interest. That is, the principal changes from period to period. The deposit would accumulate to $10,000 \times (1.10)^3 = \$10,000 \times 1.331 = \$13,310$:

	PRINCIPAL	COMPOUND INTEREST	BALANCE, END OF YEAR
Year 1	$10,000	$10,000 × 0.10 = $1,000	$11,000
Year 2	11,000	11,000 × 0.10 = 1,100	12,100
Year 3	12,100	12,100 × 0.10 = 1,210	13,310

The "force" of compound interest can be staggering. For example, the same deposit would accumulate as follows:

	AT END OF		
	10 Years	20 Years	40 Years
Simple interest:			
$10,000 + 10 ($1,000) =	$20,000		
10,000 + 20 ($1,000) =		$30,000	
10,000 + 40 ($1,000) =			$ 50,000
Compound interest:			
$10,000 × (1.10)^{10} = $10,000 × 2.5937 =	$25,937		
$10,000 × (1.10)^{20} = $10,000 × 6.7275 =		$67,275	
$10,000 × (1.10)^{40} = $10,000 × 45.2593 =			$452,593

Hand calculations of compound interest quickly become burdensome. Therefore, compound interest tables have been constructed to ease computations. (Indeed, many hand calculators contain programs that provide speedy answers.) Hundreds of tables are available, but we will use only the three most useful for capital budgeting.[1]

TABLE 1: PRESENT VALUE OF $1

How shall we express a future cash inflow or outflow in terms of its equivalent today (at time zero)? Table 1, page 728, provides factors that give the *present value* of a single, lump-sum cash flow to be received or paid at the *end* of a future period.[2]

Suppose you invest $1.00 today. It will grow to $1.06 in one year at six percent interest; that is, $1 \times 1.06 = \$1.06$. At the end of the second year its value is ($1 \times 1.06) \times 1.06 = \$1 \times (1.06)^2 = \$1.124$, and at the end of the third year it is $1 \times (1.06)^3 = 1.191$. In general, $1.00 grows to $(1 + i)^n$ in n years at i percent interest.

To determine the *present value*, you reverse this accumulation process. If $1.00 is to be received in one year, it is worth $1 \div 1.06 = \$0.9434$ today. Suppose you invest $0.9434 today. In one year you will have $0.9434 \times 1.06 = \$1.00$. Thus, $0.9434 is the *present value* of $1.00 a year hence at 6%. If the dollar will be received in two years, its present value is $1.00 \div (1.06)^2 = \$0.8900$. The general formula for

---

[1] For additional tables, see R. Vichas, *Handbook of Financial Mathematics, Formulas and Tables* (Englewood Cliffs, N.J.: Prentice-Hall, 1979).

[2] The factors are rounded to four decimal places. The examples in this text use these rounded factors. If you use tables with different rounding, or if you use a hand calculator or personal computer, your answers may differ from those given because of a small rounding error.

the present value (*PV*) of an amount *S* to be received or paid in *n* periods at an interest rate of *i* % per period is

$$PV = \frac{S}{(1+i)^n}$$

Table 1 gives factors for the present value of $1.00 at various interest rates over several different periods. Present values are also called *discounted* values, and the process of finding the present value is *discounting*. You can think of this as discounting (decreasing) the value of a future cash inflow or outflow. Why is the value discounted? Because the cash is to be received or paid in the future, not today.

Assume that a prominent city is issuing a three-year noninterest-bearing note payable that promises to pay a lump sum of $1,000 exactly three years from now. You desire a rate of return of exactly 6%, compounded annually. How much would you be willing to pay now for the three-year note? The situation is sketched as follows:

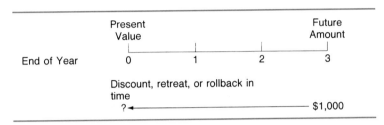

The factor in the period 3 row and 6% column of Table 1 is 0.8396. The present value of the $1,000 payment is $1,000 × 0.8396 = $839.60. You would be willing to pay $839.60 for the $1,000 to be received in three years.

Suppose interest is compounded semiannually rather than annually. How much would you be willing to pay? The three years become six interest payment periods. The rate per period is half the annual rate, or 6% ÷ 2 = 3%. The factor in the period 6 row and 3% column of Table 1 is 0.8375. You would be willing to pay $1,000 × 0.8375 or only $837.50 rather than $839.60.

As a further check on your understanding, review the earlier example of compound interest. Suppose the financial institution promised to pay $13,310 at the end of three years. How much would you be willing to deposit at time zero if you desired a 10% rate of return compounded annually? Using Table 1, the period 3 row and the 10% column show a factor of 0.7513. Multiply this factor by the future amount:

$$PV = 0.7513 \times \$13,310 = \$10,000$$

A diagram of this computation follows:

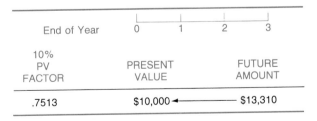

Pause for a moment. Use Table 1 to obtain the present values of

1. $1,600, at 20%, at the end of 20 years
2. $8,300, at 10%, at the end of 12 years
3. $8,000, at 4%, at the end of 4 years

Answers:

1. $1,600 (0.0261) = $41.76
2. $8,300 (0.3186) = $2,644.38
3. $8,000 (0.8548) = $6,838.40

TABLE 2: PRESENT VALUE OF AN ORDINARY ANNUITY OF $1

An *ordinary annuity* is a series of equal cash flows to take place at the *end* of successive periods of equal length. Its present value is denoted PV_A. Assume that you buy a noninterest-bearing serial note from a municipality that promises to pay $1,000 at the end of *each* of three years. How much should you be willing to pay if you desire a rate of return of 6%, compounded annually?

You could solve this problem using Table 1. First, find the present value of each payment, and then add the present values as in Exhibit B–1. You would be willing to pay $943.40 for the first payment, $890.00 for the second, and $839.60 for the third, a total of $2,673.00.

Since each cash payment is $1,000 with equal one-year periods between them, Table 2 provides a shortcut method. The present value in Exhibit B–1 can be expressed as

$$PV_A = \$1,000 \times \frac{1}{1.06} + \$1,000 \times \frac{1}{(1.06)^2} + \$1,000 \times \frac{1}{(1.06)^3}$$

$$= \$1,000 \left[\frac{1}{1.06} + \frac{1}{(1.06)^2} + \frac{1}{(1.06)^3} \right]$$

The three terms in brackets are the first three numbers from the 6% column of Table 1, and their sum is in the third row of the 6% column of Table 2: .9434 + .8900 + .8396 = 2.6730. Instead of calculating three present values and adding them, you simply multiply the PV factor from Table 2 by the cash payment: 2.6730 × $1,000 = $2,673.

This shortcut is especially valuable if the cash payments or receipts extend over many periods. Consider an annual cash payment of $1,000 for 20 years at six percent. The present value, calculated from Table 2, is $1,000 × 11.4699 = $11,469.90. To use Table 1 for this calculation, you would perform 20 multiplications and then add the twenty products.

EXHIBIT B–1

PAYMENT	END OF YEAR	0 PRESENT VALUE	1	2	3
1	$\frac{1,000}{1.06} = .9434$	$ 943.40	$1,000		
2	$\frac{1,000}{(1.06)^2} = .8900$	$ 890.00		$1,000	
3	$\frac{1,000}{(1.06)^3} = .8396$	$ 839.60			$1,000
		$2,673			

The factors in Table 2 can be calculated using the following general formula:

$$PV_A = \frac{1}{i}\left[1 - \frac{1}{(1+i)^n}\right]$$

Applied to our illustration:

$$PV_A = \frac{1}{.06}\left[1 - \frac{1}{(1.06)^3}\right] = \frac{1}{.06}(1 - .8396) = \frac{.1604}{.06} = 2.6730$$

Use Table 2 to obtain the present values of the following ordinary annuities:

1. $1,600 at 20% for 20 years
2. $8,300 at 10% for 12 years
3. $8,000 at 4% for 4 years

Answers:

1. $1,600 (4.8696) = $7,791.36
2. $8,300 (6.8137) = $56,553.71
3. $8,000 (3.6299) = $29,039.20

In particular, note that the higher the interest rate, the lower the present value.

TABLE 3: PRESENT VALUE OF ACRS DEPRECIATION

Investment in a depreciable asset results in a tax savings because each dollar of depreciation is deductible in the computation of income taxes. Most investments are depreciated by the accelerated cost recovery system (ACRS) method for tax purposes. Table 3 provides the present value of the ACRS depreciation on a $1.00 investment over 3-, 5-, 10-, and 15-year recovery periods for several different interest rates. For instance, for a 5-year asset and a 10% desired rate of return, the present value is (assuming depreciation is at the end of each year*):

YEAR	(1) DEPRECIATION	(2) PV FACTOR	(1) × (2) PRESENT VALUE OF DEPRECIATION
1	$0.40	0.9091	$0.3636
2	0.24	0.8264	0.1983
3	0.144	0.7513	0.1082
4	0.108	0.6830	0.0738
5	0.108	0.6209	0.0671
Total Depreciation	$1.00		
Present Value of $1 of Depreciation, shown in Table 3			$0.8110

To find the present value of the *tax savings* from $1.00 of investment, multiply the present value of $1 of depreciation (from Table 3) by the income tax rate. If the tax rate is 60%, the present value of the tax savings for the example is 0.60 × $0.8110 = $0.4866, or 48.66% of the acquisition cost of the asset.

---

* The year refers to a year of the asset's life. This may not correspond to a calendar (or tax) year. See footnote 2 on page 386.

TABLE 1 (Put a clip on this page for easy reference.)

Present Value of $1

$$PV = \frac{1}{(1+i)^n}$$

PERIODS	3%	4%	5%	6%	7%	8%	10%	12%	14%	16%	18%	20%	22%	24%	25%	26%	28%	30%	40%
1	.9709	.9615	.9524	.9434	.9346	.9259	.9091	.8929	.8772	.8621	.8475	.8333	.8197	.8065	.8000	.7937	.7813	.7692	.7143
2	.9426	.9246	.9070	.8900	.8734	.8573	.8264	.7972	.7695	.7432	.7182	.6944	.6719	.6504	.6400	.6299	.6104	.5917	.5102
3	.9151	.8890	.8638	.8396	.8163	.7938	.7513	.7118	.6750	.6407	.6086	.5787	.5507	.5245	.5120	.4999	.4768	.4552	.3644
4	.8885	.8548	.8227	.7921	.7629	.7350	.6830	.6355	.5921	.5523	.5158	.4823	.4514	.4230	.4096	.3968	.3725	.3501	.2603
5	.8626	.8219	.7835	.7473	.7130	.6806	.6209	.5674	.5194	.4761	.4371	.4019	.3700	.3411	.3277	.3149	.2910	.2693	.1859
6	.8375	.7903	.7462	.7050	.6663	.6302	.5645	.5066	.4556	.4104	.3704	.3349	.3033	.2751	.2621	.2499	.2274	.2072	.1328
7	.8131	.7599	.7107	.6651	.6227	.5835	.5132	.4523	.3996	.3538	.3139	.2791	.2486	.2218	.2097	.1983	.1776	.1594	.0949
8	.7894	.7307	.6768	.6274	.5820	.5403	.4665	.4039	.3506	.3050	.2660	.2326	.2038	.1789	.1678	.1574	.1388	.1226	.0678
9	.7664	.7026	.6446	.5919	.5439	.5002	.4241	.3606	.3075	.2630	.2255	.1938	.1670	.1443	.1342	.1249	.1084	.0943	.0484
10	.7441	.6756	.6139	.5584	.5083	.4632	.3855	.3220	.2697	.2267	.1911	.1615	.1369	.1164	.1074	.0992	.0847	.0725	.0346
11	.7224	.6496	.5847	.5268	.4751	.4289	.3505	.2875	.2366	.1954	.1619	.1346	.1122	.0938	.0859	.0787	.0662	.0558	.0247
12	.7014	.6246	.5568	.4970	.4440	.3971	.3186	.2567	.2076	.1685	.1372	.1122	.0920	.0757	.0687	.0625	.0517	.0429	.0176
13	.6810	.6006	.5303	.4688	.4150	.3677	.2897	.2292	.1821	.1452	.1163	.0935	.0754	.0610	.0550	.0496	.0404	.0330	.0126
14	.6611	.5775	.5051	.4423	.3878	.3405	.2633	.2046	.1597	.1252	.0985	.0779	.0618	.0492	.0440	.0393	.0316	.0254	.0090
15	.6419	.5553	.4810	.4173	.3624	.3152	.2394	.1827	.1401	.1079	.0835	.0649	.0507	.0397	.0352	.0312	.0247	.0195	.0064
16	.6232	.5339	.4581	.3936	.3387	.2919	.2176	.1631	.1229	.0930	.0708	.0541	.0415	.0320	.0281	.0248	.0193	.0150	.0046
17	.6050	.5134	.4363	.3714	.3166	.2703	.1978	.1456	.1078	.0802	.0600	.0451	.0340	.0258	.0225	.0197	.0150	.0116	.0033
18	.5874	.4936	.4155	.3503	.2959	.2502	.1799	.1300	.0946	.0691	.0508	.0376	.0279	.0208	.0180	.0156	.0118	.0089	.0023
19	.5703	.4746	.3957	.3305	.2765	.2317	.1635	.1161	.0829	.0596	.0431	.0313	.0229	.0168	.0144	.0124	.0092	.0068	.0017
20	.5537	.4564	.3769	.3118	.2584	.2145	.1486	.1037	.0728	.0514	.0365	.0261	.0187	.0135	.0115	.0098	.0072	.0053	.0012
21	.5375	.4388	.3589	.2942	.2415	.1987	.1351	.0926	.0638	.0443	.0309	.0217	.0154	.0109	.0092	.0078	.0056	.0040	.0009
22	.5219	.4220	.3418	.2775	.2257	.1839	.1228	.0826	.0560	.0382	.0262	.0181	.0126	.0088	.0074	.0062	.0044	.0031	.0006
23	.5067	.4057	.3256	.2618	.2109	.1703	.1117	.0738	.0491	.0329	.0222	.0151	.0103	.0071	.0059	.0049	.0034	.0024	.0004
24	.4919	.3901	.3101	.2470	.1971	.1577	.1015	.0659	.0431	.0284	.0188	.0126	.0085	.0057	.0047	.0039	.0027	.0018	.0003
25	.4776	.3751	.2953	.2330	.1842	.1460	.0923	.0588	.0378	.0245	.0160	.0105	.0069	.0046	.0038	.0031	.0021	.0014	.0002
26	.4637	.3607	.2812	.2198	.1722	.1352	.0839	.0525	.0331	.0211	.0135	.0087	.0057	.0037	.0030	.0025	.0016	.0011	.0002
27	.4502	.3468	.2678	.2074	.1609	.1252	.0763	.0469	.0291	.0182	.0115	.0073	.0047	.0030	.0024	.0019	.0013	.0008	.0001
28	.4371	.3335	.2551	.1956	.1504	.1159	.0693	.0419	.0255	.0157	.0097	.0061	.0038	.0024	.0019	.0015	.0010	.0006	.0001
29	.4243	.3207	.2429	.1846	.1406	.1073	.0630	.0374	.0224	.0135	.0082	.0051	.0031	.0020	.0015	.0012	.0008	.0005	.0001
30	.4120	.3083	.2314	.1741	.1314	.0994	.0573	.0334	.0196	.0116	.0070	.0042	.0026	.0016	.0012	.0010	.0006	.0004	.0001
40	.3066	.2083	.1420	.0972	.0668	.0460	.0221	.0107	.0053	.0026	.0013	.0007	.0004	.0002	.0001	.0001	.0001	.0000	.0000

TABLE 2

Present Value of Ordinary Annuity of $1

$$PV_A = \frac{1}{i}\left[1 - \frac{1}{(1+i)^n}\right]$$

PERIODS	3%	4%	5%	6%	7%	8%	10%	12%	14%	16%	18%	20%	22%	24%	25%	26%	28%	30%	40%
1	.9709	.9615	.9524	.9434	.9346	.9259	.9091	.8929	.8772	.8621	.8475	.8333	.8197	.8065	.8000	.7937	.7813	.7692	.7143
2	1.9135	1.8861	1.8594	1.8334	1.8080	1.7833	1.7355	1.6901	1.6467	1.6052	1.5656	1.5278	1.4915	1.4568	1.4400	1.4235	1.3916	1.3609	1.2245
3	2.8286	2.7751	2.7232	2.6730	2.6243	2.5771	2.4869	2.4018	2.3216	2.2459	2.1743	2.1065	2.0422	1.9813	1.9520	1.9234	1.8684	1.8161	1.5889
4	3.7171	3.6299	3.5460	3.4651	3.3872	3.3121	3.1699	3.0373	2.9137	2.7982	2.6901	2.5887	2.4936	2.4043	2.3616	2.3202	2.2410	2.1662	1.8492
5	4.5797	4.4518	4.3295	4.2124	4.1002	3.9927	3.7908	3.6048	3.4331	3.2743	3.1272	2.9906	2.8636	2.7454	2.6893	2.6351	2.5320	2.4356	2.0352
6	5.4172	5.2421	5.0757	4.9173	4.7665	4.6229	4.3553	4.1114	3.8887	3.6847	3.4976	3.3255	3.1669	3.0205	2.9514	2.8850	2.7594	2.6427	2.1680
7	6.2303	6.0021	5.7864	5.5824	5.3893	5.2064	4.8684	4.5638	4.2883	4.0386	3.8115	3.6046	3.4155	3.2423	3.1611	3.0833	2.9370	2.8021	2.2628
8	7.0197	6.7327	6.4632	6.2098	5.9713	5.7466	5.3349	4.9676	4.6389	4.3436	4.0776	3.8372	3.6193	3.4212	3.3289	3.2407	3.0758	2.9247	2.3306
9	7.7861	7.4353	7.1078	6.8017	6.5152	6.2469	5.7590	5.3282	4.9464	4.6065	4.3030	4.0310	3.7863	3.5655	3.4631	3.3657	3.1842	3.0190	2.3790
10	8.5302	8.1109	7.7217	7.3601	7.0236	6.7101	6.1446	5.6502	5.2161	4.8332	4.4941	4.1925	3.9232	3.6819	3.5705	3.4648	3.2689	3.0915	2.4136
11	9.2526	8.7605	8.3064	7.8869	7.4987	7.1390	6.4951	5.9377	5.4527	5.0286	4.6560	4.3271	4.0354	3.7757	3.6564	3.5435	3.3351	3.1473	2.4383
12	9.9540	9.3851	8.8633	8.3838	7.9427	7.5361	6.8137	6.1944	5.6603	5.1971	4.7932	4.4392	4.1274	3.8514	3.7251	3.6059	3.3868	3.1903	2.4559
13	10.6350	9.9856	9.3936	8.8527	8.3577	7.9038	7.1034	6.4235	5.8424	5.3423	4.9095	4.5327	4.2028	3.9124	3.7801	3.6555	3.4272	3.2233	2.4685
14	11.2961	10.5631	9.8986	9.2950	8.7455	8.2442	7.3667	6.6282	6.0021	5.4675	5.0081	4.6106	4.2646	3.9616	3.8241	3.6949	3.4587	3.2487	2.4775
15	11.9379	11.1184	10.3797	9.7122	9.1079	8.5595	7.6061	6.8109	6.1422	5.5755	5.0916	4.6755	4.3152	4.0013	3.8593	3.7261	3.4834	3.2682	2.4839
16	12.5611	11.6523	10.8378	10.1059	9.4466	8.8514	7.8237	6.9740	6.2651	5.6685	5.1624	4.7296	4.3567	4.0333	3.8874	3.7509	3.5026	3.2832	2.4885
17	13.1661	12.1657	11.2741	10.4773	9.7632	9.1216	8.0216	7.1196	6.3729	5.7487	5.2223	4.7746	4.3908	4.0591	3.9099	3.7705	3.5177	3.2948	2.4918
18	13.7535	12.6593	11.6896	10.8276	10.0591	9.3719	8.2014	7.2497	6.4674	5.8178	5.2732	4.8122	4.4187	4.0799	3.9279	3.7861	3.5294	3.3037	2.4941
19	14.3238	13.1339	12.0853	11.1581	10.3356	9.6036	8.3649	7.3658	6.5504	5.8775	5.3162	4.8435	4.4415	4.0967	3.9424	3.7985	3.5386	3.3105	2.4958
20	14.8775	13.5903	12.4622	11.4699	10.5940	9.8181	8.5136	7.4694	6.6231	5.9288	5.3527	4.8696	4.4603	4.1103	3.9539	3.8083	3.5458	3.3158	2.4970
21	15.4150	14.0292	12.8212	11.7641	10.8355	10.0168	8.6487	7.5620	6.6870	5.9731	5.3837	4.8913	4.4756	4.1212	3.9631	3.8161	3.5514	3.3198	2.4979
22	15.9369	14.4511	13.1630	12.0416	11.0612	10.2007	8.7715	7.6446	6.7429	6.0113	5.4099	4.9094	4.4882	4.1300	3.9705	3.8223	3.5558	3.3230	2.4985
23	16.4436	14.8568	13.4886	12.3034	11.2722	10.3711	8.8832	7.7184	6.7921	6.0442	5.4321	4.9245	4.4985	4.1371	3.9764	3.8273	3.5592	3.3254	2.4989
24	16.9355	15.2470	13.7986	12.5504	11.4693	10.5288	8.9847	7.7843	6.8351	6.0726	5.4509	4.9371	4.5070	4.1428	3.9811	3.8312	3.5619	3.3272	2.4992
25	17.4131	15.6221	14.0939	12.7834	11.6536	10.6748	9.0770	7.8431	6.8729	6.0971	5.4669	4.9476	4.5139	4.1474	3.9849	3.8342	3.5640	3.3286	2.4994
26	17.8768	15.9828	14.3752	13.0032	11.8258	10.8100	9.1609	7.8957	6.9061	6.1182	5.4804	4.9563	4.5196	4.1511	3.9879	3.8367	3.5656	3.3297	2.4996
27	18.3270	16.3296	14.6430	13.2105	11.9867	10.9352	9.2372	7.9426	6.9352	6.1364	5.4919	4.9636	4.5243	4.1542	3.9903	3.8387	3.5669	3.3305	2.4997
28	18.7641	16.6631	14.8981	13.4062	12.1371	11.0511	9.3066	7.9844	6.9607	6.1520	5.5016	4.9697	4.5281	4.1566	3.9923	3.8402	3.5679	3.3312	2.4998
29	19.1885	16.9837	15.1411	13.5907	12.2777	11.1584	9.3696	8.0218	6.9830	6.1656	5.5098	4.9747	4.5312	4.1585	3.9938	3.8414	3.5687	3.3317	2.4999
30	19.6004	17.2920	15.3725	13.7648	12.4090	11.2578	9.4269	8.0552	7.0027	6.1772	5.5168	4.9789	4.5338	4.1601	3.9950	3.8424	3.5693	3.3321	2.4999
40	23.1148	19.7928	17.1591	15.0463	13.3317	11.9246	9.7791	8.2438	7.1050	6.2335	5.5482	4.9966	4.5439	4.1659	3.9995	3.8458	3.5712	3.3332	2.5000

TABLE 3

Present Value of $1 of Declining Balance Depreciation

DISCOUNT RATE	3-YEAR	5-YEAR	7-YEAR	10-YEAR	15-YEAR	20-YEAR
3%	.9584	.9355	.9138	.8827	.8120	.7634
4%	.9453	.9156	.8879	.8487	.7613	.7035
5%	.9325	.8965	.8633	.8170	.7156	.6507
6%	.9200	.8781	.8399	.7872	.6741	.6041
7%	.9079	.8604	.8175	.7593	.6364	.5628
8%	.8960	.8433	.7963	.7331	.6021	.5260
9%	.8845	.8269	.7760	.7085	.5707	.4932
10%	.8732	.8110	.7566	.6853	.5421	.4638
12%	.8515	.7809	.7203	.6429	.4917	.4134
14%	.8308	.7528	.6872	.6050	.4490	.3722
15%	.8208	.7394	.6716	.5876	.4300	.3543
16%	.8111	.7265	.6567	.5711	.4125	.3380
18%	.7922	.7019	.6286	.5406	.3811	.3093
20%	.7742	.6788	.6027	.5130	.3538	.2849
22%	.7570	.6571	.5788	.4879	.3301	.2641
24%	.7405	.6367	.5566	.4651	.3092	.2460
25%	.7325	.6270	.5461	.4545	.2996	.2379
26%	.7247	.6175	.5359	.4443	.2907	.2303
28%	.7095	.5993	.5167	.4252	.2742	.2165
30%	.6950	.5821	.4987	.4077	.2595	.2042
40%	.6301	.5088	.4245	.3378	.2046	.1594

* Double declining balance for 3, 5, 7, and 10 year assets, and 150% declining balance for 15 and 20 year assets.

GLOSSARY

The italicized words within the definition or explanations are also described in the glossary.

ABSORPTION APPROACH (p. 72). See *absorption costing.*

ABSORPTION COSTING (p. 72). The type of product costing that assigns fixed *manufacturing overhead* to the units produced as a *product cost.* Contrast with *direct costing.*

ACCELERATED COST RECOVERY SYSTEM (ACRS) (p. 385). A system of the Internal Revenue Service that requires *depreciation* deductions to be based on arbitrary "recovery periods" instead of useful lives.

ACCELERATED DEPRECIATION (p. 384). Any pattern of *depreciation* that writes off depreciable *costs* more quickly than the ordinary straight-line method.

ACCOUNT (p. 553). Summary of the changes in a particular *asset* or *equity.*

ACCOUNTING PRINCIPLES BOARD (APB) (p. 572). The top private-sector regulatory body, which existed from 1959 to 1973, when it was succeeded by the *Financial Accounting Standards Board.*

ACCOUNTING RATE OF RETURN (p. 358). An expression of the utility of a given project as the ratio of the increase in future average annual *operating income* to the initial increase in required investment. Also called *book value method* and *unadjusted rate.*

ACCOUNTS PAYABLE (p. 550). The debts shown on the buyer's *balance sheet* when the buyer has bought goods or services on open *account.* Usually a *current liability.*

ACCOUNTS RECEIVABLE (p. 550). The claims against debtors generally arising from sale of goods or services on open account. Usually a *current asset.*

ACCRUAL BASIS (p. 555). A matching process whereby *revenue* is recognized as services are rendered and *expenses* are recognized as efforts are expended or services utilized to obtain the revenue, regardless of when cash is received or disbursed.

ACCRUE (p. 565). Accumulation of a receivable or payable during a given period even though no explicit *transaction* occurs.

ACCUMULATED DEPRECIATION (p. 603). The portion of the original *cost* of a *fixed asset* that has previously been charged as *depreciation* expense.

ACQUISITION COST (p. 131). See *historical cost.*

ACRS (p. 385). See *Accelerated cost recovery system.*

ADDBACK METHOD (p. 618). The practice of beginning a *statement of changes in financial position* with *net income* and then adding or deducting *income statement* items not affecting *working capital.*

ADJUSTING ENTRIES (p. 556). The records made of an accounting *transaction* giving effect to the correction of an error, an accrual, a write-off, a prepayment, a provision for bad debts or *depreciation*, or the like.

ADJUSTMENTS (p. 556). The key final process (before the computation of ending *account* balances) that assures the accountant that the financial effects of *transactions* are assigned to the appropriate time periods.

AGENCY THEORY (p. 313). An economic theory used to explain choices of performance measures and rewards.

ALL-COSTS APPROACH (p. 98). An approach to pricing that is based on the total *costs* of manufacturing plus the total costs of nonmanufacturing.

ALLOCATION (p. 62). See *Cost allocation*.

APB (p. 572). See *Accounting Principles Board*.

APB OPINIONS (p. 572). A series of 31 Opinions of the *Accounting Principles Board* issued during 1962–73, many of which are still in force.

ASSETS (p. 549). Economic resources that are expected to benefit future activities.

ATTENTION DIRECTING (p. 5). The function of the accountant's information-supplying task that focuses on problems in the operation of the firm or that points out imperfections or inefficiencies in certain areas of the firm's operation.

AUDIT (p. 571). See *Independent audit*.

AVOIDABLE COST (p. 101). Those *costs* that will not continue if an ongoing operation is changed or deleted.

BALANCE SHEET (p. 548). A statement of financial status at an instant of time.

BOOK VALUE (p. 131). The carrying amount in the *accounts*, net of any *contra accounts*. For example, the book value of equipment is its *acquisition cost* minus its *accumulated depreciation*.

BOOK VALUE METHOD (p. 358). See *Accounting rate of return*.

BUDGET (p. 6). A formal quantitative expression of management plans.

BUDGET VARIANCE (p. 188). The difference between an actual and a *budget* amount.

BY-PRODUCTS (p. 130). Products like *joint products* that are not individually identifiable until manufacturing reaches a *split-off point*. However, by-products have relatively insignificant sales values in comparison with joint products.

CAPACITY COSTS (p. 227). An alternate term for *fixed costs*, emphasizing the fact that fixed costs are needed in order to provide operating facilities and an organization ready to produce and sell at a planned volume of activity.

CAPITAL (p. 571). In accounting, this word is too general by itself. In most cases, capital implies *owners' equity*. Money generated by long-term debt is also often called capital.

CAPITAL BUDGETING (p. 340). Making decisions that have significant effects beyond the current year.

CAPITAL TURNOVER (p. 316). *Revenue* divided by invested capital.

CASH BASIS (p. 555). A process of accounting whereby *revenue* and *expense* recognition depend solely on the timing of various cash receipts and disbursements.

CASH BUDGET (p. 163). A schedule of expected cash receipts and disbursements.

CASH FLOW (p. 621). A term often used to mean cash provided by operations.

CERTIFICATE (p. 572). See *Independent opinion*.

CERTIFIED MANAGEMENT ACCOUNTANT (p. 18). A designation given by the Institute of Certified Management Accountants of the *National Association of Accountants* to those who pass a set of examinations and meet specified experience and continuing education requirements.

CERTIFIED PUBLIC ACCOUNTANT (p. 18). In the United States, an accountant earns this designation by a combination of education, qualifying experience, and the passing of a three-and-one-half day written national examination.

CHANGES STATEMENT (p. 612). A *statement of changes in financial position*.

CHOICE CRITERION (p. 515). Often used as a synonym for *objective function*.

CMA (p. 18). See *Certified management accountant*.

COEFFICIENT OF DETERMINATION (p. 245). A goodness-of-fit statistic, labeled r, that reveals the percentage of variation in one variable (e.g., *cost*) that is explained by another variable (e.g., volume).

COMMITTED FIXED COSTS (p. 228). Those *fixed costs* arising from the possession of plant and equipment and a basic organization and thus are affected primarily by long-run decisions as to the desired level of capacity.

COMMON COST (p. 101). *Costs* of facilities and services that are shared by user departments.

COMMON STOCK (p. 607). Stock that has no predetermined rate of *dividends* and is the last to obtain a share in the *assets* when a *corporation* is dissolved. It usually has voting power in the management of the corporations.

COMPONENT PERCENTAGES (p. 658). Analysis and presentation of financial statements in percentage form to aid comparability.

COMPTROLLER (p. 13). See *Controller*.

CONSOLIDATED FINANCIAL STATEMENTS (p. 641). Statements that combine legally separate companies as though they were a single fused *entity*.

CONSTANT DOLLARS (p. 689). Those monetary units restated so as to represent the same general purchasing power.

CONTINUITY CONVENTION (p. 579). See *Going-concern convention*.

CONTINUOUS BUDGET (p. 157). A *budget* that perpetually adds a month in the future as the month just ended is dropped.

CONTRIBUTION APPROACH (p. 73). A method of preparing *income statements* that separates *variable costs* from *fixed costs* in order to emphasize the importance of cost behavior patterns for purposes of planning and control.

CONTRIBUTION MARGIN (p. 31). Excess of sales price over variable expenses. Also called *marginal income*. May be expressed as a total, as a ratio, or on a per-unit basis.

CONTROL-FACTOR UNITS (p. 231). A measure of work accomplished used in formulating the *budget*.

CONTROLLABLE COST (p. 265). The opposite of *uncontrollable cost*.

CONTROLLER (p. 13). The chief management accounting executive. Also spelled *comptroller*.

CONTROLLING (p. 6). Obtaining conformity to plans through action and evaluation.

CONVERSION COSTS (p. 64). *Direct labor* plus *factory overhead*.

CORPORATION (p. 549). Organizations that are "artificial beings" created by individual state laws.

COST (p. 62). Sacrifice made for goods or services. May take the form of an *outlay cost* or an *opportunity cost*.

COST ACCUMULATION (p. 62). Gathering of *costs* in some organized way via an accounting system.

COST ALLOCATION (p. 62). A general label for all tracing of various *costs* to *cost objectives* such as departments or products.

COST-ALLOCATION BASE (p. 267). A common denominator used to trace the *cost* or costs in question to the *cost objectives*. Examples are direct-labor-hours and machine-hours.

COST APPLICATION (p. 283). *Allocation* of total departmental *costs* to the revenue-producing products.

COST APPROXIMATION (p. 235). See *Cost estimation*.

COST BEHAVIOR PATTERN (p. 235). See *Cost function*.

COST-BENEFIT CRITERION (p. 19). As a system is changed, its expected additional benefits usually must exceed its expected additional *costs*.

COST-BENEFIT THEME (p. 19). See *Cost-benefit criterion*.

COST CENTER (p. 261). An area of responsibility for *costs*.

COST ESTIMATION (p. 235). An attempt to specify some underlying relationship between x and y over a stipulated *relevant range* of x that may be of interest. An approximation of how a *cost* truly behaves. The approximation is usually in linear rather than nonlinear form.

COST FUNCTION (p. 235). A relationship between a *cost* and one or more variables such as the total cost of repairs in relation to miles driven

COST METHOD FOR INVESTMENTS (p. 639). The method whereby the initial investment is recorded at cost and *dividends* are recorded as income.

COST OBJECTIVE (p. 62). Any activity for which a separate measurement of *costs* is desired. Examples include departments, products, territories, etc.

COST OF CAPITAL (p. 342). As used in this book, and in many finance books, a synonym for *required rate of return*.

COST OF GOODS SOLD (p. 40). *Cost* of the merchandise that is acquired and resold.

COST OF SALES (p. 40). See *Cost of goods sold*.

COST POOL (p. 267). A group of individual *costs* that is allocated to *cost objectives* using the same *cost-allocation base*.

CREDIT (p. 282). In accounting, means one thing and one thing only—"right side," as distinguished from "left side." It typically refers to an entry in an *account* or the balance of an account.

CURRENT ASSETS (p. 598). Cash plus those *assets* that are reasonably expected to be converted to cash or sold or consumed during the normal *operating cycle*.

CURRENT COST (p. 689). The *cost* to replace an *asset*, its current market price as opposed to *historical cost*.

CURRENT-COST METHOD (p. 690). See *Current cost*.

CURRENT LIABILITIES (p. 605). Existing debts that fall due within the coming year or within the normal *operating cycle* if longer than a year.

CURRENT RATIO (p. 660). The ratio of *current assets* to *current liabilities*.

CURRENTLY ATTAINABLE STANDARDS (p. 197). Standards that can be achieved by very efficient operations.

CUTOFF RATE (p. 342). Minimum desired rate of return.

DEBENTURE (p. 606). A security with a general claim against all unencumbered *assets* rather than a specific claim against particular assets.

DEBIT (p. 582). An entry on the left side of an *account*.

DECENTRALIZATION (p. 304). The delegation of freedom to make decisions. The lower the level in the organization that decisions are made, the greater the decentralization.

DECISION MODEL (p. 91). A formal method for making a choice that often involves quantitative analysis. More generally, a decision model is any method for making a choice.

DECISION TABLE (p. 515). The combination of possible actions, *events*, and *outcomes* that can occur.

DEFERRED CHARGES (p. 602). Like *prepaid expenses* but with longer-term benefits.

DEFERRED CREDIT (p. 564). Often used a synonym for *deferred revenue* or as a description for *deferred income tax*. In its bookkeeping application, the term refers to an amount that is classified as a *liability* that will eventually be transferred as a *credit* to *revenue* or a credit to *expense*.

DEFERRED INCOME (p. 564). See *Deferred revenue*.

DEFERRED REVENUE (p. 564). *Income* received or recorded before it is earned.

DEPRECIATION (p. 559). The allocation of the *acquisition cost* of plant, property, and equipment to the particular periods or products that benefit from the utilization of the *assets*.

DIFFERENTIAL APPROACH (p. 353). A method of determining which of two alternative courses of action is preferable by calculating the difference in net cash between alternatives, and then converting these differences to their present values.

DIFFERENTIAL COST (p. 128). See *Incremental cost*.

DIRECT COSTING (p. 73). The type of product costing that charges fixed *manufacturing overhead* immediately against the *revenue* of the period in which it was incurred, without assigning it to specific units produced. Also called *variable costing* or *marginal costing*.

DIRECT LABOR (p. 64). The wages of all labor that is physically traceable to the finished goods in an economically feasible way.

DIRECT MATERIAL (p. 64). All raw material that is an integral part of the finished good and can be conveniently assigned to specific physical units.

DIRECT METHOD (p. 281). A method that ignores other *service departments* when any given service department's *costs* are allocated to revenue-producing or production departments.

Discount Rate (p. 342). As used in *capital budgeting*, the minimum desired rate of return.

Discretionary Fixed Costs (p. 229). Fixed *costs* arising from periodic, usually yearly, appropriation decisions that directly reflect top management policies. Also called *programmed costs* or *managed costs*.

Dividends (p. 569). Ordinarily distributions of *assets* that liquidate a portion of the ownership claim.

Dual Price (p. 527). See *Shadow price*.

Dysfunctional Behavior (p. 309). Actions taken in conflict with top management goals.

Earned Surplus (p. 569). A virtually archaic term for *retained income*.

Earnings (p. 554). The excess of *revenues* over *expenses*.

Earnings per Share (p. 611). *Net income* divided by the number of common shares outstanding. However, where *preferred stock* exists, the preferred *dividends* must be deducted in order to compute the *net income* applicable to *common stock*.

Economic Lot Size (p. 529). Synonym for *economic order quantity*.

Economic Order Quantity (p. 529). The best size of either a normal purchase order or a shop order for a production run.

Efficiency Variance (p. 199). The difference between the quantity of actual inputs and the quantity of inputs that should have been used for the actual output achieved multiplied by the budgeted unit price.

Efficient Capital Market (p. 664). One in which market prices "fully reflect" all information available at a given time.

Engineered Cost (p. 230). Any *cost* that has an explicit, specified physical relations with a selected measure of activity.

Entity (p. 548). A specific area of accountability that is the focus of the acc process. It may be a single *corporation*, a tax district, a department, a ing machine, or a consolidated group of many interrelated corpora

Equities (p. 549). The claims against or interest in the *assets*. The cr are *liabilities* and the owners' claims are *owners' equity* or, in th tion, *stockholders' equity*.

Equity Method (p. 639). Accounts for investments at *acquisiti the investor's share of *dividends* and *earnings* or losses of t to the date of investment.

Equivalent Units (p. 447). The expression of output in t work applied thereto.

Events (p. 515). Set of all relevant occurrences that of nature.

Expected Value (p. 518). The sum over all *eve times the *payoff* from the event.

Equity Capital (p. 571). See *owners' equity*.

Expense (p. 553). Generally a gross decrease

Expired Costs (p. 558). *Expenditures* fr an *expense*; a *cost* absorbed over or a *loss* incurred.

Explicit Transactions (p. 557). E trigger nearly all day-to-d

Factory Burden (p. 64). See

Factory Overhead (p. 64). A Also called *factory* head, and *manuf*

FASB Statements (p reporting iss Board.

FAVORABLE COST VARIANCE (p. 188). Budgeted *costs* minus actual costs when actual costs are less than budgeted costs.

FIFO (p. 680). See *First-in, first-out*.

FINANCIAL ACCOUNTING (p. 3). Is concerned mainly with how accounting can serve external decision makers, as distinguished from *management accounting*.

FINANCIAL ACCOUNTING STANDARDS BOARD (FASB) (p. 8). The primary regulatory body over accounting principles and practices. It is an independent creature of the private sector.

FINANCIAL BUDGET (p. 159). A *budget* that focuses on the effect that the operating budget and other plans (such as capital expenditures and repayments of debt) will have on cash.

FINANCIAL CAPITAL MAINTENANCE (p. 689). The quantity of financial resources (usually *historical costs*), as distinguished from physical resources or operating capability, to be recovered before *income* emerges.

FINANCIAL PLANNING MODELS (p. 168). Mathematical statements of the relationships in the organization among all the operating and financial activities, and of other major internal and external factors that may affect decisions.

FIRST-IN, FIRST-OUT (p. 680). An inventory costing method where the stock of merchandise or material that is acquired earliest is assumed to be used first; the stock

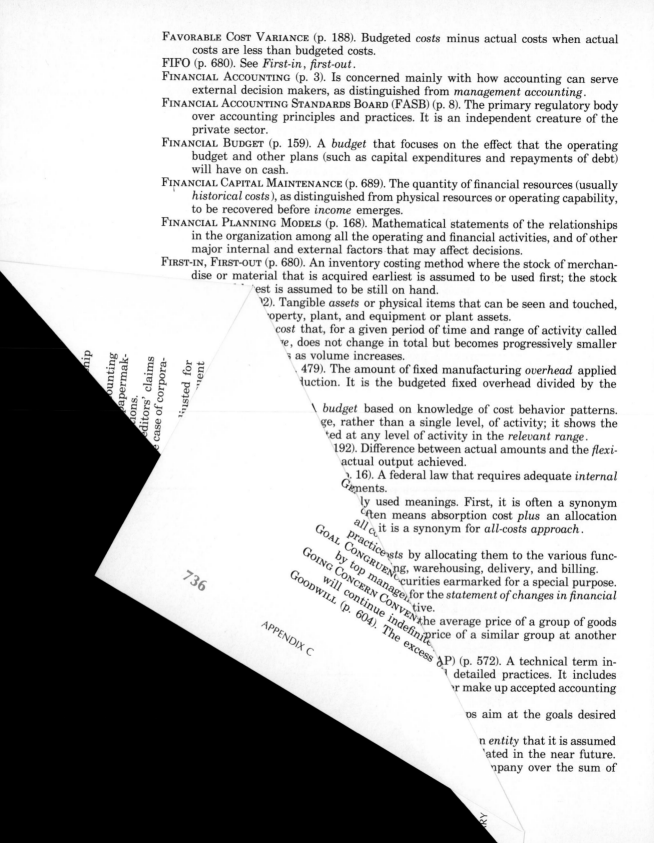

est is assumed to be still on hand.

...2). Tangible *assets* or physical items that can be seen and touched,
...operty, plant, and equipment or plant assets.

...*cost* that, for a given period of time and range of activity called
...e, does not change in total but becomes progressively smaller
...as volume increases.

...479). The amount of fixed manufacturing *overhead* applied
...luction. It is the budgeted fixed overhead divided by the

...*budget* based on knowledge of cost behavior patterns.
...ge, rather than a single level, of activity; it shows the
...ted at any level of activity in the *relevant range*.

...192). Difference between actual amounts and the *flexi-*
...actual output achieved.

...16). A federal law that requires adequate *internal*
...ments.

...ly used meanings. First, it is often a synonym
...ften means absorption cost *plus* an allocation
...it is a synonym for *all-costs approach*.

GOAL CONGRUENCE ...sts by allocating them to the various func-
...ng, warehousing, delivery, and billing.

GOING CONCERN CONVENTION ...curities earmarked for a special purpose.
...for the *statement of changes in financial*
...tive.

GOODWILL (p. 604). The excess ...the average price of a group of goods
...price of a similar group at another

...P) (p. 572). A technical term in-
...detailed practices. It includes
...make up accepted accounting

...os aim at the goals desired

...*entity* that it is assumed
...ated in the near future.
...pany over the sum of

736

APPENDIX C

the fair market values of the identifiable individual *assets* less the *liabilities*.

GROSS BOOK VALUE (p. 321). Carrying amount of an *asset* before deducting any related amounts (such as *accumulated depreciation*).

GROSS MARGIN (p. 40). Also called *gross profit*. Excess of sales over the *cost of goods sold*, that is, over the *cost* of the merchandise inventory that is acquired and resold.

GROSS PROFIT (p. 40). See *gross margin*.

HALF-YEAR CONVENTION (p. 386). A widely used custom of regarding all depreciable *assets* placed in service during the year as if they had been placed in service at the year's midpoint.

HISTORICAL COST (p. 131). The amount originally paid to acquire an *asset*.

HOLDING GAINS OR (LOSSES) (p. 692). Increases (or decreases) in the *replacement cost* (or other appropriate measure of current value) of the *assets* held during the current period.

HURDLE RATE (p. 342). Minimum desired rate of return. Also called *required rate of return*.

HYBRID COSTING (p. 426). See *Operation costing*.

IDLE TIME (p. 77). A classification of *indirect labor* that constitutes wages paid for unproductive time due to circumstances beyond the worker's control.

IMPLICIT TRANSACTIONS (p. 557). Events (like the passage of time) that are temporarily ignored in day-to-day recording procedures and that are recognized via end-of-period *adjustments*.

INCENTIVE (p. 311). Those informal and formal performance measures and rewards that enhance *goal congruence* and *managerial effort*.

INCOME (p. 554). The excess of *revenues* over *expenses*.

INCOME PERCENTAGE OF REVENUE (p. 316). *Income* divided by *revenue*.

INCOME STATEMENT (p. 548). A statement that evaluates the operating performance of the corporation by matching its accomplishments (*revenue* from customers, which usually is called sales) and efforts (*cost of goods sold* and other *expenses*).

INCREMENTAL (p. 36). Change in total results (such as *revenue*, *expenses*, or *income*) under a new condition in comparison with some given or known condition.

INCREMENTAL APPROACH (p. 353). See *Differential approach*.

INCREMENTAL COST (p. 129). The difference in total *cost* between two alternatives. Also called *differential cost*.

INDEPENDENT AUDIT (p. 571). An examination that is made in accordance with generally accepted auditing standards. Its aim is to give credibility to financial statements.

INDEPENDENT OPINION (p. 572). See *Auditor's report*.

INDIRECT LABOR (p. 76). All factory labor that is not *direct labor*.

INDIRECT MANUFACTURING COSTS (p. 64). All manufacturing *costs* other than *direct material* and *direct labor*.

INFLATION (p. 392). The decline in the general purchasing power of the monetary unit.

INTANGIBLE ASSETS (p. 604). A class of long-lived assets that are not physical in nature. Examples are *franchises*, *patents*, *trademarks*, *copyrights*, and *goodwill*.

INTERNAL ACCOUNTING CONTROL (p. 301). See *Internal control system*.

INTERNAL CONTROL SYSTEM (p. 301). Methods and procedures that are mainly concerned with the authorization of *transactions*, safeguarding of *assets*, and accuracy of the financial records.

INTERNAL RATE OF RETURN (p. 344). The *discount rate* that makes the net present value of a project equal to zero.

INVENTORY TURNOVER (p. 105). Number of times the average inventory is sold per year.

INVESTMENT CENTER (p. 261). An area of responsibility measured by *income* (*revenues* and *costs*) and the relationship between income and invested capital.

INVESTMENTS IN AFFILIATES (p. 649). Often used to describe investments in voting stock that represent 20% to 50% ownership.

INVESTMENTS IN ASSOCIATES (p. 649). Often used as synonym for *investments in affiliates*.

INVESTMENT TAX CREDIT (p. 390). Direct reductions of income taxes arising from the acquisition of depreciable *assets*.

JOB ORDER (p. 411). A document that shows the *costs* allocated to a specific batch of products.

JOB-ORDER COSTING (p. 409). The method of allocating *costs* to products that receive varying attention and effort.

JOINT COSTS (p. 126). *Costs* of manufacturing *joint products* prior to their *split-off point*.

JOINT PRODUCT COSTS (p. 126). See *Joint costs*.

JOINT PRODUCTS (p. 126). Two or more manufactured products that (1) have relatively significant sales values and (2) are not separately identifiable until their *split-off point*.

JUST-IN-TIME INVENTORY SYSTEM (p. 533). An inventory system that minimizes inventories by arranging to have materials and subcomponents arrive just as they are needed—no sooner and no later.

LAST-IN, FIRST-OUT (p. 680). A cost-flow assumption that the stock acquired earliest is still on hand; the stock of merchandise or material acquired latest is used first.

LEAD TIME (p. 531). The time interval between placing an order and receiving delivery.

LEAST SQUARES REGRESSION ANALYSIS (p. 245). An objective way of using all available data points to determine a *cost function*.

LEDGER (p. 582). A group of *accounts*.

LEGAL VALUE (p. 607). *Par* or *stated value* of corporate capital stock that is almost always far below the actual cash invested by a stockholder.

LIABILITIES (p. 549). Probable future sacrifices of economic benefits stemming from present legal, equitable, or constructive obligations of a particular enterprise to transfer *assets* or provide services to other entities in the future as a result of past *transactions* or events affecting the enterprise.

LIFO (p. 680). See *Last-in, first-out*.

LIFO INCREMENT (p. 683). *See LIFO Layer*.

LIFO LAYER (p. 683). A separately identifiable additional segment of *LIFO* inventory.

LIFO POOL (p. 683). See *LIFO layer*.

LIMITED LIABILITY (p. 608). Corporate creditors ordinarily have claims against the corporate *assets* only. Therefore the stockholders as individuals have no liability beyond their original investment in the *corporation*.

LIMITING FACTOR (p. 104). The item that restricts or constrains the production or sale of a product or service.

LINEAR PROGRAMMING (p. 523). A mathematical approach to a group of business problems that contains many interacting variables and basically involves combining limited resources to maximize *profits* or minimize *costs*.

LINE AUTHORITY (p. 10). Authority that is exerted downward over subordinates.

LONG-RANGE PLANNING (p. 157). Producing forecasted financial statements for five- or ten-year periods.

LONG-TERM LIABILITIES (p. 606). Debts that fall due beyond one year.

MANAGED COSTS (p. 229). See *Discretionary costs*.

MANAGEMENT ACCOUNTING (p. 4). Concerned mainly with how accounting can serve internal decision makers. Defined as the process of identification, measurement, accumulation, analysis, preparation, interpretation, and communication of information that assists executives in fulfilling organizational objectives.

MANAGEMENT AUDIT (p. 17). A review to determine whether the policies and procedures specified by top management have been implemented.

MANAGEMENT BY EXCEPTION (p. 7). The practice by the executive of focusing his or her attention mainly on significant deviations from expected results. It might also be called management by *variance*.

MANAGEMENT BY OBJECTIVES (MBO) (p. 322). Joint formulation by a manager and his or her superior of a set of goals and of plans for achieving the goals for a forthcoming period.

MANAGERIAL EFFORT (p. 302). Exertion toward a goal. Includes all actions (such as watching or thinking) that result in more *efficiency* and *effectiveness*.

MANUFACTURING EXPENSES (p. 64). See *Factory overhead*.

MANUFACTURING OVERHEAD (p. 64). See *Factory overhead*.

MARGINAL COSTING (p. 73). See *Direct costing*.

MARGINAL INCOME (p. 31). See *Contribution margin*.

MASTER BUDGET (p. 154). The *budget* that consolidates the organization's overall plans.

MASTER BUDGETED SALES (p. 167). See *Sales budget*.

MATCHING AND COST RECOVERY (p. 574). The procedure of accrual accounting whereby *expenses* are either directly attributed to related *revenues* (matching) of a given period or are otherwise regarded as *costs* that will not be recovered from revenue in future periods. In short, cost recovery is the justification for carrying *unexpired costs* as *assets* rather than writing them off as expenses.

MATERIAL REQUIREMENTS PLANNING (MRP) SYSTEM (p. 533). An inventory system that first specifies a production plan to meet a given output schedule and then determines what materials and subcomponents are required for the production and when they are needed. From this, purchasing schedules and subcomponent manufacturing schedules are set.

MATERIALITY (p. 576). The accounting convention that justifies the exclusion of insignificant information from financial reports. Whether an item is material (significant) is a matter of professional judgment.

MBO (p. 322). Acronym for *management by objectives*.

MINORITY INTEREST (p. 644). The total shareholder interest (other than the parent's) in a *subsidiary corporation*.

MIXED COST (p. 237). A *cost* that has both fixed and variable elements.

MODEL (p. 514). A simplified description of a device, system, or situation. It includes the factors and interrelationships most important to the user of the model; those of least importance are omitted.

MONETARY ITEMS (p. 701). A claim receivable or payable in a specified number of dollars; the claim remains fixed regardless of changes in either specific or general price levels.

MRP SYSTEM (p. 533). See *Material requirements planning system*.

NAA (p. 18). See *National Association of Accountants*.

NATIONAL ASSOCIATION OF ACCOUNTANTS (p. 18). The largest U.S professional organization of accountants whose major interest is management accounting.

NET BOOK VALUE (p. 321). Carrying amount of an *asset*, net of any related *accounts* (such as *accumulated depreciation*).

NET INCOME (p. 610). The excess of all *revenues* and gains for a period over all *expenses* and *losses*.

NET-PRESENT-VALUE METHOD (p. 342). A discounted-cash-flow approach to *capital budgeting* that discounts all expected future cash flows to the present using a minimum desired rate of return.

NET WORTH (p. 571). A synonym for *owners' equity*; no longer widely used.

NOMINAL DOLLARS (p. 689). Monetary amounts that are not restated for fluctuations in the general purchasing power of the monetary unit.

NORMAL COSTING (p. 423). The method of allocating *costs* to products using actual *direct materials*, actual *direct labor*, and predetermined overhead rates.

NORMAL COST SYSTEM (p. 423). See *Normal costing*.

OBJECTIVE FUNCTION (p. 515). Goal that can be quantified, often expressed as a maximization (or minimization) of some form of *profit* (or *cost*).

OBJECTIVITY (p. 579). Accuracy supported by convincing evidence that can be verified by independent accountants.

OBJECT OF COSTING (p. 62). See *Cost objective*.

OPERATING BUDGET (p. 159). *Budget* of the *income statement* together with supporting schedules.

OPERATING CYCLE (p. 599). The time span during which cash is spent to acquire goods and services that are used to produce the organization's output, which in turn is sold to customers, who in turn pay for their purchases with cash.

OPERATION COSTING (p. 426). System for costing goods that have some common characteristics plus some individual characteristics. Accumulates the cost of *direct labor* and *factory overhead* by operation for control purposes.

OPPORTUNITY COST (p. 124). The maximum available contribution to profit forgone by using scarce resources for a particular purpose.

ORDINARY INCREMENTAL BUDGET (p. 234). *Budget* that usually considers the previous period's *budget* and actual results as a given. The budget amount is then changed in accordance with experience during the previous period and expectations for the next period.

ORGANIZATION STRUCTURE (p. 300). The way top management has arranged the lines of responsibility within an entity.

OUTCOMES (p. 515). Measures of the consequences of the various possible actions in terms of the *objective function*.

OUTLAY COST (p. 124). A cash disbursement, as distinguished from an *opportunity cost*.

OUTSIDE STOCKHOLDERS' INTEREST IN SUBSIDIARIES (p. 644). Synonym for *minority interest*.

OVERABSORBED OVERHEAD (p. 419). See *Overapplied factory overhead*.

OVERAPPLIED FACTORY OVERHEAD (p. 419). The excess of *overhead* applied to products over actual overhead incurred.

OVERTIME PREMIUM (p. 76). A classification of *indirect labor costs*, consisting of the wages paid to *all* factory workers in excess of their straight-time wage rates.

OWNERS' EQUITY (p. 549). The interest of stockholders or other owners in the *assets* of an enterprise and, at any time, the cumulative net result of past *transactions* and other events and circumstances affecting the enterprise.

PAID-IN CAPITAL (p. 549). The *owners' equity* measured by the total amounts invested at the inception of a business and subsequently.

PARAMETER (p. 236). A constant, such as a, or a coefficient, such as b, in a model or system of equations, such as $y = a + bx$.

PARTNERSHIP (p. 570). A special form of organization that joins two or more individuals together as co-owners.

PAR VALUE (p. 607). The value printed on the face of the security certificate.

PAYBACK PERIOD (p. 357). See *Payback time*.

PAYBACK TIME (p. 357). The measure of the time needed to recoup, in the form of cash inflow from operations, the initial dollars invested.

PAYOFFS (p. 515). Synonym for *outcomes*.

PAYOFF TABLE (p. 515). See *Decision table*.

PAYROLL FRINGE COSTS (p. 77). Employer contributions to employee benefits such as social security, life insurance, health insurance, and pensions.

PERFORMANCE REPORT (p. 7). The comparison of actual results with the *budget*.

PERIOD COSTS (p. 65). Those *costs* being deducted as *expenses* during the current period without having been previously classified as *product costs*.

PERIODIC INVENTORY SYSTEM (p. 680). *Cost of goods sold* is determined by deducting the ending inventory, determined by a physical count, from the sum of beginning inventory and purchases during the period.

PERPETUAL INVENTORY SYSTEM (p. 680). Keeps a running, continuous record that tracks inventories and *cost of goods sold* on a day-to-day basis.

PHYSICAL CAPITAL MAINTENANCE (p. 689). *Income* emerges only after recovering an amount that allows physical operating capital to be maintained.

PLANNING (p. 6). Selecting objectives and the means for their attainment.

POSTAUDIT (p. 361). A performance evaluation of individual capital-budgeting projects.

PRACTICAL CAPACITY (p. 484). The maximum level at which the plant or department can realistically operate most efficiently (i.e., ideal capacity less allowances for unavoidable operating interruptions). Also called practical attainable capacity.

Preferred Stock (p. 607). Stock that has some priority over other shares regarding *dividends* or the distribution of *assets* upon liquidation.

Previous-Department Costs (p. 459). See *Transferred-in costs*.

Price Variance (p. 199). The difference between actual unit prices and budgeted unit prices multiplied by the actual quantity of goods or services purchased.

Prime Costs (p. 64). *Direct material cost* plus *direct labor cost*.

Priority Incremental Budget (p. 234). Similar to *ordinary incremental budget*. However, the budget request must be accompanied by a statement of what incremental activities or changes would occur if the *budget* were increased or decreased by a given amount or percentage.

Probabilities (p. 515). Likelihoods of occurrence of *events*.

Problem Solving (p. 5). That function of the accountant's information-supplying task which expresses in concise, quantified terms the relative advantages and disadvantages to the firm of pursuing a possible future course of action, or the relative advantages of any one of several alternative methods of operation.

Process (p. 409). A series of actions or operations leading to a definite end.

Process Costing (p. 409). The method of allocating *costs* to the products resulting from the mass production of like units.

Product Costs (p. 65). *Costs* that are identified with goods produced or purchased for resale.

Production Volume Variance (p. 483). Difference between *budgeted* fixed factory overhead and the fixed *factory overhead* applied to products.

Profit Center (p. 261). A *segment* of a business where managers are responsible for both *revenue* and *expense*.

Profit Plan (p. 159). See *Operating budget*.

Profits (p. 554). The excess of *revenues* over *expenses*.

Pro Forma Statements (p. 157). Forecasted financial statements.

Programmed Costs (p. 229). See *Discretionary costs*.

Proprietorship (p. 570). A separate *entity* with a single owner.

Prorating (p. 488). Assigning variances to the inventories and *cost of goods sold* related to the production during the period the variances arose.

Quantity Variance (p. 199). See *Efficiency variance*.

Rate Variance (p. 199). A *price variance* applied to *direct labor*.

Realization (p. 554). The recognition of *revenue*. Generally three tests must be met. First, the earning process must be virtually complete in that the goods or services must be fully rendered. Second, an exchange of resources evidenced by a market transaction must occur. Third, the *asset* received must be cash or convertible into cash with reasonable certainty.

Regression Analysis (p. 245). See *Least-squares regression analysis*.

Reinvested Earnings (p. 568). See *Retained income*.

Relevant Data for Decision Making (p. 87). See *Relevant information*.

Relevant Information (p. 87). Expected future data that will differ among alternatives.

Relevant Range (p. 28). The band of activity in which budgeted sales and *expense* relationships will be valid.

Required Rate of Return (p. 342). Minimum desired rate of return.

Reserve (p. 609). Has one of three meanings: (1) a restriction of dividend-declaring power as denoted by a specific subdivision of *retained income*; (2) an offset to an *asset*; and (3) an estimate of a definite *liability* of indefinite or uncertain amount.

Residual Income (RI) (p. 316). The *net income* of a *profit center* or *investment center*, less the "imputed" interest on the net *assets* used by the center.

Residual Value (p. 602). The predicted disposal value of a long-lived asset.

Responsibility Accounting System (p. 260). A system that measures the financial results of *responsibility centers*.

Responsibility Center (p. 260). A set of activities assigned to a manager or group of managers.

RETAINED EARNINGS (p. 550). See *Retained income*.

RETAINED INCOME (p. 550). Additional *owners' equity* generated by *profits*.

RETURN ON INVESTMENT (ROI) (p. 315). A measure of *income* or *profit* divided by the investment required to help obtain the *income* or *profit*.

RETURN ON STOCKHOLDERS' EQUITY (p. 660). The rate of return on the invested capital of the shareholders.

REVALUATION EQUITY (p. 692). That portion of *stockholders' equity* that shows all accumulated *holding gains* not otherwise shown in *retained income*.

REVENUES (p. 553). Generally, a gross increase in net *assets* from delivering goods or services. More specifically, revenues are inflows or other enhancements of *assets* of an enterprise or settlements of its *liabilities* (or a combination of both) during a period from delivering or producing goods, rendering services, or other activities that constitute the enterprise's ongoing major or central operations.

RI (p. 316). Symbol for *residual income*.

ROI (p. 315). Symbol for *return on investment*.

SAFETY STOCK (p. 532). A minimum or buffer inventory as a cushion against reasonable expected maximum usage.

SALES BUDGET (p. 167). The target level of sales resulting from decisions to create conditions that will generate a desired level of sales.

SALES FORECAST (p. 167). A prediction of sales under a given set of conditions.

SALES MIX (p. 40). The relative combination of the quantities of a variety of company products that comprise total sales.

SALES VOLUME VARIANCE (p. 191). Difference between the *flexible budget* amounts and the *static budget* amounts.

SALVAGE VALUE (p. 602). See *Residual value*.

SCARCE RESOURCE (p. 104). See *Limiting factor*.

SCOREKEEPING (p. 5). That data accumulation function of the accountant's information-supplying task which enables both internal and external parties to evaluate the financial performance of the firm.

SCRAP VALUE (p. 602). See *Residual value*.

SECURITIES AND EXCHANGE COMMISSION (SEC) (p. 572). The federal agency designated by the U.S. Congress as holding the ultimate responsibility for authorizing the *generally accepted accounting principles* for companies whose stock is held by the general investing public.

SEGMENT (p. 271). Any line of activity or part of an organization for which separate determination of *costs* or sales is wanted.

SEGMENT AUTONOMY (p. 305). Possession of decision-making power by managers of *segments* of an organization.

SENSITIVITY ANALYSIS (p. 351). Used in *capital budgeting*, it shows the financial consequences that occur if actual cash inflows and outflows differ from those expected.

SERVICE DEPARTMENTS (p. 268). Those departments that exist solely to support other departments.

SHADOW PRICE (527). Information from *linear programming* useful for *sensitivity analysis*, indicating how much the *objective function* will increase if one more unit of the limiting resource were available or decrease if there were one less unit.

SHORT-TERM INVESTMENT (p. 600). A temporary investment in marketable securities of otherwise idle cash.

SINGLE-STEP INCOME STATEMENT (p. 563). One that groups all *revenue* together (sales plus interest and rent revenues) and then lists and deducts all *expenses* together without drawing any intermediate subtotals.

SOURCE DOCUMENTS (p. 557). The original records of any *transaction*, internal or external, that occurs in the *entity's* operation.

SPECIFIC IDENTIFICATION (p. 680). This inventory method concentrates on the physical linking of the particular items sold.

SPECIFIC PRICE INDEX (p. 693). A specialized index used to approximate the *current cost* of a particular *asset*.

SPECIFICATION COSTING (p. 426). See *Operation costing*.

SPENDING VARIANCE (p. 204). See *Variable overhead spending variance*.

SPLIT-OFF POINT (p. 126). The juncture of the production where the *joint products* and *by-products* become individually identifiable.

STAFF AUTHORITY (p. 10). The authority to advise but not to command; it may be exerted laterally or upward.

STANDARD COST (p. 196). A carefully predetermined *cost* that should be attained, usually expressed per unit.

STANDARD DEVIATION (p. 519). Square root of the mean of the squared deviations from the *expected value*.

STANDARD DIRECT COSTING (p. 485). That type of product costing in which the *cost* of the finished unit is calculated as the sum of the costs of the standard allowances for the factors of production, excluding fixed factory overhead, which is treated as a *period cost*, and without reference to costs actually incurred.

STATED VALUE (p. 607). A nominal value of a stock certificate that is usually far below the actual cash invested. See *Par value*.

STATEMENT OF CHANGES IN FINANCIAL POSITION (p. 612). A basic financial statement that summarizes the financing and investment activities of the enterprise. It provides the reader with a glimpse of where resources came from during the year and where they have gone.

STATEMENT OF FINANCIAL CONDITION (p. 549). A synonym for *balance sheet*.

STATEMENT OF FINANCIAL POSITION (p. 549). A substitute term for *balance sheet*.

STATEMENT OF PROFIT AND LOSS (p. 548). The *income statement*.

STATEMENT OF RETAINED EARNINGS (p. 612). A financial statement that analyzes changes in the *retained earnings* or *retained income* account for a given period.

STATEMENT OF RETAINED INCOME (p. 612). Synonym for *statement of retained earnings*.

STATEMENT OF SOURCES AND APPLICATIONS OF FUNDS (p. 612). See *Statement of changes in financial position*.

STATES (p. 515). Synonym for *events*.

STATES OF NATURE (p. 515). Synonym for *events*.

STATIC BUDGET (p. 187). A *budget* prepared for only one level of activity and, consequently, one that does not adjust automatically to changes in the level of volume.

STEP-DOWN METHOD. (p. 281) A method for allocating *service department costs* that recognizes that service departments support the activities in other service departments as well as in revenue-producing departments. A sequence of allocations begins with the department that renders the greatest service (as measured by cost) to the greatest number of other departments. Once a department's costs are allocated to other departments, no subsequent service department costs are allocated back to it.

STEP-FUNCTION COSTS (p. 237). Those *variable costs* that change abruptly at intervals of activity because their acquisition comes in indivisible chunks.

STOCKHOLDERS' EQUITY (p. 549). The excess of *assets* over *liabilities* of a corporation.

STRAIGHTFORWARD METHOD (p. 617). The practice of beginning a *changes statement* with sales or *revenue* and then deducting only those *income statement* items affecting *working capital*.

STRAIGHT-LINE DEPRECIATION (p. 559). A method of *depreciation* that allocates the same *cost* to each year of an *asset's* useful life.

STRATEGIC PLANNING (p. 157). Setting the goals and objectives of the organization.

SUBORDINATED (p. 607). A creditor claim that is junior to other creditor claims.

SUBORDINATED DEBENTURE (p. 607). See *Subordinated* and *Debenture*.

SUBSIDIARY (p. 641). A corporation owned or controlled by a parent company, through the ownership of more than 50% of the voting stock.

SUBUNIT AUTONOMY (p. 305). See *Segment autonomy*.

SUNK COST (p. 132). A *cost* that has already been incurred and, therefore, is irrelevant to the decision-making process. Also called *historical cost*.

TANGIBLE ASSETS. (p. 602) *Assets* that can be physically observed.

TARGET RATE (p. 342). Often used in *capital budgeting* as either the minimum desired rate of return or the budgeted rate of return.

TAX SHIELD (p. 381). Usually defined as noncash items (e.g., *depreciation*) charged against *income*, thus protecting that amount from income tax.

TERMINAL VALUE (p. 602). See *Residual value*.

TIME-ADJUSTED RATE OF RETURN (p. 344). See *Internal rate of return*.

TOTAL PROJECT APPROACH (p. 353). A method of comparing two or more alternative courses of action by computing the total expected inflows and outflows of each alternative and then converting these flows to their present value by applying some predetermined minimum rate of return.

TRADITIONAL COSTING (p. 72). See *Absorption costing*.

TRANSACTION (p. 549). Any event that affects the financial position of an *entity* and requires recording.

TRANSFER PRICE (p. 306). The amounts charged by one *segment* of an organization for a product or service that it supplies to another segment of the same organization.

TRANSFERRED-IN COSTS (p. 459). In *process costing*, *costs* incurred in a previous department that have been received by a subsequent department.

TREASURY STOCK (p. 608). A *corporation's* issued stock that has subsequently been repurchased by the company and is being held for a specific purpose.

UNADJUSTED RATE OF RETURN (p. 358). See *Accounting rate of return*.

UNAVOIDABLE COST (p. 101). The opposite of *avoidable cost*.

UNCONTROLLABLE COST (p. 265). A *cost* that cannot be affected by a manager of a *responsibility center* within a given time span.

UNDERAPPLIED FACTORY OVERHEAD (p. 419). The excess of actual *factory overhead* over the factory overhead applied to products.

UNDISTRIBUTED EARNINGS (p. 568). See *Retained income*.

UNEARNED REVENUE (p. 564). See *Deferred revenue*.

UNEXPIRED COSTS (p. 558). Any *expenditures* benefiting the future; any asset, including *prepaid expenses*, normally appearing on a *balance sheet*.

UNFAVORABLE COST VARIANCE (p. 188). Actual *cost* minus budgeted costs when actual costs are greater than budgeted costs.

USAGE VARIANCE (p. 199). See *Efficiency variance*.

VARIABLE BUDGET (p. 189). See *Flexible budget*.

VARIABLE COST (p. 26). A *cost* that is uniform per unit but fluctuates in total in direct proportion to changes in the related total activity or volume.

VARIABLE-COST PERCENTAGE (p. 40). The *variable-expense ratio* expressed as a percentage.

VARIABLE COSTING (p. 73). See *Direct costing*.

VARIABLE-COST RATIO (p. 50). See *Variable-expense ratio*.

VARIABLE-EXPENSE RATIO (p. 40). All variable *expenses* divided by *revenues*.

VARIABLE OVERHEAD EFFICIENCY VARIANCE. (p. 203) The difference between actual *direct labor* hours and standard direct labor hours allowed for the actual output achieved multiplied by the standard variable overhead rate per hour.

VARIABLE OVERHEAD SPENDING VARIANCE (p. 204). The difference between actual variable overhead cost and the amount of variable overhead budgeted for the actual labor hours worked. It measures control over both usage and price of variable overhead items themselves.

VARIANCE (p. 7). The deviation of actual results from the expected or budgeted result.

VERIFIABILITY (p. 579). See *Objectivity*.

VOLUME VARIANCE (p. 480). See *Production volume variance* and *Sales volume variances*.

WEIGHTED-AVERAGE COST (p. 681). This inventory method assumes that all items available for sale during the period are best represented by their weighted-average cost.

WORKING CAPITAL (p. 613). The excess of *current assets* over *current liabilities*.

WORKING-CAPITAL CYCLE (p. 599). See *Operating cycle*.

WORKING CAPITAL PROVIDED BY OPERATIONS (p. 617). *Revenues* less all operating *expenses* requiring *working capital*.

WORK MEASUREMENT (p. 230). The systematic analysis of a task, its size, the methods used in its performance, and its efficiency.

ZBB (p. 234). Acronym for *zero-base budgeting*.

ZERO-BASE BUDGETING (ZBB) (p. 234). Budgeting from the ground up as though the *budget* were being initiated for the first time.

INDEX